Econometric Studies of Japan

Econometric Studies of Japan

Edited by
Richard Kosobud
and
Ryoshin Minami

UNIVERSITY OF ILLINOIS PRESS
Urbana Chicago London

Library of Congress Cataloging in Publication Data

Main entry under title:

Econometric studies of Japan.

Bibliography: p.
Includes index.
1. Japan — Economic conditions — Mathematical models — Addresses, essays, lectures. I. Kosobud, Richard F. II. Minami, Ryoshin, 1933-
HC462.8.E26 330.9'52'04 76-30360
ISBN 0-252-00255-5

Contents

Preface

The idea for this book arose during pauses in rather serious Ping-Pong at Hitotsubashi University. We seemed time and time again to want ready at hand some basic studies on the economy of Japan to which we could refer as we talked about current problems. Other reasons for assembling such studies followed quickly. The development of our reasons for editing this volume is more appropriately placed in the introduction, so we will say no more at this point. It does seem to us, as we look back on our editorial labors, that a significant body of quantitative work became available during the past few years when data and tools and endeavor seemed simultaneously to have come together and we have a feeling of satisfaction in having brought a sample of it together in this form.

There are several sources of studies and several kinds of acknowledgments due. A number of studies were published previously in journal literature and we are glad to acknowledge, where appropriate, permissions from the various journals, which are mentioned at the beginning of each study. Several of the studies were translated from the Japanese, and we wish to acknowledge receipt of a grant from the University of Illinois at Chicago Circle Research Board to assist in carrying out these translations. It is very pleasant to acknowledge some special debts. Professor Lawrence R. Klein provided helpful suggestions and comment, a continuation of his role in facilitating the international transfer of econometric technology. Professor Ippei Yamazawa helped the editors greatly in preparing the introduction to the studies on international trade. Mrs. Geri Kennedy provided efficient services in typing and managing the flow of materials between Chicago and Tokyo. We alone are responsible for errors and editorial judgments.

For whom is the book intended? Our definition of quantitative studies is rather wide and includes those based on econometric analysis with its emphasis on a specified model and estimations method as well as those based on a more general quantitative approach not always requiring a conclusion about the initial hypothesis. Therefore, we believe that students, research workers in Japan, and especially research workers elsewhere, and the general well-informed reader will find the following studies of interest. We provide a general guide for these readers as well as a specific guide to individual studies in the introduction.

Introduction by the Editors

A General Survey of Objectives

In the terminology of the coldly analytical social scientist, the Japanese economy has been performing a series of experiments in very rapid growth. The results of these experiments, pro and antigrowth supporters agree, have not yet been thoroughly recorded and analyzed. The process of rapid economic growth not yet being well understood and its appraisal from a welfare point of view not yet far advanced, it is important to expand and to distribute widely studies of the Japanese growth path. It is the general objective of this book to make a contribution toward this end by assembling a cross section of studies that deals with various aspects of an economy undergoing sustained rapid growth.

A quick perusal of the table of contents will reveal our interest in quantitative and positivistic studies, but the reader may be interested in more detail on our selection criteria. The editors, therefore, present in the first part of this introduction a general guide to the studies selected. In the second part, they offer a survey of individual studies, giving some highlights of their results and methodology.

What do we mean when we write that the attainment of rapid growth rates in general and the growth path of the Japanese economy, say between 1950 and 1970, are not yet well understood? Consider some general questions for which no generally acceptable answers are yet available. Was this growth path unique, a result of the singular events of the turbulent 1930s and war-perturbed 1940s, or was it an acceleration of trends in the Japanese economy which will continue to hold sway? To what extent did the sources of economic growth respond to market forces? To what extent did the various national and regional economic plans and the activities of the government agencies having primary responsibility for an industry shape economic events? Was the influence of the business community somehow differently exerted than in other capitalistic economies? What can be said about the growth rates of investment and savings; were they optimal in some sense or was the growth rate of consumption too low? Can sources of the Japanese growth path be identified and compared to those in other economies? Was technological progress a separable source in this connection, with distinct mechanisms for its production, transfer, and implementation?

What was the correspondence between growth rates of national income and its components and the growth rates of welfare and environmental quality? How did measures of income and wealth distribution change during this period? What are the appropriate roles to be given to the growth of exports compared to the growth of the domestic market in the attainment of a high overall growth rate? How did consumers, investors, and other decision units "behave" under conditions of rapid growth, and how do these decisions compare to those made in different times and in different places?

Clearly not all of these questions can be dealt with in a book of finite length (and our first selection of studies yielded a book stretching finiteness).[1] Our own interests are in studies utilizing analytical rather than description methods, and in studies with an empirical rather than purely theoretical bent. For example, we have selected studies dealing with the sources of growth rather than the issue of planning versus market direction, studies dealing with the behavior of sectors of the economy under conditions of rapid growth rather than a welfare appraisal of these conditions, and studies dealing with quantitative models for prediction purposes rather than with questions of optimal growth paths. This is not to argue that the questions we have set aside are less important. Rather, as we shall explain later, it seemed to us important to take advantage of a burst of research effort in certain areas and an enlargement of data that has recently taken place.[2] As the studies selected have the objective of providing quantitative results to rather precisely defined questions, they rarely pose general questions as we have just posed them. Yet their results contribute to the answers to these questions. In our survey of particular studies we shall attempt to relate these results to the more general questions.

There are more proximate reasons for bringing out such a volume at this time, reasons which also have guided us in selecting studies. There has been considerable research along quantitative lines which if not providing definitive answers to a wide range of questions has been an impressive increase over prior work. Our aim has been to make some of this work more generally available. One gets an impression of this increase from the burgeoning of journal literature, pamphlets, and books, and from the inauguration of one interesting journal devoted to the translation of studies from Japanese to English. As further evidence of this point, we note, though it detracts from our claims to originality, that a volume in Japanese similar in spirit to ours was recently published. Several studies included there have been translated for this work (studies by Sato, by Shinkai, by Klein and Shinkai and by Tatemoto, Uchida, and Watanabe).[3] An English volume of research on agriculture has also recently been published, which led us to exclude studies of this sector from our volume.[4]

Not unrelated to this increase in effort has been an enlargement in the quantity of data available on Japanese economic activity. Several aspects of these developments on the data front deserve further mention here. Broadly speaking, these advances may be grouped into three categories: an extension over time of selected time series; a disaggregation over time, commodity, and sector of the national income and product accounts; and increased information obtained by means of sample surveys. The estimates of long-term economic statistics of Japan since 1868 under the general editorship of Professors K. Ohkawa, M. Shinohara, and M. Umemura have opened up empirical research opportunities to obtain answers to questions formerly posed only in a speculative manner. Several of the studies included in this volume (by Yoshihara, Ohkawa, and Ueno) report on results obtained by an analysis of these valuable data.

The national income and product account data maintained by the Economic Planning Agency of the Prime Minister's office have undergone several major revisions in the period of postwar rapid growth and provide the indispensable base for the quantitative models of growth and business cycles contained in this book. A major revision is underway at the time of writing this introduction, a revision which will yield more detail on production structure, government expenditure, and implicit price deflators, among other advances. A quick perusal of the list of variables found in econometric models and measured by these social accounts as in the study of Klein and Shinkai, then in the study of Tatemoto, _et al_., and finally in the study of Shishido, _et al_., will give some idea of the expansion of these accounts.

Sample surveys have a long history in Japan. A monthly survey carried out by the Statistics Bureau in the Prime Minister's office obtains family budget data from about 10,000 households. A rotating reinterview sample yields savings data. A nationwide survey every five years has provided detailed data on consumption. The Bank of Japan obtains information from selected large enterprises, including data on borrowing plans. The Ministry of Finance obtains data on selected items in the balance sheets and profit and loss statements of a sample of all enterprises. Both the Economic Planning Agency and the Ministry of International Trade and Industry survey the business community to obtain information on investment expenditure intentions in addition to other variables. Studies in this volume by Fujino and by Sato indicate some of the research possibilities opened up by these data. It was one of our objectives to introduce these sources of data to the non-Japanese research worker who may not have been fully aware of their richness or usefulness in designing comparative studies.

Much has been made of the institutional and cultural differences which are thought to constitute pitfalls to the research worker essaying a study outside his own country and own language. We firmly believe stories of these pitfalls have too often exaggerated the difficulties and prevented fruitful enquiry, not to mention the fact that variations in institutional and cultural detail open up interesting research opportunities in their own right. Having made that point, however, we must add that overlooking these differences can vitiate the results of a well-meant research effort. Many of the studies presented here take account of these differences which become an essential feature of the research. The fact that annual and semiannual bonuses make up an important component of wage and salary income is brought out in the study by Blumenthal. The fact that checking account balances currently play little role in the balance sheets of households is clearly of importance in the study of Fujino. The heavy dependence of business upon bank credit emerges in the study of Sato. After allowance for these institutional differences, there emerge relationships inviting comparison with those of other countries; relationships which are specifications of marginal productivity theory, of the transactions demand function for money, and of the stock adjustment model of investment expenditures.

One final general point seems in order. As we write this introduction, the full details of the growth record for Japan (for the calendar year 1976) are becoming available and reveal rather low growth rates in real national income, not a good record for the past few years. Official forecasts for 1977 have been scaled down to comparatively modest goals. Some observers are proclaiming the necessity of an end to rapid economic growth, perhaps an end to positive per-capita growth rates themselves. If this should be the case, then the epoch of rapid growth will be a matter for historical research. We may, then, be entering a new epoch in which, for example, questions about the distribution of income rather than its size will come to the fore. Yet, we venture the conjecture that we may continue to have positive and even high growth rates, if we want them, and that the enchanced capacity to solve economic problems afforded by significantly high growth rates is an advantage not easily given up. The problem is one of achieving a growth path whose consequences are better understood and appraised. It is toward this latter end that we hope the selected studies contribute.

A Specific Survey of Individual Studies

In the opening study, Yoshihara brings the various tools of econometrics to bear on the Japanese consumer's allocation of income among five broad groupings of commodities. It is an example of the comprehensive nature of econometric research, including a discussion of the alternative theoretical models of consumer behavior, the application of econometric theory required to obtain quantitative results, the measurement practices utilized to obtain the data, the results themselves, and finally the implications of the results for the various models. Theoretical criteria are presented in order to appraise four leading, perhaps contending, expenditure models. A noteworthy feature of this study is the use of long-run (1905-1965) historical data on income, quantities of commodities consumed, and prices to which reference has previously been made.

Readers interested in consumer expenditure patterns will find the high (relative to other developed economies) income elasticities of expenditure for clothing and housing worth careful consideration. All four models provide estimates of these income elasticities within apparently reasonable distance of each other. Price elasticities appear relatively low, but the four models provide estimates differing markedly. No one model appears consistently superior when tested by the plausibility of its estimates or its predictive power. However, the linear expenditure and double log models do appear to have an edge in this study. A naive model set up as a benchmark does not out-perform models with theoretical (that is, maximizing) content, except for one probably not significant exception.

These results are suggestive and are likely to stimulate further work in Japan and in other countries. For example, the one instance in which Yoshihara utilizes a measure which could be interpreted as an approximation to normal or permanent income yields elasticities of demand for the commodity groups which tend to be lower than measures calculated from observable income. Further research in this area would seem rewarding. Yoshihara mentions the possible importance of structural shifts over the long period of the time series sample, and some tests of such shifts could be devised. It would be extremely interesting, finally, to try approaches other than differencing in order to handle the problem of temporal correlation of residuals. Whether consumer expenditure patters have altered in response to the expanded welfare and medical programs of the Japanese government, among other influences on consumer expenditure and saving behavior, are questions deserving research priority.

Fujino's study provides an example of the search for a single relationship between currency demanded by households and the appropriate determining variables. An alternative approach in which savings of households are allocated to an exhaustive set of asset and liability items awaits future research. Studies such as Fujino's will provide valuable help toward that general objective. A number of important issues in formulating this single demand relationship are raised by Fujino.

A characteristic of the sample period studied is that consumers bought "almost all consumption goods through the medium of currency" and rarely were found to have checking accounts. Thus, the study is interpreted by its author as an investigation of the transactions demand for money defined mainly as currency. In axamining sample survey data on household currency, income, and expenditure, the author as his point of departure considers the empirical hypothesis that the size of the income (or expenditure) elasticity of demand for currency is less than unity. This question has in various formulations stimulated a good deal of research, and the interested reader may welcome this effort to add to the body of positive knowledge on the subject by utilizing a relatively untapped source of data.

As a first test, the author formulates a model which enables him to estimate the expenditure elasticity of demand for currency from income class (cross-section) data. The result is an elasticity coefficient less than unity, an apparent confirmation of the inventory theoretic approach to currency holdings. Fujino, however, believes his first results explain average holdings of currency during the month but not the variation of cash balances held at the beginning and end of the month by households of varying income.

The facts that attracts Fujino's interest are the tendency for lower income households to hold smaller currency balances (in relation to income or consumption expenditure) at the end of the month than at the beginning. This tendency is reversed for higher income households. To explain this unexpected pattern, Fujino erects the definitional edifice of permanent and transitory components of currency balances and income. By making key behavioral assumptions that permanent balances are a constant proportion of permanent income, and transitory balances are an increasing function of transitory income, Fujino is able to develop his model to the point at which several key identifications of variables with observable entities enable him to estimate the long-run relationship between the demand for permanent cash balances and income, and the short-run relationship between transitory components. By identifying average cash balances held at the beginning of the month with permanent balances, and by identifying permanent income with the sample (geometric) mean, Fujino estimates an alternate model which yields an elasticity coefficient of unity. The reader not familiar with data reported by the Bureau of Statistics in The Survey of Consumer's Income and Expenditure may welcome this glimpse of some of the details on flow and stock items. He will also be alerted to interesting features of the data by Fujino's description of the bonus or extra wage payments which distinguish Japanese wage and salary payment practices. In recognition of the impact of this feature on the data, Fujino eliminates December figures from his study.

The availability of sample survey data over the years enables Fujino to estimate the parameters of his demand model for the years 1951 through 1960. He finds trends in his parameters indicative of cyclical variation in the velocity of money. He seeks explanations for these trends in price changes, in rationing which was in effect during 1951 and 1952, and in deviations of average sample income from permanent income during this time period. He finds these same trends in more aggregative measures of non-bank holdings of money. Fujino provides, then, in closing his study, an agenda for further research into the determinants of the demand for money.

We turn now to the demand for fixed capital goods on the part of the manufacturing sector of the business community. K. Sato has chosen to study gross investment expenditures by developing an explicit model of investment planning and implementation within the general framework of the flexible accelerator theory of investment demand originated by H. B. Chenery and L. M. Koyck. It is interesting to note that Sato presents a complete theory of investment, including an explanation of the desired level of capacity output (capital stock), a depiction of the time structure of the investment process, and an estimate of replacement investment. An indication of the completeness of the study is found in his examination of the stability properties of the investment model. For the reader lacking complete familiarity with the variety of data available on investment and related activity in Japan, this study will provide a guide to information ranging from sample survey data on investment plans to manufacturer's new orders for machinery and to indexes of manufacturing capacity.

The underlying model is of a form being actively studied and developed. Gross investment expenditure on plant and equipment is made to depend on the producer's desires to attain a specific output capacity (capital stock) at some future date. This long-run determinant is modified by short-run expectations about output fluctuations and the cost of financing investment expenditures. Departures from instantaneous formulation of investment plans and their implementation give a time structure to the investment process. Thus Sato's model provides an application of recent developments in capital theory and an attempt to penetrate the investment decision in depth. A variety of alternative specifications is possible within this framework, including alternative measures of output capacity, inclusion of output and input prices (fixed versus flexible technical coefficients), costs of external or internal finance, and the like. In making these choices, Sato keeps in mind characteristics of the Japanese economy, such as rapid growth.

The desired capacity output is a fundamental determinant of investment expenditures and is made to depend upon the anticipated growth rate of desired capacity over the planning horizon less existing capacity. The actual growth rate of capacity output during the sample period was 3.5 percent per quarter, and Sato is able to obtain plausible quantitative results using this value. This provides one piece of evidence of the strong growth orientation of investment planning. Capacity is an important concept in the model for which Sato must find an appropriate measure. A basic source is the Ministry of International Trade and Industry's indexes of manufacturing capacity.

Short-run fluctuations in output are introduced into the investment process by their influence on output expectations, which if in excess of normal output increase desired investment plans. Another short-run influence introduced is the cost of finance. There is strong support for Sato's decision to provide a measure of the cost of external finance as the relevant determinant "in view of the heavy dependence of Japanese firms on bank loans in their financing." The measure chosen, the effective interest rate on bank loans and discounts, may not reflect all aspects of the process by which commercial banks and the monetary authorities make credit available to enterprises, and Sato raises this issue as deserving of further research.

The formulation of investment plans and their implementation are developed in an explicit way by Sato, who shows that if there is imperfect adaptation of new plans to the gap between desired and existing plans, then the time structure of investment will follow a distributed lag. Alternative lag specifications are possible at this stage, and the author chooses a geometrically declining lag structure by which prior gross investment expenditure becomes a determinant of its present value.

An important consideration is whether to introduce the prices of labor and capital services into the investment process. The issue is the appropriate specification of the underlying technology and whether substitution is permitted among inputs or whether fixed coefficients are to be assumed. Sato reports that experimentation with a flexible capital output ratio did not seem to improve the results.

In specifications of the investment process involving investment plans, it is sometimes the practice to manipulate the model so as to arrive at indirect estimates of the formulation of investment plans and their implementation. Sato is able to make direct estimates of these aspects by utilization of Economic Planning Agency sample survey data on investment intentions. This more direct estimation of important parameters in the equations of the investment sector adds confidence to the interpretation of his results.

The results indicate that Sato's approach has been fruitful. A negative influence of existing capital stock on investment is detected, all the more impressive for being revealed during a period of unprecedented growth. Short-run determinants of investment expenditures are revealed to exert an influence in excess of the long-run, although this result must be put forth tentatively, as it depends on a particular formulation of the model (a formulation which gives weight to the expectation function). Costs of external finance are revealed to exert a strong influence with the appropriate negative sign. Another interesting result has to do with the stability features of the investment sector which Sato reduces to a third-degree difference equation in gross investment. When output grows exponentially, the system exhibits damped oscillations and Sato concludes that the interaction between capacity and investment alone is not the major source of cyclical fluctuations in Japan.

Looking ahead, one may venture the opinion that Sato's study will contribute to research interest into the investment process along several lines. The role of external finance approximated in this study by an interest rate appears to be capable of further development. The allocation of credit among producers is a subject for further research. The time structure of the investment process is likely to be further explored with alternative lag distributions, including those that give greater weight to the middle past rather than geometrically declining weights. And awaiting further investigation is the development of a simultaneous model incorporating not only investment decisions but also production and financial decisions.

A body of positive knowledge is being developed on the sources of economic growth in Japan. After making allowance for capital and labor input growth (and after making quality adjustments for these inputs), most recent studies find a large unexplained residual rate of growth remains. Ohkawa's study presents estimates indicating that over 50 percent of the rate of growth may be attributable to this residual source during the time periods 1955-61 and 1962-64. The author presents estimates that are lower for earlier periods. An appropriate response to these results is to endeavor to probe further into this unexplained source of growth. The author addresses his study to a decomposition of the residual rate of growth and specifically addresses his study to the questions of how much of the residual rate of growth arises because of the reallocation of labor and capital among the major sectors of the Japanese economy (structural change).

To accomplish his objective, Ohkawa develops the neoclassical production function along lines that have yielded fruitful empirical results. By assuming constant returns to scale and competitive pricing of capital and labor within (but not necessarily between) major sectors of the economy, Ohkawa decomposes residual productivity change into intrasector technological progress of the conventional sort and sectoral reallocation of labor and capital. As the author remarks, this latter concept is more precise than the former in many ways.

It is possible to conceive of efficiency gains resulting from reallocation of labor and capital starting from an initial disequilibrium situation which is slow to work itself out (a version of the well-known dualism theory of economic development). Or such efficiency gains many result from moving or shocked sectoral equilibriums to which labor and capital are adjusting continuously. The author's study is closer to the former view. Gains from reallocation of resources may be viewed as a kind of technological progress (the economy becomes more efficient), and it is plausible to think that inputs are required to bring about this reallocation (raising questions about the rate of return of expenditures facilitating such reallocation). In this sense, reallocation of resources can be viewed as an improvement in the organization of inputs bringing the benefit of increased output.

The author applies his method to long-term data on national income and expenditure, data he himself has done so much to obtain. The extent of the data enables the author to disaggregate the economy into five major sectors, including manufacturing and agriculture. Here it is of interest to note the finding that the disaggregation between agriculture and non-agriculture has the greatest significance for efficiency gains of labor and capital. Another finding is the author's demonstration that the reallocation of labor has made the largest quantitative contribution to a more efficient economy, a finding consistent with his view that the basic source of efficiency gain is disequilibrium of the labor market and not, to the same extent, of the capital market. A further finding is that the share of residual growth attributable to reallocations has been declining over time (from about one-third to about one-quarter of the residual). During the early 1960s about one-quarter of the residual rate of growth is attributed to the reallocation(mainly from agriculture) of labor and, to a lesser extent, capital. While a lively controversy has developed over the proper methodology for investigating and interpreting technological progress, Okhawa's study provides a persuasive explanation for part of the increase in efficiency of labor input.[5]

The next study of Hamada borders on several areas of research, but we have decided to place it here because the author builds upon an explicit formulation of the constant elasticity of substitution production function. The author's objective is to derive an expression for the determinants of the rate of growth of the capital stock in Japan. As he notes in his first table, the capital stock for most of the seventeen industries in his sample grew more rapidly than the associated labor force during the sample period. This rapid increase in the capital to labor ratio measured in "natural" units has characterized the current scene in Japan. At the same time the rate of growth of the cost or rental rate of capital has been less than that of the wage rate. The author attempts to assess the quantitative importance of this latter factor relative to others in bringing about the accumulation of capital.

As an intermediate step in his research plan, the author calculates estimates of the elasticity of substitution of capital for labor. His estimates tend to be over unity, a finding which is consistent with the view that as the cost of capital has declined relative to labor, the substitution of capital for labor has occurred consequently increasing the share of capital in national income. Estimates of aggregate elasticities of substitution have varied greatly, as the author is well aware, so that further study on the part of quantitative economists of production functions in Japan is deserving of a high priority.

Hamada's conclusion is that the decline in the cost of capital relative to labor was a significant stimulant to the relatively rapid growth of the capital stock. His method of approach permits him to attach quantitative estimates to the importance of this factor in various industries. He estimates that about one-third of the rate of growth of the capital stock in chemical products and fertilizers is accounted for in this way, about 20 percent in automobiles and iron and steel, and the smallest role, less than 10 percent, in paper and pulp, stone, clay and glass and cement products.

An implicit question that emerges from this study inviting further research concerns the functioning of the capital markets in Japan and the role of government policy in influencing the level and structure of interest rates. Whether capital markets were in a rough sort of equilibrium status, or whether, as we believe, they were in disequilibrium characterized by excess demand is a fascinating area for further research.

Blumenthal's study may be usefully divided into three parts. In the first, he shows that a transition from the labor surplus to the labor shortage phase took place during 1958-64 in Japan by clarifying some indexes for the excess demand for labor and for labor mobility. In the second, he measures wage differentials in the manufacturing industries for three years, 1958, 1961, and 1964, making use of analysis of variance methods. This study is an extension of his previous contribution in which he measured the wage differentials for 1961, based on the same procedure, and examined the effects on them of socioeconomic factors, such as age, sex, education, and so forth.[6] He concludes that marginal productivity theory provided only part of the answer to questions about wage differentials. His empirical results provide, for example, measures of the importance of age and sex characteristics. By introducing dummy variables to measure an "industry effect," Blumenthal finds that the dispersion of the industry coefficients increased from 1958 to 1961 and decreased in 1964. According to him, this change signifies the movement toward a more competitive structure of the labor market during 1961-64. This finding is consistent with the assertion that 1961 is the "turning point" in the Japanese economy.[7]

In the third and last part of his paper, Blumenthal confirms the structural change of the labor market in a much more exact way: he supposes that labor productivity and unionization rate affect interindustry wage differentials to a greater extent in the labor surplus economy than in the labor shortage economy. In the latter economy, for instance, the ties among firms are much closer, and each firm cannot pursue its own policy within a more or less fenced-off internal market. Under this supposition, he regressed the industry effect on labor productivity and found that both the coefficient of determination and the regression coefficients have decreased from 1958 to 1961 and from 1961 to 1964. According to him, this confirms the hypothesis that a scarcity of labor has been a major factor for the recent decrease in the wage differentials.

In his study, Watanabe considers several alternative explanations of price and manufacturing wage level changes in Japan. He chooses first to develop a model for prices, a model which depends upon a demand-supply equilibrating process in competitive markets. Because of the strong trend movement in variables characterizing the Japanese economy, he uses rates of change measures of variables in his equations. Utilizing quarterly data, he obtains significant results relating consumer price changes positively to per-capita disposable income and negatively to a labor productivity index in manufacturing industries. Watanabe experiments with a Phillips-Lipsey tradeoff model for wage rate changes and unemployment. He introduces various shift variables which may characterize this relationship in the Japanese economy. What appears to work best is the rate of change of the consumer price index with a lag, a finding which Watanabe interprets as a measure of the current strength of union bargaining over wages.

In an alternative formulation, the author considers a recursive model in which changes in wage rates are influenced by an index of excess supply in the labor market (the percentage of total employees who received unemployment insurance) and lagged price changes. Current price changes are determined by a productivity index and current wage changes. From an econometric point of view, the author attempts to avoid single equation least squares bias in the latter equation by substituting estimated wage rate changes predicted by the first equation. Watanabe concludes from his study of varied explanations of inflationary processes that both demand pull and cost push factors have been significant in current Japanese economic history.

Ichimura's paper provides estimates of export and import functions by the use of time series data. The relationships are formulated so that estimates may be obtained directly of the elasticities of Japanese exports with respect to the relative price (the ratio of domestic to world prices) and to a measure of the world's income. The elasticities of Japanese imports with respect to the relative price (imported goods vs. domestic goods in Japan) and to the Japanese income are obtained in the same way. Estimates of these elasticities provide information indispensable to an understanding of balance of trade movements during a period of economic growth. The high income elasticity of demand for Japanese exports is a significant finding of this study.

Ichimura estimates export functions by type of products (those of heavy industry, of textiles, of foods, and others) and by export area (the United States, Europe, Canada, and the rest of the world in the case of textiles exports; the United States, Canada, Europe, and the rest of the world in the case of food exports; and the United States, Canada, Europe and the rest of the world in the case of other commodity exports). As an example, let us take the export function of machinery (one of the three commodities of the heavy industry's products). In this function, the ratio of the world export price of machinery and equipment to the Japanese export price index of this commodity is introduced. Other than this, three variables are taken into consideration. The first is an increment in the world production index of this commodity which is considered to be the best substitute for the world's income in the basic export function. The second and the third variables are the foreign exchange reserves of Asian countries and reparations and loans, respectively. These variables are found to explain a considerable part of export of this commodity to Asian countries. Some unexplained variation appears to be cyclical in nature and deserving of further research attention.

Ichimura estimates four import functions: that is, the functions for rice (and barley), other foods, machinery, and materials or natural resources and related products. Take the function for raw materials and related products as an example. In this function, he introduces three variables other than seasonal dummy variables. The three variables, all significant, are the sales of manufacturing industry, the inventory stock of raw materials, and foreign reserves, all with time lags.[8] The price variable is not found to be significant in this case.

Time series estimates of price elasticities of exports and imports as Ichimura recognizes, raise difficult problems of biases. In addition to identification problems, the matter of finding the appropriate lag structure offers opportunities for further research.

In order to provide additional information on these difficulties, Shinkai has attempted to estimate the price elasticities of exports and imports by using cross-sectional data. Cross-sectional estimation of these elasticities is based on two assumptions. The first is that the price elasticities are equivalent among components of commodity aggregates. The second is that, in the case of the export function, the Japanese share in exports is not affected if the ratio of Japanese export price to the world price is constant. And, in the case of the import function, the ratio of imports to domestic production in Japan is unaltered with a constant relative price of imports to domestic products. The second assumption is equivalent to an assumption of a unitary income elasticity of demand for exports and imports. These assumptions enable the author to estimate elasticities by regressing the ratio of Japan's exports and imports to the world values on the ratio of Japan's prices to world prices. By applying cross-commodity data to import and export equations, the desired price elasticities may be estimated. Shinkai's results for imports based on cross-commodity data for another period, 1965-68, are not included in this volume, but are available elsewhere.[9] The estimation is made for finished goods, crude materials and intermediate goods, and total commodities, respectively. In this study he reached interesting conclusions: the export price elasticity is numerically larger for finished goods than crude materials and intermediate goods. Both tend to increase over time. The increase in the price elasticity very likely reflects the progressive trade liberalization in Japan. Problems of bias are not avoided completely in cross-section studies. The author presents a detailed analysis of the dangers of bias arising from the use of unit values, and the use of quantity data with errors of measurement.

Amano has set forth in his study a medium size, macroeconometric model with an emphasis on the balance of payments sector. The model places emphasis on the mutual interrelationships between the balance of payment sector and rest of the economy. That is, unlike ordinary macroeconometric models which treat mainly the influences of a change in the domestic economy upon the balance of payments situation, Amano's model has made it possible to know the effect of the changed balance of payment situation upon the domestic economy. In other words, calculation of the dynamic multipliers and simulation tests, with the balance of payments adjustment, can be made.

An an example of the above point, Amano develops an equation which shows that the official discount rate depends upon, *inter alia*, foreign exchange reserves during the period of his study. The official discount rate is assumed by the author to have been adjusted by government officials so as to maintain the external balance. The official discount rate policy has played a central role in the Japanese economy during the observation period of 1961-67. A slack in economic activity in the rest of the world, for instance, will reduce Japan's exports, deteriorate the current account balance, and cause an outflow of international reserves. A raise of the official discount rate will then be induced. This will raise the market rate of interest, depress the domestic aggregate demand, decrease the imports, and finally terminate the drain of international reserves.

Two major conclusions have been obtained by the author by means of simulation tests. First, the external equilibrium is restored in five to nine quarters with the official discount rate policy after the occurrence of an autonomous disturbance. And second, the level of dynamic multipliers is much smaller with the balance of payments adjustment mechanism. This signifies that macromodels disregarding this mechanism tend to overestimate the multiplier effect.

Chenery, Shishido, and Watanabe, in their study of economic growth, examine changes in the pattern of Japanese industrialization. Their method is to derive and to examine deviations from the "normal" pattern of industrialization, and may be divided into two types of studies. In the first type of study, which is an extension of the earlier studies by Chenery and the United Nations' group, the normal pattern of industrialization is taken as the "standard" pattern of industrialization being observed internationally during recent years.[10] Specifically, the authors estimate a relationship in which output of a particular commodity is made to depend upon per-capita income and population. The relationship is estimated from a cross section of national economies. Next, they substitute the values for per-capita income and population for Japan and obtained predicted or standard levels for commodities which may then be compared to the actual levels.

In the second type of study, comprising the main body of their paper, they assume a "proportional" or balanced expansion, which means that output, domestic demand, exports, and imports increase at the same rate. Any difference between the actual level of output and the estimated level which would be attained under the proportional expansion is called the deviation is decomposed into four deviations: deviations in domestic demand, in exports, in imports, and in residuals (technological progress). They calculuate these deviations for the period 1914-54 and appraise their relative importance.

In a recent study, Watanabe extended these studies to intervening years and to a later period.[11] His principal conclusions were that the Japanese pattern of industrialization did not change significantly between 1914 and 1935, but did reveal a spurt in heavy industry between 1935 and 1954. Technological progress was an important source of later deviations, explaining over one-third of the difference between observed and predicted values.

It is possible that prediction of future economic events and efforts to gauge the consequences of public policies on these events create more interest in Japan than elsewhere. This may explain, in part, why quantitative modeling of the Japanese economy has been so active an area of research during the past 25 years, with rapid development under the aegis of both public and private enterprises. We have selected the studies of four model-building groups because they seemed to us significant examples of models constructed for different purposes. They also reveal the fast pace of development as more detailed data became available. Quantitative or econometric model building is a continuing process, so that models remain in a constant state of alteration and extension. Nevertheless, later efforts build on earlier, and it is of great interest to have the benchmarks clearly on record. It is equally important to note that further experiments in the form of policy simulations or re-estimation of relationships are possible with earlier versions of econometric models. It was with these ends in view that we chose the four examples included in this book.

The first study by Klein and Shinkai is a pioneering work in this field. A major feature of their model is the emphasis placed on determinants of effective demand, although supply side considerations are not ignored and find expression in production and employment relationships in agricultural and nonagricultural sectors. The authors estimated their model on the basis of annual data available to them for the periods 1930-36 and 1951-58, data which we have reproduced in the appendix to their paper, although substantial revisions have occurred (and are occurring).[12] We include these data, as they could be of value to readers interested in evaluating the effects of alternative estimators and they do provide the basis for replication of parameter estimates, a desirable feature for every econometric study. The model remains, then, as a point of departure for later studies, and we shall refer to it in making some general comparisions at a later point.

In comparision with Klein and Shinkai model, the Ueno

model is a neoclassical one which focuses on the production or supply side of the economy. That is, his model is characterized by a production function with substitutability between labor and capital. The savings function determines the supply of capital stock. This feature of the model is a necessary consequence of the purpose of this study to forecast the potentiality of economic growth in the future. For this purpose, however, a simple one-sector model is not appropriate and sectoral division is necessary, because the growth potential depends upon, to a great extent, the structural changes in the Japanese economy. Because of data limitations, a sectoral division as is made in the neoclassical theory of economic growth (the consumption goods sector and the capital goods sector) is impossible. Therefore, Ueno proposes a division into primary and nonprimary sectors.

In such a two-sector model, special attention should be paid to the relationships between the two sectors. Allocation of labor force between the sectors depends upon the relative wages and the share of production. The first explanatory variable is introduced to capture the behavior of labor supply whereas the second variable is introduced to reflect the demand for labor in the two sectors. Private fixed investment in the nonprimary sector is determined by the investment function whereas the primary investment is given as a residual of the total private investment. No competitiveness is assumed between the two sectors in this market. Price indexes for the two sectors are determined independently of each other in the two respective price determination functions. This signifies the nonexistence of substitutability between the two products, unlike the ordinary theory of prices based on the competitive output market. Conclusively, the connection between the two sectors lies solely in the labor market in this model.

The two short-term econometric models which end this series of econometric studies were selected because of their special relation to the five-year plans of 1964-68 and 1967-71, and because of their significance in the continuing process of econometric model building in Japan. It is of great interest to note which features of the models have changed and which have not. Some of the reasons for changes throw light not only on the field of econometric model building but also on the policy preoccupations of the time. All these models were developed with much attention paid to the specification of policy instruments and to the policy uses of econometric models. Interest in the models before us need not be diminished by the knowledge that later, extended models will have been developed.[13]

Additional information on the background of these models will bear on these point. The Klein-Shinkai model (annual model), published early in 1962, was based on available annual data for intervals during the period 1930-59. They note several apparent structural shifts in relationships when comparing the prewar with the postwar periods, but the scarcity of observations in the latter period dictated their sample period decision. The Tatemoto-Uchida-Watanabe model (semiannual model), published about two years later, made use of six-month or semiannual data for the period 1954-62, a period during which rapid progress was made in the development of social accounting data by the Economic Planning Agency. The use of semiannual data made available extra observations and was not an artificial sectioning of time. This step in disaggregation over time was supported by the fact that the accounting period and to some extent the decision period for many Japanese enterprises is on a six-month basis (it may be noted that dummy variables representing the first and second half of the fiscal year - April to the following March - were introduced with significant results in several relationships). The Shishido-Kohno-Nagaya-Tanaka model (quarterly model) published about two years later, made use of the major revision of the national income and product accounts in 1966, which provided more quarterly data on a conceptual basis closer to that of other industrialized economies. What emerges clearly is the strong interaction between the swift pace of model development and the provision of more disaggregated social accounting data.

The policy problems being posed to model builders were another major theme during this period. The authors of the semiannual model conceived of their work as providing a consistent basis for the 1964-68 plan, the medium-term economic plan formulated by the Economic Planning Agency. This was the first of the well-known economic plans for the Japanese economy to be based upon projections of an econometric model, the prior plans having been developed from either unintegrated supply-type relationships or labor-force growth equations.[14]

The space the authors devote to an examination of the predictive accuracy of their model, both with respect to forecasts into future periods and with respect to simulating the sample period after starting up the model with lagged endogenous variables, testifies to their policy preoccupation.

The second of the short-term models is reported by the authors to have provided the basis for a "standard simulation" mostly based on the exogenous variables used for the 1967-71 plan, the economic and social development plan. Consequently, we are now considering the second econometric model to serve as a basis for an economic plan. An essential prerequisite was the publication of a significant body of quarterly time series data. Such revised, detailed data called for re-estimation and revision of econometric relationships. The slackening in the rate of growth of output in 1965 may also have given additional impetus to the elaboration of econometric models, with added emphasis on demand side factors such as will be found in the quarterly model.

Both groups of authors describe in detail their efforts to obtain estimates of parameters of their models with desirable properties. They also have been occupied with methods of practical solution of their systems, a problem due in part to complicating nonlinearities. They have also devoted more space than is customary to tests of the predictive performance of their models. These characteristics may be traced to the evident concern expressed by the authors that their models provide a plausible framework for simulation of policy decision. As an introduction to their work we have chosen to discuss and compare several of the central structural specifications of the models.

The consumption functions contain lagged consumption terms, a feature which seems essential if consumer behavior under conditions of rapid economic growth is to be appropriately represented. Such a specification is consistent with ideas about the importance of normal or permanent income, but also consistent with ideas about lags in the development of new consumption habits. The authors of the quarterly model introduce the distribution of income by distinguishing wage and salary income from property income, and they obtain a significantly lower marginal propensity to consume in the latter.

As high household saving rates have been frequently cited as one of the sources of economic growth in Japan, it is of interest to examine the implications of the estimates for these rates. We believe it is important to include a "normal" growth rate of about 10 percent in estimating the long-run marginal propensity to consume from relations with income and lagged consumption. Proceeding in this way we obtain the results shown in Table 1 based on the estimates of our authors together with the estimates of the other models discussed earlier (but excluding the long-run growth model). These estimates do indicate low consumption rates.

TABLE 1

ESTIMATES OF THE MARGINAL PROPENSITY TO CONSUME

Model	Short-run marginal propensity to consume	Long-run marginal propensity to consume
Annual model	.23	.50
Semiannual model	n.c.	.66
Quarterly model	.39	.71

(n.c. = not calculated)

The authors of the annual model believe their use of per-capita data to have lowered their estimate of the marginal propensity to consume. In their model, a general price level index was used as a deflator for consumption, which may also have tended to lower their estimate.

As more disaggregated data become available, we may look forward to estimation of consumption relations for finer and finer categories of commodities. The rapid diffusion of television sets, washing machines, and refrigerators among other durables in households during the 1960s makes up an interesting chapter in the history of consumer expenditure events, and it will be of considerable interest to study these more detailed consumption functions from a comparative point of view.

In both the annual and semiannual models, the authors concentrate on the availability of funds in the specification of the investment function. Investment expenditures are made to depend positively on profits and negatively, and significantly, upon an interest rate variable; these results appear consistent with characteristics of the Japanese capital market. Stocks and bonds are less frequently used as a source of financing, throwing the burden upon retained earnings and, to a greater extent than in other capitalistic economies, upon bank credit. During the immediate postwar years, changes in these latter sources explained a good part of the dynamics of the investment process. The cost of funds approach, however, required some modification in the 1960s, as output or sales variables emerged into more significant factors. The slackening of the rate of growth of output in 1965 may have signaled the new era. The developers of the quarterly model extended the investment function in a way that is consistent with the flexible accelerator approach as well as the capacity form of the investment function.

The lag structure of the quarterly model appears to imply a shorter appropriation (corporate decision-making process) and implementation process than found in the United States. It is likely, however, that further work on the appropriate lag structure will yield new and interesting results. It seems to us that it is possible for the appropriation process to be longer in Japan than in the United States, while the implementation process is shorter. In any case, the appropriate lag structure may require a larger weight to be given to output or sales of several quarters back rather than one-quarter back.

A comprehensive econometric model provides an explanation of the balance of payments. The models under consideration provide building blocks toward this goal and throw considerable light on current questions about the magnitudes of international price and income elasticities. Elasticity values calculated from parameters of the models are reproduced below, together with recent estimates for Japan by Professors Houthakker and Magee obtained by a different but not contradictory method for the sample period 1951-66.[15] Several comments are required before interpreting the table of elasticities. The price elasticities are given as absolute values and exhibit marked variation among the studies, a research result also reported in other studies. It is likely that the appropriate lag structure for price elasticities for Japanese imports and exports has yet to be discovered.

With respect to income elasticities, in Table 2 it may

TABLE 2
BALANCE OF TRADE ELASTICITIES

	Imports (to Japan)		Exports (from Japan)	
	Income	Price	Income	Price
Annual model			1.07	1.36
Semiannual model			1.77	1.52
Quarterly model	1.07	.23	1.87	.30
Houthakker/Magee	1.23	.72	3.55	.80

be noted on the import side that the quarterly model contains a term for inventories as well as income (output). Consequently, the elasticity coefficient 1.07 will be further increased via an inventory effect. The quarterly model estimate is thus brought closer to the Houthakker-Magee estimate. The short-term models utilize an index of world exports as the income measure on the Japanese export side. The Houthakker-Magee study utilizes an index of income of major importing economies. As the former increased about twice as rapidly as the latter during the sample period, the elasticity estimates are brought closer together if an adjustment is made. Assuming price elasticities of demand for imports and exports to be roughly equal, it may be concluded from these income elasticity results that the Japanese economy has grown and may grow more rapidly than the average of other major trading economies without experiencing undue balance of payments difficulties.

Technological change as a source of economic growth has been the special subject of several studies in this volume. The quarterly model contains a production function fitted with a significant time trend that yields a quantitative estimate of a 4 percent increase in output annually. This growth may be attributed to neutral, disembodied technological change, and is within a tolerable range of the results in the other studies in this volume. This agreement on the quantitatitive importance of technical change does not yet provide an adequate explanation of the determinants of the rate of such change. It would appear to be a matter of great importance to investigate further the allocation of resources to technical innovations and the transfer of technology, and the rates of return to such allocations.

In considering the use of these short-term models for stabilization purposes, it will be of interest to point out the specification of various policy instruments and the estimation of associated multipliers. In the semiannual model, government expenditures and tax receipts are introduced into identity equations and remain autonomous, except for three tax equations. The interest rate on bank loans appears with negative, highly significant signs in the investment equations. The authors of the semiannual model develop this relationship further in the direction of specifying policy instruments under the control of the Bank of Japan by relating the market interest rate to the rediscount rate. The rediscount rate is revealed to be significant. This result is consistent with the information that the Bank of Japan did, in fact, manipulate this policy instrument during the sample period (and did not engage significantly in measures such as open market operations or reserve requirement changes). The authors remark at the close of their study that further work on the government sector is called for in classifying expenditure and receipt components as induced or autonomous so that more precision can be obtained in studying the stabilization implications of particular government measures.

The authors of the quarterly model carry further the specification of government policy instruments, although it should be noted that data for all relevant items were not available on a quarterly basis. Variables such as a customs (duty) ratio for imported commodities are introduced to provide information on changes in a wider variety of policy measures. A major section is devoted to simulation of the model under maintained changes in selected instruments. For dynamic, nonlinear models, these multipliers can vary depending upon initial values of variables such as employment. The authors first calculate a "control solution" based on exogenous variables used for the 1967-71 plan. The multiplier effects were then evaluated by varying policy instruments and comparing the time paths of endogenous variables to the control solutions, as appraisal of these results must be couched in terms of the time profile or path of endogenous variables. The multiplier of government expenditures assumes larger values than the multiplier of transfer payments during initial periods, but this quantitative importance is reversed for later periods, a result due to the slow but continuous rise in consumption. An aspect of monetary policy is captured by tracing the time path effect on endogenous variables of a measured change in the interest rate on bank loans. The authors report a sensitive response of investment to interest rate increases with effects building up for eight quarters. These results enable the authors to detect in the tight money policies of early 1964 an important source of the slackening of the rate of growth in 1965, a slackening which was not offset by fiscal policies. The editors would like to end their remarks by noting that simulations with the quarterly model ten years later reveal in late 1974 and early 1975 remarkably similar consequences of monetary and fiscal policy upon the Japanese economy.

Notes

1. We should like to record at this point that the editors had originally intended to include studies of their own, but to reduce the size of the projected volume these were eliminated. As references have been made in other places to the fact that our studies would be available in this book, we should like to note where they have been published. The studies are available as follows: Richard Kosobud, "Measured Productivity Growth in Japan, 1952-1968," Japanese Economic Studies, Vol. II, No. 3 (Spring 1974), pp. 80-118, and Ryoshin Minami and A. Ono, Japanese Economic Studies, in press.

2. A good example of the increased attention being given to studies of the welfare appraisal of economic growth may be found in the phamphlet Measuring Net National Welfare of Japan, Report of the Net National Welfare Measurement Committee of the Economic Council of Japan (Tokyo: Ministry of Finance, 1974).

3. S. Ichimura and M. Tatemoto, Nippon Keizai no Keiryō Bunseki [Quantitative Studies of the Japanese Economy] (Tokyo: Tōyō Keizai Shinpō Sha [Oriental Economist], 1970).

4. K. Ohkawa, B. F. Johnston, and H. Kaneda, Agriculture and Growth: Japan's Experience (Tokyo: University of Tokyo Press, 1969).

5. A recent study on Japan which adopts a critical view toward interpreting the residual as technological progress is D. Jorgenson and H. Ezaki, "Measurement of Aggregate Productivity Change" (in Japanese) in K. Ohkawa and Y. Hayami, ed., Long-Terms Analysis of the Japanese Economy (Tokyo: Nikkei Newspaper Company, 1973), pp. 87-127. Further references may be found in R. Kosobud, "Measured Productivity Growth," Japanese Economic Studies, pp. 116-118.

6. Tuvia Blumenthal, "The Effect of Socio-Economic Factors on Wage Differentials in Japanese Manufacturing Industries," Kikan Riron Keizai Gaku [Economic Studies Quarterly], Vol. XVII, No. 1 (Sept. 1966), pp. 52-67.

7. E.g., Ryoshin Minami has asserted that the Lewisian turning point had been passed at the beginning of the 1960s in a study entitled "The Turning Point in the Japanese Economy," Quarterly Journal of Economics, Vol. LXXXII, No. 3 (Aug. 1968), pp. 380-402. More detailed analysis is in R. Minami, The Turning Point in Economic Development: Japan's Experience (Tokyo: Kinokuniya Shoten, 1973).

8. The export and import functions estimated in this paper will be used to explain the external sector of a big macro-econometric model. Additional studies on capital and service transactions are required to close the balance of payments. The following paper is a step in the direction of a comprehensive study of all items of external transactions: Masahiro Tatemoto and Akira Yajima, "Macro-Model ni okeru Kaigai Sector" [External Sector in the Macro-Model] in M. Tatemoto, ed., Kokusai Bōeki no Keiryō Bunseki [Quantitative Analysis of International Trade] (Tokyo: Nippon Keigai Shinbun Sha, 1969), pp. 9-61.

9. Yoichi Shinkai, "Elasticities of Substitution for the Japanese Imports," Review of Economics and Statistics, Vol. LIV, No. 2 (May 1972), pp. 198-202.

10. H. G. Chenery, "Patterns of Industrial Growth," American Economic Review, Vo. L, No. 4 (Sept. 1960), pp. 624-654.

Also, United Nations, Department of Economic and Social Affairs, A Study of Industrial Growth (New York: United Nations, 1963).

11. T. Watanabe, Sūryō Keizai Bunseki [Quantitative Economic Analysis] (Tokyo: Sōbun Sha, 1970), Chapter 2.

12. For example, estimates of national income and capital stock series for prewar years have been published in volume 1 and volume 3, respectively, of the Estimates of Long-Term Economic Statistics of Japan since 1968 (Tokyo: Tōyō Keizai Shinpō Sha, 1974 and 1966). These series for the post-war years have been prepared by the Economic Planning Agency. A basic revision of national income data was carried out in 1966 and is in process in 1975. These statistics were not available when Klein and Shinkai estimated their model.

13. The reader interested in related developments closely tied to our included studies is referred to the report by the Committee on Econometric Methods (advisory committee to the Economic Planning Agency in the Prime Minister's office): "Econometric Models for Basic Economic and Social Plan 1973-1977," Economic Planning Agency, government of Japan, July, 1973. This plan is currently under extensive revision.

14. We should note at this point that a lively controversy exists over whether these plans really constitute economic planning, or forecasts, or government intentions, or something else. This is another story to be told at another time.

15. H. S. Houthakker and Stephen P. Magee, "Income and Price Elasticities in World Trade," Review of Economics and Statistics, Vol. LI, No. 2 (May 1969), pp. 111-125.

Part I
Studies of Consumer and Investment Demand

1

The Application of Alternative Demand Models to the Japanese Expenditure Pattern

Kunio Yoshihara

Demand studies may be classified into two broad categories. One group of studies is concerned with finding a model to explain the relationships among the quantity consumed of a single commodity, its price, the prices of related commodities, and total income. Such a demand model is considered in some of those studies as a part of a system of demand functions, and hypotheses are tested to determine whether theoretical properties such as homogeneity of degree zero in prices and income are fulfilled. The other group of demand studies is concerned with the problem of allocating total expenditure to an exhaustive set of different commodities. These studies usually assume that the problem of deciding how much to consume at any given time point has been solved, and concentrate on the problem of allocation. In this paper we shall be concerned not with demand models for a single commodity, but with demand models to explain the allocation problem of a rational consumer.

In this paper we first investigate the theoretical properties of four models, and then their ability to explain the expenditure pattern in Japan over the period 1905-1965 (see Appendix for the sources of data). The parameters of the models considered in this study are assumed to be stable over the period. Therefore, when a model is derived from a utility function, it is assumed that the structure of preference is stable. Objections could be raised to this assumption when we investigate such a long-term series of data: new commodities are being produced almost every year, and it might be unnatural to assume that this does not have any impact on the preference structure. In order to account for change in preferences, R. Stone introduced a time trend in the parameters[1] whereas H. Houthakker and L. Taylor, and K. Tsujimura [2] introduced a habit formation variable. If the assumption that the parameters remain unchanged throughout the period is one extreme, the assumption that the parameters change every year seems to be the other. We grouped commodities into five categories: Food, Clothing, Housing, Fuel and Light, and Miscellaneous, and assumed that the parameters determining the choice among these groups did not change. If we were considering individual commodities, our assumption would be untenable, but when the grouping is as broad as ours, the assumption might be justified. The stability question is certainly important and should be investigated, but this task is not undertaken in this paper.

I. Alternative Demand Models

The models we shall consider in this paper are (a) the double log, (b) the Rotterdam, (c) the linear expenditure, and (d) the indirect addilog models.

The Double Log Model

$$(1.1) \quad x_i = A_i y^{a_{i0}} \prod_{j=1}^{m} p_j^{a_{ij}} \qquad i = 1, m.$$

where x_i the quantity of the ith commodity demanded, y = total expenditure, and p_j = the price of the jth good. In a logarithmic form (1.1) becomes

$$(1.1') \quad \log x_i = c_i + a_{i0} \log y + \sum_{j=1}^{m} a_{ij} \log p_j \qquad i = 1, m,$$

and the dependent and independent variables are log transformed.[3] This is the reason for calling (1.1) the double logarithmic, or double log, model.

The Rotterdam Model[4]

$$(1.2) \quad \underline{w}_i \underline{d}(\log \underline{x}_i) = \underline{B}_i(\underline{d}(\log \underline{y}) - \sum_{\underline{k}=1}^{\underline{m}} \underline{w}_k \underline{d}(\log \underline{p}_k)) + \sum_{\underline{j}=1}^{\underline{m}} \underline{C}_{ij}(\underline{d}(\log \underline{p}_j) - \sum_{\underline{k}=1}^{\underline{m}} \underline{B}_k \underline{d}(\log \underline{p}_k)) \qquad i = 1, m.$$

$\underline{w}_i = \underline{p}_i \underline{x}_i / \underline{y}$, $\underline{d}(\log \underline{x}_i)$ = the change of $\log \underline{x}_i$, $\underline{d}(\log \underline{y})$ and $\underline{d}(\log \underline{p}_j)$ are similarly defined. $\underline{B}_i$ and $\underline{C}_{ij}$ are constants satisfying

$$(1.2^*) \quad \underline{C}_{ji} = \underline{C}_{ij}$$

$$(1.2^{**}) \quad \sum_{\underline{i}=1}^{\underline{m}} \underline{B}_i = 1$$

$$(1.2^{***}) \quad \sum_{\underline{j}=1}^{\underline{m}} \underline{C}_{ij} = \psi \underline{B}_i$$

where $\psi = \frac{(\partial \log \underline{y})}{(\partial \log \lambda)}$, and λ = the Lagrangian multiplier.

By using condition (1.2***) the model can be rewritten as

$$(1.2') \quad \underline{w}_i \underline{d}(\log \underline{x}_i) = \underline{B}_i(\underline{d}(\log \underline{y}) - \sum (\underline{w}_k + \psi \underline{B}_k)\underline{d}(\log \underline{p}_k)) + \sum \underline{C}_{ij}\, \underline{d}(\log \underline{p}_j).$$

Since $\sum (\underline{w}_k + \psi \underline{B}_k)\, \underline{d}(\log \underline{p}_k)$ can be considered as the log change in some appropriate price index, the first term can be interpreted as the log change in real income. Thus, the Rotterdam model explains the log change in quantity consumed multiplied by its share in terms of the log change of real income and individual price indexes.

Since the model was developed by H. Theil and A. Barten at the Econometric Institute in Rotterdam, we shall call (1.2) the Rotterdam model.

The Linear Expenditure Model[5]

$$(1.3) \quad \underline{p}_i \underline{x}_i = \underline{p}_i \underline{c}_i + \underline{b}_i(\underline{y} - \sum_{\underline{j}=1}^{\underline{m}} \underline{p}_j \underline{c}_j) \qquad \underline{i} = 1, \underline{m}.$$

First, we notice that the expenditure on the ith commodity is a linear function of p_i and y, which is the reason for calling (1.3) the linear expenditure model.

This model has the following interpretation. The expenditure on the ith commodity is equal to a certain basic amount of consumption, c_i, valued at current prices plus a certain proportion, b_i, of total expenditure less total basic commitment. The consumer uses up a certain amount of total expenditure in acquiring the consumption vector $c = (c_1, \ldots, c_m)$ at current prices, and then distributes the remainder over the set of available commodities in a certain fixed proportion given by the elements of $b = (b_1, \ldots, b_m)$.

Since $\sum p_i x_i$ should be equal to y, the following constraint is imposed on the parameters:

$$\sum p_i x_i = \sum p_i c_i + y \sum b_i - \sum p_j c_j \sum b_i \; .$$

The condition $\sum p_i x_i = y$ is met when

$$(1.3^*) \qquad \sum b_i = 1.$$

The Indirect Addilog Model[6]

$$(1.4) \quad x_i = \frac{a_i (y/p_i)^{b_i+1}}{\sum_{j=1}^{m} a_j (y/p_j)^{b_j}} \qquad i = 1, m.$$

Unlike the preceding two models, there is no linear constraint on the parameters a_i and b_i. Because the model is based on the indirect utility function, which is additive in logarithms, the model is called the indirect addilog model.

We judge the above four models by their ability to explain the dependent variables, but we shall postpone this discussion to a later section. In the remainder of this section we shall examine the theoretical merits of each model.

A model might be considered theoretically satisfactory if the following conditions are satisfied:

(i) the adding-up conditions: $y = \sum_{i=1}^{m} p_i x_i$,

(ii) the homogeneity condition: $x_i = x_i(\lambda p_j, \lambda y)$,

(iii) the Slutsky condition: $\frac{\partial x_i}{\partial p_j} + x_j \frac{\partial x_i}{\partial y} = \frac{\partial x_j}{\partial p_i} + x_i \frac{\partial x_j}{\partial y}$.

All these conditions are satisfied by a demand model derived from a utility function.[7]

We might want to introduce another condition which a theoretically satisfactory demand function must satisfy:

(iv) $\frac{\partial x_i}{\partial y} \frac{y}{x_i} \neq 1$ for some i.

If income elasticity is one for all i, the proportion of expenditure on different goods in the total remains the same when the relative prices do not change. The change in expenditure shares might not provide a complete justification for introducing the fourth condition, since the change might be caused by the change in relative prices. But since the expenditure pattern is more likely to change when a consumer is presented with rising income and constant prices, it appears reasonable to introduce the above condition.

Then, the question of whether a model satisfies all four conditions simultaneously becomes equivalent to the problem of whether we can integrate the system of demand equations back to a nonhomogeneous utility function. That is, if we can obtain a corresponding utility function which is nonhomogeneous, the four conditions are satisfied, and the model is theoretically satisfactory: if we can not, they are not satisfied and the model is unsatisfactory.

We should explain briefly the relation between income elasticities and nonhomogeneity. This relation is given by the following theorem.

Ville's theorem: $\frac{\partial x_i}{\partial y} \frac{y}{x_i} = 1$ for all i is necessary and sufficient for the utility function to be homogeneous.[8] According to this theorem, the utility function which satisfies the fourth condition must be nonhomogeneous.

First, let us consider the double log model. We can easily verify that the Slutsky condition is not satisfied without introducing constraints on the parameters. Therefore, we cannot find a utility function leading to the double log model, since the Slutsky condition is necessary for integrability.

We might want to introduct the following constraints:

(1.1.a) $a_{i0} = 1$ $\quad i = 1, m$

(1.1.b) $a_{ii} = -1$ $\quad i = 1, m$

(1.1.c) $a_{ij} = 0$ $\quad j \neq i.$

Then the model becomes

$$(1.5) \quad p_i x_i = A_i y.$$

If we impose the constraint $\sum_{i=1}^{m} A_i = 1$, model (1.5) satisfies the first three conditions. If we integrate (1.5) back to a utility function, we obtain

$$(1.6) \quad u = \prod x_i^{A_i} .$$

But since income elasticity based on (1.5) is 1 for all i, as expected from Ville's theorem, (1.6) is a homogeneous function. Thus, model (1.5) must be judged theoretically unsatisfactory.

Constraints (1.1.a) - (1.1.c) might be too restrictive. But no matter what constraints are imposed on a_{ij} to meet the Slutsky condition, the resulting utility function must be homogeneous. This can be seen as follows. By differentiating the adding up condition, we obtain

$$(1.7) \quad 0 = \sum p_i x_i (1 - a_{i0}).$$

We restrict the values of p_i, x_i, and y to positive values. (1.1) can be written as

$$(p_i x_i / y) = (A_i \prod_{j=1}^{m} p_j^{a_{ij}} \, p_i) y^{a_{i0}-1}$$

Suppose $a_{i0} > 1$ for some i. Then, $(p_i x_i / y)$ goes to infinity as y goes to infinity. Therefore, $(p_i x_i / y)$ is greater than one for $y > y_0$, where y_0 is the level of total expenditure at which $\sum p_i x_i = y_0$. Thus, if a_{i0} is greater than 1 for even one commodity, the adding up condition is violated. Therefore, $a_{i0} < 1$ for all i. But a_{i0} cannot be less than 1 because of (1.7). Thus, $a_{i0} = 1$ for all i. But if $a_{i0} = 1$ for all i, income elasticity is 1 for all i. Thus, no matter what other constraints might be, the resulting utility function must be homogeneous.

The Rotterdam model also contains theoretical defects, in spite of the elaborate steps leading to the functional forms specified in the model.

It was shown that the model reduces, using (1.2***), to a system of partial differential equations[9]

$$(1.8) \quad \frac{\partial x_i}{\partial y} = \frac{B_i}{p_i} \qquad i = 1, m$$

$$(1.9) \quad \frac{\partial x_i}{\partial p_j} = -\frac{B_i x_j}{p_i} + [C_{ij} - \psi B_i B_j]\frac{y}{p_j} \qquad i,j = 1, m.$$

The solution of (1.8) must be of the functional form

$$x_i = B_i \frac{y}{p_i} + b_i(p_1, \ldots, p_m) \qquad i = 1, m.$$

If the model is good for all positive values of income and prices, b_i must be zero since x_i goes to 0 as y goes to 0. Then the resulting demand system is

$$(1.5) \quad x_i = \frac{B_i y}{p_i} \qquad i = 1, m.$$

That is, the Rotterdam model reduces to a special case of the double log model. Therefore, the Rotterdam model is theoretically unsatisfactory, and it might be best considered as a model of approximation.

The last two models, the linear expenditure and the indirect addilog models, have a corresponding utility function. The linear expenditure model was first derived from a general linear function with the first three conditions imposed, but later it was found that its corresponding utility function[10] is

$$(1.10) \quad u = \prod_{i=1}^{m} (x_i - c_i)^{b_i}.$$

As long as not all c_i are 0, u is not homogeneous, and the fourth condition is also satisfied.

Unlike the linear expenditure model, the indirect addilog model was derived directly from a particular form of utility function[11] in the form of indirect utility function,

$$(1.11) \quad u = \sum_{i=1}^{m} \left(\frac{a_i}{b_i}\right)\left(\frac{y}{p_i}\right)^{b_i}$$

The demand model was obtained by using Roy's theorem:[12]

$$(1.12) \quad x_i = -\frac{\frac{\partial u}{\partial p_i}}{\frac{\partial u}{\partial y}} \qquad i = 1, m.$$

Although the utility function from which the demand model was obtained is in the form of indirect utitlity, the first three conditions are satisfied.[13] Because (1.11) is the indirect utility function, we cannot verify directly whether the direct utility function is nonhomogeneous, for the transformation from the indirect function to the direct function is not simple. We can, however, check income elasticity and use Ville's theorem to determine whether the direct utility function is homogeneous.

By differentiating x_i with respect to y, we obtain

$$\frac{\partial x_i}{\partial y} = \frac{1}{y}\left[x_i + b_i x_i - x_i \frac{\sum b_j a_j \left(\frac{y}{p_j}\right)^{b_j}}{\sum a_j \left(\frac{y}{p_j}\right)^{b_j}}\right]$$

Then

$$\frac{\partial x_i}{\partial y}\frac{y}{x_i} = (1 + b_i - \sum w_i b_i),$$

where $w_i = \frac{p_i x_i}{y}$.

$\frac{\partial x_i}{\partial y}\frac{y}{x_i} = 1$ for all i only if $b_i = \sum b_j w_j$, but there is no reason to expect this condition to hold in general. Thus, income elasticities are not necessarily 1 for all i, which implies that the direct utility function is nonhomogeneous.

We can summarize the theoretical desirability of the four

models as follows. The double log and the Rotterdam models are not derived from a utility function, whereas the linear expenditure and the indirect addilog models have a correspondent nonhomogeneous utility function. If we judge a model as theoretically satisfactory when it is derived from a nonhomogeneous function, we must conclude that the last two models are theoretically satisfactory, whereas the first two are not. The first two models can be considered as models of approximation.

II. Estimation

The Double Log Model

A statistical model for the double log system is based on (1.1'):

$$(1.13)\quad \log \underline{x}_{it} = \underline{c}_i + \underline{a}_{i0} \log \underline{y}_t + \sum_{\underline{j}=1}^{m} \underline{a}_{ij} \log \underline{p}_{jt} + \underline{u}_{it}$$

$$\underline{i} = 1, \underline{m};\quad \underline{t} = 1, \underline{T}.$$

The $\underline{u}_{it}$ are introduced to represent the effect of random factors affecting the demand system. When we estimate the parameters of a model from time series data, it often happens that there is some degree of dependence among the successive errors $\underline{u}_{it}$, $\underline{u}_{it+1}$, ... The errors express the effect of factors of which no explicit account is taken in the model, either because they cannot be observed independently, or because individually they are not very important. For most economic quantities, the evaluation of these factors often manifest more regularity than a purely random series. If their effect $\underline{u}_{it}$ is positive for the $\underline{t}$th observation, then $\underline{u}_{it+1}$ tends to be positive. We assume in this study that the process of $\underline{u}_{it}$ can be approximated by

$$\underline{u}_{it} = \rho_{\underline{i}} \underline{u}_{it-1} + \underline{v}_{it},$$

where

(a) $0 < \rho_{\underline{i}} < 1$

(b) $\underline{E}(\underline{v}_{it}) = 0$ $\qquad \underline{i} = 1, \underline{m}$; $\underline{t} = 1, \underline{T}$

(c) $\underline{v}_t$ and $\underline{v}_\theta$ are stochastically independent whenever $\underline{t} \neq \theta$

(d) $\underline{V}(\underline{v}_t) = \Omega$

When the value of $\rho_{\underline{i}}$ is known, the model can be transformed to

$$(1.14)\quad (\log \underline{x}_{it} - \rho_i \log \underline{x}_{it-1})$$
$$= \underline{c}_i(1 - \rho_i) + \underline{a}_{i0}(\log \underline{y}_t - \rho_i \log \underline{y}_{t-1})$$
$$+ \sum_{j=1}^{\overline{m}} \underline{a}_{ij}(\log \underline{p}_{jt} - \rho_i \log \underline{p}_{jt-1}) + \underline{v}_{it}\,,$$

where the $\underline{v}_{it}$ satisfy the last three assumptions.

If errors $\underline{v}_{it}$ and $\underline{v}_{kt}$ relating two different commodities in the same period are independent, that is, $\Omega = \underline{I}$, it is almost obvious that the different equations of the model are independent among themselves, and that the parameters of each equation must be estimated equation by equation. But since not all factors affecting the consumer's allocation decision can be taken into account in the model, those missing factors can affect the consumer's decision in a systematic fashion and give rise to the dependence between errors $\underline{v}_{it}$ and $\underline{v}_{kt}$ relating to the same period.

The contemporaneous covariance matrix Ω represents new problems to the estimation of the parameters. If we let

$$\underline{y}_i = \begin{bmatrix} \log \underline{x}_{i2} - \rho_i \log \underline{x}_{i1} \\ \cdot \\ \cdot \\ \cdot \\ \log \underline{x}_{iT} - \rho_i \log \underline{x}_{iT-1} \end{bmatrix}, \quad \alpha_i = \begin{bmatrix} \underline{c}_i \\ \underline{a}_{i0} \\ \underline{a}_{i1} \\ \cdot \\ \cdot \\ \cdot \\ \underline{a}_{im} \end{bmatrix}, \quad \underline{v}_i = \begin{bmatrix} \underline{v}_{i2} \\ \cdot \\ \cdot \\ \cdot \\ \underline{v}_{iT} \end{bmatrix}, \text{ and}$$

$$\underline{X}_i = \begin{bmatrix} 1 - \rho_i, \ \log y_2 - \rho_i \log y_1, \ \log p_{12} - \rho_i \log p_{11}, \ \ldots, \ \log p_{m2} - \rho_i \log p_{m1} \\ \cdot \\ \cdot \\ \cdot \\ 1 - \rho_i, \ \log y_T - \rho_i \log y_{T-1}, \ \log p_{1T} - \rho_i \log p_{1T-1}, \ \ldots, \ \log p_{mT} - \rho_i \log p_{mT-1} \end{bmatrix}$$

model (1.14) can be written as

$$(1.15) \qquad y_i = X_i\alpha_i + v_i \qquad i = 1, m.$$

The trouble is that

$$(1.16) \qquad \hat{\alpha}_i = (X_i'X_i')^{-1} X_i y_i \qquad i = 1, m$$

is not the unbiased minimum variance estimator.

If we let

$$\alpha = \begin{bmatrix} \hat{\alpha_{11}} \\ \vdots \\ \alpha_{1m^*} \\ \vdots \\ \alpha_{21} \\ \vdots \\ \alpha_{2m^*} \\ \vdots \\ \alpha_{m1} \\ \vdots \\ \alpha_{mm^*} \end{bmatrix}, \quad y_t = \begin{bmatrix} y_{1t} \\ \\ \\ \\ y_{mt} \end{bmatrix}, \quad v_t = \begin{bmatrix} v_{1t} \\ \\ \\ \\ v_{mt} \end{bmatrix}$$

and

$$X_t = \begin{bmatrix} X_{11t}, \ldots, X_{1m^*t}, 0 & & \\ 0 & X_{21t}, \ldots, X_{2m^*t}, 0 \ldots & \\ & & \\ 0 & & X_{m1t}, \ldots, X_{mm^*t}, \end{bmatrix}$$

where $y_{it} = \log x_{it} - \rho_i x_{it-1}$,
$x_{i1t} = 1 - \rho_i$, $x_{i2t} = \log y_t - \rho_i \log y_t$, $X_{ijt} =$
$a_{ij}(\log p_{jt} - \rho_i \log p_{jt-1})$ for $j = 3, m^*$ and $m^* = m + 2$,

$$(1.16') \quad \text{we can write (1.15) as } y_t = X_t\alpha + v_t.$$

If we know Ω, the efficient estimator of α is

$$(1.17) \quad \hat{\alpha} = [\frac{1}{T} \sum \underline{X}_t' \Omega^{-1} \underline{X}_t]^{-1} [\frac{1}{T} \sum \underline{X}_t' \Omega^{-1} \underline{y}_t]$$

and its variance matrix is

$$\underline{v}(\hat{\alpha}) = \frac{1}{T} [\frac{1}{T} \sum \underline{X}_t' \Omega^{-1} \underline{X}_t]^{-1}$$

That is, $\hat{\alpha}$ is the minimum variance estimator among all linear unbiased estimators for any sample size.[14]

But we do not know the contemporaneous covariance matrix, and thus it must be estimated. If we can find a matrix such that plim $\underline{S}_T = \Omega^{-1}$, then $\hat{\hat{\alpha}}$ obtained by substituting $\underline{S}_T$ in (1.17) is asymptotically equivalent to $\hat{\alpha}$. The following method is suggested to obtain an asymptotically efficient estimator.[15]

(1.18)

(1) Compute $\alpha^* = (\frac{1}{T} \sum \underline{X}_t' \underline{X}_t)^{-1} (\frac{1}{T} \sum \underline{X}_t' \underline{y}_t)$,

(2) Compute $\underline{S}_T^{-1} = \underline{M}_{ee} = \frac{1}{T} \sum \underline{e}_t \underline{e}_t'$,

where $\underline{e}_t = \underline{y}_t - \underline{X}_t \alpha^*$.

(3) Compute $\hat{\hat{\alpha}} = [\frac{1}{T} \sum \underline{X}_t' \underline{M}_{ee}^{-1} \underline{X}_t]^{-1} [\frac{1}{T} \sum \underline{X}_t' \underline{M}_{ee}^{-1} \underline{y}_t]$

$\hat{\hat{\alpha}}$ is asymptotically efficient and has

$$(1.19) \quad \underline{V}(\hat{\hat{\alpha}}) = \frac{1}{T} [\frac{1}{T} \sum \underline{X}_t' \underline{M}_{ee}^{-1} \underline{X}_t]^{-1}$$

as the variance matrix of the estimator.

We are not much satisfied with the estimator, which is efficient when the sample size is infinitely large, but even if we want to settle with this type of estimator because there is no better estimation method, the problem is not yet settle. The above result is based on the assumption that we know the value of ρ_i, so that we can transform the model to the one with $\underline{v}_{it}$ which are statistically independent. But since we do not know the value of ρ_i, the estimation problem still remains. Although it is not quite certain whether the following method is the best way of dealing with the model described here with serially as well as contemporaneously correlated errors, we separated the problem of estimating ρ_i from that of estimating the parameters of the model.

First, we estimated ρ_i by the following method.

(1.) Estimate the parameters by regressing $\log x_{it}$ on $\log y_t$ and $\log p_{jt}$, and obtain v^*_{it}.

(2.) Regress v^*_{it} on v^*_{it-1} and estimate ρ_i.

We then transformed the variables using the estimate of ρ_i and computed α^* to obtain M_{ee}. Then we computed $\hat{\hat{\alpha}}$ by using (1.18). The result of estimation is shown in Table 1.1.[16]

The Rotterdam Model

We interpreted the first term in the model

$$(1.2') \quad w_i d(\log x_i) = B_i (d(\log y) - \sum (w_k + \psi B_k) d(\log p_k)) + \sum C_{ij}\, d(\log p_j)$$

as the log change in real income. But this term can not be constructed from data unless we know the parameters B_k and ψ. But in fitting the model to time series data, it has been proposed that

$$d(\log x_t) = \sum w_i\, d(\log x_{it})$$

closely approximates the first term.[17] By using this approximation we write the model as follows:

$$(1.20) \quad w^*_{it}\, d(\log x_{it}) = \sum_j C_{ij}\, d(\log p_{jt}) + B_i\, d(\log x_t) + u_{it} \qquad i = 1, m \quad t = 1, T,$$

where $w^*_{it} = (w_{it} + w_{it+1})/2$.

We assume that the error terms u_{it} satisfy the following assumptions:

(e) $E(u_{it}) = 0$.

(f) u_t and u_θ are stochastically independent

TABLE 1.1.

Estimates of the Parameters of the Double-Log Model

Commodity Group i	$\hat{\rho}_i$	$\hat{c}_i$	$\hat{a}_{i0}$	$\hat{a}_{i1}$	$\hat{a}_{i2}$	$\hat{a}_{i3}$	$\hat{a}_{i4}$	$\hat{a}_{i5}$
Food	.391	- .730	.597 (.034)	-.587 (.077)	-.408 (.062)	-.113 (.054)	.195 (.049)	-.051 (.110)
Clothing	.556	-1.991	1.602 (.190)	-.931 (.325)	-.283 (.254)	-.300 (.285)	-.055 (.300)	-.088 (.512)
Housing	.386	-2.492	1.515 (0.090)	-.524 (.199)	-.260 (.128)	-.082 (.156)	-.101 (.128)	-.459 (.280)
Fuel and Light	.426	-3.236	.916 (.093)	-.176 (.192)	-.340 (.165)	-.408 (.155)	-.594 (.146)	.635 (.297)
Miscellaneous	.250	-1.692	1.398 (.057)	-.479 (.140)	-.029 (.118)	-.355 (.109)	-.220 (.105)	-.962 (.180)

Note: Standard errors are in parentheses.

whenever $t \neq \theta$.

(g) $V(u_t) = \Omega$.

Since the variables in the model are roughly the first difference of logarithms, we assume that for this model, the u_{it} are not serially correlated.

The problem of estimation for this model is not simple. The least squares estimate of the parameters separately for each equation will not do since the parameters must satisfy the conditions

(1.2a) $C_{ji} = C_{ij}$

and

(1.2b) $\sum B_i = 1$.

Our problem is now to estimate the parameters under the above three conditions when those constraints are imposed on the parameters.

We have not found a satisfactory method of estimation for the case when the sample size is small. Even for the case of a large sample we need to introduce another major assumption:

(h) u_t is normally distributed.

If this assumption, in addition to the first three assumptions, is satisfied, the method described below is suggested to obtain an asymptotically efficient estimator.[18] But we have to bear in mind that since our sample size is not infinitely large, the estimator shown below may not be very efficient for our case. But in the absence of a better statistical method, an asymptotically efficient estimator is preferred to other estimators which are not efficient even if the sample size is not large.

The estimation procedure we used is as follows.

(i) Calculate C^*_{ij} and B^*_j by the least squares method equation by equation, ignoring the constraints, and obtain u^*_{it}.

(ii) Let

$$\underline{u}^* = \begin{bmatrix} \underline{u}^*_{1t} \\ \vdots \\ \underline{u}^*_{mt} \end{bmatrix}. \text{ Compute } \underline{M}^{*\;-1}_{\underline{uu}} = (\underline{E}_{\underline{ij}}) = (\frac{1}{T} \sum_{\underline{t}} \underline{u}^*_{\underline{t}}\, \underline{u}^{*\prime}_{\underline{t}})^{-1}.$$

(iii) Let

$$\underline{C} = \begin{bmatrix} \underline{C}_{11}, & \ldots, & \underline{C}_{1\underline{m}}, \underline{C}_{1\underline{m}'} \\ \underline{C}_{\underline{m}1}, & \ldots, & \underline{C}_{\underline{mm}}, \underline{C}_{\underline{mm}'} \end{bmatrix}, \quad \underline{M}_{\underline{zz}} = (\underline{Z}_{\underline{ij}}) = \frac{1}{T} \sum \underline{Z}_t\, \underline{Z}'_t,$$

where

$$Z_t = \begin{bmatrix} \underline{d}(\log \underline{p}_{1\underline{t}}) \\ \vdots \\ \underline{d}(\log \underline{p}_{\underline{mt}}) \\ \underline{d}(\log \underline{x}_{\underline{t}}) \end{bmatrix}, \text{ and } C^* = \begin{bmatrix} \underline{C}^*_{11}, & \ldots, & \underline{C}^*_{1\underline{m}}, \underline{C}^*_{1\underline{m}'} \\ & \vdots & \\ \underline{C}^*_{\underline{m}1}, & \ldots, & \underline{C}^*_{\underline{mm}}, \underline{C}^*_{\underline{mm}'} \end{bmatrix}$$

$\underline{m}' = \underline{m} + 1$, $\underline{C}_{\underline{im}'} = \underline{B}_{\underline{i}}$, and $\underline{C}^*_{\underline{im}'} = \underline{B}^*_{\underline{i}}$.

Find matrix $\underline{C}^{**}$ which minimizes

$$\phi = \underline{tr}\{(\underline{C}^* - \underline{C}^{**})\underline{M}^{*\;-1}_{\underline{uu}}\,(\underline{C}^* - \underline{C}^{**})\underline{M}_{\underline{zz}}\}$$

under constraints

$$\underline{C}^{**}_{\underline{ij}} = \underline{C}^{**}_{\underline{ji}}$$

and

$$\sum_{\underline{i}} \underline{C}^{**}_{\underline{im}'} = 1 .$$

We can verify that the $\underline{C}^{**}_{\underline{ij}}$ which minimize ϕ can be obtained by solving the following system of equations:

$$(1.21)\begin{cases} (1.21.1) & \sum_{k=1}^{m'} \sum_{j=1}^{m} C^{**}_{jk} E_{ij} Z_{k\ell} + g(i, \ell)\lambda_{i\ell}(1 - \delta_{i\ell}) + \theta\delta_{\ell m'} = \sum_{k=1}^{m'} \sum_{j=\ell}^{m} C^{*}_{jk} E_{ij} Z_{k\ell} & \ell = 1, m' \quad i = 1, m \\ (1.21.2) & C^{**}_{i\ell} = C^{**}_{\ell i} & i = 1, m \quad \ell > i \\ (1.21.3) & \sum_{i=1}^{m} C^{**}_{im'} = 1. & \end{cases}$$

The function $g(i, \ell) = 1$ when $i > \ell$
$= -1$ when $i < \ell$,
and $\lambda_{i\ell} = \lambda_{\ell i}$. This is a system of $(m \times m' + (m(m - 1)/2) + 1)$ equations with the same number of unknowns $(m \times m'\ C^{**}_{jk},\ (m(m - 1)/2)\lambda_{i\ell},$ and $\theta)$.

The result of computation is shown in Tables 1.2 and 1.3. Table 1.2 gives C^{*}_{ij}, the least square estimate of C_{ij}, which was obtained in the first stage of calculation. Since the parameters were estimated without taking the constraints into account, the constraints are not satisfied. Table 1.3 gives the solution of (1.21) for C^{**}_{ij}, which are the asymptotically efficient estimators of C_{ij}. Since C^{**}_{ij} must satisfy (1.21.2) and (1.21.3), the constraints are automatically satisfied.[19]

The Indirect Addilog Model

We first observe that the parameters of this model are not linear, so that we are not able to estimate them by the ordinary least squares method. There are two approaches to the estimation. The first is to transform the demand function to the function for expenditure shares:

$$(1.22) \quad \frac{p_{it}x_{it}}{y} = \frac{a_i(y_t/p_{it})^{b_i}}{\sum a_j(y_t/p_{jt})^{b_j}} \qquad i = 1, m.$$

TABLE 1.2. Unconstrained Estimates of the Parameters of the Rotterdam Model

Commodity Group *i*	C^*_{i1}	C^*_{i2}	C^*_{i3}	C^*_{i4}	C^*_{i5}	B^*_i
Food	-.157 (.037)	.006 (.034)	-.054 (.046)	.114 (.043)	.044 (.064)	.465 (.050)
Clothing	.030 (0.34)	-.005 (.031)	.041 (.042)	-.033 (.039)	.022 (.058)	.180 (.046)
Housing	.044 (0.16)	-.011 (.015)	-.034 (.020)	-.026 (.019)	.008 (.028)	.139 (.022)
Fuel and Light	.017 (.005)	-.006 (.005)	-.001 (.006)	-.023 (.006)	.018 (.009)	.009 (.007)
Miscellaneous	.066 (.024)	.016 (.022)	.048 (.031)	-.031 (.028)	-.094 (.042)	.207 (.033)

Note: Standard errors are in parentheses.

TABLE 1.3. Constrained Estimates of the Parameters of the Rotterdam Model

Commodity Group i	C^{**}_{i1}	C^{**}_{i2}	C^{**}_{i3}	C^{**}_{i4}	C^{**}_{i5}	B^{**}_{i}
Food	-.127	.022	.033	.017	.055	.467
Clothing		-.012	-.011	-.008	.009	.199
Housing			-.039	-.005	.022	.124
Fuel and Light				-0.19	.014	.012
Miscellaneous					-.099	.198

If we let $x'_{it} = \frac{p_{it}x_{it}}{y_t}$, (1.22) is a special case of the following equation:

$$x'_{it} = f_i(p_{1t}, \ldots, p_{mt}, y_t, a_1, \ldots, a_m, b_1, \ldots, b_m),$$

where a_i and b_i appear in a nonlinear fashion. That is, the effect of the exogenous variables cannot be represented by an equation linear in its parameters. We can estimate a_i and b_i by using a program designed to estimate nonlinear functions.

Appeal to the nonlinear program is not, however, the most satisfactory way of handling statistical estimation. By the nature of the problem, usually more than one set of solutions exists for given data, so that the estimates differ depending on the initial values. But if there is not any other way to get around the problem because of the constraints of the model, we must resort to nonlinear estimation. But this approach becomes quite involved when we assume that the errors are serially as well as contemporaneously correlated.

In our study we tried a second approach, which is to take the ratio of x_i of two commodity groups, and write

$$\frac{x_{it}}{x_{jt}} = \frac{a_i(y_t/p_{it})^{b_i + 1}}{a_j(y_t/p_{jt})^{b_j + 1}} .$$

By taking the logarithms of both sides of the equation, we obtain

$$(1.23) \qquad \log(x_{it}/x_{jt}) = \log(a_i/a_j) + (b_i + 1)\log(y_t/p_{it}) - (b_j + 1)\log(y_t/p_{jt}) .$$

Since there are $(m - 1)$ equations for a fixed j, we have $m(m - 1)$ equations from which we can estimate a_i and b_i. But among $m(m - 1)$ only $(m - 1)$ equations are independent, and the rest of the equations can be expressed as a linear combination of $(m - 1)$ indpendent equations. Here we took the $(m - 1)$ independent pairs as follows: the first and second commodities, the first and third commodities, the first and fourth commodities, ..., the first and last commodities. Our statistical model is

$$(1.24) \quad \log(x_{it}/x_{1t}) = \log(a_i/a_1) + \beta_i \log(y_t/p_{it}) + \beta_1 \log(y_t/p_{1t}) + u_{it} \qquad i = 2, m.$$

where $\beta_i = b_i + 1$, $\beta_1 = -(b_1 + 1)$, and u_{it} are error terms representing the effect of random terms on $\log(x_i/x_1)$.

For the same reason as in the case of the double log model, we assume that the error terms are serially correlated as follows:

$$u_{it} = \rho_i u_{it-1} + v_{it} ,$$

and retain the assumption (a) - (d).

If we know the value of ρ_i, we can transform (1.24) to

$$(1.25) \quad x'_{it} = (1 - \rho_i)\log(a_i/a_1) + \beta_i y'_{it} + \beta_1 y^i_{1t} + v_{it} \qquad i = 2, m,$$

where

$$x'_{it} = \log(x_{it}/x_{1t}) - \rho_i \log(x_{it-1}/x_{1t-1})$$

$$y'_{it} = \log(y_t/p_{it}) - \rho_i \log(y_{t-1}/p_{it-1})$$

$$y^i_{1t} = \log(y_t/p_{1t}) - \rho_i \log(y_{t-1}/p_{1t-1}).$$

If we let

$$\alpha = \begin{bmatrix} \log \frac{a_2}{a_1} \\ \vdots \\ \log \frac{a_m}{a_1} \\ \beta_1 \\ \vdots \\ \beta_m \end{bmatrix}, \quad x'_t = \begin{bmatrix} x'_{2t} \\ \vdots \\ x'_{mt} \end{bmatrix}, \quad v_t = \begin{bmatrix} v_{2t} \\ \vdots \\ v_{mt} \end{bmatrix},$$

and

$$\underline{Z}_t = \begin{bmatrix} 1-\rho_2 & \cdots & 0 & y^2_{1t} & y'_{2t} & \cdots & 0 \\ \vdots & \ddots & \vdots & \vdots & \vdots & \ddots & \vdots \\ 0 & \cdots & (1-\rho_m) & y^m_{1t} & 0 & \cdots & y'_{mt} \end{bmatrix}$$

We can write (1.25) as

$$(1.26) \qquad x'_t = Z_t\alpha + v_t.$$

Statistical problems involved in estimating α are identical with those which are discussed in the extimation of the double log model. We first estimated ρ_i from u^*_{it} by using (1.24). Then, we estimated the contemporaneous covariance from v^*_{it} by using (1.25). Finally we estimated α by using the estimate of the contemporaneous covariance. The result of computation is shown in Table 1.4.

The Linear Expenditure Model

There was a tremendous increase of expenditure in current prices during the sample period 1905-1965 (see Appendix). The increase was caused partly by the general increase of prices in the prewar period, but it was caused mainly by the rapid inflation during the war and immediate postwar years. To avoid the problem of heteroscedasticity arising in this situation, we transformed the model to the following form:

$$(1.27) \qquad \frac{p_{it}x_{it}}{p_{1t}} = c_i \frac{p_{it}}{p_{1t}} + b_i\left(\frac{y}{p_{1t}} - \sum c_j \frac{p_{jt}}{p_{1t}}\right)$$

$$i = 1, m$$
$$t = 1, T.$$

Letting $x'_{it} = \dfrac{p_{it}x_{it}}{p_{1t}}$, $p'_{it} = \dfrac{p_{it}}{p_{1t}}$ and $y'_t = \dfrac{y_t}{p_{1t}}$, and introducing error terms, we write the model as

TABLE 1.4. Constrained Estimates of the Parameters of the Indirect Addilog Model

Commodity Group i	$\hat{\rho}_i$	$\hat{\beta}_i$	$\hat{b}_i$	$\log(\frac{a_i}{a_1})$	$\frac{a_i}{a_1}$
Food		.145 (.017)	-1.145		
Clothing	.63	.652 (.206)	-.348	-1.461 (.157)	.232
Housing	.73	.845 (.098)	-.155	-1.546 (.102)	.213
Fuel and Light	.67	.511 (.101)	-.489	-2.795 (.932)	.061
Miscellaneous	.70	.797 (.130)	-.203	-0.967 (.874)	.381

Note: Standard errors are in parentheses.

$$(1.28) \qquad x'_{it} = c_i p'_{it} + b_i (y'_t - \sum c_j p'_{jt}) + u_{it} \qquad i = 1, m \quad t = 1, T .$$

As we did for the double log and the indirect addilog models, we assume that u_{it} are serially correlated and the process can be represented by

$$u_{it} = \rho u_{it-1} + v_{it},$$

where ρ lies between 0 and 1, and the v_{it} satisfy the three assumptions we listed for the two models. We should point out that for the linear expenditure model we constrain the value of ρ to be the same for every i. This assumption is more restrictive than before, but has to be introduced because of the difficulties which arise in estimation when the ρ_i are assumed to vary. But this is better than assuming that errors are not serially correlated, which is a dubious assumption when sample data come from annual observations.

If we know the value of ρ, we can transform (1.28) to

$$(1.29) \qquad x^*_{it} = c_i p^*_{it} + b_i (y^*_t - \sum c_j p^*_{jt}) + v_{it} \qquad i = 1, m \quad t = 1, T' ,$$

where

$$x^*_{it} = x'_{it} - \rho x'_{it-1}$$

$$p^*_{it} = p'_{it} - \rho p'_{it-1}$$

$$y^*_t = y'_t - \rho y'_{t-1} .$$

We note that b_i and c_i are nonlinear. There is no satisfactory way to transform (1.29) so that the parameters become linear. We have no choice other than to resort to an iterative procedure.

The problem of estimation for this model is simpler than for a model such as the indirect addilog before the transformation, for the degree of nonlinearity is slight. Rather than using the direct iterative procedure, the following three stage procedure of linear estimation is recommended:[20]

(i) Assuming that the estimate of c_i is given, estimate b_i from

$$(1.30) \qquad \hat{b}_i = \frac{\sum (x^*_{it} - \hat{c}_i p^*_{it})(y^*_t - \sum \hat{c}_j p^*_{jt})}{\sum (y^*_t - \sum \hat{c}_j p^*_{jt})^2} .$$

(ii) By using $\hat{b}_i$ obtained in (i), construct the following matrix and vector:

$$X = \begin{bmatrix} (\hat{b}_1 - 1)p^*_{11} & \cdots & \hat{b}_1 p^*_{m1} \\ \vdots & & \vdots \\ (\hat{b}_1 - 1)p^*_{1T'} & \cdots & \hat{b}_1 p^*_{mT'} \\ \vdots & & \vdots \\ \hat{b}_m p^*_{11} & \cdots & (\hat{b}_m - 1)p^*_{m1} \\ \vdots & & \vdots \\ \hat{b}_m p^*_{1T'} & \cdots & (\hat{b}_m - 1)p^*_{mT'} \end{bmatrix}$$

$$y = \begin{bmatrix} x^*_{11} - \hat{b}_1 y^*_1 \\ \vdots \\ x^*_{1T'} - \hat{b}_1 y^*_{T'} \\ \vdots \\ x^*_{m1} - \hat{b}_m y^*_1 \\ \vdots \\ x^*_{mT'} - \hat{b}_m y^*_{T'} \end{bmatrix}$$

(iii) Estimate

$$\hat{c} = \begin{bmatrix} \hat{c}_1 \\ \cdot \\ \cdot \\ \vdots \\ \hat{c}_m \end{bmatrix}$$

from

$$(1.31) \quad \hat{c} = (X'X)^{-1}X'y \ .$$

A computer program can be written to assign zero to c_i as the initial value and start the iteration. b_i computed in (i) is used to obtain $\hat{c}$ in (iii), which is, in turn, used to obtain $\hat{b}_i$ in (i). The iteration stops when the sum of absolute percentage difference between two successive estimates is smaller than some preassigned value, such as .001 for both b and c.

We should note that this double sequence of linear estimation automatically satisfies the constraint that the sum of $\hat{b}_i$ is 1.[21] For

$$\sum \hat{b}_i = \frac{\sum_i \sum_t (x^*_{it} - c_i p^*_{it})(y^*_t - \sum c_j p^*_{jt})}{\sum (y^*_t - \sum c_j p^*_{jt})^2}$$

$$= \frac{\sum (y^*_t - \sum c_j p^*_{jt}) \sum (x^*_{it} - c_i p^*_{it})}{\sum (y^*_t - \sum c_j p^*_{jt})^2}$$

$$= 1 \quad \text{if} \quad \sum (x^*_{it} - c_i p^*_{it}) = y^*_t - \sum c_j p^*_{jt} \ ,$$

or if $\quad \sum x^*_{it} = y^*_t \ .$

But

$$\sum x^*_{it} = \sum (x'_{it} - \rho x'_{it-1}) = \sum x'_{it} - \sum \rho x'_{it-1}$$

$$= y'_t - \rho y'_{t-1} = y^*_t \ .$$

We have thus far assumed that we know the value of ρ. But since we do not know it in practice, its estimate must be substituted for ρ in the estimation procedure. We obtained $\hat{\rho}$ as follows.

First we note that (1.28) can be transformed to

$$(1.32) \quad x'_{it} = \alpha_i p'_{it} - \sum_{j \neq i} \alpha_j p'_{jt} + b_i y'_t + u_{it} \qquad \begin{matrix} i = 1, m \\ t = 1, T, \end{matrix}$$

where $\alpha_i = (1 - b_i)c_i$, and $\alpha_j = b_i c_j (j \neq 1)$.

If we ignore the constraints on parameters, (1.32) is linear in α_j and b_i. We fitted (1.32) to each commodity group and obtaind u^*_{it}. Then we estimated ρ from the model,[22]

$$u^*_{it} = \rho u^*_{it-1} + v_{it} \qquad \begin{matrix} i = 1, m \\ t = 1, T. \end{matrix}$$

Table 1.5 presents the result of estimation.

III. Comparision of the Four Models

The task which confronts us now is to evaluate the four models on empirical grounds. First, we shall obtain the predicted values of x_{it}, $\hat{x}_{it}$, by using the models and investigate their relation to the actual values during the sample period.

For the double log model we could predict the logarithm of x_{it} from

$$\log \hat{x}_{it} = \hat{c}_i + \hat{a}_{i0} \log y_t + \sum \hat{a}_{ij} \log p_{jt},$$

and exponentiate $\log \hat{x}_{it}$ to obtain $\hat{x}_{it}$. But since we assumed that the error terms are generated by a first-order Markov process, we can use the error of past prediction for the current prediction. This idea leads to the following prediction formula:

$$\log \hat{\hat{x}}_{it} = \hat{c}_i + \hat{a}_{i0} \log y_t + \sum \hat{a}_{ij} \log p_{jt} + \hat{\rho}_i e_{it-1},$$

where e_{it-1} = the error of prediction in the past year.

TABLE 1.5. Constrained Estimates of the Parameters of the Linear Expenditure Model with $\hat{\rho} = .534$

Commodity Group i	b_i	c_i
Food	.261 (.008)	.362 (.011)
Clothing	.160 (.007)	.038 (.006)
Housing	.208 (.005)	.010 (.005)
Fuel and Light	.042 (.001)	.010 (.002)
Miscellaneous	.329 (.006)	.033 (.012)

Note: Standard errors are in parentheses.

Our predicted x_{it} are based on $\log \hat{\hat{x}}_{it}$ rather than $\log \hat{x}_{it}$.

Using the same line of reasoning, the predicted values of the linear expenditure model are based on

$$\hat{y}_t = \frac{\widehat{p_{it}x_{it}}}{p_{1t}} = \hat{c}_i \frac{p_{it}}{p_{1t}} + \hat{b}_i \left(\frac{y_t}{p_{1t}} - \sum \hat{c}_j \frac{p_{jt}}{p_{1t}} \right) + \rho e_{it-1}.$$

$\hat{x}_{it}$ were obtained by multiplying $\hat{y}_t$ by $\dfrac{p_{1t}}{p_{it}}$.

For the Rotterdam model we first obtained the predicted values of $w^*_{it}d(\log x_{it})$ by using the estimate of B_i and C_{ij}, and then divided the predicted values by w^*_{it} to obtain the predicted values of $\log \dfrac{x_{it}}{x_{it-1}}$ We then exponentiated $\log \dfrac{\hat{x}_{it}}{x_{it-1}}$ and obtained $\dfrac{\hat{x}_{it}}{x_{it-1}}$. The predicted values for this model were obtained from

$$\hat{x}_{it} = \frac{\hat{x}_{it}}{x_{it-1}} \; x_{it-1}.$$

For the indirect addilog model we need to transform the model for the purpose of prediction because we do not know the values of all 10 parameters. We know the value of a_i in the ration form, a_i/a_1, but we do not know each value of a_i. Thus, we divide the numerator and the denominator by a_1 and write the model as:

$$x_{it} = \frac{\left(\dfrac{a_i}{a_1}\right)\left(\dfrac{y_t}{p_{it}}\right)^{b_i + 1}}{\sum \left(\dfrac{a_j}{a_1}\right)\left(\dfrac{y_t}{p_{jt}}\right)^{b_j}}.$$

We use this formula for predicting x_{it}.

Table 1.6 shows how closely the four models predicted x_{it}. For purposes of comparison, we included the naive model, which predicts the current level of x_{it} by

$$x_{it} = x_{it-1}\left(1 + \frac{x_{it-1} - x_{it-2}}{x_{it-2}}\right).$$

TABLE 1.6. Percentage Variation Unexplained (in %)

	Model	Food	Clothing	Housing	Fuel and Light	Miscel-laneous	Unadjusted Total	Adjusted Total
1.	Naive	22.65	13.25	5.88	1.40	1.21	8.03	
2.	Double-log	1.88	3.95	.31	.70	.58	1.12	1.15
3.	Rotterdam	3.48	2.73	.59	.77	2.87	2.63	3.03
4.	Indirect addilog	6.74	9.32	3.68	3.66	1.25	4.02	4.14
5.	Linear Expenditure	2.78	3.95	.64	1.18	.87	1.64	1.71

Notes: 1. Percentage variation unexplained in group $\underline{i}$ = $100 \times \frac{\sum_t \underline{e}^2_{\underline{it}}}{\sum_t (\underline{x}_{\underline{it}} - \underline{\bar{x}}_{\underline{i}})^2}$.

2. Unadjusted total variation unexplained in $100 \times \frac{\sum\sum \underline{e}^2_{\underline{it}}}{\sum\sum (\underline{x}_{\underline{it}} - \underline{\bar{x}}_{\underline{i}})^2}$.

3. Adjusted total variation unexplained = $\frac{N \times 5}{(N \times 5 - M)}$ × "unadjusted total," where $\underline{M}$ = the number of parameters.

Since the $\underline{x}_{it}$ have a trend and all five models give a high $\underline{R}^2$, in order to make the difference in the explanatory power of the models clear, the results given in the next table are $(1 - \underline{R}^2)$, which is interpreted as the percentage variation of $\underline{x}_{it}$ left unexplained.

The first thing we notice in Table 1.6 is that there is no model which completely dominates the others in terms of explanatory ability. For example, the double log model gives the best fit to four groups, but the Rotterdam model does better than the double log model in explaining clothing consumption. But the performance of the double log model seems to be the best overall. It gives better fits than the naive, the indirect addilog, and the linear expenditure models for all five groups, and its performance is better than that of the Rotterdam model except in one commodity group.

The naive model does better than some models. For the fourth group its performance is better than the indirect addilog model. For the last group the model explains past consumption better than the Rotterdam model. But the double log and the linear expenditure models perform better than the naive model for each commodity group. If we find it objectionable for a model to do worse than the naive model even for one commodity, we have to conclude that the first two models are empirically unsatisfactory.

Some indicator of overall performance is given in the column of Unadjusted Totals. The figures can be interpreted as the average percentage of residuals in the variation of $\underline{x}_{it}$. If we rank the alternaive models by using this column, we reinforce the former conclusion that the double log model gives the best fit overall. It is of some relief to find that the naive model comes at the bottom of this ranking.

The good results for the double log model might be due to the fact that the parameters of the model are not constrained, whereas those of the other models are constrained. As a consequence, the double log model has more parameters than the other models, which gives greater flexibility in fitting. One wonders what happens to the result when the difference in the number of parameters is taken into account in comparison. In the last column we tried a crude adjustment for the difference. But for our sample size the adjustment did not produce different results.

R^2, or $(1 - R^2)$, is not the only criterion to judge the past performance of the alternative models. We might ask how well a model could predict the change of direction of x_{it}. Table 1.7 shows how many turns were predicted by the alternative models. We notice that the performance of the models is somewhat reversed in this test. The indirect addilog and the Rotterdam model predict the turns better than the double log model for each commodity group. Also, the linear expenditure model, which was poorer in R^2, seems to be doing better than the double log model.

We can consider the prediction problem from one other viewpoint. We might want to investigate whether the sign of the errors of prediction alternates frequently. When a long series of pluses is followed by a long series of minuses, it might indicate the misspecification of the model, or even a change of parameters during the sample period. Table 1.8 shows the number of runs of error terms of the four models for the five commodity groups.

The performance of the Rotterdam model is not as good as in the previous test, but the indirect addilog model continues to do well in this test. The linear expenditure model, however, does better in this test for some commodities than the indirect addilog model. The double log model comes out better than the Rotterdam model for the last group, but its overall performance is poorer than the indirect addilog and the linear expenditure models.

We can also judge the relative merits of the models by examining the implication of the estimates of the parameters. We computed in Table 1.9 income elasticities of the four models. We have some a priori ideas about the elasticities and wish to see whether the estimates violate them. First, since none of the commodities can be considered inferior goods, income elasticities should not be negative. All models satisfy this test. Second, it is generally believed that the elasticity for food should be less than 1. This is again met by all four, and fails to provide a means to discriminate among the models.

The estimates of the elasticities might be considered somewhat similar for the food, clothing, housing, and miscellaneous groups, but for the fuel and light group the estimate of the Rotterdam model is low compared with the other estimates. The estimate of the indirect addilog model is about four times

TABLE 1.7. Predictions of the Changes of Direction

	Food	Clothing	Housing	Fuel and Light	Miscellaneous	$\sum$
Number of Turns	23	19	12	16	12	83
Model						
Double log	17	8	8	8	6	47
Rotterdam	22	15	10	14	8	69
Indirect addilog	21	17	10	9	7	64
Linear expenditure	17	9	9	5	8	48

TABLE 1.8. The Number of Runs

Model	Food	Clothing	Housing	Fuel and Light	Miscellaneous	$\sum$
Double log	22	16	15	18	19	90
Rotterdam	21	28	20	23	12	104
Indirect addilog	27	20	21	27	24	119
Linear expenditure	23	25	23	20	19	110

Note: The maximum number of runs for each group = 46.

TABLE 1.9. Income Elasticities at Average Expenditure Shares

Model	Food	Clothing	Housing	Fuel and Light	Miscellaneous
Double log	.597	1.602	1.515	.916	1.398
Rotterdam	.855	1.596	1.127	.300	1.075
Indirect addilog	.594	1.391	1.584	1.250	1.536
Linear expenditure	.478	1.312	1.891	1.042	1.786

Note: The income elasticity of commodity i,

$$\frac{\partial x_i}{\partial y}\frac{y}{x_i} = a_{i0} \quad \text{for the double log model,}$$

$$= B_i/w_i \quad \text{for the Rotterdam model,}$$

$$= b_i/w_i \quad \text{for the linear expenditure model,}$$

$$= (1 + b_i - \sum b_j w_j) \quad \text{for the indirect addilog model.}$$

larger than that of the Rotterdam model. The expenditure share of this group increased only slightly during the sample period, which is indicative that the elasticity is somewhere around 1. The change of the share is certainly not a perfect indicator of income elasticity, but .300 at the average share might be considered too small. It is too small from another point of view as well. The income elasticity of the model for the food group is higher than that for the fuel and light group. This is a somewhat dubious result.

We found that all income elasticities are positive, that is, none of the goods is inferior. Therefore, it is necessary that the own price elasticities, $(\partial x_i/\partial p_i)/(p_i/x_i)$, must be negative for the own substitution term to be negative. For, since the own substitution term

$$= \frac{\partial x_i}{\partial p_i} + x_i \frac{\partial x_i}{\partial y}$$

and

$$\frac{\partial x_i}{\partial y} > 0,$$

this term can be negative when $\partial x_i/\partial p_i < 0$. Even if one does not want to go into utility analysis, it is reasonable to require that x_i decreases when its price increases and total expenditure remains the same. In Table 1.10 price elasticities are computed. But all estimates are negative, and it does not help us much in judging the relative merits of the four models.

Summary

1. First, we investigated the relationship between a utility function and a demand model. We took the stand that a model is theoretically satisfactory when it is derived from a utility function. But we did not admit any utility function: we restricted it to the class of nonhomogeneous functions. We concluded that the indirect addilog and the linear expenditure models are theoretically satisfactory, whereas the double log and the Rotterdam models are not.

2. Since a model might be considered as a model of approximation (valid for certain ranges of y and p_i), we fitted all four models to data and compared them on empirical grounds. Overall, the double log model gave the best fit, whereas the

TABLE 1.10. Price Elasticities

Model	Food	Clothing	Housing	Fuel and Light	Miscellaneous
Double log	-.587	-.283	-.082	-.594	-.962
Rotterdam	{-.195 -.320	{-.069 -.150	{-.228 -.649	{-.403 -.658	{-.350 -.762
Linear expenditure	{-.530 -.613	{-.397 -.552	{-.911 -1.10	{-.093 -.323	{-.858 -.881
Indirect addilog	{-.312 -.601	{-.798 -.713	{-.854 -.871	{-.534 -.624	{-.826 -.856

Notes: 1. In $\frac{a_1}{a_2}$, a_1 indicates the lowest price elasticity and a_2 the highest price elasticity during the sample period.

2. The price elasticity of commodity $\underline{i}$, $\frac{\partial x_i}{\partial p_i}$, $= a_{ii}$ for the double log, $= \frac{c_{ii}}{w_i}$ for the Rotterdam, $= -b_i(w_i^{-1}(1 - \sum p_i c_i / y) + \frac{c_i}{x_i})$ for the linear expenditure, and$=b_1(w_1-1)-1$ for the indirect addilog model.

indirect addilog model did the worst. But the double log model did poorly in predicting the change of direction and in the "run" test. The performance of the Rotterdam and the indirect addilog models was better in these tests than in the $\underline{R}^2$ test.

3. The estimates of the Rotterdam model have some defects. This model gives a very low estimate of income elasticity for the fuel and light group, lower than the estimate of elasticity for food. The test based on price elasticities did not discriminate among the models since all estimates had a negative sign.

4. There is no model which dominates the others in all tests. If we judge models by the criterion that a model whose explanatory power is poorer than the naive model, even for one commodity, is unsatisfactory, the choice seems to be between the linear expenditure and the double log models. If one is empirically oriented, the double log model is quite appealing since it is easy to estimate and gives a high $\underline{R}^2$. However, it is not a good model for predicting changes. If one is theoretically oriented, one would choose the linear expenditure model. Its explanatory power is not very much worse and it does even better than the double log model in predicting directional changes and avoiding consistent over- and under-estimation.

Notes

This paper was written while the author was associated with the Institute of Economic Research of the Economic Planning Agency of Japan as visiting fellow during the 1968-69 academic year. He acknowledges with appreciation the financial support from the Far Eastern Seminar at the University of Michigan and the computational assistance provided by the Institute.

1. Richard Stone, (ed.), University of Cambridge, Department of Applied Economics, _Program for Growth, The Model in Its Environment: A Progress Report_, No. 5 (London,: Chapman and Hall, 1964).

2. H. Houthakker and L. Taylor, _Consumer Demand in the United States, 1929-1970_ (Cambridge, Mass.: Harvard University Press, 1966); Kotaro Tsujimura, _Shohikozo to Bukka_ (_The Structure of Demand and Prices_) (Tokyo: Keiso Shobo, 1968); Kotaro Tsujimura and Sata Tamotsu, "Irreversibility of Consumer Behavior in Terms of Numerical Preference Fields," _Review of Economics and_

<u>Statistics</u>, 46(1946): 305-319.

3. $\underline{y}$ and $\underline{p}_j$ are considered to be independent variables. This is the traditional assumption in demand studies.

4. The theoretical discussion of the model is given in H. Theil, <u>Economics and Information Theory</u> (Chicago: Rand McNally, 1967). For its empirical application, see Richard Parks, "System of Demand Equations: An Empirical Comparision of Alternative Functional Forms," Report 6808, Center for Mathematical Studies in Business and Economics, University of Chicago, June 1968; and A. Barten, "Consumer Demand Functions Under Conditions of Almost Additive Preferences, " <u>Econometrica</u>, 32 (1964): 1-38.

5. The model was derived in L. Klein and H. Rubin, A Constant-Utility Index of the Cost of Living," <u>Review of Economic Studies</u>, 15 (1947-48): 84-87.

6. This model was proposed by H. Houthakker, "Additive Preferences," <u>Econometrica</u>, 28 (1960), 244-257.

7. J. R. Hicks, <u>Value and Capital</u> (London: Oxford University Press, 1939); 307-311.

8. See H. Wold and L. Jureen, <u>Demand Analysis</u> (New York, Wiley, 1953), exercise 55 on p. 147. This exercise summarizes J. Ville, "The Existence-Condition of a Total Utility Function," <u>Review of Economic Studies</u>, 19 (1952): 123-128.

9. D. McFadden, "Notes on Professor Theil's Demand System," Berkeley: University of California, Department of Economics (mimeographed).

10. R. C. Geary, "A Note on 'A Constant Utility Index of the Cost of Living,'" <u>Review of Economic Studies</u>, 18 (1949-50): 65-66.

11. Houthakker, "Additive Preferences," pp. 244-257, section 7.

12. René Roy, <u>De l'utilité: Contribution à la théorie de choix</u> (Paris: Herman, 1943), pp. 21-25.

13. For model (1.4), we can easily see that the adding up and homogeneity conditions are satisfied. The direct check of the Slutsky condition is given in K. Yoshihara, "Demand Functions: An Application to the Jananese Expenditure Pattern," Econometrica 37 (1969): 257-274.

14. E. Malinvaud, Statistical Methods of Econometrics (Chicago: Rand McNally, 1966), p. 285.

15. Malinvaud, Statistical Methods of Econometrics, p. 286.

16. See Malinvaud, Statistical Methods of Econometrics, p. 44. $\hat{\rho}_i$ in Table 1.1 was computed using the Durbin-Watson statistic d_i obtained in the first regression. We can show $d_i = 2(1 - \hat{\rho}_i)$. Thus $\hat{\rho}_i = 1 - (1/2)d_i$.

17. Parks, "System of Demand Equations."

18. Malinvaud, Statistical Methods of Econometrics, Chapter 9, Section 5.

19. The variance of C^{**}_{ij} can be computed from the following formulas cited in Malinvaud, Statistical Methods of Econometrics, p. 305:

$$\text{The variance of } C^{**}_{kj} = \frac{1}{T}(E_{kk}Z_{jj} + E_{jj}Z_{kk} + 2E_{kj}Z_{kj}) \qquad j = 1, m \quad k \neq j$$

$$\text{The variance of } C^{**}_{kk} = \frac{1}{T}(E_{kk}Z_{kk}) \qquad k = 1, m$$

$$\text{The variance of } C^{**}_{jm'} = \frac{1}{T}(Z_{m'm'}E_{jj}) \qquad j = 1, m$$

We computed variances by using these formulas (not shown in the table), but they were too large relative to C^{**}_{ij}. As a consequence, the precision of the estimates in Table 1.2 is not very good. The trouble is with the inverse of M^*_{uu}. Its determinant was very close to 0, and we had to do the computation of its inversion with double precision to ensure that ${M^*_{uu}}^{-1}M^*_{uu} = I$. Since the determinant was very small, each element in the inverse was very large. As a consequence, the variance turned out to be large for each estimate. If this situation arises in a rather general case, we have to look for an alternative method to obtain a consistent estimate of Ω.

20. See Malinvaud, Statistical Methods of Econometrics, pp. 310-314. An alternative method is proposed in Parks, "System of Demand Equations."

21. Note that if ρ is assumed to vary among equations, this three stage interative linear method does not automatically satisfy the constraint and gives rise to new complications.

22. $$\frac{\sum_{j}\sum_{t} u^{*}_{it}\, u^{*}_{it-1}}{\sum\sum u^{**}_{it}} = 1 - \frac{1}{2}\sum d_i \frac{\hat{\sigma}_i^2}{\sum \hat{\sigma}_i^2}$$ where

$$\hat{\sigma}_i^2 = \frac{\sum u^{*2}_{it}}{T - (m + 1)}$$

and d_i are the Durbin-Watson statistics.

Appendix

TABLE A.1.1. Per Capita Consumption in Constant Prices (in yen)

Year	Food	Clothing	Housing	Fuel and Light	Miscel-laneous
1905	325.6	32.5	20.1	9.3	75.8
1906	329.0	37.1	17.6	9.7	75.8
1907	307.8	37.9	18.5	9.9	77.6
1908	384.8	39.9	22.5	9.2	81.6
1909	386.2	43.5	26.4	9.5	82.1
1910	390.4	42.9	25.9	10.2	85.3
1911	388.5	44.4	26.6	10.6	88.7
1912	397.5	44.0	28.2	11.6	91.4
1913	411.7	45.5	28.3	12.0	90.8
1914	365.8	40.2	28.4	12.6	89.4
1915	410.2	45.7	28.0	13.5	85.3
1916	416.4	20.9	28.5	14.0	90.2
1917	421.1	60.1	31.6	14.9	97.5
1918	412.2	71.1	35.3	14.8	104.1
1919	422.9	97.2	38.4	15.9	106.4
1920	417.3	66.9	38.5	18.6	112.5
1921	476.3	84.3	34.3	15.6	105.2
1922	462.0	85.8	41.1	16.3	131.3
1923	479.9	67.7	45.1	15.7	140.8
1924	470.1	71.1	51.1	15.8	135.4
1925	485.4	64.6	53.6	16.8	138.7
1926	488.8	71.9	50.2	18.2	133.8
1927	471.8	79.9	47.7	17.4	137.2
1928	490.0	90.6	48.7	17.1	137.6
1929	481.5	76.0	50.5	17.4	135.9
1930	484.9	81.9	49.6	18.5	131.4
1931	488.9	96.8	48.7	19.1	127.9
1932	461.5	96.3	47.4	20.2	124.4
1933	495.0	92.2	47.6	19.3	143.9
1934	501.9	114.0	49.6	20.2	170.0
1935	505.0	114.9	49.3	21.3	171.0
1936	499.1	124.9	53.5	20.6	116.3
1937	505.4	145.4	56.7	21.5	171.3
1938	491.7	142.1	58.6	22.2	179.2
1952	407.8	83.4	71.5	28.9	128.7
1953	439.0	96.0	87.1	29.8	147.8
1954	446.0	97.1	90.3	30.8	165.9
1955	476.7	103.9	97.4	30.1	184.8
1956	498.1	113.6	104.8	31.2	198.8
1957	511.6	123.0	112.2	32.0	219.2
1958	529.2	124.8	123.1	32.9	234.7
1959	548.9	131.7	145.1	34.4	254.0
1960	562.8	150.6	164.0	37.4	284.5
1961	578.3	167.7	192.0	40.9	314.5
1962	600.5	184.3	215.6	45.4	358.5
1963	615.3	191.1	237.5	50.5	401.2
1964	658.8	203.4	257.7	54.5	441.0
1965	666.5	212.7	279.8	61.0	471.1

TABLE A.1.2. Per Capita Total Expenditure in Current Prices (in Yen)

Year			
1905	54.5	1930	175.7
1906	56.2	1931	156.0
1907	60.2	1932	153.2
1908	68.6	1933	167.0
1909	67.2	1934	183.5
1910	68.3	1935	188.9
1911	74.7	1936	195.3
1912	81.3	1937	218.7
1913	85.8	1938	241.4
1914	72.4	1952	43,909.7
1915	71.7	1953	51,997.6
1916	81.2	1954	56,676.8
1917	104.5	1955	59,937.7
1918	147.7	1956	64,267.5
1919	213.9	1957	69,730.7
1920	211.2	1958	73,749.8
1921	205.2	1959	79,866.7
1922	209.8	1960	89,387.6
1923	211.1	1961	101,570.8
1924	214.5	1962	117,528.2
1925	222.2	1963	134,446.1
1926	212.9	1964	151,236.8
1927	206.6	1965	169,122.4
1928	205.1		
1929	195.3		

TABLE A.1.3. Prices

	Food	Clothing	Housing	Fuel and Light	Miscel-laneous
1905	.1064	.1335	.2227	.1834	.1225
1906	.1957	.1417	.2756	.1897	.1253
1907	.1221	.1510	.2835	.2146	.1276
1908	.1145	.1384	.2442	.2562	.1304
1909	.1082	.1342	.2442	.2562	.1300
1910	.1073	.1477	.2562	.2352	.1295
1911	.1209	.1540	.2623	.2294	.1290
1912	.1314	.1535	.2662	.2411	.1318
1913	.1361	.1551	.2602	.2413	.1375
1914	.1199	.1523	.2554	.2235	.1377
1915	.1048	.1444	.2554	.2234	.1404
1916	.1108	.1749	.2644	.2311	.1513
1917	.1458	.2338	.2676	.2760	.1689
1918	.2150	.3152	.2865	.3761	.2013
1919	.3005	.4146	.3259	.4859	.2514
1920	.3125	.3934	.3500	.5217	.2777
1921	.2554	.3319	.4298	.5620	.3048
1922	.2639	.2959	.4414	.5607	.2682
1923	.2537	.3570	.4283	.5499	.2631
1924	.2653	.3553	.4184	.5219	.2573
1925	.2705	.3508	.4443	.5001	.2601
1926	.2503	.3051	.4763	.4860	.2685
1927	.2451	.2733	.5001	.5129	.2654
1928	.2274	.2662	.5026	.5100	.2643
1929	.2212	.2589	.5008	.4571	.2615
1930	.1938	.2087	.4850	.4141	.2508
1931	.1602	.1787	.4767	.3876	.2328
1932	.1690	.1770	.4632	.3560	.2328
1933	.1722	.2015	.4600	.3867	.2349
1934	.1818	.2085	.4512	.3856	.2256
1935	.1880	.2101	.4492	.3798	.2316
1936	.1966	.2142	.4379	.3993	.2330
1937	.2089	.2385	.4420	.4240	.2584
1938	.2285	.3016	.4575	.4713	.2734
1952	52.52	84.53	50.85	76.02	52.51
1953	63.86	83.39	55.32	84.87	58.24
1954	68.42	83.87	58.73	86.20	60.93
1955	66.00	80.54	61.25	87.53	62.28
1956	65.93	80.86	65.96	87.82	63.34
1957	68.21	81.44	68.56	92.86	64.54
1958	68.64	80.54	71.97	91.05	66.10
1959	68.85	79.88	77.41	89.72	67.87
1960	71.27	81.43	81.23	95.14	70.76
1961	75.41	83.96	85.46	97.62	74.66
1962	80.73	88.84	88.71	99.90	80.89
1963	88.60	94.71	92.28	99.81	86.94
1964	91.16	97.00	96.42	99.90	93.3
1965	100.00	100.00	100.00	100.00	100.00

Appendix

Sources for Tables

TABLE A.1.1:

Source: Miyohei Shinohara, Personal Consumption Expenditures, Estimates of Long Term Economic Statistics of Japan since 1968, Edited by Kazushi Ohkawa, et. al., Vol. 6. (Tokyo: Toyokeizai Shimposha, 1967), pp. 132-135; Economic Planning Agency, Annual Report on National Income Statistics, Tokyo, 1968, pp. 74-75.

Note: Miscellaneous = medical + transportation + communication + social + education and miscellaneous expenditure.

TABLE A.1.2:

Source: See Source for Table A.1.1.

TABLE A.1.3:

Source: Kazushi Ohkawa, et al., Prices, Estimates of Long-Term Economic Statistics of Japan since 1868, vol. 8, (Tokyo: Toyokeizai Shimposha, 1967), pp. 135-136.

Note: The price indexes are for urban families. The indexes including farm household by commodities were not available for the prewar period.

2

Permanent Income and the Transaction Demand for Money by Households

Shozaburo Fujino

2.1. Introduction

Since Keynes analyzed the demand for money, the traditional tendency for investigating it, whether the investigation be theoretical or empirical, has been to concentrate attention explicitly or implicitly on consumer behavior, applying the analytical result to the demand for money in the economy as a whole. Before we decide finally what kind of aggregate demand function for money we choose, however, it seems necessary that we analyze at first the demand for money by households and by business firms, respectively, because in households the key variables of various asset holdings are the demand for money and the demand for liquid assets other than money, on the one hand, while business firms are mainly concerned with physical assets holdings and money holdings, on the other; and because it seems that both economic units have different processes for adjusting their demand for money to their supply of money.[1]

The purpose of this paper is to investigate the transaction demand for money in households by examining behavior of currency holdings observed in consumer survey data in Japan, where consumers buy almost all consumption goods through the medium of currency, seldom or never holding a checking account in a bank,

[1] Hitotsubashi Journal of Economics, vol. 5, no. 1 (June 1964), pp. 38-51. Reprinted by courtesy of the author.

so that behavior of balances of currency held by them reflects very well that of transaction demand for money.

Showing, at first, our hypothesis in regard to the expenditure elasticity of transaction demand for money, we shall investigate cross-section data in the Bureau of Statistics' Survey of Income and Expenditure, making these data tell us various interesting facts regarding consumer holdings of currency. Then we shall explain these facts simultaneously by the permanent income hypothesis. In the process, however, we shall introduce not only the permanent but also the transitory components of income into our demand function for money, to explain the long term as well as the short term behavior of transaction demand for money by households.

2.2. Expenditure and the Transaction Demand for Money: Hypothesis and Facts

Households obtain money by receiving their income and then release it daily for expenditure. Therefore their demand for money for transaction motives must be closely connected with consumption expenditure. They are, in principle, able to choose freely a transaction period for income receivings or expenditure payments from possible periods for transactions. However, in practice, their choice of an employment opportunity means at the same time the designation of an income receiving period, at least under the present economic system. Therefore the transaction period will be a given condition for the current household enjoying some job opportunity, on the one hand, and there are only a limited number of payment periods, even if this household could select a period among alternatives, on the other. Accordingly, the usual hypothesis assuming a given transaction period is not always unrealistic. That is, we can assume without any fear of leaving out essential aspects of household behavior that the key variable to analyze the transaction demand for money by households is consumption expenditure.

There are three possible sizes of elasticity of demand for money in regard to consumption expenditure: greater than unity, equal to unity, and less than unity. According to W. J. Baumol's and J. Tobin's analyses, the transaction demand for money changes in proportion to the square root of turnover or expenditure, so that the ratio of cash balances to expenditure decreases with an increase in total expenditure; the expenditure elasticity of demand for money is 0.5.[2] This conclusion is derived from an application of an analysis of determination of optimal inventory[3] to that of optimal cash balances, presupposing that households and/or economic units promptly transform income received into interest-bearing assets (for instance, interest-bearing deposits), and pay expenditures by selling (or withdrawing) them. These topics will be examined later.

An alternative hypothesis is that the expenditure elasticity of demand for money equals unity. Excluding the possibility of diseconomy of large-scale utilizing of money on a priori grounds, there remain two possibilities: (1) households discover economies of scale, or (2) do not discover economies. The Baumol-Tobin model assumes the former type of behavior, and the second hypothesis the latter, which we shall choose to analyze the behavior of households' transaction demand for money in the following. Although it is possible that the ratio of currency balances held by households to their expenditure depends on variables other than expenditure and/or income, we assume that the key variable is expenditure and/or income that influences the transaction demand for money essentially. Whether it is proportional to the consumption expenditure or not, its behavior is closely related to the behavior of consumption. In consequence it will be related to income and other variables through the consumption function.

Before proceeding with our analysis, let us show a few facts regarding household's transaction demand for money. In the Bureau of Statistics' Survey of Consumer Income and Expenditure we have by income groups such items as "balances of currency at the beginning of the month" and "balances of currency at the end of the month" in addition to other items as income, expenditures and so forth. By these materials, we obtain Table 2.1, which shows the currency-income ratios as well as the currency-consumption ratios by income groups in 1953. 1953's figures are shown as the representative of those in other years, because the latter brings similar observations.[4]

Our observations obtained from Table 2.1 are as follows:

1. The ratio of balances of currency to disposable income declines as the income group moves from low to high income, whether we take balances of currency held at the beginning of

TABLE 2.1. THE CURRENCY-INCOME RATIO AND THE CURRENCY-CONSUMPTION RATIO BY INCOME GROUPS (CONSUMERS IN ALL URBAN AREAS, 1953)

Income Group (unit: yen)	The Currency-Income Ratio			The Currency-Consumption Ratio		
	$\frac{M_0}{Y}$	$\frac{M_0'}{Y}$	$\frac{\bar{M}_0}{Y}$	$\frac{M_0}{C}$	$\frac{M_0'}{C}$	$\frac{\bar{M}_0}{C}$
Average	37.28	38.56	37.92	38.91	40.25	39.58
0-3,999	1,191.24	339.44	765.34	89.37	25.47	57.42
4,000-7,999	89.75	52.64	71.20	52.18	30.61	41.40
8,000-11,999	62.29	48.62	55.46	50.00	39.03	44.52
12,000-15,999	49.63	46.87	48.25	46.40	43.82	45.11
16,000-19,999	41.46	40.90	41.18	41.31	40.75	41.03
20,000-23,999	37.56	38.97	38.26	37.99	40.14	39.07
24,000-27,999	35.55	38.51	37.03	38.06	41.23	39.65
28,000-31,999	34.75	38.10	36.42	37.31	40.91	39.11
32,000-35,999	31.55	35.63	33.59	35.04	39.57	37.31
36,000-39,999	29.64	34.67	32.16	33.55	39.24	36.40
40,000-43,999	28.65	34.00	31.32	32.93	39.08	36.01
44,000-47,999	27.44	32.59	30.02	32.10	38.13	36.12
48,000-51,999	23.24	32.09	27.67	28.13	38.85	33.49
52,000-55,999	23.73	31.37	27.55	28.79	38.07	33.43
56,000-59,999	22.05	32.38	27.22	29.10	42.73	35.92
60,000-	20.85	31.15	26.00	28.37	42.39	35.38

month $\underline{M}_0$ or those at the end of month $\underline{M}'_0$ to represent balances of currency held by consumer units.

2. In addition we observe that the ratio of balances of currency at the beginning of the month to disposable income $(\underline{M}_0/\underline{Y})$ is greater in low income groups, but is less than the ratio of balances of currency at the end of the month to disposable income $(\underline{M}'_0/\underline{Y})$ in high income groups.

3. We find in Table 2.1 a declining tendency of the ratios of average of $\underline{M}_0$ and $\underline{M}'_0$ to consumption $(\overline{M}_0/\underline{C})$ from 57.4% in the lowest to 35.4% in the highest income group, though some irregular movements are found there. The ratio $(\underline{M}_0/\underline{C})$ shows also similar behavior over various income groups.

4. The ratio $(\underline{M}'_0/\underline{C})$, however, increases at first, then turns into a diminishing tendency, as the income group moves from low to high income.

5. The ratio $(\underline{M}_0/\underline{C})$ is greater than the ratio $(\underline{M}'_0/\underline{C})$ in low income groups, but the opposite is true in high income groups.

2.3. Examination of Cross-Section Data (1)

Are the above observed facts favorable to our hypothesis or to the Baumol-Tobin hypothesis?

Now, suppose the following relationship holds to explain the behavior of the transaction demand for money $\underline{M}_T$:

$$(2.1) \qquad \underline{M}_T/\underline{C} = \underline{AC^r}.$$

And let us represent $\underline{M}_T$ by $\overline{M}_0$. According to the data shown in Table 2.1, the ratio $(\overline{M}_0/\underline{C})$ is 57.42% in the lowest and 35.38% in the highest income group, and the $\underline{C}$ which are not given in Table 2.1 are 13,382 yen and 43,785 yen per month in each of both groups, respectively. By inserting these magnitudes into (2.1) we get

$$(2.1') \qquad 0.5742 = A(13,382)^r,$$

and

$$(2.1'') \qquad 0.3538 = A(43,785)^r.$$

From these two equations, we can easily estimate the value of r, i.e.,

$$(2.2) \qquad r = -0.409.$$

It is nearly equal to -0.5,[5] corresponding closely to the consequence obtained from the Baumol-Tobin hypothesis that the transaction holdings of money are proportional to the square root of expenditure. Further examination of our observations in detail, however, attracts our attention to the fact that observation 4 of the behavior of the ratio $(\underline{M}'_0/\underline{C})$ is not yet explained by it. In addition, how does the Baumol-Tobin hypothesis illustrate observations 2 and 5?

Before advancing our examination, let us describe the Bureau of Statistics' Survey of Consumer Income and Expenditure. The survey asks consumer units picked as samples to keep accounts during six successive months. A sample is, however, not always classified into the same income group in each of the six months. Namely, samples are grouped in each month according to the size of their money income in the month, so that a consumer unit may move from an income group to another as its income changes. If a consumer unit remains in one income group so far as it continues to be in the sample, the figure of balances of currency at the end of a month should be equal to that at the beginning of the next month, apart from the fact that samples are replaced half-yearly. And it seems that there is not any systematic difference between the yearly average of currency holdings at the beginning of month $\underline{M}_0$ and that at the end of month $\underline{M}'_0$ in each income group under such classification of samples into income groups. Thus we can expect that there occurs a systematic difference between $\underline{M}_0$ and $\underline{M}'_0$, because of moving of a consumer unit among various income groups. However, observations 2 and 5 cannot yet be explained by the characteristics of the method of the survey alone.

2.4. Examination of Cross-Section Data (2)

Is there any single hypothesis by which all of the obser-

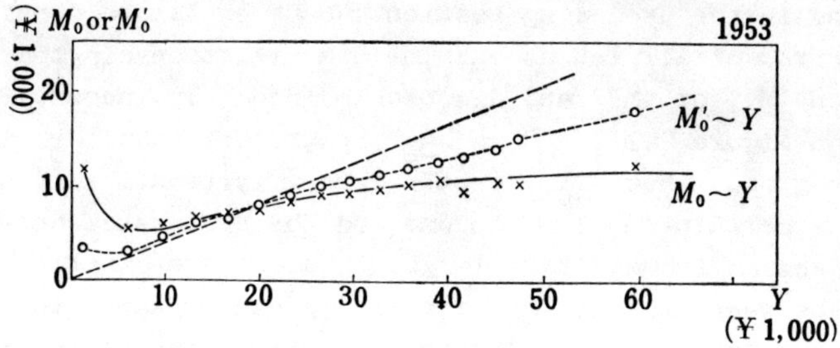

Fig. 2.1.1.

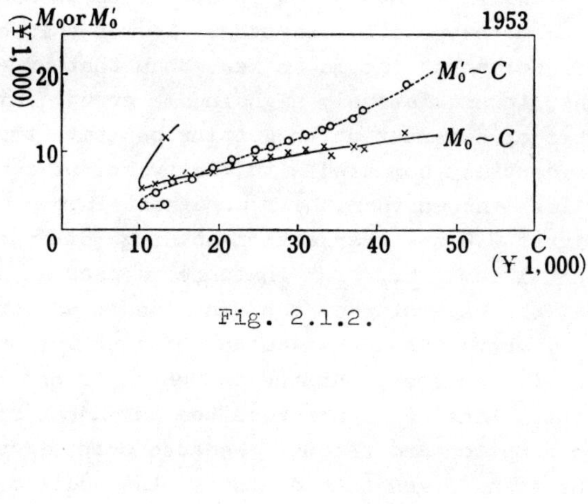

Fig. 2.1.2.

vations in the preceding section can be explained consistently?

First of all let us examine what relationship there is between $\underline{M}_0$ or $\underline{M}'_0$ and disposable income by income groups in 1953 on Figure 2.1.1. Here $\underline{M}_0$ is greater than $\underline{M}'_0$ in low income groups, but $\underline{M}'_0$ becomes larger systematically than $\underline{M}_0$ above a certain level of income and the difference between them increases as income grows larger. We observe similar relationships between $\underline{M}_0$ or $\underline{M}'_0$ and $\underline{Y}$ in other years, too, which we generalize to obtain Figure 2.2, where line $\underline{AA}$ shows the relation between $\underline{M}_0$ and $\underline{Y}$, and line $\underline{BB}$ that between $\underline{M}'_0$ and $\underline{Y}$. As mentioned above, a household does not necessarily remain at one income group, moving among various income groups from month to month. For example, it is ranked in a high income group if it happens to earn relatively large income in a month, and it is classified into a low income group in another month, when its income happens to decrease. If, in this case, the variance of permanent income is less than that of actual income, there might, in a relatively high income group, exist relatively large number of consumer units getting positive transitory income accidentally compared with the number of consumer units obtaining less income than their permanent income by chance.[6]

In Figure 2.2 the transaction holdings of money at a level of permanent income $\underline{Y}_1$, for instance, appear as currency holdings at the beginning of the month under an actual level of income $\underline{Y}_2$, where the actual amount of consumption indicated by line $\underline{C}_0$-$\underline{C}_0$ is less than the one which is spent when $\underline{Y}_2$ is permanent. Line $\underline{P}_C$ indicates the permanent relationship between consumption and income. Because part of savings will probably be transformed into deposits, the additional holdings of currency will be less than savings. At $\underline{Y}_2$, for example, savings are expressed by the distance $\underline{a'b'}$ or $\underline{ab}$. But there the addition to holdings of currency will be relatively small, as $\underline{Y}_2$ represents only the average actual income in a relatively high income group which brings a lesser consumption than when $\underline{Y}_2$ happens to be the permanent. Thus line $\underline{BB}$ lies below line $\underline{P}_M$, which shows the relationship between the permanent income and the corresponding normal cash balances. As a result we can clearly explain why in Figure 2.1.1 the straight line connecting the origin with the intersection of line $(\underline{M}_0 - \underline{Y})$ with line $(\underline{M}'_0 - \underline{Y})$ lies above line $(\underline{M}'_0 - \underline{Y})$

in high income groups. It is in the income group where line ($\underline{M}_0$ - $\underline{Y}$) intersects with line ($\underline{M}_0'$ - $\underline{Y}$) that the average actual income coincides with the average permanent income.

On the other hand, the opposite phenomena occur in low income groups. That is, the lower the level of income, the more there exist consumer units whose income falls below the permanent accidentally. Their holdings of currency at the end of the month will become less than at the beginning of the month, because part of balances of currency will be used to fill up part of the negative transitory income. They will, however, withdraw their deposits and sell their assets and/or borrow money, so that their holdings of currency at the end of the month are greater than otherwise. In Figure 2.2 deposits are drawn or assets are sold or money is borrowed by cd at $\underline{Y}_3$, and as a result line BB lies above line B'B', because the distance between line B'B' and line AA means the amount of savings. Furthermore line BB is above line $\underline{P}_M$, for actual income is lower than the permanent there, but for the former lies below line AA, because consumer units use part of balances of currency for spending without refilling it by received income.[7]

Under the above conditions we could observe a relation between cash balances and income near to that embodied in line $\underline{P}_M$, if we average holdings of currency indicated by line AA and magnitudes given by line B'B' to get holdings of currency. But when we take average of holdings of currency obtained by line AA and those of line BB, the resultant line CC lies below line $\underline{P}_M$ in higher income and above it in lower income than $\underline{Y}_0$.

Regarding behavior of line AA or line BB, a further interesting phenomenon is observed. That is, line ($\underline{M}_0$ - $\underline{Y}$) in Figure 2.1.1 corresponding to line AA in Figure 2.2, shows rather larger holdings of currency in the lowest income group than in other income groups.[8] This is because the lowest income group never includes such consumer units that happen to be pushed up from a low income group owing to positive transitory income, so that its holdings of currency become larger than those of upper but relatively low income groups, which include those consumer units whose holdings of currency are relatively low because of positive transitory income. Line ($\underline{M}_0'$ - $\underline{Y}$) in Figure 2.1.1 or the corresponding line BB in Figure 2.2 shows a similar tendency, although it is more moderate than that of line $(\underline{M}_0 - \underline{Y})$ or line $\underline{AA}$. This will be because the lowest income group will consist mainly of households that fell from upper groups, so that there will occur withdrawing of much more deposits or selling much more assets or borrowing much more money on the average than in upper groups, in order to maintain their level of consumption and therefore balances of currency.

Next let us investigate connection between currency holdings and expenditure, shown in Figure 2.1.2. We can say that it emerges from projecting the above relationship between currency holdings and income into the consumption function. For example, the span of observed consumption over the range between the lowest and the highest income groups is less than that of observed income, and comsumption is greater than income in low income groups, as indicated by line $(\underline{C}_0 - \underline{C}_0)$ in Figure 2.2. As a result,coordinates of holdings of currency and consumption lie far from the origin, compared with those of holdings of currency and income. And there appear curves turning upward and downward with a shape of a fish hook in the lowest income group, because its amount of consumption is larger than its neighbors'. Observation 4 is brought about by the existence of the curve turning downward in regard to $\underline{M}'_0$ and $\underline{C}$. In fact it is obvious in Table 2.1 that the increasing tendency of $(\underline{M}'_0/\underline{C})$ occurs in income groups with greater consumption than disposable income.

Thus, the various phenomena observed in cross-section data based on the classification of income groups by the size of income received are explainable by the permanent income hypothesis. In addition we can say that the observed bechaior of "currency holdings at the beginning of the month" and "currency holding at the end of the month" among income groups provide a new test and new support for the hypothesis.

2.5. Setting up Consumer Transaction Demand Function for Money

Since consumer demand for currency, which seems to represent consumer demand for money for transaction motives, behaves as mentioned above, we will follow M. Friedman's method used in investigating the consumption function. But a weak point existing in presuppositions of Friedman's permanent income hypothesis is to assume that the transitory components of income and consumption are uncorrelated with one another.[9] To adopt this assumption will be certainly a suitable way for finding out the most important aspect of consumer behavior surrounded with the complicated conditions of the actual world. In spite of that it seems that there exists some part of consumer behavior in the short-term which will be influenced by the transitory component of income. In addition, since nonhuman wealth is the accumulated sum of savings, which are largely influenced by the transitory component of income, it is likely to be affected by the transitory component of income in the short-term, although we can neglect its effect in the long-term owing to the play of the law of averages. Specifically, we can say as follows regarding holdings of currency as a component of nonhuman wealth. Survey of Consumer Income and Expenditure data are classified into several groups on the basis of the amount of income received, so that consumer units belonging to an income group in a month will hold balances of currency distributed at random at the beginning of the month. That is, we can expect that the transitory components of balances of currency will cancel each other within the group. Therefore, in each income group average balances of currency at the beginning of the month will be nearly equal to the average permanent balances of the income group. On the other hand, currency holdings at the beginning of the month are transformed into those at the end of the month by having superimposed upon it positive or negative influence by the transitory component included in actual income in that month, so that on the average within an income group currency holdings at the end of the month, we can say, consist of the permanent balances and the transitory balances, the latter of which depend not on all accumulated transitory components of income in the past but on the current transitory component of income. And it is observed in Figure 2.1.1 that the transitory component of income gives positive effect upon that of balances of cash, because the slope of line ($\underline{M}_0$ - $\underline{Y}$) is less than that of line ($\underline{M}'_0$ - $\underline{Y}$).

Now let us formalize the matter more exactly. At first Figure 2.3 indicates to us that relationships between $\underline{M}_0$ and $\underline{Y}$ and between $\underline{M}'_0$ and $\underline{Y}$ are log linear except for the lowest income group, which has different characteristics from

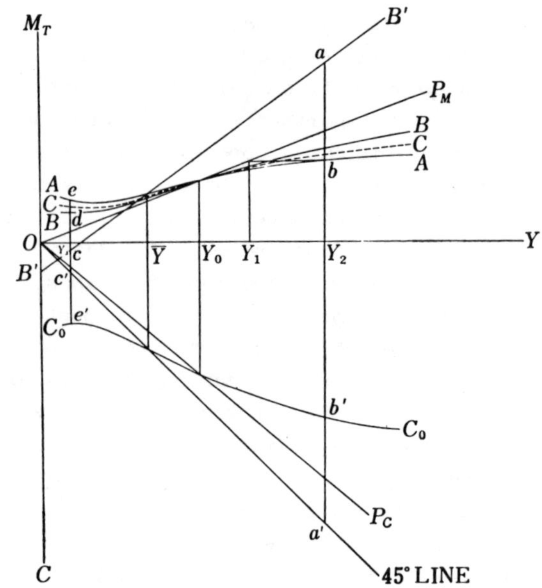

M_T
B'
a
P_M
B
C
A
b
A e
C
B d
O
Y
c
$\bar{Y}$
Y_0
Y_1
Y_2
B'
c'
e'
C_0
b'
C_0
P_C
a'
C
45° LINE

Fig. 2.2.

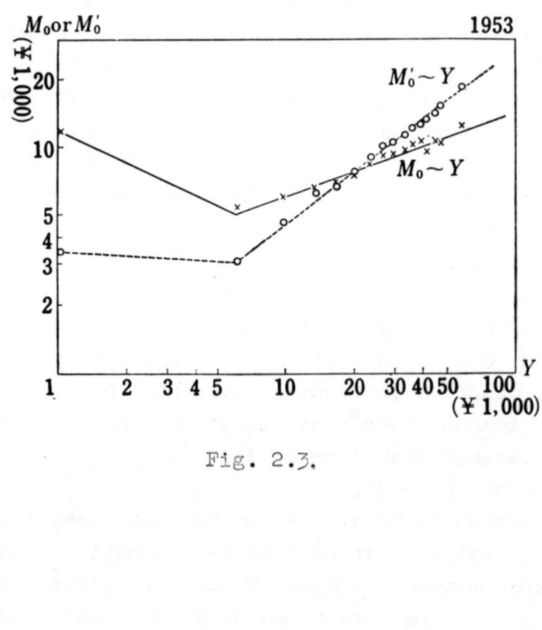

M_0 or M_0'
1953
(¥ 1,000)
20
10
5
4
3
2
$M_0' \sim Y$
$M_0 \sim Y$
Y
1
2
3
4
5
10
20
30
40
50
100
(¥ 1,000)

Fig. 2.3.

the others as mentioned above. Therefore the logarithmic values of actual balances of cash $\underline{M_T}$ and actual income $\underline{Y}$ are, we assume, composed of the permanent and the transitory component, respectively, as follows:

$$(2.3) \qquad \log \underline{M_T} = \underline{m} = \underline{m_p} + \underline{m_t},$$

and

$$(2.4) \qquad \log \underline{Y} = \underline{y} = \underline{y_p} + \underline{y_t},$$

where $\underline{m_p}$ or $\underline{y_p}$ represents the permanent and $\underline{m_t}$ or $\underline{y_t}$ the transitory component of the concerned variable. By our hypothesis that households take advantage neither of the economy nor of the diseconomy of large-scale utilizing of money, we have

$$(2.5) \qquad \underline{m_p} = \underline{k_T} + \underline{y_p},$$

where $\underline{k_T}$ is constant. On the other hand we assume that $\underline{m_t}$ is an increasing function of $\underline{y_t}$:

$$(2.6) \qquad \underline{m_t} = \gamma \underline{y_t} \qquad\qquad 0 < \gamma < 1,$$

where there is no constant term, because it seems that $\underline{m_t}$ vanishes, when $\underline{y_t}$ is zero. From (2.6) we obtain

$$(2.6') \qquad \underline{m_t} - \underline{y_t} = (\gamma - 1)\underline{y_t}.$$

And from (2.5) and (2.6') we get the following:

$$(2.7) \qquad \underline{m} - \underline{y} = \underline{k_T} + (1 - \gamma)(\underline{y_p} - \underline{y}),$$

or

$$(2.7') \qquad \underline{m} - \underline{y} = \underline{k_T} - (1 - \gamma)\underline{y_t}.$$

Second, we can assume that the average balances of cash at the beginning of the month in each income group coincide with the average permanent balances in that group, repectively, on the one hand; and that balances of cash per household at the end of the month in each income group consist, on the average, of the permanent and the current transitory component, so that we infer from Figure 2.3 the existence of the following equations:

$$(2.8) \qquad \underline{m}_p = \alpha_0 + \alpha_1(\underline{y}_p + \underline{y}_t),$$

and

$$(2.9) \qquad (\underline{m}_p + \underline{m}_t) = \beta_0 + \beta_1(\underline{y}_p + \underline{y}_t).$$

If there are no correlations between $\underline{m}_p$ and $\underline{m}_t$, between $\underline{m}_p$ and $\underline{y}_t$, between $\underline{y}_p$ and $\underline{y}_t$ and between $\underline{y}_p$ and $\underline{m}_t$, we can obtain

$$(2.10) \qquad \alpha_1 = (M_{\underline{m}_p\underline{y}_p}/M_{\underline{yy}}) = (M_{\underline{y}_p\underline{y}_p}/M_{\underline{yy}})$$

by regression of $\underline{m}_p$ on $\underline{y}$ on the one hand, and we can get

$$(2.11) \qquad \beta_1 = [M_{\underline{m}_p\underline{y}_p} + M_{\underline{m}_t\underline{y}_t}]/M_{\underline{yy}} = \alpha_1 + (M_{\underline{m}_t\underline{y}_t}/M_{\underline{yy}})$$

by regression of $\underline{m}$ on $\underline{y}$ on the other hand, where $\underline{M}$ with suffixes show covariances between the concerned variables indicated by the suffixes. From (2.1) and (2.11) we infer that if $M_{\underline{m}_t\underline{y}_t}$ is positive, then β_1 is greater than α_1, and contrarily if β_1 is greater than α_1, then $M_{\underline{m}_t\underline{y}_t}$ should be positive. We observe in Figure 2.3 that β_1 is greater than α_1, so that it is suggested that $M_{\underline{m}_t\underline{y}_t}$ is positive. This is favorable to our hypothesis that the transitory component of income has positive influence upon that of cash balances.[10]

Third, we get from equations (2.5) and (2.8)

$$(2.12) \qquad \underline{y}_p = (\alpha_0 - \underline{k}_T) + \alpha_1\underline{y}.$$

And (2.12) gives us the following equation:

$$(2.12') \qquad \underline{y} - \underline{y}_p = (1 - \alpha_1)\underline{y} - (\alpha_0 - \underline{k}_T).$$

Taking the average of both sides of (2.12') results in

$$(2.12'')\quad \bar{y} - \bar{y}_p = (1 - \alpha_1)\bar{y} - (\alpha_0 - k_T),$$

where $\bar{y}$ or $\bar{y}_p$ expresses arithmetic mean of y or y_p, respectively. Now let us define τ as follows:

$$(2.13)\quad \bar{y} = \bar{y}_p + \tau.$$

We substitute equation (2.13) into equation (2.12") to get

$$(2.14)\quad \bar{y} = \frac{1}{1 - \alpha_1}[(\alpha_0 - k_T) + \tau].$$

Rewriting (2.14) gives us

$$(2.14')\quad y - \bar{y} = \frac{1}{1 - \alpha_1}[(1 - \alpha_1)y - (\alpha_0 - k_T) - \tau].$$

Let us substitute (2.12') into (2.14') to obtain

$$(2.15)\quad y_t = (1 - \alpha_1)(y - \bar{y}) + \tau.$$

From (2.7') and (2.15) we get

$$(2.16)\quad m - y = k_T - (1 - \gamma)\tau + b(\bar{y} - y),$$

where b represents $(1 - \gamma)(1 - \alpha_1)$. If τ is equal to zero, i.e., if $\bar{y}$ coincides with $\bar{y}_p$, then (2.16) is transformed into the following:

$$(2.17)\quad m - y = k_T + b(\bar{y} - y).$$

If this is the case, we can measure the demand function for money including not only the influence of the permanent component of income but also that of the transitory component of income upon the demand for money for transaction motives. In addition we can fix the true, long-term relationship between the demand for cash balances and income, because we are able to estimate the size of k_T itself.

2.6. A Measurement of Consumer Transaction Demand Function for Money

Before proceeding to measurement, we should give a solution to the following question, referred to already in note 10. Is the transitory component of cash balances actually influenced not only by the current but also by the past transitory component of income, although we assumed in equation (2.6) that $\underline{m}_t$ depends only on the current transitory component of income $\underline{y}_t$? It could, we believe, be affected by both. But the latter effect must be relatively minor, because the concerned transaction demand for money is closely related to the amount of consumption, which is nothing but a flow variable. Furthermore, in cross-section data the magnitude of cash balances at the beginning of the month will be nearly equal to that of the permanent component of cash balances, as mentioned above. Therefore we proceed to measurement by assuming that in each income group the arithmetic average of both cash balances at the beginning and at the end of the month gives us the sum of the permanent component and the current transitory component of cash balances.

In order to measure the demand function for money, there is one more question to be solved. That is, what kind of figure should we use for representing $\bar{y}$ in equation (2.17)? First of all, the simplest way is to take the average of disposable income given by the Survey of Consumer Income and Expenditure, which is the arithmetic mean of disposable income earned by consumers surveyed, and to convert it into logarithmic value. But the method is basically related not to the geometric mean but to the arithmetic mean, so that the estimate of $\bar{y}$ obtained by it will have some bias. In addition there can occur another kind of bias, because what we take is not the population mean but the sample mean. The first bias will be removed at least partly by such calculation that transforms the sample arithmetic mean of disposable income in each income group into logarithmic value and then takes the average over all income groups. But it cannot exclude the second shortcoming. The situation is not changed even if we could compute the geometric mean over all samples.

It is, however, possible to avoid these defects and to estimate the population geometric mean of disposable income. According to many empirical analyses of income distribution, we might be safely able to assume that the distribution of income among individuals is log normal. Then we can estimate $\bar{y}$ from Survey of Consumer Income and Expenditure data. Denote by σ the standard deviation of $\underline{y}$ and by $\underline{n}$ the number of consumer units with $\underline{y}$. We assume that disposable income obeys the log normal distribution, so that

$$(2.18) \qquad \underline{n} = \frac{1}{\sqrt{2\pi}\,\sigma} e^{-\frac{1}{2\sigma^2}(\underline{y} - \bar{\underline{y}})^2} .$$

Let us define $\underline{E}$ as follows:

$$(2.19) \qquad \underline{E} = \int_{-\infty}^{\theta} \underline{ndy} = \frac{1}{\sqrt{2\pi}\,\sigma} \int_{-\infty}^{\theta} e^{-\frac{1}{2\sigma^2}(\underline{y} - \bar{\underline{y}})^2} \underline{dy}.$$

When we transform $\underline{y}$ to $\underline{t}$ by

$$(2.12) \qquad \underline{t} = \frac{\underline{y} - \bar{\underline{y}}}{\sigma} = \frac{1}{\sigma}\underline{y} - \frac{\bar{\underline{y}}}{\sigma} ,$$

we get

$$(2.21) \qquad \underline{E} = \frac{1}{\sqrt{2\pi}} \int_{-\infty}^{\theta} e^{-\frac{t^2}{2}} \underline{dt} .$$

Therefore we can estimate population parameters σ and $\bar{\underline{y}}$ by getting the value of cumulative frequency distribution $\underline{E}$ in each income group from samples, converting it into the corresponding $\underline{t}$, and calculating regression between $\underline{t}$ and $\underline{y}$. In each year of 1951-1960, data of consumer disposable income classified by the size of income received show a good fit to the log normal distribution except the first and the second group counted from the lowest income group, That is, we discover a fine linear line on the probability paper in each year. Estimates obtained are given in Table 2.2.[11] $\bar{\underline{R}}$ is the correlation coefficient, and $\bar{\underline{S}}$ is the standard error, each of them adjusted for the degree of freedom, respectively. It is interesting to observe in Table 2.2 that $\bar{\underline{Y}}$, i.e., the antilogarithmic value of $\bar{\underline{y}}$, takes near magnitude to disposable income in the income group where cash balances at the beginning of the month $\underline{M_0}$ become nearly equal to those at the end of the month $\underline{M_0'}$. The fact will be favorable to our explanation regarding the relationships between $\underline{M_0}$ and $\underline{Y}$ and between $\underline{M_0'}$ and $\underline{Y}$ shown in Figure 2.1.1 and Figure 2.2.

Using the $\bar{\underline{y}}$ thus obtained, we get the estimation of our demand function for cash shown in Table 2.3, where we do not include the lowest and the next income group to it to

TABLE 2.2. ESTIMATION OF CONSUMER INCOME DISTRIBUTION

year	$1/\sigma$	$\bar{y}/\sigma$	$\bar{R}^2$	$\bar{S}$	$\bar{y}$*	σ	$\bar{Y}$
1951	4.410	4.678	0.997	0.046	1.061	0.227	11,499 yen
1952	4.489	5.189	0.999	0.031	1.156	0.223	14,314
1953	4.657	5.797	0.998	0.045	1.245	0.215	17,564
1954	4.626	5.941	0.998	0.046	1.284	0.216	19,237
1955	4.499	5.816	0.998	0.044	1.293	0.222	19,624
1956	4.606	6.061	0.998	0.044	1.316	0.217	20,695
1957	4.288	5.754	0.998	0.047	1.342	0.233	21,972
1958	4.261	5.836	0.998	0.050	1.370	0.235	23,423
1959	4.333	6.038	0.998	0.049	1.394	0.231	24,746
1960	4.295	6.136	0.996	0.065	1.429	0.233	26,837

* Unit of $\bar{y}$ is the common logarithmic value of 10,000 yen.

TABLE 2.3. ESTIMATION OF CONSUMER TRANSACTION DEMAND FUNCTION FOR MONEY

	k_T	K_T	b	$\bar{R}^2$	$\bar{S}$	M/Y*
1951	-0.302	0.4989	0.313 (0.024)	0.935	0.016	0.4761
1952	-0.269	0.5383	0.331 (0.027)	0.944	0.016	0.5059
1953	-0.377	0.4198	0.429 (0.015)	0.983	0.013	0.3792
1954	-0.405	0.3936	0.300 (0.023)	0.908	0.023	0.3694
1955	-0.404	0.3927	0.344 (0.027)	0.906	0.028	0.3622
1956	-0.410	0.3891	0.374 (0.026)	0.920	0.027	0.3560
1957	-0.425	0.3759	0.281 (0.013)	0.964	0.014	0.3513
1958	-0.429	0.3724	0.293 (0.014)	0.959	0.016	0.3456
1959	-0.404	0.3942	0.365 (0.018)	0.968	0.019	0.3573
1960	-0.398	0.3998	0.354 (0.028)	0.925	0.028	0.3629

*M/Y indicates the cash-income ratio calculated from sample means of cash balances and income.

estimate the demand function, because they have the bias already noted. The figure within parentheses under the estimate of $\underline{b}$ expresses its standard error. $\underline{K}_T$ represents the antilogarithmic value of $\underline{k}_T$. It remains stable around the level of 39% except in 1951 and 1952, where it is irregularly high. The high value of $\underline{K}_T$ in 1951 and 1952 will be investigated later. Let us assume that income is paid once a month and that consumer units spend a certain constant amount every day. Then the ratio of average cash balances to consumption should be 50%, and the ratio of the former to income is equal to 50% times the consumption-income ratio. If $\underline{K}_T$ is 40% under the assumed conditions, the consumption-income ratio should be 80%. But the normal consumption-income ratio of 80% seems to be low. Thus, when we assume that it is greater than 80%, the normal cash-income ratio of 40% will indicate either the consumers' income periods are on the average less than a month, or that consumers spend much more immediately after they receive income than later, or both. In Japan, consumer units are usually paid their income once a month, so that the second reasoning will be, we infer, stronger to interpret the level of normal cash-income ratio.

Although $\underline{K}_T$ stays close to 40% after 1953, there is a slightly declining tendency until 1958 and then it turns upward, if we investigate its behavior in detail. These tendencies seem to result from the fact that $\bar{\underline{y}}$ does not always coincide with $\bar{\underline{y}}_p$ in every year. Let us define

$$(2.22) \qquad \underline{k}'_T \equiv \underline{k}_T - (1 - \gamma)\tau .$$

Then it is obvious from (2.16) that if τ is not equal to zero, i.e., if $\bar{\underline{y}}$ does not equal $\bar{\underline{y}}_p$, the estimate of the constant term obtained from the regression of $(\underline{m} - \underline{y})$ on $(\bar{\underline{y}} - \underline{y})$ is not that of $\underline{k}_T$ but that of $\underline{k}'_T$. And if τ is positive, it will be less than $\underline{k}_T$, and <u>vice versa</u>. Therefore, it seems that τ was increasing during the period 1953-1958 and began to decrease after 1958 and that such gaps between $\bar{\underline{y}}$ and $\bar{\underline{y}}_p$ will explain the tendencies observed in the estimates of $\underline{K}_T$.

Now let us turn our attention to the behavior of $\underline{K}_T$ before 1953. As shown in Table 2.3, the cash-income ratio was so high before 1953 that it seems to have behaved in a different manner in this period compared with that after 1953. The shift was probably brought about by factors other than those considered so far. In Table 2.4 we can compare the ratio of currency holdings outside banks to national income (or consumption) in the economy as a whole $(\underline{M}_1/\underline{NI})$ (or $\underline{M}_1/\underline{CO}$) with the currency-disposable income (or consumption) ratio $(\overline{M}_0/\underline{Y})$ (or $\overline{M}_0/\underline{C}$) calculated from the <u>Survey of Consumer Income and Expenditures</u>.[12] Since the former ratio reflects behavior of currency holdings by consumer units as well as by nonconsumer units, and since there are great differences between the former and the latter, we can infer that the amount of currency held by business firms, to which we do not refer here will play an important role on explaining behavior of $(\underline{M}_1/\underline{NI})$.[13] However the movement of $(\overline{M}_1/\underline{NI})$ or $(\overline{M}_1/\underline{CO})$ corresponds well to that of consumer ratio $(\overline{M}_0/\underline{Y})$ or $(\overline{M}_0/\underline{C})$. Therefore we might assume that the former represents the latter. Then how can we explain its declining tendency in the immediate postwar days? The weight of consumption in national income was very great in those days, as clearly shown by Table 2.4. It will partly illustrate why the concerned ratio was high. But even the ratio of nonbank public holdings of currency to consumption was large and declining so that we need other factors than it to interpret the concerned phenomenon. There could be several hypotheses for it.

Hypothesis 1. Generally speaking, inflation makes the total holdings of money, including not only currency holdings but also balances of deposits, decrease, other things being equal. (See $(\underline{M}_2/\underline{NI})$ in Table 2.4.) But on the other hand, it makes the demand for physical goods increase, with the result that the propensity to hold those liquid assets, which have the highest convertability into them, will be strengthened. Thus, even if the ratio of deposits to income decreases in the process of inflation, the currency-income ratio will increase.

Hypothesis 2. The abnormal conditions of the war as well as of the immediate postwar period decreased the demand for holdings of deposits and increased the demand for currency, because they intensified safety motives.

Hypothesis 3. This is a specific form of Hypothesis 2. The period when the currency-income ratio was high and declining coincides with that where necessaries were put on ration or where the control for rationing was gradually being abolished. Transaction through the black market throve in the

TABLE 2.4. THE ANNUAL RATIO OF CURRENCY HOLDINGS TO INCOME ETC. IN THE POSTWAR PERIOD (IN %)

Year	$\frac{M_1}{NI}$*	$\frac{M_1}{CO}$*	$\frac{CO}{NI}$*	$\frac{M_2}{NI}$*	$\frac{M_0}{Y}$	$\frac{M_0}{C}$	$\frac{C}{Y}$
1946	18.62	20.17	92.30	6.12			
1947	16.98	17.97	94.54	9.97			
1948	13.38	15.07	88.76	13.48			
1949	10.63	12.87	82.60	15.19			
1950	9.80	13.82	70.89	15.64			
1951	8.96	13.43	66.70	15.60			
1952	8.84	12.22	72.35	18.42	3.91	4.09	95.63
1953	8.67	11.46	75.71	19.62	2.98	3.17	94.20
1954	8.30	10.55	78.71	19.77	2.94	3.18	92.56
1955	7.69	10.09	76.18	20.13	2.84	3.13	90.80
1956	7.60	10.53	72.13	21.68	2.77	3.13	88.23
1957	7.48	10.36	72.17	21.32	2.71	3.09	87.53
1958	7.65	10.36	73.88	23.29	2.67	3.06	87.35
1959	7.45	10.85	68.51	23.13	2.76	3.20	86.09
1960	7.39	11.44	64.64	23.38	2.76	3.25	85.11
1961	7.57	11.98	63.18	23.83			

Note: M_1 = currency in circulation outside banks. M_2 = balances of deposits excluding interbank deposits, where deposits cover current deposits, ordinary deposits, deposts at notice, and special deposits. Source of data of both M_1 and M_2 for 1954-1961 is Bank of Japan: *Economic Statistics of Japan* (Tokyo, 1954-1961), and data for 1946-1953 were estimated by the author. NI = national income. CO = consumption. Souce of data of NI and CO is Economic Planning Agency, *Report on National Income* (Tokyo, 1961).

* The figures are for the fiscal year.

economy under the rationing, and the public were used to taking advantage of chances to buy necessaries whenever they found them. In such a situation the demand for currency would become relatively large to consumption or income, because they attempted always to be ready to buy necessaries. As the economy continued to recover and the rationing was abolished, such demand for currency decreased.

Hypothesis 4. All of the above three hypotheses implicitly assume that the demand for and supply of currency were in equilibrium in each year concerned. But we can suppose that until about 1952, there was an excess supply of currency which was later absorbed into rising prices.

These four hypotheses will be combined to interpret the behavior of the cash-income ratio in the post-war period. When comparing ratio (M_1/NI) or ratio (M_1/CO) with the rate of change in prices, we find a positive correlation between them. The postwar inflation was related to the abnormal conditions of the economy in those days and obliged the rationing begun in wartime to remain, so that we can say that Hypotheses 1, 2, and 3 are reflected in the positive correlation, and at the same time the phenomenon observed can be at least partly explained by Hypothesis 4.

Notes

The author wishes to express his thanks for comments given by Professor Hiroshi Kawaguchi when this study was reported at the 1961 meeting of the Japan Association of Theoretical Economics. The author also studied firms' demand for money in his article "The Demand for Money in Business Firms," Economic Review, January 1962 (in Japanese).

1. The author investigated these points in Cyclical Growth and and Balance of Trade," Economic Review, April 1960, pp. 148-159 (in Japanese).

2. W. J. Baumol, "The Transaction Demand for Cash: An Inventory Theoretic Approach," Quarterly Journal of Economics, 56 (1952): 545-556; "Marginalism and the Demand for Cash in Light of Operations Research Experience," Review of Economics and Statistics, 40 (1958): 209-214; J. Tobin, "The Interest

Elasticity of Transactions Demand for Cash," Review of Economics and Statistics, 38 (1956): 241-247.

3. See, for example, T. M. Whitin, The Theory of Inventory Management (Westport, Conn.: Greenwood, 1957).

4. In postwar Japan, consumer income in urban areas in December was several times as high as that in other months, because of payments of bonuses from firms to employees, including white-collar workers. This practice became generalized among various parts of the economy that these payments lost their original meaning of bonus payments and became wage payments rather than distribution of special profits earned to workers. Thus income ranges for grouping households were different in December from other months in some years, so that in the following we shall use averages of various data in January through November in each income group.

5. If we take in equation (2.1) total expenditures including nonconsumption expenditures like tax payments instead of consumption expenditures, we get -0.459 as the magnitude of r in the same year.

6. M. Friedman, A Theory of the Consumption Function (Princeton: Princeton University Press, 1957); pp. 34-35.

7. In Figure 2.2 we should note that there are positive savings at Y_0, where line AA intersects with line BB, so that Y_0 is greater than $\bar{Y}$, where there are no savings at all. Assume for simplicity that line $C_0 - C_0$ is straight in the neighborhood of its intersections with both 45° line and with line P_C. That is, assume the following observed consumption income line for a moment:

$$* \qquad C = a_0 + a_1 Y \qquad 0 < a_1 < 1.$$

Furthermore we assume that the permanent component of consumption C_p is expressed by

$$** \qquad C_p = \alpha Y_p \qquad 0 < \alpha < 1,$$

where Y_p is the permanent component of income and α is

greater than $\underline{a}_1$. 45^0 line on the consumption income space is nothing but the following:

$$*** \quad \underline{C} = \underline{Y}.$$

$\bar{\underline{Y}}$, where there are no savings, is the solution of equation * and ***, so that

$$\underline{Y} = \underline{a}_0/(1 - \underline{a}_1).$$

On the other hand, $\underline{Y}_0$, where actual consumption happens to coincide with the permanent component of consumption, so that line $\underline{AA}$ intersects with line $\underline{BB}$, is obtainable to solve simultaneously both equations * and **, i.e.,

$$\underline{Y}_0 = \underline{a}_0/(\alpha - \underline{a}_1).$$

By our assumptions

$$1 > \alpha > \underline{a}_1 > 0,$$

so that

$$(1 - \underline{a}_1) > (\alpha - \underline{a}_1) > 0.$$

Thus

$$\underline{Y}_0 = \underline{a}_0/(\alpha - \underline{a}_1) > \underline{a}_0/(1 - \underline{a}_1) = \bar{\underline{Y}}.$$

Because we assume that α is less than unity, we get positive savings at $\underline{Y}_0$. The author at first thought that savings are zero at $\underline{Y}_0$. Mr. H. Kawaguchi suggested to me that savings could be positive at $\underline{Y}_0$, where line $\underline{AA}$ intersects with line $\underline{BB}$. Owing to this suggestion, I examined the matter again and came to the elaborated analysis of relationships among consumption, holdings of currency, and income shown in Figure 2.20.

8. In some years of 1951-1960 not only the lowest but also the next to the lowest income group shows a similar tendency.

9. Friedman, A Theory of the Consumption Function, pp. 26-29.

10. There could occur a question on identifying average cash balances at the beginning of the month in each income group with the permanent component of cash balances, because the transitory components of income in the past are projected into the stock variable, although the flow variable has no projection of the past transitory components. We shall discuss this point later.

11. In the estimation we use common logarithms instead of natural logarithms. And the lowest and the next income group to it are excluded from calculation to estimate parameters. We can estimate $(1/\sigma)$ and $(\underline{y}/\sigma)$ by regression of $\underline{t}$ on $\underline{y}$ or regression of $\underline{y}$ on $\underline{t}$. Figures given in Table 2.2 are the average of the two estimates.

12. Although figures to calculate the ratios $(\underline{M}_0/\underline{Y})$ and $(\underline{M}_0/\underline{C})$ are those in the calendar year, $(\underline{M}_1/\underline{NI})$ and $(\underline{M}_1/\underline{CO})$ are computed from yearly averages of currency holdings outside banks and national income in the fiscal year, which begins in April and ends the following March.

13. Regarding the demand for money by business firms, see S. Fujino, "<u>Demand for Money in Business Firms</u>," <u>op. cit</u>.

3

A Model of Investment Behavior: Fixed Investment and Capacity in Japanese Manufacturing, 1952-1963

Kazuo Sato

3.1 Introduction

This paper develops a model to explain quarterly investment behavior and applies it to Japanese manufacturing for the period 1952-1963. In a number of econometric studies of the investment function, the mechanism of investment decision-making behind the investment function is not necessarily clearly specified. Under such circumstances, it is difficult to judge whether particular coefficient estimates are realistic or not. The model to be presented below is intended to rectify this state of affairs by explicitly introducing the process of investment planning and implementation into the model. It makes it clear that the lagged investment variable is an essential factor in the quarterly investment function. As for investment demand itself, the model adopts the stock adjustment version of the acceleration principle, which makes investment demand a function of the capacity requirement. The interaction between investment and capacity is one of the central features of the growth process. This interaction is of a dual character. Current investment increases capacity, while expanded capacity exerts a depressing effect on future investment. The model considers this chain of causative relations.[1]

Economic Studies Quarterly, June 1966, pp. 1-21. Reprinted by courtesy of the author.

The Japanese economy displayed extremely strong internal growth forces during the period under study, frustrated only by recurring balance-of-payments difficulties. Fixed investment played the key role in this growth process by creating effective demand on the one hand and productive capacity on the other. To explain this process in econometric terms is an important undertaking for the sake of the *ex post* analysis and of the prediction of further growth potentials of the Japanese economy. In particular, it is interesting to see whether investment functions usually met in literature can explain the behavior of fixed investment in this period.[2] The alleged phenomenon of investment creating further investment opportunities was often emphasized in Japanese literature on the basis of the seemingly positive effect of capital stock on investment. It has led to the conviction among some Japanese economists that the stock adjustment or capacity version of the acceleration principle did not operate in the Japanese economy in the 1950s. I hope that the econometric exercise of the present paper may shed some light on these issues. Among other things, the present study clearly shows the negative effect of capital accumulation upon investment.

The model is presented in section 3.2. Its statistical estimation is given in section 3.3. Some economic implications of the model are discussed in section 3.4. The appendix presents statistical data employed.

3.2. The Model

Important variables and parameters appearing in the model are listed below.

Variables:

I_t Manufacturers' gross expenditure on plant and equipment in the quarter t

I_t' Manufacturers' new plant and equipment installed in the quarter t

$\underline{C}_t$ Manufacturers' provisional construction accounts at the end of the quarter $\underline{t}$

$\underline{N}_t$ Volume of manufacturers' new investment plans made at the beginning of the quarter $\underline{t}$

$\underline{B}_t$ Outstanding volume of manufacturers' investment plans at the beginning of the quarter $\underline{t}$

$\underline{A}_t$ Desired level of manufacturers' investment plans at the beginning of the quarter $\underline{t}$

$\underline{X}_t$ Manufacturing output in the quarter $\underline{t}$

$\underline{X}_t^{\underline{c}}$ Manufacturing capacity at the end of the quarter $\underline{t}$

$\underline{i}_t$ Effective rate of interest on bank loans and discounts in the quarter $\underline{t}$ (percent per annum)

Parameters:

α The proportion of the <u>new</u> investment plans which are to be implemented in the current quarter

β The proportion of the <u>outstanding</u> investment plans which are to be implemented in the current quarter

μ The adaptation coefficient of investment plans

σ The proportion of current investment expenditure which is to be installed in the current quarter

σ' The proportion of the provisional construction accounts which are to be installed in the current quarter

δ The capacity retirement ratio per quarter

κ The incremental capital-output ratio (ICOR)

γ The expected normal growth rate of capacity per quarter

$\underline{n}$ The length of the planning horizon

ρ The normal degree of capacity utilization

3.2.1. Productive Capacity. Productive capacity or potential output is defined as the volume of output which can be produced if existing plant and equipment are fully operated under normal conditions.[3] A certain fraction of the existing capacity is retired from productive service every quarter, and newly installed plant and equipment adds to capacity. Let X_t^c be the productive capacity existing in the quarter t. Denote by κ the incremental capital-output ratio and by δ the rate at which capacity is retired per quarter. I_t' represents the new plant and equipment installed by manufacturers during the quarter t. Then, we have the following identity:[4]

$$(3.1) \qquad X_t^c = (1 - \delta)X_{t-1}^c + \frac{1}{\kappa} I_t'.$$

3.2.2. Installation of Plant and Equipment. Current investment expenditure does not necessarily increase productive capacity at once. Capacity expands only when new plant and equipment is installed. There are certain time lags between spending on and installation of plant and equipment, which represents the gestation period.[5] Such time lags may be unstable, varying from project to project.[6] However, there may be some stability for the aggregate of investment projects. Denoting by σ_i the proportion of investment expenditure i quarters ago "gestating" this quarter, we have

$$(3.2) \qquad I_t' = \sigma_0 I_t + \sigma_1 I_{t-1} + \ldots + \sigma_T I_{t-T} = \sum_{i=0}^{T} \sigma_i I_{t-i},$$

$$\text{all} \quad \sigma_s > 0$$

where $\sum_{i=0}^{T} \sigma_i = 1$. T represents the maximum period of construction.[7] This lag structure may be of the form of an inverted **V**: new investment gestates gradually but there may be a peak at which its predominant portion is completed. In fact, a substantial portion of new investment is likely to be installed within the first two quarters.[8] Thus, we may approximate this lag structure by the following geometrically distributed lag structure.[9]

$$\sigma_0 = \sigma, \quad \sigma_1 = \sigma'(1 - \sigma), \quad \sigma_2 = (1 - \sigma')\sigma'(1 - \sigma),$$

$$\sigma_3 = (1 - \sigma')^2\sigma'(1 - \sigma), \ldots$$

Then, it is easy to derive the following relations from (3.2):

$$(3.2.1) \quad \underline{I}_t' - (1 - \sigma')\underline{I}_{t-1}' = \sigma\underline{I}_t + (\sigma' - \sigma)\underline{I}_{t-1} \quad \text{and}$$

$$(3.2.2) \quad \underline{I}_t' = \sigma\underline{I}_t + \sigma'\underline{C}_{t-1}$$

where

$$\underline{C}_{t-1} = \sum_{\underline{i}=-\infty}^{t-1} (\underline{I}_t - \underline{I}_t').$$

$\underline{C}_t$ represents the total of investment spending which still remains to be completed at the end of the quarter $\underline{t}$, i.e. the provisional construction accounts in Japanese statistical nomenclature. We have

$$(3.3) \quad \underline{C}_t = \underline{C}_{t-1} + \underline{I}_t - \underline{I}_t'.$$

According to (3.2.2), 100σ % of the current investment expenditure $\underline{I}_t$ immediately adds to productive capacity, while $100\sigma'$ % of $\underline{C}_{t-1}$ is to be completed this quarter.

3.2.3 Investment Plans and Implementation. We shall now turn to a function governing manufacturers' decisions to invest. Business firms first formulate investment programs before implementation. This process must be taken into account. Let $\underline{N}_t$ be the volume of new investment plans (net of cancellations) at the beginning of the quarter $\underline{t}$,[10] $\underline{B}_t$ the outstanding volume of investment plans carried over from the preceding quarter, and $\underline{A}_t$ the desired level of total investment plans at the beginning of the quarter $\underline{t}$.

First, we have the identity

$$(3.4) \qquad \underline{B}_t = \underline{B}_{t-1} + \underline{N}_{t-1} - \underline{I}_{t-1}.$$

Let us assume that constant proportions of new and outstanding investment plans are implemented in each quarter, i.e.

$$(3.5) \qquad \underline{I}_t = \alpha\underline{N}_t + \beta\underline{B}_t.$$

α and β would fall between 0 and 1. They are not necessarily identical.[11] Furthermore, we shall assume that new investment plans are formulated in proportion to the gap between the desired and the outstanding volumes of investment plans at the beginning of the quarter $\underline{t}$, i.e.

$$(3.6) \qquad \underline{N}_t = \mu(\underline{A}_t - \underline{B}_t),$$

where μ is the adaptation coefficient of investment planning. The total volume of investment plans existing at the beginning of the quarter $\underline{t}$ is thus given as a weighted average of $\underline{A}$ and $\underline{B}$,[12]

$$(3.7) \qquad \underline{N}_t + \underline{B}_t = \mu\underline{A}_t + (1 - \mu)\underline{B}_t.$$

If $\mu = 1$, the existing plans are always perfectly adapted to the desired program. The value of μ between 0 and 1 represents imperfect adaptation of plans, which seems to be a more realistic case. On the other hand, once investment plans have been adopted and are being implemented, it is not easy to alter them in any substantial way without impairing the program's efficiency. On the other hand, there is a decision lag in formulating new investment plans, even when there is a considerable gap between the desired and outstanding volumes of investment plans.

Eliminating $\underline{N}_t$ from (3.5) and (3.6), we obtain

$$\underline{I}_t = \alpha\mu\underline{A}_t + (\beta - \alpha\mu)\underline{B}_t.$$

Because of (3.4) and (3.6),

$$\underline{B}_t - \underline{B}_{t-1} = \mu(\underline{A}_{t-1} - \underline{B}_{t-1}) - \underline{I}_{t-1}.$$

Eliminating $\underline{B}$ from these two equations, we get

$$(3.8) \qquad \underline{I}_t = (1 - \mu - \beta + \alpha\mu)\underline{I}_{t-1} + \alpha\mu\underline{A}_t + (\beta - \alpha)\mu\underline{A}_{t-1}.$$

If $\alpha = \beta$ is assumed, (3.8) is simplified into

$$(3.9) \qquad \underline{I}_t = (1 - \alpha)(1 - \mu)\underline{I}_{t-1} + \alpha\mu\underline{A}_t.$$

Henceforth, we employ (3.9)[13]. On the quarterly basis, α and μ are likely to be substantially less than unity. Therefore, (3.8) and (3.9) show why the lagged value of investment expenditure is an important determinant of its current value.

We may note here that there is a simple relation among α, μ, and the planning horizon $\underline{n}$ if plans are consistent in their formulation and implementation. Consider a hypothetical case where both $\underline{I}$ and $\underline{A}$ remain stationary. Then, $\underline{N}$ and $\underline{B}$ also remain stationary. In fact, $\underline{N}$ is equal to $\underline{I}$. If the planning horizon is $\underline{n}$ quarters, producers plan to implement their desired investment program $\underline{A}$ by the end of $\underline{n}$ quarters. Hence, $\underline{A} = \underline{nN}$ in this case. We can readily derive the following relation:

$$\frac{1}{\alpha} + \frac{1}{\mu} = \underline{n} + 1.$$

Both α and μ must lie between $1/\underline{n}$ and 1.

3.2.4. Fixed Investment Function. With the introduction of a function specifying the desired level of investment plans, (3.9) becomes our basic investment functions. In this regard, we must consider the fact that $\underline{A}_t$ is under the influence of long-term as well as short-term factors.

First, the desired volume of investment plans depends on the capacity requirement over the planning horizon. Suppose that the producer looks $\underline{n}$ quarters ahead in formulating his investment plans. He anticipates a normal growth rate of $\underline{r}$ per quarter for the productive capacity. Then, the desired capacity at the quarter $\underline{t} + \underline{n}$ is equal to $\epsilon\underline{X}_{t-1}^{\underline{c}}$ where $\epsilon = (1 + \underline{r})^{\underline{n}}$. The difference between the desired capacity and the existing capacity (including the provisional construction accounts) plus replacement needs should be covered by the investment plans. This component is equal to

$$\kappa[\epsilon \underline{X}_{t-1}^{c} - (1 - \delta')\underline{X}_{t-1}^{c} - \frac{\underline{C}_{t-1}}{\kappa}]$$

where δ' is the capacity retirement ratio for the planning period as a whole. δ' is somewhat larger than $\underline{n}\delta$.[14]

Second, $\underline{A}_t$ is also subject to short-term variations caused by short-term changes in demand and monetary conditions. The expected level of output in the quarter $\underline{t}$, $\underline{X}_t^{e}$, deviates from the capacity level which the producer considers as normal, $\rho \underline{X}_{t-1}^{c}$, ρ being the normal degree of capacity utilization.[15] The deviation $(\underline{X}_t^{e} - \rho \underline{X}_{t-1}^{c})$ should have a positive influence on investment decisions. For the expectation function, we may assume that

$$\underline{X}_t^{e} = \underline{X}_{t-1} + \underline{h}(\underline{X}_t - \underline{X}_{t-1}), \qquad 0 \leq \underline{h} \leq 1.$$

Short-term changes in monetary conditions should have a strong negative effect on investment decisions in view of the heavy dependence of Japanese firms on bank loans in their financing. This factor is represented by the effective interest rate on bank loans and discounts, $\underline{i}$, lagged one quarter.[16] As the influence of the interest rate is likely to be proportional to the economic scale, we represent it by $(\underline{i}_{t-1} - \bar{\underline{i}})\underline{X}_{t-1}^{c}$ where $\bar{\underline{i}}$ is the average over the period.

Thus, all combined, we have

$$(3.10) \quad \underline{A}_t = \kappa[\epsilon \underline{X}_{t-1}^{c} + \gamma\{\underline{X}_{t-1} + \underline{h}(\underline{X}_t - \underline{X}_{t-1}) - \rho \underline{X}_{t-1}^{c}\} - \eta(\underline{i}_{t-1} - \bar{\underline{i}})\underline{X}_{t-1}^{c} - (1 - \delta')\underline{X}_{t-1}^{c} - \frac{\bar{\underline{C}}_{t-1}}{\kappa}].$$

For the signs of the coefficients, we expect $\epsilon > 1$ (for $\underline{r} > 0$), $\gamma > 0$, $1 \geq \underline{h} \geq 0$, $\eta > 0$ and $\delta' > \underline{n}\delta > 0$. (3.10) is substituted into (3.9) to produce

$$(3.11) \quad \underline{I}_t = (1 - \alpha)(1 - \mu)\underline{I}_{t-1} + \alpha\mu\kappa[\gamma\{\underline{X}_{t-1} + \underline{h}\Delta\underline{X}_t\} + \{\epsilon - \gamma\rho - (1 - \delta')\}\underline{X}_{t-1}^{c} - \eta(\underline{i}_{t-1} - \bar{\underline{i}})\underline{X}_{t-1}^{c} - \frac{\underline{C}_{t-1}}{\kappa}].$$

We can note that the effect of capacity or capital accumulation upon investment plans is positive or negative according as the long-term growth factor (ϵ) exceeds or falls short of the sum of the short-term response factor $(\gamma\rho)$ and the past capital accumulation factor (after adjusting for required replacements) $(1 - \delta')$. The capacity effect is positive only if the producer has extremely high growth expectations, low short-term responses to changes in current production, and a low degree of capacity utilization which is considered to be normal.

3.3. Statistical Estimation

Our model presented in section 3.2, is applied to Japanese manufacturing for the period beginning the middle of 1952 and ending in 1963, which covers three full cycles. Because of a number of statistical problems not fully resolved, the following exercise should be viewed as an attempt to derive broadly consistent rather than exact coefficient estimates.

Basic data and their sources are given in the Statistical Appendix. The quarterly series of investment expenditure and installations refer to manufacturing corporations. Investment expenditure is defined as purchases of new fixed tangible assets (excluding land but including expenditures on provisional construction accounts). Sales and purchases of second-hand capital goods are not included. Output and capacity indexes are derived from seasonally adjusted official MITI (Ministry of International Trade and Industry) indexes for all manufacturing. The fact that the output index is expressed with 1955 = 100 should be kept in mind in interpreting statistical results.

3.3.1. Productive Capacity. Equation (3.1) is rewritten as

$$(\underline{X}_t^{\underline{c}} - \underline{X}_{t-1}^{\underline{c}}) + \delta \underline{X}_{t-1}^{\underline{c}} = \frac{\underline{I}_t'}{\kappa} .$$

Summing this equation from $\underline{t} = 1$ to $\underline{T}$, we have

$$\underline{X}_T^{\underline{c}} - \underline{X}_0^{\underline{c}} + \delta \sum_1^{\underline{T}} \underline{X}_{t-1}^{\underline{c}} = \frac{1}{\kappa} \sum_1^{\underline{T}} \underline{I}_t' .$$

Denote the left-hand side by ξ_T. Then, the incremental capital output-ratio (ICOR), κ, between the quarters 1 and T can be obtained as $\sum_1^T I_t'/\xi_T$.

Given the retirement rate δ, we can readily estimate the ICOR. However, we do not have any well established estimate of δ. The value of δ depends on the manner in which the existing capital goods lose productive efficiencies. Suppose that capital goods have a fixed lifetime, say of T years, during which their efficiencies remain unimpaired. In this case, the capacity retired this year is the part associated with capital goods installed T years ago. On this assumption, δ is closely analogous to the replacement ratio of conventionally defined gross fixed capital stock. The EPA (Economic Planning Agency) study[17] estimates that 2.1% of gross fixed capital stock was replaced per annum on the average during the 1950s. This replacement amounted to 22.2% of the total gross investment installed.

On the other hand, corresponding to the concept of net capital stock, we may assume that wear and tear exponentially reduces efficiencies of capital goods over time. In this case, δ represents not physical withdrawals of capital goods but deterioration in productive efficiencies. Assume that δ is fairly well represented by the declining-balance depreciation rate. The EPA study[18] gives $\delta = 11.3\%$ per annum for the net capital stock in manufacturing. These two types of estimates probably provide the minimum and maximum values of δ. Hence, we get $0.0050 \leq \delta \leq 0.027$ per quarter.

Table 3.1 presents the estimates of the ICOR computed for selected values of δ. As the period may be separated into three subperiods, during each of which the ICOR is roughly constant, the ICOR is computed between the terminal quarters of each subperiod and the entire period. (See Figure 3.1 comparing $\sum_1^T I_t'$ and ξ_T for $\delta = 0.0050$.)

The fact that these estimates of δ are reasonable is corroborated by the MITI study of manufacturing capacity[19] which estimates the ICOR at 1.25 in 1959-61,[20] which is a ratio of the book value of installed fixed assets less that of

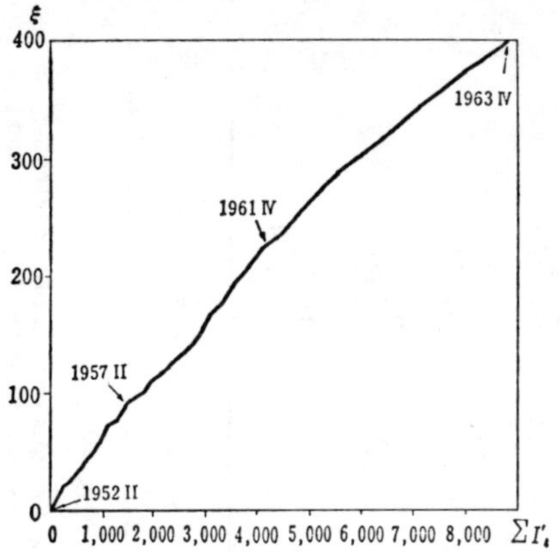

Fig. 3.1. The Capital-Output Relation, 1952 IIQ-1963 IVQ, δ = 0.0050 per quarter

retired ones during the one year to the increase in capacity (in 1960 prices) in the same year. If the book value of installed assets is taken instead as the denominator, the ICOR is 1.33 and, when price changes are corrected, 1.16.[21] Note that this estimate corresponds to the case of $\delta = 0$ in Table 3.1.

In all cases considered, there are similar rising trends in κ. However, the actual rise in κ is probably not as much as the table suggests for any constant value of δ because there is reason to believe that δ has been increasing. The rapid rate of technical progress observed in the period under study must have increased the proportion of obsolete equipment, especially toward the end of our sample period.[22]

We have no reliable information on the particular value of δ. Judging from the replacement ratio implied by the value of δ,[23] we tentatively choose $\delta = 0.010$ and $\kappa =$ 20 (ICOR(1)).

3.3.2 Installation of Plant and Equipment. Using the series of $\underline{C}$, obtained by cumulating the differences $\underline{I} - \underline{I}'$ from 1950 IQ, we have obtained the following regression for equation (3.2.2) for 1952 IIQ-1963 IVQ:

$$\text{(R.1)} \qquad \underline{I}_t' = \underset{(0.054)}{0.325}\,\underline{C}_{t-1} + \underset{(0.079)}{0.528}\,\underline{I}_t + 7.7,$$

$$\underline{R}^2 = 0.9245 \qquad \text{d.f.} = 43$$

TABLE 3.1. INCREMENTAL CAPITAL -OUTPUT RATIOS, 1952 IIQ-1963 IVQ*

Subperiod	δ	0	0.005	0.0075	0.010	0.020	0.027
1. 1952 IIQ-1957 IIQ	(1)	17.90	15.55	14.60	13.75	11.16	9.86
	(2)	0.884	0.768	0.721	0.679	0.551	0.487
2. 1957 IIQ-1961 IVQ	(1)	24.03	21.41	20.30	19.30	16.14	14.47
	(2)	1.187	1.057	1.002	0.953	0.797	0.714
3. 1961 IVQ-1963 IVQ	(1)	30.68	28.95	27.05	25.38	20.30	17.89
	(2)	1.663	1.430	1.336	1.253	1.002	0.883
1+2+3. 1952 IIQ-1963IVQ	(1)	25.22	22.12	20.83	19.69	16.16	14.35
	(2)	1.245	1.092	1.029	0.972	0.798	0.709
Ratio of replacement to gross increase in capacity (%)+		0	12.3	17.4	21.9	35.9	43.3

*1. The units are $\underline{I}'$ in billions of 1955 yen and ξ built up from $\underline{X}^{c}$ (index).

2. (1) expressed as the conventional ICOR. Corporate value added (in the Census of Manufactures definition) was 2025 billion yen in 1955 according to Corportate Enterprise Statistics (annual). Hence, (2) = (1) ÷ 20.25 represents the ICOR on the annual basis.

+ $\delta \sum_{1}^{\underline{T}} \underline{X}_{\underline{t}-1}^{\underline{c}}/\xi_{\underline{T}}$.

Some experimentation shows that the regression coefficients are fairly stable.[24] We have $\sigma = 0.528$ and $\sigma' = 0.325$; the average gestation period is estimated at 2.45 quarters. The constant term is negligibly small.

3.3. Investment Plans. For the values of α and β, we may consult estimates directly derived from the surveys of investment intentions which have been conducted semiannually by the EPA since 1957.[25] Table 3.2 presents such estimates of α and β for all industry.

Inspection of the table suggests that there is no significant difference between α and β, apart from random errors. Therefore, setting $\alpha = \beta$, we obtain semiannual and quarterly estimates of $\alpha = \beta$. Comparing them with the degree of capacity utilization, we find a positive correlation. Regressing the quarterly estimates of $\alpha = \beta$ on the average of X_t/X_t^c in the half year to which the survey refers (denoted by $\bar{x}$), we obtain

$$\text{(R.2)} \qquad \alpha = \underset{(0.062)}{0.245}x + 0.0015, \qquad R^2 = 0.5951, \quad s_u = 0.012,$$

for the 13 observations in Table 3.2 (both α and x expressed in percent) (see Figure 3.2). It indicates that corporations

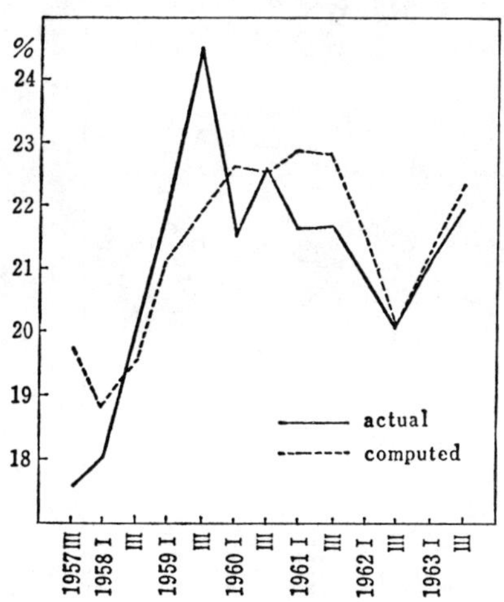

Fig. 3.2. Quarterly Estimates of $\alpha = \beta$

TABLE 3.2. ESTIMATES OF α AND β

Time of Survey	Semiannual Basis α (1)	β (2)	α = β (3)	Quarterly Basis α = β (4)
1957	0.392	0.313	0.325	0.175
1958 IIIQ	0.327	0.322	0.323	0.181
IIIQ	0.311	0.358	0.348	0.197
1959 I Q	0.290	0.399	0.363	0.217
IIIQ	0.395	0.446	0.435	0.244
1960 I Q	0.339	0.371	0.362	0.214
IIIQ	0.438	0.402	0.409	0.224
1961 I Q	0.315	0.383	0.362	0.215
IIIQ	0.371	0.392	0.388	0.215
1962 I Q	0.407	0.362	0.371	0.208
IIIQ	0.416	0.360	0.369	0.200
1963 I Q	0.383	0.364	0.368	0.210
IIIQ	0.432	0.389	0.397	0.219

Source: computed from EPA, Hojin Kigyo Toshi Yosoku Chosa Hokoku (Survey of Corporate Investment Intentions) (Tokyo, biannual issues).

The survey covers two quarters immediately after the quarter the survey is made (e.g. the survey conducted in 1957 IIIQ refers to the half year covering 1957 IVQ and 1958 IQ). Let I_N, I_B, and I represent the planned investment expenditures out of new, outstanding, and total investment plans during the half-year period. Then, $\alpha = I_N/N$, $\beta = I_B/B$, and $\alpha = \beta = I/(N + B)$ on the half-year basis. To convert the last one into the quarterly basis, we employ the formula $\alpha = \beta = \frac{I/2}{B + N/2}$ on the assumption that N and I are evenly distributed.

plan to implement a larger proportion of their investment plans when demand is expected to press against capacity. Note that these estimates of α and β are obtained from planned rather than actual investment expenditure. However the EPA notes that the difference between anticipations and realizations in investment spending has largely been seasonal; realizations tend to exceed anticipations in the third quarter survey and fall short in the first quarter survey.[26] Thus, we may take these estimates of α and β as the coefficients of plan implementation. We take the sample mean $\alpha = \beta = 0.209$, as its normal value. From the regression equation above, we see that its standard deviation is 0.012 after eliminating the capacity effect. Instead of taking an explicit account of the short-term variation in the rates of plan implementation, we may take $\alpha = \beta$ as a constant and assign all short-term influences to $\underline{A}_t$.

3.3.4. Fixed Investment Function, In statistical estimation of (3.11), the $\underline{C}_{t-1}$ term creates trouble if included as a separate term because of its high collinearity with $\underline{I}_{t-1}$. As its effect is small (provided that α and μ are small), its omission does not affect other coefficients in any significant manner. For the regression purpose, (3.11) is divided through by $\underline{X}_{t-1}{}^{\underline{c}}$ in order to eliminate multicollinearity among independent variables with strong trends and heteroscedasticity in residuals.[27] With the addition of a disturbance term, (3.11) then takes the following form:[28]

$$(3.12)\qquad \frac{\underline{I}_t}{\underline{X}_{t-1}{}^{\underline{c}}} = (1-\alpha)(1-\mu) + \alpha\mu\underline{x}\Big[\gamma\underline{h}\,\frac{\underline{X}_t}{\underline{X}_{t-1}{}^{\underline{c}}} + \gamma(1-\underline{h})\,\frac{\underline{X}_{t-1}}{\underline{X}_{t-1}{}^{\underline{c}}} - \eta(\underline{i}_{t-1} - \bar{\underline{I}}) + \{\epsilon - \gamma\rho - (1-\delta')\}\Big] + \underline{u}_t\ .$$

Even then, however, it has turned out that regression coefficients are rather unstable. Hence, we cannot put too much faith in particular coefficient estimates; they nevertheless give good indications of general orders of magnitude.

We have seen that the ICOR, κ, showed some rising trend during the period under study. However, we take κ as a constant in (3.12). This is because an attempt to make κ a variable parameter failed to produce any significant improvement.[29]

(i) $\underline{h} = 0$. This assumption makes all independent variables predetermined. Applying the ordinary least-squares method, we obtain the following regression over the period 1952 IVQ - 1963 IVQ:

$$\text{(R.3)} \qquad \frac{\underline{I}_t}{\underline{X}_{t-1}^{\underline{c}}} = \underset{(0.090)}{0.466}\, \frac{\underline{I}_{t-1}}{\underline{X}_{t-1}^{\underline{c}}} + \underset{(0.355)}{1.697}\, \frac{\underline{X}_{t-1}}{\underline{X}_{t-1}^{\underline{c}}} - \underset{(0.0358)}{0.1433}\,(\underline{i}_{t-1} - \bar{\underline{i}}) - 0.906,$$

$$\underline{R}^2 = 0.9467, \quad \text{d.f.} = 41, \quad \frac{\delta^2}{\underline{S}^2} = 1.669$$

where $\bar{\underline{i}} = 8.68$. The von Neumann ratio indicates no autocorrelation of residuals at the 5% significance level (the critical value is 1.555). Figure 3.3 compares the actual and computed values of the dependent variable in (R.3). There appear large discrepancies between the two at quarters immediately following the upper turning points, namely 1954 IIIQ,

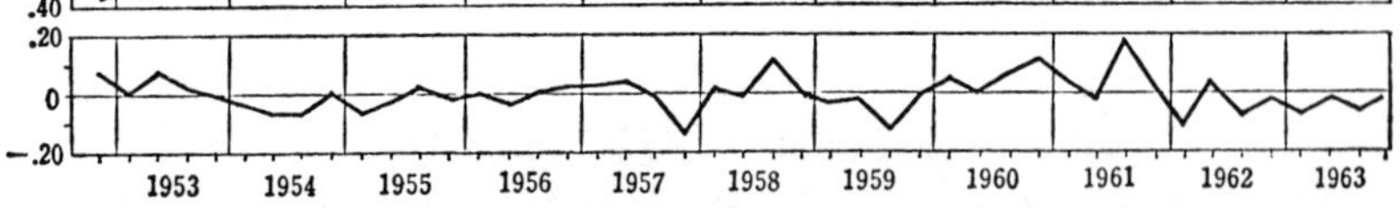

Fig. 3.3. Actual and Computed Values $\underline{I}_t/\underline{X}_{t-1}^{\underline{c}}$, (R.3), 1952 IVQ-1963 IVQ

1957 IVQ, and 1962 IQ. It strongly indicates that manufacturers tend to curtail investment extenditure more drastically at the beginning of slack periods. In order to take this factor into account, a dummy variable D is introduced. D is 1 at these three quarters and 0 in all other quarters. For the same period, the new regression is as follows:

$$(R.4)\qquad \frac{\underline{I}_t}{\underline{X}_{t-1}^c} = \underset{(0.079)}{0.551}\, \frac{\underline{I}_{t-1}}{\underline{X}_{t-1}^c} + \underset{(0.304)}{1.676}\, \frac{\underline{X}_{t-1}}{\underline{X}_{t-1}^c} - \underset{(0.0323)}{0.1021}\,(\underline{i}_{t-1} - \bar{\underline{i}}) - \underset{(0.036)}{0.143}D - 0.949,$$

$$\underline{R}^2 = 0.9619,\quad d.f. = 40,\quad \frac{\delta^2}{\underline{S}^2} = 1.987$$

Figure 3.4 compares computed and actual values of the dependent variable in (R.4) with the three components shown separately.

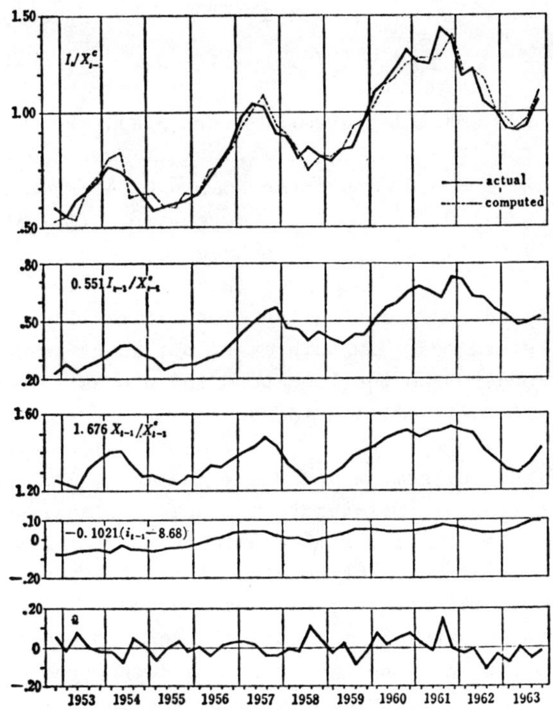

Fig. 3.4. Actual and Computed Values of $\underline{I}_t/\underline{X}_{t-1}^c$, (R.4), 1952 IVQ-1963 IVQ

From the coefficient estimate of the first independent variable, we get $\hat{\mu} = 0.30$, provided that $\hat{\alpha} = 0.21$. If we take our tentative estimate of $\hat{\kappa} = 20$, then we have $\alpha\hat{\mu}\kappa = 1.22$. This leads to the following estimates: $\hat{\gamma} = 1.37$, $\hat{\eta} = 0.084$, and $\epsilon - \gamma\hat{\rho} - (1 - \delta') = -0.078$. If we assume that $\hat{\delta}' = 0.08$ and $\hat{\rho} = 0.80$,[30] then $\hat{\epsilon} = 1.24$.[31] The result broadly suggests that short-term and long-term influences on the desired level of investment are of comparable strength. The negative constant term in (R.3) and (R.4) is also indicative of the negative effect of capital accumulation upon investment.[32]

(ii) $\underline{h} > 0$. Now freeing $\underline{h}$ but still applying the least squares method,[33] we obtain the following regression:

$$\text{(R.5)} \quad \frac{\underline{I}_t}{\underline{X}_{t-1}^{c}} = \underset{(0.082)}{0.634} \frac{\underline{I}_{t-1}}{\underline{X}_{t-1}^{c}} + \underset{(0.294)}{1.524} + \underset{(0.362)}{0.893} \frac{\underline{X}_{t-1}}{\underline{X}_{t-1}^{c}}$$

$$- \underset{(0.0351)}{0.0592} (\underline{i}_{t-1} - \bar{\underline{i}}) - \underset{(0.0356)}{0.1165} \underline{D} - 0.923$$

$$\underline{R}^2 = 0.9671, \quad \text{d.f.} = 39, \quad \frac{\delta^2}{\underline{S}^2} = 2.11$$

which shows a small improvement over (R.4). We find that $\underline{h} = 0.59$, i.e. $\underline{X}_t^{c} = 0.4\, \underline{X}_{t-1} + 0.6\, \underline{X}_t$. Provided that $\hat{\alpha} = 0.21$, we get $\hat{\mu} = 0.20$ and hence $\alpha\hat{\mu}\kappa = 0.84$. From this it follows that $\hat{\gamma} = 1.81$, $\hat{\eta} = 0.70$, and $\epsilon - \gamma\hat{\rho} - (1 - \delta') = -1.10$. If $\hat{\delta}' = 0.10$ and $\hat{\rho} = 0.80$, we have $\hat{\epsilon} = 1.25$. The estimates differ from those obtained from (R.4) in lower $\hat{\mu}$ and higher $\hat{\gamma}$. An interesting point is the close similarity of $\hat{\epsilon}$ in the two regressions. In this case, the short-term influences appear stronger than the long-term influences. The negative capacity effect is still evident.

3.3.5. Fixed Investment and Anticipations. In this paper, fixed investment is related to producers' plans, which are in turn formulated on producers' anticipations of future production. Anticipations are subject to violent fluctuations in response to changes in internal and external factors. Investment expenditure is strongly affected by such unpredictable anticipatory variables, especially in the neighborhood of turning points, which can be evidenced by our failure to predict the intensity of downturns in investment at the upper turning points.

It has been recognized that predictions can be improved by the explicit introduction of anticipatory variables. In the case of fixed investment expenditure such anticipatory variables are firms' investment intentions and sales forecasts. However, the semiannual government survey of business investment intentions (including sales forecasts) has yet a short history beginning at the latter half of 1957. Therefore, we take the series of new orders for machinery, which is available monthly since April 1953. It is known that new orders have a few months' lead on actual investment expenditure. This fact implies that firms make forecasts on their own activities three to six months ahead.[34] Thus, manufacturers' new orders for machinery may be used as an anticipatory variable in our model.

Assume that manufacturers have to place orders for new machinery in the quarter $\underline{t} - 1$ if they plan to purchase machinery during the quarter $\underline{t}$. New orders for machinery are naturally tied in with investment plans, new and outstanding. We may describe this situation as follows:

$$(3.13) \qquad O_{\underline{t}-1} = \alpha' \underline{N}_{\underline{t}} + \beta' \underline{B}_{\underline{t}}$$

where O is manufacturers' new orders for machinery. In our model where $\alpha = \beta$ is assumed, we can easily obtain the following relation:

$$(3.14) \qquad \underline{I}_{\underline{t}} = (1 - \alpha)(1 \quad \frac{\beta'}{\alpha'})\underline{I}_{\underline{t}-1} + \frac{\alpha}{\alpha'} O_{\underline{t}-1} \ .$$

For the series O, we take manufacturers' new orders for machinery placed with a panel of 127 machine producers.[35] A quick comparison of this series of total fixed investment expenditure reveals an apparent downward bias over time in it, most probably because of the gradual loss of representativeness by the fixed panel of machine producers. To compensate for the bias, a time trend is added to the coefficient of O_{t-1} in (3.14).[36] (3.14) is also divided through by $\underline{X}_{\underline{t}-1}{}^{\underline{c}}$. The resulting regression is as follows for the period from 1953 IIIQ to 1963 IVQ:

$$(R.6) \qquad \frac{\underline{I}_{\underline{t}}}{\underline{X}_{\underline{t}-1}{}^{\underline{c}}} = \underset{(0.067)}{0.608} \frac{\underline{I}_{\underline{t}-1}}{\underline{X}_{\underline{t}-1}{}^{\underline{c}}} + \underset{(0.140)}{0.375} \frac{O_{\underline{t}-1}}{\underline{X}_{\underline{t}-1}{}^{\underline{c}}}$$

$$+ \underset{(0.0246)}{0.0923t} \frac{\underline{O}_{t-1}}{\underline{X}_{t-1}^{c}} + 0.1791,$$

$$\underline{\bar{R}}^2 = 0.9571, \quad \text{d.f.} = 38$$

($\underline{t}$ is 0 in 1953 IIIQ and increases by 1/4 per quarter). Figure 3.5 compares actual and computed values of the dependent variable in (R.6). We may note that contraction in investment expenditure at the upper turning points is more accurately predicted.

Since $\underline{O}$ refers only to machinery, while $\underline{I}$ covers both structures and machinery, we cannot put much economic meaning into the coefficient estimates. However, the coefficient of $\underline{I}_{t-1}$ suggests that α' may be substantially higher than β'. New orders for machinery are likely to be more strongly influenced by new investment plans than outstanding ones.

The present analysis suggests that new investment plans $\underline{N}_t$ are formulated during the quarter $\underline{t}$ - 1. Thus, even $\underline{\bar{X}}_{t-1}$ is not exactly known at the time manufacturers make their new investment plans. This indicates an important role of short-term anticipations in making investment decisions.

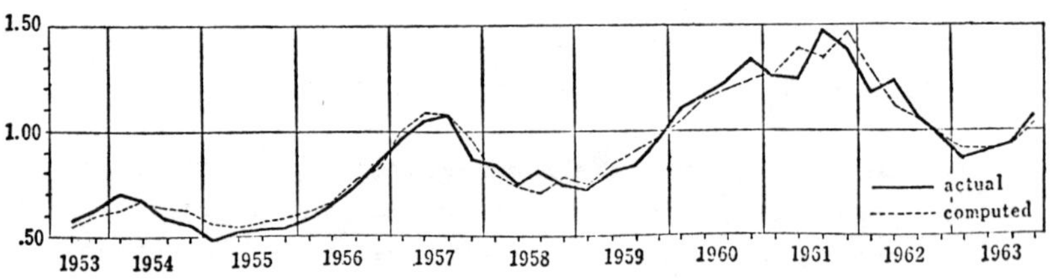

Fig. 3.5. Actual and Computed Values of $\underline{I}_t/\underline{X}_{t-1}^{c}$, (R.6), 1953 IIIQ-1963 IVQ

3.4. Some Economic Implications

3.4.1. Interaction of Capacity and Investment. A meaningful analysis of interaction between capacity and investment, implied by our model, is possible only within a complete model in which the repercussions of investment on effective demand can be analyzed. Here we limit ourselves to a more modest task. We shall see what sort of behavior investment and capacity would follow when output grows exponentially. Our question is whether the model produces cyclical solutions or not.

For the sake of simplicity, let us assume that $i_t = \bar{i}$ and $h = 0$. Then, our model consists of the following four equations:

$$(3.1) \qquad X_t^c = (1 - \delta)X_{t-1}^c + \frac{1}{\kappa} I_t',$$

$$(3.2.2) \qquad I_t' = \sigma I_t + \sigma' C_{t-1},$$

$$(3.3) \qquad C_t = C_{t-1} + I_t - I_t',$$

$$(3.11) \qquad I_t = (1 - \alpha)(1 - \mu)I_{t-1} + \alpha\mu\kappa[\gamma X_{t-1} + (\epsilon - \gamma\rho - (1 - \delta'))X_{t-1}^c - \frac{1}{\kappa}C_{t-1}].$$

Given the time path of X, the model generates time paths of all other variables. The solution consists of general and special solutions. The general solution is obtained by finding a solution to the homogeneous system exclusive of X. First, eliminating I_t' from the first three equations, we have

$$\kappa X_t^c - (1 - \delta)\kappa X_{t-1}^c = \sigma I_t + \sigma' C_{t-1},$$

$$C_t = (1 - \sigma')C_{t-1} + (1 - \sigma)I_t.$$

Dropping X_{t-1} from (3.11), we obtain the following system of equations:

$$\begin{bmatrix} 1 & 0 & -\sigma \\ 0 & 1 & -(1-\sigma) \\ 0 & 0 & 1 \end{bmatrix} \begin{pmatrix} \kappa \underline{X}_t{}^{\underline{c}} \\ \underline{C}_t \\ \underline{I}_t \end{pmatrix} =$$

$$\begin{bmatrix} 1-\delta & \sigma' & 0 \\ 0 & 1-\sigma' & 0 \\ -\alpha\mu(1-\delta'+\gamma\rho-\epsilon) & -\alpha\mu & (1-\alpha)(1-\mu) \end{bmatrix} \begin{pmatrix} \kappa\underline{X}_{t-1}{}^{\underline{c}} \\ \underline{C}_{t-1} \\ \underline{I}_{t-1} \end{pmatrix}$$

Putting $\epsilon - \gamma\rho + \delta' = \nu$, we can transform it into

$$\begin{pmatrix} \kappa \underline{X}_t{}^{\underline{c}} \\ \underline{C}_t \\ \underline{I}_t \end{pmatrix} =$$

$$\begin{bmatrix} (1-\delta)-\alpha\mu\sigma(1-\nu) & \sigma'-\alpha\mu\sigma & (1-\alpha)(1-\mu) \\ -\alpha\mu(1-\sigma)(1-\nu) & (1-\sigma')-\alpha\mu(1-\sigma) & (1-\alpha)(1-\mu)(1-\sigma) \\ -\alpha\mu(1-\nu) & -\alpha\mu & (1-\alpha)(1-\mu) \end{bmatrix}$$

$$\begin{pmatrix} \kappa\underline{X}_{t-1}{}^{\underline{c}} \\ \underline{C}_{t-1} \\ \underline{I}_{t-1} \end{pmatrix}.$$

Denoting the matrix on the right-hand side by A, we have the characteristic equation $|\underline{A} - \lambda\underline{E}| = 0$ where $\underline{E}$ is the identity matrix. It can be simplified as follows:

$$\begin{vmatrix} (1-\delta)-\lambda & \sigma' & \sigma\lambda \\ 0 & (1-\sigma')-\lambda & (1-\sigma)\lambda \\ -\alpha\mu(1-\nu) & -\alpha\mu & (1-\alpha)(1-\mu)-\lambda \end{vmatrix} = 0,$$

which is expanded into

$$\begin{aligned} \underline{f}(\lambda) = {} & [(1-\delta)-\lambda][(1-\sigma')-\lambda][(1-\alpha)(1-\mu)-\lambda] \\ & + \alpha\mu\lambda[(1-\nu\sigma)(1-\lambda) - \{\sigma'(1-\nu)+\delta(1-\sigma)\}] = 0. \end{aligned}$$

It is easy to see that the moduli of the three roots of $\underline{f}(\lambda) = 0$ are less than one for plausible parameter values.[37] Thus, if output continues to grow along a smooth curve, the solution would be convergent to another smooth curve with the same growth rate. Though there is some possibility of oscillations, the interaction between capacity and investment alone is not the major source of cyclical fluctuations.

3.4.2. An Alternative Interpretation of the Model. In many econometric models, investment is assumed to be a function of past profits, which represent availability of internal funds or a proxy for future profitability. Such investment functions are quite close to ours. To see this, let us assume that the particular investment function is given by a distributed lag equation:

$$\underline{I}_t = \lambda[\underline{P}_{t-1} + (1 - \lambda')\underline{P}_{t-2} + (1 - \lambda')^2\underline{P}_{t-3} + \ldots]$$

where $\underline{P}$ stands for profits. Then

$$\underline{I}_t = (1 - \lambda')\underline{I}_{t-1} + \lambda\underline{P}_{t-1}.$$

It is well known that $\underline{P}$ is positively related to capacity utilization. Thus, assume that

$$\underline{P}_t = \underline{a}[\underline{X}_t - \underline{bX}_t{}^{\underline{c}}]$$

where $\underline{b}$ represents the break-even point. Then, the investment function is given by

$$(3.15) \quad \underline{I}_t = (1 - \lambda')\underline{I}_{t-1} + \underline{a}\lambda(\underline{X}_{t-1} - \underline{bX}_{t-1}{}^{\underline{c}}).$$

The function is comparable with (3.11), though the interpretation of coefficients is now different. If we take ($\underline{R}$.4) as the estimate of (3.15), we find $\hat{\lambda}' = 0.449$, $\hat{a\lambda} = 1.676$, and $\hat{\underline{b}} = 0.566$ (assuming $\underline{i} = \bar{\underline{i}}$).

For the profit determination in Japanese manufacturing, we obtain

$$(\text{R.7}) \quad \frac{\underline{P}_t}{\underline{X}_t{}^{\underline{c}}} = \underset{(0.254)}{3.442}\frac{\underline{X}_t}{\underline{X}_t{}^{\underline{c}}} + \underset{(0.0351)}{0.0366}\,\underline{Q}_1 - \underset{(0.0351)}{0.0163}\,\underline{Q}_2$$

$$+ \underset{(0.0351)}{0.0438}\,\underline{Q}_3 - 1.869, \qquad \underline{R}^2 = 0.8425$$

for the period from 1952 $\underline{IQ}$ to 1961 $\underline{IVQ}$. ($\underline{P}$ is the gross profits before depreciation, deflated by the output price index, in billions of 1955 yen and $\underline{Q}_{\hat{i}} = 1$ in the i-th quarter and 0 in other quarters). Eliminating the seasonal factors, (R.7) reduces to

$$\underline{P}_{\underline{t}} = 3.442(\underline{X}_{\underline{t}} - 0.539\ \underline{X}_{\underline{t}}^{\underline{c}}),$$

indicating the break-even point at 54%, which is almost identical with the one derived from (R.5). Putting $\hat{\underline{a}} = 3.442$, we obtain $\hat{\lambda} = 0.487$, which is close to $\hat{\lambda}'$.

3.4.3. The Response Speed of Investment. A change in the desired level of investment plans is transmitted to changes in actual investment expenditure according to (3.8) or (3.9). For instance, a change in the interest rate at quarter ($\underline{t}$ - 1) leads to a change in $\underline{A}_{\underline{t}}$ and hence induces a change in $\underline{I}_{\underline{t}}$ equal to $\alpha\mu\Delta\underline{A}_{\underline{t}}$.[38] The latter will in turn lead to a further change in $\underline{I}_{\underline{t+1}}$ equal to $(1 - \alpha)(1 - \mu)\alpha\mu\Delta\underline{A}_{\underline{t}}$ and so on. Thus, the cumulative effect is given by

$$\sum_{\tau=0}^{\infty} \Delta\underline{I}_{\underline{t}+\tau} = \frac{\alpha\mu\Delta\underline{A}_{\underline{t}}}{1 - (1 - \alpha)(1 - \mu)} = \frac{\alpha\mu}{\alpha + \mu - \alpha\mu}\Delta\underline{A}_{\underline{t}} = \frac{1}{\underline{n}}\Delta\underline{A}_{\underline{t}}.$$

This total effect is asymptotically approached; by ($\underline{t} + \tau$), $[1 - (1 - \alpha)^{\tau}(1 - \mu)^{\tau}]$ of the total effect will have been completed. If $(1 - \alpha)(1 - \mu) = 0.551$ as in (R.4), 91% of the total effect is to be completed within a year. Hence, if the interest rate remains at the new level for a year, 91% of its total effect is to be realized by the end of the year.[39]

Statistical Appendix

		(1) I_t	(2) I_t'	(3) C_t	(4) p_I	(5) p_I'	(6) X_t	(7) X_t^c	(8) i_t	(9) O_t	(10) P_t
1952	I	77.5	80.1	36.1	105.6	103.0	66.9	88.4	9.525	...	59.8
	II	60.6	63.9	32.8	103.4	103.2	65.6	91.3	9.493	...	39.1
	III	40.5	36.7	36.6	102.1	102.6	70.7	94.9	9.523	...	64.9
	IV	47.7	39.3	45.0	102.2	102.4	72.1	98.5	9.382	...	46.7
1953	I	45.5	41.3	49.2	102.3	102.3	74.5	102.2	9.312	...	67.1
	II	54.1	48.7	54.6	101.9	102.1	82.3	105.3	9.270	17.9	93.2
	III	61.9	56.9	59.6	104.8	103.4	87.2	107.9	9.256	20.2	110.2
	IV	69.4	61.1	67.9	105.7	104.5	92.6	110.5	9.254	20.6	105.2
1954	I	78.0	80.3	65.6	104.7	104.6	94.6	113.1	9.188	18.8	112.8
	II	78.6	78.6	65.6	101.7	103.2	92.7	116.2	9.264	14.3	81.1
	III	71.1	74.3	62.4	98.2	100.7	90.1	119.8	9.293	12.3	94.7
	IV	68.6	83.0	48.0	96.8	98.7	93.3	123.4	9.291	11.8	82.8
1955	I	60.2	61.0	47.2	99.6	99.1	95.3	126.9	9.294	16.8	98.4
	II	63.8	71.3	39.7	98.9	99.0	96.5	130.1	0.269	19.3	93.8
	III	67.8	66.4	41.1	99.6	99.3	101.9	133.6	0.114	21.4	117.5
	IV	72.5	74.3	39.3	101.9	100.6	106.2	138.4	9.024	27.5	95.8
1956	I	81.2	70.2	50.3	105.8	103.2	113.1	142.5	8.823	31.3	138.5
	II	93.8	79.8	64.3	109.6	106.4	118.8	149.0	8.683	43.9	141.7
	III	111.0	91.0	84.3	117.4	111.9	126.9	155.8	8.530	50.8	153.9
	IV	132.1	97.2	119.2	121.7	116.8	133.8	158.4	8.477	67.8	147.5
1957	I	154.4	128.4	145.2	122.0	119.4	141.7	165.3	8.435	73.2	164.4
	II	173.3	131.2	187.3	122.4	120.9	151.2	173.5	8.491	63.0	191.3
	III	182.5	158.0	211.8	117.9	119.4	150.6	177.4	8.635	30.4	182.7
	IV	153.7	158.6	206.9	115.6	117.5	144.4	180.4	8.819	24.8	162.6

Statistical Appendix. Continued

1958	I	152.1	146.5	212.5	111.1	114.3	144.8	186.9	8.833	22.6	156.1
	II	142.2	168.8	185.9	109.8	112.1	142.6	193.3	8.834	21.3	156.1
	III	156.7	150.1	192.5	106.9	109.5	148.2	196.3	8.684	29.1	153.3
	IV	150.0	161.0	181.5	107.3	108.4	154.6	202.9	8.508	30.2	178.2
1959	I	149.4	169.6	161.3	110.2	109.3	166.2	209.0	8.427	51.2	214.3
	II	169.6	146.1	184.8	110.7	110.0	179.5	214.7	8.305	54.5	232.0
	III	179.1	184.8	179.1	111.2	110.6	191.6	224.6	8.263	71.3	265.5
	IV	216.5	178.5	217.1	114.0	112.3	202.5	235.1	8.278	71.7	301.6
1960	I	262.1	217.8	261.4	113.4	112.8	218.3	245.6	8.385	80.5	324.1
	II	288.3	253.6	296.1	112.3	112.5	235.2	261.2	8.416	90.7	339.4
	III	324.6	277.5	343.2	111.5	112.0	247.3	272.6	8.406	84.9	344.9
	IV	364.4	348.0	359.6	113.8	112.9	257.1	290.6	8.286	91.7	335.7
1961	I	368.6	324.2	404.0	115.4	114.2	271.3	301.7	8.190	126.9	387.7
	II	377.6	340.8	440.8	117.6	115.9	290.5	319.1	8.090	130.8	381.9
	III	467.3	375.5	532.6	119.4	117.7	303.1	332.3	8.150	133.0	416.3
	IV	460.1	383.5	609.2	121.7	119.7	314.3	345.9	8.350	84.3	391.3
1962	I	407.6	395.3	621.5	118.0	118.9	321.3	356.0	8.390	77.5	...
	II	434.3	420.6	635.2	116.5	117.7	322.1	374.7	8.420	52.6	...
	III	392.0	435.2	592.0	115.3	116.5	320.5	386.4	8.440	55.7	...
	IV	381.6	341.7	631.9	115.3	115.9	319.1	397.8	8.370	50.8	...
1963	I	358.2	390.2	599.0	115.3	115.6	324.2	409.8	8.160	66.4	...
	II	370.2	394.4	574.8	115.6	115.6	343.1	420.6	7.900	75.8	...
	III	397.9	389.2	583.5	115.6	115.6	370.1	430.8	7.900	96.0	...
	IV	456.4	446.4	593.5	117.0	116.3	391.9	441.3	7.880	100.0	...

(1) (2) (3) (9) (10): billions of 1955 yen (4) (5) (6) (7): $\underline{P}_I$ 1955 = 100, X. 1955 = 100

(8) = % p.a.

Sources of Data

(1) $\underline{I}_t$ Investment expenditures by manufacturing corporations in constant 1955 prices. The seasonally adjusted quarterly series of investment expenditures by manufacturing corporations is taken from the EPA[40] for the period 1950 IQ - 1961 IQ. The series is extended to cover later quarters by the author from data given in the Ministry of Finance,[41] the original source of the EPA study. The current price series is deflated by the price index given in (4) below. It is judged from other available statistics that the series seriously overestimates investment expenditures until 1952 IQ, probably because of insufficient allowances made for revaluations of fixed assets which were included in figures of increases in values of fixed assets reported in the original source.

(2) $\underline{I}_t'$ New plant and equipment installed by manufacturing corporations. The current price series is taken from the same source as (1) up to 1961 IQ and extended to later quarters by the author. The series is deflated by the price index given in (5) below.

(3) $\underline{C}_t$ The constant-price series of provisional construction accounts existing at the end of quarter $\underline{t}$. This series is obtained as the cumulated sum of $(\underline{I} - \underline{I}')$, i.e.

$$\underline{C}_t = \sum_{\underline{i}=1}^{\underline{t}} (\underline{I}_{\underline{i}} - \underline{I}_{\underline{i}}') + \underline{C}_0.$$

We arbitrarily set $\underline{C}_0 = 0$ at $\underline{t} = 0$ (1950 IQ).

(4) $\underline{p}_I$ The price index of investment goods, 1955 = 100. This index is a weighted average of the output price index of heavy manufacturing industries and the standard construction cost. It is prepared by the Institute of Social and Economic Research, Osaka University, in connection with

its econometric model project.

(5) $\underline{p_I}'$ The deflator of $\underline{I}'$. It is obtained as a geometrically weighted average of $\underline{p_I}$ according to

$$\underline{p_{I_t}}' = \frac{1}{2}(\underline{p_{I_t}} + \underline{p_{I_{t-1}}}'),$$

to account for the distributed lag character of $\underline{I}'$.

(6) $\underline{X_t}$ Index of manufacturing production (excluding tobacco), seasonally adjusted, with 1955 value-added weights, 1955 = 100. Tobacco, produced by a government monopoly, is excluded from the index. The official MITI index of manufacturing production[42] is available up to 1962 IIQ and then replaced by a new index with 1960 weights. The new 1960 base index ($\underline{X}'$, 1960 = 100) is converted into the 1955 base index ($\underline{X}$, 1955 = 100) according to

$$\underline{X}(1) = 2.70\underline{X}' - 29.4,$$

which holds for the overlapping period (1959-1962, 1st half). A similar conversion is applied to the 1960 base production index ($\underline{X}''$) corresponding to the capacity index (to be discussed in (7)) according to

$$\underline{X}(2) = 2.72\underline{X}'' - 31.6$$

$\underline{X}(1)$ and $\underline{X}(2)$ show very close movements. The index adopted finally here is as follows:

up to 1959 IIQ:	$\underline{X}$
1959 IIIQ to 1961 IIIQ	$\underline{X}(2)$
1961 IVQ and later:	$\underline{X}(1)$.

(7) $\underline{X_t}^c$ Index of manufacturing capacity existing in the middle of quarter $\underline{t}$. This index corresponds to the index of production so that $\underline{X_t}/\underline{X_t}^c$ is the degree of capacity utilization. The index is based on

the MITI indexes of manufacturing capacity accompanied by the corresponding indexes of production, which are available for (i) each March from 1950 to 1957 (with 1950 valued-added weights), (ii) the last month of each quarter from 1955 IQ to 1962 IVQ (with 1955 valued-added weights), and (iii) the middle month of each quarter, from 1959 IIQ on (with 1960 valued-added weights). Capacity is defined as the level of production which is possible under "normal" working conditions in the reporting month and production refers to production in the reporting month in (i) and (ii) and in the reporting quarter in (iii). Industry indexes of capacity and output are constructed from a sample of selected commodities ((i) 66, (ii) 76, and (iii) 127) combined with respective valued-added weights. For concepts and methods employed for the capacity indexes, see note 43. The capacity index used here is derived as follows: Because of undercoverage in the earlier series (i) and (ii), it is necessary to adjust the indexes to correspond to all manufacturing (excluding tobacco). First, output indexes of individual industries covered by the capacity indexes are adjusted to their official MITI indexes of production (used in (6) above), together with corresponding adjustments on the capacity indexes. Second, on an assumption that the degree of capacity utilization is the same in uncovered industries as in covered industries at the peak levels of production, the aggregate index of capacity is obtained for benchmark quarters and then intrapolated by the total capacity index. The index is averaged for two adjoining quarters to represent mid-quarter capacity. For (iii), the index of production (X'', 1960 = 100) which accompanies the capacity index ($X^{c''}$, 1960 = 100) is transformed so as to correspond to the official MITI index of production (X', 1960 = 100) according to

$$\underline{X}' = 1.008\ \underline{X}'' - 0.8 \quad \text{for 1959 IIQ - 1961 IVQ}$$
$$\underline{X}' = 0.974\ \underline{X}'' + 3.5 \quad \text{for 1961 IVQ - 1964 IVQ.}$$

The capacity index ($\underline{X}^{c\prime}$, 1960 = 100) corresponding to $\underline{X}''$ is derived by substituting $\underline{X}^{c\prime\prime}$ for $\underline{X}''$ in these two equations. Then, following the conversion of $\underline{X}'$ (1960 = 100) to $\underline{X}$ (1955 = 100), $\underline{X}^{c\prime}$ is again transformed to $\underline{X}^{c}$ according to

$$\underline{X}^{c} = 2.70\ \underline{X}^{c\prime} - 29.4$$

(Note $\underline{X}^{c}$ is now an index with 1960 = 100). Then $\underline{X}^{c}$ is linked to the capacity index derived from (ii) at 1959 IIQ. For the source, see note 44.

(8) $\underline{i}_t$ The effective rate of interest on bank loans and discounts, percent per annum. Weighted averages of interest rates paid on bank loans and discounts were computed from tables entitled "Outstanding Loans and Discounts of All Banks by Interest Rates," see note 45.

(9) $\underline{O}_t$ Manufacturers' new orders for machinery in constant 1955 prices. The current-value quarterly series, obtained from the monthly series of new orders for machinery received by 55 machine producers (old series available since April 1953) and by 127 producers (new series available since October 1957), are deflated by the wholesale price index of machinery (the Bank of Japan index of wholesale prices of machinery, 1955 = 100). The new series ($\underline{O}$) is extrapolated by the old series ($\underline{O}'$) for 1953 IIQ - 1957 IIIQ according to

$$\underline{O}_t = 1.2644\ \underline{O}_t' + 0.0915 \quad \text{(in billion yen),}$$

which is obtained for the period 1957 IIIQ - 1960 IVQ ($\underline{R}^2 = 0.999$).

(10) $\underline{P}_t$ Manufacturers' gross profits (including deprecia-

tion charges) in constant 1955 prices. The series in current value is deflated by the output price index of manufacturing. Both series are prepared by the Institute of Social and Economic Research, Osaka University.

Notes

The ideas contained in this paper were initially developed during the author's participation in the construction of a quarterly econometric model of the Japanese economy at the Institute of Social and Economic Research, Osaka University. Acknowledgment is made of the referee's detailed comments on an earlier draft of the paper.

1. The present paper owes much to three earlier studies: H. B. Chenery, "Overcapacity and the Acceleration Principle," Econometrica, 20(January 1952): 1-28 for the capacity principle; EPA (Economic Planning Agency), Shihon Sutokku to Keizai Seicho (Capital Stock and Economic Growth) (Tokyo, 1962) for the relation of capacity to investment and the distinction between investment outlays on and installation of new plant and equipment; and F. de Leeuw, "The Demand for Capital Goods by Manufacturers: A Study of Quarterly Time Series," Econometrica, 30 (July 1962): 407-423 for the interrelation between investment plans and investment expenditures. For a convenient and concise summary of empirical studies of the acceleration principle and for various statistical problems which have close relevance to the present paper, see D. Smyth, "Empirical Evidence on the Acceleration Principle," Review of Economic Studies, 31 (June 1964): 185-202.

2. A large number of econometric studies which contain the investment function have appeared in the Japanese literature in recent years. For a survey of these studies, see MITI (Ministry of International Trade and Industry), Nihon Keizai no Kyoshiteki Keiryo Keizai Moderu, (Econometric Macromodels of the Japanese Economy) (Tokyo, 1964); and S. Tanaka "Kigyo Ryudosei to Toshi Katsudo" (Business Liquidity and Investment Activities), Keizai Bunseki, EPA, no. 14 (March 1965): pp. 25-60).

3. For discussion of the concept of capacity, see F. de Leeuw, "The Concept of Capacity," Journal of the American Statistical Association, 57 (December 1962): 826-840); and MITI (Ministry of International Trade and Industry), Wagakuni Seizokogyo no Seisan Noryoku to Shihon Kozo (Productive Capacity and Capital Structure in Japanese Manufacturing) (Tokyo, 1963).

4. The concept of capacity is closely analogous to that of gross capital stock. Let K_t be the manufacturers' gross capital stock available for service at the quarter t. Then, corresponding to (3.1), we have

$$(3.1.1) \quad K_t = (1-\delta)K_{t-1} + I_t' .$$

Obviously, δ depends on the time distribution of fixed investment in the past and the frequency distribution of mortality of fixed assets. On this topic, see R. W. Goldsmith, The National Wealth of the United States in the Postwar Period (Princeton, 1962). It may be noted that δ is influenced more by the rate and direction of technical progress since economic obsolescences may be predominant in the retirement of capital goods. However, the transfer of second-hand machinery and equipment from larger to smaller firms which was in extensive practice during the 1950s makes this factor less important in Japanese manufacturing during the period under study.

5. The gestation period of investment expenditure played an important role in the business cycle models of Kalecki and Goodwin.

6. For instance, in construction of large buildings and integrated plant, investment expenditures "gestate" only after a long period has elapsed. On the other hand, small machines increase capacity immediately upon their purchase.

7. The gestation period may be defined as the average length of time that it takes for new investment to be installed, i.e.,

$$T_i = \sum_{i=0}^{T} i\sigma_i$$

(excluding the quarter when spending is made).

8. There are usually one-year backlogs of unfilled orders for machinery. Because new orders for machinery lead spending by one quarter or more, the lag between spending and delivery is three quarters at most. Thus, the average lag may be taken as two quarters. The proportion of machinery and plant in manufacturing investment has been 3:1 on the average. Thus, even though the gestation period is much longer for construction, the average lag cannot be very much higher than two quarters.

9. We have $T_g = \frac{\sigma}{1 - \sigma'}$.

10. This implies that the new plans N_t are formulated during the quarter $t - 1$.

11. More rigorously, we must add a stochastic term in (3.5). There is a relation analogous to (3.2), which describes the process of implementation, i.e.,

$$I_t = \alpha_0 N_t + \alpha_1 N_{t-1} + \ldots + \alpha_T N_{t-T} = \sum_{i=0}^{T} \alpha_i N_{t-1}.$$

When the lag structure is a geometrically distributed one,

$$\alpha_0 = \alpha,\ \alpha_1 = \beta(1 - \alpha),\ \alpha_2 = (1 - \beta)\beta(1 - \alpha),$$
$$\alpha_3 = (1 - \beta)^2\beta(1 - \alpha),\ \ldots$$

it reduces to (3.5). de Leeuw, "The Demand for Capital Goods by Manufacturers," argues that distributed lags assume an inverted V form in U. S. manufacturing investment. A more recent study, S. Almon, "The Distributed Lag between Capital Appropriations and Expenditures," Econometrica, 33 (January 1965): 178 - 196), proves de Leeuw's contention on data of capital appropriations and investment expenditures. This finding may apply to the Japanese data. However, it is likely that with very rapid growth it is difficult to distinguish the forms of lags.

12. The total volume of the existing plans, $N_t + B_t$, must be nonnegative, i.e., A_t cannot fall below $-(1 - \mu)\bar{B}_t$.

13. In the general case, equation (3.8) may be transformed into

$$\underline{I}_t = \alpha\mu\underline{A}_t + (1 - \alpha)(\frac{\beta}{\alpha} - \mu)[\underline{I}_{t-1} + (\frac{\alpha-\beta}{\alpha})\underline{I}_{t-2} + (\frac{\alpha-\beta}{\alpha})^2\underline{I}_{t-3} + \ldots].$$

It may be noted that insofar as α and β are fairly close to each other, all lagged investment terms except the first two would be negligibly small. There is nothing against including $\underline{I}_{t-1}$ and $\underline{I}_{t-2}$ together in the regression equation, but the high degree of multicollinearity results in unstable coefficient estimates. Note also that the coefficient of $\underline{I}_{t-2}$ is negative if $\beta > \alpha$. (D. Jorgensen, "Capital Theory and Investment Behavior," American Economic Review, Papers and Proceedings, 53 (May 1963): 247-259) employs lags extending more than one quarter in his investment function.

14. Expected replacements are given by

$$\delta[\underline{X}_{t-1}{}^{\underline{c}} + \ldots + \underline{X}_{t+n-2}{}^{\underline{c}}] = \delta[\frac{(1+\underline{r})^{\underline{n}}-1}{\underline{r}}]\underline{X}_{t-1}{}^{\underline{c}}.$$

Hence

$$\delta' = \delta[\frac{(1+\underline{r})^{\underline{n}} - 1}{\underline{r}}] > n\delta.$$

15. See Chenery, "Overcapacity and the Acceleration Principle", and F. Hamada, "Nihon Keizai no Toshi Kodo no Keiryo Bunseki" (Econometric Analysis of Investment Behavior in the Japanese Economy), Economic Studies Quarterly, 13 (September 1962): 15-23.

16. What are the most relevant monetary variables in the investment function is still not answered satisfactorily. The bank rate of interest is not necessarily the best variable to choose, especially in view of the disequilibrium in the capital market of Japan. It is taken here, however, as an indicator of the tightness of the money market. On the subject of liquidity and fixed investment, see Tanaka, "Kigyo Ryudosei to Toshi Katsudo."

17. EPA, Shihon Sutokku to Keizai Seicho, p. 54.

18. EPA, Shihon Sutokku to Keizai Seicho, pp. 38 - 39.

19. MITI, Wagakuni Seizokogyo no Seisan Noryoku to Shihon Kozo.

20. See MITI, Wagakuni Seizokogyo no Seisan Noryoku to Shihon Kozo, pp. 36-40. The ICOR is defined as

$$\frac{p'_{It} I_t}{p_{1960}(X_t^c - X_{t-1}^c)} .$$

For t = 1959, 1960, and 1961, it is 1.237, 1.223, and 1.275 with the denominator being investment expenditure minus book value of retired fixed assets.

21. The ICOR is 1.322, 1.285, and 1.372. Multiplying the estimates by p_{1960}/p'_{I_t} = 0.896, 0.862, and 0.847 for t = 1959, 1960, and 1961, we get κ = 1.19, 1.11, and 1.16.

22. One evidence is the diminishing importance of second-hand capital goods transferred from large establishments to smaller, less efficient establishments. Such transfers decreased from a little more than 10% of total new investment in 1954-56 to a little less than 4% in 1960-1962.

23. The book value of retired assets was 7% of that of installed assets according to the data given in MITI, Wagakuni Seizokogyo no Seisan Noryoku to Shihon Kozo. Note that the former is the depreciated value.

24. If $\sigma = \sigma'$, (3.2.1) reduces to $I_t' = \sigma I_t + (1 - \sigma) I_{t-1}'$. Fitting this equation in the same period, we get

$$I_t' = \underset{(0.187)}{0.498} I_t + \underset{(0.205)}{0.493} I_{t-1}' - 0.3 \qquad R^2 = 0.8773, \text{ d.f.} = 43$$

Coefficient estimates are less stable.

25. The survey is a sample survey of corporations with equity capital more than 100 million yen. However, the share of such large corporations is close to 80% of total fixed investment of corporations with equities more than 2 million yen. Therefore, we can consider it as representative of investment behavior of corporate firms as a whole.

26. EPA (Economic Planning Agency), Hojin Kigyo Toshi Yosoku Chosa Hokoku (Survey of Corporate Investment Intentions) (Tokyo, biannual issues).

27. This procedure is justifiable only if (3.11) is homogeneous, i.e., if it has no constant term. If this condition is not satisfied, regression estimates would be biased. I do not think that such a bias is a serious one in our case.

28. Without the inclusion of the lagged investment term, the regression residuals have turned out to be strongly autocorrelated. It indicates that both α and $\beta < 1$. However, then the disturbance term $\underline{u}_t$ in (3.12) is serially correlated. To see this, let us spell out the original equations with disturbance terms as follows:

$$\underline{I}_t = \alpha(\underline{N}_t + \beta_t) + \underline{v}_t, \qquad \underline{N}_t = \mu(\underline{A}_t - \underline{B}_t) + \underline{w}_t,$$

$$\underline{B}_{t+1} = \underline{B}_t + \underline{N}_t - \underline{I}_t,$$

Solving them, we get $\underline{u}_t = \underline{v}_t - (1 - \mu)\underline{v}_{t-1} + \alpha\underline{w}_t$. If both $\underline{v}_t$ and $\underline{w}_t$ are not serially correlated and are independent of each other, then $\underline{E}(\underline{u}_t\underline{u}_{t-1}) = -(1 - \mu)\underline{E}(\underline{v}_{t-1}^2)$. Thus, $\underline{u}_t$ is likely to be negatively autocorrelated. As Smyth, "Empirical Evidence on the Acceleration Principle," p. 191, points out, negative serial correlation of the disturbance term biases the coefficient estimate of $\underline{I}_{t-1}$ toward zero in large samples. For a given value of α, this means that μ tends to be overestimated. For a concise discussion of other related statistical problems, see Smyth, "Empirical Evidence on the Acceleration Principle."

29. This has been done by introducing a dummy variable. In this connection, we may note that when relative prices change, κ in (3.11) should be replaced by $(\frac{\underline{p}}{\underline{p}_I})^{\kappa}$. From 1952 to 1963, $(\frac{\underline{p}_I}{\underline{p}})$ was as follows: 96.8, 98.5, 97.8, 100.0, 107.6, 111.6, 109.9, 111.0, 111.7, 117.3, 117.4, 115.8. The relative rise of $\underline{p}_I$ offsets the rise of κ to some extent. When κ is variable, a more complete analysis requires an explicit introduction of the underlying production function.

30. We get $\hat{n} = 7.1$ from the relation $\frac{1}{\alpha} + \frac{1}{\mu} = \underline{n} + 1$. Assuming $\delta = 0.01$, we get $\hat{\delta}' = 0.08$ on the basis of $r = 3.5\%$ per quarter, which is the historical growth rate of capacity between 1952 and 1963. The degree of capacity utili-

zation, averaged over cycles from trough to trough, is 78.3% (1953 IQ-1955 IQ), 80.6% (1955 IIQ-1958 IIQ), and 85.3% (1958 IIIQ-1963 IQ). We have taken their rough average, 80%, as the normal degree of capacity utilization.

31. Note that we expect that ε is equal to $(1 + \underline{r})^{\underline{n}} = 1.28$ for $\underline{r} = 3.5\%$ and $\underline{n} = 7.1$.

32. Given the value of α, we can run a number of regressions for different values of μ. This exercise reveals that an increase in μ is associated with decreases in estimated values of γ and $\gamma\rho + (1 - \delta') - \varepsilon$. However, the constant term is negative in all cases.

33. Because $\underline{X}_{\underline{t}}$ and $\underline{I}_{\underline{t}}$ are simultaneously determined, the ordinary least squares method produces biased estimates.

34. One important factor responsible for this lead is the lag from orders to deliveries.

35. Before September 1957, the series was extrapolated backward by the series of new orders for machinery received by 55 machine producers.

36. Without the time trend, the regression residuals exhibit a high degree of autocorrelation.

37. Note that δ, σ, σ', α, and μ are all positive and less than 1. We can easily see that

$$\underline{f}(\lambda) < \underline{f}(1) < 0 \quad \text{for all} \quad \lambda > 1$$
$$\text{and } \underline{f}(\lambda) > \underline{f}(0) > 0 \quad \text{for all} \quad \lambda < 0.$$

Therefore, there is at least one positive real root, say λ_1, which is less than unity. If the other two roots, λ_2 and λ_3, are real, they obviously fall between 0 and 1. If they are complex, their modulus is less than 1 if λ_1 is more than $(1 - \delta)(1 - \sigma')(1 - \alpha)(1 - \mu)$, which is equal to $\lambda_1\lambda_2\lambda_3$. This condition seems to be usually satisfied. As an illustration let $\sigma = 0.528$ and $\sigma' = 0.325$ (see R.1)). Based on (R.4), we have $\alpha = 0.21$, $\mu = 0.30$, $\delta = 0.080$, and $\nu = 0.22$. In this case, we have

$$\underline{f}(\lambda) = 0.342 - 1.463\lambda + 2.091\lambda^2 - \lambda^3.$$

We get $\underline{f}(0) = 0.342$ and $\underline{f}(;) = -0.030$. Because $\underline{f}(0.342) = 0.046 > 0$, λ_1 is larger than 0.342. Hence, the modulus of λ_2 and λ_3 is less than unity. We have $\lambda_1 \approx 0.65$, λ_2 and $\lambda_3 \approx 0.72 \pm 0.08\underline{i}$. It can be easily seen that $\underline{f}(\lambda)$ is very flat and close to the λ-axis when approaching $\lambda = 1$ from the left. This implies that the solutions are sensitive to changes in parameter values.

Based on (R.5), we have $\alpha = 0.21$, $\mu = 0.20$, $\delta = 0.10$, and $\nu = -0.10$ and

$$\underline{f}(\lambda) = 0.385 - 1.574\lambda + 2.165\lambda^2 - \lambda^3.$$

As $\underline{f}(0) = 0.385$, $\underline{f}(1) = -0.024$, and $\underline{f}(0.385) = 0.043 > 0$, we have $\lambda_1 > 0.385$ and the modulus of λ_2 and λ_3 less than unity. We have $\lambda_1 \approx 0.77$, λ_2 and $\lambda_3 \approx 0.70 \pm 0.12\underline{i}$.

38. The interest elasticity of the desired level of investment plans $\underline{A}$ is given by

$$\underline{e}_{\underline{A}} - \frac{\underline{i}}{\underline{A}} \frac{\partial \underline{A}}{\partial \underline{i}} .$$

Evaluating $\underline{e}_{\underline{A}}$ at $\underline{i} = \bar{\underline{i}}$, $\underline{h} = 0$ and $\underline{X}/\underline{X}^{\underline{c}} = \rho$, we get

$$\underline{e}_{\underline{A}} = \frac{\bar{\underline{i}}}{\varepsilon - (1-\delta')} .$$

We obtain $\underline{e}_{\underline{A}} = 2.3$ for (R.4) and 1.7 for (R.5).

39. It must be noted, however, that the adjustment speed of investment is highly sensitive to the lag structure involved.

40. EPA, Shihon Sutokku to Keizai Seicho, pp. 182-185.

41. MITI (Ministry of International Trade and Industry), Kokogyo Shisu Soran (Industrial Production Indexes) (Tokyo, 1961).

42. MITI, Kokogyo Shisu Soran; MITI, Tsusan Tokei Geppo (Monthly Bulletin of Statistics) (Tokyo).

43. MITI, Wagakuni Seizokogyo no Seisan Noryoku to Shihon Kozo.

44. MITI, Kokogyo Shisu Soran; MITI, Seisan Dotai Junen no Ayumi (Ten Years' Progress in Production Statistics)(Tokyo, 1958);

MITI, Tsusan Tokei Geppo (Monthly Bulletin of Statistics).

45. Bank of Japan, Japanese Economic Statistics (Tokyo, annual issues).

Part II
Studies of Production and Total Factor Productivity Growth

4

Effects of Structural Change on Productivity Growth: A Long-Term Measurement

Kazushi Ohkawa

4.1. Introduction

Ever since 1957 I have been observing the significance of the effects of structural changes on productivity growth of the Japanese economy. Noting that a sum of sectoral productivity growth rates turned out to be smaller by aggregate measurement than the productivity growth rate, I suggested that the effect of structural changes was contained in the latter.[1] What I developed at that time was a simple formula for a two-sector economy (sectors 1 and 2) as follows:

$$(4.1) \qquad G_y = (X_1 G_{y1} + X_2 G_{y2}) + [(X_1 - V_1) G_{L1} + (X_2 - V_2) G_{L2}],$$

where L = labor, X = sectoral share of output, V = sectoral share of labor, y = partial productivity of labor, and G = rate of growth. The corresponding formula for capital is

$$(4.2) \qquad G_h = (X_1 G_{h1} + X_2 G_{h2}) + [(X_1 - W_1) G_{K1} + (X_2 - W_2) G_{K2}],$$

where K = capital, W = sectoral share of capital, and h = partial productivity of capital.

In (4.1) and (4.2), the first term is for the productivity growth proper and the second term measures the effects of changes in the industrial structure. If, for example, in 4.1 the rate of labor increase is the same for both sectors,

$\underline{G}_{L1} = \underline{G}_{L2}$, the latter term will be zero, as $\underline{X}_1 + \underline{X}_2 = 1$ and $\underline{V}_1 + \underline{V}_2 = 1$. If the sectoral shares of output and labor are equal for both sectors, $\underline{X}_1 = \underline{V}_1$ and $\underline{X}_2 = \underline{V}_2$, the second term will be zero, implying an equal partial productivity of labor for both sectors. Each case shows no change in the industrial structure.

Later, in 1963, when analyzing the Japanese economic growth based on the revised data, this simple formula was applied to the case of labor by a 3-sector treatment. The effect of structural change was found significant, particularly for the postwar period.[2]

It took several years more to prepare the data which are indispensable to the total productivity approach. I tried to extend a formula of measuring the effect of structural change in terms of marginal productivity, and it was applied to the postwar period for the case of labor.[3] The result of measurement suggested that the effect of structural change appears to be significant also in the total productivity approach, though this finding was preliminary and illustrative. Since then I and my colleagues have made considerable progress in revising the data so that the same formula could be applied to a longer term period, 1905-1965, retaining the two-sector approach. We confirmed our view that the effect of structural changes is one of the most important items in minimizing the total productivity growth or the residual crudely measured.[4]

Based on these previous works, this paper is intended to present a more systematic approach with an aim of establishing the quantitative significance of the effect of structural changes in the measurement of productivity growth. The following points, among others, are specifically aimed at (1) to treat the case of capital as well as that of labor in order to compare both cases and to arrive an estimate of total effects; (2) to examine both swing and trend patterns in the longer time series data now available; and (3) to disaggregate data into five broad industrial sectors in order to clarify the sectoral characteristics in contributing, positive or negative, to the total effects of structural changes.

The major results of measurements and their implications will be described in section 4.2. In section 4.3, some observations will be developed with concluding remarks.

4.2. The Formula and Measurements

If the conditions of competitive determination of factor prices, constant return to scale, and disembodied technological progress of Hicksian neutrality can approximately be assumed, the total productivity growth rate, G_T, in aggregate measurement is given by

$$G_T = G_Y - \alpha G_K - \beta G_L, \tag{4.3}$$

where Y stands for output and α, β for relative income shares ($\alpha + \beta = 1$). This formula can be applied respectively to all sectors composing the economy if all the conditions mentioned above are approximately valid despite the sectoral breakdown.

The relation between the aggregate measurement and disaggregated approach is given by

$$G_T = (\Sigma X_i G_{Ti}) + [\Sigma X_i \alpha_i (G_{Ki} - G_K) + \Sigma X_i \beta_i (G_{Li} - G_L)]. \tag{4.4}$$

The first term is a sum of sectoral total productivity growth weighted by the sectoral shares of output, whereas the second terms, in brackets, represents tht total effect of structural changes, the first for capital and the second for labor.[5] Considering $\alpha + \beta = 1$, the second term, which is denoted by G_E, is transformed to

$$G_E = \Sigma X_i (G_{Ki} - G_K) + \Sigma X_i \beta_i [(G_K - G_L) - (G_{Ki} - G_{Li})]. \tag{4.4'}$$

Corresponding to (4.1) and (4.2) stated in the preceding section, G_E can be expressed as follows for a two-sector case, if α and β are assumed equal respectively for both sectors:

$$\beta[X_1 (G_{L1} - G_L) + X_2 (G_{L2} - G_L)] \tag{4.5}$$

and

$$\alpha[X_1 (G_{K1} - G_K) + X_2 (G_{K2} - G_K)]. \tag{4.6}$$

The term in brackets in (4.5) is equivalent to (4.1) if

we introduce a relation $\underline{G}_L = \underline{V}_1\underline{G}_L + \underline{V}_2\underline{G}_{L2}$, considering $\underline{X}_1 + \underline{X}_2 = 1$. The same holds for capital. Therefore, the simpler formula of the partial productivity approach composes the important part of the measurement of $\underline{G}_E$, and it is to be noted that the three conditions mentioned at the outset of this section with respect to (4.4) have nothing to do with this part.

The major formula is (4.4) in our measurement, but others will be used additionally. Empirical examination of the three conditions assumed above is required before the application of the formula. This task is, however, extremely difficult. My judgment is that these can be allowed as a first approximation. After measurement, the results will be investigated in section 4.3. Use of income shares as a proxy for output elasticities of capital and labor is required in this procedure. When this assumption appears not to be valid, special consideration will be paid to actual measurement of output elasticities.

Before describing the major results of measurement, certain preliminaries need to be mentioned.

1. Long-term observation is our aim, so that the original annual time series of output, labor, and capital estimated for 1905-1965 (an abnormal period; 1941-1952 is excluded) are all smoothed by a moving average of 7 years for the prewar period and 5 years for the postwar period) in order to eliminate the effects of fluctuations mostly caused by short-term business cycles. Measurement has been done first on an annual basis by use of these smoothed series (in terms of the rates of changes in output, capital, and labor). Second, in view of the findings of long swings, the entire period has been demarcated in five phases. For each phase, the results will be presented as averages of the annually calculated series.

2. The industrial structure is represented by five broad sectoral groups: M, F, C, S, and A. M is manufacturing with mining included because a reliable breakdown of prewar capital series cannot be given as yet. F is the so-called facilitating industries, which cover transportation, communication, and public utilities. This grouping intends, among others, to represent the industries whose capital-labor ratio is particularly high. C is construction. As will be noted in the following discussion, the shares of construction, both in output

and input, appear to be too small to be treated as an independent sector. The category is retained, however, because its characteristics seem to be different from other industries. A is agriculture, forestry, and fishing. Finally, S includes services and commerce, and in addition all industries other than those grouped above. Admittedly, this group is too big, but limitations of data, particularly those of prewar capital series, do not allow a further breakdown as yet.

All these data are arranged to exclude government activities in order to represent the private sector. In this respect no serious problem exists. As will be discussed in section 4.3, however, there remains a problem pertaining to the dualistic growth of the Japanese economy. In most of the sectors classified above, there exist both the modern and traditional enterprises, although their proportion not only varies from one sector to another but also changes over time. Since the data do not allow us to make a general breakdown into modern and traditional sectors, we will make a rough approximation by equating the traditional sector to agriculture.

3. In applying formula (4.4) and the like, the data reliability of relative income shares is crucial because use of these shares makes the total productivity approach basically different from the partial productivity approach. For the postwar years we estimated these shares for the five sectors classified above. The estimation was done for corporate and unincorporated sectors separately for each industrial group because the latter requires "imputation" in order to divide the so-called mixed income into the two categories of capital's share and labor's share of income. For each industrial sector a weighted sum was calculated from these two kinds of income shares, corporate and unincorporated. For the prewar years, however, the data are not yet available for estimating such sectoral income shares and proxies were made. Because aggregate income shares for the nonagricultural sector are available, they are estimated by use of the postwar ratios obtained between sectoral and aggregate values. The prewar income shares are accordingly less reliable. (With respect to agriculture, we cannot use income shares and special treatment is required, as will be mentioned in later pages.) These are all used in period averages of annual series.

4. Whether to use data "net" or "gross" of capital

depreciation is a controversial issue in measuring productivity growth. Output, capital, and relative share are all used in gross terms here. This is not the place to dwell upon the reasons for this choice. One thing specifically requiring statement here is that the competitive equilibrium which underlies formula (4.4) can be assumed in theory, we believe, for the case of growth terms.

5. Finally, both capital and labor series are used in crude terms in the sense that no adjustment is made for changes or differences in the rate of utilization and the quality of production factors. This is not an accurate presentation of our measurement. If the data are reliable enough these adjustments should of course be done. Even for an aggregate approach, however, this is not yet easy for a long-term study of Japan. Regarding the sectoral approach, therefore, use of crude terms is unavoidable at present.[6]

Now, as has been suggested in section 4.1, our aim is not only to measure the total magnitude of the effects of structural changes, denoted by $\underline{G_E}$, but also to clarify the individual performance of the major components of $\underline{G_E}$. I believe this is highly desirable in order to interpret the result of measurement in the light of structural changes which have actually taken place during modern economic growth. Let us begin with stating the historical pattern of sectoral allocation of capital and labor. Sectoral rates of growth of capital and labor are shown in Table 4.1 in terms of their difference from the aggregate rate (column T). These are the measurement of $(\underline{G_{Ki}} - \underline{G_K})$ and $(\underline{G_{Li}} - \underline{G_L})$ in (4.4).

The periodization is based on long swings in private capital investment. The performance of aggregate capital growth shown in column T does not necessarily coincide with it. Particularly the aggregate rate of capital growth for 1962-1964 is very high. Further explanation will be given at a later point in connection with additional data presented in Table 4.3. At any rate a very clear tendency is seen throughout the entire period for both capital and labor growth, almost irrespective of the swings of the economy. The rate of capital accumulation was slower in the sectors of services and agriculture, whereas in other sectors, M, F, and C, it was higher than the aggregate rate of growth with slight exceptions. The negative figure of agriculture is far bigger

TABLE 4.1. SECTORAL RATES OF GROWTH OF CAPITAL AND LABOR (ANNUAL RATES, %)

PERIOD	Difference from the Aggregate Rate M	F	C	S	A	T
Capital						
1909-17*	2.90	4.59	3.40	-0.05	-3.08	4.03
1918-31	-1.10	3.10	1.77	-0.21	-2.45	3.75
1932-38	5.67	-0.46	6.67	-0.22	-3.19	3.70
1955-61	3.94	3.42	11.15	-2.86	-5.18	8.65
1962-64	2.75	-0.63	10.88	-1.01	-6.11	11.01
Labor						
1908-17	2.39	1.18	1.40	1.32	-0.97	0.46
1918-31	1.59	0.36	0.72	1.09	-0.96	0.70
1932-38	2.91	-0.32	0.53	0.65	-1.03	0.78
1955-61	3.38	3.65	5.36	2.10	-4.23	1.89
1962-64	2.21	4.28	3.38	2.32	-5.51	1.79

*1908 is omitted because of lack of data, but this shorter period is assumed to be comparable to the period 1908-1917 utilized in the case of labor.

(in an absolute sense) than that of services. The rate of increase in the labor force employed is also shown in terms of the difference from the rate of aggregate increase, column T, in the table. It is clear, however, that labor had continued to decrease absolutely in agriculture at a low rate during the prewar years and at a higher rate during the postwar years, whereas it increased in all other sectors. What is distinctly different from the case of capital is that the rate of increase of labor employed in services was larger than in the aggregate.

The corresponding performance of capital-labor ratio or capital intensity, which appeared in formula (4.4') above in terms of growth rate, can easily be examined from the figures in Table 4.1 by calculating $(G_K - G_L) - (G_{Ki} - G_{Li})$: the difference of sectoral rate of growth of the capital-labor ratio from the aggregate one was again negative for services and agriculture, whereas for other sectors it was positive with slight exceptions.

The terms $\Sigma X_i \beta_i$ and $\Sigma X_i \alpha_i$ are other indicators of structural changes in our formula. With components, X_i and β_i, the figures are shown in Table 4.2.

First, regarding the long-term trend of sectoral shares of output, we see an increase in M and C, a decrease in A, and a small change in S and F. These are almost universal phenomena internationally. What is characteristic to Japan's case is the very speedy tempo of these changes. Second, labor's income share varies rather widely among sectors: among the nonagricultural sector it is small in M and F and large in C and S, whereas A has a very small value. The reservation made in the preliminary description should be noted here for the nonagricultural sector, and yet we can say that sectors M and F are capital intensive while sectors C and S are labor intensive in their technologies adopted. For agriculture, a directly measured output elasticity with respect to labor is adopted because use of income shares is less reliable. The output elasticity is derived from production function measurements based on cross-section data.[7]

Finally, the "weighted shares" in the table are intended to give proxies of weighted sectoral output elasticities with respect to labor. If β is the same for all the sectors, the weighted share would be affected only by the output shares in panel X_i. The actual variation of the β_i does affect them considerably, as illustrated by examples. The weighted share of agriculture in its percentage to the aggregate in 1913 is 18.5% as against 32.3% in the case of output share, whereas the weighted share of services in its percentage relation to the aggregate in 1958 is 43.1 as against 35.6 in the case of output share. No table is needed for the case of capital for $\alpha + \beta = 1$ except for agriculture, for which the output elasticity with respect to capital is estimated to be .286 for the prewar and .328 for the postwar years.

Now, information on the component terms of our formula may be sufficiently accurate, I hope, to determine the performance

TABLE 4.2. SECTORAL OUTPUT SHARES AND RELATIVE INCOME SHARES OF LABOR (%)

Year	M	F	C	S	A	T
Output Shares (X_i)						
1913	16.0	5.7	2.0	44.0	32.3	100.0
1924-25	18.7	11.0	1.8	44.3	24 2	100.0
1935	30.0	10.3	2.6	38.1	19.0	100.0
1958	34.3	7.0	4.6	35.6	18.5	100.0
1963	32.7	8.3	5.5	43.0	10.5	100.0
Income Shares of Labor (β_i)						
1913	48.3	47.3	66.5	63.2	28.0	
1924-25	58.0	56.8	79.9	75.9	28.0	
1935	55.1	53.9	75.8	72.0	28.0	
1958	65.9	60.9	88.0	83.0	43.0	
1963	59.0	55.6	81.3	79.3	43.0	
Weighted Shares (X_i β_i)						
1913	7.7	2.7	1.3	27.8	9.0	48.5
1924-25	19.8	6.3	1.4	33.6	6.8	58.9
1935	16.5	5.6	1.9	27.4	5.3	56.7
1958	22.6	4.3	4.0	29.5	8.0	68.4
1963	19.3	4.6	4.5	34.1	4.5	67.0

Remarks: The mid-year of each period is selected. With respect to the figures of "income shares" for agriculture, see the explanation in the text.

of structural changes which took place during Japan's modern economic growth since around the turn of the century. Let us proceed to the discussion of our main subject.

First, Table 4.3 presents a summary of the measured results of the total productivity approach.

TABLE 4.3. EFFECTS OF STRUCTURAL CHANGES: A SUMMARY (ANNUAL RATE OF INCREASE, %)

Period	Output Growth	Total Productivity	Structural Terms			Share of Structural Term
			Labor	Capital	Sum	
	(1)	(2)	(3)	(4)	(5)	(6) = (5)/(2)
1908-17	4.20	1.84	0.51	0.11	0.62	34.0
1918-31	2.61	0.67	0.50	-0.08	0.42	63.9
1932-38	5.51	3.41	0.60	0.59	1.19	34.8
1955-61	11.23	7.21	1.53	0.17	1.70	26.3
1962-64	11.42	6.58	1.32	0.41	1.73	26.2

See text for data and method of measurements.

The rate of output growth, column (1), is given to illustrate the swing performance of demarcated periods. 1908-17, 1932-38, and 1955-61 are phases of higher growth rate, while 1918-31 is a phase of lower growth rate. 1962-64 is too short, but it is included to show another downward phase in terms of investment swings, although output growth does not slow down. Through swings, a trend of acceleration of the output growth rate appears to exist, although confirmation of it requires detailed examination which would need separate treatment.

The effects of structural change are shown in columns (3), (4), and (5) which are measured by formula (4.4). The labor term is 0.5-0.6% during the prewar years, being relatively stable despite the swings of output growth, whereas it shows a distinct increase toward the postwar years to a high of 1.3-1.5%. This appears to be associated with the postwar high rate of output growth. The capital term is generally much lower than the labor term, with the exception of 1932-38. A negative value even is seen for a downward phase of 1918-31. No positive association is seen between the capital term and the output growth pattern.

The sum of labor and capital terms, shown in column (5),

however, appears to change somehow in a positive association with the output growth rate, ranging from 0.4% to 1.7%. The total productivity growth is shown in column (2) for reference. This is an aggregate measurement by a simple formula, using the sum of weighted income shares shown in Table 4.2. It shows a swing-wise movement in a positive association with the rate of output growth, ranging widely from 0.7% to 7.2%. The share of the effect of structural change, summed in column (5), in the total productivity growth is shown in column (6). It ranges from about 26% to 35% if an exceptionally high figure for 1918-38 is excluded. This very high percentage suggests that the effect of structural change is a most significant item in explaining the source of total productivity growth.

The long-term performance of this percentage, column (6), appears not to show a distinct pattern, but at least the following can be said. The swing-wise changes in the sum of structural terms, column (5), tends to be much less as compared with those of total productivity growth, and this may explain the reason why the sum of structural terms tends to be smaller for the phases of higher growth rates of output.

From the observation of the results of our measurement, three major mutually interrelated points may be summarized as follows: (1) The magnitude of the effect of structural change seems to be significant both in absolute and relative terms. (2) The long-term performance of structural change appears to be swing-wise but seems to be more stable as compared with that of total productivity. (3) Between labor and capital terms, sizable differences appear recognizable, differences such as the average magnitude and long-term performance.

Second, detailed examination by sectoral breakdown will be developed with an aim of exploring further these points. To begin with the labor term, the measured values of $\underline{X_i}\ \beta_i(\underline{G_{Li}}-\underline{G_L})$ are shown in Table 4.4. These may conveniently be called "sectoral contributions" to the total effect of structural change. The following two points are noted. First, throughout the entire period under review, agriculture's contribution is negative whereas all other sectors' contributions are positive with only a few exceptions. As a matter of fact, this can be expected from the data given in Table 4.1. Second, regarding the nonagricultural sectors, the contribution of manufacturing and services is of major importance. This is mostly caused by

TABLE 4.4. DISAGGREGATED LABOR TERMS
(ANNUAL RATE OF CHANGE, %)

Period	M	F	C	S	A	T
1908-17	0.193	0.034	0.017	0.356	-0.087	0.513
1918-31	0.172	0.023	0.010	0.366	-0.065	0.506
1932-38	0.479	-0.018	0.011	0.178	-0.055	0.600
1955-61	0.874	0.157	0.214	0.620	-0.338	1.527
1962-64	0.427	0.197	0.152	0.791	-0.248	1.319

The weighted shares for midyear shown in Table 4.2 are used.

the bigger output weights of these two categories, sectoral difference of the rates of increase in the labor force employed being not so significant. The long-term performance of the contribution of these two sectors requires particular attention. Manufacturing shows a distinct swing-wise movement with a trend of increase. Services reveal a more pronounced swing for the downward phases with a less distinct trend of increase. Both the output weight and the difference in the rate of increase in the labor force employed explain this contrast between the two sectors. Point (2), regarding to the swing performance of the structural term, can mostly be explained by this finding.

Table 4.5 presents the corresponding figures for the case of capital. The following points are to be noted. First, unlike the case of labor, a negative contribution is found not only for agriculture but also for services during the entire period under review with the minor exception of 1918-31. For manufacturing, facilitating industries, and construction, the contribution is positive except for two slight negative values for manufacturing in 1918-31 and facilitating industries in 1932-38. These are of course to be expected from the data given in Table 4.1, and are relevant in explaining the relative smallness of capital terms. Second, the major positive contribution is given by manufacturing and facilitating industries during the prewar period both for 1909-17 and alternately for 1918-31 and 1932-38, whereas for the post-

TABLE 4.5. DISAGGREGATED CAPITAL TERMS
(ANNUAL RATE OF CHANGE, %)

Period	M	F	C	S	A	T
1909-17*	0.242	0.138	0.024	-0.008	-0.284	0.112
1918-31	-0.087	0.149	0.007	0.023	-0.170	-0.078
1932-38	0.765	-0.022	0.040	-0.024	-0.172	0.586
1955-61	0.500	0.092	0.067	-0.174	-0.3.6	0.169
1962-64	0.496	0.022	0.109	-0.009	-0.207	0.411

The weighted shares for midyear given in Table 4.2 are used.

*1909-17 is substituted for 1908-17 because of lack of data.

war period manufacturing is the only major sector contributing positively to the capital term, though construction is beginning to increase its positive contribution. Third, the swing movement of the sectoral capital terms appear to be much less distinct as compared with the previous case of labor. Historical change in the industrial structure seems to be more relevant. The major positive contribution of facilitating industries during the first two prewar phases, which is followed by manufacturing during the subsequent periods, seems to present an illustrative example of this phenomenon, in addition to the previously noted features of the services sector. These are relevant to the point (3) mentioned above.

Point (1) remains to be examined further, and this can better be done in connection with presenting the result of the partial productivity approach. To begin with formula (4.1), it is transformed to $\Sigma \underline{X_i}(\underline{G_{Li}} - \underline{G_L})$. The estimated figures are shown in Table 4.6.

First of all, what draws our particular attention is the long-term performance of the labor term presented in column (3). This shows a pattern which is very similar to the pattern of the labor term previously found in the total productivity approach (see column (3) in Table 4.3). Clearly the latter is much influenced by the former, the effects of β

TABLE 4.6. LABOR TERMS IN THE PARTIAL PRODUCTIVITY APPROACH (ANNUAL RATE OF CHANGE, %)

Period	$\Sigma X_i G_{Li}$	G_L	Labor Term	$G_Y - G_L$	Share
	(1)	(2)	(3) = (1) - (2)	(4)	(5) = (3)/(4)
1908-17	1.18	0.46	0.72	3.74	19.2
1918-31	1.29	0.70	0.59	1.91	30.9
1932-38	1.69	0.78	0.91	4.73	19.1
1955-61	3.52	1.89	1.63	9.34	17.4
1962-64	3.47	1.79	1.68	9.65	17.4

The output weight X of the midyear shown in Table 4.2 is used.

being less influential. And the magnitude of this term in turn is affected by a fact that the rate of increase in the labor force employed tends to be higher in the sector of greater output weight. Second, this structural effect does not tend to increase as the aggregate rate of labor productivity growth increases: the percentage of the labor term calculated to the latter, shown in column (5), appears to have no distinct tendency over the long term, showing narrow differences except for a big share for the prewar downswing phase.

The corresponding figures are presented in Table 4.7 for the case of capital.

The following points are noted. The long term performance of the capital term, presented in column (3), can be understood to be not entirely different from the pattern we previously found in column (4) in Table 4.3, although 3 of 5 cases show negative figures in the former. As is shown in column (4), the aggregate rate of capital productivity growth moves in association with the swings of economic growth, probably with a trend of increase. The capital term of the effect of structural change appears not far from this. Unlike the previous case of labor, however, the share of (3) to (4) would fluctuate

TABLE 4.7. CAPITAL TERMS IN THE PARTIAL PRODUCTIVITY APPROACH (ANNUAL RATE OF CHANGE, %)

Period	$\Sigma X_i GK_i$ (1)	G_K (2)	Capital Term (3) = (1) - (2)	$G_Y - G_K$ (4)
1909-17*	3.79	4.03	-0.23	0.17
1918-31	3.33	3.75	-0.42	-1.14
1932-38	4.80	3.70	1.10	1.81
1955-61	8.78	8.65	0.13	3.58
1962-64	10.80	11.01	-0.21	0.42

The output weight X of the midyear shown in Table 4.2 is used.

* 1909-17 is substituted for 1908-17 because of lack of data.

widely if mechanically calculated. The magnitude of the rate of change in capital productivity at any rate tends to be much lower than that of labor productivity, and this is partly responsible for the wide fluctuations of the ratio. In sum, we can say that in the case of capital the difference between column (1) and (2) tends to be much smaller as compared with labor, and this may mainly be responsible for the smallness of the capital term which we found in the total producitivity approach.

What we have thus examined with respect to the partial productivity approach can help explain point (1) in addition to giving further information for point (3). As a matter of fact, this can reasonably be expected from what has been pointed out in Section 4.1 that the "structural terms" in partial productivity measurement do compose the important part of the effect of structural change to be measured by the total productivity approach. It is particularly to be noted for the case of labor that the "partial productivity part" is influential despite a wide range of sectoral variance of the output elasticities. The partial productivity measurement can be a fairly good approximation in approaching the effects of structural changes in a long-term growth process when reliability of the output elasticity data appears to be low.

4.3. Observations and Remarks

What has been measured in the preceding section can be examined further from various points of view. The formula we adopted is not the only one. In addition, it is subject to several qualifications. Other approaches are possible also. International comparisons are desirable in order to evaluate correctly the Japanese case. Our grouping of industrial sectors may be too broad and a more detailed breakdown may be needed in order to verify the results of our measurement. In this section, while examining some of these issues, we will focus our observation on the characteristics of the broad sectors into which we classified the private economy. The results of measurement have been described in some detail in the preceding section, and some of the sectoral characteristics have already been discussed there. It is intended here to develop them further, mostly in terms of a dichotomy: agriculture and nonagriculture.

First, let us begin with stating one of our most important observations, that is, that the effect of structural change is most significant between the two sectors agriculture and nonagriculture. One may say that this is obvious and no further investigation is needed, but we would not agree with that statement. As a matter of fact, even within the nonagricultural sector wide differentials of productivity and wages have been recognized during the historical process of Japan's modern economic growth. A sustained existence of these differentials is of course relevant to the effect of structural change, and it is quite natural to expect a considerable magnitude of that effect within the nonagricultural sector. The measurement turned out, however, to show that the magnitude is rather small in the case of labor for this sector, although in the case of capital this is not necessarily so. In giving evidence for this finding, we shall apply first the same formula as has been used in the preceding section, and then a different kind of formula. Table 4.8 presents the summary result of the former approach both for labor and capital.

TABLE 4.8. EFFECTS OF STRUCTURAL CHANGES IN THE NONAGRICULTURAL SECTOR (ANNUAL RATE OF CHANGE, %)

Period	M	F	C	S	T
Labor					
1908-17	0.075	-0.019	-0.013	-0.169	-0.126
1918-31	0.039	-0.040	-0.010	-0.103	-0.114
1932-38	0.363	-0.090	-0.037	-0.164	0.072
1955-61	0.111	0.034	0.122	-0.319	-0.052
1962-64	-0.044	0.052	0.050	-0.087	-0.029
Capital					
1909-17*	0.058	0.095	0.010	-0.600	-0.437
1918-31	-0.307	0.075	0.001	-0.236	-0.463
1932-38	0.792	-0.072	0.005	-0.151	0.574
1955-61	0.436	0.082	0.071	-0.277	0.312
1962-64	0.284	0.046	0.147	-0.355	0.122

The data are all the same as for the previous case of aggregate estimation.

*is the same as for the previous tables for the case of capital.

The total effect in the case of labor, shown in column $\underline{T}$, shows a small magnitude throughout all periods. Its correspondence to the total effect shown in Table 4.3 is very minor for the last three periods, although it is small in the first two periods in both cases. Why is this so? The major reason is that a positive effect of manufacturing is almost canceled by a negative effect of services, the last period only being an exception. This is a combined result of three factors. First, within the nonagricultural sector, $(\underline{G}_{Li} - \underline{G}_L)$ tends to be always positive for manufacturing whereas it tends to be negative for services, though only slightly. Second, the output share $\underline{X}_i$ tends to increase in manufacturing while services retain its large share almost unchanged. Third, the labor's income share β is larger for services than for manufacturing. In addition, two points may be worth mentioning. Both facilitating industries and construction show a shift from the prewar negative to the postwar positive, and this may have contributed to minimize the total effect of structural changes toward the postwar years. The postwar downswing phase, 1962-64, though too short, appears to suggest a future pattern when the tempo of industrialization will slow down.

Regarding the case of capital, a contrast is also seen between the positive contribution of manufacturing (with an exception for the prewar downswing phase) and the negative contribution of services, but the total effect is much bigger than that of the case of labor. The negative effect for the first two periods and the positive effect for the last three periods appear to be relevant to the long-term performance of the capital term presented in column (4) in Table 4.3.

Now, as has been suggested before, a few results from another approach will be tested with respect to labor (no data are available for capital). The formula we have used in this paper pertains in essence to the sustained existence of marginal productivity differentials of production factors. Therefore, a direct approach by use of wage differentials would, of course, be possible under the identical assumptions so that the marginal productivity of factors can be approximated by actual wage rates, or at least by their ratios. It is a widely known fact that there have been wide differentials of wages in the Japanese economy in terms of the modern and traditional sectors and/or enterprises. A few illustrative figures will be discussed for the postwar years.

Corporate (C) vs. unincorporated sectors (U). Excluding agriculture, the economy is broken down into these two sectors for 1955 and 1961. Taking the total average as 100, the wage differential estimated by yearly wage earnings was 116.2 (C) : 68.0 (U) in 1955 and 111.1 (C) : 72.5 (U) in 1961, showing a tendency of narrowing differential. The proportion of the number of workers changes from 66.4 : 33.6% in 1955 to 72.1 : 27.9% in 1961.[8] Use of the 1955 weight gives an annual average rate of increase of 0.40% and use of the 1955-61 average weight gives 0.34% in the change of marginal productivity of labor.

Corporate vs. unincorporated sectors for manufacturing. Within the nonagricultural sector the effect may vary from one to the other. A bigger effect is expected for manufacturing, and the exactly corresponding calculation for manufacturing as before gives the following results. The wage differential was 115.2 (C) : 64.1 (U) in 1955 and 106.2 (C) : 23.3% (U) in 1955 and 81.9 (C) : 18.1% (U) in 1961. Use of the 1955 weight gives 0.98% and use of the 1955-61 weight 0.66% as the annual average rate of increase in the marginal productivity of labor. These differentials are much higher than the preceding ones.

Large-scale vs. small-scale establishments in manufacturing. Differentials of wages and proportional distribution of the number of workers are shown in Table 4.9 for 1955 and 1961.

TABLE 4.9. WAGE EARNINGS AND DISTRIBUTION OF WORKERS BY ESTABLISHMENT SCALE IN MANUFACTURING, 1955 AND 1961

Number of Workers	Wage Earning Differentials		Distribution of Workers	
	1955	1961	1955	1961
4 - 9	54.5	55.7	11.08	7.68
10 - 29	68.9	72.9	23.93	20.64
30 - 99	83.3	86.5	20.72	20.77
100 - 499	109.4	101.0	20.50	23.48
500 - 999	135.7	120.2	7.54	8.16
1000 and over	168.8	151.7	16.23	19.27
Average or Total	100.0	100.0	100.0	100.0

Source: Ministry of International Trade and Industry, The Census of Manufactures (Kōgyō Tōkei-hyō), (Tokyo)

Use of 1955 relatives of wages with the 1961 distribution proportion of workers gives an annual rate of 0.85%, while another combination of 1961 wage relatives with 1955 proportion gives 0.69%. The average of the two is 0.77%. These are close to the second case above.

Now, with these examples, we can say that the effects of structural change on productivity growth are small so far as the nonagricultural sector is concerned. The two examples of manufacturing appear to suggest sizable effects at a first glance, but viewed from the nonagricultural aggregate, they are rather small. For example, an apparent effect of 0.8% in manufacturing is actually 0.32% when weighted by 0.4, labor's share of this sector in the aggregate. However, even so these examples of the direct approach appear to suggest something more than what has been measured by our formula with respect to the nonagricultural sector shown in Table 4.8. The data for making a direct approach is limited, and our test covers only one postwar phase, 1955-1961, so that it would be risky to interpret the difference between the results of the two approaches. In this connection, examinations by industrial breakdowns of each sectoral group are also desirable.[9]

Having examined the nonagricultural sector, let us discuss the peculiar nature of agriculture as compared with the non-agricultural sector in general. Three factors are relevant. First, in Table 4.1, we saw that agriculture is the only sector whose rate of labor increase is negative compared with a positive aggregate. It also has a historical tendency to increase its (absolute) negative magnitude: from about -0.1 to -5.5%. Its negative contribution to the total structural term must tend to increase to a great extent so far as this tendency is concerned. Second, however, its output share has a reverse tendency and particularly in Japan's case this was very speedy. To this extent, the negative contribution of agriculture tended to decrease rapidly. Third, its output elasticity with respect to labor continued to be much smaller as compared with those of other sectors. This implies a very low marginal productivity of labor in agriculture because its average productivity of labor is considerably lower than those of other sectors. There has existed a long-term pattern of widening the gap. Our estimation shows that its output elasticity did increase considerably from prewar to postwar years, and yet it remains considerably lower as compared with those of other sectors. This has the effect of making its negative contribution comparatively small. These three features characterize agriculture distinctly, and so long as these characteristics are sustained, the effect of structural changes on the aggregate productivity growth will continue to be sizable.

Finally, I would like to discuss further three points

bearing on this conclusion, these points being relevant to what we call differential structure.[10]

1. It is a notable fact that the output elasticities of labor and capital vary systematically in the differential structure. In a comparison between small-size, low-productivity enterprises and large-size, high-productivity enterprises, labor's income share is bigger in the former than in the latter; the reverse is true for capital's income share. This is almost universal in the nonagricultural sector. Under a competitive condition, this implies differentials of output elasticities, and viewed from the pattern of technologies, we can say that a low-productivity enterprise of small size is labor intensive whereas a high-productivity enterprise of large size is capital intensive. This is not the sole explanation, but it is relevant to the actual difference of income shares between the broad sectors which we have discussed previously.

As compared with this universal phenomenon in the nonagricultural sector, agriculture has its distinct feature basically because of its technological nature of using the land as a basic factor of production. With a condition of constant return to scale, the output elasticity with respect to land is very high, particularly in the traditional agriculture. This implies smaller output elasticities for labor and capital in agriculture as compared with other sectors of the economy. The existence of disguised unemployment or excess employment in agriculture it has long been asserted, is the basic source which enables such structural changes as have been discussed in this paper. However, what I want to emphasize here is that what is characteristic of agriculture cannot fully be understood without recognizing the unique contribution of land in this sector. If we suppose an economy where β differs only to a minor extent between agriculture and the nonagricultural sector, the phenomena which I have described could take place only with a tendency of increasing returns to scale in agriculture.

2. In connection with the above, let us pay attention to an approach which divides the economy into two sectors: competitive and noncompetitive (or much less competitive) in determining factor prices, particularly in the case of labor. This view assumes that the wage differentials which exist in the former sector reflect solely the quality differentials of labor, whereas in the latter sector an "excess labor employment" exists,

the marginal productivity of labor of which is lower than the prevailing wage level. In theory I am sympathetic with this two-sector model, but for empirical measurement such an approach, I believe, may be less reliable than our formula if it is applied in general to the entire economy. There are two reasons. One is simply a data limitation. The self-employment sector must be included in practice in the latter sector, and this raises very difficult measurement problems, particularly in long-term series. The other reason is substantial. In the light of Japanese experience, the wage differentials in the former sector cannot be entirely attributed to the quality differentials. Evidence can be given by the fact that the wage differential tended to narrow, as we have seen in the previous discussion, during the postwar growth, which can be explained by the changes in demand-supply situations. Therefore, another kind of two-sector model approach in terms of agriculture vs. nonagriculture can be a good proxy for the competitive-noncompetitive one. This is suggested from the entire results of our previous examination.[11]

3. With respect to the quality differentials, I would say the required adjustment is actually very minor for the effect of structural changes we have measured by crude terms. It is estimated to be as low as 0.1% at the largest. This is proved as follows. Let $\underline{G}_{\underline{q}}$ stand for the rate of growth of labor quality. The effect of labor quality differentials, which is denoted by $\underline{Q}$, can be measured by a similar formula as (4.4) stated in section 4.1. For simplicity, for a two-sector case, we have

$$(4.7) \qquad \underline{Q} = \underline{X}_1\beta_1(\underline{Q}_{\underline{q}_1} - \underline{G}_{\underline{q}}) + \underline{X}_2\beta_2(\underline{G}_{\underline{q}2} - \underline{G}_{\underline{q}}).$$

Considering a relation, $\underline{G}_{\underline{q}1}\underline{V}_1 + \underline{G}_{\underline{q}2}\underline{V}_2 = \underline{G}_{\underline{q}}$, (4.7) is transformed to

$$(4.8) \qquad \underline{Q} = (\underline{X}_1\underline{V}_2\beta_1 - \underline{X}_2\underline{V}_1\beta_2)(\underline{G}_{\underline{q}1} - \underline{G}_{\underline{q}2}).$$

Substantially, this formula can safely be applied to a two-sector model of agriculture and nonagriculture, the crucial value being the gap between the rates of quality increase in the two sectors. It is to be regretted that no time series are available for $\underline{G}_{\underline{q}1}$ and $\underline{G}_{\underline{q}2}$, but we have fairly reliable data for G_q, which is estimated to be 0.49 - 0.66% for prewar periods and 0.36 - 0.43% for postwar periods in terms of period averages of our standard periodization. The difference between the two sectors may be 0.5% at the largest. On the other hand, the term $(X_1V_2\beta_1 - X_2V_1\beta_2)$ is estimated to be 0.10 - 0.20% so that the value of Q may probably range from 0.05% to 0.10%. Therefore, no serious qualifications would be needed with regard to the labor quality problem.

With respect to the other points about the crudeness of the measurement as well as the assumed conditions for applying our formula, it is not possible to make quantitative comments except to say the following. The total productivity growth denoted by G_T, to which the effect of structural changes is compared, is a residual - a sum of unspecified contributions. In this sense, our measurement can be justified as a first approximation.

4.4. Concluding Remarks

1. The effect of structural changes on productivity growth is measured in this study over the long term of Japan's modern economic growth, 1908-1964, with a sectoral breakdown into five broad industrial groups. Five phases are demarcated in terms of long swings in order to examine the long term performance of the effects in both aggregate and sectoral terms.

2. The total magnitude of structural change is confirmed to be significant both in absolute terms and in relation to total productivity growth. The effect produced between the two major sectors, agriculture and nonagriculture, is recognized to be dominant, whereas within the nonagriculture sector it is minor.

3. The total effect of structural changes appears to move somehow swingwise, but it is more stable than total productivity growth. This suggests that the structural change goes on to a certain extent independently of output growth swings. The characteristics of the service sector seem to be related to this fact.

4. Between the two measurements, one in terms of labor allocation and the other in terms of capital allocation, notable differences are confirmed. It is particularly to be emphasized that the magnitude is far bigger for the former than in the latter, and that the long-term performance of the total effect

is thereby greatly affected by the former.

5. There remain still weak or unsolved points to be explored further along the line of this or similar approaches. A major bottleneck is the limitation of data. Further efforts to obtain additional data deserve high priority, especially because the effect of structural changes is most clear-cut in concept among the various sources of productivity growth.

Notes

1. Kazushi Ohkawa and others, The Growth Rate of the Japanese Economy since 1878, Economic Research Series no. 1, Institute of Economic Research, Hitotsubashi University (Tokyo: Kinokuniya, 1957); pp. 19-25. The phenomenon has been called by various authors with different terms such as shift, transfer, or reallocation effects. I have also used these terms interchangeably since then. However, in this paper I prefer the more general term "structural change" in order to avoid possible misunderstanding. The effects of actual shift or flow of labor and capital from one sector to another are an important component of our measurement. A flow oflabor force hitherto engaged in agriculture to the nonagricultural sector is a typical example of such an actual shift. But this is not our exclusive aim of measurement. Even if no such actual shift of factors should take place, the industrial structure could change over time by way of sectoral allocation of the new labor force and/or new capital investment.

2. K. Ohkawa and H. Rosovsky, "Recent Japanese Growth in Historical Perspective," Americal Economic Review, May 1963; pp. 578-588. For 1953-60, for example, the productivity growth proper was 5.8% and the effect of structural change 1.3% Professor Hugh Patrick rightly criticized us, among other things, that the paper gives no information on the effects measured in terms of marginal productivity.

3. K. Ohkawa, "Makuro Seisansei Jōshō eno Seisan-yōso Haibun-hendō no Kōka" ("Effects of Changes in the Sectoral Distribution of Production Factors on the Increase in the Macroproductivity"), Keizai Kenkyū (The Economic Review), vol. 18, no. 4 (October 1967); pp. 346-350.

4. Contained in K. Ohkawa and H. Rosovsky, Japanese Economic Growth: Trend Acceleration in the Twentieth Century (Stanford, California: Stanford University Press, 1973).

5. For the details of deriving this formula, see Ohkawa, "Makuro Seisansei Jōshō eno Seisan-yōsō Haibun-hendō no Kōka". This is in essence equivalent to what Massel first developed; see B. F. Massel, "A Disaggregated View of Technical Change, " Journal of Political Economy, December 1961.

6. All the original data relevant to these preliminary descriptions from (1) to (5) have been published with explanations of their estimating procedures in Kazushi Ohkawa et al., Kokuminshotoku (National Income) (Tokyo: Tōyō Keizai Shinpō-sha, 1974).

7. Because of the data limitation both for prewar and postwar periods, no long-term change is presented, but this may not be a serious defect. For the details of this procedure, see K. Ohkawa and H. Rosovsky, Japanese Economic Growth: Trend Acceleration in the Twentieth Century (Stanford, California: Stanford University Press, 1973), Chapter 4.

8. The original data are more or less consistent with the national income statistics. For sector U, the average wages earned by the workers employed in this sector are taken assuming that these can be imputed to the nonhired workers in this sector. The wage differentials for the two years are deflated by 1960 output prices.

9. Regarding the manufacturing sector, T. Watanabe measured the "shift effect" by breaking it down into 14 industries and found that 0.25% for labor and 0.12% for capital as an average of annual calculations for 1952-1961. The formula is the same as our (4.4). These are very small particularly as compared with the case of the United States as measured by B. Massel. See T. Watanabe, Sūryō Keizai Bunseki (Quantitative Economic Analysis) (Tokyo: Sōbun-sha, 1970); Chapter 4, pp. 123-128), and Massel, "A Disaggregated View of Technical Change,"

10. For its concept and application, see Kazushi Ohkawa, Differential Structure and Agriculture: Essays on Dualistic Growth, Economic Research Series, no. 13, Institute of Economic Research, Hitotsubashi University (Tokyo: Kinokuniya, 1972).

11. Denison made an elaborate calculation by use of an agriculture and nonfarm self-employment sector, assuming such a two-sector model in theory. See E. F. Denison, Why Growth Rates Differ: Postwar Experience in Nine Western Countries, Brookings Institution Economic Studies (Washington D.C., 1967). It is interesting to compare our measurement with his result. "The combined contributions to growth rates of the shifts of resources from agriculture and from self-employment" for the 1950-62 range from a low of 0.10 for United Kingdom to a high of 1.26 for Italy. For northwestern Europe as a whole, the share of this shift effect in total productivity is most significant in parallel with the effect of economies of scale.

5

Growth in Capital Stock in the Postwar Japanese Manufacturing Industries

Fumimasa Hamada

This paper attempts to decompose the actual rate of growth in fixed capital stock into three components: production expansion, change in the price of capital relative to labor, and technical progress. W. E. G. Salter, R. M. Solow, and others have, recently, developed measures of technological change. It seems, however, very important to consider the mechanism generating growth in fixed capital which can be taken not only as a measure of increases in production capacity, but also as that of capital intensity. As far as I know, no attempt has ever been made to consider the problem of which of those three factors described above contributes most to actual growth in fixed capital stock in the light of econometric analysis.

For simplicity's sake, we assume that (1) there exists a single homogeneous product and two productive factors[1] - fixed capital and labor; (2) the production function is of the CES type with linear homogeneity,[2] (3) the markets for the product and the productive factors are perfectly competitive, and an entrepreneur makes a decision regarding the input level of fixed capital and labor with the output level and the prices given; and (4) the price of capital relative to that of labor affects the substitution of fixed capital for labor in the long run so as to cover the short run booms and recessions.

Review of Economics and Statistics, vol. 49, no. 4 (November 1967), pp. 630-635. Reprinted by courtesy of the Review of Economics and Statistics and the author.

Assumption (2) is supported by the empirical evidence shown in Table 5.1, where the estimates of the coefficient of elasticity of substitution seem to be different from the unity[3]. We also assume that technical progress is neutral in the sense of Professor J. R. Hicks - that the ratio of marginal productivity of fixed capital to that of labor remains unchanged with the capital-labor ratio given. This means that, in our production function, only the efficiency parameter is submitted to shift through technical progress. If, in our observation period, capital-using technical progress has prevailed, i.e., an increasing trend in the distribution parameter in the production of the CES type, we would have underestimated the negative effect of neutral technical progress on the growth of fixed capital stock.

Assumption (3) is intended to aid analysis of the actual growth in fixed capital stock from the demand side, in order to avoid many complex problems regarding mechanism of price formation. Assumption (4) implies that the entrepreneur has such a long planning period or "horizon of expectation" as to cover the periods in short-run recession. Consequently, the investment behavior observed in the short run is supposed to be the short-run adjustment process to optimal production capacity.[4]

5.1. The Model

The assumptions stated above will lead to the basic relation between the optimal rate of growth in fixed capital stock and the factors which may regulate it through the rational behavior of the entrepreneur. Suppose, with the planned level of output, prices of fixed capital goods, the interest rate, the rate of depreciation, and the wage rate given, the entrepreneur minimizes his total cost under the constraint of the technological relationship between output and inputs. Then the optimal volume of fixed capital can be deduced.

The CES production function can be written as follows:

$$(5.1) \qquad \underline{V} = \gamma[\delta\underline{K}^{-\rho} + (1 - \delta)\underline{L}^{-\rho}]^{-\frac{1}{\rho}}$$

where $\underline{V}$ is volume of output, $\underline{K}$, that of fixed capital; $\underline{L}$, labor employment; γ, the efficiency parameter; δ, the distribution parameter; and ρ, the substitution parameter. Since the raw materials input is assumed to be proportional to the level of output with assumption (1), the cost of production to be minimized, $\underline{C}$, may be defined as:

$$(5.2) \qquad \underline{C} = \underline{p}_1(\underline{i} + \epsilon)\underline{K} + \underline{p}_2\underline{L}$$

where $\underline{p}_1$ is the average price of fixed capital goods; $\underline{i}$, the interest rate; ϵ, the rate of depreciation; and $\underline{p}_2$, the wage rate. Equation (5.2) implies that the cost of production is composed of wage payments and capital costs. The latter involves fixed rates of depreciation ($\epsilon\underline{p}_1\underline{K}$) and of interest costs ($\underline{i}\underline{p}_1\underline{K}$) imputed both to the external and the internal funds. The rate of depreciation, ϵ, may have to include both the rate of replacement and a risk premium for obsolescence of existing fixed tangible assets. This may be particularly true in the postwar Japanese manufacturing industries, where extreme competition in borrowing technology from abroad prevailed among business corporations.

Minimization of the production cost, defined with equation (5.2), subject to the technological relationship (5.1), leads to the necessary condition:

$$(5.3) \qquad \partial\underline{V}/\partial\underline{K}/\underline{p}_1(\underline{i} + \epsilon) = \partial\underline{V}/\partial\underline{L}/\underline{p}_2$$

and consequently, the optimal ratio of fixed capital to labor χ^* is

$$(5.4) \qquad \chi^* = \left(\frac{\underline{K}}{\underline{L}}\right)^* = \left(\frac{\delta}{1-\delta}\right)^{\frac{1}{1+\rho}} \left\{\frac{\underline{p}_1(\underline{i}+\epsilon)}{\underline{p}_2}\right\}^{\frac{-1}{1+\rho}}$$

This expression can be rewritten in the form of relative rate of change:

$$(5.5) \qquad \frac{\chi^{*\prime}}{\chi^*} = \frac{-1}{1+\rho} \cdot \frac{\bar{\underline{u}}_{12}'}{\bar{\underline{u}}_{12}}$$

where

$$\bar{\underline{u}}_{12} \equiv \frac{\underline{p}_1(\underline{i}+\epsilon)}{\underline{p}_2}\ ; \quad \chi^{*\prime} \equiv \frac{d\chi^*}{\underline{dt}}\ ; \quad \bar{\underline{u}}_{12} \equiv \frac{d\bar{\underline{u}}_{12}}{\underline{dt}}\ .$$

Differentiating equation (5.1) with respect to time $\underline{t}$, and arranging terms, we have

$$(5.6) \qquad \frac{K'}{K} = -\frac{\gamma'}{\gamma} + \frac{V'}{V} + (1-\delta)\left(\frac{Z}{\gamma}\right)^{\rho} \cdot \frac{\chi'}{\chi}$$

where $Z = V/L$; $\chi = K/L$.

From equation (5.1),

$$(5.7) \qquad \left(\frac{Z}{\gamma}\right)^{\rho} = \left[\delta\left(\frac{K}{L}\right)^{-\rho} + (1-\delta)\right]^{-1}.$$

Substituting (5.7) into equation (5.6) and combining with equation (5.4), the optimal rate of growth in fixed capital stock is given as follows:

$$(5.8) \qquad \frac{K^{*\prime}}{K^{*}} = -\frac{\gamma'}{\gamma} + \frac{V'}{V} - \frac{1-\delta}{1+\rho} \cdot \frac{\bar{u}_{12}'}{\bar{u}_{12}} \left\{1 - \delta\left[1 - \left(\frac{1-\delta}{\delta}\,\bar{u}_{12}\right)^{\frac{\rho}{1+\rho}}\right]\right\}^{-1}.$$

Equation (5.8) implies that the optimal rate of growth in fixed capital stock can be decomposed into three components, the effects of neutral technical progress (negative), production expansion, and change in the price of capital relative to that of labor. The more rapid production expansion is, and the greater the decline in the rate of change in the relative price is, the higher is the rate of growth in fixed capital stock. If the neutral technical progress were not negligible, however, fixed capital would grow more slowly.

5.2. Sample and Variables

Before presenting the empirical results, the sample and variables used in this study should be made clear in some detail. Data on the relevant variables are available from "Analysis of Financial Statements of Main Industrial Corporations in Japan" (Statistics Department, Bank of Japan). Companies selected in this survey are represented in each industry among the listed business corporations in Japan. The sample is almost fixed during the periods of the first half of 1956 through that of 1963. Therefore, we can exclude some difficulties caused by the behavior of marginal producers in product market. A few industries were excluded because of lack of the corresponding price deflators or the transforming multiplier which converts the initial net stock of fixed capital into the gross stock.

Data processing for the relevant variables was as follows:

1. Gross stock of fixed capital. The initial (latter half of 1955) gross stock of fixed capital was estimated through the process (a) subtract the asset value of land from the value of tangible fixed assets at the end of the latter half of 1955, (b) adjust it to the value of 1960 constant million yen, and (c) convert it into the gross stock, making use of a transforming multiplier which is estimated by Economic Research Institute, Economic Planning Agency. The gross stock of fixed capital in each (half year) period was obtained, adding up to real investment in tangible fixed assets except in land.[5]

2. Labor employment. The total number of employees working in factories and in offices is included because of indivisibility of the available data. Our data cover the regular worker employment.

3. Real output. Sales deflated with product price indices were obtained, since sales and output would expand parallel to each other in the long run.

4. Relative price of capital to labor. p_1 corresponds to a price index of fixed capital goods; i is the ratio of interest burden (equals (Interest and Discount Paid + Premium on Bonds Amortized + Interest on Debenture and Mortgage Bonds Paid) divided by (Average Total Liabilities both at the end of this period and of the preceding period)]; ϵ is the ratio of depreciation; and p_2 is the average wage per worker.

5.3. Empirical Results

The average percentage increases in the observation periods in real sales, gross stock of fixed capital, labor employment, and the relative price were calculated from the estimates of semilogarithmic regression equation:

$$\log_e Y = a_0 + a_1 t$$

where Y is the variable in question and t, a time variable in half-year units. Table 5.1 gives the average half-year increases in gross stock of fixed capital, real sales, labor employment, and the price of capital relative to that of labor. There were a few industries for which the correlation coefficients of the regressions were comparatively low: -0.48 for the regression of $\log \bar{u}_{12}$ on t in automobiles; -0.56, -0.49, and 0.64 for the regressions of $\log L$ on t in textile products, cotton products, and fertilizer, respectively. The figures in Table 5.1 are impressive concerning two points, the relative rate of change in the gross stock of fixed capital is greater than that of labor employment, and the relative rate of change in the price of capital relative to that of labor is negative in all industries.

In order to estimate the three components, shown in equation (5.8), we have to obtain the estimates of the distribution parameter δ and the substitution parameter ρ in advance. The substitution parameter, ρ, (and consequently, the coefficient of elasticity of substititution σ), can be estimated from equation (5.5), by dividing $(\frac{K'}{K} - \frac{L'}{L})$ by $\frac{\bar{u}_{12}'}{\bar{u}_{12}}$. The estimates are listed in column (6) of Table 5.1. Since the estimates of the average percentage increase in K, L, and $\bar{u}_{12}$, which can be derived from the estimates of a_1s, are almost significant at the 5% level, the estimates of the substitution parameter ρ, and consequently the coefficient of elasticity of substitution σ, could be stable in the observation period. Elasticity of substitution appears to be greater than unity in almost all the industries except paper and pulp; stone, clay, and glass products; and cement. The estimate in automobiles seems to be very high, being influenced by the increasing rate of depreciation which prevented the price of capital relative to labor from decreasing during the observation period. This strong upward trend could never be found in the other industries.

Making use of the estimates of σ, we can get the estimates of the distribution parameter δ, with the relation below:

TABLE 5.1. ESTIMATES OF THE COEFFICIENT OF ELASTICITY OF SUBSTITUTION AND THE DISTRIBITION PARAMETER[a]

	Industries	$\frac{K'}{K}$	$\frac{L'}{L}$	$\frac{\bar{u}_{12}'}{\bar{u}_{12}}$	$\frac{S'}{S}$	$\frac{\chi^{*\prime}}{\chi^{*}}$	σ	δ
1.	Food and Kindred Products	7.64	3.746	-3.714	5.328	3.889	1.048	0.4051
2.	Textiles Products	4.81	-0.053	-3.772	5.579	4.863	1.289	0.3099
3.	Cotton Products	3.04	-0.624	-3.281	4.409	3.666	1.117	0.2992
4.	Chemical Fibers Products	6.95	1.135	-5.077	8.849	5.817	1.146	0.4262
5.	Paper and Pulp	3.51	2.072	-2.353	5.908	1.434	0.609	0.8941
6.	Chemical Products	9.01	1.866	-3.414	7.635	7.146	2.093	0.2826
7.	Fertilizers	8.09	0.481	-3.438	5.943	7.610	2.213	0.3008
8.	Rubber Products	7.93	4.772	-2.421	7.677	3.155	1.303	0.2347
9.	Stone, Clay and Glass Products	5.50	2.284	-3.928	6.617	3.211	0.817	0.9596
10.	Cement	4.70	0.926	-4.905	6.820	3.145	0.641	0.8994
11.	Iron and Steel	8.91	3.133	-4.523	7.953	5.780	1.278	0.4392
12.	Nonferrous Metals	5.79	1.574	-2.738	7.350	4.219	1.541	0.3601
13.	Fabricated Metal Products	8.96	4.194	-2.084	7.842	4.766	2.287	0.2105
14.	General Machines and Tools	8.91	4.207	-2.683	10.620	4.702	1.753	0.2676
15.	Electric Machines and Tools	12.54	6.887	-1.638	12.417	5.649	3.449	0.1869
16.	Transportation Machines and Tools	9.56	2.953	-2.232	10.265	6.608	2.960	0.1616
17.	Automobiles	14.17	5.046	-0.521	13.796	9.119	17.517	0.2682
18.	Manufacturing (total)	6.28	3.096	-3.430	7.905	3.186	0.929	0.4487

[a]The observation period covers the first half of 1956 through the first half of 1963. All figures, except those in the last two columns, are shown in the form of an average half-year percentage increase.

$$(5.9)\qquad \delta = \frac{\underline{\bar{u}}_{12}(\underline{K}/\underline{L})^{\frac{1}{\sigma\dagger}}}{1 + \underline{\bar{u}}_{12}(K/L)^{\frac{1}{\sigma\dagger}}}$$

which can be deduced from equation (5.4). If the hypothesis of Hicks-neutral technical progress were acceptable, the estimates of δ from equation (5.9) would be stable throughout the observation period. Moreover, from equation (5.4), we have the ratio of the relative share of capital to labor:

$$(5.10)\qquad \frac{\underline{p}_1(\underline{i}+\epsilon)\underline{K}}{\underline{p}_2\underline{L}} = \left(\frac{\delta}{1-\delta}\right)^{\sigma} \underline{\bar{u}}_{12}{}^{1-\sigma} .$$

This expression is equivalent to equation (5.9). Equation (5.9) could be used to examine the hypothesis of Hicks-neutral technical progress and, at the same time, to discover how well the estimated production functions could reproduce the distributive facts. Fig. 5.1 shows the variations of the estimates of δ by industry. The strong stability of the estimated series in each industry seem to ensure the constancy of this parameter. Now, it may be possible to estimate the average values of δ making use of equation (5.11):

$$(5.11)\qquad \delta = \frac{\text{Av.}(\underline{\bar{u}}_{12})[\text{Av.}(\underline{K}/\underline{L})]^{1/\sigma\dagger}}{1 + \text{Av.}(\underline{\bar{u}}_{12})[\text{Av.}(\underline{K}/\underline{L})]^{1/\sigma\dagger}}$$

where Av. is mean value of a variable in the observation period. The estimates of δ are also listed in the last column of Table 5.1. The numbers in Table 5.2 were computed from those in Table 5.1 with the computational formulae given in the footnote to the table. The estimate of Hicks-neutral technical progress is higher in textile products, cotton products, chemical fibers products, chemical products, nonferrous metals, general machines and tools, electric machines and tools, transportation machines and tools, and automobiles than in manufacturing (total). This fact seems to be closely related to the fact that the market for each of these industries is highly competitive and the exploitation of new products is remarkable.

There remains another test to be made on the stability of the estimated production functions. In order to know how well the estimated production functions reproduce the variations of the input and output of the industries in question, we make a check on the stability of the initial value of efficiency parameter γ, that is γ_0. In our case, the production function can be rewritten as below:

$$(5.12)\qquad \underline{S}_t = \gamma_0(1+\gamma_1)^{\underline{t}}[\delta \underline{K}_t^{-\rho} + (1-\delta)\underline{L}_t^{-\rho}]^{-1/\rho}$$

where γ_0 is the initial value of γ, γ_1 is the relative rate of increase in γ, the estimates of which are listed in the second column (2) of Table 5.2. Since the figures in Tables 5.1 and 5.2 give the estimates of σ, δ, and γ_1, it is possible to estimate the right-hand side of equation (5.12) except for γ_0. Dividing the observed values of $\underline{S}_t$ by the estimates of the right-hand side of (5.12) except γ_0, can give the estimated series of γ_0, which should be constant throughout the observation period. Figure 5.2 shows that the estimated series of γ_0 seems to be considerably stable, but displays short-run fluctuations, which might be attributed to changes in the degree of utilization of the industries in question. 1956 was the boom period, ending in the first half-year of 1957. After the severe recession, the economy moved to the recovery in 1959. This was stimulated by the so-called "Income-Doubling Plan" of the Japanese government which started in December of 1960. The second big recession period began in 1962. A large sum for investment in plants and equipment induced by the strong expectation for the future economy which was warranted by the "Plan" brought about a drastic fall of the degree of utilization in manufacturing industries. The estimated series of γ_0 in each industry appears to be dominated by the cyclical fluctuations briefly stated above.

5.4. Concluding Remarks

The relative contribution of the three components are given in the last three columns of Table 5.2. All the figures are percentages of the absolute value of each component to the sum of absolute values of the three. It is interesting that the effect of production expansion is the highest of the three in all industries. The effect of the price of capital relative to labor is higher in eight industries than the absolute effect of neutral technical progress. However, it is not acceptable

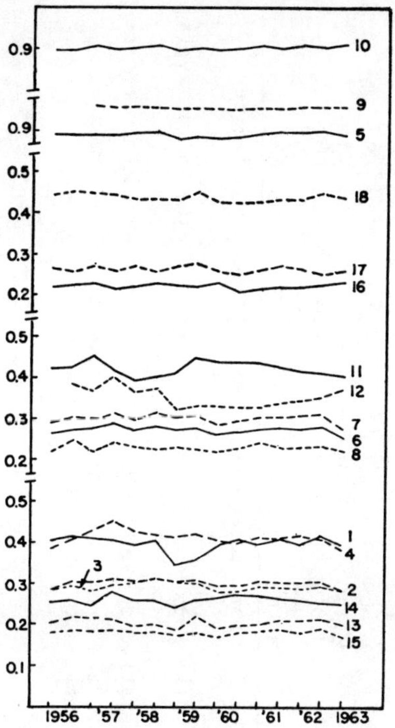

Fig. 5.1. Variations of the Estimates of δ

The number attached to each curve is of industries listed in Table 5.1.

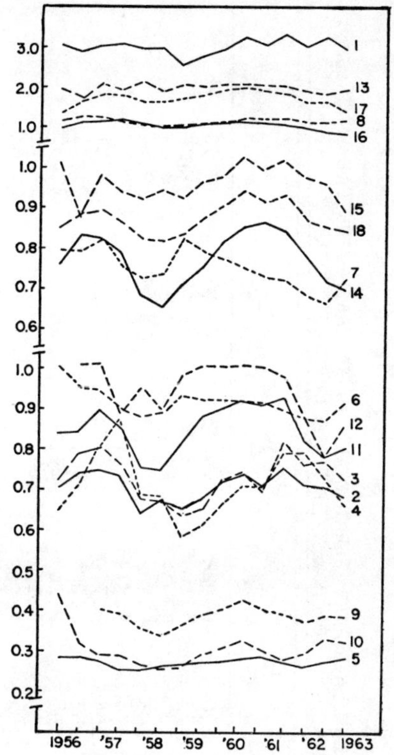

Fig. 5.2. The Estimated Series of γ_0

The number attached to each curve is of industries listed in Table 5.1.

TABLE 5.2. THE COMPONENTS DUE TO CHANGE IN RELATIVE PRICE AND TO NEUTRAL TECHNICAL PROGRESS, AND THEIR RELATIVE CONTRIBUTION TO GROWTH IN FIXED CAPITAL STOCK[a]

	Industries	R^b	$\frac{\gamma'}{\gamma}$	A	B	C
1.	Food and Kindred Products	2.290	-0.022	69.73	29.97	0.30
2.	Textile Products	3.335	4.104	42.86	25.62	31.52
3.	Cotton Products	2.585	3.954	40.27	23.61	26.12
4.	Chemical Fibers Products	3.203	5.102	51.59	18.67	29.74
5.	Paper and Pulp	0.376	2.774	65.22	4.15	30.63
6.	Chemical Products	5.154	3.779	46.08	31.11	22.81
7.	Fertilizers	5.152	3.004	42.15	36.54	21.31
8.	Rubber Products	2.358	2.108	63.22	19.42	17.36
9.	Stone, Clay and Glass Products	0.029	1.151	84.87	0.37	14.76
10.	Cement	0.782	2.902	64.93	7.44	27.63
11.	Iron and Steel	2.981	2.024	61.38	23.00	15.62
12.	Nonferrous Metals	2.551	4.111	52.46	18.21	29.33
13.	Fabricated Metal Products	3.436	2.318	57.68	25.27	17.05
14.	General Machines and Tools	3.388	5.098	55.59	17.73	26.68
15.	Electric Machines and Tools	5.263	5.140	54.41	23.06	22.53
16.	Transportation Machines and Tools	5.310	3.015	47.54	24.60	27.86
17.	Automobiles	5.237	4.958	57.29	22.12	20.59
18.	Manufacturing (total)	1.825	3.450	59.98	13.85	26.17

[a] Figures of the first two columns are in the form of average half-year percentage increases.

[b] $\underline{R} = \frac{1-\delta}{1+\rho} \cdot \frac{\bar{\underline{u}}_{12}}{\bar{\underline{u}}_{12}} \{1 - \delta[1 - (\frac{1-\delta}{\delta} \text{Av}.\bar{\underline{u}}_{12})^{\frac{\rho}{1+\rho}}]\}^{-1}$; $\frac{\gamma'}{\gamma} = \frac{S'}{\underline{S}} + \underline{R} - \frac{K'}{\underline{K}}$, where $\text{Av}.\bar{\underline{u}}_{12}$ is the average value of $\bar{\underline{u}}_{12}$. A, B, and C are the relative contributions of production expansion, change in the relative price of capital to labor, and neutral technical progress to the growth in fixed capital stock, in the form of percentages of the total absolute effect.

to conclude that, even in industries other than paper and pulp; cement; and stone, clay and glass products, the relative contribution of a change in the price of capital relative to labor to the growth in fixed capital stock is so small, compared with that of neutral technical change.

In this study, we have found that the downward tendency of the price of capital relative to that of labor contributed greatly in fixed capital stock in the postwar Japanese manufacturing industries. We have assumed that there is no bias in technical progress, but it may be easy to overestimate the effect of the price of capital relative to labor, or underestimate the negative effect of neutral technical progress. The estimate of the coefficient of elasticity of substitution, σ, is strongly dependent on the relative rate of change of the capital-labor ratio and that of the price of capital relative to labor, in other words, the relative income share of labor. If the biased (capital-intensive) technical progress were remarkable, and at the same time, the relative price were decreasing in our observation period, then the effect of the relative price on growth in fixed capital stock would be overestimated, but it might be thought to be the problem of selecting a hypothesis in the first approach to the actual growth in fixed capital stock. The same thing could be true for a hypothesis with the so-called "capital-and/or labor-embodied technical progress."

Notes

The paper was first presented at the First Far Eastern Meeting of the Econometric Society in Tokyo, Japan, July 2, 1966. The author's thanks for useful comments and suggestions are due to Kazushi Okawa, Kôtaro Tsujimura, Keiichiro Obi, Iwao Ozaki, Yuichi Shionoya, and others. This study was supported by the funds of the Institute of Management and Labor Studies, Keio University. Computation was performed fo Keio Computation Center.

1. W. E. G. Salter, Productivity and Technical Change, (Cambridge, 1960), pp. 30-35; R. M. Solow, "Technical Change and the Aggregate Production Function," Review of Economics and

Statistics, 39 (August, 1957), 312-320; and C. E. Ferguson, "Time-Series Production Functions and Technological Progress in American Manufacturing Industry," Journal of Political Economy, 73 (April, 1965), 135-147.

2. K. Arrow, H. B. Chenery, B. S. Minhas, and R. M. Solow, "Capital-Labor Substitution and Economic Efficienty," Review of Economics and Statistics, 43 (August, 1961), 225-250.

3. Our estimating method, different from the ordinary one, is based on assumption (4), since we assume that the average period of adjustment to subsequent equilibria of production capacity is long enough to cover short-term economic fluctuations.

4. J. R. Meyer and R. R. Glauber, Investment Decisions, Economic Forecasting, and Public Policy (Boston, 1964), gives a proper exposition of this statement. See also J. R. Meyer, and E. Kuh, The Investment Decision: An Empirical Study (Cambridge, 1957).

5. This process would lead to overestimation of real gross stock, because we have neglected the requirements for replacement which should have been subtracted from gross investment. But reliable data on these requirements were not available. The ratio of replacement to the gross stock, which had been tentatively estimated by the Economic Research Institute, Economic Planning Agency, was about 2% in each industry in our observation period.

Part III

Studies of Market Clearing and Price Formation

6

Scarcity of Labor and Wage Differentials in the Japanese Economy, 1958-1964

Tuvia Blumenthal

6.1. Introduction

The Japanese labor market has undergone a considerable change during the postwar period. Prior to this change, Japan was regarded as a country having abundant and cheap labor, with one of the main characteristics of the Japanese economy being its "unlimited" or at least "highly elastic" supply of labor. This picture has changed from the end of the '50's, and Japan has been facing a problem of labor shortage. Although short periods when labor was scarce are not unknown in the economic history of modern Japan,[1] the present change seems to be of a more permanent nature and will undoubtedly have an important effect on various phases of the Japanese economy, including its future rate of growth.

The present paper is concerned with the impact of this structural change on wage differentials in manufacturing industries during the period 1958-1964. Although this is a relatively short period, a considerable change in wage differentials, which can be regarded as a direct consequence of the changing

Economic Development and Cultural Change, vol. 17, no. 1 (October 1968), pp. 15-32. Reprinted by courtesy of the University of Chicago Press and the author.

conditions in the labor market, is found to have taken place. This raises the more general question of the relation between the structure of the labor market (as far as labor abundance and scarcity are concerned) and wage differentials, to which I shall turn in the last part of the paper.

6.2. Labor Scarcity and Labor Mobility

The term labor scarcity must be understood in a relative sense, as a faster increase in the demand for labor than in its supply. During the period 1958-1964, there has been a continuous outflow of people from the agricultural sector to the nonagricultural sector of the economy and an absolute decrease in the agricultural labor force.[2] Thus, the reason for the "tight" labor market must lie in the fact that the increase in demand was much more rapid than the increase in the supply of labor.

A process of "tightening" of the labor market is reflected in various phenomena, not all of which are revealed in the published statistical data. There are fewer applications from workers for existing vacancies; there is an increased time lag between the opening of vacancies and the hiring of workers to fill them;[3] workers have to be recruited in far districts; there is a rise in recruitment costs; and various acts of "labor piracy" are committed by firms.

One indicator which comes to mind as a measure of the conditions in the labor market is the rate of unemployment. Since unemployment exists also in "tight" labor markets, and the rate of unemployment cannot take negative values, this in itself cannot be a measure of labor scarcity. However, total unemployment is known to be composed of several types, including "frictional" unemployment, which is unlikely to disappear even under conditions of severe shortage. We can, therefore, regard a certain level of unemployment as representing an equilibrium position, and any divergence from it as indicating excess demand or supply.

The first column of Table 6.1 gives the unemployment rate for the period 1955-1964. This data, taken from the Labor Force Survey, is based on a very narrow definition of unemploy-

TABLE 6.1. MEASURES OF EXCESS DEMAND AND MOBILITY

Year	Unemployment rate (%) (1)	Job seekers ÷ openings (2)	Turnover rate (%)[a] (3)
1955	1.8	3.6	3.6
1956	1.7	2.6	4.1
1957	1.4	2.1	4.2
1958	1.4	2.6	4.0
1959	1.5	2.0	4.7
1960	1.1	1.4	4.9
1961	1.0	1.0	5.6
1962	0.9	1.0 (0.7)[b]	4.9
1963	0.9	0.6	4.8
1964	0.8	0.6	5.4

[a]In manufacturing industries for establishments with 30 employees or more.

[b]There has been a change of definition since the 1962 survey. The number in parentheses is the new figure to be compared to later years.

Sources: Column (1) - Office of the Prime Minister, Labor Force Survey; column (2) - Ministry of Labor, Employment Security Statistics; column (3) - Ministry of Labor, Monthly Survey of Labor Statistics.

ment. Every worker who was employed for at least one hour during the week of the survey was defined as employed;[4] thus the low absolute values. However, there is a clear downward trend, and the unemployment rate in 1964 is less than half of that of 1955.

Another indicator of supply-demand conditions in the labor market is the relation between workers looking for jobs and firms looking for workers through employment centers. This data, given in column 2, shows that at the beginning of the period there were more than three times as many job seekers as openings, while at the end of the period the situation has reversed, and there were almost two openings for every job seeker.

Before turning to a detailed examination of wage dif-

TABLE 6.2. PERCENT OF VOLUNTARY SEPARATIONS OUT OF TOTAL SEPARATIONS

Year	500+[a]	100-499	30-99
1958	54.3	60.4	66.9
1959	63.3	69.9	75.6
1960	65.2	80.7	90.0
1961	75.1	78.7	87.6
1962	74.1	82.8	80.4
1963	76.8	86.2	86.4
1964	83.5	87.2	88.4

Source: Ministry of Labor, Labor Turnover Survey

[a]Employment size of firm.

ferentials, let us take a look at another element in the labor market, namely mobility. One of the characteristics of the postwar Japanese economy is said to be a low rate of mobility, which, according to one view, is a reflection of the dual structure of the labor market. Large-scale and medium-small-scale firms obtain their employees from different sources, and there is almost a total absence of labor mobility from the former to the latter.[5] Looking at column 3, we find an increase in the turnover rate, which is defined here as the sum of the accession and separation rates.[6] There is also evidence for a considerable increase in the mobility rate in the medium- and large-scale firms toward the end of the period.[7]

A better insight into the composition of the workers who changed jobs can be gained from looking at the reasons for separation from work, presented in Table 6.2. Voluntary separation is inversely related to the size of the firm, but for all scales there has been an increase in voluntary separations and a decrease in discharges. This indicates that more workers left their working places of their own will under the changing conditions in the labor market.

6.3. Measuring Wage Differentials

One way to define wage differentials is by the variance

(or some other measure of dispersion) among averages of subgroups in the population. For instance, if we are interested in interindustry wage differentials, we can measure the dispersion among the average wages of the different industries. The problem here is that the average wage of an industry is influenced to a large extent by the composition of the workers in this particular industry, and when we find an industry with a low average wage, we cannot tell whether this is caused by an intrinsic characteristic of the industry or by the composition of its workers. For example, the fact that the textile industry has a low average wage must be partially attributed to the fact that the proportion of women employed in it is larger than in most other industries. To put the matter differently, we do not know if equal workers get different wages in different industries, or if the difference in average wage stems from the fact that the composition of the workers is different.

There are various statistical devices to cope with this problem in order to identify the "true" wage differentials caused by different factors. One method is to take a "standard population" and compute the average wage of each industry, had all the industries had the same composition of workers as the "standard population."[8] In the present study, the purpose is to analyze the wage differentials according to several factors such as age, sex, industry, scale, type of work, and education, and to identify the effect attributed to each factor separately. For this purpose the variance analysis method can be utilized, though with a different emphasis than that common in statistical studies.

The statistical framework is presented elsewhere in detail,[9] so there is no need of an elaborate description, and a short summary will suffice. The crux of this method is in regarding the wage of every worker as the sum of several effects which represent the impact of socioeconomic factors. (The term "factor" is used to denote such categories as age, sex, etc., while "effect" is the numerical value related to a certain level of the factor, such as age: 20-24; sex: male, etc.) Since the effects may vary according to the level of the other factors present, interactions are also considered. For instance, there may be an interaction between age and sex, so that the effect of the age group 20-24 on male workers is different from that on female workers. For the actual computations dummy variables are defined, one for each level of the factors except for the first level, which has the effect 0.[10] A variable is also attached to each level of the interactions except those where the first level of any factor is involved. Each dummy variable takes the value 1 for observations belonging to the group represented by this variable and 0 for all other observations. Thus, if $\underline{X}_3$ is the variable corresponding to the age group 30-39, a worker in the age group 30-39 will have the value 1 for this variable and one not belonging to this group the value 0.

Two additional remarks must be made. The data at our disposal are not the wages of individual workers but the averages of subgroups of the workers' population, cross-classified according to the levels of the different factors. The numerical results are obtained by taking the weighted regression of the dependent variable (average wage of each subgroup) on the independent variables (the dummy variables), the weights being the number of workers of each subgroup in the population. This causes some problems in the calculation of standard errors, but the estimate of the coefficients is not affected.[11] In the present study we shall not present standard error estimates and will deal only with the coefficients themselves. The second remark has to do with the use of variance analysis in the present study, as compared with the more common use made of it in statistical analysis. Usually the problem is to test the significance of various effects and interactions, namely, to determine the existence or absence of these effects, rather than to estimate the coefficients. Here the emphasis is reversed. Since we are concerned with the changes in wage differentials over the period, we are mainly interested in the magnitude of the coefficients, rather than in the significance of the effects.[12]

The following factors are considered in the present study (the figures in parentheses are the number of levels of each factor): age (6); sex (2); scale (3); education (2); type of employment (2); and industry (19). To this the following interactions are added: age and sex; age and scale; sex and scale; scale and education; scale and type; and type and education.

Most of the factors are self-explanatory. Scale is

measured by the number of regular workers in the establishment, and only establishments with 10 workers or more are considered. Education is divided into "elementary" - workers who completed the elementary school under the prewar system or the junior high school of the postwar system, and "higher" - workers who completed the prewar middle school or the postwar senior high school or more. Type of employment is divided into "wage earners" - workers performing physical work directly connected with the establishment's main productive purpose, and "salaried employees"-all other workers.

The maximum number of observations (the number of "cells" created by the classification according to the factors) is 2,736, but some of these "cells" may be empty in a particular year. Since the first level of each factor is 0 by definition, and no dummy variable is attached to it, the total number of dummy variables in this analysis is 50.

6.4. Numerical Results

The analysis of variance coefficients for the three years 1968, 1961, and 1964 are presented in Table 6.3. Since there has been a change in the absolute level of wages during the period, both the 1968 and the 1964 coefficients have been "deflated" to the 1961 level. The increase of average wages in manufacturing industries was 24.0 percent and 25.9 percent from 1958 to 1961 and 1961 to 1964, respectively.

According to our formulation, the entries in the table give the difference between each level and the initial level of each factor. When factors are interacted with others, the entries for single factors in the table stand for the effect of the respective factor when interacted with the first level of the other factors. For example, the figure in the raw "age 18-19" (711 in 1958) represents the effect of this age level when it is interacted with the first level of sex (female) and scale (10-99).

The presence of interactions makes it somewhat difficult to draw conclusions about the change in wage differentials directly from Table 6.3, but, as can be readily seen, the effect of the interactions on wages, particularly those of

TABLE 6.3. ANALYSIS OF VARIANCE COEFFICIENTS 1958, 1961, 1964 (YEN)

			1958	1961	1964
Constant Term			6,173	7,339	7,925
Age	18-19		711	398	645
	20-24		2,001	1,380	1,726
	25-29		2,556	2,072	2,241
	30-39		1,481	543	1,083
	40+		144	-654	237
Sex	Male		-31	-257	522
Scale	100-999		-397	-800	-222
	1,000 +		971	-683	-261
Type	Salaried employee		2,482	2,750	3,448
Education	Higher		196	369	1,006
Industry					
18	Food		-433	-607	-824
20	Textile		334	446	601
21	Apparel		0	0	0
22	Lumber and wood		-3,245	-3,393	-3,092
23	Furniture		5	-596	136
24	Paper and pulp		2,427	1,226	806
25	Publishing and printing		3,507	3,454	3,485
26	Chemical products		766	406	506
27	Petroleum and coal products		4,228	3,544	2,649
28	Rubber products		536	771	909
29	Leather		1,409	1,886	1,053
30	Ceramic		800	388	-42
31	Iron and steel		4,276	6,131	5,053
32	Nonferrous metal		1,220	2,432	1,630
33	Fabricated metal		2,238	2,439	2,200
34	Machinery		1,291	2,349	1,953
35	Electrical machinery		1,023	1,014	289
36	Transportation and equipment		1,911	2,282	1,994
37	Precision machinery		3,297	2,885	2,088
Sex and Age					
	Male	18-19	1,910	2,398	2,331
		20-24	4,238	4,999	4,988
		25-29	8,124	8,798	8,746
		30-39	13,897	14,695	13,529
		40 +	16,387	17,079	14,928

TABLE 3 (continued)

			1958	1961	1964
Scale and Age					
	100-999	18-19	-55	13	-577
		20-24	-195	78	-911
		25-29	956	923	-451
		30-39	3,379	3,428	1,603
		40 +	6,143	5,844	3,644
	1,000 +	18-19	-787	-277	-489
		20-24	-577	-268	-1,285
		25-29	2,138	1,485	-713
		30-39	7,240	7,884	4,961
		40 +	15,391	16,020	12,739
Type and Education	Salaried employee	Higher	1,907	1,362	636
Education and Scale	Higher	100-999	135	135	-86
		1,000 +	1,365	871	409
Sex and Scale	Male	100-999	1,094	834	22
		1,000 +	467	578	-409
Type and Scale	Salaried employee	100-999	1,551	726	382
		1,000 +	2,985	2,092	277
R^2			0.931	0.928	0.918

age-sex and age-scale, is very important. This means that the effect of these factors depends on other factors with which they are combined.

In order to see explicitly the effect of each factor, the difference between consecutive levels of the factor can be computed for all other factors with which it has interactions. This serves also to eliminate an element of arbitrariness in Table 6.3., i.e., that all wage differentials are measured from the first level. These computations for the factors age, sex, and scale are presented in the Appendix tables.

6.4.1. Age

There was no clear-cut change from 1958 to 1961 in the

interage wage differentials. Among female workers there has been a contraction of differentials in the 100-999 scale group, but no one-sided change in the other two groups. The picture for males is ambiguous in all scale groups. From 1961 to 1964 the direction of change is much clearer. For male workers there is a reduction in differentials for all subgroups except for the two first levels of scale 10-99, and for females the reduction is somewhat smaller but is seen to be an almost general phenomenon. Although the absolute differentials with regard to age are still considerable, particularly in large-scale firms, there has been a marked reduction in interage differentials during the second subperiod.

6.4.2. Sex

There is a clear difference between the behavior of the intersex differentials in the two subperiods. In the first there was a general tendency for them to increase in all scale groups and all age groups except the first. This pattern has been reversed in the second subperiod, where differentials tend to decrease. This tendency is not the same for all scales: for large- and medium-scale workers the gap diminishes for all age groups, while for the small-scale workers, only for the last two age groups.

6.4.3. Scale

The scale factor is of great interest in the Japanese economy. As mentioned above, one of the peculiar features of this economy is said to be its dual structure, where a modern sector and a premodern sector are functioning side by side. One of the expressions of the dual structure is in large wage and productivity differences between large-scale and medium-small-scale enterprises.

During the whole period there has taken place a process of reduction in differentials (except for a few cases). In most of the groups up to age 29, there has actually been a reversal of the differentials, as the workers in the smaller-scale firms get higher wages than in larger firms.

It can be said that as far as interscale wage differentials are concerned, the dual economy is heading to a gradual disappearance. Although there are still considerable differentials in wages in the high age groups, they show a marked tendency to diminish.

6.4.4. Type of Employment

It was possible to divide this and the next factor into two levels only, so that their impact is not fully revealed.

As to workers with higher education there is a reduction of differentials between salaried employees and wage earners. The picture is less clear as to workers with elementary education, where differentials have been reduced in large firms but increased in small ones.

6.4.5. Education

For salaried employees there is a reduction in the effect of education for all scales. For wage earners there is an increase in differentials for small- and medium-scale and no visible trend for large-scale firms.

6.4.6. Industry

Wage differentials among industries, as measured by the dispersion of their average wage, can be attributed to two sources. One is the different composition of workers in the various industries as far as age, sex, scale, education, and type of employment are concerned. The second is the industry effect *per se*, namely, the effect on similar workers of their being in different industries. Under conditions of perfect competition, with perfect labor mobility, these interindustry differentials should disappear. The existence of such inter-industry differentials indicates the absence of an open labor market, and the change in them can indicate the movement to a more competitive structure.

The question has been raised how to distinguish empirically between the two components of the dispersion of average wages of industries,[13] and the method presented here gives at least a partial answer. We cannot claim that all "distribution" effects have been eliminated from the industry effect. On the one hand, there are some factors (such as skill) which were not introduced at all, while on the other hand, a more refined division of the factors which have been introduced is desirable. It can also not be claimed that our results are an upper bound to the true industry effect, since the missing elements may be "competitive" or "complementary" to the ones that were introduced. By complementary we mean two factors that reinforce each other in their effect on average industrial wage (if, for instance, industries with more male workers have also more workers in high age groups, these two factors are complementary), whereas two factors in which those levels that cause high wages do not appear together are competitive.

A comparison of the industry effect which emerges from the variance analysis with the industry's average wage shows that the dispersion of the former is considerably smaller than the latter. The standard deviation of the industry effect is 1,794, 2,026, and 1,729 yen for 1958, 1961, and 1964, respectively, while that of the industry's average wage is 4,898, 4,716, and 3,779 for the same years. This indicates that the other factors which were introduced into the analysis are complementary rather than competitive. It also suggests that introducing more factors will reduce the interindustry differentials even more.

Turning now to the magnitude of the effect for different industries, we find that the general pattern, as represented by the rank, was fairly stable during the period; there are exceptions as to a few industries whose relative positions have changed.[14]

As was already mentioned, the industry effect cannot be regarded as an ideal indicator of the pure impact of this factor. However if we can assume that there was no significant change in other factors which were not introduced into the analysis, we can take the magnitude of the dispersion of the industry effect as an indicator of the degree of diversity from a competitive market. There was an increase in the dispersion from 1958 to 1961 and a decline to 1964, the 1964 value being lower than that of 1958. This may indicate the movement toward a more competitive structure of the economy in the second subperiod and to confirm the proposition according to which 1961 can be regarded as the turning point in the labor market's structural change.

6.5. Scarcity of Labor and Wage Differentials

We can summarize the results of the empirical study as follows. During the period 1958-1964 there was a process of "tightening" in the Japanese labor market. This resulted in an increase in mobility among firms and in an over-all reduction in wage differentials. Whereas up to 1961 the reduction has been mainly manifested in interscale wage differentials, from 1961 there has also been a considerable reduction in interage and interindustry differentials. Thus, we find an inverse relation between scarcity of labor and wage differentials during this period in the Japanese economy, which raises the more general question of the relation between the conditions in the labor market and wage differentials. Why do we find the large wage differentials before, and why did differentials shrink when scarcity of labor occurred? Under conditions of surplus of labor the general wage level is pressed downward, but there seems no reason why large-scale companies should pay higher wages to workers when similar workers in the market receive lower wages. As indicated in this study, the difference in wage levels between scales and industries was not caused only because different types of workers were employed, but also because the same workers received different wages. As to the low rate of mobility, this can be well understood from the worker's point of view: under circumstances of labor abundance he will be reluctant to leave the firm, not being sure that he can find other work. But this does not explain why the firm will not lay off workers and employ cheaper labor. Since we are dealing here with supply-demand relations, we must look at the empirical evidence from both sides.

In recent years the concept of an internal labor market has been put at the center of several studies of labor relations.[15] In contrast to the neoclassical theory, in which labor is being hired from a pool of workers where workers are perfectly mobile at every stage of the occupational ladder and therefore wages of homogeneous workers must be equal throughout the economy, the new theory puts the emphasis on the intraplant wage policy. There are only a limited number of "ports of entry" through which workers enter into the firm, and these are generally at the base of the occupational ladder. The rise in this ladder is to a great extent the consequence of training, formal or informal, within the plant and is done according to criteria which consist of a mixture of economic and institutional elements. Likewise, there are "ports of exit" through which the workers leave the firm, either to the external labor market or out of the labor force.

The Japanese labor market seems to be most appropriate for this model,[16] since, especially in large firms, the principle of "lifetime commitment" is the rule. This is a very "closed" internal market, where there is only one port of entry, at the bottom of the occupational ladder, through which the worker enters the firm after having finished his formal education, and almost only one port of exit to retirement. As to the promotion system, seniority plays an important role, and the connection between the worker's remuneration and the length of service is very strong. This is reflected in the present study by the age factor and the age and scale interaction, which show the considerable impact of age, especially in the large-scale establishments.

Although the firm is to some extent an autonomous unit which has considerable discretion, it is not altogether independent of its surroundings, the external labor market, and changes in the latter can be expected to produce changes in the internal labor market.

A "tightening" of the labor market, such as the one that occurred in the period under study, can be expected to influence the internal market both as to the ports of entry and exit and the rules for advancement within the plant.[17] Under labor scarcity the ties among firms are much closer, and each firm cannot pursue its own policy within a more or less fenced internal market.

A more basic question concerns the factors which determine the firm's discretionary policy in fixing wages. Tradition, custom, and responsibility toward employees may be important in formulating these decisions. However, some attempts have been made to link the wage differentials to measurable variables, such as productivity and labor unions,[18] and these factors were found to explain a certain part of wage variability.

If the preceding analysis is correct, it can be expected that the changing conditions in the labor market have brought about a change in the impact of productivity and unionization on wage differentials. In particular, the impact of these factors should have been reduced under a more competitive market structure.

Since there is a high correlation between labor productivity and unionization rate in a cross-section of industries (caused partially by the fact that both are associated with the scale of firms), it is not possible to obtain statistically significant results by introducing both variables into a regression equation. Productivity seems to have the greater impact, so a regression of the industry effect, derived from the previous analysis, on value-added productivity (value added in each industry divided by the number of employees) has been computed. The wage data (monthly wage, in yen) refers to April of each year, while the productivity data (in 100,000 yen) refers to the calendar year; therefore the productivity data of the preceding year have been used in the regression.[19] Both variables are deflated by the change in the average value of the variable compared to 1961.

TABLE 6.4.

Year	Regression Coefficient[a]	R^2 [b]
1958	302.04 (95.23)	0.2979
1961	211.95 (98.61)	0.1212
1964	193.43 (117.35)	0.0364

[a]The numbers in parentheses are standard errors.
[b]Corrected for degrees of freedom.

The results of the computations are given in Table 6.4. It is evident that there has been a great reduction in the impact of productivity on the interindustry wage effect as seen both by the coefficient of determination and the regression coefficients. This seems to confirm the hypothesis about the connection between scarcity of labor and wage differentials.

Appendix

TABLE 6.A.1. WAGE DIFFERENCES BETWEEN CONSECUTIVE AGE GROUPS (YEN) 1958, 1961, 1964

	1000+			100-999			10-99		
Age Groups	1958	1961	1964	1958	1961	1964	1958	1961	1964
Male									
18-19 minus -17	1,834	2,519	2,487	2,566	2,809	2,399	2,621	2,796	2,976
20-24 minus 18-19	3,828	3,592	2,942	3,478	3,648	3,404	3,618	3,583	3,738
25-29 minus 20-24	7,156	6,244	4,845	5,592	5,336	4,733	4,441	4,491	4,273
30-39 minus 25-29	9,800	10,767	9,299	7,121	6,873	5,679	4,698	4,368	3,625
40+ minus 30-39	9,304	9,323	8,331	3,917	3,603	2,594	1,153	1,187	553
Female									
18-19 minus -17	-76	121	156	656	411	68	711	398	645
20-24 minus 18-19	1,500	991	285	1,150	1,047	747	1,290	982	1,081
25-29 minus 20-24	3,270	2,445	1,087	1,706	1,537	975	555	692	515
30-39 minus 25-29	4,027	4,870	4,516	1,348	976	896	-1,075	-1,529	-1,158
40+ minus 30-39	6,814	6,939	6,932	1,427	1,219	1,195	-1,337	-1,197	- 846

TABLE 6.A.2. WAGE DIFFERENCES BETWEEN MALES AND FEMALES (YEN) 1958, 1961, 1964

Scale	Year	-17	18-19	20-24	25-29	30-39	40+
1000+	1958	436	2,346	4,674	8,560	14,333	16,823
	1961	321	2,719	5,320	9,119	15,016	17,400
	1964	113	2,444	5,101	8,859	13,642	15,041
100-999	1958	1,063	2,973	5,301	9,187	14,960	17,450
	1961	577	2,975	5,576	9,375	15,272	17,656
	1964	544	2,875	5,532	9,290	14,073	15,472
10-99	1958	-31	1,879	4,207	8,093	13,866	16,356
	1961	-257	2,141	4,742	8,541	14,438	16,822
	1964	522	2,853	5,510	9,268	14,051	15,450

TABLE 6.A.3. INTERSCALE WAGE DIFFERENTIALS (YEN) 1958, 1961, 1964

Type	Education	Year	-17	18-19	20-24	25-29	30-39	40+
Scale: 1,000 + minus 100-999								
Male								
Wage Earner	Elementary	1958	741	9	359	1,923	4,602	9,989
		1961	-139	-429	-485	423	4,317	10,037
		1964	-470	-382	-844	-732	2,888	8,625
	Higher	1958	1,971[a]	1,239	1,589	3,153	5,832	11,219
		1961	597[a]	307	251	1,159	5,053	10,773
		1964	25[a]	113	-349	-237	3,383	9,120
Salaried Employee	Elementary	1958	2,175	1,443	1,793	3,357	6,036	11,423
		1961	1,227	932	881	1,789	5,683	11,403
		1964	-575	-487	-949	-837	2,783	8,520
	Higher	1958	3,405[a]	2,673	3,023	4,587	7,266	12,653
		1961	1,963[a]	1,673	1,617	2,525	6,419	12,139
		1964	-80[a]	8	-454	-342	3,278	9,015

CONTINUED ON NEXT PAGE

Appendix Table 3 (continued)

Type	Education	Year	-17	18-19	20-24	25-29	30-39	40+
Female								
Wage Earner	Elementary	1958	1,368	636	986	2,550	5,229	10,616
		1961	117	-173	-229	679	4,573	10,293
		1964	-39	49	-413	-301	3,319	9,056
	Higher	1958	2,598[a]	1,866	2,216	3,780	6,459	11,846
		1961	853[a]	563	507	1,415	5,309	11,029
		1964	456[a]	544	82	194	3,814	9,551
Salaried Employee	Elementary	1958	2,802	2,070	2,420	3,984	6,663	12,050
		1961	1,483	1,193	1,137	2,045	5,939	11,659
		1964	-144	-56	-518	-406	3,214	8,951
	Higher	1958	4,032[a]	3,300	3,650	5,214	7,893	13,280
		1961	2,219[a]	1,929	1,873	2,781	6,675	12,395
		1964	351[a]	439	-23	89	3,709	9,446

CONTINUED ON NEXT PAGE

Appendix Table 3 (continued)

Type	Education	Year	-17	18-19	20-24	25-29	30-39	40+
Scales 100-999 minus 10-99								
Male								
Wage Earner	Elementary	1958	697	642	502	1,653	4,076	6,840
		1961	34	47	112	957	3,462	5,878
		1964	-200	-777	-1,111	-651	1,403	3,444
	Higher	1958	832[a]	777	637	1,788	4,211	6,975
		1961	169[a]	182	247	1,092	3,597	6,013
		1964	-286[a]	-863	-1,197	-737	1,317	3,358
Salaried Employee	Elementary	1958	2,248	2,193	2,053	3,204	5,627	8,391
		1961	760	773	838	1,683	4,188	6,604
		1964	182	-395	-729	-269	1,785	3,826
	Higher	1958	2,383[a]	2,328	2,188	3,339	5,762	8,526
		1961	895[a]	908	973	1,818	4,323	6,739
		1964	96[a]	-481	-815	-355	1,699	3,740
Female								
Wage Earner	Elementary	1958	-397	-452	-592	559	2,982	5,746
		1961	-800	-787	-722	123	2,628	5,044
		1964	-222	-799	-1,133	-673	1,381	3,422

CONTINUED ON NEXT PAGE

Appendix Table 3 (continued)

Type	Education	Year	-17	18-19	20-24	25-29	30-39	40+
	Higher	1958	-262[a]	-317	-457	694	3,117	5,881
		1961	-665[a]	-652	-587	258	2,763	5,179
		1964	-308[a]	-885	-1,219	-759	1,295	3,336
Salaried Employee	Elementary	1958	1,154	1,099	959	2,110	4,533	7,297
		1961	-74	-61	4	849	3,354	5,770
		1964	160	-417	-751	-291	1,763	3,804
	Higher	1958	1,289[a]	1,234	1,094	2,245	4,668	7,432
		1961	61[a]	74	139	984	3,489	5,905
		1964	74[a]	-503	-837	-377	1,677	3,718

[a]Actually there are no workers in this category. Nevertheless we get the figure from the analysis.

Notes

This paper is based on a part of a Ph.D. dissertation completed at Osaka University. I wish to express my gratitude to the Japanese Ministry of Education for a scholarship during my stay in Japan and to the Institute of Social and Economic Research, Osaka University, for the use of its facilities and financial aid. My foremost thanks go to Professor S. Ichimura, M. Morishima, M. Saito, and I. Sugiura for their help and encouragement. All remaining errors are, of course, my responsibility.

1. Kazushi Ohkawa and Henry Rosovsky, "A Century of Japanese Economic Growth." In W. W. Lockwood (ed.), The State and Economic Enterprise in Japan (Princeton University Press, 1965), p. 79.

2. The average yearly increase in the nonagricultural labor force reached 980,000 during the period 1958-1964 (Labor Force Survey). See also R. Minami, "Population Migration Away from Agriculture in Japan," Economic Development and Cultural Change, vol. 15, no. 2, part I (January 1967).

3. This point is stressed in M. Reder, "The Theory of Occupational Wage Differentials," American Economic Review, vol. 45, no. 5 (December 1955).

4. The difference in definitions compared to the United States lies mainly in the unpaid workers category. In the United States a person belonging to this group is considered employed if he has worked at least 15 hours during the week of the survey; in Japan if he has worked one hour or more.

5. Miyohei Shinohara, Growth and Cycle in the Japanese Economy (Tokyo: Kinokuniya, 1962), pp. 17-19.

6. The turnover rate in the United States was 8.1 in 1960. See U. S. Department of Labor, Employment and Earnings, vol. 13, no. 7 (January 1967), p. 80.

7. Ministry of Labor, Labor White Paper 1965, (Tokyo), p. 32.

The problem of labor mobility and its relation to the traditional social values of the Japanese, specifically loyalty on the part of the employee and responsibility on the part of the employer, gave rise to an interesting controversy. See James G. Abegglen, The Japanese Factory (Glencoe, Ill: Free Press, 1958); and K. Taira, "The Characteristics of Japanese Labor Markets," Economic Development and Cultural Change, vol. 10, no. 2, part I (January 1962). Abegglen emphasized the role of traditional concepts, such as loyalty and mutual responsibility, as a cause for the strong ties between the employee and the company. Taira argued that the low rate of mobility is a postwar phenomenon and that the prewar rate was not different from that of the United States, thus rejecting the former interpretation.

8. This device was used by Akira Ono in "Rōdō Kumiai to Sangyōkan Chingin Kakusa" ("Labor Unions and Interindustry Wage Differentials"), Economic Studies Quarterly, vol. 12, no. 1, (September 1966): pp. 15-26.

9. D. B. Suits, "Use of Dummy Variables in Regression Equations," Journal of the American Statistical Association 52 (December 1957): pp. 548-551; F. G. Adams, "The Size of Individual Incomes: Socioeconomic Variables and Chance Variation," Review of Economics and Statistics, vol. 40, no. 4 (November 1958): pp. 390-398; T. P. Hill, "An Analysis of the Distribution of Wages and Salaries in Great Britain," Econometrica, vol. 27, no. 3 (July 1959); pp. 355-380; G. H. Orcutt et al., Microanalysis of Socioeconomic Systems (New York: Harper, 1961); L. Johansen, "A Note on Regression with Dummy Variables," Nordisk Tidsskrift for Industriel Statistik, ving 7, haefte 4 (1962); T. Blumenthal, "The Effect of Socioeconomic Factors on Wage Differentials in Japanese Manufacturing Industries," Economic Studies Quarterly, vol. 17 no. 1 (September 1966); pp. 53-67.

10. This is so because if we define a nonzero variable for each level, we encounter the problem of singularity of the independent variables' matrix, and there is no single solution for the coefficients. Additional constraints must be added, and one set of such constraints is to define the first level of

each factor to be zero. Thus, all other coefficients represent the difference between the respective level and the first. Using this method has the additional advantage of reducing the number of variables.

11. This can be shown as follows. Let $\underline{w}(\underline{n} \times 1)$ be the vector of wages of individual workers and $\bar{\underline{w}}(\underline{m} \times 1)$ the vector of mean wages in groups. Let $\underline{Z}(\underline{n} \times \underline{k})$ be the matrix of predetermined variables for individual workers, and $\bar{\underline{Z}}(\underline{m} \times \underline{k})$ be the respective matrix for the means. Note that the value of the predetermined variables is the same for all workers in a group.

$$\underline{V} = \begin{bmatrix} \underline{n}_1 & & & & 0 \\ & \underline{n}_2 & & & \\ & & \cdot & & \\ & & & \cdot & \\ 0 & & & & \underline{n}_m \end{bmatrix}$$

where $\underline{n}_{\underline{i}}$ is the number of workers in the $\underline{i}^{th}$ group. The two models are:

$$(1) \qquad \underline{w} = \underline{Z}\beta + \underline{u}$$

$$(2) \qquad \bar{\underline{w}} = \bar{\underline{Z}}\bar{\beta} + \bar{\underline{u}}$$

The respective estimates are:

$$\beta = (\underline{Z}'\underline{Z})^{-1}\underline{Z}'\underline{w}$$

$$\bar{\beta} = (\bar{\underline{Z}}'\underline{V}\bar{\underline{Z}})^{-1}\bar{\underline{Z}}'\underline{V}\bar{\underline{w}}$$

But $\underline{Z}'\underline{Z} = \bar{\underline{Z}}'\underline{V}\bar{\underline{Z}}$ and $\underline{Z}'\underline{w} = \bar{\underline{Z}}'\underline{V}\bar{\underline{w}}$, so $\beta = \bar{\beta}$.

12. The sample on which the study is based is the Basic Survey of Wage Structure (Ministry of Labor, 1958 Chingin Kōzō Kihon Chōsa Tokyo, 1959, 1961 Chingin Jittai Sōgō Chōsa, Tokyo, 1962, and 1964 Chingin Kōzō Kihon Tōkei Chōsa, Tokyo, 1965). This survey covers between one-eighth and one-fourth of all workers and can be regarded as highly representative of the population.

13. Konoske Odaka, "Rationalizing Inter Industry Wage Differentials: An Analytical Framework," Hitotsubashi Journal of Economics, June 1966.

14. Thus, the paper and pulp and the ceramics industries show great changes in their relative industry effect. The shortness of the period does not allow us to draw conclusions, but the present method can be used for analyzing changes in the industrial structure over time.

15. Clark Kerr, "The Balkanization of Labor Markets," in E. W. Bakke et al., Labor Mobility and Economic Opportunity (Cambridge: MIT Press, 1954), P. B. Doeringer and M. J. Piore, "Internal Labor Markets, Technological Change, and Labor Force Adjustment" (Washington, D.C.: U. S. Department of Labor, October, 1966).

16. It is interesting to note that in his book, Abegglen regards the Japanese factory as the antithesis of the Western type (see note 7). The internal labor market hypothesis regards both as belonging to the same type, although the motives behand the firms' discretionary actions may be different.

17. There is also an effect on other aspects of the firm's policy, such as substitution of capital for labor, increase in overtime work, nonwage benefits, etc.

18. Ono, "Rōdō Kumiai to Sangyōkan Chingin Kakusa"; Blumenthal, "The Effect of Socioeconomic Factors on Wage Differentials in Japanese Manufacturing Industries." See also T. W. Garbarino, "A Theory of Interindustry Wage Structure Variations," Quarterly Journal of Economics, vol. 64, no. 2 (May 1950).

19. The source for the date on productivity is the Ministry of International Trade and Industry, Census of Manufactures.

7

Price Changes and the Rate of Change of Money Wage Earnings in Japan, 1955-1962

Tsunehiko Watanabe

7.1. Introduction

This study is an attempt to shed light on changes both of money wage earnings in manufacturing industries and of consumer prices and their interrelations during the period 1955-1962, for since 1960 the trend of consumer prices, which was relatively stable during the 1950s has been sharply upward and has become a new headache for the Japanese economy. The consumer price index increased sharply after 1960 and reached the so-called Western countries' level, although other price indexes, i.e., the wholesale price index and the export price index, remained relatively stable (Table 7.1). For example, in 1962 the consumer price index reached 120.1, quite similar to indexes in Western countries, as shown in Table 7.2. Furthermore, the 8 percent increase per annum of this index for the past three years is large enough to offset the increase in the rate of economic growth (i.e., around 9 percent per annum in real terms of GNP for the past ten years) from a consumer's viewpoint. As might be expected from past experiences in other countries, this sharp rise in consumer prices has produced very controversial problems, both economic and political in nature. The purpose of the present study is to provide a feasible answer to this problem of rising consumer prices from an economist's (not from a politician's) viewpoint.

TABLE 7.1. MOVEMENTS OF PRICE INDEXES IN JAPAN

	C.P.I.	W.P.I.	E.P.I.
1954	100.0	100.0	100.0
1955	98.9	98.2	93.6
1956	99.3	102.5	96.6
1957	102.3	105.5	100.3
1958	101.9	98.7	95.5
1959	103.0	99.7	95.3
1960	106.7	100.8	97.5
1961	112.4	101.8	94.7
1962	120.1	100.1	92.3
1963 (June)	130.4	102.0	93.9

Source: C.P.I. (Consumer's Price Index) from Central Statistical Bureau, Prime Minister's Office, W.P.I. (Wholesale Price Index) from Bank of Japan, and E.P.I. (Export Price Index) from Ministry of Finance.

Note: The base is 1954 for all indexes

TABLE 7.2. CONSUMER'S PRICES IN WESTERN COUNTRIES

	1959	1962
Belgium	109	112
Canada	110	113
France	129	145
West Germany	110	119
Italy	110	120
Japan	104	122
Netherlands	115	121
Norway	116	126
Sweden	119	132
United Kingdom	117	128
United States	102	113

Source: U.N. Statistical Yearbook, Monthly Bulletin of Statistics, and I.M.F. International Financial Statistics.

Note: The base is 1954 for all countries

Specifically, there are three major problems which will be investigated below, i.e., (i) the varying pace of the rise in consumer prices; (ii) the relation between unemployment and the rate of change of money wage earnings as affected by other possible variables, such as the rate of change of the profit rate, of price increases, etc. - the applicability of the Phillips-Lipsey hypothesis to Japanese data will be tested as an important objective; and (iii) the simultaneous relation between the change of consumer prices and that of money wage earnings.

It should be noted here that the following discussion is based entirely on short-term observations because of the lack of suitable statistical information. The model for explaining changes in consumer prices and the statistical results derived from this model through the use of Japanese data are discussed in section 7.2. The Phillips-Lipsey hypothesis in the Japanese economy is examined in section 7.3, together with alternative hypotheses. In section 7.4, the effect of prices on wages and of wages on prices is investigated. A fuller description and discussion of the data are reserved for the Appendix. The concluding section sums up the results of the study and evaluates briefly their implications for present-day inflation in Japan.

7.2. Determinants of Price Changes

There are at least two important models for explaining determinants of price changes, i.e., the formulations based on the demand-supply mechanism in the competitive market and those based on the mark-up (or the cost-determined) principle. On the other hand, there is an important restriction in applying these two formulations to Japanese data, i.e., the empirical specifications of the variables. If the price level is taken as the variable to be explained, even a very crude approach yields quite good results in a statistical sense: the coefficients of determination between the level of income per capita and the level of consumer prices (either in the aggregate or in the disaggregate breakdown) for the period of this study is 0.95.[1] But the goodness of fit of this relationship is largely determined by the strong upward trends in both of the variables considered; almost any series of Japanese data expressed in nominal money terms would have a similar high correlation caused by a fairly rapid economic growth in the postwar period.

The model which is derived from the demand-supply relation is largely implicit in the standard reference of economics.[2] Let us define the demand and the supply equations respectively as

$$(7.1) \qquad \underline{q}^D = \underline{f}(\underline{p},\underline{y})$$

$$(7.2) \qquad \underline{q}^S = \underline{g}(\underline{p},\underline{z})$$

where the notations are

$\underline{q}^D$ = amount of demand
$\underline{q}^S$ = amount of supply
$\underline{p}$ = price
$\underline{y}$ = the variable indicating a shift of the demand curve, e.g., income per capita
$\underline{z}$ = the variable indicating a shift of the supply income, e.g., an increase of labor productivity

It is hardly possible to estimate these two equations directly from the observable sample without imposing an equilibrium condition, especially on the aggregate levels. The equilibrium condition can be introduced in two ways, i.e., (i) the speed of adjustment in the market is infinite within the specified observation period (e.g., a quarter), which corresponds to the equality between $\underline{q}^D$ and $\underline{q}^S$, and (ii) the speed of adjustment is finite, which means that the difference between $\underline{q}^D$ and $\underline{q}^S$ is not equal to zero. According to the former condition, the path of price changes can be traced through the following reduced form, i.e., solving equations (7.1) and (7.2) together with the condition of $\underline{q}^D = \underline{q}^S$ with respect to $\underline{q}^D$, $\underline{q}^S$, and $\underline{p}$ at each period,

$$(7.3) \qquad \underline{p} = \underline{h}(\underline{y},\underline{z})$$

which can be called a comparative static approach. On the other hand, the latter condition can specify the path of price changes as a dynamic adjustment process, i.e.,

$$(7.4) \qquad \frac{dp}{dt} = m(q^D - q^S).$$

The transformation of these theoretically derived models into statistically operational ones can be made as follows: taking the annual relative difference of all variables concerned using quarterly data (which is expressed as the percentage change with respect to the level in the preceding year, e.g., $(p_t - p_{t-4})/p_{t-4}$),[3] either a straight linear form or a log-linear form is used, i.e., for equation (7.3),

$$(7.5) \qquad \left(\frac{p_t - p_{t-4}}{p_{t-4}}\right) = \alpha_0 + \alpha_1\left(\frac{y_t - y_{t-4}}{y_{t-4}}\right) + \alpha_2\left(\frac{z_t - z_{t-4}}{z_{t-4}}\right) + \epsilon_1$$

$$(7.6) \qquad \log\left(\frac{p_t}{p_{t-4}}\right) = \beta_0 + \beta_1 \log\left(\frac{y_t}{y_{t-4}}\right) + \beta_2 \log\left(\frac{z_t}{z_{t-4}}\right) + \eta_t$$

and for equation (7.4),

$$(7.7) \qquad \frac{p_t - p_{t-4}}{p_{t-4}} = \theta_0 + \theta_1 \left(\frac{J_t - J_{t-4}}{J_{t-4}}\right) + \epsilon_t^*$$

where ϵ_t, η_t, and ϵ_t^* are random disturbances, the family of α, β, and θ are parameters to be estimated, and $J_t = q_t^D - q_t^S$.[4] Among these equations, the last one presents a serious problem, i.e., it is almost impossible to define the amount of J_t quantitatively, since aggregate amounts of demand and also of supply corresponding to the overall consumer price index include services and perishable goods (they are approximately 40 percent of total goods and services covered in the Japanese consumer price index). In order to overcome this difficulty and also the multicollinearity appearing in explanatory variables, equation (7.7) has to be alternatively expressed by the second-order difference, i.e.;[5]

$$(7.8) \qquad \Delta^2 p_t = \delta_0 + \delta_1 \Delta p + \delta_2 \Delta y + \delta_3 \Delta z + \eta_t'.$$

The following data were used: (i) the overall consumer price index was used for price, (ii) gross domestic product per capita and the labor productivity index in manufacturing industries were used for the variable z, and (iii) personal disposable income per capita, the money wage earnings index in manufacturing industries,[6] and personal consumption expenditure per capita were used for the variable $\underline{y}$. Data are given in Table 7.3 below.

TABLE 7.3. DATA SERIES

		(1)	(2)	(3)	(4)	(5)	(6)
		$\frac{\Delta \underline{p}_t}{\underline{p}_{t-4}}$	$\frac{\Delta \underline{x}_t}{\underline{x}_{t-4}}$	$\frac{\Delta \underline{w}_t}{\underline{w}_{t-4}}$	$\frac{\Delta \underline{y}_t}{\underline{y}_{t-4}}$	$\frac{\Delta \underline{c}_t}{\underline{c}_{t-4}}$	$\underline{U}_t$
1956	4	0.41	13.72	13.13	10.00	8.39	2.7
1957	1	1.25	12.15	11.55	9.15	7.57	3.0
	2	1.84	11.28	9.20	8.35	7.42	2.8
	3	2.85	8.61	7.82	9.65	7.81	2.8
	4	3.12	4.72	4.32	10.20	8.42	3.0
1958	1	2.52	1.73	4.29	9.10	8.69	4.1
	2	1.64	-2.63	3.83	7.53	7.91	4.2
	3	0.15	-4.56	4.92	5.15	6.46	4.4
	4	-0.49	-2.85	5.21	4.53	5.32	3.9
1959	1	-0.33	0.60	6.75	5.58	5.28	3.9
	2	0.06	5.70	7.15	7.75	5.89	3.1
	3	0.68	9.90	8.96	10.35	4.86	2.8
	4	1.15	11.84	9.85	12.35	8.16	2.3
1960	1	1.81	14.26	10.16	12.75	9.26	2.6
	2	2.58	14.20	10.84	13.85	9.74	2.1
	3	3.23	13.51	10.11	13.93	10.74	2.2
	4	3.58	12.60	9.92	14.20	11.97	1.9
1961	1	3.72	10.75	10.11	14.43	11.82	2.6
	2	3.69	10.95	11.80	14.60	12.73	2.0
	3	4.10	11.3	13.52	15.75	13.04	2.0
	4	5.37	12.44	15.53	16.88	14.02	1.7
1962	1	6.27	12.88	15.90	17.35	15.81	2.5
	2	7.42	10.66	14.71	17.78	17.07	2.2
	3	7.85	8.59	13.52	16.48	13.57	2.6
	4	6.87	2.85	10.40	14.90	16.57	2.5

The price equations (7.5) and (7.6), estimated by the single stage least squares method, using quarterly data during 1955 and 1963 are:

$$(7.9) \quad \frac{\Delta \underline{p}_t}{\underline{p}_{t-4}} = \underset{(1.52)}{-2.14} - \underset{(0.06)}{0.22} \frac{\Delta \underline{x}_t}{\underline{x}_{t-4}} + \underset{(0.10)}{0.68} \frac{\Delta \underline{w}_t}{\underline{w}_{t-4}} \qquad \bar{R} = 0.82$$

$$(7.10)\quad \frac{\Delta p_t}{p_{t-4}} = \underset{(0.73)}{-1.29} - \underset{(0.05)}{0.25}\,\frac{\Delta x_t}{x_{t-4}} + \underset{(0.07)}{0.58}\,\frac{\Delta y_t}{y_t} \qquad \bar{R} = 0.80$$

$$(7.11)\quad \log \frac{p_t}{p_{t-4}} = \underset{(0.74)}{1.03} - \underset{(0.02)}{1.158}\,\log \frac{x_t}{x_{t-4}} + \underset{(0.04)}{0.64}\,\log \frac{y_t}{y_{t-4}} \qquad \bar{R} = 0.96$$

$$(7.12)\quad \log \frac{p_t}{p_{t-4}} = \underset{(0.74)}{1.10} - \underset{(0.05)}{0.24}\,\log \frac{x_t}{x_{t-4}} + \underset{(0.09)}{0.69}\,\log \frac{w_t}{w_{t-4}} \qquad \bar{R} = 0.83$$

$$(7.13)\quad \log \frac{p_t}{p_{t-4}} = \underset{(0.72)}{1.09} - \underset{(0.02)}{0.14}\,\log \frac{x_t}{x_{t-4}} + \underset{(0.04)}{0.59}\,\log \frac{c_t}{c_{t-4}} \qquad \bar{R} = 0.96$$

where the following notation has been used:

x_t = labor productivity index,
w_t = average wage earnings index in manufacturing industries,
p_t = overall consumer price index,
y_t = personal disposable income per capita,
c_t = personal consumption expenditure per capita,
Δ represents the first-order difference with respect to the corresponding level in the previous year, e.g., $\Delta p_t = p_t - p_{t-4}$,
$\bar{R}$ represents the correlation coefficient adjusted by the degree of freedom (here its size was 25).

It may be possible to draw the following tentative conclusions from these statistical results:

1. A 1 percent change in personal income per capita or in the money wage earnings index gives rise to about 0.6 percent increase in consumer prices. Similarly a change of 1 percent in labor productivity appears to lead a negative change of about 0.2 percent in consumer prices.

2. There may be no significant differences between straight

linear and log-linear specifications, although the correlation coefficients in the latter case are slightly higher than in the former.

3. The effect of personal disposable income per capita, personal consumption expenditure per capita and money wage earnings per capita, as a shifting variable in the demand curve are all in comparable order, i.e., the regression coefficients with respect to these variables center around 0.6.

4. Since the estimates of constant term in every equation are not statistically significant, it is almost impossible to identify the long-term implications. In other words, the short-term clearance mechanism in the market may have sufficient explanatory powers for price determination.

Two important problems remain to be investigated here: (i) are the time-lag effects important, and (ii) can money wage earnings be considered only from the demand side as stated above? Let us consider possible effects caused by time-lags in the variables.

Different time-lags or initial delay periods were experimented with for both income and productivity variables. First of all, substitution of the above variables with the variables lagged by more than two periods failed to provide reasonable results, i.e., either the estimated regression coefficients were not statistically significant, or the expected sign conditions (the positive for the income variable and the negative for the productivity variable) were not obtained.

On the other hand, the use of the variable lagged one period gave generally good and comparable results, for example, the substitution of $\Delta \underline{x}_t/\underline{x}_{t-4}$ with $\Delta \underline{x}_{t-1}/\underline{x}_{t-5}$ into equation (7.10) was:

$$\frac{\Delta \underline{p}_t}{\underline{p}_{t-4}} = \underset{(1.10)}{-1.77} - \underset{(0.06)}{0.16} \frac{\Delta \underline{x}_{t-1}}{\underline{x}_{t-5}} + \underset{(0.08)}{0.59} \frac{\Delta \underline{y}_t}{\underline{y}_{t-4}} \qquad \bar{\underline{R}} = 0.76.$$

The use of a sequence of lagged variables (e.g., a simultaneous introduction of $\Delta \underline{x}_t/\underline{x}_{t-4}$ and $\Delta \underline{x}_{t-1}/\underline{x}_{t-5}$ into equation (7.10) however, gave no sensible results because of the existence of multicollinearity among the lagged variables. According to these experiments, we may say that effects caused by the initial delay periods were not positively identified, although the use of a much shorter sample period, e.g., a monthly basis may produce different results.

The remaining problem, which may be much more important for the present investigation than for the first one, concerns the dual character of money wage earnings, i.e., whether this factor affects the demand side as an income variable or the supply side as a cost variable. The above conclusion 1, that shows similar effects with other income variables, may partly confirm a hypothesis that it plays its part primarily as an income variable. It would be desirable to make a direct test, however. Different types of wage cost indexes were experimented with for this purpose, i.e., average wage cost indexes (total wage bill paid/total output) in manufacturing industries, nonagricultural industries (manufacturing plus service industries), wholesale and retail trade, services, and small-scale sectors, were constructed and tested with productivity variables. None of them gave satisfactory results in the sense that either the sign conditions or the statistical significance with respect to explanatory variables were not fulfilled. For example, the wage cost index in nonagricultural industries was:[7]

$$\frac{\Delta \underline{p}_t}{\underline{p}_{t-4}} = 2.84 + \underset{(0.10)}{0.13} \frac{\Delta \underline{x}_t}{\underline{x}_{t-4}} + \underset{(0.19)}{0.33} \frac{\Delta \underline{w}_t}{\underline{w}_{t-4}} \qquad \bar{R} = 0.69$$

where $\underline{w}_t$ represents the above wage cost index. Although the tests may not be perfectly satisfactory because of the exclusion of cyclical considerations,[8] we may say that the role of money wage earnings appears to be most important on the demand side, confirming conclusion 1 above.

As a final remark, it will be mentioned here that a statistical testing of equation (7.8) does not provide any sensible results, since three explanatory variables on the right-hand side of the equation already have a high statistical correlation as shown in equation (7.10). (If the third-order difference is introduced to avoid this difficulty, it is seriously disturbed by computational errors appearing in the process of constructing the original price index.)

7.3. The Phillips-Lipsey Hypothesis

Since much discussion has been stimulated recently both in the United Kingdom and elsewhere, by the Phillips-Lipsey hypothesis of a reasonably stable "adjustment mechanism" in the labor market, it may not be necessary to add further explanation here.[9] The present section, therefore is concerned only with the application of this hypothesis to recent Japanese data.

The basic model in question is implicit for the most part in Phillips' work, amended by Lipsey. In outline, it suggests that the rate of change of money wages is a function of the level of excess supply (demand) in the market. As a sufficient approximation, a linear form between the percentage change in money wages and the percentage of supply in excess of labor was proposed by Lipsey. Along with his suggestions, the basic model can be written as:

$$(7.14) \quad \frac{dw}{dt} = 1\left(\frac{L^s - L^D}{L^s}\right) + u(F)$$

where the notations are:

w = the rate of money wages
L^s = supply of labor
L^D = demand of labor
F = a suitable variable which may represent effects caused by institutional forces (e.g., trade union power) or to the aggregation of individual markets. (Further specifications will be discussed below.)

Before going into the estimation procedure, there are a few problems to be considered about empirical specifications of variables. First of all, an indicator for the excess supply (demand) in the labor market must be established. As is already well recognized, the level of unemployment may not be a sufficiently suitable indicator for this hypothesis, since the level of unemployment never has a negative value by the nature of its definition. Construction of other indicators, e.g., "pressure of demand for labor" by Dow and Dicks-Mirreaux,[10] will be very desirable in principle, especially if statistical information about unplaced applicants and unfilled vacancies is available. After making trial observations with Japanese data, the number of persons who received unemployment insurance has been found to produce quite a similar pattern to the above two factors combined (they are available only on an annual basis), while the rate of unemployment reported in the labor force survey is not a satisfactory indicator.[11]

The next point to be considered here concerns a specification of the variable $\underline{F}$. From the viewpoint of statistical techniques, the variable $\underline{F}$ has to fluctuate independently of the unemployment variable, in order to avoid disturbances caused by multicollinearities among explanatory variables. The possible candidates which were suggested in the previous studies for this variable may be the level of profits and its rate of change, the rate of change of the level of unemployment, and the rate of change in the cost of living index.[12] Among these variables, the last one can be further identified as the relative percentage change of consumer prices, which was investigated in the previous section.

The last problem concerns the length of the observation period for which the relative difference will be defined. In the previous section, this was mainly decided by the need for eliminating seasonal fluctuations. Since experiences with wage negotiations in Japan during the postwar period have indicated that the most important item in wage negotiations is the determination of the annual increase in the money wage rate, it might be logical to take the annual change in money wage earnings as the basic objective in a wage adjustment mechanism.

Statistical results, estimated by the single-stage least squares method, are

$$(7.15)\quad \frac{\Delta \underline{w}_t}{\underline{w}_{t-4}} = 17.60 - \underset{(0.60)}{3.23}\,\underline{U}_t + \underset{(0.20)}{0.40}\,\frac{\Delta \underline{p}_{t-1}}{\underline{p}_{t-5}} \qquad \bar{\underline{R}} = 0.82$$

$$(7.16)\quad \frac{\Delta \underline{w}_t}{\underline{w}_{t-4}} = 17.07 - \underset{(0.52)}{3.07}\,\underline{U}_t + \underset{(0.39)}{1.26}\,\frac{\Delta \underline{p}_{t-1}}{\underline{p}_{t-2}} \qquad \bar{\underline{R}} = 0.86$$

$$(7.17)\quad \frac{\Delta \underline{w}_t}{\underline{w}_{t-4}} = 37.85 - \underset{(0.86)}{5.86}\,\underline{U}_{t-1} - \underset{(0.25)}{0.58}\,\frac{\Delta \underline{P}_t}{\underline{P}_t} \qquad \bar{\underline{R}} = 0.81$$

$$(7.18) \quad \frac{\Delta \underline{w}_t}{\underline{w}_{t-4}} = 18.05 - \underset{(0.86)}{3.95}\, \underline{U}_{t-1} + \underset{(0.024)}{0.016}\, \frac{\Delta \underline{U}_{t-1}}{\underline{U}_{t-4}} \qquad \bar{\underline{R}} = 0.73$$

where the notations are:

$\underline{w}$, $\underline{p}$, and $\bar{\underline{R}}$ = defined in the previous sections
$\underline{U}$ = the percentage of total employees who re-received unemployment insurance
$\underline{P}$ = the ratio of profit (including depreciation) to net worth of own capital in nonagricultural industries

$$\Delta \underline{p}_{t-1} = \underline{p}_{t-1} - \underline{p}_{t-5}, \qquad \tilde{\Delta} \underline{p}_{t-1} = \underline{p}_{t-1} - \underline{p}_{t-2}$$

$$\Delta \underline{U}_{t-1} = \underline{U}_{t-1} - \underline{U}_{t-5}, \qquad \Delta \underline{P}_{t} = \underline{P}_{y+1} - \underline{P}_{t-1} \, .$$

It should be noted here that these four equations were selected from experiments which tested different time lags and different combinations of explanatory variables and other types of specification of the profit variable (e.g., the ratio of profit to total output). Among these four equations (7.15) and (7.16) satisfy our expectations both theoretically and statistically. From these results, it may be possible to draw the following conclusions:

1. The applicability of the Phillips-Lipsey hypothesis to Japanese data is generally quite high.[13]

2. The Phillips-Lipsey hypothesis in Japan tells us that the level of unemployment which completely stabilizes the rate of change of money wage earnings, i.e., the case of $\Delta \underline{w}_t = 0$ is around 5.5 percent, which is quite similar to experience in other countries.[14]

3. In general, the cost-of-living index or the rate of change of consumer prices plays an active role in wage adjustments, and this variable may well be interpreted as a strategic indicator of union power during the period considered here.

4. Specifically, the effects of the change of consumer prices, with either one year lag or one quarter lag, are almost comparable (taking account of the size of standard errors with

respect to the corresponding coefficients), although the effect with one quarter lag is considerably more stable in a statistical sense.

5. Shifts of the Phillips-Lipsey schedule may well be explained by addition of the price variable, though the length of sample period here may not be sufficient. This implies that the Phillips-Lipsey schedules during different periods, e.g., the prewar and the postwar years,have to be observed with suitable additional variables, though this conjecture was not positively confirmed with Japanese data because of the lack of statictical information in the prewar period.

7.4. The Simultaneous Relations Between Prices and Wages

So far, our discussions have been concerned only with individual equations, i.e., price and wage equations, without taking into account the mutual feedback mechanism between these two variables. Furthermore, from the viewpont of statistical techniques, the procedures followed in the previous sections are insufficient, since biases caused by the single equation estimate may well be introduced. In what follows two types of mutual interactions between prices and wages, i.e., a pure simultaneous determination and a successive (or a recursive) determination, will be investigated.

A straightforward formulation of the mutual feedback mechanism can be expressed as the following simultaneous equations system:

$$\begin{aligned} \frac{\Delta \underline{p}_{\underline{t}}}{\underline{p}_{\underline{t}-4}} &= \underline{a}_0 + \underline{a}_1 \frac{\Delta \underline{x}_{\underline{t}}}{\underline{x}_{\underline{t}-4}} + \underline{a}_2 \frac{\Delta \underline{w}_{\underline{t}}}{\underline{w}_{\underline{t}-4}} \\ \frac{\Delta \underline{w}_{\underline{t}}}{\underline{w}_{\underline{t}-4}} &= \underline{b}_0 + \underline{b}_1 \underline{U}_{\underline{t}} + \underline{b}_2 \frac{\Delta \underline{p}_{\underline{t}}}{\underline{p}_{\underline{t}-4}} \end{aligned} \qquad (7.19)\ ,$$

where the notations are already defined in the previous sections. This system implies that economically there exists no one-way causal relation,i.e., neither from price to wage nor from wage to price. Here, both the price and the wage variables are assumed to be endogeneous, while both the productivity and the unemployment variables are exogeneous. A statistical estimation with regard to this simultaneous equation system was made by the two-stage least squares method and the result is:

$$(7.20)\quad \begin{aligned} \frac{\Delta \underline{p}_t}{\underline{p}_{t-4}} &= -4.96 - \underset{(0.18)}{0.35}\ \frac{\Delta \underline{x}_t}{\underline{x}_{t-4}} + \underset{(0.37)}{1.12}\ \frac{\Delta \underline{w}_t}{\underline{w}_{t-4}} \qquad \bar{R} = 0.59 \\ \frac{\Delta \underline{w}_t}{\underline{w}_{t-4}} &= 24.10 - \underset{(1.43)}{4.63}\ \underline{U}_t - \underset{(0.73)}{0.52}\ \frac{\Delta \underline{p}_t}{\underline{p}_{t-4}} \qquad \bar{R} = 0.79 \end{aligned}$$

This result suggests that the hypothesis of a simultaneous determination between price and money wage earnings cannot be supported empirically, since the sign condition of the price variable in the wage equation became negative, in addition to general declines of the coefficients of determination. Economically, it may not be so difficult to explain this situation, although it may be tentative empirically. The original intention of adding the price variable into the wage equation, as discussed in section 7.3, was to explain the effect of the existence of union power in wage negotiations, i.e., the greater the increase of consumer prices, the easier the increase of money wages. Under this assumption, it may not be possible to use the price variable, since the information on the change of prices, which is available at the period of wage negotiations, belongs usually to past experience. We may conclude, therefore, that the simultaneous determination of prices and money wage earnings is not applicable, at least to Japanese data.

An alternative formulation of this simultaneous system can be characterized by the introduction of a successive determination system. This system will be constructed from two stages; i.e., in the first stage, the change of money wage earnings will be determined by both the rate of unemployment and the change of consumer prices at the end of the previous period, and in the second stage, the change of consumer prices will be determined by both the change of labor productivity and the <u>estimated</u> change of money wage earnings from the first stage. The fundamental difference between the present procedure and the single equation approaches of the previous two sections is in the use of the estimated value of money wage earnings in the price equation.

The successive determination system can be written as:

$$(7.21)\quad \begin{aligned} \frac{\Delta \underline{w}_t}{\underline{w}_{t-4}} &= \underline{b}_0^* + \underline{b}_1^* \underline{U}_{t-1} + \underline{b}_2^* \frac{\tilde{\Delta}\underline{p}_{t-1}}{\underline{p}_{t-2}} \\ \frac{\Delta \underline{p}_t}{\underline{p}_{t-4}} &= \underline{a}_0^* + \underline{a}_1^* \frac{\Delta \underline{x}_t}{\underline{x}_{t-4}} + \underline{a}_2^* \left(\frac{\Delta \underline{w}_t}{\underline{w}_{t-4}}\right)_{est.} \end{aligned}$$

where most of the notations are already defined in the previous sections, except $\left(\frac{\Delta \underline{w}_t}{\underline{w}_{t-4}}\right)_{est.}$ = the estimated values of $\frac{\Delta \underline{w}_t}{\underline{w}_{t-4}}$ from the above equation.

Since, in this system, the variables $\underline{U}_t$ and $\tilde{\Delta}\underline{p}_{t-1}/\underline{p}_{t-2}$ in the wage equation and also the variables $\Delta \underline{x}_t/\underline{x}_{t-4}$ and $(\Delta \underline{w}_t/\underline{w}_{t-4})_{est.}$ in the second price equation can be assumed as exogeneous variables respectively, the single-stage least squares method can be applied in each equation.

The statistical result is:

$$(7.22)\quad \begin{aligned} \frac{\Delta \underline{w}_t}{\underline{w}_{t-4}} &= 16.73 - \underset{(0.54)}{2.97}\, \underline{U}_{t-1} + \underset{(0.40)}{1.36} \frac{\tilde{\Delta}\underline{p}_{t-1}}{\underline{p}_{t-2}} \qquad \bar{\underline{R}} = 0.85 \\ \frac{\Delta \underline{p}_t}{\underline{p}_{t-4}} &= -2.72 - \underset{(0.06)}{0.18} \frac{\Delta \underline{x}_t}{\underline{x}_{t-4}} + \underset{(0.17)}{0.70} \left(\frac{\Delta \underline{w}_t}{\underline{w}_{t-4}}\right)_{est.} \qquad \bar{\underline{R}} = 0.81 \end{aligned}$$

where it is easily seen that the estimated results here are quite similar to those in the previous sections - all of which implies a constancy of the regression coefficients.

From these findings, we may summarize the present discussion as follows:

1. The relation between the change of consumer prices and of money wage earnings can be said to be a successive determination system, originating from the wage side, instead of the simultaneous system.

2. If the rate of unemployment remains 3 percent and the increase of consumer prices during the previous period is 1.5 percent, the money wage earnings in this period will increase about 10 percent. As a result of this increase in money wages,

consumer prices in this period will increase about 3.5 percent compared with the level in the previous year, assuming an annual increase of 7 percent in labor productivity.

3. An open question to be investigated in the future will be the compatibility between 3 percent unemployment and 7 percent annual increase in labor productivity.

7.5. Conclusion

The findings derived in the present paper can be summarized:

1. The change of consumer prices can be explained by the mechanism of a comparative static equilibrium in the market, i.e., by the change of labor productivity (on the supply side) and of income per capita or money wage earnings (on the demand side).

2. The role of a change of money wage earnings can be identified more clearly as an income variable rather than a cost variable, although this finding is less reliable than the others.

3. The Phillips-Lipsey hypothesis has considerable explanatory application to Japanese data, and shifts of this schedule are also explained by the change of consumer prices.

4. The change of consumer prices can be explained primarily by an induced demand effect originating from the rise in money wage earnings through a successive determination system.

The most controversial aspect of the recent inflation in Japan has been its causes, especially as related to demand-pull versus cost-push pressures. It is almost impossible to identify these two forces apart from empirical observations. Rather a mixture of these two approaches can be an important clue for explaining real situations. For example, significant induced (not autonomous) demand effects have resulted from increases in money wage earnings in manufacturing industries, where the highest rate of growth has been achieved in the postwar period. And in the process of fairly rapid industrialization, unbalanced productivity increases among the first, second, and third sectors have widened, as shown in the following diagram. Thus, adjustments necessary for fulfilling the induced demands in these lagging sectors without rising prices may well become difficult.

Fig. 7.1. Productivity Increases

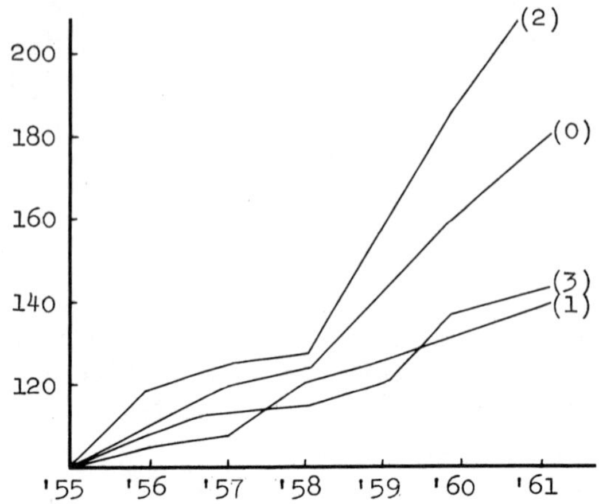

Source: Economic White Paper, 1963, Economic Planning Agency. (1), (2), (3), and (0) represent the first, second, third and overall industries respectively.

Appendix

The main series used in the earlier analysis are presented in Table 7.3. A brief description of their derivation and sources follows. Overall consumer prices were derived from figures for the consumer price index published by the Statistical Bureau, Prime Minister's Office, where the basic year is 1960.

The number of persons who received unemployment insurance and the money wage earnings index were derived from the report published by the Ministry of Labor.

The figures for labor productivity were calculated from the labor productivity index, prepared by the Japan Productivity Center.

Personal disposable income per capita and also personal consumption expenditure per capita were derived from National Income and Expenditure, 1955-63, published yearly by the Economic Planning Agency.

All figures listed in Table 7.3 are the percentage relative differences defined in the main text, except the one for unemployment.

Notes

The author would like to thank Professor S. Ichimura, Kyoto University, and I. Ozaki, Keio University; and Mr. S. Sasaki, Economic Research Institute, Economic Planning Agency, for their invaluable comments at all stages in the preparation of this paper.

1. For example,

$$p = 65.57 + \underset{(0.03)}{0.43w} - \underset{(0.02)}{0.12}\,(V/L) + \underset{(0.007)}{0.02D} \qquad \bar{R} = 0.995$$

where p = consumer price, w = money wage earnings, V = GNP (real), L = total employees, and D = dummy variable (0 for the first six months and 100 for the remaining six months). All data, except price, are derived from Economic Planning Agency, National Income Statistics (Tokyo), on a biannual basis from 1954 to 1962.

2. See, for example, P. A. Samuelson, Foundations of Economic Analysis (Cambridge, Mass.: Harvard University Press, 1947).

3. The relative difference with respect to the previous year's level was used mainly to avoid the seasonal fluctuation in the quarterly data, although there is an economic reason for this type of definition in the money wage variable (see section 7.3).

4. It has to be noted here that equation (7.5) is only one type of statistically operational equation which can be derived from the theoretical model of equation (7.3). For example, the equation $p_t = \alpha_t' + \alpha_t' y_t + \alpha_2' z_t + \epsilon_t$ also belongs to this group. Because of the existence of high correlation between y and z, however, it is desirable to use the difference equation.

5. Derivation of equation (7.8) (assuming the linear demand and supply equation) is:

$$q^D = \alpha_0 + \alpha_1 p + \alpha_2 y \quad \text{and} \quad q^S = \beta_0 + \beta_1 p + \beta_2 z;$$

equation (7.4) will be written as:

$$\frac{d\underline{p}}{dt} = m'\{\alpha_0 - \beta_0 + (\alpha_1-\beta_1)\underline{p} + \alpha_2\underline{y} - \beta_2\underline{z}\};$$

then,

$$\Delta^2 p_t = \delta_0 + \delta_1\Delta\underline{p} + \delta_2\Delta\underline{y} + \delta_3\Delta\underline{z}.$$

6. The money wage earnings index may have dual characteristics; i.e., the variable which affects the demand side as an income factor may also affect the supply side as a cost factor. This point will be discussed in the latter part of this section.

7. Without taking the relative difference in these variables, the estimated results were significantly disturbed by the multicollinearity among explanatory variables.

8. Some effort might be made to separate effects of changes of cost items into two periods; i.e., recession periods and boom periods. At present, however, such separation is impossible since the available sample period in Japan is too small.

9. See A. W. Phillips, "The Relation between Unemployment and the Rate of Change of Money Wage Rates in the United Kingdom, 1861-1957," Economica, N. S. 25 (November 1958); R. D. Lipsey, "The Relation between Unemployment and Rate of Change of Money Wage Rates in the United States, 1861-1957: A Further Analysis," Economica, N.S. 27 (February 1960); S. F. Kaliski, "The Relation between Unemployment and the Rate of Change of Money Wages in Canada," International Economic Review, vol. 5 (January 1964).

10. J. C. R. Dow and L. A. Dicks-Mirreax, "Excess Demand for Labor," Oxford Economic Papers, vol. 10 (February 1958).

11. Two important defects exist in the Japanese labor force survey: (i) the conceptual definition of unemployment is too broad for the present discussion, e.g., the persons who worked only one hour during a specified week per month are counted as part of the active labor force; and (ii) the definition with respect to population is not uniform throughout the survey.

Detailed discussions will be found in K. Tsujimura and S. Sasaki, Employment Structure and Business Fluctuations, Economic Bulletin no. 2, (Tokyo: Economic Planning Agency, July 1959).

12. R. J. Bhatia, "Profits and the Rate of Change in Money Earnings in the United States, 1935-1959, "Economica, N.S. 29 (August 1962); O. Eckstein and T. A. Wilson, "The Determination of Money Wages in American Industry," Quarterly Journal of Economics, 76 (August 1962); R. G. Lipsey and M. D. Steur, "The Relation between Profit and Wage Rates," Economica, N.S. 28 (May 1961).

13. Nonlinear type of specification for the Phillips-Lipsey hypothesis also gave similar results:

$$\frac{\Delta w_t}{w_{t-4}} = \underset{(1.20)}{-0.46} + \underset{(4.49)}{23.37}\,\frac{1}{U_t} + \underset{(0.36)}{1.26}\,\frac{\tilde{\Delta} p_{t-1}}{p_{t-2}} \qquad \bar{R} = 0.84$$

$$\frac{\Delta w_t}{w_{t-4}} = \underset{(1.33)}{-0.93} + \underset{(5.02)}{24.67}\,\frac{1}{U_t} + \underset{)0.21)}{0.40}\,\frac{\Delta p_{t-1}}{p_{t-5}} \qquad \bar{R} = 0.80$$

where the notations are the same as those in the text. Furthermore, additions of other variables, e.g., profits, failed to be significant. These results, however, were not taken into our considerations positively because the introduction of nonlinearity would disturb the simultaneous approach in section 7.4.

14. Lipsey, "The Relation between Unemployment and the Rate of Change of Money Wage Rates in the United States, 1861-1957"; Phillips, "Relation between Unemployment and Rate of Change of Money Wage Rates in the United Kingdom, 1861-1957"; P. A. Samuelson and R. Solow, "Analytical Aspects of Anti-Inflation Policy," American Economic Review, 50 (May 1960).

Part IV
Studies of International Trade

8

An Econometric Analysis of Japanese Exports and Imports

Shinichi Ichimura

8.1. Introduction

Japan is very much an open economy, so that the foreign component of final demand must be treated in any econometric model with great care. I shall treat different components of exports and imports by separate equations in the disaggregated forms.

There are four import equations - rice and barley, other food, machinery, and materials and other products. Rice imports depend on domestic food consumption, domestic agricultural production, and the rural-urban population distribution. Other food imports depend on food consumption and the relative price of domestic vs. imported food. The comparative importance of rice and other foods in the Japanese diet is changing, and our import functions should reflect this change. Machinery imports depend on domestic capital formation, and material imports depend largely on manufacturing output.

Exports are split into two groups: type of product, and export area. The area classification is particularly important for certain commodities for which there are regional quotas for Japanese exports, regional discrimination against Japanese exports, or regional preference for Japanese exports. The product classification is fourfold -- heavy industry, textiles, food, and other. The residual category corresponds closely with "other" manufacturing in the producing sectors of the model.

Heavy industry exports are further subdivided into ships, machinery, and steel and other metal products. Shipbuilding for export depends upon orders for ships, which in turn depend on world tonnage requirements and relative prices -- Japanese vs. rest of the world in heavy industry products. Machinery exports are a function of world production of machinery, reparation payments to Asian countries, the foreign exchange reserve position of Asian countries, and relative price. These same variables, applying specifically to external steel trade and prices, determine the demand for Japanese steel exports.

Textile exports to the United States depend on the quota limitation for such exports, in addition to U.S. consumption and relative textile prices (Japanese vs. the United States). Textile exports to Europe and Canada and to the rest of the world depend on the same kind of activity and relative price variables, with appropriate adjustments for the region involved. In the case of textiles, export price is regarded as a separate endogenous variable, depending on the domestic textile price and the world textile price. In all the export equations, overseas activity and foreign price variables are regarded as exogenous.

Food exports are also divided by regions, but Canada is grouped with the United States instead of with Europe. This natural regional grouping was not used for textiles because of the importance of the U.S. quota. Food exports to Europe and to the rest of the world are separately determined as functions of income levels and relative prices in each of the two areas, respectively. In the case of textiles there was an equation of export price determination, but agricultural export prices are not endogenously generated within the model.

A residual group of exports, all commodities except heavy industry products, textiles, and food is determined by two separate equations, one covering the United States, Canada, and Europe, the other covering the rest of the world. As in the other export equations, overseas activity and relative prices are the explanatory variables. An equation relating the export price of this residual group to the domestic price of "other" manufacturing and the world price of such goods is also included.

The estimation of the equations in this study was made by the two-stage least squares method using data over the period 1952-1961.

The current quarterly model of the Japanese economy includes a large number of variables. A considerable portion of statistical data for these variables was taken from published government and semigovernment sources with little further processing, but it was necessary in many cases to construct our own time series on the basis of official and private data. Considerable time had to be spent in such exercises, though our output was not necessarily without the need of further improvement.[1] We have found time and again serious inconsistencies among related statistics. Almost all series relating to the manufacturing sector, which provides the pivot of our model, were constructed by us. Because the model covers the entire economy, the most important single source was the White Paper on National Accounts of the Economic Planning Agency. Recent annual issues of this publication give quarterly series of national accounts from the first quarter of 1955 and annual series before 1955. For earlier years, such quarterly series published in earlier White Papers were not officially revised by the Economic Planning Agency except for large aggregates now available in the summary table appearing in the White Paper for the period beginning with the second quarter of 1951. Earlier quarterly series were taken from a mimeographed report circulated by the Economic Planning Agency. In some cases, series for earlier years were reconstructed according to the method of data estimation fairly well explained in the 1958 edition of the White Paper.[2]

In constructing time series on our own, especially extensive use was made of the Census of Manufactures, Annual and Quarterly Report of Corporate Enterprise Statistics, Establishment Census, National Wealth Survey, Summary Report on External Trade, and Bank of Japan, Wholesale Price Annual, to cite only a few among a larger number of statistical sources. A list of major statistical sources is given below. The English translation of titles is based mostly on Prime Minister's Office, Supplement to the Monthly Statistics of Japan, Explanatory Note, January issue, which gives a concise general review of government and semigovernment statistical sources.

The value series were expressed in hundred billion yen unless otherwise specified. The price indexes were expressed with 1955 = 1.00. In general, no seasonal adjustment was performed on the series.[3]

8.2. List of Time Series and Symbols

8.2.1. Series of Values of Imports (c.i.f.) at Current Prices (hundred billion yen)

$\underline{B}$	Total commodity imports
$\underline{B}_{f1}$	Imports of rice and barley
$\underline{B}_{f2}$	Imports of other foodstuffs
$\underline{B}_{h2}$	Imports of machinery and equipment
$\underline{B}_{m}$	Imports of other goods

8.2.2. Series of Exports (f.o.b.) at Current Prices (hundred billion yen)

$\underline{E}$	Total commodity exports
$\underline{E}_{h1}$	Exports of ships
$\hat{\hat{\underline{E}}}_{h1}$	Outstanding orders for ships (export)
$\hat{\underline{E}}_{h1}$	New orders for ships (export)
$\underline{E}_{h2}$	Exports of machinery and equipment
$\underline{E}_{h3}$	Exports of steel and other metal products
$\underline{E}_{t}^{i}$	Exports of textiles to the ith region, where $\underline{i}$ = $\underline{U}$ (the United States and Canada), $\underline{E}$ (Europe) and $\underline{A}$ (the rest of the world)
$\underline{E}_{a}^{i}$	Exports of food to the ith region, where $\underline{i}$ = $\underline{U}$ (the United States and Canada), $\underline{E}$ (Europe) and $\underline{A}$ (the rest of the world)
$\underline{E}_{o}^{i}$	Exports of other goods to the ith region, where $\underline{i}$ = $\underline{UE}$ (the United States, Canada, and Europe),and $\underline{A}$ (the rest of the world).

8.2.3. Series of Import Price Indexes (1955 = 1.00)

$\underline{P}_{f1}^{\underline{b}}$	Import price index of rice and barley
$\underline{P}_{f2}^{\underline{b}}$	Import price index of other foodstuffs

P_{h2}^{b}	Import price index of machinery and equipment
P_{i}^{bm}	Import price index of raw materials for the ith industry where $i = h$, t, and o
P_{m}^{b}	Import price index of goods other than foodstuffs and machinery

8.2.4. Series of Export Price Indexes (1955 = 1.00)

P_{h1}^{e}	Export price index of ships
P_{h2}^{e}	Export price index of machinery and equipment
P_{h3}^{e}	Export price index of steel and other metal products
P_{t}^{e}	Export price index of textiles
P_{a}^{e}	Export price index of food
P_{o}^{e}	Export price index of other goods
P_{h1}	Index of contract prices of exported ships
P_{h1}'	Moving average of P_{h1}

8.2.5. Miscellaneous External Series (all indexes 1955 = 1.00)

μ	Freight tonnage as proportion of merchant tonnage (percent)
P_{i}^{w}	World export price index of the ith commodity group, where $i = h_1$ (ships), h_2 (machinery and equipment), h_3 (steel), and o (other goods)
P_{t}^{i}	Price index of textiles in the ith region, where $i = U$ (the United States), E (Europe and Canada), and A (the rest of the world)
P_{a}^{i}	Price index of food in the ith region, where $i = U$ (the United States and Canada), E (Europe), A (the rest of the world), and w (world average).
x_{i}^{w}	World production index, weighted by Japan's exports of the ith commodity group, where $i = h_2$ and h_3

x_t^A	Production index of developing regions, weighted by Japan's exports of textiles
R_i^A	Foreign exchange reserves of Asian countries weighted by exports of the *i*th commodity group where $i = h_2$ and h_3 (hundred million dollars)
R^E	Foreign exchange reserves of the United Kingdom (hundred million dollars)
A	Reparations and loans (million dollars)
Q^U	U.S. quota of textile imports from Japan (percent)
y^E	European personal consumption (hundred billion dollars)
y^U	U.S. personal consumption (hundred billion dollars)
y^{UE}	Personal consumption of the United States, Canada, and Europe (weighted average, hundred billion dollars)
y^A	Exports of developing regions (hundred billion dollars)

8.2.6. Series Relating to the Balance of Payments Accounts (hundred million dollars)

E'	Exports of goods in the balance of payments
B'	Imports of goods in the balance of payments
E'_{inv}	Invisible exports
B'_{inv}	Invisible imports
B_k	Net capital imports
R	Foreign exchange reserves
η'	Adjustment idem for foreign exchange reserves
η	Noncommodity balance in external transactions constant-price value (hundred billion yen)
$\frac{\eta}{P_\eta}$	Noncommodity balance in external transactions current-price value (hundred billion yen)

8.2.7. Other Variables Mainly Related to the Rest of the Economy

C_f	Private consumption of food, beverage, and tobacco

P_f^c	Consumer price index of food
X_A	Value added of the agricultural sector
P_A	Output price index of agricultural commodities
N_I	Employment in the industrial sector
N_A	Employment in the agricultural sector
P_M^m	Implicit deflator of total imports
I_p	Fixed investment by the industrial sector
P_k	Fixed investment goods price index
X_h	Sales of heavy industry
P_h	Output price index of heavy industry
h	Degree of capacity utilization index in heavy industry
X_t	Sales of textile industry
P_t	Output price index of textile industry
X_o	Sales of other industry
P_o	Output price index of other industry
H_m	Manufacturers' inventory stock of raw materials
G_1	Surplus of foreign exchange fund
G_2	Surplus of foodstuff control account
G_3	Surplus of other treasury account
V	Loans of the Bank of Japan to private banks
Y	Net national product at factor cost
P_m	Implicit deflator of manufacturers' output
i^*	Official discount rate of the Bank of Japan
L_a	Loans of private banks to the private sectors
L_2	Deposit currency at the end of quarter
L_3	Time and saving deposits at the end of quarter
Q_i	Dummy variables for quarterly adjustment

8.3. Import and Export Functions

8.3.1.

(i:1) Import Functions

(i:1-f-1) Rice and Barley

$$\frac{B_{f1}}{p_{f1}^{b}} = \underset{(0.0398)}{0.03656} \sum_{-1}^{-4} \frac{C_f/p_f^{c}}{4} - \underset{(0.0325)}{0.003888} \left(\frac{X_A}{p_A}\right)_{IV,-1}$$

$$- \underset{(0.489)}{1.119} \sum_{-1}^{-4} \frac{N_I}{N_A} + \underset{(0.0842)}{0.007389}\, Q_1 + \underset{(0.105)}{0.07046}\, Q_2$$

$$- \underset{(0.0717)}{0.01433}\, Q_3 + \underset{(0.169)}{0.4580}$$

$$\bar{R}^2 = 0.48 \qquad \delta^2/S^2 = 1.33$$

(i:1-f-2) Other Food

$$\frac{B_{f2}}{p_{f2}^{b}} = \underset{(0.0127)}{0.07179} \sum_{-1}^{-4} \frac{C_f/p_f^{c}}{4} + \underset{(0.0774)}{0.1200} \frac{p_A}{p_{f2}^{b}} + \underset{(0.0216)}{0.1677}\, Q_1$$

$$+ \underset{(0.0215)}{0.02513}\, Q_2 + \underset{(0.0213)}{0.03280}\, Q_3 - \underset{(0.0683)}{0.2023}$$

$$\bar{R} = 0.72 \qquad \delta^2/S^2 = 2.59$$

(i:1-h-2) Machinery

$$\frac{B_{h2}}{p_{h2}^{b}} = \underset{(0.00892)}{0.08596} \left(\frac{I_p - B_{h2}}{p_k}\right)_{-2} - \underset{(0.0174)}{0.001980}\, Q_1 + \underset{(0.0174)}{0.009289}\, Q_2$$

$$+ \underset{(0.0169)}{0.01096}\, Q_3 + \underset{(0.0211)}{0.008627}$$

$$\bar{R}^2 = 0.76 \qquad \delta^2/S^2 = 1.02$$

(i:1-m) Materials and Others

$$\frac{B_m^{\ b}}{p_m} = \underset{(0.0238)}{0.1366}\left(\frac{X_h}{p_h} + \frac{X_t}{p_t} + \frac{X_o}{p_o}\right)_{-1} - \underset{(0.0712)}{0.1701}\left(\frac{H_m^{\ m}}{p_M}\right)_{-2}$$

$$+ \underset{(0.0317)}{0.05409}\,\frac{R_{-3} + R_{-4}^{\ b}}{2p_{m-3}} + \underset{(0.132)}{0.1353}\,Q_1 + \underset{().131)}{0.302}\,Q_2$$

$$+ \underset{(0.128)}{0.02896}\,Q_3 - \underset{(0.345)}{0.04246}$$

$$\bar{R}^2 = 0.84 \qquad \delta^2/S^2 = 0.55$$

8.3.2.

(i:2) Export Functions of Heavy Industry's Products

(i:2-1-i) Ships

$$\frac{E_{h1}^{\ e}}{p_{h1}} = \underset{(0.0284)}{0.03592} + \underset{(0.0198)}{0.2086}\left(\frac{\hat{\hat{E}}_{h1}}{p_{h1}^{\ \prime}}\right)_{-2}$$

$$\bar{R}^2 = 0.82 \qquad \delta^2/S^2 = 2.57$$

(i:2-1-ii)

$$\Delta\frac{\hat{\hat{E}}_{h1}}{p_{h1}^{\ \prime}} = \underset{(0.182)}{0.9701}\,\frac{\hat{E}_{h1}}{p_{h1}} - \underset{(0.147)}{0.6008}\,\frac{E_{h1}^{\ e}}{p_{h1}}$$

$$\bar{R}^2 = 0.53$$

(i:2-1-iii)

$$\frac{\hat{E}_{h1}}{p_{h1}} = \underset{(0.0725)}{0.07662}\ \mu > \underset{(0.441)}{0.6486}\,\frac{p_{h1}^{\ W}}{p_{h1}} - 0.9966$$

$$\bar{R}^2 = 0.65 \qquad \delta^2/S^2 = 1.32$$

(i:2-2) Machinery

$$\frac{E_{h2}^{\ e}}{p_{h2}} = \underset{(0.149)}{0.3169}\,\Delta x_{h2}^{\ W} + \underset{(0.0865)}{0.3101}\,\frac{p_{h2}^{\ W}}{p_{h2}^{\ e}} + \underset{(0.00784)}{0.02460}\,\frac{R_{h2}^{\ A}}{p_{h2}^{\ e}}$$

$$+ \underset{(0.0137)}{0.1244}\,\frac{A}{p_{h2}^{\ e}} - \underset{(0.107)}{0.3521}$$

$$\bar{R}^2 = 0.95 \qquad \delta^2/S^2 = 1.33$$

(i:2-3) Steel and Other Metal Products

$$\frac{E_{h3}}{p_{h3}^{e}} = \underset{(0.0743)}{0.07042}\, x_{h3}^{W} + \underset{(0.0913)}{0.1747}\, \frac{p_{h3}^{W}}{p_{h3}^{e}} + \underset{(0.00997)}{0.01428}\, \frac{R_{h3}^{A}}{p_{h3}^{e}}$$

$$+ \underset{(0.0169)}{0.01933}\, \frac{A}{p_{h3}^{e}} - \underset{(0.108)}{0.1675}\, \rho_h + \underset{(0.0984)}{0.5898}\, \left(\frac{E_{h3}}{p_{h3}^{e}}\right)_{-1}$$

$$- \underset{(0.0168)}{0.07057}\, Q_1 - \underset{(0.0153)}{0.03823}\, Q_2 - \underset{(0.0168)}{0.03526}\, Q_3 - \underset{(0.126)}{0.03403}$$

$$\bar{R}^2 = 0.90 \qquad \delta^2/S^2 = 2.92$$

8.3.3.

(i:3) Export Functions of Textile Products

(i:3-U) Textile Exports to the United States

$$\frac{E_t^{U}}{p_t^{e}} = \underset{(0.269)}{1.397}\, y^{U} + \underset{(0.0440)}{0.05057}\, \frac{p_t^{U}}{p_t^{e}} + \underset{(0.148)}{0.4063}\, \left(\frac{E_t^{U}}{p_t^{e}}\right)_{-1}$$

$$+ \underset{(0.0264)}{0.05567}\, Q_t^{U} - \underset{(0.144)}{0.7465}$$

$$\bar{R}^2 = 0.94 \qquad \delta^2/S^2 = 1.69$$

(i:3-E) Textile Exports to Europe and Canada

$$\frac{E_t^{E}}{p_t^{e}} = 0.2475\, y^{E} + \underset{(0.0366)}{0.008102}\, \frac{p_t^{E}}{p_t^{e}} + \underset{(0.144)}{0.8083}\, \left(\frac{E_t^{E}}{p_t^{e}} - 2.475\, y^{E}\right)_{-1}$$

$$- \underset{(0.00675)}{0.02249}\, Q_1 - \underset{(0.00667)}{0.006590}\, Q_2 - \underset{(0.00664)}{0.009659}\, Q_3$$

$$+ \underset{(0.0383)}{0.002604}$$

$$\bar{R}^2 = 0.68 \qquad \delta^2/S^2 = 2.37$$

(*i*:3-*A*) Textile Exports to the Rest of the World

$$\frac{E_t^A}{p_t^e} = \underset{(0.122)}{0.2795}\, x_t^A + \underset{(0.260)}{0.08732}\,\frac{p_t^A}{p_t^e} + \underset{(0.186)}{0.4440}\left(\frac{E_t^A}{p_t^e}\right)_{-1}$$

$$- \underset{(0.0342)}{0.1295}\,Q_1 - \underset{(0.0317)}{0.08461}\,Q_2 - \underset{(0.0316)}{0.09133}\,Q_3 - \underset{(0.211)}{0.04364}$$

$\bar{R}^2 = 0.87$ $\delta^2/S^2 = 2.18$

(*i*:3-*p*) Textile Export-Price Determination

$$p_t^e = \underset{(0.140)}{0.7037}\, p_t + \underset{(0.504)}{0.4199}\, p_t^W - \underset{(0.411)}{0.09159}$$

$\bar{R}^2 = 0.72$ $\delta^2/S^2 = 0.70$

8.3.4.

(*i*:4) Export Functions of Food

(*i*:4-*U*) Food Exports to the United States and Canada

$$\frac{E_a^U}{p_a^e} = \underset{(0.125)}{0.06634}\,(1-0.7432)\, y^U + \underset{(0.0361)}{0.03711}\,\frac{p_a^U}{p_a^e}$$

$$+ \underset{(0.135)}{0.7432}\left(\frac{E_a^U}{p_a^e}\right)_{-1} + \underset{(0.00546)}{0.0003095}\,Q_1 + \underset{(0.00540)}{0.004698}\,Q_2$$

$$+ \underset{(0.00532)}{0.009850}\,Q_3 - \underset{(0.0344)}{0.03478}$$

$\bar{R}^2 = 0.57$ $\delta^2/S^2 = 2.76$

(*i*:4-*E*) Food Exports to Europe

$$\frac{E_a^E}{p_a^e} = 0.1200\, y^E + \underset{(0.0576)}{0.1250}\,\frac{p_a^E}{p_a^e} - \underset{(0.127)}{0.4016}\,\Delta\,\frac{p_a^E}{p_a^e}$$

$$+ \underset{(0.00107)}{0.003201}\,\frac{R^E}{p_a^e} - \underset{(0.0509)}{0.1930}$$

$\bar{R}^2 = 0.51$ $\delta^2/S^2 = 1.73$

(i:4-A) Food Exports to the Rest of the World

$$\frac{E_a^A}{p_a^e} = \underset{(0.0204)}{0.04299}\, y^A + \underset{(0.0268)}{0.03719}\, \frac{p_a^A}{p_a^e} - \underset{(0.00431)}{0.004575}\, Q_1$$

$$- \underset{(0.00433)}{0.005579}\, Q_2 + \underset{(0.00437)}{0.002126}\, Q_3 - \underset{(0.0252)}{0.03142}$$

$$\bar{R}^2 = 0.28$$

8.3.5.

(i:5) Export Functions of Other Commodities

(i:5-UE) Other Commodities Exports to the United States, Canada and Europe

$$\frac{E_o^{UE}}{p_o^e} = \underset{(0.539)}{1.413}\, y_o^{UE} + \underset{(0.150)}{0.3202}\, \frac{p_o^W}{p_o^e} + \underset{(0.165)}{0.6643}\left(\frac{E_o^{UE}}{p_o^e}\right)_{-1}$$

$$+ \underset{(0.0202)}{0.007736}\, Q_1 - \underset{(0.0205)}{0.02779}\, Q_2 + \underset{(0.0191)}{0.01441}\, Q_3$$

$$- \underset{(0.329)}{0.9370}$$

$$\bar{R}^2 = 0.94 \qquad \delta^2/S^2 = 2.39$$

(i:5-A) Other Commodities Exports to the Rest of the World

$$\frac{E_o^A}{p_o^e} = \underset{(0.111)}{0.3452}\, \frac{Y^A}{p_o^e} + \underset{(0.127)}{0.6181}\left(\frac{E_o^A}{p_o^e}\right)_{-1} - \underset{(0.0113)}{0.04839}\, Q_1$$

$$+ \underset{(0.0117)}{0.03469}\, Q_2 - \underset{(0.0136)}{0.004138}\, Q_3 - \underset{(0.0537)}{0.1274}$$

$$\bar{R}^2 = 0.96 \qquad \delta^2/S^2 = 2.28$$

(i:5-p) Other Commodities Export-Price Determination

$$p_o^e = \underset{(0.314)}{0.6508}\, p_o + \underset{(0.127)}{0.4012}\, p_o^W - \underset{(0.0204)}{0.3161}\, Q_1 - \underset{(0.0206)}{0.03156}\, Q_2$$

$$- \; 0.003648 \, Q_3 \; - \; 0.08363$$
$$(0.0202) \qquad (0.265)$$
$$\bar{R}^2 = 0.57 \qquad \delta^2/S^2 = 0.99$$

8.3.6.

(j:1) Commodity-to-Exchange Conversion

(j:1-e) Export

$$E' = \underset{(0.0579)}{2.632} \, E + \underset{(0.117)}{0.5283} \, Q_1 + \underset{(0.116)}{0.3784} \, Q_2 + \underset{(0.115)}{0.3622} \, Q_3 - \underset{(0.273)}{0.2361}$$
$$\bar{R}^2 = 0.99 \qquad \delta^2/S^2 = 2.16$$

(j:1-b) Import

$$B' = \underset{(0.125)}{2.355} \, B - \underset{(0.231)}{0.1545} \, Q_1 + \underset{(0.232)}{0.2434} \, Q_2 + \underset{(0.230)}{0.1019} \, Q_3 - \underset{(0.582)}{0.1330}$$
$$\bar{R}^2 = 0.93 \qquad \delta^2/S^2 = 1.53$$

8.3.7.

(k) Some Related Equations

(k:1) $E = E_b + E_t + E_a + E_o$

(k:2) $B = B_{f1} + B_{f2} + B_{h2} + B_{m+c}$

(k:3) $E_h = E_{h1} + E_{h2} + E_{h3}$

(k:4) $E_t + E_t^U + E_t^E + E_t^A$

(k:5) $E_a = E_a^U + E_a^E + E_a^A$

(k:6) $E_o + E_o^{UE} + E_o^A$

(k:7) $\Delta R = E' - B' + E_{inv}' - B_{inv}' + B_k + \eta'$

(k:8)
$$G_1 = \underset{(0.0824)}{0.4431} \, \Delta R - \underset{(0.219)}{3.691} \, Q_1 - \underset{(0.218)}{2.085} \, Q_2$$
$$- \; \underset{(0.217)}{2.510} \, Q_3 + \underset{(0.454)}{2.152}$$
$$\bar{R}^2 = 0.91 \qquad \delta^2/S^2 = 1.85$$

(k:9) $$\Delta V_g = \underset{(0.147)}{0.7934\, G_n} + \underset{(0.643)}{0.3680\, Q_1} - \underset{(0.444)}{1.477\, Q_2}$$

$$- \underset{(0.464)}{0.3695\, Q_3} + \underset{(0.647)}{0.3839}$$

$$\bar{R}^2 = 0.91 \qquad \delta^2/S^2 = 2.92$$

(k:10) $$G_n = G_1 + G_2 + G_3$$

(k:11) $$V = -3.2879 + \underset{(0.14532)}{0.13795\, V_{-1}} + \underset{(0.05488)}{0.095198\, Y_{-1}}$$

$$- \underset{(7.288)}{44.370\, \Delta p_m} + \underset{(0.08442)}{0.39681\, R_{-4}} - \underset{(0.38393)}{0.61791\, \Delta i^*}$$

$$+ \underset{(0.10447)}{0.28952}\, [L_a - 1.112\, (L_2 + L_3)] + \underset{(0.3196)}{0.18779\, Q_1}$$

$$+ \underset{(0.3113)}{0.41718\, Q_2} + \underset{(0.3181)}{0.44439\, Q_3}$$

$$\bar{R}^2 = 0.879 \qquad \delta^2/S^2 = 1.14$$

(k:12) $$X_M = X_h + X_t + X_o$$

(k:13) $$p_M = X_M / (X_h/p_h + X_t/p_t + X_o/p_o)$$

8.4. Exposition and Analysis of Import and Export Equations

8.4.1. Import Function

(i) Import of Food and Forage

The import of food was subdivided into (i) rice and barley and (ii) other food and forage because the two time series show completely opposite movement. The former simply decreases, whereas the latter steadily increases from 1952 to 1961. The import of rice and barley is related positively to food consumption but negatively to the domestic production of food. The term N_I/N_A is also introduced to explain the shift of demand from traditional rice and barley to bread and other flour products in the urban area as urbanization progresses. By the comparison of different time lags in regressions it was found that imports have a one-quarter lag in all explanatory variables. The price effect was found to be insignificant.

The import of other food was taken as dependent also on consumption and relative price. The two import functions taken together seem to imply that the increase of food consumption induces 10.8% of imports. The elasticities are:

	consumption	X_A/P_A	N_I/N_A	P_A/p_{f2}^b
B_{f1}/p_{f1}^b	1.481	-0.130	-3.277	
B_{f2}/p_{f2}^b	1.18			0.284

It should be noted that rising consumption induces higher import of food, but urbanization reduces the import of rice and barley. There seems to be an increasing import of other food and forage as the consumption level goes up.

(ii) Import of Materials and Others

The imports of raw materials and consumption goods were not distinguished from one another because of the difficulty in commodity classification. This is not too serious up to 1959, because until then imports were relatively small. The import of raw materials was taken as dependent on the levels of production in the manufacturing sector with a one-quarter time lag. The relative importance of imported materials in one sector compared with those in another is ignored. Since it is known that the inventory stocks of imported materials are important in total materials stocks, it is expected that the current import of materials should be negatively correlated with the inventory stocks H_m/P_M^m. Quantitative restrictions have been imposed on the import of some materials when foreign exchange reserves decreases. Thus $(R_{-3} + R_{-4})/2p_{m-3}^b$ was introduced as a predetermined variable. The time lag was determined so as to give the highest $\bar{R}^2$. The elasticities are:

	X_M/p_M	H_m/p_M^m	F Exchange Res.
B_m/p_m^b	1.264	-0.415	0.297

Notice here that the elasticity with respect to the production level is greater than unity, implying that as the production increases, the propensity to import is likely to go up.

(iii) Import of Machinery

The underlying hypothesis is that the amount of imported machines keeps a stable relationship with investment in domestically produced machines. The regression equation shows that the proportion is about 8.6%. The elasticity is 0.924.

8.4.2. Export Functions

(i) General remarks

Corresponding to the classification sectors in our large model, to be referred as the Institute of Social and Economic Review (ISER) model hereafter, we need the export functions of heavy, textile, and other manufacturing industries' products, and of food. However, since the behavior of E_{h1}, E_{h2}, and E_{h3} within heavy industry's products was considerably different over time, a separate equation was set up for each of these functions. The export functions of textile and other manufacturing industries' products and food gave poor results unless they are disaggregated by destinations. By doing so, we could select more appropriate explanatory variables and obtain plausible values for elasticities.

The export prices were taken as endogenous variables, but except for p_t^e and p_o^e, good equations were not obtained. To obtain similar good results in p_{hi}^e and p_a^e, the breakdowns of heavy industry and agriculture in the other parts of the ISER model were needed but not made here.

It should be emphasized that, as Table 8.1 shows, the elasticity values are very high with respect to the indexes of both foreign economic activities and relative prices. No wonder that Japanese exports increased about three times as rapidly as did world trade.

(ii) Ships

The gestation period of shipbuliding is long; most ships take more than a year to build. Hence, we must distinguish among new orders $\hat{E}_{h1}$, backlog orders $\hat{E}_{h1}$, and realized exports E_{h1}. Clearly the prices are also different, corresponding to them. Thus we used p_{h1}, p_{h1}' and p_{h1}^e, respectively.

TABLE 8.1. ELASTICITY VALUES FOR DIFFERENT CATEGORIES OF EXPORTS

Category	Income or Real Variable	Relative Price	Foreign Exchange Reserve	Reparation and Loans	Other Variables	Multiplier for Long-Term Effect
Ships	3.99	3.35				
Machinery	1.81*	1.63	0.71	0.42		
Iron and Metal	0.34	0.60	0.32	0.05	-0.63(ρ_h)	1.70
Textiles to United States	5.72	0.36			-0.12(Q_t^v)	2.46
Textiles to Europe	2.08+	0.11				1.24
Textiles to Other Areas	0.64	0.18				2.25
Other imports to United States and Europe	2.61	1.29				1.51
Other imports to Other Areas	0.89	0.89				1.62
Food to United States	0.19	0.69				1.35
Food to Europe	0.98	2.45**	1.56			
Food to Other Areas		1.31				

*The elasticity of E_{h2}/p_{h2}^e with respect to x_{h2}^w alone, while keeping $x_{h2,-1}^w$ unchanged. Notice here that x_{h2}^w is an index of production.

+The elasticity is computed with respect to y^E and p_a^E/p_a^e, respectively, while keeping its ratio to y_{-1}^E and $(p_a^E/p_a^e)_{-1}$, respectively, fixed at the value of ratios of their means.

p_{h1}' was computed as the moving average of p_{h1} over the average period during which backlog orders are held. Monthly data are available for $\hat{E}_{h1}$ and p_{h1} for 55 representative companies. (i:2-1-ii) should read $\Delta\hat{E}_{h1} = \hat{E}_{h1} - E_{h1}$ if data were exact, apart from price index problems. (i:2-I-iii) was adopted after comparing this equation with another which included the freight rate f as an additional explanatory "real" variable. However, since f is theoretically a function of μ, we did not use it.

(iii) Machinery

x_{h2}^{w} was computed as the weighted average of production indexes in four main continents: North America, Latin America, Asia (excluding Japan), and Europe. The weights are their average shares in Japanese machinery exports over the observed period: 0.639, 0.093, 0.171, 0.097. Though we computed the equations with x_{h2}^{w} and Δx_{h2}^{w}, it is of interest that this equation had a slightly higher $\bar{R}^2$. This seems to mean that the machinery exports, being capital goods, are demanded according to the acceleration principle. The elasticity computed as mentioned above is very high. It would mean that the export of machinery is more likely to expand than steel and metal products if world production keeps the same rate of increase.

p_{h2}^{w} is the weighted average of machinery export prices of the United States, the United Kingdom, and Germany; the weights are their shares in Asian countries' imports of machinery (India, Indonesia, Burma, Thailand, Taiwan, Pakistan, the Philippines): 0.49682: 0.35404: 0.14910.

The foreign exchange reserve of the above mentioned Asian countries are weighted by their shares in Japanese machinery exports and taken as a variable to influence the imports of those countries, together with A, government loans (including reparations) to Asian countries. Notice that the effect of A is far greater than that of R.

(iv) Steel and Other Metal Products

x_{h3}^{w}, R_{h3}^{A}, and p_{h3}^{w} are constructed similarly to the averages for machinery. The coefficients of x_{h3}^{w} and p_{h3}^{w}/p_{h3}^{e} are not statistically significant, though the signs are satisfactory. This would probably mean that the export market is not yet well established for $(\underline{h3})$. $\rho_{\underline{h}}$ is introduced to show the effect of the so-called "drive to export" in recessions. If ρ is low, $\underline{E}_{\underline{h3}}$ increases. ρ seems to be the best variable to take the effect into account.

The coefficient of $\underline{A}$ is smaller here than in section 8.2. It means that $\underline{A}$ is more closely tied with the exports of machinery.

$\underline{x}_{\underline{h3}}{}^{\underline{w}}$ rather than $\Delta\underline{x}_{\underline{h3}}{}^{\underline{w}}$ is the explanatory variable in section 8.30. Steel and other metals are mostly the intermediary products used as raw materials to produce finished products, so that they are related to the level of economic activity rather than to its rate of change.

The lagged value of $\underline{E}_{\underline{h3}}/\underline{p}_{\underline{h3}}{}^{\underline{e}}$ was introduced to express the point that when Japan is cutting in the foreign markets, the short-term effect must be clearly distinguished from the long-term effect.

The weights for $\underline{x}_{\underline{h3}}{}^{\underline{w}}$ are 0.100 (North America); 0.310 (Latin America); 0.497 (Asia); and 0.093 (Europe).

(v) Textiles

The difficult problem confronting Japanese textile exports is the fact that an important part of the total export is restricted by a quota imposed in 1956. To take into account the effect of the quota, we introduced a dummy variable, $\underline{Q}_{\underline{t}}{}^{\underline{U}}$ which expresses the quota in the following way. The quota is imposed on cotton products. The maximum rate of growth in the export of cotton products for 1952-1959 is 49.1 percent in 1954-1955. We compare the growth rate of quotas with this value, and define $\underline{Q}_{\underline{t}}{}^{\underline{U}}$ as the growth rate of quota -49.1. For example, if the quota is increased by 5 percent, $\underline{Q}_{\underline{t}}{}^{\underline{U}} = -44.1$. The absolute value of 49.1 is not important in this treatment of quotas, but since $\underline{Q}_{\underline{t}}{}^{\underline{U}}$ is defined in terms of growth rates, $\underline{Q}_{\underline{t}}{}^{\underline{U}}$ decreased year after year unless quotas are increased at the rate of 49.1 percent a year.

Remember that the income elasticity is very high. Japanese textiles are very much demanded by American consumers. The large multiplier for long-term elasticity would mean that still further penetration into the U.S. markets is possible in time.

As for the textile exports to Europe and Canada, $\underline{y}^{\underline{E}}$ is the weighted sum of the OEEC figure of Europe's personal consumption and Canada's personal consumption; the weights being 0.7745 and 0.2255, which are the shares in Japanese exports. The parameter 2.475 was obtained by multiplying the proportion of textile consumption to total consumption by the income elasticity of clothing consumption, measured by Houthakker.[4]

Here the distributed lag was assumed for the price effect only. If $D = \alpha y + \beta p + \beta\lambda p_{-1} + \beta\lambda^2 p_{-2} + \ldots,$ then $D - \alpha y = \lambda(D - \alpha y)_{-1} + \beta p + \ldots$. This is the one estimated there, so that the long-term elasticity is meaningful for the price elasticity only. This procedure was adopted because y in Europe was derived from annual figures so that the quarterly fluctuations of y were averaged out in the near past.

The price elasticity is higher to Europe than to the United States in both the short and the long terms.

The income elasticity is approximately equal to the original elasticity assumed. The original was taken from England. This seems to have kept the income elasticity lower than the true value. Japanese textiles are expanding the market in Europe, so that the value may be expected to be higher. This is partly proved by the high value of the long-term elasticity multiplier.

Textile exports to the rest of the world are related to x_t^A and relative prices. Their dependence on foreign exchange reserves was not significant. x_t^A (the sum of exports of Asia, Africa, and Latin America), was adopted because E_t^A/p_t^e was explained with better statistical significance by x_t^A than by Y_t^B.

Compared with the other areas, both elasticities are lower to this area. This is because the competitive capacity of the Japanese textile industry is declining against the rising world industry.

p_t^e is highly correlated with domestic price rather than the world price.

(vi) Food

The coefficients of income variables were computed in the same way as 2.475 for textile exports to Europe and Canada. The original values of elasticities were taken from Stone and Prais and Houthakker.[5] Here the United States and Canada are treated together. The disaggregation was necessary because we could not obtain plausible coefficients for price variables. The elasticities are low for exports to Europe and Asia but very high for exports to the United States.

(vii) Other Commodities

Y^{uE} is the weighted sum of personal consumption in the United States, Canada, and Europe; the weights being 0.7688, 0.0957 and 0.1354. p_o^{uE} was similarly computed. As for exports to the rest of the world, we could not obtain a suitable equation separating real activity and price variables in it. Y^B is the sum of exports of the rest of the world. This form of equation assumes that we have the same elasticity with respect to income and price.

p_o^e is more highly correlated with the world price than with the domestic price, contrary to the case of p_t^e.

8.4.3. Some Related Equations

Apart from some identities which are self-explanatory, there are some equations that are important in describing the links of the foreign trade sector with the rest of the economy. (j:1-e) and j:1-b) simply convert exports and imports evaluated at the Customs-House to those appropriate in the Foreign Exchange Account. It may be noted here that neither $E - B$ nor $E' - B'$ is the balance in the National Income Account. The external account officially published by the Economic Planning Agency may be expressed by $E - B + \eta$. η here comprises the balance in invisible trade, special procurements by the U.S. armed forces, and other statistical discrepancies.

(k:3) relates the change in foreign exchange reserve to the balance of payments and capital transactions. Despite the tight control of foreign exchange by the government, the published figures of ΔR shows a significant deviation from $E' - B' + E_{inv}' + B_k$. The difference is simply shown by η', which seems to show somewhat cylical movement. An attempt was made to obtain an empirical equation for this, but it was thought better to regard it as an exogenous variable. This foreign exchange reserve R has an impact on the cost of the economy via two channels: one by influencing the balance of foreign exchange funds in the Ministry of Finance's Special Account and thereby the Bank of Japan's loans to the government as expressed by (k:8), (k:9), and (k:10), another by giving the effect on the Bank of Japan's loans to commercial banks as expressed by (k:11). It implies that the position of foreign exchange reserve has a significant influence on the control bank's loan policy. Finally, R has the important effect on the import of raw materials because of direct control of government when foreign exchange reserve is short, as demonstrated by (i:1-m).

Notes

The author is Professor of Economics at the Center for Southeastern Asian Studies, Kyoto University. The paper was written as part of a large econometric model of postwar Japanese economy, 1952-1961 when he was at the Institute of Social and Economic Research, Osaka University. The first version of the model of export functions was published in Japanese as a joint paper by Eiichi Eguchi and this author in The Economic Studies Quarterly, February 1964. The present version, including the other sectors, is available as Discussion Papers of the Center for Southeast Asian Studies, Kyoto University.

1. Since the preparation of data for our sample period was completed, several new publications became available that could have been profitably consulted. These include inter alia the 1966 revision of National Accounts for the years from 1951 (see Economic Planning Agency, Annual Reports on National Income Statistics, Tokyo, 1966); the National Wealth Survey of 1960 (see Economic Planning Agency, Report on the 1960 National Wealth Survey, Tokyo, December 1964); the interindustry table of 1960; and unpublished statistical data compiled for the Medium-Term Economic Plan (on this, see Economic Planning Agency, The Medium-Term Economic Plan, Tokyo, 1965).

2. A mimeographed version, prepared by the Economic Planning Agency, which describes the estimation in more detail, was also consulted. Another useful material was the EPA's publication, National Income Data (Kokumin Shotoku Shiryo). Our reference here is to the pre-1966 state of national account statistics. In 1966, the Economic Planning Agency published new national income statistics going back to 1951. The revision made use

of new benchmarks and introduced new methods of estimation for individual series. The title, White Paper, has been superseded by Annual Report.

3. The details of the compilation of data are explained in the discussion paper; "An Econometric Analysis of the Postwar Japanese Economy: Chapter VI, The Compilation of Data," by S. Ichimura, L. R. Klein, S. Koisumi, K. Sato, and Y. Shinkai (Kyoto University, Center for Southeast Asian Studies, 1969). This chapter was written by S. Ichimura and K. Sato.

4. H. S. Houthakker, "An International Comparison of Household Expenditure Patterns, Commemorating the Centenary of Engel's Law," Econometrica, 25 (1957): 532.

5. R. Stone, The Measurement of Consumers' Expenditure and Behavior in the United Kingdom, 1920-1938. (vol. 1 (Cambridge: Cambridge University Press, 1954), pp. 315-317; S. J. Prais and H. S. Houthakker, The Analysis of Family Budgets (Cambridge: Cambridge University Press, 1955), 106-107.

9

Price Elasticities of Japanese Exports: A Cross-Section Study

Yoichi Shinkai

9.1. Introduction

The purpose of this paper is twofold, namely, to present a cross-sectional estimate of the price elasticities of Japanese exports, broken down into commodity groups as well as the total, on the one hand, and on the other to assess the reliability of the quantity (unit value) data used in the present study. It is well-known that Japanese exports have been growing rapidly, and it will be instructive to examine the contribution of the price competitiveness to Japan's export performance. Estimates so far produced of the price elasticities of Japanese exports,[1] some results of which will be quoted below, are based on time-series data, and their findings may profitably be compared with our cross-sectional results.

Except for a limited number of standardized commodities, no price data quoted in the world market are available, and the only price series that can be used in our study is that of unit values (value divided by quantity). It is well known that unit values give poor estimates of price movements.[2] This is related partly to the aggregation problem (i.e., any commodity

---

Review of Economics and Statistics, vol. 50, no. 2 (May 1968), pp. 368-273. Reprinted by the courtesy of the Review of Economics and Statistics and the author.

group is made up of heterogeneous goods), and partly to possible measurement errors in the quantity data (customs house officials are not very particular about quantities). We will examine in what follows some implications of the aggregation and measurement error problems.

After a brief description in section 9.2 of the data used, we will present our estimates of the price elasticities and of what we call level elasticities in sections 9.3 and 9.4. The latter are supposed to express an effect of the habit formation: With the price competitiveness equal, exports will be larger if more of the same goods have been exported before. It will be seen that the effect of the habit formation works more or less independently of the price differentials. In section 9.5 the reliability of our unit value series will be examined, as well as a possible bias in our estimates. It will be argued in section 9.6 that if the quantity (or unit value) series are measured with error while the value series are accurate, the estimated price elasticities will be biased toward -1. A short remark on our results in section 9.7 concludes the paper.

9.2. Commodity Classification and Data

The data used for estimating the elasticities were taken from two major sources: the Japanese Finance Ministry's Boeki Nempyo[3] (Yearbook of Japan's Foreign Trade), and the United Nations' Commodity Trade Statistics.[4] As will be explained in the next section, we will need cross-sectional series on the world import values and quantities. These can be obtained from the Commodity Trade Statistics by adding up entries, for each commodity, through about fifty countries. This would, however, be a very tedious job, and I would not have undertaken the present study had it not been for G. Alon's World Commodity Imports 1965-1964.[5] Alon's "recomputerized statistics" provide just what we need, and our series on the values and quantities of world imports by commodity are, in most cases, taken wholly from this source.

Both the Japanese and the United Nations figures are recorded according to the Standard International Trade Classification (SITC). Because of the availablity of the world imports data, we base our study on the 4-digit series; our "commodity" is actually an aggregate comprising a number of more or less heterogeneous commodities. As already indicated, this procedure raises a serious problem of aggregation, and we propose to examine the reliability of the 4-digit data by utilizing what little information is available for the 5-digit world imports series. Note, however, that even the 5-digit data are far from being homogeneous; the Japanese data, for example, are available on a 6-digit basis.

There are thousands of entries, even on the 4-digit basis, recorded in the Japanese exports table. The numbers involved and the availability of the corresponding figures for world imports make it impossible to deal with each item as a separate commodity. We therefore confined our attention to those exports whose value exceeded one billion yen (approximately $2.8 million in 1964). From among these exports further selection had to be made; a commodity was included in the sample of exports if the quantity is recorded by weight (not by number, for example), and if the corresponding data on the world imports are available. Thus it must be admitted that our sample was not drawn through a probability mechanism of any sort.

We are left with about 130 observations, classified into the commodity groups as follows:

Total
One digit (SITC)
- 0 -- food and live animals
- 5 -- Chemicals
- 6 -- Manufactured goods classified chiefly by materials
- Others

Two digits (SITC)
- 51 -- Chemical elements compounds
- 52-59 -- Other chemicals
- 62-64 -- Rubber, wood cord, and paper
- 65 -- Textile yarn fabrics articles
- 67 -- Iron and steel
- Others

9.3. Estimates of Price Elasticities

Let us take a Japanese export commodity and regard it as a substitute for the same class of goods exported by other countries. The world demand for the Japanese commodity may then be written as

$$\log q_J = \alpha \log \frac{p_J}{p_W} + \beta \log y_W + u,$$

where q_J is the quantity of exports, p_J and p_W the prices of Japanese exports and world exports, respectively, y_W is the world's real income, α and β price and level (habit) elasticities to be estimated. If we assume that with the relative prices unchanged, the demand for the Japanese commodity increases or decreases proportionately with the demand for the competitive world exports, we will obtain from the above equation[6]

$$\log q_J = \alpha \log \frac{p_J}{p_W} + \log q_W + u,$$

where q_W stands for the world export (equals, of course, the world import) of the commodity in question.

Our estimation, therefore, is based on the equation

$$\log \frac{q_J}{q_W} = \alpha \log \frac{p_J}{p_W} + u.$$

Estimates of the relative price elasticity a of the demand for a Japanese export are shown in Table 9.1 for the total as well as for commodity group exports. The computer program and the format of input data were such that the coefficients of determination could not be obtained, and we record the estimated standard deviation of u as well as the mean of $\log (q_J/q_W)$.

Two of the two-digit estimates are statistically insignificant, both in 1964 and 1965, though they do have the correct sign. All the remaining estimates seem to be acceptable, and it may be thought reassuring that the estimated elasticities are of the same order of magnitudes as between the two periods. A general impression one obtains from Table 9.1 is that the relative price (or substitution) elasticities of Japanese

TABLE 9.1. ESTIMATED PRICE ELASTICITIES OF JAPANESE EXPORTS, 1964 AND 1965

SITC	1964				1965			
	a	s_a	s_e	q	a	s_a	s_e	q
Total	-1.247	0.123	0.198	-0.990	-1.374	0.151	0.205	-0.961
One Digit								
0	-1.875	0.506	0.326	-1.358	-1.492	0.435	0.302	-1.519
5	-1.455	0.340	0.149	-1.254	-1.166	0.307	0.129	-1.127
6	-0.995	0.140	0.150	-0.871	-1.099	0.249	0.198	-0.837
Others	-1.384	0.168	0.187	-1.005	-1.651	0.323	0.192	-0.916
Two Digits								
51	-1.726	0.517	0.220	-1.214	-1.548	0.500	0.164	-1.071
52-59	-1.019*	0.522	0.113	-1.283	-0.790*	0.399	0.110	-1.170
62-64	-0.771*	0.619	0.230	-1.260	-0.490*	0.929	0.196	-1.196
65	-0.830	0.172	0.091	-0.761	-1.176	0.492	0.254	-0.856
67	-0.914	0.296	0.087	-0.858	-0.857	0.362	0.073	-0.585
61,66 68,69	-1.449	0.269	0.146	-0.788	-1.513	0.347	0.131	-0.819

*Not significant at 5% level

a: price elasticity; s_a: standard error of a; s_e: standard error of estimate;

q: mean of the dependent variable

exports are neither very large nor very small; a few estimates fall slightly below unity while none exceeds 2 (numerically). These results may reflect the reality that confronts Japanese exports, but the fact that all the estimates obtained are distributed around -1 casts some doubt as to the reliability of our procedure. To this problem we will return in later sections of the paper.

Let us briefly compare our estimates with the results obtained so far from time-series studies. Table 9.2 contains two representative estimates of the relative price elasticities of Japanese exports. The time-series estimates here indicate larger numerical elasticities than might be inferred from our findings. However, Eguchi's estimates, which record some very large elasticity values, are based on price series that are <u>not</u> unit values.

TABLE 9.2 TIME-SERIES ESTIMATES

	Quarterly		
	Eguchi[7]	1953 II - 1959 I	
Ships	-0.349	Textiles (to United States	-5.457*
Machinery	-1.978	Textiles (to other countries)	-0.922*
Producers' Goods excluding Textiles	-1.621*		
Foods	-2.185	Durable Consumers' Goods and Miscellaneous	-4.135
	Annual		
	Shishido[8]	**1953 - 1962**	
Foods	-0.824	Metals	-2.924
Textiles	-0.862	Machinery	-0.027
Chemicals	-2.301	Other Macufacturers	-1.770

*"Long-run elasticities" in the context of a distributed lag model.

9.4. Habit Formation

There will certainly be factors other than relative prices that influence Japan's share in world exports. Within the framework of our cross-sectional study, however, we can consider factors of only very general character, and we may summarize them in the records of past export performance.

If the export performance of a commodity has been good, customers will be better acquainted with it than otherwise; and with the prices equal, Japan's share will be larger. This supposition may be cast in the form

$$\log \frac{q_J}{q_W} = \alpha \log \frac{p_J}{p_W} + \beta \log (q_J)_{-1} + u.$$

As the equation stands, α measures the influence of the relative price on Japan's share, while β measures that of the level of the past exports.[9]

The result of regression is shown in Table 9.3. Estimates of the habit elasticity b are of poorer quality than those of the price elasticity, 5 out of 11 estimates being insignificant at a 5% level. Besides, its numerical magnitudes are not easy to interpret. Let it suffice here to note that the habit effect is positive and that it exerts an influence more or less independently of the prices, as may be seen by comparing the estimates of a in Table 9.3 with those in Table 9.1.[10]

9.5. How Good Are Unit Values?

In this section we will consider how good the estimates of price movements are that the unit value indices yield.[11] Our sample consists of SITC 4-digit values and quantities, and it is these quantity series that are possibly affected by aggregation. There are available some (though not systematic) series of world import data on a 5-digit basis. Our procedure will be to regard those 5-digit figures as correct, and construct alternative 4-digit price indices.

Let the 5-digit values, quantities, and prices be v_i, q_i, and p_i $(= v_i/q_i)$. Assuming that these are free from aggregation bias, the 4-digit unit values are calculated as

TABLE 9.3. EFFECT OF HABIT FORMATION: JAPANESE EXPORTS 1965

SITC	a	s_a	b	s_b	s_e	q
Total	-1.352	0.142	0.222	0.052	0.180	-0.961
One Digit						
0	-1.232	0.480	0.311*	0.264	0.290	-1.519
5	-1.192	0.248	0.274	0.078	0.084	-1.127
6	-1.143	0.235	0.208	0.066	0.176	-0.837
Others	-1.622	0.324	0.176*	0.175	0.192	-0.916
Two Digits						
51	-0.976*	0.481	0.466	0.207	0.109	-1.071
52-59	-1.200	0.369	0.253	0.102	0.075	-1.170
62-64	-0.386*	1.106	-0.072*	0.351	0.220	-1.196
65	-1.205	0.500	0.135*	0.194	0.260	-0.856
67	-0.927	0.406	0.063*	0.143	0.077	-0.585
61,66 68,69	-1.420	0.321	0.251	0.118	0.111	-0.819

*Not significant at 5% level

a: price elasticity; s_a: standard error of a; b: habit elasticity; s_b: standard error of b; s_e: standard error of estimates; q: mean of the dependent variable.

$$\text{unit value} = \frac{v_1 + v_2 + v_3 + \cdots}{q_1 + q_2 + q_3 + \cdots} = \frac{q_1p_1 + q_2p_2 + q_3p_3 + \cdots}{q_1 + q_2 + q_3 + \cdots} .$$

It is seen that the 4-digit unit value is actually a weighted average of the 5-digit prices, the weights being 5-digit quantities. Since the summation of quantities is very questionable, we may instead construct a value-weighted price, namely,

$$\text{value-weighted price} = \frac{v_1p_1 + v_2p_2 + v_3p_3 + \cdots}{v_1 + v_2 + v_3 + \cdots} .$$

We actually computed the series for the commodities in SITC 5, and the result of the regression analysis is presented in Table 9.4. Comparison of unit values with value-weighted prices paints different pictures as between 1964 and 1965. The two price series are more or less comparable in 1964, the estimated elasticities being -1.649 and -1.601. However, they give widely different results in 1965.

It may be interesting to note, in passing, that the regression with disaggregated 5-digit unit values gives a numerically lower estimate of the price elasticity than the regression with the 4-digit unit values. Since the more aggregated data conceal some of the substitutions that may take place within a class,[12] one would have expected a higher estimate with the 5-digit series.

If the 5-digit data are sufficiently reliable, an orthodox method of constructing 4-digit price indices will be to use the Japanese or the world quantities as weights and arrive at relative prices:

$$\frac{p_J}{p_W} = \frac{q_{1J}p_{1J} + q_{2J}p_{2J} + \cdots}{q_{1J}p_{1W} + q_{2J}p_{2W} + \cdots}$$

$$\frac{p_J}{p_W} = \frac{q_{1W}p_{1J} + q_{2W}p_{2J} + \cdots}{q_{1W}p_{1W} + q_{2W}p_{2W} + \cdots}$$

Fig. 9.1 shows these two indices for the commodities in SITC 5, together with the relative unit values. Though we did not compute elasticity estimates with the data of Fig. 9.1, the reader may be in a position to judge the reliability of the unit

TABLE 9.4. EFFECTS OF AGGREGATION: JAPANESE EXPORTS, SITC 5

		a	s_a	s_e	q
1. Regression with 4-digit data (unit values)	1964	-1.649	0.401	0.165	-1.314
	1965	-1.515	0.381	0.131	-1.200
2. Regression with 5-digit data (unit values)	1964	-0.959	0.231	0.690	-1.585
	1965	-1.136	0.131	0.497	-1.374
3. Regression with value-weighted prices, 4-digit classification	1964	-1.601	0.298	0.151	1.595
	1965	-0.990	0.115	0.150	-0.946

a: price elasticity; s_a: standard error of a; s_e: standard error of estimates;

q: mean of the dependent variable.

Fig. 9.1a.
Japan's Export Price/
World Import Price (SITC 5)

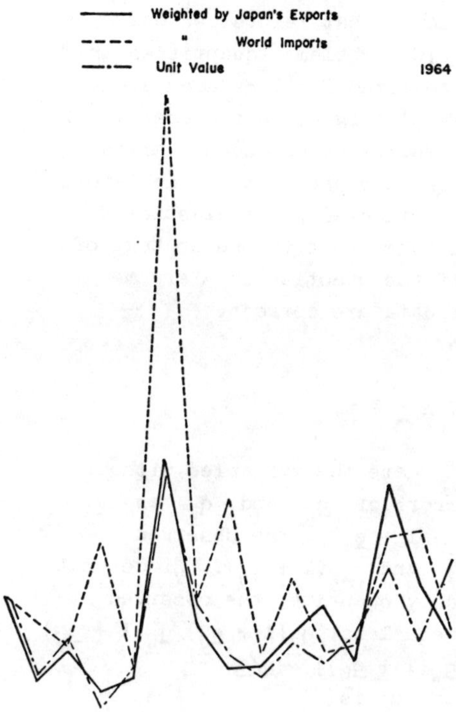

Fig. 9.1b.
Japan's Export Price/
World Import Price (SITC 5)

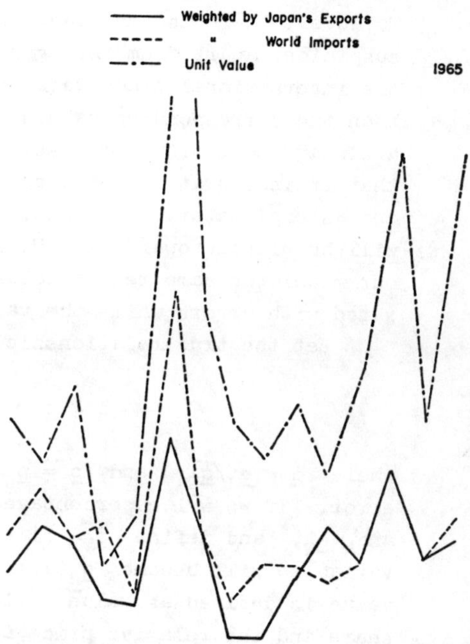

value series from materials already presented.

9.6. Errors in the Quantity Measurement and a Possible Bias

We have seen that there are reasons to suspect the reliability of the aggregated 4-digit quantity (or unit value) data. Moreover, there is one reason at least that reinforces our suspicion, apart from the aggregation problem: quantities in the international trade data are measured far less accurately than the corresponding values. Kemp[13] argues in the context of a linear model with the level of imports as dependent variable that if inaccurately measured prices are used both as deflators and as explanatory variables, the estimated price elasticity will be biased toward -1. We will show that in the context of our model the same result holds if the quantity data are measured with errors while the value data are correct.

Let the true relationship be

$$\log q = \alpha \log p + u,$$

where $q = q_J/q_W$ and $p = p_J/p_W$ are the variables without error. If we write percentage errors of q_J and q_W as e_J and e_W, and define $e = (1 + e_J)/(1 + e_W)$, the observed variables will become $q_J(1 + e_J)$ and $q_W(1 + e_W)$. Since unit value is defined as value divided by quantity, the observed share and the relative price are equal to $q_J(1 + e_J)/q_W(1 + e_W) = q \cdot e$ and $[v_J/q_J(1 + e_J)]/[v_W/q_W(1 + e_W)] = p/e$.

The least squares estimate of α is

$$\alpha = \frac{\sum (\log p - \log e - k)(\log q + \log e - \ell)}{\sum (\log p - \log e - k)^2},$$

where k and ℓ are appropriate constants. On the assumption that the expected values of $\sum (\log p - k)u$, $\sum (\log p - k)\log e$, $\sum (\log e)u$, and $\sum (\log e)$ are all zero, the expectation of

$\underline{a}$ becomes,

$$\underline{a} = \alpha - (1 + \alpha)\underline{d},$$

where $\underline{d} = \sum (\log \underline{e})^2/[\sum (\log \underline{p} - \underline{k})^2 + \sum \log \underline{e})^2]$ is the ratio of the variance of log $\underline{e}$ to the sum of the variances of log $\underline{p}$ and log $\underline{e}$. If the error variance is very large,[14] $\underline{d}$ becomes nearly equal to unity, and of course $\underline{d}$ is zero if the errors are absent.

The relationship among the true elasticity α, the expected estimate of it $\underline{a}$, and the variance of the observation errors relative to the variance of the price, is shown in Fig. 9.2. It is seen immediately that with positive $\underline{d}$, $\underline{a}$ is biased toward -1.

9.7. Conclusion

We have found, on the assumption of unitary elasticity with respect to the volume of world imports, that the relative price elasticities of the demand for Japanese exports are neither very large nor very small numerically. Taken at face value, this suggests that a decrease in Japanese export prices (through productivity rise or currency devaluation) will result in a moderate increase in the value of exports. The analysis is based on cross-sectional value and quantity series, and it is conceivable that the quantity data, from which our unit value series are constructed, contain a fair margin of errors. The reliability of unit values with respect to the aggregation problem is examined, and measurement errors in the quantity series may have biased our estimates of elasticities toward -1. Since it is often the case that the estimation of price elasticities in international trade has to rely on unit value series, we maintain that bias caused by inaccurate quantity data should be taken seriously.

Fig. 9.2.

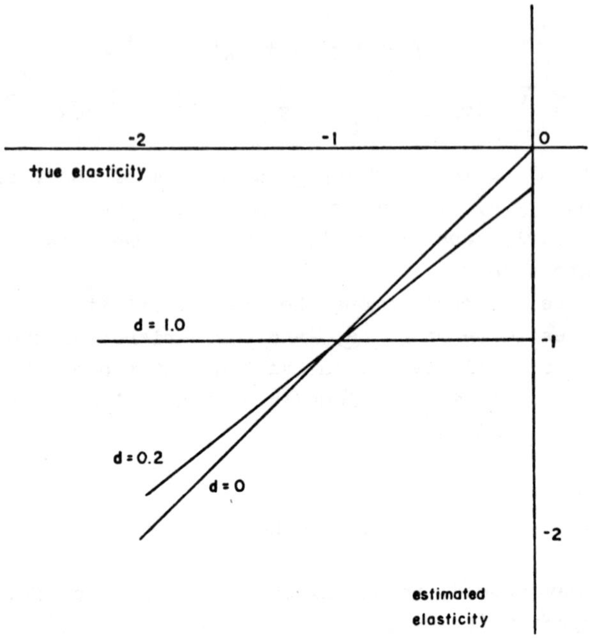

Notes

The author thanks Professor Masahiro Tatemoto for his valuable comments and the Japan Economic Research Center for financial support.

1. H. Eguchi, "A Note on the Export Function in Postwar Japan" (in Japanese) Keizai Kenkyu, vol. 12(1961); S. Ichimura, et al., "A Quarterly Econometric Model of Japan, 1952-1959," Osaka Economic Papers, vol. 12 (1964).

2. R. G. D. Allen and J. E. Ely, International Trade Statistics (New York: Wiley, 1953), especially Chapter 10.

3. Okura-sho (The Ministry of Finance), Boeki Nempyo (Yearbook of Japan's Foreign Trade)(Tokyo, annually).

4. United Nations, Commodity Trade Statistics, (New York, annually).

5. G. Alon, World Commodity Imports 1965-1964 (New York: Budd, 1967, 10 vols.)

6. With constant prices, $\log q_J = \beta \log y_W$ and $\log q_W = \beta' \log y_W$. If $\beta = \beta'$, $\log q_J = \log q_W$, with constant terms being omitted because they have no part to play in what follows.

7. H. Eguchi, "A Note on the Export Function in Postwar Japan" (in Japanese), Keizai Kenkyu, vol. 12 (1961).

8. S. Shishido, "An Analysis of Japanese Export Competitiveness by Means of Classified Export Functions" (in Japanese), Nippon-Keizai Chosa-Kyogikai, International Competitiveness of Japanese Industries (Tokyo, 1966).

9. Though the context is very different, it may be comparable in character with Chenery's size elasticity. See H. B. Chenery, "Patterns of Industrial Growth," American Economic Review, vol. 50 (1960).

10. The result is substantially the same if we replace $(\underline{q}_J)_{-1}$ by $(\underline{p}_J\underline{q}_J)_{-1}$.

11. An example of utilizing unit values to estimate foreign trade (import) elasticities may be found in L. B. Krause, United States Imports, 1947-1958," Econometrica, vol. 30 (1962).

12. That a cross-sectional analysis is sensitive to the degree of aggregation is well known. A good account of the nature of the problem may be found in M. Michaely, Concentration in International Trade (Amsterdam: North-Holland, 1962). On this score S. J. Prais, "Econometric Research in International Trade: A Review," Kyklos, vol. 15 (1962), goes so far as to state that cross-section estimates are of no value.

13. M. C. Kemp, The Demand for Canadian Imports 1926-1955 (Toronto: University of Toronto Press, 1962), appendix IV.

14. $\mathrm{Var}(\log \underline{e}) = \mathrm{Var}(\log 1 + \underline{e}_J) + \mathrm{Var}(\log 1 + \underline{e}_W) - 2\mathrm{cov}(\log 1 + \underline{e}_J)(\log 1 + \underline{e}_W)$ and the last term may safely be neglected.

10

Japan's Balance of Payments and Its Adjustment: A Quarterly Econometric Model, 1961-1967

Akihiro Amano

10.1 Introduction

The balance of payments has always been a major factor affecting the Japanese policy formulation. In the past 13 years from 1955 to 1968, Japan has experienced balance of payments difficulties for four times, in 1957, 1961, 1964, and 1967. In each period Japanese authorities pursued a tight-money policy including a raise in the official discount rate. Such restrictive measures, of course, reduced the rate of economic growth temporarily, but in every case the adjustment in the balance of payments was accomplished within a relatively short period and it did not leave prolonged and detrimental effects to the long-run growth of the economy. The principal concern of the present study is to analyze the balance of payments adjustment mechanism of the Japanese economy in the period from 1961 to 1967.

In section 10.2 we shall first give a brief outline of our model, and then present the entire system of equations. After testing the traceability of the estimated system of the actual data by means of a final simulation test in section 10.3, we shall analyze the balance of payments adjustment process in section 10.4 by means of a dynamic multiplier analysis.

10.2 The Model and Its Estimation

10.2.1. A Brief Outline of the Model

Our model is of a simple Keynesian aggregative type, which may conveniently be divided into the following three sectors: the domestic expenditure sector, the balance of payments sector, and the monetary sector. These three sectors are of course mutually interdependent; and an important link between the first and the second sectors is provided by the income determination mechanism, through which various domestic expenditures affect and are affected by the current account balance of international transactions. The third sector, on the other hand, furnishes a key factor in the Japanese balance of payments adjustment mechanism in the period under consideration.

Under the variable exchange rate system, imbalances in the external accounts are directly reflected in foreign exchange rate changes, which in turn affect the relative price situation between the domestic and the foreign countries, and which therefore will correct the imbalances as long as the system is stable. Under the fixed exchange rate system, however, the external imbalances are first reflected in changes in the official holdings of international reserves. Whether and how these changes in international reserves influence the following course of the economy mainly depends on the objectives of economic policy. A country may leave the external adjustment to policies affecting the long-run changes in productivities and prices, and/or direct and indirect controls of international transactions, thus reserving other policy tools for domestic objectives. Or it may divert some of the latter policy tools to cope with the external imbalance, thus temporarily postponing the attainment of domestic objectives. Monetary policy has long been used for this purpose since the regime of the international gold standard; and as we have stated above the official discount rate policy appears to have played a central role in the Japanese economy during the period from 1961 through 1967.

The following flow chart depicts the gist of the interrelationships among the three sectors of our model. Variables put into circles are endogenous, while those in squares are exogenous. (The actual model involves further disaggregation,

Fig. 10.1. Simplified Flow Chart of the Model

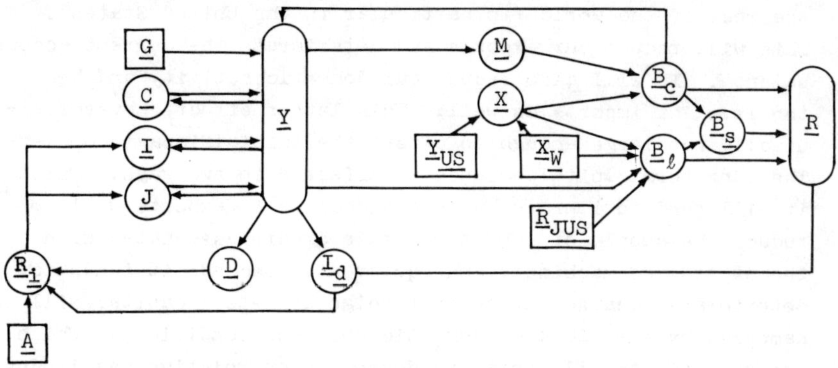

A = supply of cash currency

B_c = balance on current account

B_ℓ = balance on long-term capital account

B_s = balance on short-term capital account

C = personal consumption expenditures

D = demand for money (cash and deposit currency)

G = government expenditures

I = private fixed investment expenditures

I_d = official discount rate

J = inventory investment

M = imports

R = gold and foreign exchange reserves

R_i = interest rate

R_{JUS} = long-term interest rate differential between Japan and the United States

X = exports

X_W = total world exports

Y = gross national product

Y_{US} = gross national product of the United States

additional endogenous and exogenous variables, empirically determined lags, and so on.)

Suppose that there has been a slack in economic activity in the rest of the world (in particular in the United States). This will reduce our exports and deteriorate the current account balance. It will also reduce our domestic activity and hence the level of imports as well. This latter effect, however, is usually not large enough to offset the initial impact completely. The long-term capital balance is affected in two ways. First, it will tend to improve because a decline in exports will reduce the supply of long-term trade credit associated with the exports of machinery and equipment. Second, it tends to deteriorate because inflow of foreign long-term capital will be hampered by the slack of domestic business conditions. Which of the two effects will dominate depends upon relative magnitudes of various parameters, but other long-run factors are likely to be more important in determining the long-term capital flows, so that the net effect will not be very large. The deterioration in the current account balance will therefore cause an outflow of international reserves, although the extent of deficit may be somewhat mitigated by an opposite movement in the balance of short-term capital account.

A tight money policy including a rise of the official discount rate will then be followed, which will in turn raise the market rate of interest. A higher interest rate tends to depress the domestic aggregate demand through its impact upon investment expenditures. It may also affect the level of imports directly by raising the carrying costs of imported inventories. When international short-term capital movements are sensitive to interest rate differentials, a higher domestic interest rate will cause the short-term capital balance to improve. These forces are expected to terminate the drain of international reserves. We believe that the above somewhat orthodox, or textbook style adjustment mechanism is the one that has been operating in the Japanese economy during the 1960s, and the main purpose of this paper is to verify it by estimating and working a medium-size macroeconometric model.

The size of our model was determined primarily as a consequence of compromising the following somewhat conflicting objectives: namely to isolate as many individual components as possible of the adjustment mechanism, on the one hand, and to abstract the major causal relations as clearly as possible, on the other hand. The model thus contains 39 behavior and statistical equations (18 in the domestic expenditure sector, 18 in the balance of payments sector, and 3 in the monetary sector), and 11 nonstochastic equations (5 in the domestic expenditure sector, 6 in the balance of payments sector), which then determine 50 endogenous variables in terms of 32 exogenous variables.

The equations presented below were estimated from seasonally unadjusted quarterly data for the period 1961.I-1967.IV. The choice of this sample period was inevitable, because systematic balance of payments statistics were available only for this period when this research was initiated. The ordinary least squares (OLS), two-stage least squares with principal components (TSLSPC), and the three-pass least squares (3PLS) methods have been used in estimation. In some equations the method of ordinary least squares has been applied recursively. Thus, a variable in parentheses followed by the letter E indicates that the values of the variable are estimated by other equations. In the first stage of the two-stage least squares method, we used principal components of the least squares residuals of the regressions of the excluded predetermined variables on the predetermined variables included in the equation to be estimated.[1] In general, satisfactory results have been obtained when the number of principal components is set one or two greater than the number of explanatory endogenous variables of the equation, though in some cases larger numbers have been required.

In each equation the standard errors of the coefficients are given in parentheses below the coefficients. RR denotes the coefficient of determination adjusted by the degree of freedom, SE the standard error of estimate, and DW the Durbin-Watson test statistic. In the equation where the three-pass least squares method is used, $\hat{u}_{-1}$ indicates a consistent estimate of the residuals (lagged one period) of the original equation that can be obtained at the second stage of the three-pass least squares method. Finally, all the elasticities given in the comments on individual equations that are linear in parameters are evaluated at the sample means of the respective variables.

The variables are defined in the Appendix.

10.2.2. Estimated Equations

(i) National Income Accounts

(i)1 Domestic Expenditures

Private consumption

$$\text{(10.1)}\quad \underline{CP}/\underline{N} = \underset{(0.01072)}{0.28142}\ \underline{YPS}/(\underline{PCP}\cdot\underline{N}) + \underset{(0.02007)}{0.66426}\left(\frac{1}{4}\sum_{\underline{i}=1}^{4}(\underline{CP}/\underline{N})_{-\underline{i}}\right)$$
TSLSPC

$$-\underset{(13.5)}{115.4}\ \underline{Q1} - \underset{(13.3)}{143.1}\ \underline{Q3} + 133.7$$

$$\underline{SE} = 27.6,\quad \underline{DW} = 1.59.$$

Private fixed investment in machinery and equipment

$$\text{(10.2)}\quad \underline{IPE} = \underset{(0.09809)}{0.58543}[(\underline{SC} + \underline{CCA})/\underline{PIPE}]_{-1} - \underset{(348.068)}{823.179}\ \underline{RBL}_{-3}$$
OLS

$$-\underset{(26.9)}{88.3}\ \underline{Q2} + \underset{(30.0)}{131.3}\ \underline{Q3} + 2398.6$$

$$\underline{RR} = 0.9336,\quad \underline{SE} = 58.0,\quad \underline{DW} = 1.10.$$

Private fixed investment in dwellings

$$\text{(10.3)}\quad \underline{IRC} = \underset{(0.015875)}{0.080169}\ \underline{YPD}/\underline{PIRC} - \underset{(49.002)}{95.008}\ \underline{RBL}_{-2}$$
TSLSPC

$$+\underset{(0.12833)}{0.37356}\ \underline{IRC}_{-1} + \underset{(26.9)}{112.1}\ \underline{Q1} + \underset{(14.9)}{127.2}\ \underline{Q2}$$

$$+\underset{(18.8)}{117.3}\ \underline{Q3} + 16.5$$

$$\underline{SE} = 11.0,\quad \underline{DW} = 2.01.$$

Inventory investment

$$\text{(10.4)}\quad \underline{II} = \underset{(0.02480)}{0.47342}\ \underline{GNP}/\underline{PGNP} + \underset{(246.82)}{891.01}\ (\underline{GNP}/\underline{PGNP})/(\underline{GNP}/\underline{PGNP})_{-4}$$
TSLSPC

$$-\underset{(291.843)}{507.470}\ \underline{RBL}_{-1} - \underset{(0.01844)}{0.38025}\ (\underline{KI}/\underline{PII})_{-1} - \underset{(38.0)}{44.9}\ \underline{Q1}$$

$$+ \underset{(39.8)}{241.3}\ \underline{Q2} + 79.6$$

$$\underline{SE} = 67.0, \quad \underline{DW} = 1.15.$$

Depreciation allowance

(10.5) OLS

$$\underline{CCA}/\underline{PIPE} = \underset{(0.001423)}{0.041422}\ (\underline{KPE}/\underline{PIPE})_{-1} + \underset{(1.0290)}{4.3939}\ \underline{RHO}_{-1}$$

$$- \underset{(13.7)}{122.7}\ \underline{Q1} - \underset{(13.6)}{123.3}\ \underline{Q2} - \underset{(13.6)}{72.5}\ \underline{Q3} - 290.4$$

$$\underline{RR} = 0.9836, \quad \underline{SE} = 25.4, \quad \underline{DW} = 1.52.$$

Consumption is estimated on a per capita basis as a function of personal disposable income and the arithmetic mean of the level of consumption of the past four quarters. The short-run marginal propensity to consume in equation (10.1) is 0.281, and the long-run marginal propensity to consume is 0.838. The short-run and the long-run marginal propensities to consume out of personal disposable income obtained by other writers for the Japanese economy are: 0.230 and 0.542 by Klein and Shinkai[2] for the period 1930-1936 and 1951-1958; 0.367 and 0.737 by Ichimura, et al.[3] for the period 1952-1959 (computed from their estimates on an assumption that the distribution of income is held constant); and 0.394 and 0.741 by Tatemoto, Uchida, and Watanabe[4] for the period 1953-1963. Compared with these results our estimate of the long-run marginal propensity seems to give a rather higher value. The difference may largely be caused by differences in the specification of consumption function. But it may also be the case, as the above quotation happens to exemplify, that the marginal propensities to consume have become larger in the more recent period.

Domestic investment expenditures are divided into three components: private investment in machinery and equipment, private investment in dwellings, and inventory investment. Private investment in machinery and equipment is assumed as a function of gross corporate savings and the interest rate (average lending rate by all banks), while residential investment is a function of personal disposable income and the interest rate. The inventory investment function is estimated based on the simple, flexible accelerator model. The implied interest elasticities are -1.53 for investment in machinery and equipment, -0.73 (short-run) and -1.17 (long-run) for residential investment, and -4.53 for inventory investment.

Depreciation allowances are related to the private fixed capital stock and the operating ratio of the manufacturing industries.

(i)2 Personal Income

Personal income

(10.6) TSLSPC

$$\underline{YP} = \underset{(0.01619)}{0.70639}\ \underline{GNP} - \underset{(78.9)}{864.1}\ \underline{Q1} - 83.5$$

$$\underline{SE} = 177.7, \quad \underline{DW} = 1.89.$$

Personal income taxes and charges

(10.7) TSLSPC

$$\underline{TP} = \underset{(0.001578)}{0.065939}\left(\frac{1}{2}\sum_{\underline{i}=0}^{1}\underline{YP}_{-\underline{i}}\right) + \underset{(13.2)}{131.1}\ \underline{Q1} + \underset{(13.3)}{31.4}\ \underline{Q2} + \underset{(13.2)}{102.8}\ \underline{Q3} - 122.5$$

$$\underline{SE} = 24.4, \quad \underline{SW} = 2.71.$$

Personal transfers

(10.8) TSLSPC

$$\underline{TRP} = \underset{(0.001582)}{0.083050}\left(\frac{1}{3}\sum_{\underline{i}=0}^{2}\underline{YP}_{-\underline{i}}\right) + \underset{(5.6)}{33.0}\ \underline{Q1} + \underset{(5.6)}{62.5}\ \underline{Q3} - 132.3$$

$$\underline{SE} = 11.9, \quad \underline{DW} = 1.56.$$

By definition personal disposable income is personal income less income taxes and transfer payments such as social security contributions. Equation (10.6) gives a statistical relation between personal income and gross national product at current prices, and equations (10.7) and (10.8) explain personal income tax and transfer payments, respectively, as a function of personal income.

(i)3 Corporate Income

Corporate income

(10.9) TSLSPC

$$\underline{YC/YN} = \underset{(0.10647)}{0.26976}\,(\underline{IPE} + \underline{IRC})/(\underline{GNP}/\underline{PGNP}) + \underset{(0.033749)}{0.066413}\,(\underline{GNP}/\underline{PGNP})/(\underline{GNP}/\underline{PGNP})_{-4} + \underset{(0.18240)}{0.42235}\,(\underline{YC}/\underline{YN})_{-1} + \underset{(0.00671)}{0.04902}\,\underline{Q1} + \underset{(0.00310)}{0.02190}\,\underline{Q2} - 0.07956$$

$$\underline{SE} = 0.00633, \quad \underline{DW} = 1.83.$$

Corporate taxes and charges

(10.10) TSLSPC

$$\underline{TC} = \underset{(0.04181)}{0.35182}\,\left(\frac{1}{3}\sum_{\underline{i}=0}^{2} \underline{YC}_{-\underline{i}}\right) - \underset{(16.1)}{56.5}\,\underline{Q1} - \underset{(15.9)}{85.1}\,\underline{Q3} + 72.1$$

$$\underline{SE} = 34.3, \quad \underline{DW} = 2.73.$$

Corporate transfers to private sector

(10.11) OLS

$$\underline{YDIV} = \underset{(0.02147)}{0.92738}\,\underline{YDIV}_{-2} + \underset{(3.2)}{19.2}\,\underline{Q2} - \underset{(3.3)}{11.7}\,\underline{Q3} + 10.4$$

$$\underline{RR} = 0.9923, \quad \underline{SE} = 6.4, \quad \underline{DW} = 1.80.$$

According to the neo-Keynesian, or Kaldorian, theory of income distribution, the share of profit in national income is an increasing function of investment ratio, i.e., the ratio of investment to national income. Moreover, business cycle theories suggest that there will be a shift of income in favor of profits in the upswing of the cycle, and vice versa. Thus, equation (10.9) relates the share of corporate income in national income to the proportion of gross private fixed investment in gross national product, and to the rate of growth of gross national product.

Corporate income tax is estimated as a function of corporate income. The marginal rate of income tax on corporate income is about 35 percent, which may be compared with 7 percent on personal income (see equation (10.7)). In the dividend payments equation (10.11), the corporate income variable turned out to be insignificant. Thus the equation becomes a simple difference equation with the average, quarterly stationary value equal to 169 billion, which is about 1.6 times as large as the sample mean.

(i)4 Implicit Deflators

Consumption expenditure deflator

$$\text{(10.12) OLS} \quad PCP/PCP_{-4} = \underset{(0.07521)}{0.26305}\,((GNP/PGNP - II)/(GNP/PGNP - II)_{-4})_{-3}$$

$$+ \underset{(0.11307)}{0.21193}\, PMGR/PMGR_{-4}$$

$$+ \underset{(0.13646)}{0.64203}\,(PCP/PCP_{-4})_{-1} - 0.126$$

$$RR = 0.5136, \quad SE = 0.012, \quad DW = 1.93.$$

Investment in machinery and equipment deflator

$$\text{(10.13) OLS} \quad PIPE/PIPE_{-4} = \underset{(0.017749)}{0.055063}\,(IPE/IPE_{-4})E$$

$$+ \underset{(0.14399)}{0.47180}\,(PIPE/PIPE_{-4})_{-1} + 0.475$$

$$RR = 0.6664, \quad SE = 0.010, \quad DW = 1.71.$$

Investment in dwellings deflator

$$\text{(10.14) OLS} \quad PIRC/PIRC_{-4} = \underset{(0.69560)}{2.43785}\,(PIPE/PIPE_{-4})E$$

$$+ \underset{(0.17913)}{0.27206}\,(PIRC/PIRC_{-4})_{-1} - 1.694$$

$$RR = 0.7346, \quad SE = 0.028, \quad DW = 1.45.$$

Inventory investment deflator

$$\text{(10.15) OLS} \quad PII - PII_{-1} = \underset{(0.000006610)}{0.000029124}\,((GNP/PGNP)_{-1} - (GNP/PGNP)_{-2})$$

$$+ \underset{(0.00034885)}{0.00063002}(W_{-1} - W_{-2}) - \underset{(0.010)}{0.053}\,Q1$$

$$+ \underset{(0.018)}{0.056}\,Q2 - 0.002$$

$$RR = 0.5853, \quad SE = 0.008, \quad DW = 1.77.$$

GNP deflator

(10.16) OLS

$$\underline{PGNP} - \underline{PGNP}_{-1} = \underset{(0.17104)}{0.37663}(\underline{PCP} - \underline{PCP}_{-1})E + \underset{(0.19030)}{0.73761}(\underline{PII} - \underline{PII}_{-1})E - \underset{(0.007)}{0.048}\,\underline{Q1} - \underset{(0.007)}{0.040}\,\underline{Q2} - \underset{(0.007)}{0.044}\,\underline{Q3} + 0.039$$

$\underline{RR} = 0.7934$, $\underline{SE} = 0.012$, $\underline{DW} = 1.26$.

Implicit deflators were estimated either by a growth rate form or by a first difference form. They are explained either directly by the rate of growth of effective demand and other factors or indirectly by other deflators.

(i)5 Statistical Equations and Identities

National income

(10.17) TSLSPC

$$\underline{YN} = \underset{(0.01408)}{0.79893}\,\underline{GNP} - \underset{(68.6)}{695.0}\,\underline{Q1} + 204.9$$

$\underline{SE} = 154.6$, $\underline{DW} = 2.12$.

Seasonally adjusted GNP

(10.18) TSLSPC

$$\underline{GNPS} = \underset{(0.00729)}{1.00260}\,\underline{GNP}/\underline{PGNP} + \underset{(25.2)}{1349.3}\,\underline{Q1} + \underset{(25.7)}{1654.1}\,\underline{Q2} + \underset{(24.3)}{1401.2}\,\underline{Q3} - 1124.8$$

$\underline{SE} = 40.4$, $\underline{DW} = 1.62$.

Personal disposable income

(10.19) $\underline{YPD} = \underline{YP} - \underline{TP} - \underline{TRP}$

Corporate savings

(10.20) $\underline{SC} = \underline{YC} - \underline{TC} - \underline{YDIV}$

Fixed capital stock

(10.21) $\underline{KPE}/\underline{PIPE} = \underline{IPE} - \underline{CCA}/\underline{PIPE} + (\underline{KPE}/\underline{PIPE})_{-1}$

Inventory stock

(10.22) $\underline{KI}/\underline{PII} = \underline{II} + (\underline{KI}/\underline{PII})_{-1}$

Income determination

(10.23) $\underline{GNP} = \underline{PCP}\cdot\underline{CP} + \underline{PIPE}\cdot\underline{IPE} + \underline{PIRC}\cdot\underline{IRC} + \underline{PII}\cdot\underline{II} + \underline{G} + 0.36\underline{BPC}$

Equations (10.17) and (10.18) provide the statistical relations to complete the model, and equations (10.19)-(10.23) are self-explanatory.

(ii) Balance of Payments Accounts

(ii)1 Merchandise Exports

Exports of machinery and equipment

(10.24) OLS

$$LN(\underline{XGM}/\underline{PXGM}) = \underset{(0.17724)}{1.77757}\ LN(\underline{XTW}/\underline{PXGM}) + \underset{(0.24841)}{0.64728}\ LN(\underline{RHO}) + \underset{(0.04727)}{0.28649}\ \underline{QXC} + \underset{(0.04956)}{0.12366}\ \underline{QVN} - \underset{(0.03754)}{0.08968}\ \underline{Q1} - \underset{(0.03437)}{0.12636}\ \underline{Q2} + \underset{(0.03640)}{0.05131}\ \underline{Q3} - 18.08435$$

$\underline{RR} = 0.9873$, $\underline{SE} = 0.06092$, $\underline{DW} = 1.39$.

Exports of other commodities

(10.25) OLS

$$LN(\underline{XGO}/\underline{PXGO}) = \underset{(0.12136)}{1.88877}\ LN(\underline{GNPAS}/\underline{PXGO}) - \underset{(0.14372)}{0.36661}\ LN(\underline{RHO}) - \underset{(0.03050)}{0.05011}\ \underline{QXC} + \underset{(0.01808)}{0.12827}\ \underline{QSS} - \underset{(0.01955)}{0.18506}\ \underline{Q1} - \underset{(.01917)}{0.06859}\ \underline{Q2} - \underset{(0.01888)}{0.5502}\ \underline{Q3} - 3.40219$$

$\underline{RR} = 0.9818$, $\underline{SE} = 0.03474$, $\underline{DW} = 1.12$.

Total merchandise exports are here divided into two groups: machinery and equipment, and other commodities. Since the balance of payments table gives only total merchandise exports on the balance of payments basis, we split them into the above two categories using the proportions given by the customs clearance statistics. This division is made mainly because it was expected that the first component would play an important role in explaining Japan's long-term loans to other countries (see equation (10.36) below).

Each export function was estimated by a double-logarithmic form using the foreign activity variable, the relative price variable, and the index of operating ratio of Japanese manufacturing industries as main explanatory variables. In every estimation, however, the coefficient of the relative price variable was statistically insignificant and/or of wrong sign. The operating ratio variable was statistically significant in both equations, but unexpectedly it has a positive sign in the export function of machinery and equipment (10.24). A possible explanation for this may be that a higher operating ratio strengthens the international competitiveness by reducing the average fixed costs.

The dummy variable QVN represents the effect of the Vietnam war, and QSS the effect of an expectation of a steel strike in the United States lasting from the autumn of 1964 to September 1965. Finally, the dummy variable QXC is introduced to account for a change in the commodity classification of export data.

The elasticity of exports with respect to the foreign activity variable is almost 2 in either equation, which seems to be the single most important factor that makes it possible for the Japanese economy to sustain a high rate of economic growth without causing secular balance of payments difficulties under the stable exchange rates system.

(ii)2 Merchandise Imports

Imports of raw material and mineral fuel

$$\underset{\text{TSLSPC}}{(10.26)}\quad \underline{MGR}/\underline{PMGR} = \underset{(0.01472)}{0.15585}\,(\underline{GNP}/\underline{PGNP} - \underline{II}) + \underset{(0.19003)}{0.43177}\,\underline{II} - \underset{(23.2)}{50.3}\,\underline{QMC} + \underset{(155.6)}{437.1}\,\underline{Q1} + \underset{(108.0)}{457.6}\,\underline{Q2} + \underset{(132.0)}{398.4}\,\underline{Q3} - 351.9$$

$$\underline{SE} = 43.0, \quad \underline{DW} = 2.40.$$

Imports of other commodities

$$\underset{\text{TSLSPC}}{(10.27)}\quad \underline{MGO}/\underline{PMGO} = \underset{(0.06529)}{0.19454}\,\underline{CP} + \underset{(0.12928)}{0.24979}\,(\underline{IPE} + \underline{IRC}) + \underset{(23.8)}{160.7}\,\underline{Q1} + \underset{(22.6)}{170.4}\,\underline{Q2} + \underset{(37.3)}{92.8}\,\underline{Q3} - 444.4$$

$$\underline{SE} = 33.0, \quad \underline{DW} = 1.71.$$

Merchandise imports are also disaggregated into two categories: raw materials and mineral fuel, and other merchandise. The method of disaggregating total balance of payments imports is the same as that applied to exports. Each category of imports was estimated as a function of the relative price of imports and various components of domestic expenditures. It turned out, however, that the price coefficients were not statistically significant. The dummy variable QMC in equation (10.26) accounts for the changes in import control policy by means of import collateral adjustments adopted in the early 1960s.

In equation (10.26) the coefficient of inventory investment is much larger than that of final sale, and the difference between them is significant at the 5 percent level. Similarly, in equation (10.27) the coefficient of private fixed investment is larger than that of private consumption, but the difference is not quite significant. Since domestic expenditures are measured by billions of yen and imports by millions of dollars, we can obtain the ordinary marginal import coefficients by multiplying these coefficients by 0.360.

(ii)3 Transportation and Insurance Transactions

Receipts from transportation and insurance

$$\underset{\text{OLS}}{(10.28)} \quad \underline{XSTI} = \underset{(0.00430)}{0.10267}(\underline{XGM} + \underline{XGO})E + \underset{(0.17707)}{0.21320}\,\underline{FR} - \underset{(8.2)}{18.8}\,\underline{QSMS}$$

$$+ \underset{(5.8)}{27.6}\,\underline{Q1} + \underset{(5.7)}{12.3}\,\underline{Q2} + \underset{(5.6)}{10.9}\,\underline{Q3} - 48.5$$

$$\underline{RR} = 0.9703, \quad \underline{SE} = 10.2, \quad \underline{SW} = 1.25.$$

Payments for transportation and insurance

$$\underset{\text{TSLSPC}}{(10.29)} \quad \underline{MSTI} = \underset{(0.01463)}{0.27324}(\underline{MGF} + \underline{MGO}) + \underset{(16.3)}{66.7}\,\underline{QSMS} - \underset{(12.5)}{46.3}\,\underline{QLF}$$

$$- \underset{(10.1)}{18.0}\,\underline{Q1} - \underset{(10.1)}{21.0}\,\underline{Q2} - 81.1$$

$$\underline{SE} = 21.5, \quad \underline{DW} = 1.39.$$

Receipts and payments on transportation and insurance accounts are mainly explained by the value of merchandise exports and imports, respectively. The index of tramper freight rate was not significant in the payments equation and is significant only at the 15 percent level in the receipts equation. The dummy variable QSMS is to account for the effects of the strike by the seamen's union which broke out at the end of 1965. Both receipts and payments were affected unfavorably by this strike, and its effect is estimated as the net worsening of the balance by about \$86 million. The other dummy variable QLF in equation (10.29) represents the effect of import liberalization of crude oil in October 1962. As a result of this liberalization, the yen sales of oil in bond have increased, with the effect of reducing our payments for port disbursements.

The estimated coefficients in equations (10.28) and (10.29) indicate that a simultaneous expansion of merchandise exports and imports by \$100 million will worsen the balance on the service account by about \$17 million.

(ii)4 Income on Foreign Investment and Other Services

Receipts from income on direct investment

$$\underset{\text{TSLSPC}}{(10.30)} \quad \underline{XSID} = \underset{(0.001138)}{0.006810}\,\underline{KDJW} + \underset{(0.5)}{5.4}\,\underline{Q1A} + \underset{(0.5)}{4.7}\,\underline{Q3A} - 0.9$$

$$\underline{SE} = 1.1, \quad \underline{DW} = 2.49.$$

Receipts from income on other investments

$$\text{(10.31)}\quad \underline{XSLO} = \underset{(0.001558)}{0.023014}\,(\underline{KLJW} + \underline{KOJW})_{-2} + \underset{(2.6)}{7.9}\,\underline{Q1} + \underset{(2.5)}{7.0}\,\underline{Q3} + 15.5$$

OLS

$\underline{RR} = 0.8920,\quad \underline{SE} = 5.5,\quad \underline{DW} = 1.97.$

Payments for income on direct investment

$$\text{(10.32)}\quad \underline{MSID} = \underset{(0.002867)}{0.014908}\,\underline{KDWJ}_{-2} + \underset{(2.0)}{4.1}\,\underline{QLR64} + \underset{(1.1)}{3.9}\,\underline{Q2B} - \underset{(1.1)}{2.0}\,\underline{Q3C} + 5.2$$

OLS

$\underline{RR} = 0.7768,\quad \underline{SE} = 1.7,\quad \underline{DW} = 1.79.$

Payments for income on other investments

$$\text{(10.33)}\quad \underline{MSIO} = \underset{(0.001680)}{0.034105}\,(\underline{KLWJ} + \underline{KOWJ})_{-3} + 33.8$$

OLS

$\underline{RR} = 0.9383,\quad \underline{SE} = 6.5,\quad \underline{DW} = 0.85.$

Payments for other services

$$\text{(10.34)}\quad \underline{MSO} = \underset{(0.001007)}{0.027451}\,\underline{GNP} + \underset{(5.9)}{66.9}\,\underline{Q1} + \underset{(6.0)}{70.9}\,\underline{Q2} + \underset{(5.8)}{64.1}\,\underline{Q3} - 83.2$$

TSLSPC

$\underline{SE} = 10.0,\quad \underline{DW} = 1.46.$

Income on foreign investment is explained by the relevant stock variable, i.e., cumulated foreign investment measured from an arbitrary origin (the fourth quarter of 1960). Seasonal dummy variables and the lags were selected experimentally. Inspection of the data on XSID and MSID reveals clear shifts of seasonality, which are probably caused by changes in the compilation of reported data. Quarterly dummy variables are therefore adjusted accordingly. The dummy variable QLR64 in equation (10.32) represents the liberalization of remittance of investment income in April 1964.

Payments for other services is estimated as a function of gross national product. Receipts from other services is treated as exogenous, since it mostly consists of government transactions (especially, military transactions) which, on average, amount to approximately 70 percent of the total receipts from other services for the period concerned.

(ii)5 Long-Term Capital Movements

<u>Cumulated direct investment to other countries</u>

(10.35) OLS

$$\underline{KDJW} = \underset{(0.00030890)}{0.00081239}\ \underline{XTW} - \underset{(8.6858)}{24.8600}\ \underline{RLJA}$$

$$- \underset{(44.4242)}{94.4491}\ (\underline{GNP}/\underline{GNP}_{-4} - \underline{XTW}/\underline{XTW}_{-4})$$

$$+ \underset{(9.04750)}{0.83060}\ \underline{KDJW}_{-1} + 17.6$$

$$\underline{RR} = 0.9968,\quad \underline{SE} = 10.3,\quad \underline{DW} = 1.78$$

<u>Cumulated long-term loans to other countries</u>

(10.36) OLS

$$\underline{KLJW} = \underset{(0.07539)}{0.11815}\ (\underline{XGM})E + \underset{(0.04287)}{0.98835}\ \underline{KLJW}_{-1} + 7.8$$

$$\underline{RR} = 0.9976,\quad \underline{SE} = 27.5,\quad \underline{DW} = 1.53.$$

<u>Cumulated other long-term investments to other countries</u>

(10.37) 3PLS

$$\underline{KOJW} = - \underset{(14.9766)}{76.6008}\ \underline{RLJA} - \underset{(53.358)}{175.265}\ (\underline{GNP}/\underline{GNP}_{-4} - \underline{XTW}/\underline{XTW}_{-4})$$

$$+ \underset{(0.05579)}{0.85888}\ \underline{KOJW}_{-1} + \underset{(0.24408)}{0.56348}\ \hat{\underline{u}}_{-1} + 245.8$$

$$\hat{\underline{u}}_{-1} = \underline{KOJW}_{-1} - 0.80827\ \underline{KOJW}_{-2} + 53.3840\ \underline{RLJA}_{-1}$$

$$+ 103.297\ (\underline{GNP}/\underline{GNP}_{-4} - \underline{XTW}/\underline{XTW}_{-4})_{-1} - 174.8$$

$$\underline{RR} = 0.9969,\quad \underline{SE} = 12.2,\quad \underline{DW} = 1.59.$$

<u>Cumulated direct investment from other countries</u>

(10.38) TSLSPC

$$\underline{KDWJ} = \underset{(0.019807)}{0.019412}\ \underline{GNPS} + \underset{(12.7038)}{19.6569}\ \underline{RLJA} + \underset{(6.1)}{22.0}\ \underline{QLR63}$$

$$+ \underset{(0.13120)}{0.88706}\ \underline{KDWJ}_{-1} - 128.8$$

$$\underline{SE} = 5.9, \quad \underline{DW} = 1.90.$$

Cumulated other long-term investments from other countries

(10.39) 3PLS

$$\underline{KLWJ} + \underline{KOWJ} = \underset{(14.9640)}{14.4295}\ \underline{RLJA} + \underset{(32.9)}{167.9}\ \underline{QLR63}$$

$$+ \underset{(0.02083)}{1.08069}\ (\underline{KLWJ} + \underline{KOWJ})_{-1}$$

$$+ \underset{(0.10836)}{0.73070}\ \hat{\underline{u}}_{-1} + 75.9$$

$$\hat{\underline{u}}_{-1} = (\underline{KLWJ} + \underline{KOWJ})_{-1} - 1.14809\ (\underline{KLWJ} + \underline{KOWJ})_{-2}$$

$$- 51.0351\ \underline{RLJA}_{-1} - 175.1\ \underline{QLR63}_{-1} + 41.0$$

$$\underline{RR} = 0.9974, \quad \underline{SE} = 31.7, \quad \underline{DW} = 1.84.$$

The estimation of long-term capital transactions to and from other countries is based on the familiar stock adjustment theory. The desired stock of foreign investment is assumed as a function of some activity variable, the long-term interest rate differential, and the growth rate differential. The last variable is to approximate the differences in expected profitability. The actual stock of foreign investment is assumed to adjust to the desired level according to the partial adjustment scheme.

The long-term interest differential (the difference between Japan and the United States) and the growth rate differential are both significant in equations (10.35) and (10.37), but not in other equations. Equation (10.36) demonstrates that the supply of long-term loans from Japan is significantly explained by Japanese exports of machinery and equipment. The dummy variable QLR63 in equations (10.38) and (10.39) represents the liberalization of remittance of capital invested in stocks in April 1963, which seems to explain the large inflow of long-term capital in the second quarter of 1963.

(ii)6 Short-Term Capital Movements and Changes in International Reserves

Balance on short-term capital account

(10.40) TSLSPC

$$\underline{BPS} = - \underset{(0.13544)}{0.64682}\ \underline{BPB} - \underset{(43.6)}{132.5}\ \underline{Q3} + 52.9$$

$$\underline{SE} = 89.6, \quad \underline{DW} = 1.37.$$

Changes in international reserves

(10.41) TSLSPC

$$\underline{GFE} - \underline{GFE}_{-1} = \underset{(0.10058)}{0.97553}\ (\underline{BPO} + \underline{BPOAD}) + \underset{(11.5)}{25.1}\ \underline{Q2} - 5.6$$

$$\underline{SE} = 22.6, \quad \underline{DW} = 2.15.$$

In the official publication of Japan's balance of payments the balance on short-term capital accounts excludes the commercial banking sector, the latter being included in the balance of monetary movements. Short-term capital movements conducted by the commercial banking sector, however, are governed by the same factors as those influencing other short-term capital movements such as import usances and borrowings in foreign currency. Therefore, these two categories of short-term capital movements are here combined under one heading.

Equation (10.40) confirm the interesting finding by Ezekiel and Patel that Japan's short-term capital movements have a high inverse relationship with its basic balance of payments.[5] The short-term interest rate differential, however, was not found to be a significant factor. This may be explained by the fact that the Japanese short-term interest rates have been considerably higher than those in other advanced countries during most of the sample period. There has been a tendency, however, for the Japanese short-term interest rates to decline, and in 1965 there were some instances indicating interest-rate sensitivity of short-term capital movements. A further study of this topic is needed.

Equation (10.41) represents a statistical relation between changes in official holdings of international reserves and the balance of official monetary movements. The variable BPOAD is to account for major discrepancies between the balance of official monetary movements and the changes in gold and foreign exchange reserves. It consists of the special borrowings of the Bank of Japan from U.S. commerical banks in the period 1961-1962 and of the inclusion of gold transche into the foreign exchange reserves in March 1963.

(ii)7 Identities

Balance of trade

$$BPG = XGM + XGO - MGR - MGO \qquad (10.42)$$

Balance on service account

$$BPI = XSTI - MSTI + XSID + XSIO - MSID - MSIO + XSO - MSO \qquad (10.43)$$

Current account balance

$$BPC = BPG + BPI \qquad (10.44)$$

Balance on long-term capital account

$$BPL = KDWJ - KDWJ_{-1} + (KLWJ + KOWJ) - (KLWJ + KOWJ)_{-1} - KDJW + KDJW_{-1} - KLJW + KLJW_{-1} - KOJW + KOJW_{-1} \qquad (10.45)$$

Basic balance of payments

$$BPB = BPC + BPT + BPL \qquad (10.46)$$

Balance of official monetary movements

$$BPO = BPB + BPS + BPE \qquad (10.47)$$

(iii) The Monetary Sector

Demand for Money

(10.48) TSLSPC

$$D = \underset{(0.13079)}{0.20043}\,GNP + \underset{(0.09694)}{0.87128}\,D_{-1} - \underset{(339.4)}{826.4}\,Q1 - \underset{(344.1)}{520.3}\,Q2 - \underset{(298.6)}{513.8}\,Q3 + 364.9$$

$$SE = 234.5 \quad DW = 1.44.$$

Interest rate on bank loans

(10.49) TSLSPC

$$\underline{LN(RBL)} = \underset{(0.012201)}{0.018152}\ LN(\underline{D} - \underline{CC}) + \underset{(0.03970)}{0.15384}\ LN(\underline{ROD}) + \underset{(0.06467)}{0.83979}\ LN(\underline{RBL})_{-1} - \underset{(0.00391)}{0.00515}\ \underline{Q1} + \underset{(0.00384)}{0.00168}\ \underline{Q2} - 0.00397\ \underline{Q3} - 0.31719$$

$\underline{SE} = 0.00710$, $\underline{DW} = 1.77$.

Official discount rate

(10.50) TSLSPC

$$\underline{ROD} = -\underset{(0.0007606)}{0.0018577}\ \underline{GFE} + \underset{(1.2899)}{1.1348}\ (\underline{GNP}/\underline{PGNP})/(\underline{GNP}/\underline{PGNP})_{-4} + \underset{(0.16225)}{0.50838}\ \underline{ROD}_{-1} + \underset{(0.0009492)}{0.0016261}\ \underline{BPOAD} + 5.330$$

$\underline{SE} = 0.236$, $\underline{DW} = 1.65$.

The monetary sector consists of the demand and supply functions of money and a monetary policy equation which determines the official discount rate. The demand for money, i.e., cash currency plus deposit currency outstanding, is considered as a function of the interest rate (the average lending rate by all banks) and gross national product at current prices. In equation (10.48), however, the interest rate variable was not retained as a significant explanatory variable. The supply function of money, on the other hand, was estimated in an inverted form, that is by using the interest rate as a dependent variable. Thus the rate of interest is positively related to the supply of deposit currency and to the official discount rate, which determines the cost of borrowing of commercial banks from the Bank of Japan.

As to monetary policy, Japanese monetary authorities have relied on two major policy tools, the discount rate policy and the credit rationing. Known as the "window regulation," credit rationing operates through administrative guidance and controls the amount of commercial credits to the public. Since it is difficult to quantify the latter policy because of lack of data, we postulate here that in the period under consideration the official discount rate has been geared to the two target variables, the rate of growth of gross national product at constant prices and the level of international reserves. In other words, the official discount rate is assumed to have been adjusted so as to maintain stable economic growth and external balance.

Although the coefficient of growth rate variable is not statistically significant in equation (10.50), the result supports the view that the discount rate policy followed rather closely the rules of the game of "gold standard." The long-run coefficient of international reserves is -0.00378, which means that a reduction of international reserves by $132 million will lead to a rise of the official discount rate by 0.5 percent.

10.3 Simulation Test of the Model

Before we proceed to the discussion of multipliers and the balance-of-payments adjustment periods, it will be necessary to evaluate how our model traces the behavior of actual data within the sample period. For this purpose we run a so-called final simulation test; that is, a simulation using observed values of the exogenous variable and values of lagged endogenous variables generated within the model.

Although there are various nonlinearities in the present model, an examination of the system reveals that it has the following simple structure. Let the vector of endogenous variables be divided into subvectors, $\underline{y}_1$, $\underline{y}_2$, and $\underline{y}_3$, with $\underline{n}_1$, $\underline{n}_2$ and $\underline{n}_3$ elements, respectively. In each period variables in the first block can be determined recursively, given the values of predetermined variables:

$$\underline{y}_{11} = \underline{f}_{11}(\underline{z}),$$

$$\underline{y}_{1\underline{i}} = \underline{f}_{1\underline{i}}(\underline{y}_{11},\ldots,\underline{y}_{1,\underline{i}-1};\ \underline{z}),\quad \underline{i} = 2,\ldots,\underline{n}_1,$$

where $\underline{z}$ is the vector of predetermined variables.

Variables in the second block must be solved simultaneously. But fortunately it turns out that the equations in the second block have the following form:

$$A\underline{y}_2 = \underline{f}_2(\underline{y}_1;\ \underline{z})$$

where A is a coefficient matrix whose elements depend only upon $\underline{y}_1$ and $\underline{z}$. Since the current values of A and $\underline{f}_2$ can be computed, we can solve the above system as

$$\underline{y}_2 = A^{-1}\underline{f}_2$$

for each period.

Finally, variables in the third block can again be determined recursively once $\underline{y}_1$ and $\underline{y}_2$ are known:

$$\underline{y}_{31} = \underline{f}_{31}(\underline{y}_1, \underline{y}_2;\ \underline{z})$$

$$\underline{y}_{3\underline{i}} = \underline{f}_{3\underline{i}}(\underline{y}_{31}, \ldots, \underline{y}_{3,\underline{i}-1}, \underline{y}_1, \underline{y}_2; \underline{z}), \quad \underline{i} = 2, \ldots, \underline{n}_3.$$

In the present model, these three blocks involve 16, 17, and 17 endogeneous variables, respectively. They are:

Block 1: XGM, XGO, XSTI, XSIO, MSID, MSIO, KLJW, IPE/PIPE KPE/PIPE, CCA/PIPE, PIPE, PIRC, PCP, PII, PGNP, YDIV;

Block 2: CP/PCP, IRC/PIRC, II/PII, MGR, MGO, MSTI, MSO, XSID, KDJW, BPG, BPI, BPC, GNP, YP, TP, TRP, YDP;

Block 3: YN, YC, TC, SC, GNPS, KDWJ, KLWJ+KOWJ, KOJW, BPL, BPB, BPS, BPO, GFE, KI, D, RBL, ROD.

In Figs. 10.1-10.8, we exhibit the comparison of actual and simulated values of various subsections of the balance of payments. As is well known, estimation of a net balance from separate estimation of its components is generally not very successful, because a relatively small percentage error in the first component will result in a large percentage error in the balance. Moreover, when the individual component has a strong upward trend, the same percentage error in the individual component will become more serious in later periods. The final simulation results presented in Figs. 10.1-10.8 seem to indicate that, in spite of the above difficulties, our model reproduces the general pattern of the actual time path of the economy to a tolerable extent. The model traces fairly well the cyclical movements of various balances. However, it underestimates the

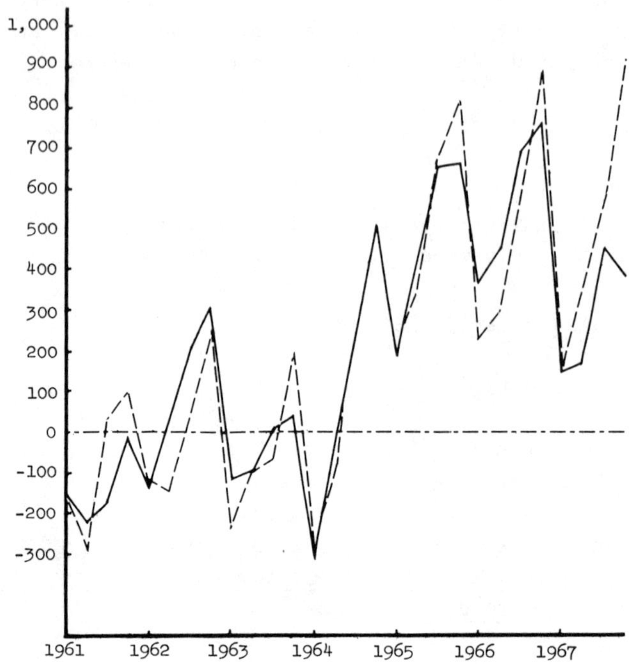

Fig. 10.2. Balance on Goods Account ($ million)
——— Actual, ----- Computed

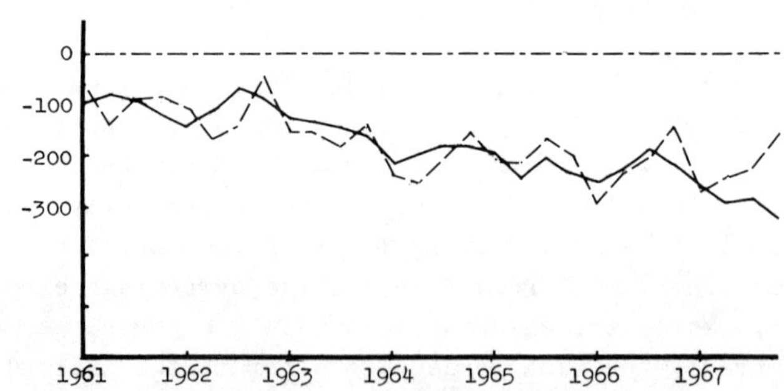

Fig. 10.3. Balance on Service Account ($ million)
——— Actual, ----- Computed

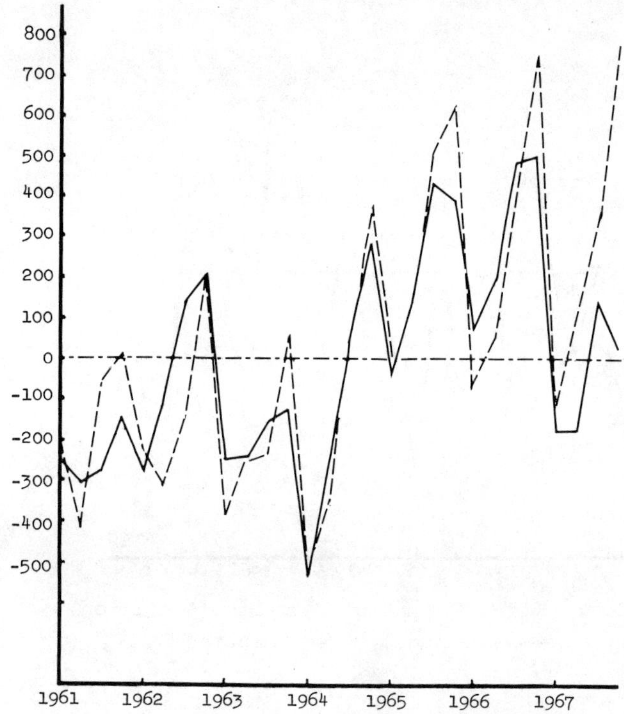

Fig. 10.4. Balance on Current Account ($ million)
——— Actual, ----- Computed

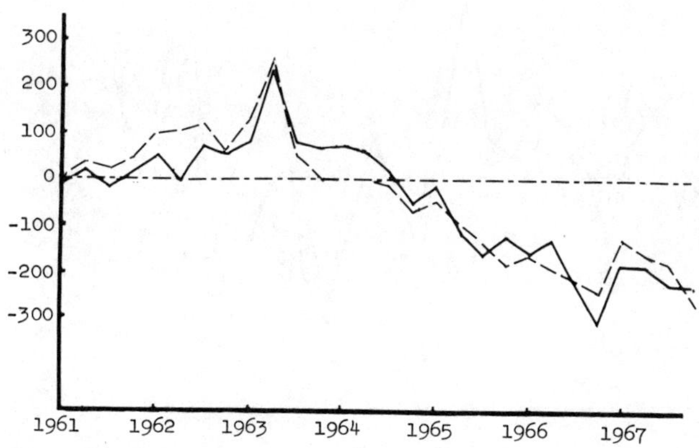

Fig. 10.5. Balance on Long-Term Capital Account ($ million)
——— Actual, ----- Computed

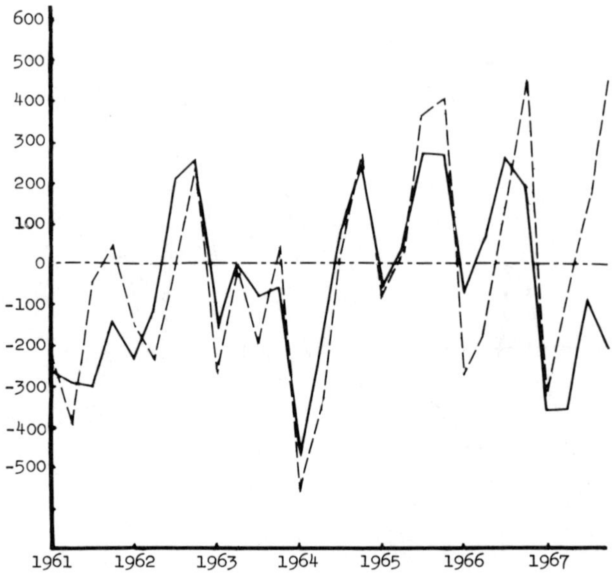

Fig. 10.6. Basic Balance of Payments ($ million)
——— Actual, ----- Computed

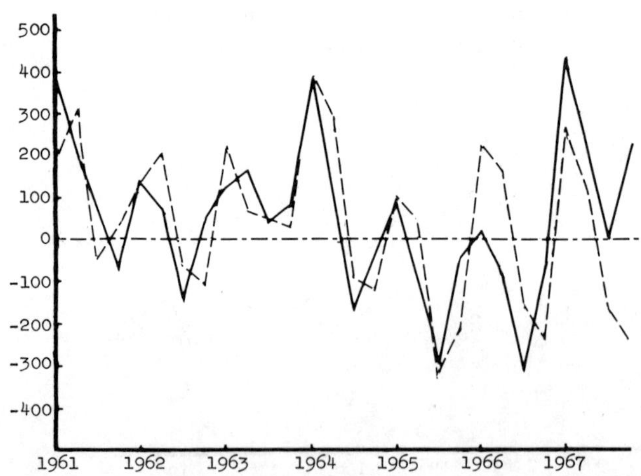

Fig. 10.7. Balance on Short-Term Capital Account ($ million)

——— Actual, ----- Computed

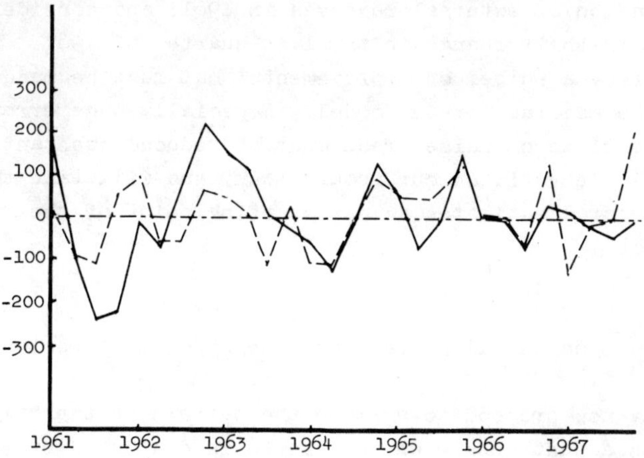

Fig. 10.8. Balance of Official Monetary Movements
($ million)
—— Actual, ----- Computed

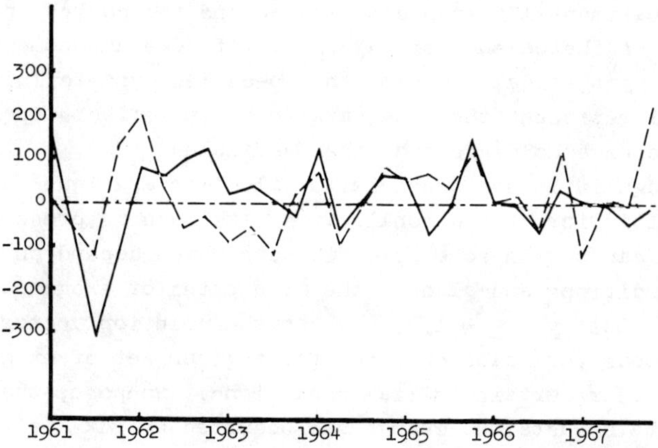

Fig. 10.9. Changes in Gold and Foreign Exchange
Reserves ($ million)
—— Actual, ----- Computed

sharp reduction of external reserves in 1961, and considerably overestimates their change in the last quarter of 1967. There is, of course, a number of improvements that must be made to increase the accuracy of our model. Especially, the errors in the balance of merchandise trade must be reduced substantially. But we shall leave it as our future task, and will take the above structural estimates as our starting point of the further exploration.

10.4 Dynamic Multipliers and the Adjustment Periods

We may now proceed to examine the pattern of the balance of payments adjustments when the system is disturbed by some autonomous change. In the actual economy the time paths of exogenous variables are highly varied, and it is impossible to identify one single cause of external imbalance or to observe the process of adjustment confined to that particular disturbance. Once the model structure is estimated, however, we can isolate experimentally each disturbance and the corresponding adjustment of the balance of payments. If some autonomous change is hypothetically given, the so-called dynamic multipliers will represent the time pattern of its effects upon the external reserve holdings and other variables.

Although it is not possible to calculate a unique set of dynamic multipliers for a nonlinear system such as present model, one can obtain some specific sets which depend on the initial conditions and also on the time paths of exogenous variables. Let y_t ($t = 1,2,\ldots$) be the solution vector of the endogenous variables obtained for a given set of exogenous variables under certain initial conditions. Suppose, then, that a certain sustained change has occurred by Δx (a scalar), which may be a sustained change in some exogenous variable (or an autonomous shift in some function). Let y_t^* ($t = 1,2,\ldots$) be the corresponding solution vector obtained under the same initial conditions but for the adjusted set of exogenous variables (or the modified constant term). Then, the dynamic multiplier effects of this autonomous change can be computed as

$$(y_{it}^* - y_{it})/\Delta x \qquad i = 1,2,\ldots,n \quad t = 1,2,\ldots .$$

We used the sample period, final simulation as our control solution, and computed dynamic multiplier effects of various autonomous changes for two alternative systems: a system in which the official discount rate is treated as exogenous, on the one hand, and one in which the discount rate policy is endogenized according to our estimated equation, on the other. Table 10.1 presents these two sets of dynamic multiplier effects of selected autonomous changes upon the gross national product <u>at constant prices</u> and the gold and foreign exchange reserves.

As can be seen from the table, when the official discount rate is geared to the balance of payments situation, external equilibrium will be restored (in the sense that the original change in international reserves will be terminated) in 5-9 quarters after the occurence of autonomous disturbance. The length of the adjustment period in the above sense depends on the character of the disturbance: 5 quarters for <u>II</u>, 6 quarters for <u>G</u> and <u>IPE</u>, 7 quarters for <u>IRC</u>, <u>TC</u>, and <u>TP</u>, 8 quarters for <u>CP</u> and <u>BPT</u>, and 9 quarters for <u>XGM</u>, <u>XGO</u>, <u>MGR</u>, and <u>MGO</u>. Generally speaking, the disturbance originating in the domestic sector (except for a shift of the consumption function) is adjusted in a relatively shorted period (5-7 quarters) than the one originating in the external sector (8-9 quarters). It is interesting to note that the adjustment process exhibits a damped oscillation, and that the effects of the changes in the official discount rate are such that they not only terminate the changes in international reserves caused by the disturbance but also regain the initial level of international reserves in an additional round of the adjustment period.

Another important finding of this study is that there exist sharp differences between the dynamic multipliers computed with and without the balance of payments adjustment mechanism. The multipliers computed from macroeconometric models usually disregard the balance of payments adjustment.[6] Comparing the multiplier effects of various autonomous changes upon real GNP in the two systems given in Table 10.1, however, it can be seen that the multipliers disregarding the balance of payments adjustment tend to overestimate the multiplier effects to a considerable extent if the relevant autonomous changes induce the balance of payments deficit, and vice versa.

TABLE 10.1. DYNAMIC MULTIPLIER EFFECTS OF VARIOUS AUTONOMOUS CHANGES UPON THE GROSS NATIONAL PRODUCT AT CONSTANT PRICES AND CHANGES IN INTERNATIONAL RESERVES

Figures represent the effects of an autonomous increase in each variable by ¥ 100 billion. Changes in gross national product are measured by ¥ 100 billion, and those in international reserves by $1 million.

	G				IPE				IRC			
	ROD exogenous		ROD endogenous		ROD exogenous		ROD endogeneous		ROD exogenous		ROD endogenous	
Period	GNP	ΔGFE	GNP	ΔGFE	GNP	ΔGFE	GNP	ΔGFE	GNP	ΔGFE	GNP	ΔGFE
1	2.26	-28.6	2.26	-28.6	2.19	-38.6	2.19	-38.6	2.10	-37.7	2.10	-37.7
2	1.90	-23.7	1.84	-22.5	2.10	-37.6	2.03	-36.2	2.89	-53.0	2.82	-51.7
3	2.84	-42.0	2.70	-39.2	3.23	-58.4	3.05	-54.9	4.22	-78.2	4.01	-74.3
4	2.02	-28.2	1.63	-21.1	2.40	-45.7	1.92	-36.2	4.12	-79.9	3.58	-69.1
5	2.48	-41.1	1.81	-28.7	3.08	-61.6	2.21	-45.2	4.58	-90.2	3.52	-70.0
6	1.45	-20.0	0.40	- 0.3	1.92	-37.7	0.51	-11.3	3.59	-70.2	1.77	-36.2
7	0.75	- 8.3	-0.73	19.1	1.51	-31.3	-0.54	6.5	3.05	-62.0	0.29	-11.1
8	0.73	- 4.9	-0.83	26.1	1.00	-19.9	-1.27	25.2	2.11	-42.8	-1.11	20.8
9	0.60	- 3.2	-1.24	33.1	1.19	-24.5	-1.57	30.1	2.13	-44.4	-1.91	35.2
10	1.58	-19.7	-0.11	13.8	1.99	-37.2	-0.78	18.0	2.82	-54.4	-1.50	31.2
11	1.05	- 9.1	-0.74	27.8	1.67	-31.6	-1.43	32.2	2.43	-48.7	-2.53	52.6
12	1.74	-24.8	0.60	1.4	2.16	-44.0	-0.23	9.8	3.02	-62.6	-1.08	29.0
13	1.67	-23.6	0.45	3.6	2.38	-48.4	-0.29	10.0	3.30	-68.5	-1.26	31.7
14	1.86	-29.0	0.79	- 6.4	2.67	-54.6	0.11	- 0.9	3.94	-80.0	-0.47	12.4
15	1.54	-22.0	0.54	- 1.4	2.43	-49.0	-0.15	4.4	3.62	-72.5	-0.84	19.2
16	0.94	-11.3	0.20	3.7	1.68	-36.0	-0.41	7.5	3.03	-62.6	-0.48	10.2
17	1.27	-17.1	0.22	3.5	2.21	-44.9	-0.42	7.4	3.42	-68.3	-0.86	16.3
18	0.99	-11.2	-0.24	12.5	1.97	-39.1	-0.95	17.4	3.31	-64.2	-1.34	24.5
19	1.11	-12.8	-0.02	8.9	2.11	-41.5	-0.69	13.4	3.20	-62.0	-1.25	23.7
20	0.86	- 7.4	-0.02	9.9	1.61	-32.0	-0.70	14.5	2.69	-51.8	-0.90	18.3
21	1.24	-15.8	0.34	2.6	2.29	-46.5	-0.24	5.2	3.25	-64.8	-0.72	14.2
22	1.33	-17.7	0.58	- 2.5	2.39	-48.1	-0.01	0.8	3.54	-69.3	-0.28	5.7
23	1.20	-15.6	0.75	- 6.3	2.34	-47.9	0.36	- 7.0	3.36	-66.6	0.26	- 5.1
24	1.10	-13.8	0.95	-11.2	1.99	-41.5	0.62	-13.3	3.13	-61.7	1.08	-22.1
25	1.11	-14.2	0.88	- 9.7	2.31	-48.0	0.70	-14.9	3.38	-67.3	1.06	-21.6
26	1.23	-16.2	0.94	-10.6	2.51	-50.7	0.71	-14.8	3.89	-74.6	1.35	-25.7
27	1.03	-12.1	0.77	- 7.1	2.31	-46.9	0.67	-13.9	3.53	-67.7	1.35	-25.6
28	0.94	-10.8	0.64	- 4.8	2.00	-42.1	0.45	-10.3	3.29	-64.4	1.31	-25.5

TABLE 10.1. CONTINUED

Period	CP				TC				TP			
	ROD exogenous		ROD endogenous		ROD exogenous		ROD endogenous		ROD exogenous		ROD endogenous	
	GNP	ΔGFE	GNP	ΔGFE	GNP	ΔGFE	GNP	ΔGFE	GNP	ΔGFE	GNP	ΔGFE
1	2.11	-35.4	2.11	-35.4	0.00	0.0	0.00	0.0	-0.74	12.6	-0.74	12.6
2	2.18	-37.6	2.12	-36.4	-1.24	22.2	-1.24	22.2	-0.80	14.0	-0.77	13.5
3	3.49	-61.7	3.32	-58.3	-1.20	21.6	-1.16	20.9	-1.23	22.1	-1.17	20.9
4	3.22	-59.7	2.76	-50.5	-1.65	31.9	-1.55	29.9	-1.13	21.2	-0.96	17.9
5	4.31	-81.2	3.45	-64.8	-1.43	25.9	-1.17	20.9	-1.44	27.4	-1.12	21.4
6	3.71	-67.3	2.25	-39.9	-1.43	27.9	-0.94	18.8	-1.17	21.6	-0.63	11.6
7	3.59	-66.2	1.37	-24.9	-1.41	27.5	-0.59	12.3	-1.08	20.6	-0.24	5.3
8	3.15	-57.8	0.51	- 5.5	-0.50	11.1	0.57	- 9.9	-0.87	16.5	0.12	- 2.9
9	3.47	-63.8	0.06	3.5	-0.93	18.9	0.47	- 8.3	-0.91	17.5	0.37	- 7.4
10	4.34	-77.9	0.57	- 2.9	-0.75	14.7	0.80	-15.7	-1.20	21.9	0.15	- 4.6
11	3.92	-71.7	-0.63	21.0	-1.02	20.5	0.79	-16.0	-1.01	18.9	0.58	-13.4
12	4.19	-82.1	0.17	7.5	-0.80	16.2	0.69	-16.9	-1.19	23.7	0.10	- 5.2
13	4.54	-87.9	-0.13	14.9	-1.21	25.0	0.38	-10.0	-1.24	24.5	0.21	- 7.5
14	5.11	-98.9	0.35	2.0	-1.44	28.7	0.03	- 2.1	-1.44	28.5	-0.04	- 1.2
15	4.67	-88.5	-0.40	17.6	-1.31	26.5	0.15	- 3.8	-1.28	24.7	0.15	- 5.3
16	3.84	-73.8	-0.43	18.0	-1.13	23.6	-0.02	0.4	-1.01	20.2	0.13	- 4.3
17	4.72	-86.8	-0.49	19.5	-1.16	23.8	0.22	- 3.6	-1.23	23.4	0.20	- 5.6
18	4.92	-89.7	-0.74	22.3	-1.24	25.1	0.28	- 4.1	-1.21	22.5	0.36	- 8.3
19	4.81	-87.3	-0.94	27.3	-1.07	21.5	0.41	- 7.4	-1.19	22.1	0.36	- 8.7
20	4.16	-75.1	-0.73	24.5	-0.88	17.9	0.36	- 6.7	-0.97	17.7	0.31	- 8.3
21	5.06	-93.6	-0.54	21.3	-1.16	23.7	0.26	- 5.0	-1.23	23.3	0.22	- 6.5
22	5.35	-99.9	-0.25	13.2	-1.24	25.3	0.15	- 2.7	-1.29	24.4	0.12	- 4.1
23	4.88	-91.8	-0.26	13.5	-1.23	25.2	-0.06	1.2	-1.17	22.4	0.02	- 2.2
24	4.30	-79.9	0.32	1.2	-1.01	21.2	-0.19	4.4	-1.02	19.3	-0.19	2.4
25	4.83	-89.5	0.28	2.8	-1.25	26.1	-0.31	7.0	-1.12	21.2	-0.18	2.1
26	5.33	-97.9	0.51	- 3.3	-1.33	27.0	-0.33	7.2	-1.24	23.2	-0.26	3.8
27	4.76	-86.6	0.42	- 1.0	-1.24	25.3	-0.37	8.0	-1.08	19.8	-0.25	3.6
28	4.39	-80.9	0.72	- 7.4	-1.05	22.3	-0.27	6.5	-0.99	18.4	-0.29	4.7

TABLE 10.1. CONTINUED

Period	II				XGM				XGO			
	ROD exogenous		ROD endogenous		ROD exogenous		ROD endogenous		ROD exogenous		ROD endogenous	
	GNP	ΔGFE	GNP	ΔGFE	GNP	ΔGFE	GNP	ΔGFE	GNP	ΔGFE	GNP	ΔGFE
1	1.95	-36.9	1.95	-36.9	2.49	62.7	2.49	62.7	2.49	74.0	2.49	74.0
2	1.11	-22.6	1.05	-21.4	2.10	68.2	2.11	67.9	2.10	79.4	2.12	78.9
3	1.64	-32.4	1.50	-29.6	3.14	48.3	3.25	46.3	3.14	59.2	3.27	56.5
4	0.53	-12.2	0.16	- 4.9	2.23	63.3	2.48	58.3	2.22	73.8	2.55	67.2
5	0.70	-20.0	0.10	- 8.5	2.75	49.6	3.35	38.0	2.73	59.9	3.50	45.1
6	-0.26	0.9	-1.16	17.6	1.62	73.6	2.72	52.6	1.60	83.5	2.98	57.3
7	-0.97	14.0	-2.16	35.8	0.86	86.8	2.76	50.9	0.83	96.4	3.17	52.4
8	-0.44	8.6	-1.56	30.7	0.84	90.8	3.38	40.1	0.81	100.1	3.87	39.0
9	-0.67	12.6	-1.86	36.3	0.71	92.9	4.26	21.8	0.67	101.9	4.90	17.3
10	0.36	- 5.5	-0.48	11.5	1.78	75.2	6.33	-15.8	1.74	83.8	7.07	-22.5
11	-0.07	3.9	-0.78	19.2	1.19	87.1	6.95	-29.9	1.16	95.4	7.82	-40.0
12	0.72	-13.4	0.59	- 9.6	1.95	70.3	7.76	-57.1	1.92	78.2	8.52	-66.6
13	0.47	- 8.7	0.38	- 6.3	1.88	71.8	8.50	-72.0	1.84	79.5	9.32	-82.9
14	0.39	- 8.9	0.38	- 8.8	2.09	66.3	8.98	-77.0	2.04	73.7	9.77	-86.8
15	0.25	- 5.3	0.33	- 7.4	1.74	74.2	8.73	-69.5	1.69	81.3	9.46	-78.2
16	-0.22	3.5	-0.16	1.0	1.08	86.4	6.75	-33.6	1.04	93.1	7.29	-38.8
17	-0.03	- 0.1	-0.11	0.6	1.45	80.3	7.56	-42.1	1.40	86.7	8.14	-47.9
18	-0.38	7.3	-0.57	10.4	1.16	86.9	7.13	-29.1	1.10	93.2	7.69	-34.5
19	-0.12	2.7	-0.18	3.5	1.28	85.4	6.77	-21.6	1.22	91.4	7.22	-25.1
20	-0.15	4.0	-0.11	2.9	1.00	91.7	5.05	12.1	0.95	97.2	5.31	11.9
21	0.05	- 0.5	0.20	- 3.7	1.43	82.8	5.98	- 7.3	1.36	88.1	6.24	- 7.7
22	0.10	- 1.4	0.42	- 7.9	1.53	80.9	5.85	- 3.1	1.46	86.0	6.01	- 1.9
23	0.08	- 1.4	0.56	-11.3	1.39	83.5	4.99	12.5	1.32	88.3	5.00	16.4
24	-.13	- 2.8	0.65	-14.0	1.27	86.0	3.76	37.9	1.21	90.4	3.64	44.5
25	0.01	- 0.4	0.49	-10.6	1.29	85.8	4.22	28.1	1.22	89.9	4.10	34.3
26	0.01	- 0.3	0.41	- 8.6	1.43	83.7	4.59	22.5	1.36	87.7	4.44	28.6
27	-0.07	1.5	0.23	- 4.7	1.21	88.6	3.87	36.4	1.13	92.2	3.66	43.3
28	-0.05	1.2	0.07	- 1.1	1.11	90.4	3.43	43.7	1.04	93.6	3.24	50.0

TABLE 10.1. CONTINUED

Period	MGR				MGO				BPT			
	ROD exogenous		ROD endogenous		ROD exogenous		ROD endogenous		ROD exogenous		ROD endogenous	
	GNP	ΔGFE	GNP	ΔGFE	GNP	ΔGFE	GNP	ΔGFE	GNP	ΔGFE	GNP	ΔGFE
1	-2.87	-85.5	-2.87	-85.5	-2.87	-85.5	-2.87	-85.5	0.00	95.7	0.00	95.7
2	-2.41	-91.9	-2.45	-91.3	-2.41	-91.9	-2.45	-91.3	0.00	95.7	0.09	94.0
3	-3.59	-69.0	-3.74	-66.0	-3.59	-69.0	-3.74	-66.0	0.00	95.7	0.27	90.4
4	-2.55	-85.7	-2.91	-78.5	-2.55	-85.7	-2.91	-78.5	0.00	95.7	0.69	81.8
5	-3.14	-69.7	-3.99	-53.7	-3.14	-69.7	-3.99	-53.7	0.00	95.7	1.40	69.2
6	-1.86	-96.2	-3.39	-67.8	-1.86	-96.2	-3.39	-67.8	0.00	95.7	2.40	50.9
7	-0.91	-111.3	-3.55	-62.8	-0.91	-111.3	-3.55	-62.8	0.00	95.7	3.82	25.3
8	-0.86	-116.7	-4.25	-49.9	-0.86	-116.7	-4.25	-49.9	0.00	95.7	4.61	5.0
9	-0.54	-121.6	-5.23	-29.2	-0.54	-121.6	-5.23	-29.2	0.00	95.7	6.02	-22.8
10	-2.06	-96.3	-7.68	14.9	-2.06	-96.3	-7.68	14.9	0.00	95.7	6.74	-37.6
11	-1.19	-113.5	-8.29	30.3	-1.19	-113.5	-8.29	30.3	0.00	95.7	7.99	-66.5
12	-2.38	-87.6	-9.22	63.4	-2.38	-87.6	-9.22	63.4	0.00	95.7	7.06	-59.9
13	-2.16	-92.0	-10.10	81.0	-2.16	-92.0	-10.10	81.0	0.00	95.7	7.85	-74.6
14	-2.52	-82.2	-10.63	86.6	-2.52	-82.2	-10.63	86.6	0.00	95.7	7.91	-68.0
15	-2.06	-92.3	-10.66	84.6	-2.06	-92.3	-10.66	84.6	0.00	95.7	7.85	-64.5
16	-1.19	-107.3	-8.03	39.5	-1.19	-107.3	-8.03	39.5	0.00	95.7	6.25	-34.8
17	-1.66	-99.1	-9.35	57.9	-1.66	-99.1	-9.35	57.9	0.00	95.7	7.08	-44.4
18	-1.14	-109.8	-8.38	33.1	-1.14	-109.8	-8.38	33.1	0.00	95.7	7.13	-41.6
19	-1.40	-105.9	-8.36	32.6	-1.40	-105.9	-8.36	32.6	0.00	95.7	6.50	-30.2
20	-0.98	-115.0	-5.84	-17.8	-0.98	-115.0	-5.84	-17.8	0.00	95.7	4.76	2.8
21	-1.59	-101.7	-7.59	20.0	-1.59	-101.7	-7.59	20.0	0.00	95.7	5.31	- 9.2
22	-1.71	-99.4	-7.56	15.8	-1.71	-99.4	-7.56	15.8	0.00	95.7	4.90	0.5
23	-1.57	-101.4	-6.65	1.3	-1.57	-101.4	-6.65	1.3	0.00	95.7	3.83	20.5
24	-1.46	-103.3	-5.20	-29.2	-1.46	-103.3	-5.20	-29.2	0.00	95.7	2.44	49.9
25	-1.43	-103.5	-5.75	-15.6	-1.43	-103.5	-5.75	-15.6	0.00	95.7	2.91	39.4
26	-1.61	-100.4	-6.44	- 4.5	-1.61	-100.4	-6.44	- 4.5	0.00	95.7	3.18	34.9
27	-1.29	-106.9	-5.10	-30.6	-1.29	-106.9	-5.10	-30.6	0.00	95.7	2.60	45.7
28	-1.20	-108.2	-4.49	-41.1	-1.20	-108.2	-4.49	-41.1	0.00	95.7	2.34	49.7

The above analysis thus indicates that under the fixed exchange rate system, export expansion is of primary importance in stimulating economic growth. First, it expands the aggregate demand to a larger extent than other domestic expenditures through its direct and indirect effects (by indirect effect I mean an expansion of effective demand stimulated by the accumulation of external reserves); second, through this indirect effect it accelerates domestic capital formation; and finally, an expansion of exports contributes to enlarge the national wealth through an induced increase in foreign long-term investments. We may therefore conclude that the above consideration clarifies the deep-rooted tendency of the post-war Japanese economic policy toward export-oriented expansion.

Appendix 10A. List of Variables

10A.1 Endogenous Variables

BPB = basic balance of payments ($ million)

BPC = current account balance ($ million)

BPG = balance of trade ($ million)

BPI = balance on service accounts ($ million)

BPL = balance on long-term capital accounts ($ million)

BPO = balance of official monetary movements ($ million)

BPS = balance on short-term capital account, including commercial banking sector ($ million)

CCA = provisions for the consumption of fixed capital (¥ billion)

CP = personal consumption expenditures at constant prices (¥ billion)

D = total money supply (cash currency plus deposit money), end of period (¥ billion)

GFE = gold and foreign exchange reserves ($ million)

GNP = gross national product (¥ billion)

GNPS = seasonally adjusted gross national product at constant prices (¥ billion)

II = inventory investment at constant prices (¥ billion)

IPE = private investment in machinery and equipment at constant prices (¥ billion)

IRC = private investment in dwellings at constant prices (¥ billion)

KDJW = cumulated direct investment to other countries ($ million)
KDWJ = cumulated direct investment from other countries ($ million)
KI = inventory stock (¥ billion
KLJW = cumulated long-term loans to other countries ($ million)
KLWJ
+ KOWM = cumulated long-term investment from other countries other than direct investment ($ million)
KOJW = cumulated other long-term investments to other countries ($ million)
KPE = fixed capital stock (¥ billion)
MGO = imports of commodities other than raw material and material fuel ($ million)
MGR = imports of raw material and mineral fuel ($ million)
MSID = payments on investment income account, direct investment ($ million)
MSIO = payments on investment income account, other investments ($ million)
MSO = imports of other services ($ million)
MSTI = payments on transportation and insurance account ($ million)
PCP = implicit deflator for private consumption expenditure (base year = 1960)
PGNP = implicit deflator for gross national product (base year = 1960)
PII = implicit deflator for investory investment (base year = 1960
PIPE = implicit deflator for private investment in machinery and equipment (base year = 1960)
PIRC = implicit deflator for private investment in dwellings (base year = 1960)
RBL = average interest rate on loans of all banks (Sen (= one-hundredth yen) per diem)
ROD = official discount rate, end of period (% per annum)
SC = savings of private corporations (¥billion)
TC = direct taxes and charges on private corporations (¥ billion)
TP = direct taxes and charges on personal income (¥ billion)
TRP = current personal transfers (¥ billion)
XGM = exports of machinery and equipment ($ million)
XGO = exports of other commodities ($ million)

XSID = receipts on investment income account, direct investment ($ million)

XSIO = receipts on investment income account, other investments ($ million)

XSTI = receipts on transportation and insurance account ($ million)

YC = corporate income (¥ billion)

YDIV = corporate transfers to private sector (¥ billion)

YN = national income (¥ billion)

YP = personal income (¥ billion)

YPD = personal disposable income (¥ billion)

10A.2. Exogenous Variables

BPE = net errors and omissions in the balance of payments ($ million)

BPOAD = variable explaining major discrepancies between the balance of official monetary movements and the changes in gold and foreign exchange reserves, consisting of the special borrowings of the Bank of Japan from the U.S. banks in 1961-1962 and of the inclusion of gold transche into the foreign exchange reserves in March 1963 ($ million)

BPT = balance on transfer account ($ million)

CC = cash currency outstanding, end of period (¥ billion)

FR = the index of tramper freight rate (1960 = 100)

G = government expenditures (¥ billion)

GNPAS = gross national product of the United States at current prices, seasonally adjusted annual rate ($ billion)

N = total population (100 million)

PMGO = import price index of other commodities (1965 = 1.000)

PMGR = import price index of raw materials and mineral fuel (1965 = 1.000)

PXGM = export price index of machinery and equipment (1965 = 1.000)

PXGO = export price index of other commodities (1965 = 1.000)

Q1 = seasonal dummy variable, taking the value 1 for the first quarter and 0 for the other quarters

Q2 = seasonal dummy variable, taking the value 1 for the second quarter and 0 for the other quarters

Q3 = seasonal dummy variable, taking the value 1 for the third quarter and 0 for the other quarters

Q1A = seasonal dummy variable, taking the value 1 for the first quarter in the years 1961-1964, 1 for the second quarter in the years 1965-1967, and 0 for the other quarters

Q3A = seasonal dummy variable, taking the value 1 for the third quarter in the years 1961-1964, 1 for the fourth quarter in the years 1965-1967, and 0 for the other quarters

Q2B = seasonal dummy variable, taking the value 0 for the years 1961-1963 and being identical to Q2 for the rest of the years

Q3C = seasonal dummy variable, being identical to Q3 for the years 1961-1963 and taking the value 0 for the rest of the years

QLF = dummy variable which represents the import liberalization of crude oil, taking the value 1 from the quarter 1962.IV on and 0 for the previous quarters

QLR63 = dummy variable which represents the liberalization of remittance of principal, taking the value 1 for the quarter 1963.II and 0 for the other quarters

QLR64 = dummy variable which represents the liberalization of remittance of investment income, taking the value 1 for the quarter 1964.II and 0 for the other quarters

QMC = dummy variable which represents the changes in import collateral policy

QSMS = dummy variable which represents the strike of seamen's union, taking the value 1 for the quarters 1965.IV-1966.I and 0 for the other quarters

QSS = dummy variable which represents an abnormal expansion of exports caused by the expectation of steel strike in the United States, taking the value 1 for the quarters 1964.III-1965.III and 0 for the other quarters

QVN = dummy variable which represents the effect of Vietnam war, taking the value 1 for the quarters 1964.II-1967.IV and 0 for the other quarters

QXC = dummy variable which represents the alteration of export classification, taking the value 1 for the quarters 1966.I-1967.IV and 0 for the other quarters

RHO = index of operating ratio of manufacturing industries (1965 = 100)

RLJA = long-term interest rate differential between Japan and the United States (long-term bond yield, Japan minus United States) (% per annum)

W = cash earning index of regular workers in the manufacturing industries (1965 average = 100)

XSO = exports of other services ($ million)

XTW = value of total world exports ($ million)

Notes

The present paper was written on the basis of the following two articles by the author: "Japan's Balance of Payments and Its Adjustment: A Quarterly Econometric Model," Discussion Paper no. 52, The Institute of Social and Econometric Research, Osaka University (May 1969); and "A Statistical Model of the Japanese Balance of Payments," a paper distributed at the London meeting of Project LINK (September, 1970). The author is indebted to Professor Michio Morishima for valuable comments on earlier drafts. He is also grateful to Mr. K. Nakagawa and Mrs. K. Matsuura for computational assistance.

1. See L. R. Kloek, and L. B. M. Mennes, "Simultaneous Equations Estimation Based on Principal Components of Predetermined Variables," Econometrica, vol. 28, no. 1 (January 1960).

2. L. R. Klein and Y. Shinkai, "An Econometric Model of Japan, 1930-1959," International Economic Review, vol. 4, no. 1 (January 1963), Chapter 12 in this volume.

3. S. Ichimura, L. R. Klein, S. Koizumi, K. Sato, and Y. Shinkai, "A Quarterly Econometric Model of Japan, 1952-1959," Osaka Economic Papers, vol. 12 (2), no. 23 (March 1964).

4. M. Tatemoto, T. Uchida, and T. Watanabe, A Stabilization Model for the Postwar Japanese Economy: 1954-1962," International Economic Review, vol. 8, no. 1 (February 1964). Chapter 14 this volume.

5. See Hannan Ezekiel and Chandrakant Patel, "Fluctuations in Japan's Balance of Payments and the Role of Short-Term Capital Flows, 1959-1966," IMF Staff Papers, vol. 14, no. 3 (November 1967), esp. pp. 421-422. These authors offer two explanations of this negative correlation. First, Japan's exports are generally financed by Japanese banks, while its imports are generally financed by foreign banks. Second, Japanese banks tend to use foreign funds to meet their need for boom periods at a time when the basic balance usually tends to deteriorate, and vice versa. The high rate of export financing by Japanese banks is primarily caused by the fact that the Bank of Japan has supplied credits required to finance exports at a very low interest rate to commercial banks in order to encourage Japanese exports.

6. Rhomberg's model in R. R. Rhomberg, "A Model of the Canadian Economy under Fixed and Fluctuating Exchange Rates," Journal of Political Economy, vol. 72, no. 1 (February 1964) is a notable exception.

Part V
Studies of Growth Models

11

The Pattern of Japanese Growth, 1914-1954

Hollis B. Chenery, Shuntaro Shishido, and Tsunehiko Watanabe

The paper presents a comprehensive method for analyzing structural change in a developing economy. The total change in output in each sector is expressed by means of an interindustry model as a function of four factors: (i) the change in the composition of domestic demand; (ii) the change in the volume of exports; (iii) the change in the volume of imports; and (iv) changes in technology and organization. The model is then applied to explain the process of industrialization in Japan from 1914 to 1954, during which period its economy was transformed from that of a typical underdeveloped country to that of an advanced society. The results show that less than a quarter of the increase in the share of industry in total output is due to in-

---

Econometrica, vol. 30, no. 1 (January 1962), pp. 98-139. Reprinted by courtesy of the Econometric Society and the authors

creases in exports and changes in domestic demand, while more than three quarters is traceable to changes in supply conditions, including substitution of domestic manufactures for both imported manufactures and primary products. Changes in technology and in labor productivity are also examined briefly.

11.1. Introduction

As the first Asiatic country to industrialize, Japan has great interest for the student of economic growth. In its present economic structure, as in many other aspects, Japan combines features of a modern industrial society with those of an underdeveloped economy. Since its per capita income is still relatively low, Japan does not fit many of the generalizations concerning the relation between income level and the structure of output and employment.

It is the purpose of this paper to present a method for the comparative study of growth patterns and to use it to explain some of the features of Japanese growth. There are two main characteristics of the proposed method. The first is the identification of "normal growth patterns" from a detailed statistical analysis of recent production and trade data for a large number of countries.[1] The second feature is the use of an interindustry model to specify the determinants of output and employment in each sector of the economy and to measure their effects.

These analytical tools are combined as follows in the study of Japan. We first determine the structure of the Japanese economy at twenty-year intervals - 1914, 1935, and 1954 - using the conceptual framework of the interindustry model. We then compare Japan's 1914 structure to the present normal pattern of production and trade for the levels of income and population then prevailing-$113 per capita income and 52 million inhabitants. The result is to show that in 1914 Japan was not very dissimilar to present day underdeveloped countries of the same income level and hence that most of the peculiarities of its economic structure have developed since that time.

The next part of the study (sections 11.3 and 11.4) uses an interindustry model to relate the observed changes in output and employment to changes in three sets of elements that are taken as autonomous: domestic demands, imports, and exports. This procedure has the effect of separating the internal effects of income growth, in which Japan is similar to other countries, from the external effects, which reflect its particular resource endowment. These measures, together with the normal growth pattern, provide a basis for analyzing the recent course of Japan's industrial development.[2]

The last part of the study is concerned with the effects of technological change and substitution. Here the empirical evidence is much less accurate, but several general relations can be identified. The interindustry analysis provides a measure of the total effect of technological change and substitution on each sector of production. Its main feature is the substitution of manufactured goods for primary products. Finally, a study of labor productivity shows a substantial difference between the evolution of the pattern of output and the pattern of employment, which is partially explainable by changes in foreign trade.

Our study does not get at the more basic determinants of growth: the level of savings, the adoption of new technology, the effects of specific resource endowments, or the importance of national policy. These factors enter the analysis only by inference. In limiting ourselves to the more directly measurable features, we hope to have demonstrated the advantages of an econometric approach to the study of the interdependent changes that comprise economic development. Our results may also help in the interpretation of some current theoretical concepts, such as "balanced growth" and "leading sectors."

11.2. The Structure of the Japanese Economy in 1914

The starting point of our analysis is nearly fifty years after the Meiji restoration of 1868 and at the end of a period which Rostow identifies as the Japanese "takeoff into sustained growth."[3] As Fig. 11.1 indicates, 1910 was the middle of a sixty-year span of steady growth in national income. Per capita income increased $2\frac{1}{2}$ times from 1880 to 1910, and

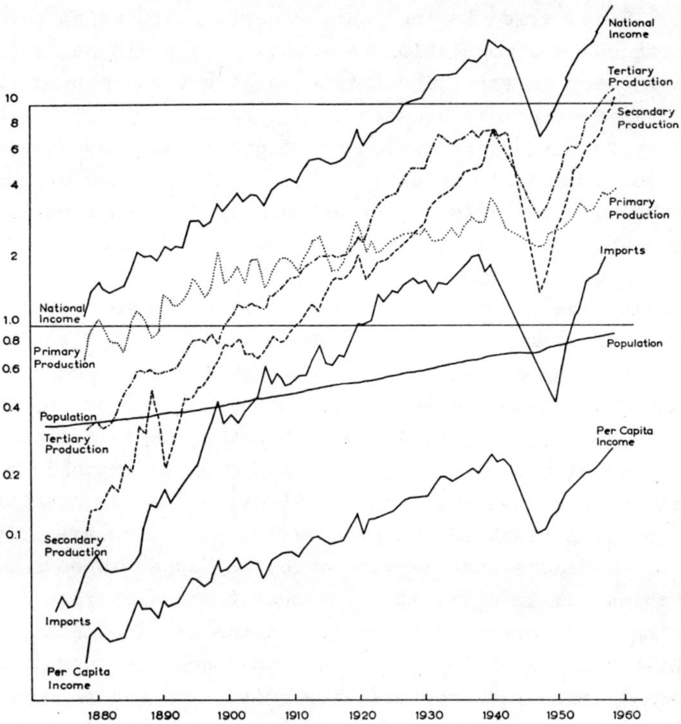

Fig. 11.1.

this performance was repeated from 1910 to 1940.[4]

Underlying the even progress in total output was a substantial variation in the growth rates of individual sectors. Until 1910, agriculture made a larger contribution than industry to the growth of total output,[5] although, as Fig. 11.1 shows, the annual growth rate in industry was 6.7 percent against 2.7 percent in agriculture. After 1910, however, there was a marked decline in agricultural growth, while industrial growth continued unchecked until 1940. 1914 therefore represents a period of transition from fairly balanced growth of industry and agriculture to one in which industry increasingly predominated.

We now wish to compare the economic structure that had evolved in Japan by 1914 to that of other countries at a similar stage in their growth. To make this comparison, we utilize a statistical analysis of production data in 14 sectors of industry and 38 countries in the postwar period,[6] in which per capita income and population were used to explain per capita output in each sector. The existence of uniform growth patterns (varying in some sectors with size of country) was confirmed by the high correlation coefficients and low standard errors for almost all industries. A parallel study of imports, using the same variables, gave an equally good explanation. Here the effects of size are more pronounced, since imports are a smaller fraction of total supply.[7]

These results provide a standard to which we can compare Japan in 1914. This is done in Table 11.1 by substituting Japan's per capita income and population for that year in the regression equations to determine the normal output for each sector. This method provides a much better basis for comparison than the usual approach of selecting one or two roughly similar countries, since the regression analysis is based on a large number of countries and the peculiarities of each are eliminated.

For the large sectors of production, Japan appears to be close to normal in agriculture, somewhat above average in manufacturing, and correspondingly low in the service sectors.

With the few exceptions, the comparisons of output in individual industrial sectors show quite a normal pattern. In column (2), the total output data is corrected to include only factory output, corresponding to the census data on which the regression equations are based. The comparison of these levels to the standard output (column 4) shows values above standard in six sectors and below standard in six, with the total for all manufacturing being 26 percent above normal. These variations are consistent with the hypothesis that Japan had a normal economic structure for her size and income level in 1914, since only one industry deviates from normality by more than one standard deviation and none by more than two.

Two corrections can be made to make Japan of 1914 more comparable to a present-day country of its income level. In the first place, the proportion of small-scale production in Japan was higher than is now typical. Allowance for this factor makes sectors like wood products and printing appear quite normal.[8] Secondly, the relatively high values of output in textiles and paper result from exports of these products. They become normal when the effect of exports is removed.

TABLE 11.1. COMPARISON OF ACTUAL AND STANDARD OUTPUTS, 1914

	Sector	Total Output (1)	Factory Output (2)	Present Standard Output (3)	Ratio (2)/(3) (4)
Factory Production (Value added)					
4.	Food, Beverages and Tobacco	14.52	6.45	5.28	1.22
5.	Textiles and Clothing	4.64	4.00	3.03	1.32
6.	Wood and Wood Products	.99	.27	.50	.54
7.	Pulp and Paper	.36	.30	.13	2.31
8.	Printing and Publishing	.64	.39	.52	.75
9.	Rubber Products	.08	.07	.16	.44
10.	Chemicals	1.53	1.28	.98	1.31
11.	Coal and Petroleum Products	.12	.12	.23	.52
12.	Non-metallic Mineral Products	.53	.41	.62	.66
13.	Metals	.91	.78	.89	.87
14.	Machinery	1.33	.97	.20	4.85
15.	Transport Equipment	1.40	1.14	.36	3.17
	Total Output	27.05	16.28	12.90	1.26
Aggregate Sectors (Net Product)[a]					Ratio (1)/(3)
1.	Agriculture	40.53		38.57	1.05
2-17.	Mining and Manufacturing	30.56		28.27	1.08
18-23.	Services	41.91		46.14	.91
	Per Capita Income	113.00		113.00	

[a]Standard net product in aggregate sectors was predicted from the equations in H. B. Chenery, "Patterns of Industrial Growth," American Economic Review, September 1960. The total is made to add to the actual net national product by multiplying each component by 1.08.

Source: Actual output from Table 11A.2, Appendix. Standard output derived from regression equations in H. B. Chenery, "Patterns of Industrial Growth," American Economic Review, September 1960, using national income of $113 and population of 52.58 million.

With these corrections, there are only four sectors in which significant differences from the standard remain. Rubber and petroleum refining are low because of the technological changes of the past fifty years and the rise in demand for their products in low income countries. The two high ones, machinery and transport equipment, are the only industries that show evidence of abnormal development resulting from government policy.

The import comparison given in Table 11.8 below also bears out the impression of normality. In marked contrast to later years, Japan in 1914 imported chemicals, paper, and metals in excess of the quantities that would be standard today; agricultural imports were substantially above normal due largely to raw cotton. The composition of Japanese imports in 1914 was therefore fairly normal for her income level, while imports as a whole were considerably higher than the present-day standard.[9]

It is in the pattern of exports that Japan in 1914 diverged most from the present low-income countries. Since there is great diversity in export patterns, a meaningful norm can be stated only in terms of large categories, such as primary and secondary products. Primary products (agricultural and mineral) typically comprise over 80 percent of exports in countries of less than $200 per capita income. In Japan, on the contrary, primary products have never accounted for as much as half of total exports. In 1914, textiles (mainly raw silk and cotton yarn) were about half of total exports, while primary products were less than 15 percent.[10] This difference is much less important than it might appear, however, because most of the manufactured exports (apart from cotton textiles) are the products of hand industry. Like many types of primary production, these handicrafts have labor as their main input and they purchase relatively little from other sectors of the economy. The same is true of raw silk production.

The early development of textile exports was one of the most significant features of the Japanese economy. They made up for the lack of exportable primary products and permitted greater than normal imports of both manufactured goods and foodstuffs. Without these extraordinary exports, the level of textile production would have been close to the standard.

The industrialization policy which the government had pursued for forty years prior to 1914 is shown by this analysis to have brought Japan up to a level of industrial output that is now the normal for the income level of $115 that then existed but not significantly above the normal. In only two sectors - machinery and transport equipment (mainly shipbuilding and railroad cars) - did government investment and subsidies result in abnormally high levels of output. The excess output in these two sectors is only about 10 percent of total factory production.

From this comparison, we conclude that in 1914 the factors which now make the Japanese economy so different from that of the underdeveloped countries had not yet had much effect. Deviations from the present normal patterns of production and imports were then no greater than would be found in a country chosen at random.[11]

11.3. The Analysis of Structural Change

We now seek to analyze the changes in output of individual sectors which took place during two twenty year periods, 1914-1935 and 1935-1954. We shall express the total change in production in each sector as a function of four component changes: (i) the change in the composition of domestic demand; (ii) the change in the volume of exports; (iii) the change in the volume of imports and (iv) changes in technology and organization. We take as a basis of comparison a growth pattern in which each element of supply and demand expands proportionately. Our procedure is first to measure the observed deviations from proportionate growth in production by sector and then to break them down into the effects of deviations in the four factors listed.

11.3.1. Basic Data.[12] The very detailed interindustry tables compiled in the Japanese Ministry of International Trade and Industry for the years 1951 and 1954 (summarized in Table 11A.8 of the Appendix) provide the basis for an interindustry analysis of earlier years. For 1935 and 1914, we estimated the outputs, imports, and elements of final demand for several hundred commodities on the same basis and then aggregated the data to a uniform 22-sector classification. The results are given in Tables 11A.1,2,3, and 4 of the Appendix. The logic of the input-output framework and a knowledge of the present uses of these commodities provides a basis for allocating commodities to intermediate or final use when other information is not available. Wherever possible, the estimates of various elements of domestic demand were made independently and then reconciled with the supply data.

The accuracy of the results can be evaluated only in general terms. The 1935 estimates are based mainly on census figures and seem reasonably accurate for the commodity-producing sectors, less so for the remainder. The import and export data for 1913-1915 are comparable in quality, but the production and use figures are much cruder. It can be said, however, that the input-output framework provides a number of checks on the consistency of estimates and hence makes the best use of data available from different sources.

11.3.2. The Model. The modified Leontief input-output model which is used here can be stated as follows:[13]

$$X_i^t - \sum_j a_{ij}^t X_j^t = Y_i^t + E_i^t - M_i^t \qquad (11.1)$$

$$(i = 1, \ldots, n;\ t = 1, 2, 3)$$

where

X_i^t is the output of commodity i in period t;

M_i^t is the import of commodity i in period t;

E_i^t is the export of commodity i in period t;

Y_i^t is the domestic final demand for commodity i in period t;

a_{ij}^t is the input coefficient for commodity i used in sector j in period t;

$\sum_j a_{ij}^t X_j^t$ is the intermediate use of commodity in all sectors of production.

The solution to (11.1) is of the form:[14]

$$(11.2) \qquad \underline{X}_{\underline{i}}^{\underline{t}} = \sum_{\underline{j}} \underline{r}_{\underline{ij}}^{\underline{t}}(\underline{Y}_{\underline{j}}^{\underline{t}} + \underline{E}_{\underline{j}}^{\underline{t}} - \underline{M}_{\underline{j}}^{\underline{t}}) \qquad (\underline{i} = 1,\ldots,\underline{n}).$$

To determine the solution corresponding to the assumption of proportionate growth between periods 1 and 2, we define the ratio of total domestic demand in the two periods as[15]

$$\lambda^{12} = \frac{\sum_{\underline{i}} \underline{Y}_{\underline{i}}^{2}}{\sum_{\underline{i}} \underline{Y}_{\underline{i}}^{1}} .$$

Given the properties of the Leontief model, if each of the three autonomous elements in (11.2) is multiplied by λ, the corresponding solution for each production level $(\underline{X}_{\underline{i}}^{\underline{p}})$ is λ times the initial level of output:

$$(11.3) \qquad \underline{X}_{\underline{i}}^{\underline{p}} = \lambda\underline{X}_{\underline{i}}^{1} = \sum_{\underline{j}} \underline{r}_{\underline{ij}}^{1}(\lambda\underline{Y}_{\underline{j}}^{1} + \lambda\underline{E}_{\underline{j}}^{1} - \lambda\underline{M}_{\underline{j}}^{1}).$$

We shall define the difference between the actual values in period 2 and values given by proportionate expansion of the system between periods 1 and 2 as

$$\delta\underline{X}_{\underline{i}}^{12} = \underline{X}_{\underline{i}}^{2} - \lambda\underline{X}_{\underline{i}}^{1},$$

$$\delta\underline{Y}_{\underline{i}}^{12} = \underline{Y}_{\underline{i}}^{2} - \lambda\underline{Y}_{\underline{i}}^{1},$$

$$\delta\underline{E}_{\underline{i}}^{12} = \underline{E}_{\underline{i}}^{2} - \lambda\underline{E}_{\underline{i}}^{1},$$

$$\delta\underline{M}_{\underline{i}}^{12} = \underline{M}_{\underline{i}}^{2} - \lambda\underline{M}_{\underline{i}}^{1}.$$

These differences will be called the <u>deviations from proportional expansion</u>, or "deviations" for short.

Using these definitions, the following expression can be derived for the deviations in production levels as a function of the deviations in the autonomous elements:[16]

$$(11.4) \qquad \delta\underline{X}_{\underline{i}}^{12} = \sum_{\underline{j}} \underline{r}_{\underline{ij}}^{2}(\delta\underline{Y}_{\underline{j}}^{12} + \delta\underline{E}_{\underline{j}}^{12} - \delta\underline{M}_{\underline{j}}^{12} - \lambda\underline{T}_{\underline{j}}^{12})$$

$$(\underline{i} = 1,\ldots,\underline{n})$$

where $\underline{T}_j^{12}$ is the change in intermediate use of commodity $\underline{j}$ in period 2 due to the change in technology between periods 1 and 2.

In this way, the deviation of production in each sector from proportional growth between periods 1 and 2 can be expressed as the sum of four terms:

(i) the effect of deviations in domestic demand:

$$\sum_{\underline{j}} \underline{r}_{\underline{ij}}^{2} \delta \underline{Y}_{\underline{j}}^{12};$$

(ii) the effect of deviations in exports:

$$\sum_{\underline{j}} \underline{r}_{\underline{ij}}^{2} \delta \underline{E}_{\underline{j}}^{12};$$

(iii) the effect of deviations in imports:

$$- \sum_{\underline{j}} \underline{r}_{\underline{ij}}^{2} \delta \underline{M}_{\underline{j}}^{12};$$

(iv) the effect of technological change:

$$-\lambda \sum_{\underline{j}} \underline{r}_{\underline{ij}}^{2} \underline{T}_{\underline{j}}^{12}, \quad \text{where} \quad \underline{T}_{\underline{j}}^{12} = \sum_{\underline{k}} (a_{\underline{jk}}^{1} - a_{\underline{jk}}^{2}) \underline{X}_{\underline{k}}^{1}.$$

11.3.3. An Example. The meaning of this breakdown of the variation in output levels can be clarified by means of a simple example. Assume a two-sector division of the economy into (1) primary production and (2) secondary production. The input coefficients are $a_{12} = .5$, $a_{21} = .25$ in period 1 and $a_{12} = .4$, $a_{21} = .3$ in period 2, giving the Leontief matrices shown in Table 11.2. Domestic demands, exports, and imports are given for the two periods. The production levels consistent with these assumptions are shown in line (6).

To analyze the change in production according to equation (11.4), we first compute λ, the ratio of the increase in domestic demands, which is 480/300 or 1.6. We then multiply all the variables in period 1 by this magnitude, as shown in Columns (3) and (4) in parentheses, to get the pattern of proportionate expansion. The deviations of the actual pattern from this standard are shown in the last two columns of Table

TABLE 11.2. EXAMPLE OF ANALYSIS OF DEVIATIONS IN PRODUCTION

	Elements	Period 1		Period 2[a]		Deviations	
		Sector 1 (1)	Sector 2 (2)	Sector 1 (3)	Sector 2 (4)	Sector 1 (5)	Sector 2 (6)
(1)	Leontief Matrix (I-A)	1.00 -.25	-.50 1.00	1.00 -.30	-.40 1.00		
(2)	Domestic Demand (Y)	200	100	280 (320)	200 (160)	-40	40
(3)	Exports (E)	74.7	0	0 (119.4)	110.0 (0)	-119.4	110.0
(4)	Imports (M)	45.4	29.3	72.0 (72.6)	38.0 (46.9)	-.6	-8.9
(5)	Technological Change (T)					-23.4	24.2
(6)	Production (X)	302.5	146.4	360.0 (483.9)	380.0 (234.2)	-123.9	145.8
	Analysis of Changes						
(7)	Inverse of Leontief Matrix $(L^2)^{-1}$			1.136 .341	.455 1.136		
(8)	Domestic Demand Effect					-27.3 (22%)	31.8 (22%)
(9)	Export Effect					-85.7 (68%)	84.3 (58%)
(10)	Import Effect					4.7 (-4%)	10.3 (7%)
(11)	Effect of technological change					-15.6 (13%)	19.5 (13%)
(12)	Total autonomous effects					-123.9	145.9

a Figures for $\lambda = 1.6$ are given in parentheses.

11.2. The fourth autonomous element, the effect of technological change, shows that with the new technology less of commodity 1 is required for the given combination of final outputs and more of commodity 2.

The second step in the analysis is to substitute these four autonomous deviations in equation (11.4) and to calculate their separate contributions to the total deviation in output. This requires a multiplication of each of them by the corresponding column in the inverse matrix for period 2 (row 7 in Table 11.2). The results are shown in the remainder of the Table. A check is provided by the fact that they add up to the previously computed total deviation in output in each sector.

Even in this extremely simple example, the relative importance of the several elements[17] is not intuitively obvious from the original data. Because of the opposite signs of the deviations in all elements except imports, the total effect of domestic demand and exports on production levels is less than the individual deviations in demand, for example. The contribution of each element in percentage terms to the total deviation in production is given in parentheses. It is apparent that when a large number of interrelated sectors is considered, a partial analysis is not likely to estimate the separate effects with any degree of accuracy.

11.3.4. Application to Japanese Data. For the Japanese case with which we are dealing, the calculation of the separate effects on output was made in the same way as in the example with one exception. Since we possess an input-output table only for the final period, 1954, it is not possible to calculate the changes in individual input coefficients. The total effect of these changes can be estimated, however, by comparing the actual intermediate demand in the earlier periods to the demand resulting from the use of 1954 technology with production levels of the first period (either 1914 or 1935).[18]

The main drawback to this procedure is that we are unable to distinguish between errors of estimation and technological change, since the latter is determined as a residual. Our only check on the calculation, therefore, comes from an evaluation of the "reasonableness" of the implied effects of technological change.

The method which is suggested is analogous to the removal of trend in analyzing cyclical variation. Here we are concerned with deviations from proportional expansion, since they produce the changes in the composition of output. Our proposal is to treat each variable as being composed of two parts, a proportional element and a deviation. The proportional elements are eliminated from the analysis, and we concern ourselves only with the relations among the deviations. The results can readily be translated into the original variables by adding the proportional elements, as is done in Table 11.6 below.

11.4. The Changing Pattern of Production and Trade

11.4.1. The General Course of Development. The four determinants of sector growth played very different roles in the two periods under consideration. In the first period, 1914-1935, domestic income was rising steadily at about 4.5 percent per year, and exports were increasing even more rapidly. By contrast, in 1954 the national income was only 17 percent above its 1935 level and per capita income was actually lower. In this second period the changes in the composition of production were almost as pronounced as in the first, but they represented the adaptation of the economy to a substantial fall in exports, to the loss of colonial supplies of raw materials, and to the change from military preparation to peace-time demands. We shall now trace the effects of these forces in each period and evaluate their importance for the whole forty-year span.[19]

In the period 1914-1935, the changes in the pattern of production were due almost entirely to the growth of domestic and foreign demand. Favorable competitive conditions in export markets, resulting from the European war of 1914-1918 and the Japanese devaluation of 1931, led to an annual growth of 7 percent in exports and prevented any shortage of imported goods despite the rapid growth of income.

The pattern of growth and its causes are summarized in Tables 11.3 and 11.4, in which the 22 productive sectors have been aggregated to seven. The slower growth of agriculture and food processing and the faster growth of finished manu-

TABLE 11.3. GROWTH IN SECTOR OUTPUT, 1914-1954 (BILLIONS OF 1951 YEN)

Sector[a]	1914			1935			1954			Indexes		
	Production (1)	Value Added (2)	% of (2) (3)	Production (4)	Value Added (5)	% of (5) (6)	Production (7)	Value Added (8)	% of (8) (9)	1935/1914	1954/1935	1954/1914
I. Primary Production												
A. Agriculture	1,016	784	36	1,397	1,079	22	1,502	1,160	17	138	108	147
B. Mining	150	92	4	267	164	3	425	256	4	178	156	278
Total Primary	1,166	876	40	1,664	1,242	26	1,927	1,416	21	142	114	162
II. Manufacturing												
A. Food	552	244	11	779	345	7	1,211	536	8	141	155	220
B. Textiles	420	78	4	2,012	373	8	2,123	392	.6	479	105	503
C. Other Finished Goods	390	117	5	1,753	537	11	2,146	661	10	458	85	564
D. Intermediate Products	316	59	3	1,497	267	6	3,329	595	9	450	223	1,004
Total Manufacturing	1,678	499	23	6,041	1,522	31	9,809	2,184	33	305	144	438
III. Services	1,264	737	34	3,195	1,884	39	4,371	2,785	42	256	148	378
Unallocated	246	74	3	655	197	4	1,042	313	5	266	159	423
TOTAL	4,354	2,186	100	11,554	4,844	100	16,508	6,698	100	222	138	307

[a] Sectors are aggregated as follows from Table 11.A.1, Appendix:
1A Agriculture (1) IIA Food (4) IIC Other Finished Goods (6,8,14,15,16,17)
1B Mining (2,3) IIB Textiles (5) IID Basic Industries (7,9,10,11,12,13)
III Services (18,19,20,21,22)

Source: Table 11A.2, 3, and 4, Appendix. Since 1954 value added ratios are assumed throughout; the value added in 1935 is understated by 15% and in 1914 by 7% on the average.

TABLE 11.4. RELATIVE IMPORTANCE OF CHANGES IN FINAL DEMAND AND TRADE, 1914-1935 and 1935-1954 (BILLIONS OF 1951 YEN)

	Direct and Indirect Effects of Deviations in:							
	Final Demand		Exports		Imports		Net Deviation[a]	
	14-35 (1)	35-54 (2)	14-35 (3)	35-54 (4)	14-35 (5)	35-54 (6)	14-35 (7)	35-54 (8)
I A. Agriculture	-929	50	170	-268	-100	397	-859	179
I B. Mining	96	-43	45	-48	-133	62	8	-29
II A. Food	-466	123	46	-86	-29	8	-449	45
II B. Textiles	382	-16	715	-807	29	93	1,126	-730
II C. Other Finished Goods	632	-113	138	-81	-1	44	769	-150
II D. Intermediate Products	534	-271	443	-280	82	535	1,059	-16
III Services	-110	378	383	-451	-45	152	228	79
Total Absolute Deviations	3,149	994	1,940	2,021	419	1,291	5,508	4,306
Relative Weight	(.57)	(.23)	(.35)	(.47)	(0.8)	(.29)	(1.00)	(1.00)
Index of Expansion	2.22	1.21	4.16	.68	2.72	.78		

[a]The "net deviation" from proportional growth is the sum of columns (1), (3), and (5) for 1914-1935 and of columns (2), (4), and (6) for 1935-1954.

<u>Source</u>: Condensed from Table 11A.6 in the Appendix with unallocated production and technological change omitted.

factured goods were due mainly to the differences in income elasticities of domestic demand for these commodities. Foreign demand was the dominant factor in the rapid growth of textiles, although domestic demand also expanded more than proportionately and accounted for a third of the total deviation. The growth of intermediate goods, which was also very rapid, was due to the indirect effects of the expansion of domestic and export demand in fairly equal proportions.

In 1914-1935 import substitution was relatively unimportant because of the rapid increase in exports and Japan's easy access to mainland sources of raw materials. Overall, the share of imports in total supply increased substantially; only in a few basic industries - chemicals, metals and machinery - was import substitution a significant cause of growth.

During the second period of war and postwar recovery, 1935-1954, the relative importance of the several factors in causing changes in output changed completely, and supply limitations became the dominant elements. In all sectors, the effects of the fall in per capita final demand were in the opposite direction from the first period, but their relative weight was much smaller (Table 11.4, column 2). Exports fell in absolute terms in practically all sectors, with textiles the most heavily affected. The drop in exports accounted for almost half of the deviations from proportionate growth in production. Import substitution was also very pronounced (Table 11.4, column 6), and in agriculture, mining, and intermediate goods it more than offset the fall in exports.

The combined effects of deviations in demand and trade between 1935 and 1954 were largely compensating in all major sectors except textiles (Table 11.4, column 8). The effects of technological change were quite substantial in this period, however. It accelerated growth in some of the basic industrial sectors while reducing the requirements for agricultural inputs - notably textile fibers - through substitution. This factor is discussed in the next section.

In summary, the second period of war and loss of export markets reversed most of the trends of the earlier period of growth. In basic industrial sectors and services there was no reversal, however, because import substitition and technological change replaced increased demand as a source of expansion.

The developments over the whole forty-year period 1914-1954 are summarized in Tables 11.3 and 11.5. A surprisingly large part of the total deviations from proportional growth is shown to be due to technological change (which includes commodity substitution). In all sectors except for food and mining, the variation in output is substantially greater than would be predicted by the use of the same input coefficients in 1914 as in 1954. The fact that technological change works in the same direction as the deviations in the autonomous elements in all sectors except food suggests that there has been a fall in relative prices in sectors of most rapid expansion, which has led to substitution effects. The importance of substitution and technological change appears to be about as great as that of the change in the composition of domestic final demand, but it is impossible to say what proportion of the former is actually due to shortcomings of the data.

Although the Second World War has greatly changed the course of Japanese growth, the final outcome is probably not so different from what it would have been in the long run without this cataclysm. The wartime destruction and postwar redirection of resources set back the growth of per capita income by about ten years. It is most unlikely, however, that even with no war the growth pattern of 1914-1935 could have been continued without substantial alteration. Textile exports would almost certainly have declined in the face of increased production elsewhere, while Japan's limited natural resources would have required increasing substitution of domestic production for imports of manufactured goods to permit the expanded importation of primary products. Thus the general direction of structural change over the past twenty years appears to have been inevitable. The temporary cessation of growth, the drop in exports, and the loss of colonial sources of imports have merely accelerated the rate of change.

11.4.2. The Causes of Industrialization. The principal virtue of the method of interindustry analysis is to show explicitly the interdependence of growth rates in different sectors of the economy. It is therefore of special value in trying to unravel the causes of the set of complex changes which is loosely called "industrialization." Since industry

TABLE 11.5. CAUSES OF DEVIATIONS FROM PROPORTIONAL EXPANSION OF OUTPUT, 1914-1935

Sector	Final Demand		Exports		Imports		Technological Change		Total Direct Deviation[c]	Total Deviation in Output[d]
	Direct Deviation[a] (1)	Total Effect[b] (2)	Direct Deviation[a] (3)	Total Effect[b] (4)	Direct Deviation[a] (5)	Total Effect[b] (6)	Direct Deviation[a] (7)	Total Effect[b] (8)	(9)	(10)
I. Agriculture	-1,030	-1,036	-58	-69	194	280	-720	-561	-1614	-1386
II. Mining	-15	69	-36	5	-144	-94	-212	15	-407	-5
III. Food	-322	-422	-27	-33	-45	-27	66	122	-328	-360
IV. Textiles	250	432	25	29	49	127	97	338	421	926
V. Other Finished Goods	559	627	70	81	13	43	163	287	805	1,038
VI. Basic Materials	16	355	90	239	303	629	509	1,198	918	2,421
VII. Services	133	250	-16	-3	7	100	478	788	602	1,135
Unallocated	-13	33	-52	-30	7	55	120	283	62	341
Absolute Total	2,338	3,224	374	489	762	1,355	2,365	3,592	5,839	8,660
Relative Weight	(.42)	(.38)	(.07)	(.06)	(.14)	(.15)	(.38)	(.42)	(1.00)	(1.00)

[a] "Direct deviation" is the change from proportional expansion of each autonomous element

[b] "Total effect" includes the direct deviation plus indirect effects of deviations in other sectors from eq. (11.4) above.

[c] "Total direct deviation" is the sum of columns (1), (3), (5), and (7).

[d] "Total deviation in output" is derived from eq. (11.3). Except for rounding errors, it is equal to the sum of columns (2), (4), (6), and (8).

Source: Table 11.A.5, Appendix.

has been the main source of Japanese growth in the period under study, the explanation of the causes of industrial expansion is largely synonymous with the explanation of growth as a whole.

Rostow's classification of sources of sector growth provides a useful starting point for our analysis.[20] He divides sectors, somewhat arbitrarily, into three categories: (i) primary growth sectors; (ii) supplementary growth sectors; and (iii) derived growth sectors. The primary growth sectors acquire their momentum from changes on the supply side, such as innovation, an improved competitive position in export markets, or the development of natural resources. The supplementary sectors develop as suppliers of the primary sectors or because of external economies supplied by the latter. The expansion of the derived growth sectors comes from the increase in total income and is not dependent on the nature of the primary sectors.

To adapt this framework to our statistical measurements, it must first be recognized that sector growth is usually influenced by several factors simultaneously. With this proviso, the three sources of growth can be related to elements of our analysis as follows:

Sources of Sector Growth

I Autonomous (primary) changes
- (a) Increased exports
- (b) Import substitution
- (c) Technological change (including all substitution for domestic products)

II Indirect effects on Producers
- (a) Indirect demands stemming from changes in exports and imports and from technological change in other sectors
- (b) External economies (reduced costs) resulting from production increases in other sectors

III Income (Derived) Effects
- (a) On consumption
- (b) On investment
- (c) On government expenditure

(i) Since we are trying to explain the increasing share of industry in total output, we take the autonomous elements of trade to be the deviation from proportional expansion rather than the absolute change in exports or imports. With this modification, the primary changes can be identified with our autonomous factors, omitting final demand changes.

(ii) The measurable part of category II consists of part (a), the indirect demands generated by primary changes. Part (b), the effect of external economies, will appear as one of the causes of autonomous change, since it cannot be identified directly.

(iii) Category III includes the direct and indirect effects of nonproportional growth in final demand, which coincides with Rostow's concept except for the shift from absolute increases to deviations.

An application of this analysis to sector growth in Japan from 1914 to 1954 is given in Table 11.6. Since it is not possible in most cases to classify sectors with any accuracy according to a single growth factor, we have grouped the sectors into four categories according to similarities in the relative importance of each factor:

Group A. Manufacturing Industry. With the exception of food, the manufacturing sectors all include important elements of Rostow's "primary growth sectors" as indicated by the autonomous changes. For the whole group, the three elements - autonomous change, indirect producer effects, and income effects - are about equally important.[21]

Group B. Auxiliary Sectors. Electric power, transport, and trade approximate the pure type of "supplementary growth sectors," since their growth depends mainly on expansion of manufacturing.

Group C. Derived Growth Sectors. Food, beverages, and tobacco (sector 4), and consumer services (sectors 20, 22) depend mainly on the growth of total income and hence correspond closely to Rostow's third category.

Group D. Resource-Limited Sectors. In Japan, growth in agriculture and mining is limited by the increasing cost of production as output increases. These primary sectors therefore comprise a fourth category whose growth rate is lower than demand conditions would indicate.

In each group, sectors are ranked according to their total growth from 1914 to 1954. All of the first 17 sectors in the overall ranking fall into the first two categories. The manufacturing sectors (group A) and auxiliary sectors (group B) both increase more than twice as fast as total output. It is somewhat surprising to find that technological change has been as important a source of growth for the auxiliary sectors as for manufacturing.[22]

In most of the sectors in groups A and B, income elasticities of demand are greater than one (indicated by the positive direct income effects), so that the total income effects augment the autonomous changes in all sectors except two.

In contrast to the first two groups, the sectors in category C expand somewhat more slowly than total income because the low income elasticity of food outweighs the higher elasticities for some of the services. Technological change and substitution seem to be relatively insignificant in these sectors.

In the resource-limited sectors (group D), the indirect effects of the expansion of manufacturing would make for higher rates of growth. They are more than offset, however, by the low income elasticity of consumer demand for agricultural products and the composite effects of rising costs shown by the autonomous elements: reduced exports, increased imports, and lowered inputs of primary products per unit of manufactured output.[23]

The importance of the several factors in the growth of each group can now be summarized. Groups B and C can be said to depend mainly on the growth of A and D, the auxiliary sectors via indirect producer effects and the derived growth sectors via income effects. The growth of groups A and D, therefore, determines the total growth of income. In Japan, the autonomous factors are in striking contrast in these two groups although in a resource-rich country the pattern would be quite different. In group A, both price changes and technological change work to produce increased exports, reduced imports, and increased use of manufactured goods,[24] while in group D they produce reduced exports, increased imports, and decreased use of primary products. These changes which are considered autonomous in the present analysis (as in Rostow's) account for 30-40 percent of total deviations from proportional growth in both group A and group D.[25]

TABLE 11.6. AUTONOMOUS AND INDUCED ELEMENTS IN INDUSTRIAL GROWTH, 1914-1954[a] (VALUE ADDED IN BILLIONS OF 1951 YEN)

Sector	Rank	I Autonomous Changes			
		Exports (1)	Imports (2)	Tech. Change (3)	Total (4)
(A) Manufacturing Industry					
11 Petroleum and Coal Products	2	0	-9	23	14
7 Pulp and Paper	3	-5	3	22	20
9 Rubber Products	4	1	*	6	7
13 Metals Manufacturing	5	10	10	19	39
10 Chemicals	6	6	70	20	96
12 Non-metallic Mineral Products	7	3	*	12	15
14 Machinery	8	15	-3	6	18
17 Construction	9	3	0	11	14
8 Printing and Publishing	10	*	*	14	14
5 Textiles, Clothing and Leather	12	6	11	22	39
16 Miscellaneous	14	2	0	0	2
6 Wood Products	16	-7	2	5	0
15 Transport Equipment	17	8	4	16	28
Total (A)		42	88	176	306
(B) Auxiliary Sectors					
18 Electricity and Gas	1	0	0	38	38
19 Trade	11	-1	0	178	177
21 Transport	13	-19	2	65	48
Total (B)		-20	2	281	263
(C) Derived Growth Sectors					
20,22 Services	18,19	8	2	17	27
4 Food	20	-12	-20	29	-3
Total (C)		-4	-18	46	24
(d) Resource-Limited Sectors					
2,3 Mining	21,15	-22	-42	-129	-193
1 Agriculture	22	-44	148	-549	-445
Total (D)		-66	106	-678	-638
TOTAL EFFECTS		-48	178	-175	-45

[a]Derived by applying value-added ratios to the output deviations of Table 11A.4.

[b]Proportional expansion is equal to output in 1913-1915 from Table 11A.2 multiplied by 2.895.

[c]Total output computed in column (14) differs slightly from the actual output in 1954 in Table 11A.4 because of small errors in calculation.

II Indirect Effects				III Income Effects		Total Deviation		Pro-portional Expan.[b]	Total Output[c] (12)+(13)	Pro-duction Index
Ex-ports (5)	Im-ports (6)	Tech. change. (7)	To-tal (8)	Di-rect (9)	To-tal (10)	Di-rect (11)	To-tal (12)	(13)	(14)	(15)
2	5	10	17	4	7	18	36	6	42	20.21
-3	6	31	34	4	18	24	72	17	89	17.81
0	1	2	3	4	4	11	14	4	18	12.64
17	17	48	82	0	34	39	155	43	198	11.19
0	37	24	61	-9	-27	87	130	73	203	7.50
2	2	7	11	-5	11	10	37	25	62	7.29
3	2	7	12	62	70	80	100	63	163	7.22
-1	3	7	9	116	113	130	136	106	242	6.55
0	1	5	6	19	19	33	39	31	70	6.40
1	18	54	73	56	97	95	209	222	431	5.05
0	0	2	2	1	3	3	7	19	26	4.40
0	2	8	10	-2	11	-2	21	47	68	4.09
0	1	6	7	-13	-14	15	21	67	88	3.76
21	95	211	327	237	346	543	977	723	1700	6.67
0	4	19	23	24	28	62	89	6	95	42.23
8	18	41	67	232	237	409	481	457	938	5.92
1	16	59	76	37	62	85	186	316	502	4.41
9	38	119	166	293	327	556	756	779	1535	5.67
0	17	57	74	-189	-161	-162	-60	1315	1255	2.74
-2	8	25	31	-142	-186	-145	-158	693	535	2.19
-2	25	82	105	-331	-347	-307	-218	2008	1790	2.75
23	-16	137	144	-10	41	-203	-8	262	254	2.83
-9	65	121	177	-785	-790	-1230	-1058	2227	1169	1.47
14	49	258	321	-795	-749	-1433	-1066	2489	1423	1.78
42	207	670	919	-596	-423	-641	449	5999	6448	2.84

Our analysis so far provides a reasonable explanation of the mechanism of industrialization - the increasing share of industry in total output - but not of growth itself. In Japan, the rise of industry and relative decline of primary production have been exceptionally rapid because of the limitations to expanded primary output, as we shall show in the next section. More than in most countries, therefore, the overall rate of growth hinges on the growth of industry. The interindustry analysis explains the demand side of the growth of industry, but it tells us little about the rate of capital formation, the sources of skills, and other supply factors.

Table 11.6 shows that the increased demand for domestic manufactured goods is generated in roughly equal degree by autonomous changes, their indirect effects on other sectors, and income effects. Our choice of concepts understates the importance of import substitution in this group, however. Since total demand for industrial output expands twice as fast as income, a growth of imports that was only proportional to income would represent a substantial decline in the fraction imported. If import substitution is defined instead as the effect of reducing the ratio of imports to domestic production, then the effect of import substitution is about twice as large as indicated here and income effects must be reduced by the same amount. On these assumptions, the relative importance of the four elements in explaining the increased share of industrial output is roughly as follows:

Technological change and substitution	40%
Import substitution	38%
Export changes	6%
Income effects	16%

In other words, if there had been no changes in the trade pattern or in input coefficients, the rise in income in Japan would have required very much less industrial development than has actually taken place.[26] Conversely, without the industrial development, resource limitations would have restricted growth much more than they did.

The relation between our results and the total growth of output is shown in columns (13) and (14) of Table 11.6 in which the proportional element is added to the deviation to give the total output in 1954.

11.4.3. Increasing Deviation from Normal Growth Patterns. The pattern of growth which we have just outlined can be put into better perspective by comparing it to the standard patterns of output and trade for a country of Japan's size and income. This is done in Tables 11.7 and 11.8, using the same methods as for 1914.

Although agriculture had started to fall behind the normal output level by 1935, on the whole the productive structure in that year showed deviations from the standard similar to 1914. The development of textiles was much more pronounced because of the export boom resulting from devaluation. Machinery and transport equipment were maintained at relatively high levels by military preparations (much of the transport equipment is naval shipbuilding). The substantial development of other sectors such as metals, building materials, petroleum, and chemicals is shown to be quite normal for this income level. The import pattern also remained much the same in 1935 as in 1914, and the total increased relative to the standard.

By the time of the postwar recovery in 1954, the comparison to the standard production levels is quite different. Since per capita income had not yet recovered its 1935 level, the standard levels are somewhat lower, but only textiles and machinery have a lower per capita output. Total factory output per capita increased by 21 percent, so that Japan had reached a level of industrial output 94 percent above that normal to her income level. This was the largest positive deviation of any of the 38 countries examined.[27]

The failure of agriculture to keep up with the expanding population is quite noticeable when compared to the standard level. Between 1935 and 1954, agriculture dropped from 89 percent to 67 percent of the standard. The economy of Japan in 1954 was thus a combination of an agricultural sector typical of a per capita income of about $150 with an industrial sector appropriate to an income level of about $275. The remaining service sectors were quite normal for her actual income of $190. Mining and manufacturing accounted for 36 percent of the national product instead of the 29 percent which would be normal for

TABLE 11.7. COMPARISON OF ACTUAL AND STANDARD OUTPUTS, 1935 AND 1954[a]

Sector	1935			1954			
	Actual Output (1)	Standard Output (2)	Ratio (1)/(2) (3)	Actual Output (4)	Standard Output (5)	Ratio (4)/(5) (6)	Equiv. Income[b] (7)
Factory Production (Valued Added)							
4. Food, Beverages and Tobacco	13.17	10.48	1.26	15.30	9.67	1.58	311
5. Textiles and Clothing	16.47	8.59	1.92	13.43	8.16	1.65	310
6. Wood Products	1.07	1.52	.70	2.19	1.33	1.65	254
7. Pulp and Paper	.84	.99	.85	3.79	.71	5.34	357
8. Printing and Publishing	1.17	1.57	.75	2.43	1.42	1.71	265
9. Rubber Products	.35	.61	.57	.62	.57	1.09	200
10. Chemicals	3.54	2.92	1.21	6.81	2.70	2.52	340
11. Coal and Petroleum Products	.45	.42	1.07	1.45	.35	4.14	294
12. Non-metallic Mineral Products	1.67	1.75	.95	2.16	1.59	1.36	231
13. Metals	3.28	3.76	.87	6.01	3.44	1.75	248
14. Machinery	5.71	1.33	4.29	5.63	1.05	5.36	350
15. Transport Equipment	3.68	1.62	2.27	3.11	1.41	2.21	270
Total Factory Output	51.40	35.56	1.45	62.93	32.40	1.94	
Aggregate Sectors							
1. Agriculture	46.78	52.60	.89	33.27	49.54	.67	
2-17. Mining and Manufacturing	71.95	61.70	1.17	69.97	55.78	1.25	
18-23. Services	90.27	94.92	.95	88.85	86.67	1.02	
Per Capita Income	209.00	209.00		192.00	192.00		
Population	69.24			88.20			

a: Source: Actual output from Tables IIA.3 and 4, Appendix: Standard output derived from regression equations in H. B. Chenery, "Patterns of Industrial Growth," *American Economic Review*, September 1960, using national income of $113 and population of 52.58 million.

b: Income at which actual output would be standard.

c: The standard output was multiplied by 1.12 in both years in order to make the components add to total income.

TABLE 11.8. ACTUAL AND STANDARD IMPORTS PER CAPITA, 1914, 1935, 1954[a]

Sector	1914		1935		1954		Ratio of Actual to Standard		
	Actual (1)	Standard (2)	Actual (3)	Standard (4)	Actual (5)	Standard (6)	1914 (7)	1935 (8)	1954 (9)
Manufactures									
4. Food, Beverages, and Tobacco	.55	.83	1.87	1.38	2.14	1.16	0.7	1.4	1.8
5. Textiles and Clothing	.80	.90	.70	1.09	.12	.92	0.9	0.6	0.16
6. Wood Products	.12	.18	.05	.34	.02	.28	0.7	0.15	0.1
7. Pulp and Paper	.44	.26	1.18	.47	.40	.39	1.7	2.5	1.2
8. Printing and Publishing	.02	.02	.03	.05	.04	.04	1.0	0.6	1.0
9. Rubber	.01	.11	.02	.13	.01	.11	0.1	0.15	0.1
10. Chemicals	4.29	.67	2.58	1.08	.93	.91	6.4	2.4	1.2
11. Petroleum Products	.09	.48	1.08	.79	1.21	.66	0.2	1.4	2.2
12. Non-metallic Mineral Products	.05	0.002	.41	0.003	.07	0.003	*	*	*
13. Metals	1.50	.76	3.62	1.49	.48	1.28	2.0	2.4	0.5
14. Machinery	.64	1.39	1.51	2.28	1.28	1.93	0.5	0.7	0.8
15. Transport Equipment	.39	.70	.45	.99	.31	.82	0.6	0.5	0.4
Total Manufactures	8.90	8.55	13.50	10.09	7.01	8.50	1.0	1.3	0.82
Total Imports	22.53	14.44	46.59	24.96	28.96	20.97	1.6	1.9	1.4
Ratio to National Income	.20		.18		.15				

*Standard imports close to zero

[a]Computed from regression equations in H. B. Chenery, "Patterns of Industrial Growth," <u>American Economic Review,</u> September 1960, Table 4.

Japan's income and size.

Although the level of industry as a whole appears more abnormal than before the war, the differences among sectors compared to the standard have tended to decrease. In no industrial sector is Japan now below the standard level, in contrast to the six below it in 1935. Factory production has replaced small-scale production in some cases and imports in others, while the range of exports has broadened. Although in some sectors (textiles, wood, rubber, metals) high domestic production makes up for low import levels, in others (food products, pulp and paper, chemicals, petroleum) both production and import levels are high. In large part, these high demands stem from the high level of industrial output, but in manufactured foodstuffs and printing consumer demand also appears abnormally high.[28] (The high value added in foodstuffs may be partially due to high indirect taxes in this sector.)

11.5. Changes in Technology and Labor Use

Over time, the effects of technological change and substitution become inextricably mixed, and it would take a much more detailed analysis than ours to sort them out. We can, however, indicate some of the ways in which the two factors have operated and their effects on intermediate demand and employment.

The results of technological change and substitution can be classified by the inputs or outputs affected although a single change may have several such effects. In our data, we can distinguish the following:

(a) The introduction of new products, which causes a substitution of new for old intermediate goods as well as a change in the composition of an industry's output.

(b) Increases in the efficiency of use of given commodities.

(c) The substitution of capital for labor, which appears as a rise of labor productivity.

For the two factors affecting the demand for intermediate goods, we can merely present the quantitative results and give examples of the causes. For labor productivity, however, we shall show a close relation to changes in foreign trade.

11.5.1. Effects of Technological Change. The effects of technological change and substitution on intermediate demand in each sector are summarized in Table 11.9. For the two earlier dates, we have calculated the intermediate demand that would have existed if 1954 technology had been used in all sectors of the economy. The difference between this estimate and the actual intermediate demand measures the combined effects of changes in the input coefficients.

The nature of these changes is remarkably uniform. There is a very pronounced decrease in the use of agricultural and mineral products and an approximately equal increase in the requirement for manufactured goods for intermediate use. These trends can be seen in each individual sector of commodity production for both periods (except construction in 1935-1954). Trade and service inputs also appear to increase substantially over time, but the data on these elements are less reliable.

We have illustrated technological developments underlying these results in Table 11.10, which gives a few inputs for which we could secure measurements in physical units. Notable changes in the earlier period are the substitution of synthetic for natural fibers and the rise in the use of machinery, electric power, rubber, and paper. These trends continue with reduced force in the second period, while the substitution of wheat flour for rice, of petroleum products for coal, and the increasing use of fertilizer are accelerated.

Innovations affecting final demand cannot be taken into account in this analysis because they are not separable from the effects of rising income. However, the development of road transportation, of new types of housing, and other innovations in consumer goods are part of the explanation of the increased input requirements for metals, nonmetallic minerals, and other materials per unit of final output.

11.5.2. Labor Productivity and Foreign Trade. There are very great differences in the rate of growth of labor productivity among different sectors of the economy as shown in Table 11.11. Between 1914 and 1954, these range from prac-

TABLE 11.9. EFFECTS OF TECHNOLOGICAL CHANGE AND SUBSTITUTION ON INTERMEDIATE DEMAND

Sector	1914 Actual Intermediate Demand (1)	1914 Excess of Calculated Demand (2)	1914 (2) as % of (1) (3)	1935 Actual Intermediate Demand (4)	1935 Excess of Calculated Demand (5)	1935 (5) as % of (4) (6)
I. Primary Production						
1. Agriculture	574.5	-253.2	-44	1370.0	-478.1	-35
2. Coal and Crude Oil	77.3	-50.5	-65	187.0	-66.2	-35
3. Other Minings	61.4	-24.0	-39	200.4	-37.0	-19
Total	713.2	-327.7	-46	1757.4	-581.3	-33
IIA,B.						
4. Processed Food	197.4	23.1	12	295.1	116.3	39
5. Textiles	246.2	34.1	14	996.6	113.8	11
Total	443.6	57.2	13	1291.7	230.1	18
IIIC. Other Finished Goods						
14,15. Mach. and Transp. Equip.	42.8	25.9	60	189.0	52.3	28
6,8,16. Other Manufacturing	62.7	19.3	30	196.6	59.3	30
17. Construction	35.0	12.4	35	143.9	-38.0	-26
Total	140.5	57.6	41	529.5	73.6	14
IID. Basic Materials						
7. Lumber and Wood Products	15.7	34.4	219	106.0	72.9	69
9. Rubber Products	6.0	14.6	243	46.8	13.0	28
10. Chemicals	154.9	24.5	16	254.7	180.1	71
11. Petroleum and Coal Products	9.1	37.5	412	82.9	54.3	66
12. NMM Products	16.0	12.5	78	90.0	21.2	24
13. Metal Products	145.0	54.7	38	711.5	184.8	26
Total	346.7	178.2	51	1291.9	526.3	41
III. Utilities and Services						
18. Elec. Gas and Water	2.2	30.8	1400	57.3	37.8	66
19,20,21,22,23. Trade and Ser.	424.5	179.3	42	1092.8	551.5	50
TOTAL	2071.6	175.4	9	6020.6	838.0	14

Source: Tables 11A.2 and 11A.3, Appendix

TABLE 11.10. EXAMPLES OF CHANGES IN INPUT COEFFICIENTS[a]

		Indicators		
A. Substitution of Processed for Crude Materials	Ratio of	1914	1935	1954
Synthetic fibers for raw cotton	Raw cotton to textile products	.42	.18	.11
Synthetic fibres for raw silk	Raw silk to textile products	9.3	5.8	1.9
Petroleum products for coal	Petroleum to coal in total energy supply	----	.069	.339
Wheat flour for rice	Wheat flour to rice		.17	.67
B. Fall due to increased efficiency of use				
Iron ore	Iron ore to pig iron (tons)	2.00	2.11	1.33
Scrap iron	Scrap to steel (tons)	2.00	1.24	1.17
C. Rise due to changes in technology or product mix				
Electric power for industry use	Electricity to total energy		.23	.36
Chemical fertilizers	Chemical fertilizer to output of rice	.015	.029	.051

[a]The classifications are merely suggestive and not mutually exclusive.

TABLE 11.11. INDEX OF CHANGE IN LABOR PRODUCTIVITY AND TRADE[a]

Sector[b]	Labor Productivity, (l^2/l^1)			Production	Exports, (e^2/e^1)			Imports, (m^2/m^1)		
	1914-54 (1)	1914-35 (2)	1935-54 (3)	1954-1914	1914-54 (4)	1914-35 (5)	1935-54 (6)	1914-54 (7)	1914-35 (8)	1935-54 (9)
18. Electricity, Gas	9.97	5.69	1.75	42.23	--	--	--	--	--	--
7. Pulp and Paper	9.10	3.75	2.43	17.81	.15	.25	.13	.12	.81	.15
5. Textiles and Leather	6.09	3.36	1.81	5.05	.61	1.19	.51	.05	.26	.18
13. Metal Mfg.	5.36	2.67	2.01	11.19	.56	.79	.71	.06	.68	.09
12. Non-metallic Min.	5.02	4.31	1.16	7.29	.65	1.20	.54	.10	.54	.17
6. Wood Products	4.78	3.17	1.51	4.09	.29	.40	.74	.08	.16	.50
16. Misc. Industry	4.57	2.54	1.80	4.90	--	--	--	--	--	--
9. Rubber	3.79	4.80	.79	12.64	.93	1.19	.38	.10	.43	.22
10. Chemicals	3.25	2.02	1.61	7.50	.82	2.45	.34	.09	.39	.24
11. Petroleum Prod.	3.11	2.74	1.14	20.21	.50	2.63	.18	1.09	1.74	.63
19. Trade	2.88	2.67	1.08	5.92	--	--	--	--	--	--
3. Mining	2.67	1.90	1.41	4.34	.71	1.16	.60	1.94	3.05	.64
21. Transportation	2.27	1.85	1.23	4.41	--	--	--	--	--	--

TABLE 11.11. CONTINUED

Sector[b]	Labor Productivity, (l^2/l^1)			Production	Exports, (e^2/e^1)			Imports, (m^2/m^1)		
	1914-54 (1)	1914-35 (2)	1935-54 (3)	1954-1914	1914-54 (4)	1914-35 (5)	1935-54 (6)	1914-54 (7)	1914-35 (8)	1935-54 (9)
14. Machinery	1.85	2.99	.62	7.22	2.16	1.91	1.12	.51	.55	.93
17. Construction	1.73	3.14	.55	6.55	--	--	--	--	--	--
4. Food	1.58	1.04	1.52	2.19	.91	1.65	.54	2.71	2.88	.94
8. Printing and Publishing	1.47	1.72	.85	6.40	.29	.97	.32	.57	.64	.89
1. Agriculture	1.39	1.48	.94	1.47	.52	.91	.54	1.33	1.67	.80
15. Transp. Equip.	1.33	2.00	.67	3.76	.06	5.45	1.00	.37	.32	1.16
2. Coal and Petroleum	1.03	1.60	.64	1.93	.16	.30	.54	4.33	3.58	1.21
22. Services	1.00	1.04	.96	2.79	--	--	--	--	--	--
20. Real Estate	.84	.92	.91	2.31	--	--	--	--	--	--
All Sectors	2.63	2.26	1.17		.75	1.57	.48	.78	1.10	.71

[a]The ratios are defined in equation (8).

[b]Sectors are given in order of the change in productivity from 1914-1954.

tically no change in services and coal mining to an increase of over 800 percent in pulp and paper and in electricity and gas. These differences reflect the fact that modernization has affected the economy very unequally. Some sectors have been completely transformed in technology and organization while others maintain their traditional structure to a large degree.

Differences in the growth in productivity are significantly correlated with differences in growth of output.[29] It is notable, however, that in sectors in which there is little or no international trade productivity increased less than would be expected from this relationship.

To explain these sectoral differences in productivity growth we should consider the incentives and obstacles to modernization. In exports, for example, there is a pressure to increase efficiency in order to meet foreign competition. In the introduction of new products, such as electric power, new techniques are used because there is no existing alternative. In the production of import substitutes, both foreign competition and new techniques raise productivity so long as trade is relatively free.

Where the incentives given by new products and the pressure of competition are absent, the adoption of labor-saving methods is likely to proceed at a slower pace. In part this is due to imperfections of the market, and in part to the varying technological possibilities for substituting capital for labor. It is probable, however, that even the optimal allocation of a limited amount of investment resources would lead to differences in productivity growth considerably larger than those experienced in advanced countries, where the gap between existing and "best" techniques is smaller.

Among the factors leading to high growth in productivity, the only one for which we can apply a quantitative test is the change in exports and imports. Here we assume that changes in the fraction of production that is exported or the fraction of supplies that are imported will be associated with changes in labor productivity. For purposes of regression analysis, this relation is expressed in terms of the differences from the average changes in these three magnitudes:

$$\left(\frac{\ell^2}{\ell^1} - \frac{\bar{\ell}^2}{\bar{\ell}^1}\right) = \alpha_0 + \alpha_1\left(\frac{m^2}{m^1} - \frac{\bar{m}^2}{\bar{m}^1}\right) + \alpha_2\left(\frac{e^2}{e^1} - \frac{\bar{e}^2}{\bar{e}^1}\right) .$$

Here $\underline{l} = \underline{X}/\underline{N}$ is labor productivity, $\underline{e} = \underline{E}/\underline{X}$ is the fraction of production exported, and $\underline{m} = \underline{M}/(\underline{X} + \underline{M})$ is the fraction of total supplies imported. The superscripts 1, 2 refer to time periods and the barred values are the averages for all sectors.

This equation was fitted to the data in Table 11.11 for the two periods of our analysis, with the following results:

$$1914\text{-}1935: \quad \frac{\ell^{35}}{\ell^{14}} = 3.45 - \underset{(.14)}{.79}\left(\frac{\underline{m}^{35}}{\underline{m}^{14}}\right) + \underset{(.12)}{.55}\left(\frac{\underline{e}^{35}}{\underline{e}^{14}}\right), \qquad \underline{R}^2 = .78$$

$$1935\text{-}1954: \quad \frac{\ell^{54}}{\ell^{35}} = 1.37 - \underset{(.18)}{1.29}\left(\frac{\underline{m}^{54}}{\underline{m}^{35}}\right) + \underset{(.26)}{1.30}\left(\frac{\underline{e}^{54}}{\underline{e}^{35}}\right), \qquad \underline{R}^2 = .83.$$

For both periods, the changes in the export and import ratios "explain" about 80 percent of the variance in the labor productivity ratios, and all the coefficients are highly significant. The regression coefficients for the second period are almost twice as large as those for the first, however; for this reason, the fit for the period as a whole is less good.

The causal nature of this relationship between trade and labor productivity is not clear. In our previous reasoning, we assumed that competitive pressures in imports and exports lead to modernization and rising productivity. It is equally plausible to think of rising productivity as determining the sectors in which imports will be replaced or exports expanded.[30] We can say only that the two sets of factors are highly correlated.

11.5.3. Changes in the Pattern of Employment. Because of the large differences in productivity, the pattern of employment does not change in the same way as the pattern of output. The extent of this deviation is shown in Table 11.12. The overall increase in output of over 200 percent was achieved by an increase in productivity of 113 percent and an increased labor input of 44 percent.

The varying effects of productivity change are shown by the breakdown in columns (4) and (5). Column (4) gives the increase in employment that results from the increase in output alone, using the most recent labor input ratios. Against this increase is offset the labor saving on 1914 production levels due to increased productivity, which is shown in column

TABLE 11.12. CHANGES IN EMPLOYMENT, 1914-1954

	1914 Employment ($\underline{N}^{14}$)	Labor Input: 1914 ($\underline{n}^{14}$)	Labor Input: Change 1914-54 ($\Delta\underline{n}$)	Changes in Employment: From Increased Output	Changes in Employment: From Increased Productivity	Changes in Employment: Total Change	1954 Employment ($\underline{N}^{54}$)	Index of Increase in: Output	Index of Increase in: Employment	Index of Increase in: Productivity
	(1)	(2)	(3)	(4)	(5)	(6)	(7)	(8)	(9)	(10)
I. Primary										
A. Agriculture	15,816	15.57	-4.38	5,443	-4,443	1,000	16,816	147	106	139
B. Mining	273	1.82	- .39	270	- 58	212	485	278	178	156
Total I	16,089	13.80	-4.81	5,713	-4,501	1,212	17,301	162	108	150
II. Manufacturing										
A. Food	453	.82	- .30	342	- 167	175	628	220	139	158
B. Textiles	1,599	3.81	-3.18	1,063	-1,336	- 273	1,326	503	83	508
C. Other Finished Goods	1,957	5.02	-2.89	3,952	-1,126	2,826	4,783	564	244	231
D. Intermediate Products	747	2.36	-1.85	1,405	- 586	819	1,566	1,004	210	478
Total II	4,756	2.85	-1.91	6,762	-3,215	3,547	8,303	438	175	250
III. Services	5,077	4.02	-1.39	8,718	-2,077	6,641	11,718	378	231	164
Total	25,922	5.95	-2.25	21,193	-9,793	11,400	37,322	307	144	213

Sources and definitions:
(1),(2),(3) from Table 11A.7, Appendix. (4) $\underline{n}^{54}(\underline{X}^{54} - \underline{X}^{14})$, where $\underline{n}^{54}$ is the labor input in 1954. (5) $\Delta\underline{n}\ \underline{N}^{14}$ = (1) × (3) (6)= (4) + (5) = $\Delta\underline{N}$ (7) = (1) + (6). (Results differ slightly from totals in Table 11A.7 because of rounding.) (8) From Table 11.3. (9) $\underline{N}^{54}/\underline{N}^{14}$ = [(7) ÷ (1)] × 100. (10) [(8) : (9)] × 100.

(5). This factor reduces the total employment increase from 21 million to 11 million, but its effect varies greatly by sector. In agriculture the output increase in almost completely offset by a modest productivity increase (39 percent) applied to a large initial output. In services the productivity increase is somewhat larger (64 percent), but even so there is a 130 percent growth in employment in services. In manufacturing, on the other hand, a much higher growth in productivity (150 percent) offsets the higher growth in output, and the increase in employment is more moderate (75 percent).

In summary, the observed changes in labor productivity result from the interplay of positive factors - investment and technological change - and negative factors - limited resources and surplus labor. Although we do not have a direct measure of investment by sector over time, it is probable that there has been a greater increase in capital per worker in most branches of manufacturing than in other sectors. Indirect evidence for this conclusion is given by Watanabe's findings[31] that Japanese capital-labor ratios are much closer to U.S. ratios in manufacturing than they are in agriculture or services.[32]

An increase in underemployed labor since the war is implied by the fall in productivity in a number of sectors between 1935 and 1954. These are mainly services and industries such as printing and publishing that do not compete with foreign producers. Since resource limitations prevent the employment of many more people in agriculture and competition limits handicraft production, services now seem to provide the main outlet for surplus labor. The rapid rise in employment in the service sectors is therefore due less to increased demand than to the ease of entry and lack of alternative employment.

11.6. Summary and Conclusions

1. The pattern of growth is measured here by comparison to a constant pattern in which each element of demand and supply expands proportionately. An interindustry model is used to explain the deviations from proportional growth in output in each of 22 sectors of the economy. Deviations from propor-

tional expansion in domestic demand, in exports, and in imports are taken as autonomous factors. After allowing for their effects, the remaining variation in output is attributed to technological change and substitution.

2. The dominant feature of the growth pattern is the very rapid rise of industry. Although in 1914 Japan was a fairly typical underdeveloped country with relatively little industry, by 1954 she had a volume of industrial output far above the normal for her income level of $200 per capita.

3. The main cause of the rise of industry has been Japan's need to overcome her limited endowment of natural resources. For this reason she has had to develop the trade pattern of an advanced country, exporting manufactured goods and importing raw materials. Although industrialization is usually attributed to changes in demand, more than 75 percent of Japan's industrial growth is traceable to changes in supply conditions. These include substitution of domestic for imported manufactured goods, substitution of manufactured goods for primary products, and other technological changes. Although increased exports were of some importance up to 1935, increases in domestic and foreign demand together account for less than a quarter of the rise in the share of industry in GNP from 1914 to 1954.

4. The growth of employment has not followed the growth of production very closely because of uneven changes in productivity. Large investments, technological change, and the pressure of foreign competition have led to high productivity increases in many branches of industry, but the pressure of population and limited resources have kept down productivity growth in agriculture and services.

5. The pattern of Japanese growth differs from the earlier European patterns in several respects, notably in the development of industry at a low income level, the importance of import substitution, and the unevenness of technological advance. Rostow's suggestions as to the role of different sectors in the growth process can, however, be applied to the analytical framework used here; they result in the four-fold sector classification given in Table 11.6.

6. The present methodology may provide a basis for comparable studies of economic development in other countries. A comparison of the results of such studies should give a

firmer empirical basis for theories of economic development and should help to separate general features from those that are peculiar to individual countries.

Appendix 11A.[33] Principal Statistical Sources[34]

11A.1. General

1. Statistics Bureau, Prime Minister's Office: Japan Statistical Yearbook (1913-1915, 1934-1936, 1957)*
2. Asahi Shimbunsha: Economic Statistics.
3. Tōyōkeizaishimposha (Oriental Economist Inc.).
4. H. Ouchi, ed.: Japan Economic Statistics for Meiji, Taisho and Showa Eras.
5. K. Ohkawa: Growth Rate of the Japanese Economy.**
6. Y. Yamada: National Income in Japan.
7. Bank of Japan: Economic Statistics of Japan, 1956.
8. Ministry of Finance: Annual Report on Financial Statistics (Kinyujiko Sankosho 1913-1915, 1934-1936).

1951 and 1954

9. Ministry of International Trade and Industry (MITI): Interindustry Analysis of the Japanese Economy.**
10. MITI: Input-Output Studies for Households, 1951.
11. MITI: Input-Output Studies for Domestic Production (Control Totals), 1951.
12. Economic Planning Board: National Wealth Census, 1955.

1913-1914 and 1934-1936

13. Economic Planning Board (EPB): National Income and the Japanese Economy, 1954.
14. EPB: National Income, 1957.**
15. Ministry of Agriculture: Statistical Yearbook for Agriculture, Forestry and Fishing.
16. MITI: Statistical Yearbook of Mining.
17. MITI: Annual Report of Manufacturing Census (1914, 1934-1936, 1951, 1954).*
18. Ministry of Finance: Foreign Trade Statistics (1934-

1936, 1951, 1954.)*

19. Toyokeizaishimposha: Foreign Trade of Japan, A Statistical Survey (Boekiseiran).*
20. Government of Korea: Foreign Trade Statistics (1934-1936).*
21. Government of Taiwan: Foreign Trade Statistics (1934-1936).*
22. Government of Sakhalin: Foreign Trade Statistics (1934-1936).*
23. Ministry of Finance: Technical Report on Foreign Trade Quantity Index.
24. U.N.: International Trade Statistics (1954).**
25. EPB: Report on Household Consumption (1957).
26. Statistics Bureau of the Prime Minister's Office: Family Income and Expenditures for Post-war Japan, 1946-1955.
27. Ministry of Agriculture: Report on Farm Household Economic Survey (1934-1936, 1951).
28. Toyokeizaishimposha: Statistics of Public Finance for Meiji and Taisho Eras.
29. Toyokeizaishimposha: History of Public Finance for Showa Era (Showazaiseishi) vol. 3, vol. 4.
30. Toyokeizaishimposha: History of Industry for Showa Era (Showasangyoshi) vols. 1-3.
31. Building Society: Building Economics.

TABLE 11A.1. SECTOR CLASSIFICATION

Sector	U.N. International Standard Industrial Classification	Aggregated Classification
1. Agriculture, Forestry, Fishing	01,02,03,04	I A
2. Coal Mining and Crude Petroleum	11,13	I B
3. Metal and Non-metallic Mining	12,14,19	I B
4. Food Manufacturing	20,21,22	II A
5. Manufacturing of Textiles and Leather	23,24,29	II B
6. Lumber and Wood Products	25,26	II C
7. Paper and Derivatives	27	II D
8. Printing and Publishing	28	II C
9. Rubber Manufacturing	30	II D
10. Chemicals	31	II D
11. Petroleum and Coal Products	32	II D
12. Nonmetallic Mineral Products	33	II D
13. Metal Manufacturing	34,35	II D
14. Machinery and Electrical Equipment	36,37	II C
15. Transport Equipment	38	II C
16. Industry n.e.c.	39	II C
17. Construction	40	II C
18. Electricity, Gas and Water	51,52	III
19. Trade	61	III
20. Real Estate	64	III
21. Transport and Communication	71,72,73	III
22. Services	62,63,81,82,83,84,90	III

TABLE 11A.2. STRUCTURE OF THE JAPANESE ECONOMY IN 1914-1916

Sectors	Demand (1) Consumption	(2) Government Expenditures	(3) Fixed Capital Formation	(4) Changes in Inventory	(5) Exports
1. Agriculture	704.5	.8		-5.1	27.6
2. Coal and Petroleum	.7	9.0		.6	14.1
3. Other Mining	.6			3.8	.4
4. Food	316.4	1.9		18.8	31.0
5. Textiles and Leather	64.7	3.4	.1	14.3	110.3
6. Wood	9.9	.7	1.1	1.9	14.5
7. Pulp and Paper	2.5	.9		.7	11.6
8. Printing and Publishing	16.2	.9		1.0	.4
9. Rubber Products	1.7	1.3		.3	.4
10. Chemicals	17.7	16.6		4.1	6.1
11. Coal and Petroleum Products	3.0	.3		.4	.2
12. Nonmetallic Mineral Products	3.5	*	.2	.8	5.2
13. Metal Manufacturing	3.2	5.4	.9	9.3	22.6
14. Machinery	4.9	2.4	38.8	3.3	3.4
15. Transport Equipment	1.7	43.0	32.6	1.6	1.6
16. Miscellaneous	8.9	1.0		1.2	4.3
17. Construction		14.1	66.9		
18. Electricity and Gas	2.5	.5			
19. Trade	135.7	2.9	10.4	3.3	25.2
20. Real Estate	64.3	4.6			
21. Transportation	43.2	10.9	.7	2.1	72.9
22. Service	581.2	21.1	8.0		14.2
23. Unallocated		65.1			29.0
Value Added[a]	(28.1)	(37.8)			
Total	2015.1	244.6	159.7	62.4	395.0

[a]Contents of Value Added are import duties. Unit is billion of yen at 1951 prices.

[b]Final demand equals the total of columns (1) to (5)

[c]Total demand equals (6) + (7)

[d]Total supply equals total demand.

Demand			Supply[d]		Technological Changes		
(6)	(7)	(8)	(9)	(10)	(11)	(12)	(13)
Total Final Demand[b] (6)	Total Intermediate Demand (7)	Total Demand (8)	Total Production (9)	Imports (10)	Calculated Intermediate Demand (11)	(11) minus (7) (12)	Value Added (13)
727.8	574.5	1302.3	1015.6	286.7	321.3	-253.2	784.2
24.4	77.3	101.7	93.9	7.8	26.8	-50.5	59.7
4.8	61.4	66.2	56.0	10.2	37.4	-24.0	32.4
268.1	197.4	565.5	551.8	13.7	220.5	23.1	244.2
192.8	246.2	439.0	420.2	18.8	280.3	34.1	78.0
28.1	32.2	60.3	57.3	3.0	37.8	5.6	16.6
15.7	15.7	31.4	21.1	10.3	50.1	34.4	6.1
18.5	10.5	29.0	28.6	.4	23.4	12.9	10.9
3.7	6.0	9.7	9.5	.2	20.6	14.6	1.4
44.5	154.9	199.4	98.7	100.7	179.4	24.5	25.8
3.9	9.1	13.0	10.9	2.1	46.6	37.5	2.0
9.7	16.0	25.7	24.6	1.1	28.5	12.5	8.7
41.4	145.0	186.4	151.3	35.1	199.7	54.7	15.3
52.8	30.5	83.3	68.2	15.1	36.6	6.1	22.3
80.5	12.3	92.8	83.3	9.2	32.1	19.8	23.5
15.4	20.0	35.4	35.4		20.8	.8	6.7
81.0	35.9	116.9	116.9		48.3	12.4	37.3
3.0	2.2	5.2	5.2		33.0	30.8	2.0
177.5	52.5	230.0	230.0		144.4	91.9	160.9
68.9	14.1	83.0	83.0		20.7	6.6	71.7
129.8	70.6	200.4	197.7	2.7	108.5	37.9	111.8
624.5	127.5	752.0	748.0	4.0	128.1	.6	290.6
94.1 (65.9)	159.8	253.9	246.0	7.9	202.1	42.3	73.8
2810.9	2071.6	4882.5	4353.5	529.0	2247.0	175.4	2185.9

TABLE 11A.3. STRUCTURE OF THE JAPANESE ECONOMY IN 1934-1936

Sectors	Demand				
	Consumption (1)	Government Expenditure (2)	Fixed Capital Formation (3)	Change in Inventory (4)	Exports (5)
1. Agriculture	803.4	2.6		.4	34.7
2. Coal and Petroleum	3.8	14.0		8.0	7.1
3. Other Mining	1.0			2.3	.9
4. Food	453.0	5.8		10.6	72.5
5. Textiles and Leather	326.6	10.8	.6	67.6	631.4
6. Wood	10.9	2.3	6.1	3.6	18.4
7. Pulp and Paper	9.4	2.9		2.1	18.1
8. Printing and Publishing	75.5	3.1		2.4	1.4
9. Rubber Products	26.8	4.1		-.1	8.8
10. Chemicals	42.8	31.4		28.4	49.9
11. Coal and Petroleum Products	8.7	17.5		4.6	4.1
12. Nonmetallic Mineral Products	16.5		.9	1.9	32.9
13. Metal Manufacturing	22.5	10.4	5.2	39.4	90.1
14. Machinery	13.3	3.9	263.9	27.2	40.4
15. Transport Equipment	6.6	138.5	130.1	39.4	32.6
16. Miscellaneous	25.4	3.6	.3	1.0	28.0
17. Construction		50.8	357.4		
18. Electricity and Gas	26.0	1.6			
19. Trade	461.0	9.4	57.1	14.0	107.1
20. Real Estate	66.5	14.3			
21. Transportation	131.3	35.2	3.6	8.9	205.8
22. Service	1035.6	66.1	43.9		141.7
23. Unallocated		202.7			120.5
Value Added[a]	(44.2)	(129.9)			
Total	3610.8	760.9	869.1	261.7	1646.4

[a]Contents of Value Added are import duties. Unit is billion of yen at 1951 prices.

[b]Final demand equals the total of columns (1) to (5).

[c]Total demand equals (6) + (7).

[d]Total supply equals total demand.

Demand			Supply[d]		Technological Changes		
Total Final Demand[b]	Total Intermediate Demand	Total Demand[c]	Total Production	Imports	Calculated Intermediate Demand	(11) minus (7)	Value Added
(6)	(7)	(8)	(9)	(10)	(11)	(12)	(13)
841.1	1370.0	2211.1	1396.9	814.2	891.9	-478.1	1078.6
32.9	187.0	219.9	158.6	61.3	120.8	-66.2	100.9
4.2	200.4	204.6	108.6	96.0	163.4	-37.0	62.7
541.9	295.1	837.0	779.2	57.8	411.4	116.3	344.9
1037.0	996.6	2033.6	2011.9	21.7	1110.4	113.8	373.4
41.3	143.7	185.0	183.5	1.5	135.8	-7.9	53.3
32.5	106.0	138.5	101.9	36.6	178.9	72.9	29.5
82.4	22.3	104.7	103.8	.9	54.5	32.2	39.7
39.6	46.8	86.4	85.6	.8	59.8	13.0	12.4
152.5	254.7	407.2	327.4	79.8	434.8	180.1	85.5
34.9	82.9	117.8	84.6	33.2	137.2	54.3	15.7
52.2	90.0	142.2	129.8	12.4	111.2	21.2	45.8
167.6	711.5	879.1	767.4	111.7	896.3	184.8	77.7
348.7	114.4	463.1	416.6	46.5	144.0	29.6	136.1
347.2	74.6	421.8	408.1	13.7	97.3	22.7	114.8
58.3	30.6	88.9	88.9		65.6	35.0	16.7
408.2	143.9	552.1	552.1		105.9	-38.0	176.3
27.6	57.3	84.9	84.9		95.1	37.8	32.8
648.6	291.4	940.0	940.0		357.0	65.6	657.6
80.8	31.2	112.0	112.0		47.5	16.3	96.7
384.8	139.4	524.2	516.6	7.6	312.1	172.7	292.2
1287.3	276.9	1564.2	1541.0	23.2	376.7	99.8	804.6
323.2	353.9	677.1	655.0	22.1	551.0	197.1	196.5
(174.1)							
6974.8	6020.6	12995.4	11554.4	1441.0	6858.6	838.0	4844.4

TABLE 11A.4. STRUCTURE OF THE JAPANESE ECONOMY IN 1954

Sectors	Demand			
	Consumption (1)	Government Expenditure (2)	Fixed Capital Formation (3)	Change in Inventory (4)
1. Agriculture	926.3	2.3		33.0
2. Coal and Petroleum	3.0	10.3		2.3
3. Other Mining	1.2			10.2
4. Food	619.6	7.7		9.9
5. Textiles and Leather	454.4	5.9	.8	23.5
6. Wood	23.5	2.4	5.6	-.3
7. Pulp and Paper	14.8	3.1		9.4
8. Printing and Publishing	94.6	2.4		3.9
9. Rubber Products	34.7	4.2		.8
10. Chemicals	67.1	.9		9.2
11. Coal and Petroleum Products	19.3	5.7		3.8
12. Nonmetallic Mineral Products	9.9		.8	-11.9
13. Metal Manufacturing	35.3	3.0	6.9	6.8
14. Machinery	39.2	23.8	255.3	8.7
15. Transport Equipment	10.4		169.0	
16. Miscellaneous	33.9	.9	.2	1.7
17. Construction		7.4	593.5	
18. Electricity and Gas	63.0	1.2		
19. Trade	698.4	7.3	61.4	6.8
20. Real Estate	114.0	12.4		
21. Transportation	196.9	18.4	4.0	4.4
22. Service	1223.9	153.3	102.6	
23. Unallocated		172.2		
Value Added[a]	(18.4)	(212.4)		
Total	4701.8	657.2	1200.1	122.2

[a]Contents of Value Added are import duties. Unit is billion of yen at 1951 prices.

[b]Final demand equals the total of columns (1) to (5).

[c]Total demand equals (6) + (7).

[d]Total supply equals total demand.

Demand				Supply[d]		
Exports	Total Final Demand[b]	Total Intermediate Demand	Total Demand[c]	Total Production	Imports	Value Added
(5)	(6)	(7)	(8)	(9)	(10)	(11)
20.5	982.1	1141.5	2123.6	1502.2	621.4	1159.9
4.4	20.0	254.3	274.3	181.7	92.6	115.5
1.2	12.6	333.7	346.3	243.0	103.3	140.4
61.2	698.4	597.0	1295.4	1211.2	84.2	536.0
339.0	823.6	1303.9	2127.5	2122.8	4.7	392.0
17.3	48.5	186.9	235.4	234.4	1.0	68.1
8.7	36.0	355.6	391.6	376.0	15.6	108.7
.8	101.7	82.8	184.5	183.0	1.5	69.9
4.7	44.4	76.0	120.4	120.1	.3	17.4
38.1	115.3	661.3	776.6	740.2	36.4	193.4
1.9	30.7	237.1	267.8	220.3	47.5	41.0
24.4	23.2	158.8	182.0	179.2	2.8	63.2
141.9	193.9	1518.4	1712.3	1693.5	18.8	171.5
53.3	380.3	162.8	543.1	492.5	50.6	160.9
32.8	212.2	114.5	326.7	314.5	12.2	88.5
25.8	62.5	94.4	156.9	155.8	1.1	29.3
8.1	609.0	156.5	765.5	765.5		244.5
	64.2	155.4	219.6	219.6		84.7
71.2	845.1	517.1	1362.2	1362.2		953.0
	126.4	65.5	191.9	191.9		165.7
177.2	400.9	474.1	875.0	871.1	3.9	492.7
55.2	1535.0	558.8	2093.8	2085.8	8.0	1089.0
30.3	202.5	854.4	1056.9	1041.8	15.1	312.5
	(230.8)					
1118.0	7568.5	10060.8	17629.3	16508.3	1121.0	6697.8

TABLE 11A.5. CAUSES OF DEVIATIONS FROM PROPORTIONAL EXPANSION OF OUTPUT, 1914-1954

	Final Demand		Exports	
	Direct Deviation[a] (1)	Total Effect[b] (2)	Direct Deviation[a] (3)	Total Effect[b] (4)
1. Agriculture, Forestry, and Fishing	-1,030	-1,036	-58	-69
2. Coal and Petroleum	-14	21	-36	-30
3. Other Mining	-1	48	0	35
4. Food	-322	-422	-27	-33
5. Textiles and Leather	250	432	25	29
6. Wood	-8	39	-24	-25
7. Pulp and Paper	16	78	-24	-34
8. Printing and Publishing	49	49	-*	*
9. Rubber Products	30	30	4	5
10. Chemicals	-32	-97	21	22
11. Coal and Petroleum Products	18	33	1	9
12. Nonmetallic Mineral Products	-14	32	10	14
13. Metal Manufacturing	-2	279	78	223
14. Machinery	187	209	44	53
15. Transport Equipment	-45	-51	28	30
16. Miscellaneous	5	20	14	16
17. Construction	371	361	8	7
18. Electricity and Gas	56	65	0	1
19. Trade	341	349	-1	11
20. Real Estate	-70	-71	0	*
21. Transport and Communications	62	103	-30	-31
22. Service	-256	-196	15	16
23. Unallocated	-13	33	-52	-30
Total	-422	308	-4	219

[a]The direct deviation is the change from proportional expansion in each autonomous element.

[b]The total effect includes indirect effects of deviations in other sectors

[c](1) + (3) + (5) + (7)

[d](2) + (4) +(6) + (8).

Imports		Technological Change		Total Direct Deviations[c]	Total Deviations in Output[d]
Direct Deviation[a]	Total Effect[b]	Direct Deviation[a]	Total Effect[b]		
(5)	(6)	(7)	(8)	(9)	(10)
194	280	-720	-561	-1,614	-1,386
-70	-65	-144	-15	-264	-89
-74	-29	-68	30	-143	84
-45	-27	66	122	-328	-360
49	127	97	338	421	926
8	14	16	44	-8	72
14	40	98	233	104	317
-*	3	37	50	86	102
*	5	42	53	76	93
250	379	70	155	309	459
-42	-17	107	158	84	183
*	6	36	56	32	108
81	216	156	543	313	1,261
-8	-4	17	40	240	298
14	19	56	79	53	77
-1	2	2	18	20	56
0	9	35	56	414	433
0	9	88	130	144	205
0	27	261	322	601	709
0	2	19	25	-51	-44
4	29	108	206	144	307
3	33	2	105	-236	-42
7	55	120	283	62	341
384	1,113	501	2,470	459	4,110

TABLE 11A.6. CAUSES OF DEVIATIONS FROM PROPORTIONAL EXPANSION OF OUTPUT, 1935-1954

	Final Demand		Exports	
	Direct Deviation (1)	Total Effect (2)	Direct Deviation (3)	Total Effect (4)
1. Agriculture, Forestry and Fishing	18	50	-20	-268
2. Coal and Petroleum	-15	-19	-4	-37
3. Other Mining	8	-24	*	-12
4. Food	88	123	-24	-86
5. Textiles and Leather	10	-16	-400	-808
6. Wood	4	14	-4	-17
7. Pulp and Paper	11	27	-13	-69
8. Printing and Publishing	6	9	-1	-11
9. Rubber Products	4	-3	-6	-16
10. Chemicals	-43	-57	-20	-138
11. Coal and Petroleum Products	-7	-15	-3	-27
12. Nonmetallic Mineral Products	-24	-12	-14	-21
13. Metal Manufacturing	-39	-210	37	-11
14. Machinery	-34	-61	6	-6
15. Transport Equipment	-189	-210	-5	-19
16. Miscellaneous	1	7	-7	-17
17. Construction	123	130	8	-11
18. Electricity and Gas	32	26	-	-22
19. Trade	140	135	-54	-120
20. Real Estate	32	37	-	-6
21. Transport and Communications	14	22	-64	-123
22. Service	139	158	-111	-179
23. Unallocated	-65	-60	-111	-197
Total	214	51	-810	-2221

Imports		Technological Change		Total Direct Deviations	Total Deviations in Output
Direct Deviation (5)	Total Effect (6)	Direct Deviation (7)	Total Effect (8)	(9)	(10)
331	396	-559	-311	-230	-132
-21	-1	-78	51	-117	-6
9	63	-43	89	-27	116
-17	8	136	255	184	300
21	93	133	498	-236	-232
1	8	-9	15	-8	20
27	60	85	239	111	257
-*	3	38	61	43	62
1	7	15	32	14	20
57	137	211	415	205	357
-9	17	64	142	45	117
12	19	25	41	-1	27
112	296	216	719	326	794
4	10	35	62	11	5
4	9	27	57	-164	-163
1	3	41	59	34	52
--	11	-45	-10	87	119
--	13	44	103	76	120
--	53	77	194	163	262
--	3	19	28	51	61
5	35	202	332	158	266
19	49	117	255	165	283
11	74	231	457	66	275
568	1,366	982	3,783	956	2,980

TABLE 11A.7. EMPLOYMENT AND LABOR INPUTS BY SECTOR

	1913-1915		1934-1936	
	N	n	N	n
1. Agriculture, Forestry, and Fishing	15,816	15,573	14,749	10,558
2. Coal and Petroleum	187	1,991	198	1,248
3. Other Mining	86	1,536	88	810
4. Food	453	821	615	789
5. Textiles and Leather	1,599	3,805	2,280	1,133
6. Wood and Wood Products	670	11,693	678	3,695
7. Pulp and Paper	97	4,597	125	1,227
8. Printing and Publishing	66	2,308	139	1,339
9. Rubber Products	4	421	45	526
10. Chemicals	133	1,348	219	669
11. Coal and Petroleum Products	6	550	17	201
12. Nonmetallic Mineral Products	204	8,923	269	2,072
13. Metal Manufacturing	303	2,003	576	751
14. Machinery	221	3,240	452	1,085
15. Transport Equipment	136	1,627	332	814
16. Miscellaneous	213	6,017	211	2,373
17. Construction	651	5,569	980	1,775
18. Electricity and Gas	38	7,308	109	1,284
19. Trade	2,364	10,278	3,623	3,854
20. Real Estate	17	205	25	223
21. Transportation and Communications	893	4,517	1,261	2,441
22. Services	1,765	2,360	3,495	2,268
23. Unallocated	0	0	0	0
Total	25,922	5,954	30,486	2,638

N: Employment in 1000 persons.

n: Labor coefficient - employment per billions yen of gross production.

1951		1954	
N	n	N	n
16,293	11,892	16,822	11,198
444	2,357	353	1,943
160	675	140	576
564	687	629	519
1,257	917	1,327	625
570	2,947	574	2,449
166	717	190	505
206	2,016	287	1,568
80	933	80	666
313	650	307	415
32	229	39	177
295	1,989	319	1,780
603	465	633	374
715	1,895	862	1,750
346	1,468	384	1,221
191	1,830	205	1,316
2,043	3,331	2,472	3,229
161	1,046	161	733
3,988	4,155	4,865	3,571
33	264	47	245
1,722	2,839	1,731	1,987
4,293	3,404	4,926	2,362
0	0	0	0
34,475	2,923	37,353	2,263

TABLE 11A.8. INPUT-OUTPUT TABLE FOR THE JAPANESE ECONOMY, 1954[a]

	1	2	3	4	5	6	7	8	9	10	11	12	13	14	15	16	17	18	19	20	21	22	23
1. Agriculture	369	280	70	2096	2205	4300	674	23	3482	1111	*	64	25	----	*	277	188	34	30	*	23	362	----
2. Coal and Petroleum	2	196	39	58	39	2	162	76	54	267	5093	975	36	17	15	7	1	1890	5	2	259	20	----
3. Other mining	33	52	48	7	----	*	188	*	149	283	39	733	1507	21	*	20	236	*	*	*	3	3	67
4. Food	162	97	5	1696	47	16	54	----	7	267	18	61	23	63	*	35	*	56	136	*	63	1119	627
5. Textiles and Leather	158	15	11	40	4144	22	142	44	2301	44	6	78	25	37	123	362	22	16	---	*	140	53	3025
6. Wood and Wood Products	16	100	23	45	8	1349	47	----	15	23	8	185	23	110	245	187	1033	1598	44	----	80	13	175
7. Pulp and Paper	11	*	----	128	173	16	4029	3574	26	139	24	587	6	92	21	1333	40	9	149	*	37	25	38
8. Printing and Publishing	*	4	----	----	4	*	96	*	5	9	*	*	---	2	-----	721	5	4	2	2	32	187	225
9. Rubber Products	62	61	80	7	22	1	43	28	201	36	16	50	9	47	364	---	37	24	66	---	106	20	80
10. Chemicals	609	168	89	23	295	166	282	309	1432	2618	168	359	25	109	123	920	151	27	*	*	29	276	1276
11. Coal and Petroleum Products	110	64	66	34	25	10	42	97	115	245	37	367	393	49	81	144	87	490	9	----	711	21	111
12. Nonmetallic Mineral Products	12	21	7	75	2	27	6	----	----	77	13	857	77	106	103	27	1232	40	---	*	16	29	----
13. Metal Manufacturing	27	520	332	127	18	58	116	62	----	276	184	246	5413	3462	2722	253	1782	408	87	*	319	31	707
14. Machinery	20	152	4	----	38	3	7	53	1	5	----	2	36	1018	1176	23	155	68	29	----	1130	110	32
15. Transport Equipment	10	*	*	*	*	*	*	*	*	*	*	*	*	*	1057	*	*	*	*	*	173	139	342
16. Miscellaneous Manufactures	--	18	15	14	31	6	19	*	10	26	9	8	1	6	23	637	113	25	234	10	62	94	----
17. Construction	101	231	21	22	37	10	72	244	8	89	20	14	35	41	41	3	25	254	82	1062	181	160	132
18. Electricity and Gas	15	427	56	62	47	117	160	70	47	172	824	222	92	69	67	33	2	115	14	4	114	59	310
19. Trade	371	102	2666	161	198	106	233	330	360	294	112	233	110	292	397	503	564	172	76	2	127	385	775
20. Real Estate	22	9	13	7	4	*	6	*	6	12	7	2	2	3	2	---	6	13	116	*	17	193	*

TABLE 11A.8 - CONTINUED

	1	2	3	4	5	6	7	8	9	10	11	12	13	14	15	16	17	18	19	20	21	22	23
21. Transportation and Comm.	58	308	58	169	95	407	380	260	203	282	299	449	127	184	122	181	408	415	525	51	329	325	1001
22. Services	15	200	44	96	153	93	229	690	54	366	42	126	99	193	72	112	778	174	704	202	416	542	1062
23. Unallocated	193	737	606	519	163	462	726	314	68	551	666	961	693	698	428	2874	*	1242	896	31	637	801	*

[a]Each coefficient is equal to $(X_{ij}/X_j) \times 10^4$, where X_{ij} is the input from industry i to sector j and X_j is production of sector j at producers' prices of 1951.

*indicates zero

--indicates value less than .5.

Notes

The research reported here has been done as part of the program of the Research Center in Economic Growth, Stanford University. We have received financial support from the Ford Foundation and the Rockefeller Foundation through the Stanford Committee on East Asian Research and the Stanford-Tokyo Committee. A large amount of supplementary analysis of basic statistical materials was carried out for us by the Japanese Ministry of International Trade and Industry. We are very grateful for the assistance provided by these institutions. Statistical calculations at Stanford were done by M. Tanaka and J. Biemans.

1. This study is reported in detail in H. B. Chenery, "Patterns of Industrial Growth," American Economic Review (September 1960); only the statistical results are used here.

2. Among economic historians, Lockwood has come closest to analyzing the set of problems raised here, and we have relied heavily on his study; see W. Lockwood, The Economic Development of Japan (Princeton: Princeton University Press, 1954) for historical background. He frequently indicates the need for a quantitative analysis of the interdependent factors which determine the pattern of growth.

3. W. W. Rostow, "The Take-Off into Self-Sustained Growth," Economic Journal (March 1956), p. 31, considers that the end of the transitional period when self-sustaining growth was firmly established may be dated somewhere between 1900 and 1914; he prefers the earlier date.

4. In the comparison of S. Kuznets,"Quantitative Aspects of the Economic Growth of Nations: Parts I and II," Economic Development and Cultural Change (October 1956 and July 1957) of long-term data for 17 advanced countries, Japan between 1880 and 1952 has the highest overall rate of growth observed, even with the setback caused by the last war.

5. According to K. Ohkawa, The Growth Rate of the Japanese Economy since 1878 (Tokyo: Kinokuniya, 1957), p. 17, primary

production (excluding mining) increased by 1130 million yen from 1880 to 1910 while secondary production increased by 890 million.

6. H. B. Chenery, "Patterns of Industrial Growth," American Economic Review (September 1960).

7. Earlier studies wuch as those of Colin Clark and Kuznets, treat manufacturing as a single sector of the economy and are therefore less useful for the present analysis.

8. We have no standard of comparison for hand production, so this allowance cannot be made in any precise way.

9. Since size of country is so important, it is difficult in the absence of multiple regression analyses to determine whether the normal ratio of trade to income has been declining over time or not, but it seems likely that it has done so.

10. The percentages are taken from Lockwood, The Economic Development of Japan, p. 354 rather than from our estimates because the latter are at producers' prices with trade and transportation shown separately.

11.Even the development of simple manufactured goods for export instead of primary products can be observed in a few low-income countries like India.

12. The basic data are given in the Appendix. 1914 was taken as the starting point because it was the year of the second census and the first on modern lines. The first census of 1909 was much less comparable to the later industrial classifications.

13. This differs from the formulation of W. W. Leontief, Studies in the Structure of the American Economy, New York, Oxford University Press, 1953, p. 18 in treating imports as autonomous elements. This form of input-output model is discussed in H. B. Chenery and P. Clark, Interindustry Economics (New York: Wiley, 1959), p. 23.

14. The coefficients $\underline{r}_{ij}$ are the elements of the inverse to the Leontief matrix, $[\underline{I}-\underline{A}]^{-1} = \{\underline{r}_{ij}\}$.

15. If trade is balanced, this ratio is the growth in GNP.

16. In matrix notation, the derivation is as follows: Let $\underline{X}$, $\underline{Y}$, $\underline{E}$, and $\underline{M}$ be the vectors of production, domestic demand, exports, and imports, and $\underline{L} = (\underline{I} - \underline{A})$ be the Leontief matrix. Equation (11.2) is then:

$$(11.2a) \quad \underline{X}^t = \underline{L}^{-1}(\underline{Y}^t + \underline{E}^t - \underline{M}^t).$$

The vector of deviations in production is defined as

$$(11.5) \quad \delta\underline{X}^{12} = \underline{X}^2 - \lambda\underline{X}^1 = (\underline{L}^2)^{-1}\underline{F}^2 - \lambda(\underline{L}^1)^{-1}\underline{F}^1$$

where $\underline{F} = (\underline{Y} + \underline{E} - \underline{M})$, the vector of combined autonomous elements. Equation (11.5) can be rewritten as

$$(11.6) \quad \delta\underline{X}^{12} = (\underline{L}^2)^{-1}\delta\underline{F}^{12} + [(\underline{L}^2)^{-1} - (\underline{L}^1)^{-1}]\lambda\underline{F}^1.$$

The second term in equation (11.6) is the vector of changes in the intermediate demands for inputs resulting from the technological change from $\underline{L}^1$ to $\underline{L}^2$. This may be rewritten as

$$\begin{aligned}(11.7) \quad [(\underline{L}^2)^{-1} - (\underline{L}^1)^{-1}]\lambda\underline{F}^1 &= -(\underline{L}^2)^{-1}(\underline{L}^2 - \underline{L}^1)(\underline{L}^1)^{-1}\lambda\underline{F}^1 \\ &= -(\underline{L}^2)^{-1}(\underline{L}^2 - \underline{L}^1)\lambda\underline{X}^1 \\ &= -(\underline{L}^2)^{-1}\lambda\underline{T}^{12}\end{aligned}$$

where $\underline{T}^{12} = (\underline{L}^2 - \underline{L}^1)\underline{X}^1$.

17. These elements are initially considered autonomous in order to separate their effects on output. Their interrelations are taken up in later sections.

18. In equation (11. 7), we therefore substitute the following expression for $\underline{T}_j$: $\underline{T}_j^{12} = \sum_{\underline{k}} \underline{X}_{jk}^1 - \sum_{\underline{k}} \underline{a}_{jk}^2\underline{X}_k^1$, where the first

term on the right is the actual total intermediate demand, whose breakdown by using sector is unknown.

19. In the first instance, we omit the effects of technological change, which cannot be satisfactorily separated from the errors in the basic statistics. This factor will be taken into account in evaluating the total change.

20. Given in Ohkawa, The Growth Rate of the Japanese Economy since 1878, and in more detail in L. H. Dupriez (ed.), Economic Progress: Papers and Proceedings of a Round Table Held by the International Economic Association (Paris: Institut de Recherches Economiques et Socials, 1955), pp. 369-377.

21. Only in wood products does the income effect account for as much as half of the total deviation from proportional growth in this group.

22. Indirect effects of the primary growth sectors account for more of the expansion in group B, however, since the "income effect" on trade is only a result of input-output accounting conventions and should be considered an indirect effect.

23. The increased proportion of agricultural imports in total supply is concealed by the measure of autonomous change as the deviation from proportionality because total agricultural demand grew more slowly than income.

24. Substitution is in part factory output for hand production.

25. In group A, all effects are additive, but in group D indirect effects offset the other two.

26. On this hypothesis, exports would have to increase by a large amount and this would cause some growth of industry but less than that caused by import substitution.

27. H. B. Chenery, "Patterns of Industrial Growth."

28. One factor explaining high consumption is the high degree of urbanization for the level of income. Second, the use of a lower yen-dollar exchange rate would somewhat reduce the deviations from the standard in both industry and agriculture. Although incomes of the countries from which the regression equations are derived are generally undervalued at actual exchange rates, the difference may be somewhat greater for Japan than for most. T. Watanabe and R. Komiya, "Findings from Price Comparisons, Principally Japan vs. the U.S.," *Weltwirtschaftliches Archiv*, October 1958, found a consumer purchasing power 1.9 times that given by the official rate, a ratio somewhat higher than the values found by M. Gilbert and I. Kravis, *An International Comparison of National Product and the Purchasing Power of Currencies* (Paris: OEEC, 1954) for Western Europe. No calculations are available for other low-income countries.

29. For the two periods, the regression of productivity growth on output growth is:

$$(1914\text{-}1935) \quad \log \frac{\ell^2}{\ell^1} = \underset{(.086)}{.667} \log \frac{x^2}{x^1}, \qquad R^2 = .77;$$

$$(1935\text{-}1954) \quad \log \frac{\ell^2}{\ell^1} = -0.1 + \underset{(.230)}{.758} \log \frac{x^2}{x^1}, \qquad R^2 = .37.$$

30. The regressions based on this assumption give poorer results, however.

31. T. Watanabe, "A Note on the Japanese Capital-Output Ratio," mimeographed (Stanford, Calif.: Stanford Project for Quantitative Research in Economic Development, July 1957).

32. Fixed capital stock per employee (in thousands of dollars) in Japan and the United States, classified roughly according to our divisions are as follows:

		U.S.	Japan	Ratio J/US
IA	Agriculture	19.58	.37	.02
IB	Mining	2.11	.75	.36
IIA	Food Products	5.07	.55	.11
IIB	Textiles	2.78	.57	.21
IIC	Finished Goods	4.59	.42	.10
IID	Int. Products	7.44	1.23	.17
III	Services	28.45	2.14	.07
	Transport	15.57	3.61	.23
	Trade	6.18	.40	.07

33. A mimeographed appendix describing the statistical procedures followed in assembling the data and giving some further statistical detail is available from the Research Center in Economic Growth, Stanford University, Stanford, California.

34. References in English are marked **; those in Japanese and English*; others are in Japanese only.

12

An Econometric Model of Japan, 1930-1959

L. R. Klein and Y. Shinkai

12.1. Introduction

There are probably more econometric models (in existence or far along in the process of construction) of Japan than of any other country in the world. The reason for proposing the present scheme therefore needs explanation. A very major model construction project that may have practical use in suggesting the lines of economic policy has been under way among the Osaka group for some time. This is perhaps the largest and most ambitious econometric project ever undertaken. It is a detailed quarterly model covering the postwar period. A model of the scope being considered cannot be estimated, tested, revised, and successfully applied in a short period of time. There is even some uncertainty as to its ultimate workability since it is such a massive scheme and nothing of comparable size or detail is known to exist in use elsewhere.

We thus thought it useful to have a companion model, in parallel, that is more aggregative over the dimensions of time and commodities. Our model in this paper is an aggre-

---

International Economic Review, vol. 4, no. 1 (January 1963), pp. 1-28. Reprinted by courtesy of the International Economic Review and the authors.

gative annual model. It is not unlike similar annual models of the United States, Canada, the United Kingdom, and Holland that have been in use for some time. It is meant to serve as a companion piece and checking device for the larger system. After a relatively short period of time (about six months), it has become available for trial applications. It is also informative, at this early stage, on some structural characteristics of the Japanese economy. While it belongs to the same general class of models as its foreign predecessors, it bears many distinctive characteristics of the Japanese economy apart from the numerical values of its estimated parameters.

The detailed quarterly model must of necessity be limited to a sample period of the era after World War II. Actually, the Japanese economy is not suitable for the types of study that we propose in this period until after the start of the Korean War and the end of the Occupation. Quarterly data are not available in large measure before the postwar period. Annual data do exist, however, for a period beginning in 1930. This makes possible the investigation of a problem that is avoided in work on the postwar quarterly model, namely, the study of structural change between the 1930's and 1950's. To many observers it may appear self-evident that behavior and technology have radically changed as a result of the impact of World War II. There is often much that is basic in economic structure, transcending even the disruptive effects of a major catastrophe such as war. We shall attempt to isolate some of the changing and the stable characteristics of the Japanese structure in the period 1930-1958. We do not, however, include the years 1937-1950 in our sample.[1] It would be possible to extend some of our related annual series beyond 1930, say to the end of World War I, but we have decided to rely on the efforts of Professor Ueno of Nagoya University for a model extending back to 1919.

12.2. Rationale of the Model

Essentially, the system is the Keynesian type model of

effective demand for an open economy. There are consumption and investment equations, with the national income-national product accounting identities. There are export and import propensity equations, production functions, and wage-price determination equations. A main feature of the Japanese economy is the relation between the primary or agricultural sector and the rest of the economy. This is brought out in our model by two separate production functions, a relationship between food imports and domestic agricultural production, and an equation on the shift of labor between the two sectors. There is a birth and death population process as well as a liquidity preference equation.

Features of many preceding models have naturally affected our choice of other equations in the system, but the open economies of Holland and the United Kingdom provided some of the closest analogies. To account for possible structural change, we introduced additive "dummy" variables (0,1), which assumed zero values for prewar years and unit values for postwar years. In cases where scatter diagrams showed changes in slope as well as level of relationships, we introduced "dummy" variables in products with variables with respect to which the slope changed.

12.2.1. Consumption. We made use of the ordinary aggregate consumption function in our model, but we explicitly took into account the effects of population size, taxes, lags, and income distribution. Since the equation is expressed in real terms, we might say that we also took into account the price level. As can be seen in equation (12.1), our income and consumption variables are measured per capita; this brings population into the equation. The income variable is disposable income; therefore taxes and transfer payments are introduced. By writing current consumption as a function of last year's consumption we have lag effects, and it is well known that this form is a transformation of a distributed lag of the Koyck type.[2]

Income distribution is represented through our use of a factor share ratio — property income divided by wage income.

12.2.2. Investment. The propensity to invest, as expressed in our model, resembles similar relationships used in many mathematical models of the trade cycle.[3] Investment, capital stock, property income, and interest rate are the familiar variables used. We relate the percentage rate of expansion of fixed capital (investment divided by the stock of capital) to the rate of return on capital (property income as a percent of fixed capital). The rate of interest as a cost factor deterring investment has been unsuccessfully explored in many econometric models. In principle this is an important variable in the investment process linking the real and monetary sectors. For the Japanese economy the principle may turn out to be significant in practice because rates are relatively high and fluctuate by a wide margin. There is much bank borrowing and comparatively less internal financing for investment than in the United States and other countries. In this aggregative model we have not separated working and fixed capital investment.

12.2.3. Exports. Japanese sales abroad are made to depend on two main variables, world activity and relative prices. The activity variable could be an index of world income, or an index of world trade. We have chosen world trade for our variable. It is probably more accurately measured over the span of our sample than are the other possible variables. We assume implicitly that Japan enjoys some marginal share of the world market. Exports could also be affected by relative price which we measure by the ratio of an index of world export prices to an index of Japanese export prices. Both indexes are expressed in gold, to take devaluations into account automatically.

12.2.4. Imports. Three categories of imports are distinguished. They are food, materials, and all other. Food imports are singled out for separate study because they are, in Japan, related to domestic food production as a supplement. When domestic agricultural output is high, food imports tend to be low and vice versa. This is particularly true for rice, the dominant food crop. Our equation posits an inverse relation between real per capita food imports and real per capita agricultural output. Another relevant variable is the relative rice price. Not only the physical production situation, but also the economic advantage of foreign compared with domestic rice will affect imports. This allows for the fact that foreign rice may be considered to be of inferior quality, for the strength of reaction to the relative rice price depends on Japanese tastes.

Materials are, for the most part, imported to be used in manufacturing. We, therefore, related material imports to the level of nonagricultural output. Other imports are used throughout the economy, and we related these to the level of aggregate national product. In all the import equations, real magnitudes and relative prices are used. Relative price variables were considered in all import equations, but the only significant effect of prices was found in the case of food imports.

These equations complete the endogenous components in the make-up of national product. We now turn to the group of equations dealing with supply, market prices,and population.

12.2.5. Production. Nonagricultural output is, as usual, made to depend on labor and capital as input factors. Technological trends were also considered but later dropped in the statistical estimate of coefficients.

In agriculture, we do not have separate capital input data. We related output per agricultural worker to important factors that affect farm production. One of these is natural conditions, expressed in the form of a regularly published series on damaged crop area as a result of adverse growing conditions. Such conditions may cover weather, pestilence, and other natural phenomena. A negative association is to be expected between output and this variable. A positive association is introduced through the use of a variable showing the quantity of fertilizer input. A final factor to consider is an upward technological trend. Significant technical progress is, in fact, found in this case.

12.2.6. Prices and Wages. In the U.K. and Dutch models, price mark-up equations for the open economy have been used.[4] These equations show the mark-up of final price over prime unit costs. The main prime costs are wages and import prices. The U.S. and Canadian models differ by using equations for labor's share.[5] These might be interpreted as marginal productivity conditions if the production relations can be approximated by equations of the Cobb-Douglas type. The literature of theoretical economics also has these distinctions, for the case of full-cost pricing, or mark-up over costs, is considered to be a practical alternative to marginalist pricing theory. The equation of labor's share may be transformed from

$$wN_e = \alpha pY$$

to

$$p = \frac{1}{\alpha} w \frac{N_e}{Y},$$

in which p = price of output, Y = volume of output, w = wage rate, and N_e = employment.

Our mark-up equation is a slight generalization of this form since p is made to be a linear combination of

$$w\frac{N_e}{Y} \quad \text{and} \quad p_i\frac{M}{Y}.$$

p_i = price of imports

M = import volume.

We can interpret this equation as saying that price is marked up over prime unit costs, w and p_i, but that the mark-up is modified by productivities of labor and imports. As these inputs become more productive, there is need for only a smaller margin of mark-up to reach a given level of profit.

The equation of wage determination states that wages adjust to changes in final prices but that labor's bargaining position is affected by the state of demand in the labor market. The latter variable is represented by unemployment. All variables in this relation are expressed in percentage terms - percent change in wage rates, percent change in price level, and percent of labor force unemployed. Similar equations have been estimated for the U.S. and U.K. models.[6]

12.2.7. Liquidity Preference. The Keynesian theory of demand for cash is a generalization over the classical quantity theory in that velocity (or its reciprocal) is not assumed to be constant. It is assumed to be variable and dependent on the rate of interest. In its most general form, this theory expresses the nominal amount of cash as a joint function of money income and interest rate. This theory is based on the assumption that assets may be held in two forms, cash or securities (bonds). We have broadened the scope of possible asset forms to include goods, or in a sense, equity investments. The desirability of holding goods or equities against either money or bonds is indicated by prospective price changes which show the extent to which capital gains can be made. We follow A. J. Brown, who pioneered in statistical research on liquidity preference, by including a price change and an interest rate variable in our explanation of cash holdings.[7] We have transformed the dependent variable to the reciprocal of the velocity ratio rather than the level of cash holding itself.

12.2.8. Population. In most econometric models, population is considered to be exogenous. An important exception is the work of Valavanis-Vail on an American growth model.[8] He starts from the identity

$$N_t = N_{t-1}(1 + b_t - d_t - e_t),$$

which states that population (N_t) of period t is equal to population of period (t - 1) augmented by births and decreased by deaths and net emigration. The rates of birth, death, and emigration for the basic time unit considered are b, d, and e. We have used this identity and attempted to find explanatory equations for b_t and d_t. Net emigration is regarded as negligible, as far as Japan is concerned. The birth rate is assumed to depend on per capita income and the death rate to be a declining trend function of time.

12.2.9. Labor Supply. Two aspects of labor supply are given explicit treatment in the model. Both are significant in the Japanese scene. Following our prior explanation of population development, we want an expression to show how many of the population are available for productive effort. We have a labor force participation rate - the ratio of labor force to population - which is a simple function of time. The rate of participation is slowly growing, apart from a wartime setback.

The other important aspect of Japanese labor supply is its distribution between agriculture and industry, emphasized by the modern shift from rural to urban areas. We make the ratio of employment in the two sectors depend on the level of the real wage rate. This is essentially the wage rate paid in the nonagricultural sector, and this equation shows the pull of workers from agriculture, the attraction being high income rates in industry.

12.2.10. Identities and Restrictions. We have completed the analysis of the content of our model in terms of behavior or technological equations. The system is not closed, however, without some identities. We have the equality between national product and national income, or, what is the same thing, total output expressed as a sum of expenditures and also as a sum of income flows, adjusted for indirect taxes and subsidies. Unemployment is the difference between labor force and employment. Net investment is the rate of change of capital stock, and the aggregate wage bill is the product of wage rate and employment. Both indirect and direct taxes are used in the model as separate variables. Under conditions of existing tax laws they could be approximately expressed as functions of total income or product. Such equations would act as restrictions on the system. We have not explicitly shown such restrictions in this writing of the model.

12.2.11. The Variables.

$*\underline{C}$ = consumption (billions of 1934-1936 yen)

$*\underline{N}$ = population (millions of persons)

$*\underline{Y}-\underline{T}_d$ = deflated disposable income (billion of 1934-1936 yen)

$*\underline{P}$ = deflated nonwage income (billions of 1934-1936 yen)

$*\underline{W}$ = deflated wage income (billions of 1934-1936 yen)

$*\underline{I}$ = net investment (billions of 1934-1936 yen)

$*\underline{K}$ = year end capital stock (billions of 1934-1936 yen)

$\underline{i}$ = interest rate

$*\underline{F_e}$ = exports (billions of 1934-1936 yen)

$\underline{T_w}$ = index of world trade

$\underline{p_w}$ = index of world export prices

$\underline{p_j}$ = index of Japanese export prices

$*\underline{F_{ij}}$ = food imports (billions of 1934-1936 yen)

$*\underline{Y_f}$ = domestic food production (billions of 1934-1936 yen)

$\underline{p_d}$ = domestic rice price

$\underline{p_m}$ = imported rice price

$*\underline{F_{im}}$ = material imports (billions of 1934-1936 yen)

$*\underline{Y}$ = net national product (billions of 1934-1936 yen)

$*\underline{F_{io}}$ = "other" imports (1934-1936 yen)

$*\underline{N_e}$ = nonagricultural employment (millions of persons)

$*\underline{N_f}$ = agricultural employment (millions of persons)

$\underline{F}$ = index of fertilizer input

$\underline{H}$ = damaged area of cultivated land (ten million cho)

$\underline{t}$ = trend, in years, beginning with unity in 1930 (× 1/10)

$*\underline{p}$ = index of price level (1934-1936: 1.00)

$\underline{p_i}$ = index of import prices

$*\underline{w}$ = wage rate (thousands of current yen)

$*\underline{M}$ = total imports (billions of 1934-1936 yen)

$*\underline{U}$ = unemployment rate

$*\underline{L}$ = cash balances (billions of current yen)

$*\underline{b}$ = birth rate

$*\underline{d}$ = death rate

$\underline{e}$ = net emigration rate

$*\underline{N_L}$ = labor force (millions of persons)

$\underline{G}$ = government current expenditures (billions of 1934-1936 yen)

$\underline{T_i}$ = indirect taxes less subsidies (billions of 1934-1936 yen)

$\underline{D}$ = prewar-postwar shift variable (zero in prewar and unity in postwar period)

Endogenous variables in this list are marked with an

asterisk (*). For purposes of statistical estimation, taxes are not treated as endogenous. Disposable income in the above list is marked endogenous, but Y is regarded as endogenous, while T_d is not; thus one must take account of this fact in counting equations and variables. We have denoted L as endogenous and i as predetermined. The usual practice in business cycle theory is the opposite, but our procedure appears to be more realistic. We have provided no explanation of Japanese rice, or total export prices; hence these are not treated as endogenous. Considering the role of government agricultural policy it is not unrealistic to treat the rice price as predetermined.

A flow chart of our specification is presented in Fig. 12.1.

12.2.12. The Estimated Equations. Our sample consists of yearly observations for the period 1930-1936 and 1951-1958. The method of estimation is Theil's "two-stage-least-squares."[9]

$$\frac{C}{N} = 0.055 + \underset{(0.072)}{0.230}\,\frac{Y - T_d}{N} + \underset{(0.069)}{0.576}\left(\frac{C}{N}\right)_{-1} - \underset{(0.0049)}{0.0191}\,\frac{P}{W} \qquad R^2 = 0.96 \tag{12.1}$$

$$\frac{I}{K} = -0.005 + \underset{(0.140)}{0.478}\,\frac{P}{K} - \underset{(0.244)}{0.678}\,i + \underset{(0.0108)}{0.0561}\,D \qquad R^2 = 0.94 \tag{12.2}$$

$$F_e = -2.92 + \underset{(0.731)}{3.917}\,T_w + \underset{(0.417)}{2.457}\,\frac{p_w}{p_j} - \underset{(0.40)}{3.37}\,D \qquad R^2 = 0.85 \tag{12.3}$$

$$\frac{F_{if}}{N} = 0.00396 - \underset{(0.0473)}{0.0618}\,\frac{Y_f}{N} + \underset{(0.00032)}{0.000463}\,\frac{p_d}{p_m} + \underset{(0.00067)}{0.00405}\,D \qquad R^2 = 0.88 \tag{12.4}$$

$$F_{im} = -1.27 + \underset{(0.029)}{0.260}\,(Y - Y_f) - \underset{(0.231)}{1.163}\,D \qquad R^2 = 0.87 \tag{12.5}$$

Fig. 12.1. Flow Chart of the Klein-Shinkai Model

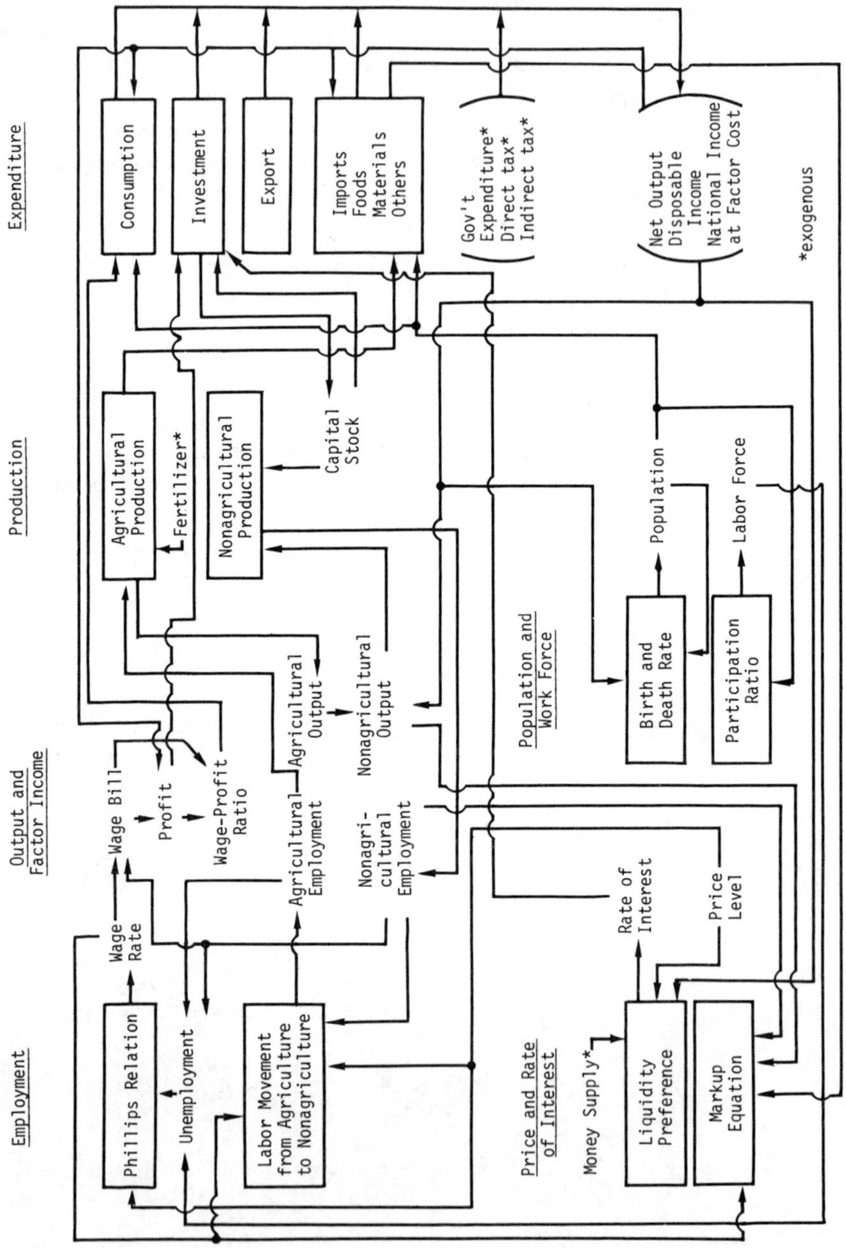

$$\underline{R}^2 = 0.87$$

$$(12.6) \quad \underline{F}_{i0} = 0.96 + \underset{(0.0132)}{0.0563}\,\underline{Y} - \underset{(0.122)}{1.713}\,\underline{D} \qquad \underline{R}^2 = 0.97$$

$$(12.7) \quad \underline{Y} - \underline{Y}_f = -6.46 + \underset{(0.083)}{0.770}\,\underline{N}_6 + \underset{(0.048)}{0.106}\,\underline{K} \qquad \underline{R}^2 = 0.89$$

$$(12.8) \quad \frac{\underline{Y}_f}{\underline{N}_f} = 0.114 + \underset{(0.0224)}{0.0590}\,\underline{F} - \underset{(0.0387)}{0.0986}\,\underline{H} + \underset{(0.0102)}{0.0269}\,\underline{t} \qquad \underline{R}^2 = 0.90$$

$$(12.9) \quad \underline{p} = 0.370 + \underset{(0.083)}{0.995}\,\underline{w}\,\frac{\underline{N}_e}{\underline{Y} - \underline{Y}_f} + \underset{(0.25)}{0.73}\,\underline{p}_i\,\frac{\underline{M}}{\underline{Y}} + \underset{(13.2)}{124.4}\,\underline{D} \qquad \underline{R}^2 = 0.99$$

$$(12.10) \quad \frac{\underline{w} - \underline{w}_{-1}}{\underline{w}_{-1}} = 0.260 + \underset{(0.183)}{0.746}\,\frac{\underline{p} - \underline{p}_{-1}}{\underline{p}_{-1}} - \underset{(10.8)}{16.98}\,\underline{U} \qquad \underline{R}^2 = 0.64$$

$$(12.11) \quad \frac{\underline{L}}{\underline{pY}} = 0.229 - \underset{(0.000368)}{0.000867}\,(\underline{p} - \underline{p}_{-1}) - \underset{(0.104)}{0.214}\,\underline{Di} \qquad \underline{R}^2 = 0.59$$

$$(12.12) \quad \log_{10}(\underline{b} - 0.015) = -0.414 - \underset{(0.565)}{6.491}\,\frac{\underline{Y}}{\underline{N}} - \underset{(0.0332)}{0.3045}\,\underline{D} \qquad \underline{R}^2 = 0.98$$

$$(12.13) \quad \log_{10}(\underline{d} - 0.005) = -1.775 - \underset{(0.004)}{0.277}\,\underline{t} \qquad \underline{R}^2 = 0.99$$

$$(12.14) \quad \frac{\underline{N}_e}{\underline{N}_f} = -0.241 + \underset{(0.59)}{3.799}\,\frac{\underline{w}}{\underline{p}} + \underset{(0.049)}{0.191}\,\underline{D} \qquad \underline{R}^2 = 0.92$$

$$(12.15)\quad \frac{\underline{N}_L}{\underline{N}}\ 0.442 + \underset{(0.0143)}{0.0398\,\underline{t}} - \underset{(0.0314)}{0.0822\,\underline{D}} \qquad \underline{R}^2 = 0.30$$

$$\underline{C} + \underline{I} + \underline{G} + \underline{F}_e - \underline{M} = \underline{Y}$$

$$\underline{P} + \underline{W} = \underline{Y} - \underline{T}_i$$

$$\underline{F}_{if} + \underline{F}_{im} + \underline{F}_{io} = \underline{M}$$

$$\underline{K} - \underline{K}_{-1} = \underline{I}$$

$$\frac{\underline{w}}{\underline{p}}(\underline{N}_e) = \underline{W}$$

$$\underline{U} = \frac{\underline{N}_L - \underline{N}_e - \underline{N}_f}{\underline{N}_L}$$

$$\underline{N} = \underline{N}_{-1}(1 + \underline{b} - \underline{d} - \underline{e})$$

12.3. Some Properties of the System

In this section we shall discuss some of the interesting properties of our system from the point of view of each equation.

12.3.1. Consumption. Our consumption function can be rewritten in the form

$$\underline{C} = 0.055\underline{N} + 0.230\,\underline{Y}_d + 0.576\left(\frac{\underline{C}}{\underline{N}}\right)_{-1}\underline{N} - 0.0191\left(\frac{\underline{P}}{\underline{W}}\right)\underline{N},$$

where $\underline{Y}_d = \underline{Y} - \underline{T}_d$ stands for disposable income. It is seen immediately that the short run marginal propensity to consume is 0.23. This value may be compared with findings by other economists: 0.346 by H. Ueno; 0.313 by T. Uchida and K. Mori; 0.373 by H. Eguchi.[10] Our value appears to be low. This may be due to the fact (1) that our function is estimated in per capita terms while the other functions are not, (2), that our sample periods extend to prewar years, in some of which $\partial\underline{C}/\partial\underline{Y}_d$ assumes negative values.

If we put $\underline{C}/\underline{N} = (\underline{C}/\underline{N})_{-1}$ in the above equation, we get a sort of long run marginal propensity to consume, which turns out to be 0.542. The comparable findings by other economists are 0.749 by H. Ueno; 0.616 by T. Uchida and K. Mori; 0.777 by H. Eguchi. The average propensity to consume at the point of sample means is 0.899, which is calculated simply as

$\sum_t C_t / \sum_t (Y_d)_t$. The Japanese people as individual consumers have been saving about 10 percent of their income in real terms.

The reader will notice that the share of nonwage income in the total national income has a negative effect on consumption, as would be expected. The magnitude of this effect may be expressed by means of an "elasticity" coefficient which assumes the value -0.0877 in the year 1958.[11] This means that a 10 percent rise in the ratio of nonwage to wage income reduces real consumption by roughly one percent.

As regards our remark above that $\partial C/\partial Y_d$ assumes negative values in some of the prewar years, it must be noted that in our estimated equation (12.1) the contribution of Y_d in the explanation of C/N is rather small, and that the lagged per capita consumption $(C/N)_{-1}$ has a coefficient which is more than twice as large. (This may be the reason why the pre-postwar shift variable turned out insignificant here.) Thus the total correlation coefficient is high in spite of the bad fit between Y_d/N and C/N in the prewar years.

12.3.2. Investment. The investment function can be rewritten as

$$I = -0.005\,K + 0.478\,P - 0.678\,iK \qquad \text{for prewar years,}$$
$$I = 0.051\,K + 0.478\,P - 0.678\,iK \qquad \text{for postwar years.}$$

If we regard i as "the" rate of interest, and assume that it is roughly equal to the rate of profit, then $P = iK$. In that case net investment becomes negative in the prewar equation; this means that when excess profits $(P - iK)$ are zero, entrepreneurs will not only stop net investment, but let the existing stock of capital decumulate. This is what would have happened in the prewar years.

In the postwar period, on the other hand, if we put $P = iK$ and substitute the average value of postwar i, the investment function becomes $I/K = 0.0341$. After the war we have observed a very high rate of growth in the Japanese economy. The above finding suggests that capital in the Japanese economy would have been growing at an annual rate of 3.4 percent even if excess profits had been zero. One is tempted to attribute this to an optimistic and spirited outlook on the part of Japanese entrepreneurs.

The contribution of interest rate is fairly large in explaining the variable $\underline{I/K}$. Our finding that the rate of interest has a significant effect on investment behavior is to be expected because in the Japanese economy the financing of capital is said to draw heavily on the money market, financing by accumulated profits being much less important than in Western countries.

12.3.3. Exports. It is noted that the coefficient of the shift variable is negative, and its magnitude 3.37 is rather large as compared with the average value of exports, which is 3.30. This means that with same levels of world trade and the relative price of world and Japanese exports, Japanese exports would have been much larger in the prewar years than in the postwar years. It is commonly believed that the abnormally high level of Japanese exports in the prewar period was due, in part at least, to her effort for political reasons to increase exports to her colonies, especially to Manchuria.[12] Some attribute it to the fact that in these periods Japan was depreciating her rate of exchange very rapidly.[13] This was of course true. However, since we have accounted for changes in the rate of exchange in our data processing, the explanation of the negative coefficient on the shift variable must be found elsewhere.

The elasticities of exports with respect to the two independent variables, $\underline{T_w}$ and $\underline{p_w}/\underline{p_j}$, are 1.068 and 1.360. They are evaluated at the average level of each variable. It is to be noted that both elasticities exceed unity, implying that a one percent rise in the volume of world trade or in relative prices would increase Japanese exports by more than one percent.

12.3.4. Imports. As for the import function of foods, the coefficient of the shift variable is rather big because the average level of the explained variable is 0.00477. An explanation of this large positive shift may be as follows: In the postwar period, the price of rice has been under control so that the observed values of $\underline{p}_d$ have been smaller than they would have been in the absence of price control. The portion of the postwar imports of rice that should have been explained by higher $\underline{p}_d/\underline{p}_m$ must therefore be explained by something else. Hence a positive coefficient on the shift variable.

A referee has pointed out that our series on food imports may show too much of an increase between pre- and postwar periods. Some estimates indicate that the food share in total imports fell from 1934-1936 to 1957. Our figures are based on aggregation of individual food imports. Lacking more definitive data on revised estimates of imports by type, we cannot decide whether our series are incorrect.

A remarkable thing in the import function of materials and of other things is that neither relative prices nor the holdings of gold and foreign currencies turned out to be significant. It is also noticeable that the shift variables have negative coefficients. In the case of material imports this may be explained by a technological improvement that led to material savings in the production of nonfood goods. In the case of other imports an explanation is found in the increased supply potential of final products in postwar Japan.

Combining the three import functions, we get total imports as a function of domestic production

$$\underline{M} = 0.3167\ \underline{Y} - 0.3222\ \underline{Y}_f + (\text{a function of } \underline{p}_d/\underline{p}_m,\ \underline{N},\ \text{and } \underline{D}).$$

As the average level of $\underline{Y}_f/\underline{Y}$ is 0.167, this function may be rewritten

$$\underline{M} = 0.2629\ \underline{Y} + \text{something}.$$

The marginal propensity to import is thus about 0.26 in real terms.

12.3.5. Nonagricultural Production. The production elasticities are calculated as 1.006 (with respect to labor) and 0.418 (with respect to capital). They add to 1.424, a value significantly larger than unity. Thus the production of nonfood goods takes place under increasing returns to scale. This might be due to fairly remarkable improvements in the technique of production. It also indicates the industrial youth of Japan.

That there have been steady technological improvements can be seen from the fact that both output per man and the output-capital ratio have been rising. On the other hand, the contribution of labor in equation (12.7) is larger and that of capital is smaller in the postwar periods than in the prewar periods. It may be that destruction of capital stock during the war made it necessary to produce a given output with less capital and more labor than before the war. But the dislocation in the modes of production during and after the war was not serious enough to make the shift variable statistically significant in this equation.

12.3.6. Agricultural Production. The trend variable, t, expresses the effect of technological improvements on agricultural productivity. To assess, in some way, the relative importance of this factor and of fertilizer input, we have calculated the "elasticities"; 0.322 with respect to F, and 0.215 with respect to t. Interpreting this equation, it should be noted that the prewar H series refers to damages by weather, but the postwar H includes damages due to other causes.

12.3.7. Price. The general price level in our model, the implicit GNP deflator, is made a function of the two main components of prime costs, the value productivity of nonagricultural labor and that of imports. These indices are not directly comparable; so we have calculated the "elasticities" with respect to the two variables in order to assess mark-up coefficients of the general price over prime costs. The result is 0.514 with respect to labor productivity and 0.873 with respect to import productivity. These figures can be compared with corresponding findings in the U.K. and the Dutch models: 0.421 and 0.216 in the U.K. and 0.48 and 0.16 in the Dutch model.[14]

In the U.K. and Dutch models general price is a function of wage rate and import price, not of productivities. It should be also noted that there are included other explanatory variables that may affect the values of the mark-up coefficients. Nevertheless, we remain convinced from the results cited above that in Japan the mark-up coefficients are significantly higher, the contribution of import productivity being especially larger. This may sustain the commonly held view that a strong inflationary tendency is inherent in the Japanese economy and that the movement of the price level is very sensitive to that of import prices.

12.3.8. Wage. Our wage rate determination equation shows that a 10 percent rise in the general price level induces a 7.5 percent increase in the wage rate within the same year. Can it be said that a three quarters adjustment of wages to prices within the same year is fairly rapid? If this is so, and if we consider the large mark-up coefficients of prices over costs discussed in the preceding paragraph, we must conclude that our findings testify to a strong inflationary tendency in the Japanese economy.

Putting $\Delta \underline{w} = 0$ and $\Delta \underline{p} = 0$ in equation (12.10), we find the level of unemployment consistent with stable wages and prices. The calculation shows that this value is about 0.0153; that is to say, we have to accept 1.53 percent unemployment if we are to have wage and price stability. Since the average level of unemployment in the sample period is 1.18 percent and the highest level is 1.69 (in 1932), it can be argued that the level of unemployment required for stable growth is fairly high. In this connection, the reader may question the plausibility of our unemployment figures, for the average level of 1.18 percent is abnormally low on Western standards. This is due to the fact that the unemployment data we used exclude all those who were employed part-time or in "disguised" employment. It is sometimes said that one percent unemployment according to these data corresponds to 4 or 5 percent in Western countries.

12.3.9. Liquidity. In the liquidity function, as it stands, the sampling errors are tolerable although the total correlation coefficient is low. If the prewar series of interest rates were taken into account, the sampling error for the coefficient of interest rate would become intolerably large. It must be recalled in this connection that in equation (12.2) the rate of interest as a cost element in investment decisions is found significant in the prewar as well as postwar periods. This may be explained by referring to the "low interest policy" of the government and monetary authorities in the prewar years that kept the rate of interest lower than it would otherwise have been, thus invalidating the liquidity function. On the other hand, the investment decisions are made according to the given rate of interest, whatever it may be, so that our prewar investment is explained significantly by interest rate fluctuations.

12.3.10. Birth and Death Rates. Although birth and death rates will be affected by various factors, economic and non-economic, we have found simple equations that fit well for our sample period. In the case of birth rate, per capita income and a shift varible explain most of the observed variations. A negative coefficient for the shift variable means that there was a once-for-all decrease in the birth rate after the war. This was apparently due to a change in the attitude of people towards birth control, which had been regarded as "unpatriotic" before the war but is now encouraged. The decrease in the death rate reflects progress in medical science.

Birth and death rates in the post sample years deviate from past trends; both rates seem to show upward trends, or they are not falling as fast as in the past. Improvements in the standard of living may have changed the minds of people for more children; or rapid industrial expansion has increased occupational diseases and accidents. Anyway, we did not think that our equations (12.12) and (12.13) would do well for forecasting purposes, and decided to treat population as a predetermined variable for forecasting.

12.3.11. Labor Supply. The ratio of nonagricultural to agricultural labor shows an upward trend in the postwar period. This trend may have started during the war partly because of the accelerated increase in industrial production and partly because of a rise in agricultural productivity. This may explain a positive coefficient for the shift variable. As to the sensitivity of the N_e/N_f ratio to the real wage rate, calculations show that a one percent increase in the real wage rate brings about a one percent rise in the N_e/N_f ratio. In the case of total labor supply, a 10 percent increase in the trend variable induces a 1.3 percent increase in the labor force participation ratio.

12.4. Extrapolation to 1959

As explained in section 12.2, the model was fit to sample data terminating with the year 1958. Subsequently, data became available for 1959, and we extrapolated the model to that year, given approximately current values of predetermined variables at the time of the extrapolation. These were not forecasts, prepared in advance of the event.

A much simpler problem than extrapolation of the entire system, is the computation of residuals for the fitted equations in 1959. This is a prior step to extrapolation of the whole model since it may show where individual components of the system are malfunctioning. Most of the equations fit well in 1959 except the investment function, the industrial production function, the cost mark-up equation, the wage determination equation, the birth rate equation and the death rate equation.

Investment and production are underestimated in their respective equations. The results are symptomatic of the investment boom and the technical changes that are going on in present-day Japan. The equations of the model dealing with price and wage formation have similarly underestimated the inflationary pressure generated by this expansionary boom. Birth rates are underestimated and death rates overestimated, giving rise to a faster population growth than our equations suggest. Birth rates have been low in postwar Japan, but we have exaggerated that tendency. There is no sign yet of a basic reversal in this trend of the birth rate. Residuals were computed for the last sample years, since 1956, as well as for 1959, to see if there are systematic biases in the equations (one-signed residuals, year after year), but we found no cause for revising our equations on this account . Residuals for the whole sample period are given in Table 12A.2.

The model is nonlinear, and this makes the simultaneous solution for extrapolation algebraically complicated. If we fix some of the variables that are associated with the large residuals noted above, for 1959, we can enormously simplify the system by nearly reducing it to a set of linear equations. We might fix the value for population on the assumption that we can extrapolate directly from past trends more accurately than by using our birth and death rate equations that are in error for 1959. We similary fixed the value for the price level on the basis of our judgment of continued inflationary pressures. For 1959, this judgment did not have to be exercised, but for 1960 and 1961 it did. The interest rate is also fixed in advance for the extrapolation period.

The factorial income distribution ratio, P/W, is a nonlinear element in the consumption equation, but this term was fixed at its 1959 value. Nonlinear expressions, wN_e and N_e/N_f were approximated by a Taylor's expansion, with linear terms only, about the previous year's values. The relationship between disposable and total income was approximated by the linear equation

$$Y_d = -3.56 + 0.92\, Y.$$

The following variables were assigned their observed levels in 1959.[15] $(C/N)_{-1}$, T_w, p_w/p_j, p_d/p_m, F, H, N_L, N, T_i, G, K_{-1}, i, p. In Table 12.1 we give the results of the extrapolation, and in Table 12.2 we present values of the predetermined variables used in the extrapolation.

The largest error is in the estimation of investment as we might have guessed on the basis of fit of the individual equations. The error in total production is considerably smaller, in percentage terms, because investment is not the largest component of national product. Material imports are poorly estimated, and these are large in the total import bill; therefore total imports are estimated with almost as large a percentage error as materials; however total imports are estimated more accurately than is investment. The wage rate and unemployment variables are very near the actual levels.

Absolute standards of precision cannot be set, but if all variables could be estimated within 5 percent of the true value we would undoubtedly be pleased. In most cases we have been within 10 percent of the true value. This leaves much room for improvement. Nevertheless, we do find that the model is functioning in the general neighborhood of the true values of the endogenous variables. This is our principal conclusion

TABLE 12.1. EX POST EXTRAPOLATION TO 1959

Variable	Observed value	Estimated value	Percentage error
$\underline{C}$	19.6	19.1	2.4
$\underline{I}$	7.43	5.26	29.2
$\underline{F}_{\underline{im}}$	4.11	3.50	14.8
$\underline{F}_{\underline{if}}$	0.588	0.571	3.0
$\underline{F}_{\underline{io}}$	0.882	0.773	12.4
$\underline{Y}$	29.7	27.1	8.7
$\underline{Y}_{\underline{f}}$	4.03	4.34	-7.7
$\underline{N}_{\underline{e}}$	28.3	26.7	5.8
$\underline{N}_{\underline{f}}$	15.4	17.1	-10.8
$\underline{w}$	174.7	170.8	2.2
$\underline{U}$	0.0130	0.0133	-2.3
$\underline{P}$	12.9	11.4	11.2
$\underline{W}$	13.6	12.4	8.3
$\underline{F}_{\underline{e}}$	4.89	4.68	4.0

from the extrapolation to 1959.

Some consequences of the error in estimation of investment can be seen in further calculations. We reduced the system to two linear equations relating $\underline{I}$ and $\underline{Y}$. One of these two equations is a direct transformation of the investment equation, and the other is a "partially reduced form" derived from algebraic substitution and elimination of all the other equations of the system. We then shifted each of these two linear equations by a constant amount so that they intersected at the actual values for $\underline{I}$ and $\underline{Y}$ in 1959. This necessitated a large adjustment to the investment equation and a small adjustment to the "partially reduced form."

An important result follows from this adjustment. The adjusted calculation gives a higher rate of growth for output (the actual growth rate, in fact) for 1958-1959 and in so doing generates a balance of trade deficit. Before adjustment, our calculations show

$$\underline{F_e} - \underline{F_{im}} - \underline{F_{if}} - \underline{F_{io}} = + 275 \text{ billion yen,}$$

calculated at current prices. In real terms, our extrapolation had underestimated total imports. After adjustment for higher investment and more rapid growth, we get

$$\underline{F_e} - \underline{F_{im}} - \underline{F_{if}} - \underline{F_{io}} = -26 \text{ billion yen,}$$

calculated at current prices. Our model suggests that the cost of rapid growth is a strain on the balance of trade.

12.5. Prospects for Japanese Development in the Light of the Model

Two genuine (or ex ante) forecasts have been made - for 1960 and 1961. The calculations were started in the latter part of 1960, and statistics for the year were not yet known, although we knew, in a general way, how the economy was functioning in months just preceding the work on the predictions. For 1961, there was no advance indication of the actual statistics. Even though the model did not extrapolate well in all departments to 1959, we felt that it could be used to show internal (within model) changes from 1959 to 1960 and from 1960 to 1961. We compare values computed for 1960 with those computed for 1959 and those computed for 1961 with those computed for 1960. Lagged values of variables used in the 1960 extrapolations were taken to be actual and not computed values for 1959.

The values of predetermined variables used in the extrapolation are shown in Table 12.2. From these, we can see the a priori presumptions that are built into the calculations. These values must be taken into account in evaluating our appraisal of the near term prospects for Japanese development. Steady growth in population, world trade, fertilizer input, the price level, and government spending are projected. Interest rates are expected to fall by a small amount between 1960 and 1961.

TABLE 12.2. PREDETERMINED VARIABLES USED IN THE EXTRAPOLATIONS

Variables	1959	1960	1961
$(C/N)_{-1}$	0.200	0.211	0.212
T_w	1.39	1.54	1.61
p_w/p_j	2.09	2.07	2.07
p_d/p_m	2.09	2.09	2.09
F	1.80	1.85	1.90
H	0.469	0.455	0.455
N	93.0	93.9	94.8
T_i	3.25	3.56	4.35
G	3.34	3.50	4.12
i	0.0790	0.0790	0.0750
p	365.08	371.25	384.24
N_L	44.3	endogenous	endogenous

The estimated values for major variables in 1960 and 1961 show a steady rate of economic growth over the 1959 estimates. The 1959-1960 growth in total output is approximately known from preliminary estimates, and our 1960 extrapolations understate both the level and rate of growth. Again investment appears to be underestimated. Consumption in 1960 is estimated fairly close to a preliminary value of the actual figure, 19.9 as compared with 20.1.

The estimated growth rates in real output are 4.7 and 6.5 percent for 1959-1960 and 1960-1961 respectively. These are low figures compared with 12.9 for 1958-1959 and with a presumption that the rate did not fall between 1960 and 1961. Our estimated growth rates in total output and the associated components of the national product indicate a balance-of-trade surplus in 1960 and in 1961. The figures are 212 billion yen and 188 billion yen at current prices.

In the 1959 extrapolations, as explained above, we adjusted the model so that the investment equation and the

TABLE 12.3. PREDICTIONS OF ENDOGENOUS VARIABLES, 1960 AND 1961

Variable	Estimate 1960	Percentage increase 1959-1960	Estimate 1961	Percentage increase 1960-1961
C	19.9	5.2	20.7	3.0
I	5.48	4.2	6.08	10.9
F_{im}	3.80	8.6	4.25	11.8
F_{if}	0.677	18.6	0.567	-16.2
F_{io}	0.848	9.7	0.950	12.0
Y	28.4	4.7	30.2	6.5
Y_f	4.51	3.9	4.59	1.8
N_e	27.4	2.6	28.8	5.1
N_f	17.3	1.2	17.2	-0.6
w	175.2	2.6	212.6	21.3
U	0.0146	9.8	0.0043	-70.5
N_L	45.3	2.3	46.2	2.0
P	12.0	5.3	12.4	3.3
W	12.9	4.0	13.5	4.7
F_e	4.83	2.9	5.10	5.6

residual relation between I and Y intersected at the observed values of these two variables. We did not make a new adjustment for 1960 or 1961 values, but we did use the 1959 adjustments to the constant terms of the two equations in extrapolating the model to 1960 and 1961. This adjustment increases the 1959-1960 estimated growth rate (6.2 percent) but not the 1960-1961 estimated rate (3.6 percent). The level of investment is raised in 1960 and in 1961 with this adjustment, but apparently not enough to make the model estimates grow as fast as the economy actually did grow. These adjustments for higher levels of investment and output turn the estimated balance-of-trade surpluses into deficits, -129 billion yen in 1960 and -84 billion yen in 1961.

Our model suggests that the ambitious plan of growth for Japan - doubling of real national product between 1960 and 1970, implying a rate of growth of 7.2 percent per annum - is faster than the pattern that would evolve from historical relationships. The main features of disagreement between our model and the rapid growth of the first years of this decade are in capital formation and foreign trade. We obtain lower values for investment and a balance-of-trade surplus. If the economy grows much faster through a greater investment program, the trade balance appears to suffer. Unless large amounts of foreign capital can be obtained, it would appear that actual growth rate - in excess of those suggested by our model - will generate a balance-of-payments disequilibrium. Most of the 1960-1970 decade lies in the future, and the experience of the first years has not assured that the 7.2 percent rate can be maintained as a decade average. Our model serves as a device to emphasize clearly and quantitatively the areas of expansion and stress in this development program.

12.6. Data Appendix

12.6.1. The Basic Time Series and General Comments. The National Income White Paper[16] published yearly by the Economic Planning Agency (EPA) presents consistent figures of the national income and product flows. On the product side, our series of consumption, gross investment, government current expenditures, exports and total imports are taken bodily from the constant price national product series listed in the White Paper. For the classification of imports into foods, materials, and other imports we had to use different sources, as specified below.

On the income side, constant price series are not prepared by the EPA. We first construct wage income, nonwage income, primary industry income, and personal disposable income from the White Paper. We then use the implicit price deflator of the national product to obtain deflated series for the income flows. Indirect taxes and subsidy figures, and book value depreciation figures are also corrected by the implicit price deflator. Our net investment series are obtained simply by deducting the book value depreciation in constant prices from the gross investment series. Our figures on food production are real incomes in primary industry.

The currently published EPA series are available from 1930.[17] The 1929 values of income and product variables which enter the model as initial lags are derived from tables prepared by Dr. K. Ohkawa.[18]

12.6.2. The Basic Time Series and Specific Comments. Our series on the stock of capital is obtained by cumulating net investment. For the benchmarks of the prewar and the postwar series, respectively, we use the National Wealth Statistics figures for 1930 and 1955, deflated by the EPA index of producer-good prices. Thus we assume that the increase or decrease in capital stock during the war period is explained by the difference between the two national wealth estimates.

The indices of the volume of world trade and world import prices are taken from the Review of World Trade (League of Nations) for the prewar years, and from the Statistical Yearbook (United Nations) for the postwar years. In order to make the prewar and postwar series comparable, we adjusted the League of Nations figures by the ratio of the 1938 UN figure to the 1938 LN figure.

The prewar series of Japanese export prices is the gold-dollar price of the Japanese exports listed in the Review of World Trade. The postwar series is the unit price of exports prepared by EPA. It is not easy to link the two series in this case; so we left the gap between them to be explained by a shift variable in the export function (after making a rough adjustment parallel to the one in the world trade series).

We constructed series on the values of food imports and materials imports from the Ministry of Finance Trade Statistics. Price indices of imported foods and of imported materials are constructed by calculating the weighted average of the unit prices of principal import commodities. Our series of food imports and material imports in constant prices are obtained from the value and price series. Our series of the remaining import items is obtained as a residual by deducting the above two import series in constant prices from total import figures listed in the White Paper.

The series on fertilizer inputs is constructed by calculating the weighted averages of chemical fertilizer inputs, the weights being the relative prices of fertilizers.

A postwar series on the rate of unemployment is taken from the Labor Force Survey by the Prime Minister's office. A prewar series is calculated from the monthly reports by the Ministry of Home Affairs. To make the two series comparable, we adjusted the prewar series so that the average level of prewar unemployment is equal to that of postwar unemployment.

12.6.3. Sources of Data

C	Economic Planning Agency, National Income White Paper
$Y-T_d$	"
P	"
W	"
I	"
F_e	"
Y_f	"
Y	"
M	"
G	"
T_i	"
K	"
i	Bank of Japan, Economic Statistics of Japan
T_w	League of Nations, Review of World Trade and United Nations, Statistical Yearbook
p_w	"
p_j	League of Nations, Review of World Trade and Economic Planning Agency, National Income White Paper
F_{if}	Ministry of Finance, Trade Statistics
F_{im}	"
F_{io}	"
p_d	H. Ouchi (ed.), Collection of Japanese Economic Statistics (Tokyo: Nippon Hyoron, 1958)
p_w	"

N	Bank of Japan, Economic Statistics of Japan
N_L	Y. Tamada (ed.), Estimates of the Japanese National Income (Tokyo: Toyekeizai, 1957) and Prime Minister's Office, Labor Force Survey
N_e	"
N_f	"
U	Ministry of Home Affairs, Monthly Report and Prime Minister's Office, Labor Force Survey
F	Ministry of Agriculture and Fishery, Yearly Statistical Tables
H	"
p	Economic Planning Agency, National Income White Paper
w	"
p_i	"
L	Bank of Japan, Economic Statistics of Japan
b	"
d	"
e	"

12.6.4. Sources of Data for Extrapolation and Forecasting. In this section we will briefly indicate the general nature of the material used in making estimates of the values of exogenous variables and of lagged endogenous variables for the forecast period.

The government current expenditure and indirect taxes, including central and local government items, are estimated from fiscal budget figures of the central government by assuming that the share of the central government in the total expenditure and tax absorption is constant or is changing "smoothly."

Variables in the export function are estimated from the UN Monthly Bulletin of Statistics and Bank of Japan Statistical Monthly. For 1961 values, the volume of world trade is extrapolated from the postwar trends, while the relative price of world and Japanese goods is assumed to remain unchanged.

The average yield on private long-term bonds is taken from Bank of Japan Statistical Monthly, and its 1961 value is assumed to fall by one percent, as indicated by the monetary authorities.

TABLE 12A.1. SAMPLE DATA

	Y	C[a]	I	G	p[b]	F_e	M
1930	12.8	10.9	0.79	1.67	1.03	2.52	3.13
1931	13.1	10.8	0.81	2.31	0.90	2.89	3.72
1932	13.1	10.8	0.64	2.52	0.93	2.87	3.70
1933	13.5	10.8	0.63	2.62	0.98	2.98	3.59
1934	15.1	11.1	1.78	2.52	0.97	3.48	3.78
1935	15.4	10.7	1.91	2.61	1.01	4.21	4.05
1936	15.9	11.0	2.09	2.62	1.04	4.47	4.34
1951	16.8	10.6	4.09	1.73	288.00	2.15	1.79
1952	18.5	12.5	3.53	2.27	300.00	2.30	2.08
1953	20.1	13.9	4.17	2.26	319.00	2.67	2.92
1954	20.7	14.5	3.69	2.56	331.00	3.00	3.06
1955	22.9	15.4	4.53	2.72	329.00	3.48	3.24
1956	24.2	16.5	5.24	2.71	340.00	3.92	4.18
1957	26.0	17.4	6.50	2.85	350.00	4.27	5.05
1958	26.3	18.4	4.63	3.29	344.00	4.32	4.34

	F_{im}	F_{if}	F_{io}	W	P	Y_f	T_d
1930	1.46	0.21	1.46	4.83	6.59	1.78	1.85
1931	1.66	0.27	1.80	4.98	6.68	1.86	1.95
1932	1.65	0.21	1.84	4.92	7.28	2.19	1.62
1933	1.80	0.18	1.62	4.93	7.77	2.53	2.75
1934	1.87	0.19	1.72	5.48	8.13	2.30	2.79
1935	1.98	0.20	1.87	5.46	8.88	2.61	2.48
1936	2.17	0.20	1.96	5.76	9.22	2.89	2.40
1951	1.23	0.41	0.14	6.31	8.78	3.44	4.60
1952	1.37	0.50	0.21	7.41	9.29	3.72	4.26
1953	1.95	0.52	0.45	8.40	9.49	3.46	5.14
1954	1.84	0.63	0.58	9.01	9.29	3.50	4.79
1955	2.01	0.62	0.62	9.58	10.40	4.16	5.38
1956	3.16	0.57	0.45	10.58	11.19	3.82	5.73
1957	3.87	0.55	0.63	11.57	11.93	3.80	6.31
1958	2.99	0.59	0.76	12.73	11.68	3.96	5.18

1929 values: a 11.5 b 1.25

TABLE 12A.1. CONTINUED

	T_i	K	w^c	T_w	p_w/p_j	p_d/p_m	p_i
1930	1.35	57.4	0.33	0.75	1.12	2.28	0.8
1931	1.46	58.2	0.32	0.69	1.16	3.28	0.6
1932	0.90	58.9	0.32	0.60	1.58	2.70	0.7
1933	0.77	59.5	0.32	0.59	1.58	2.54	0.9
1934	1.44	61.3	0.33	0.62	1.68	1.82	1.0
1935	1.05	63.2	0.33	0.65	1.68	3.84	1.0
1936	0.86	65.3	0.38	0.68	1.74	3.34	1.0
1951	1.74	44.7	90.70	0.95	1.84	1.46	399.0
1952	1.77	48.2	106.20	0.94	1.94	1.24	347.0
1953	2.22	52.3	120.20	1.00	2.07	1.28	299.0
1954	2.36	56.0	128.60	1.05	2.13	1.63	289.0
1955	2.89	60.6	130.60	1.14	2.26	1.82	281.0
1956	2.46	65.8	141.60	1.24	2.21	2.01	289.0
1957	2.49	72.3	150.90	1.31	2.22	2.13	307.0
1958	1.92	76.9	157.80	1.29	2.20	2.21	265.0

	N^d	N_L	N_e	N_f	U	b	d
1930	63.9	30.0	14.9	14.7	0.0129	0.0324	0.0189
1931	64.9	29.4	14.2	14.8	0.0146	0.0322	0.0190
1932	65.9	29.7	14.4	14.8	0.0169	0.0329	0.0177
1933	66.9	30.2	15.0	14.8	0.0140	0.0315	0.0177
1934	67.7	31.2	16.0	14.8	0.0123	0.0300	0.0181
1935	68.7	31.8	16.7	14.7	0.0115	0.0317	0.0168
1936	69.6	31.2	16.3	14.5	010107	0.0300	0.0175
1951	84.5	36.6	20.1	16.2	0.0108	0.0253	0.0099
1952	85.8	37.8	20.9	16.4	0.0126	0.0234	0.0089
1953	87.0	39.9	22.3	17.2	0.0114	0.0215	0.0089
1954	88.2	40.6	23.2	16.8	0.0148	0.0200	0.0082
1955	89.3	42.0	24.1	17.2	0.0165	0.0194	0.0078
1956	90.3	42.7	25.4	16.8	0.0152	0.0185	0.0080
1957	91.1	43.7	26.9	16.3	0.0123	0.0172	0.0083
1958	92.0	44.0	27.7	15.7	0.0131	0.0179	0.0074

1929 values: c 0.40 d 62.9

TABLE 12A.1. CONTINUED

	i	L	F	H	t
1930	0.0636	2.96	0.46	0.021	0.1
1931	0.0624	2.73	0.47	0.077	0.2
1932	0.0649	2.91	0.55	0.041	0.3
1933	0.0512	3.13	0.62	0.031	0.4
1934	0.0460	3.33	0.66	0.215	0.5
1935	0.0441	3.36	0.85	0.136	0.6
1936	0.0438	3.66	1.01	0.030	0.7
1951	0.0901	867.00	1.29	0.253	2.2
1952	0.0902	1116.00	1.01	0.170	2.3
1953	0.0898	1201.00	1.21	0.418	2.4
1954	0.0904	1198.00	1.26	0.554	2.5
1955	0.0882	1392.00	1.55	0.327	2.6
1956	0.0738	1809.00	1.65	0.477	2.7
1957	0.0791	2003.00	1.70	0.450	2.8
1958	0.0788	2149.00	1.56	0.469	2.9

The deflators are estimated from the same source, and in the absence of reasons to make changes, we have assumed that there will be no change.

Fertilizer input is extrapolated from its past trend, and estimates of the damaged area of cultivated land are put at the average of the past five years. Estimates of population published by the Institute of Population Study are fairly reliable, and we have used them in estimated lagged per capita consumption for 1959 and 1960. As for the lagged endogenous variables for 1961, we used the values of endogenous variables estimated by extrapolations to 1959 and 1960.

Notes

The research upon which this study was based was initiated during the visit of L. R. Klein to the Institute of Social and Economic Research of Osaka University. Thanks are due to the Rockefeller Foundation for support of this visit under its grant to Osaka University, and to the staff members of the

TABLE 12A.2. RESIDUALS FROM STRUCTURAL EQUATIONS

	Equation number				
	(12.1)	(12.2)	(12.3)	(12.4)	(12.5)
1930	-0.003	0.0069	-0.25	-0.00004	-0.13
1931	0.000	0.0062	0.26	0.00038	-0.01
1932	0.001	0.0006	-0.44	0.00006	0.08
1933	0.006	-0.0124	-0.29	-0.00011	0.23
1934	0.001	0.0016	-0.16	0.00012	-0.17
1935	-0.005	-0.0023	0.46	-0.00043	-0.08
1936	-0.001	-0.0006	0.45	-0.00002	0.05
1951	-0.004	0.0073	0.20	-0.00128	0.17
1952	0.003	-0.0090	0.14	-0.00011	-0.03
1953	0.003	0.0030	-0.04	-0.00015	0.06
1954	-0.005	-0.0032	-0.06	0.00086	-0.21
1955	-0.002	0.0013	-0.25	0.00095	-0.43
1956	0.002	-0.0027	-0.08	0.00003	0.38
1957	0.001	0.0135	-0.03	-0.00038	0.52
1958	0.000	-0.0102	0.15	0.00004	-0.41
	(12.6)	(12.7)	(12.8)	(12.9)	(12.10)
1930	-0.22	-0.1	-0.021	0	-0.082
1931	0.10	0.7	-0.013	0	0.041
1932	0.14	0.1	-0.002	0	0.009
1933	-0.10	-0.5	0.013	0	-0.051
1934	-0.09	0.4	0.011	0	-0.031
1935	0.04	-0.3	0.010	0	-0.095
1936	0.11	0.0	0.010	0	0.001
1951	-0.05	-0.3	-0.11	-3	0.003
1952	-0.08	0.0	0.008	-3	0.070
1953	0.07	0.4	-0.008	2	0.005
1954	0.17	-0.1	0.007	3	0.029
1955	0.08	0.1	-0.001	8	0.039
1956	-0.16	0.3	-0.009	4	0.052
1957	-0.08	0.3	-0.012	0	-0.011
1958	0.03	-0.5	0.014	-8	0.019

	Equation number				
	(12.11)	(12.12)	(12.13)	(12.14)	(12.15)
1930	-0.005	-0.047	-0.054	0.03	0.023
1931	0.002	-0.039	-0.024	-0.13	0.003
1932	0.010	-0.041	-0.041	-0.09	-0.003
1933	0.009	-0.065	-0.010	0.01	-0.007
1934	0.000	0.031	0.031	0.03	-0.001
1935	-0.012	0.091	0.013	0.12	-0.003
1936	-0.007	0.070	0.069	0.02	-0.022
1951	0.003	0.024	0.074	0.09	-0.015
1952	0.002	0.038	0.003	-0.02	-0.011
1953	-0.007	0.031	0.031	-0.08	0.004
1954	-0.025	-0.063	-0.027	-0.05	0.001
1955	-0.027	0.023	-0.058	-0.06	0.007
1956	0.017	0.002	-0.030	-0.02	0.006
1957	0.017	-0.089	0.070	0.05	0.009
1958	0.020	0.037	-0.042	0.08	0.003

Institute, who patiently gave their guidance and advice to the development of this project.

1. The normality of economic life during the period 1951-1955 is certainly questionable. We might have given special treatment to these years, by means of a dummy variable, but treating them as we did, on an equal footing with other observation periods, we did not obtain unusual residuals for these years (see Table 12A.2).

2. L. M. Koyck, Distributed Lag and Investment Analysis (Amsterdam: North Holland, 1954).

3. The well-known models of Kalecki and Kaldor are the best examples of systems with such investment relationships. M. Kalecki, "A Macrodynamic Theory of Business Cycles," Econometrica 3 (July 1935): 327-344. N. Kaldor, "A Model of the Trade Cycle," Economic Journal, 50 (March 1940): 78-92.

4. L. R. Klein, et al., *An Economic Model of the U.K.* (Oxford: Blackwell, 1961); *Scope and Methods of the Central Planning Bureau* (The Hague: Central Planning Bureau, 1956).

5. L. R. Klein and A. S. Goldberger, *An Econometric Model of the United States, 1929-1952* (Amsterdam: North-Holland, 1955).

6. Klein and Goldberger, *An Econometric Model of the United States, 1929-1952*; Klein (et al.), *An Econometric Model of the U.K.*

7. A. J. Brown, "Interest, Prices and the Demand Schedule for Idle Money," *Oxford Economic Papers*, 2(May 1939): 46-69.

8. S. Valvavanis-Vail, "An Econometric Model of Growth: U.S.A., 1869-1953," *American Economic Review*, *Papers and Proceedings*, 45 (May 1955): 208/221.

9. Predetermined variables used in the first stage of the "two-stage-least-squares" estimates proceduaes were $(C/N)_{-1}$, D, p_d/p_m p_w/p_j, F,H, p_i, T_w, G, and T_d.

10. H. Ueno, *Econometric Analysis of the Japanese Economy* (Tokyo: Toyokeizai, 1961); p. 167; T. Uchida and K. Mori, "A Simulation Analysis of the Japanese Economy," M. Morishima, M. Shinohara, and T. Uchida (Eds.), *New Economic Analysis* (Tokyo: Sobunsha, 1960); p. 214; H. Eguchi, "An Econometric Model of the Japanese Economy," (mimeographed), November 1959.

11. By "elasticity" we mean $[\partial C/\partial(P/W)](P/W)/C$. For the sake of brevity we shall refer throughout this section to the magnitude $(\partial y/\partial x)x/y$ as the "elasticity" of y with respect to x.

12. Note that our series on exports includes exports of goods and services from the Japanese Mainland to the colonies.

13. W. W. Lockwood, *The Economic Development of Japan* (Princeton: Princeton University Press, 1954), pp. 64-77.

14. L. R. Klein and R. J. Ball, "Some Econometrics of the Determination of Absolute Prices and Wages," *Economic Journal*,

69 (September 1959): 465-482, and J. Tinbergen, Economic Policy: Principles and Design (Amsterdam: North-Holland, 1956), p. 110.

15. In 1959, N_L was assigned its observed value for the solution. In later extrapolations this variable was treated as endogenous.

16. Referred to here as the White Paper.

17. As of February, 1961.

18. K. Ohkawa (Ed.), National Income (Tokyo: Shunjusha, 1960).

13

A Long-Term Model of Japanese Economic Growth, 1906-1968

Hiroya Ueno

13.1. Introduction

The Japanese economy has grown steadily since the establishment of the capitalistic system in the Meiji era, though there have been minor cyclical fluctuations. The average annual growth rate of real gross domestic product for the prewar period, 1906-1937, was 3.8 percent, and for the postwar period, 1954-1958, the average growth rate was as high as 10.8 percent. For the two periods the output of the primary and of the nonprimary sectors (the secondary and tertiary industries) rose at an average rate of 1.8 and 3.7, and 4.9 and 11.9 percent, respectively. This growth pattern of the Japanese economy is expected to continue for some time to come.

The purpose of this study is to present a long-term growth model of the Japanese economy, 1906-1968 (excluding 1938-1953), to explain the process of its development, and to provide perspectives of its future growth potential. Simulation experiments with the model may be useful to project a consistent national economic plan and to give a guidepost for economic policies. The model follows existing economic theory such as neoclassical growth theory and empirical studies to

International Economic Review, vol. 13, no. 3 (October 1972), pp. 619-643. Reprinted by courtesy of the International Economic Review and the author.

explain the historical process of Japanese economic development.

In contrast to a short-run stabilization model, which is demand-determined, it is necessary in a long-run model to cover the entire era of capitalistic development under the free enterprise system and more specifically to formulate supply factors in the economy. Also, in the long-run it is desirable to explain changes in the industrial structure in terms of sector shares of gross domestic product and labor and capital allocations. In view of this requirement, the long-term model must be composed of some major sectors, and the behavioral relationships in the model must be disaggregated by industrial sector.

In Japan, long-term model building has not proceeded as rapidly as the building of short-term quarterly models, because of a lack of adequate statistical data. In fact, there are no data available for the detailed components of the national income accounts for the prewar period. It is very difficult to obtain comprehensive and consistent annual data on capital stock and labor by industrial sector over a long period for prewar Japan.

Historical annual series of the relevant data for the model have been specifically prepared. The postwar data are from the official national income statistics, and the prewar data from the Long-Term Economic Statistics Project at the Institute of Economic Research, Economic Planning Agency (EPA), assisted by staff members at the Institute of Economic Research at Hitotsubashi University. The data are preliminary and have not yet been completely integrated into the national income accounting base.

Since our basic data depend on two different sources for the prewar national income data, the problem of data consistency arises. The values added in the primary and the nonprimary sectors were derived by the production approach, and in such categories as personal consumption, expenditure, capital formation, and government expenditure, by the commodity flow approach and the expenditure approach. Moreover, the data for the postwar period were derived by the income approach.

Data on gross capital stocks in the prewar period come from the Hitotsubashi and the EPA projects, and in the postwar period, from the EPA project. Estimates have been made independently from the national income accounting estimates. Also, methods of estimation have varied by sector: the stock method has been used for the primary sector, and the perpetual inventory method for the nonprimary sector. As for labor force, there was no census on labor force by sector before 1920, when the first population census was taken.

Several data problems are left unsolved, and their improvement is one of the most important tasks of the future.

13.2. The Structure of the Model

Unavailability of appropriate data imposed restrictions on constructing a multisector model. Consequently, our long-term model is a two sector model: The primary sector consists of agriculture, forestry, and fishing, and the nonprimary sector - secondary and tertiary industries - consists of manufacturing, construction, transportation, and service industries. This division is designed to observe sectoral trends and the changes in their role in the economy and to clarify their influences on the aggregate growth of the whole economy. The model reveals the change in Japan's industrial structure.

13.2.1. Production Function. The model is a growth model essentially built up from an aggregate savings function and two sectoral production functions. The two production functions determining the sectoral output levels are assumed to be a function of capital and labor input.

The production function of the primary sector is assumed to be a Cobb-Douglas type allowing for netural and continuous technical progress. Assuming that the production function is homogeneous of degree one, the equation is written with labor productivity as a function of capital input per labor input. In the primary sector labor input is represented by employment, and as a capital input we take not only private capital stocks into consideration, but also public capital stocks for irrigation and land improvement to measure their productive effect on agricultural production. Cultivated land (arable area and pasture) is introduced into the production function because of the importance of agriculture in the primary sector. We also introduce a weather condition variable into the production function. Weather condition series were prepared by the author on the basis of agricultural meteorological statistics. Productions of rice, barley, wheat, and naked barley are correlated with average temperatures, total precipitation, and hours with sunshine. A single measure of weather conditions was computed on the basis of these data.

The production function of the nonprimary sector is assumed to be a Cobb-Douglas type allowing for improvements in the quality of the capital stock and in the quality of the labor force. Assuming that the production function is homogeneous of degree one, the equation is also written with labor productivity as a function of capital input per labor input.

Solow suggested that the ordinary Cobb-Douglas production function did not take account of the complementarity between technical change and investment and that one of the factors that has contributed to the growth of total factor productivity has been advances in technology which have improved the productivity of new capital goods. He built the vintage model on the assumption that all technical progress is uniform and approximately exponential over time, and that new capital goods embody all the latest knowledge. The Solow vintage model with improved labor quality can be written:

$$
\begin{aligned}
(13.1)\qquad V_t &= Be^{\gamma t}(L_{\nu,t})^{\alpha}(K_{\nu,t})^{1-\alpha} \\
&= Be^{\gamma t}(L_t q_{L,t})^{\alpha}(K_t q_{K,t})^{1-\alpha} \\
&= Be^{\gamma t}(L_t e^{\omega})^{\alpha}(K_t e^{\nu})^{1-\alpha} \\
&= Be^{\gamma t}(L_t e^{\mu_0+\mu t})^{\alpha}(K_t e^{\xi_0+\xi t})^{1-\alpha},
\end{aligned}
$$

where V_t stands for the output produced at time t using equipment of vintage ν; $K_{\nu,t}$, the units of capital of vintage ν in existence at time $t \geq \nu$; $L_{\nu,t}$ the labor to be allocated to vintage ν capital; q_L, the quality index of labor; q_K, the quality index of capital; L, the labor input; K, the capital input; and γ, the rate of disembodied technical progress.

In order to estimate the quality index of capital q_K

or the vintage index v first, we consider the following relationship between total capital stock and investment in equipment:

$$(13.2) \quad \underline{K}_{\underline{t}} = \underline{I}_{\underline{t}} + (1-\delta_{\underline{t}})\underline{K}_{\underline{t}-1},$$

where $\underline{K}$ represents the real value of capital stock; $\underline{I}$, real gross investment; δ, the rate of depreciation; and $\underline{t}$, time.

The total capital stock in equation (13.2) cannot be identified with the total stock of capital equipment of different type and age in existence unless an adequate deflator to represent the value of capital stock in terms of efficiency units is available; we cannot count, for example, a 1950 open-hearth converter and a 1965 oxygen converter with equal weight. It is clear that capital equipment of different types, different makes, or of different ages cannot be treated as equivalent.

If we follow the formulation expressed in equation (13.2), we compute the total stock of capital equipment by adding together all installed equipment for past years back to some specific year, depending on the average length of life of such capital equipment. This implies that capital equipment does not depreciate at all up to a certain point and then becomes valueless.

If we assume a constant percentage rate of depreciation over time, we may derive the total stock of capital equipment, adjusted for the age composition of the stock, from an index of past investments in new equipment derived in a way to adjust for differences in make and type.

Let $\underline{K}_{v,t}$ be the stock of capital equipment during period $\underline{t}$, adjusted for age composition; $\overline{\delta}$ the constant rate of depreciation; and $\underline{I}_{\underline{t}}$ new investment during period $\underline{t}$. Then we have

$$(13.3) \quad \underline{K}_{v,\underline{t}} = \underline{I}_{\underline{t}} + (1-\overline{\delta})\underline{I}_{\underline{t}-1} + (1-\overline{\delta})^2\underline{I}_{\underline{t}-2} + \ldots$$

From (13.3) it is clear that the stock of capital equipment adjusted for age composition, $\underline{K}_{v,\underline{t}}$, is just new investment during $\underline{t}$ plus $(1-\delta)$ times the stock in the previous period, $\underline{t} - 1$:

$$(13.4) \quad \underline{K}_{\nu,\underline{t}} = \underline{I}_{\underline{t}} + (1-\bar{\delta})\underline{K}_{\nu,\underline{t}-1}.$$

$\underline{K}_{\nu,\underline{t}}$ is gross capital of vintage ν remaining at time $\underline{t}$. We can calculate the quality index of capital or the vintage index from equation (13.2) and (13.3) on the above assumptions. The rate of improvement in capital quality in the nonprimary sector was 2.2 percent a year for 1906-1921, roughly constant for 1922-1937, and 5.3 percent for the postwar period 1954-1968.

The quality index of capital is defined in terms of the quality of new capital. On the other hand, the quality index of labor, $\underline{q}_{\underline{L}}$, is defined in terms of the average quality of all labor. Improvement in the average quality of labor is related to increase in the average number of years of schooling per person in the work force, increase in the length of the school year, and change in the age-sex composition of the work force. The rate of improvement in labor quality in the nonprimary sector was 1.0 percent a year for the prewar period, 1906-1937, and 0.5 percent for the postwar period, 1954-1968.

In the nonprimary sector, labor input is represented by man-hours. As a capital input measure we take not only capital stocks into account, but also the rate of capacity utilization. The rate of capacity utilization is exogenously determined in this system, so that the characteristic of the model as a policy model can be preserved. Public capital stocks for such items as transportation, communication, and roads, is also introduced into the production function in order to measure their effect on nonprimary production. In addition, we include a dummy variable in the production function to distinguish the prewar and the postwar observations. This dummy variable is introduced into most of the equations listed below.

In the estimation of these production functions, we found an intercorrelation between the private capital stock and the public capital stock variables. In our primary production function, therefore, we estimated the productive effect of land and of irrigation and land improvement by use of information on their direct effects from the Land Improvement Survey for 1953-1959 which was made by the Ministry of Agriculture and Forestry. In the nonprimary production function, we used a method of mixed linear estimation in which the a priori information is used to eliminate part of the coefficients to be estimated, rather than the ordinary least squares procedure, which is based on observational data alone, in order to obtain a satisfactory or plausible result in economic and statistical respects. As a priori information on output elasticity with respect to public capital input, we used the mean of coefficients estimated on the basis of regional data.

13.2.2. The Wage Rate Determination Equation. We start with the following Cobb-Douglas production function for the nonprimary sector.

$$(13.5) \quad V_2 = Ae^{\gamma t}(hq_L L_2)^{\alpha}(\rho q_K K_{p2,-1})^{\beta 1}(K_{g2,-1})^{\beta 2},$$

where V_2 stands for gross value added; L_2, employment; K_{p2}, private capital stock; K_{g2}, public capital stock; h, work hours; ρ, the rate of capacity utilization; q_L, the quality index of labor; q_K, the quality index of capital; and γ, the rate of disembodied technical progress.

Given a Cobb-Douglas production function, the marginal productivity of labor is

$$(13.6) \quad \partial V_2/\partial(hq_L L_2) = \alpha \cdot V_2/hq_L L_2.$$

If we determine the desired real wage rate (the long-run equilibrium real wage rate) on the marginal productivity basis, we have

$$(13.7) \quad (w_2/p_2)^* = \alpha V_2/hq_L L_2,$$

where $(w_2/p_2)^*$ is the desired real wage rate.

Furthermore, if we assume a dynamic adjustment process so that the rate of adjustment of actual real wage rate toward a long-run equilibrium wage rate depends on the difference between the equilibrium wage rate and the actual wage rate, we may have the following adjustment relation:

$$(13.8) \quad (w_2/p_2)_t - (w_2/p_2)_{t-1} = \theta[(w_2/p_2)^*_t - (w_2/p_2)_{t-1}],$$

where $\underline{w}_2$ is the money wage rate and $\underline{p}_2$ is the price index in the nonprimary sector.

From equations (13.7) and (13.8), we can derive

$$(13.9) \quad (\underline{w}_2/\underline{p}_2)_{\underline{t}} = \theta\alpha(\underline{V}_2/\underline{hq}_{\underline{L}}\underline{L}_2) + (1-\theta)(\underline{w}_2/\underline{p}_2)_{\underline{t}-1}.$$

13.2.3. The Labor Allocation Function. In the Japanese economy, which has had an excess supply of labor in the primary sector, employment in the nonprimary sector, which is modern industry, has been determined first, and that in the primary sector has been a residual of the total labor force. In the long-run, the labor share of each sector may depend on the share of production in each sector. However, if agricultural prices, which are determined for the most part by governmental policy on the basis of the agricultrual price support system and the protective trade system, are high relative to the wage rate of the nonprimary sector, which is derived from its wage rate determination equation, labor mobility of the primary sector to the nonprimary sector may be discouraged.

Thus, the sectoral allocation of labor is formulated as

$$(13.10) \quad \log_{\underline{e}}(\underline{L}_1/\underline{L}_2) = \alpha_{30} + \alpha_{31}\log_{\underline{e}}(\underline{w}_2/\underline{p}_1) + \alpha_{32}\log_{\underline{e}}(\underline{V}_1/\underline{V}_2)_{-1},$$

where $\underline{L}_1$ is employment in the primary sector; $\underline{L}_2$, employment in the nonprimary sector; $\underline{w}_2$, money wage rate in the nonprimary sector; $\underline{p}_1$, price index of the primary sector; $\underline{V}_1$, gross value added in the primary sector; and $\underline{V}_2$, gross value added in the nonprimary sector. If the total labor force is determined by taking into account changes in the supply of labor caused by such factors as changes in age composition of population and a change in women's participation, employment in the primary and in the nonprimary sector are determined endogenously.

13.2.4. The Gross Domestic Savings Function. The gross domestic savings function determines the domestic supply of new capital. This savings function is considered to be a function of gross domestic product, savings for the previous year, and the total tax revenue (including social security contributions) divided by the gross domestic product ratio. The first explanatory variable in this form corresponds to the level of income, and the second to the consumer's habit or the ratchet effect indicating irreversibility of consumer behavior. The third variable is introduced into the function in order to show the effect of the tax burden, that is, the relative importance of the total tax revenue.

13.2.5. Investment in Personal Residential Construction. We start with a hypothesis that the economy has a desired level of capital stock in personal residential construction or a long-run equilibrium capital stock, $K^*_{h,t}$, and that the desired level is determined by the expected level of output (capacity output), V^*_t. If we assume a linear functional relationship, this hypothesis can be expressed as

$$(13.11)\quad K^*_{h,t} = \alpha_{50} + \alpha_{51}V^*_t.$$

Since the long-run equilibrium capital stock cannot be observed, this equation cannot be estimated statistically. In order to derive a relationship that can be estimated statistically, we assume a dynamic adjustment process by which the rate of adjustment of actual capital stock toward a new equilibrium position depends on the difference between the equilibrium stock and the actual stock. We may write this adjustment relation as:

$$(13.12)\quad K_{h,t} - K_{h,t-1} = \beta[K^*_{h,t} - K_{h,t-1}],$$

where β is the adjustment coefficient. Further, if we assume a depreciation rate, δ_h, to be constant over time, the actual stock $K_{h,t}$ is given by

$$(13.13)\quad K_{h,t} = I_{h,t} + (1 - \delta_h)K_{h,t-1},$$

where I_h is gross investment in personal residential construction.

From equations (13.11) and (13.13), we can derive

$$(13.14)\quad I_{h,t} = \beta\alpha_{50} + \beta\alpha_{51}V_t^* - (\beta-\delta_h)K_{h,t-1},$$

$$(13.15)\quad I_{h,t} = \beta\alpha_{50}\delta_h + \beta\alpha_{51}V_t^* - \beta\alpha_{51}(1-\delta h)V_{t-1}^* + (1-\beta)I_{h,t-1}.$$

If this equation is fitted statistically, for example by use of a search method, estimates of the coefficients permit us to estimate the appropriate rate of depreciation δ_h and the constant of proportionality β. We can also estimate the parameters of α_{50} and α_{51}.

13.2.6. Public Capital Formation for the Human Environment. As the urbanization is pushed forward by industrialization, people's desire for improvement in the human environment may be greatly increased. The movement of public capital formation for the human environment over a long period is formulated in the same manner as the residential investment function. The hypothesis is that over the long run, the economy has a desired level of capital stock for the human environment, K_{gs}^*, which is determined by the expected level of output (capacity output), V^*, and the degree of urbanization, DID/N. We assume that the equation for desired stock is:

$$(13.16)\quad K_{gs,t}^* = e^{\alpha_{60}}(V_t^*)^{\alpha_{61}}\ (DID/N)_t^{\alpha_{62}}\quad ,$$

or in logarithmic form

$$\log_e K_{gs,t}^* = \alpha_{60} + \alpha_{61}\log_e V_t^* + \alpha_{62}\log_e\ (DID/N)_t,$$

where K_{gs}^* is the desired level of capital stock for the human environment such as educational facilities, or public health facilities, and DID/N is the ratio of the number of population in densely inhabited areas to that of total population, which is an index representing the degree of urbanization.

The actual level of capital stock for the human environment K_{gs}, is given by

$$(13.17)\quad K_{gs,t} = \prod_{\theta=0}^{n-1} I_{gs,t-\theta}^{(1-\delta_{gs})^{\theta}} \cdot K_{gs,t-n}^{(1-\delta_{gs})^{n}}\ ,$$

or

$$\log_e K_{gs,t} = \log_e I_{gs,t} + (1-\delta_{gs}) \log_e K_{gs,t-1},$$

where K_{gs} is the actual capital stock for human environment; I_{gs}, gross public capital formation for human environment; and δ_{gs}, the depreciation rate. If we introduce the following adjustment process:

$$(13.18) \quad K_{gs,t}/K_{gs,t-1} = (K^*_{gs,t}/K_{gs,t-1})^{\lambda}; \qquad 0 < \lambda < 1,$$

or

$$\log_e K_{gs,t} - \log_e K_{gs,t-1} = \lambda[\log_e K^*_{gs,t} - \log_e K_{gs,t-1}],$$

where λ is the adjustment coefficient, we can derive

$$(13.19) \quad \log_e I_{gs,t} = \lambda\alpha_{60} + \lambda\alpha_{61}\log_e V^*_t + \lambda\alpha_{62}\log_e (DID/N)_t - (\lambda-\delta_{gs})\log_e K_{gs,t-1},$$

or

$$(13.20) \quad \log_e I_{gs,t} = \alpha_{60}\lambda\delta_{gs} + \alpha_{61}\lambda\log_e V^*_t - \alpha_{61}\lambda(1-\delta_{gs})\log_e V^*_{t-1} + \alpha_{62}\lambda\log_e (DID/N)_t - \alpha_{62}\lambda(1-\delta_{gs}) \log_e (DID/N)_{t-1} + (1-\lambda)\log_e I_{gs,t-1}.$$

This equation is estimated by the search method.

13.2.7. The Private Investment Function and Investment Allocation. The ratio of public investment to private investment is determined exogenously. This ratio works as a policy variable, since in our model the desired ratio between the social overhead capital stock and the private capital stock is assumed to be determined by policy consideration from a long-term point of view. If public investment is assumed to be determined autonomously from the standpoint of policy, then it could be given exogenously and no equation of investment allocation would be needed.

Private investment behavior in the nonprimary sector is also formulated in the same way as public capital formation for the human environment. We start with a hypothesis that firms have a desired level of capital stock, K^*_{p2}, which is determined by the expected level of output V^*_2. If we assume a linear functional relationship, this hypothesis can be expressed as:

$$(13.21)\quad K^*_{p2,t} = bV^*_{2,t}.$$

The actual level of capital stock is

$$(13.22)\quad K_{p2,t} = I_{p2,t} + (1-\delta_2)K_{p2,t-1},$$

where I_{p2} is gross investment and δ_2 is the depreciation rate. If we introduce the following adjustment process:

$$(13.23)\quad K_{p2,t} - K_{p2,t-1} = \lambda_1[K^*_{p2,t} - K_{p2,t-1}] + \lambda_2[K^*_{p2,t-1} - K_{p2,t-2}],$$

where λ_1 and λ_2 are the adjustment coefficients, and $\lambda_1^2 - 4\lambda_2 \geqq 0$ and $2 > \lambda_1 > 0$, we can derive

$$\begin{aligned}(13.24)\quad I_{p2,t} &= \lambda_1 b[V^*_{2,t} - V^*_{2,t-1}] + \lambda b[V^*_{2,t-1} - V^*_{2,t-2}] \\ &\quad + (1-\lambda_1)I_{p2,t-1} + \{\delta_2\lambda_1 bV^*_{2,t-1} \\ &\quad \div \delta_2\lambda_2 bV^*_{2,t-2} - \lambda_2 I_{p2,t-2}\} \\ &= \lambda_1 b\Delta V^*_{2,t} + \lambda_2 b\Delta V^*_{2,t-1} + (1-\lambda_1)I_{p2,t-1} \\ &\quad + \{\delta_2\lambda_1 bV^*_{2,t-1} + \delta_2\lambda_2 bV^*_{2,t-2} \\ &\quad - \lambda_2 I_{p2,t-2}\}.\end{aligned}$$

Moreover, if we assume $V^*_t = V_{t-1}$, we have

$$(13.25)\quad \underline{I}_{\underline{p}2,\underline{t}} = \lambda_1\underline{b}\Delta\underline{V}_{2,\underline{t}-1} + \lambda_2\underline{b}\Delta\underline{V}_{2,\underline{t}-2} + (1-\lambda_1)\underline{I}_{\underline{p}2,\underline{t}-1}$$
$$+ \{\delta_2\lambda_1\underline{b}\underline{V}_{2,\underline{t}-2} + \delta_2\lambda_2\underline{b}\underline{V}_{2,\underline{t}-3} - \lambda_2\underline{I}_{\underline{p}2,\underline{t}-2}\}$$
$$= \underline{A}_1\Delta\underline{V}_{2,\underline{t}-1} + \underline{A}_2\Delta\underline{V}_{2,\underline{t}-2} + \underline{A}_3\underline{I}_{\underline{p}2,\underline{t}-1} + \underline{A}_0,$$

where $\underline{V}_2$ is the actual level of output in the nonprimary sector.

If investment in the nonprimary sector is determined by equation (13.25), investment in the primary sector is necessarily determined as a residual of the total private investment.

13.2.8. The Food Consumption Function. When we take up domestic demand for food, we should consider both an income effect and a consumer habit effect. Food consumption expenditure is treated as a function of gross domestic product minus gross domestic savings, which nearly corresponds to the level of personal consumption expenditure, and food consumption expenditure for the previous year which represents the effect of consumer habit.

13.2.9. The Export Function. When we treat the demand for Japanese exports in the world market, we should consider an income or activity effect and a relative price effect. A measure of composite world activity is the index of world exports. Since world trade was not normal in the period 1914-1923, because of World War I, we dropped this period from the sample period.

A single measure of the relative price variable should be a price index of Japanese exports divided by an index of export prices of competing countries weighted by their share in the total world export. The relative price variable should be adjusted for changes in the exchange rates. However, since there are no reliable data on such overseas prices, we took an index of relative labor productivity, which is expressed as the labor productivity index of Japan divided by the labor productivity index of competing countries such as the United States or West Germany as a proxy for the relative price variable.

13.2.10. Import Functions. Total imports are divided into three main components: (1) imports of food; (2) imports of raw materials and fuels; and (3) imports of other goods and services (mainly consisting of capital and conumer goods). We treat food imports as a function of food consumption and domestic food production, because food imports have essentially supplemented domestic food production. Imports are generally assumed to be a function of an income or activity variable and of a relative price variable. Japan is compelled to import primary raw materials such as raw cotton, iron ore, and crude petroleum. We assume that import demand for raw materials and fuels depends exclusively upon industrial production activity and not upon relative prices. Finally, since other imports consist of capital goods, consumer perishable and durable goods, and services, we relate them to the level of total output.

13.2.11. Price Determination Equations. Primary sector prices are determined essentially by governmental policy on the basis of the agricultural price support system and the protective trade system such as tariff wall and import quotas. The price variable of the primary sector may be, therefore, a policy variable which is determined exogenously from the point of view of economic policy. Prices may be considered to be set in terms of food imports divided by the total food consumption ratio, the relative labor productivity of the primary sector, and nonprimary sector prices to explain government economic policy.

The price determination equation for the nonprimary sector is essentially of the cost markup type. The prices are considered to be marked up over unit labor costs and to be adjusted to the price level of the primary sector.

13.2.12. Demand for Money. If output (real GDP) and price level (GDP deflator) are determined in the model, the quantity equation or income velocity equation would give the demand for money (cash and demand deposits).

Our model is a growth model consisting of two blocks: the first block is built centering on the production functions and determines GDP directly. The second block, centering on the savings function, determines the supply of capital. In the first block, the two production functions determine the sectoral levels of potential output by the capital stocks of the preceding year and the labor inputs of the given year. The total labor force is given exogenously and its sectoral allocation is determined by the labor allocation function, which is related to the production function in the nonprimary sector. Consequently, in the process of applying iteration methods, GDP and the sectoral allocation of labor are determined simultaneously. The level of GDP determined by the production functions determines the aggregate supply of capital by the savings function in the second block. Since in the long-run a state of full employment and full utilization of capital is assumed, three factors -- the available capital supply, the allocation of labor and capital, and improvements in labor and capital quality -- and the rate of disembodied technical progress determine the growth potential.

The growth pattern of sectoral outputs, as well as the growth rate of the total output, is of importance in the sense that it affects the balance of trade, which in turn influences the rate of growth of total output through the equilibrium condition of savings-investment. The growth rate of the primary sector output influences the movement of food imports, whereas that of the nonprimary sector affects imports of raw materials and fuels and other imports. On the other hand, the rate of increase in the labor productivity of the nonprimary sector, together with the overseas economic situation, will influence Japan's exports. For example, in the case of a growth pattern in response to allocation of a larger amount of capital to the primary sector, the growth rate of total output would be smaller, and food imports would be smaller as a result of an accelerated rate of growth of the primary sector. Similarly, in the case of a larger rate of increase in the labor productivity of the nonprimary sector because of allocation of a larger amount of capital to the sector, Japan's exports would be larger, and food imports would also be larger.

13.3. Estimates of the Model

Our system of equations has been estimated by the method

of ordinary least squares from a sample of 47 annual observations for the period 1906-1968 (excluding 1938-1953). For each computed equation we present two statistics: a measure of goodness of fit, the multiple determination coefficient adjusted for degrees of freedom, $\bar{R}^2$, and a measure of serial correlation, the Durbin-Watson coefficient, D-W. The figures in parentheses below the corresponding estimates of parameter are standard errors of parameter estimates.

We list the definitions of variables used in the system below for ease of reference in studying estimates.

13.3.1. List of Variables. Variables below are expressed in billions of 1965 yen, except when specifically expressed otherwise. Endogenous variables in this list are marked with an asterisk (*) on the upper left-hand side.

- *V = Gross domestic product
- *V_1 = Gross value added in the primary sector (agriculture, forestry and fishing)
- *V_2 = Gross value added in the nonprimary sector (other industries)
- L = Total labor force in thousands of persons, on the Labor Force Survey basis
- *L_1 = Employment in the primary sector in thousands of persons, on the Labor Force Survey basis
- A = Cultivated land (arable area and pasture) in thousands of hectare
- Q = Index of weather condition (1955 = 100)
- ρ = Index of capacity utilization in the nonprimary sector (1961 = 100)
- h = Average daily hours worked per regular worker in the nonprimary sector
- q_K = Quality index of capital in the nonprimary sector
- q_L = Quality index of labor in the nonprimary sector
- *V_n = Gross domestic product in billions of current yen
- *V_{n1} = Gross value added in the primary sector, billions of current yen

$*V_{n2}$ = Gross value added in the nonprimary sector, billions of current yen
$*S$ = Gross domestic savings excluding change in inventories
$*I_p$ = Gross fixed investment by private enterprises
$*I_{p1}$ = Gross fixed investment by private enterprises in the primary sector
$*I_{p2}$ = Gross fixed investment by private enterprises in the nonprimary sector
$*I_g$ = Gross fixed investment by government
$*I_{g1}$ = Gross fixed investment for the primary sector by government
$*I_{g2}$ = Gross fixed investment for the nonprimary sector by government
$*I_{gs}$ = Gross fixed investment for the human environment by government
$*I_h$ = Personal residential construction
$*\bar{K}_p$ = Private capital stock
$*\bar{K}_{p1}$ = Private capital stock in the primary sector
$*\bar{K}_{p2}$ = Private capital stock in the nonprimary sector
$*\bar{K}_g$ = Public capital stock
$*\bar{K}_{g1}$ = Public capital stock in the primary sector
$*\bar{K}_{g2}$ = Public capital stock in the nonprimary sector
$*\bar{K}_{gs}$ = Public capital stock for the human environment
$*\bar{K}_h$ = Personal residential stock
$*\bar{C}_f$ = Food consumption
$*\bar{E}$ = Total exports of goods and services
$*M$ = Total imports of goods and services
$*M_f$ = Food imports
$*\bar{M}_m$ = Imports of raw materials and fuels
$*\bar{M}_0$ = Other imports
$*P$ = GDP deflator (1965 = 100)
$*P_1$ = Price index of the primary goods (1965 = 100)
$*P_2$ = Price index of the nonprimary goods (1965 = 100)
$*w_2$ = Index of money wage rate in the nonprimary sector (1965 = 100)
T_w = World exports in millions of 1963 U.S. dollars
$V_w/\bar{L}_w$ = Labor productivity index of six advanced countries (United States, Canada, West Germany, United Kingdom, France, and Italy) (1913 = 100)

V_{2w}/L_{2w} = Labor productivity index of the nonprimary sector of six advanced countries (1963 = 100)

T = Ratio of total tax revenue (including social security contributions) to GDP in current prices

$*B$ = Net exports of goods and services

$*DID$ = Population in densely inhabited areas in thousands of persons

$*M_s$ = Cash and demand deposits in billions of current yen

N = Total population in thousands of persons

β_1 = Ratio of I_g to I_p

β_2 = Ratio of I_{g1} to I_{g2}

δ_1 = Depreciation rate of private capital stock in the primary sector

δ_2 = Depreciation rate of private capital stock in the nonprimary sector

δ_{g1} = Depreciation rate of public capital stock in the primary sector

δ_{g2} = Depreciation rate of public capital stock in the nonprimary sector

δ_{gs} = Depreciation rate of public capital stock for human environment

δ_h = Depreciation rate of personal residential stock

$*O$ = Production index of manufacturing industry (1965 = 100)

Z = Dummy variable (zero in prewar and unity in postwar period)

Z' = Dummy variable (unity in prewar and zero in postwar period)

t = Time trend in years

A simplified flow chart of the specification of the model is presented in Fig. 13.1.

13.3.2. The Estimated Equations.

(i) Production functions

$$(13.26)\quad \log_e V_1/L_1 = -1.381 + \underset{(0.062)}{0.325} \log_e K_{p1,-1}/L_1$$
$$+ \underset{(0.063)}{0.447}[0.194 \log_e K_{g1,-1}/L_1$$

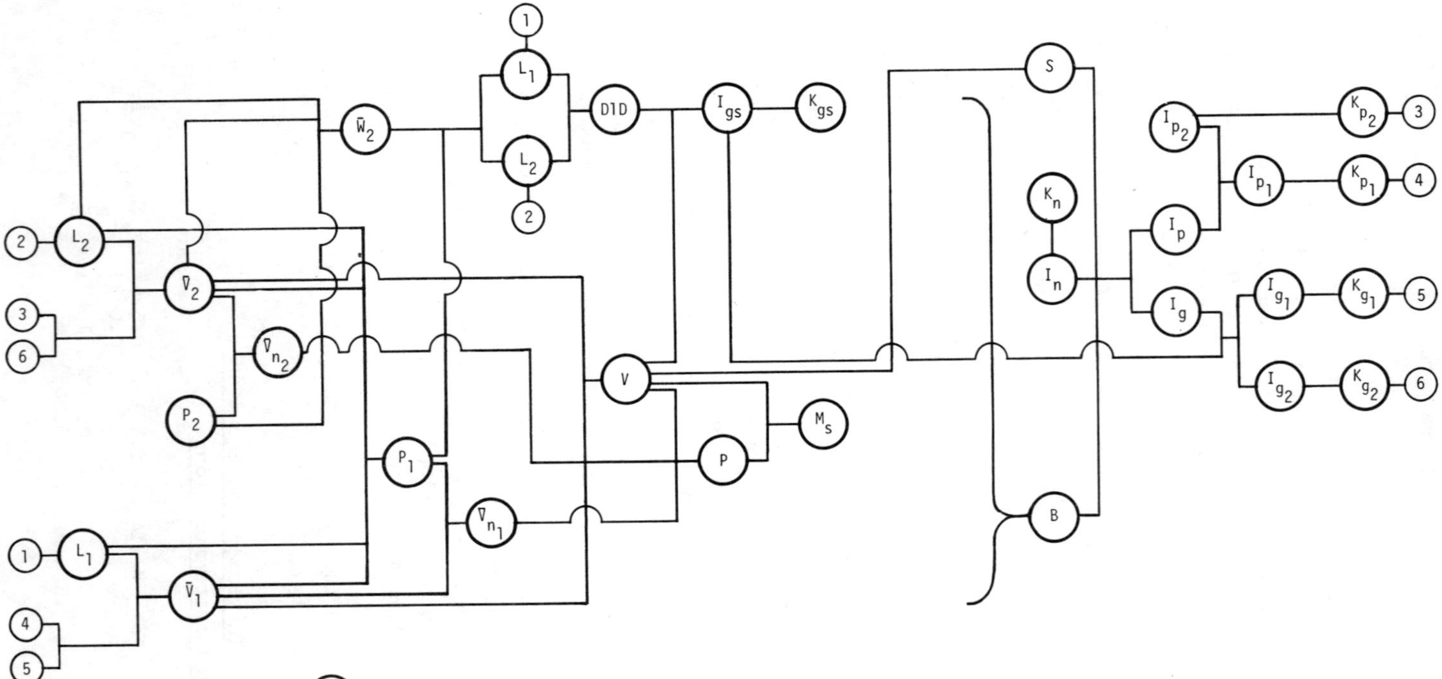

○ = endogenous variable

Some endogenous variables are omitted in this chart.

Fig. 13.1. Simplified Flow Chart of the Ueno Model

$$+ 0.806 \log_e A/L_1] + \underset{(0.001)}{0.005}\, Q$$

$$+ \underset{(0.0007)}{0.0045}\, Z_t$$

$$\bar{R}^2 = 0.986, \quad \bar{S} = 0.048, \quad D\text{-}W = 1.473$$

$$(13.27) \quad \log_e V_2/hq_L L_2 = -4.033 + \underset{(0.024)}{0.369} \log_e \rho q_K K_{p2-1}/hq_L L_2$$

$$+ 0.100Z \log_e K_{g2,-1}/hq_L L_2$$

$$+ \underset{(0.001)}{0.008t} + \underset{(0.001)}{0.019}\, Zt$$

$$\bar{R}^2 = 0.986, \quad \bar{S} = 0.053, \quad D\text{-}W = 0.858$$

(ii) Wage Rate Determination Equation

$$(13.28) \quad w_2/p_2 = 0.021 + \underset{(0.686)}{3.391}\, V_2/hq_L L_2 + 0.076\, (w_2/p_2)_{-1}$$

$$+ \underset{(0.020)}{0.092}\, Z$$

$$\bar{R}^2 = 0.983, \quad \bar{S} = 0.036, \quad D\text{-}W = 1.693$$

(iii) Labor Allocation Function

$$(13.29) \quad \log_e L_1/L_2 = 0.449 - \underset{(0.079)}{0.234} \log_e w_2/p_1$$

$$+ \underset{(0.064)}{0.723} \log_e (V_1/V_2)_{-1} - \underset{(0.051)}{0.147}\, Z$$

$$\bar{R}^2 = 0.980, \quad \bar{S} = 0.086, \quad D\text{-}W = 0.980$$

(iv) Gross Domestic Savings Function

$$(13.30) \quad S = -159.460 - \underset{(17.637)}{84.381}\, ZT + \underset{(0.038)}{0.148}\, V$$

$$+ \underset{(0.033)}{0.132}\, ZV + \underset{(0.136)}{0.350}\, S_{-1}$$

$$\bar{R}^2 = 0.996, \quad \bar{S} = 229.5, \quad D\text{-}W = 1.650$$

(v) Personal Residential Construction

$$(13.31) \quad I_h = 463.912 + \underset{(0.008)}{0.095}\, V - \underset{(0.018)}{0.084}\, K_{h,-1}$$

$$\bar{R}^2 = 0.980, \quad \bar{S} = 88.7. \quad D\text{-}W = 0.555$$

(vi) Public Capital Formation for the Human Environment

$$(13.32)\quad \log_e I_{gs} = 2.591 + \underset{(0.497)}{1.019} \log_e V + \underset{(1.081)}{1.465} \log_e DID/N - \underset{(0.285)}{0.534} \log_e K_{gs,-1}$$

$$\bar{R}^2 = 0.983,\quad \bar{S} = 0.069,\quad D\text{-}W = 1.599$$

$$(13.33)\quad \log_e DID/N = -0.227 + \underset{(0.148)}{1.908} \log_e L_2/L$$

$$\bar{R}^2 = 0.868,\quad S = 0.149,\quad D\text{-}W = 1.635$$

(vii) Private Investment Function

$$(13.34)\quad I_{p2} = 66.045 + \underset{(0.043)}{0.481} \Delta V_{2,-1} + \underset{(0.063)}{0.116} \Delta V_{2,-2} + \underset{(0.049)}{0.719} I_{p2,-1}$$

$$\bar{R}^2 = 0.994,\quad \bar{S} = 148.7,\quad D\text{-}W = 2.104$$

(viii) Food Consumption Function

$$(13.35)\quad \log_e C_f = 0.302 + \underset{(0.066)}{0.190} \log_e (V-S) + \underset{(0.051)}{0.765} \log_e C_{f,-1}$$

$$\bar{R}^2 = 0.996,\quad \bar{S} = 0.033,\quad D\text{-}W = 2.295$$

(ix) Production Index of Manufacturing

$$(13.36)\quad O = -2893 + \underset{(0.0002)}{0.0029} V_2 + \underset{(0.0002)}{0.0011} ZV_2 - \underset{(1.1939)}{6.4531} Z$$

$$\bar{R}^2 = 0.998,\quad \bar{S} = 1.561,\quad D\text{-}W = 0.874$$

(x) Export Function

$$(13.37)\quad \log_e E = -2.732 + \underset{(0.448)}{1.306} \log_e T_w - \underset{(0.285)}{3.094} Z \log_e \frac{V_w}{L_w} / \frac{V}{L} - \underset{(0.779)}{0.968} Z \log_e \frac{V_{2w}}{L_{2w}} / \frac{V_2}{L_2} - \underset{(0.663)}{4.685} Z$$

$$\bar{R}^2 = 0.950,\quad \bar{S} = 0.228,\quad D\text{-}W = 1.936$$

(xi) Import Function

$$(13.38)\quad \log_e M_f = 0.464 + \underset{(0.396)}{0.837} \log_e C_f - \underset{(0.569)}{0.768} \log_e V_{1,-1} + \underset{(0.090)}{0.747} \log_e M_{f,-1}$$

$$\bar{R}^2 = 0.953,\quad \bar{S} = 0.190,\quad D\text{-}W = 1.936$$

$$(13.39)\quad M_m = 11.812 + \underset{(1.768)}{38.750}\, O - \underset{(1.653)}{21.425}\, ZO$$

$$\bar{R}^2 = 0.994,\quad \bar{S} = 47.5,\quad D\text{-}W = 1.353$$

$$(13.40)\quad \log_e M_O = -3.415 + \underset{(0.195)}{0.676} \log_e V + \underset{(0.118)}{0.552} \log_e M_{O,-1} - \underset{(0.210)}{0.500}\, Z$$

$$\bar{R}^2 = 0.934,\quad \bar{S} = 0.184,\quad D\text{-}W = 2.193$$

(xii) Price Determination Equations

$$(13.41)\quad \log_e P_1 = 0.281 - \underset{(0.086)}{0.175} \log_e (M_f/C_f)_{-1} - \underset{(0.248)}{0.360} \log_e \frac{V_1}{L_1} / \frac{V_2}{L_2} + \underset{(0.134)}{1.250} \log_e P_{2,-1} - \underset{(0.780)}{1.149}\, Z$$

$$\bar{R}^2 = 0.997,\quad \bar{S} = 0.158,\quad D\text{-}W = 0.862$$

$$(13.42)\quad P_2 = 0.023 + \underset{(0.107)}{0.231} (w_2 L_2/V_2)_{-1} + \underset{(0.164)}{0.737} P_{1,-1}$$

$$\bar{R}^2 = 0.938,\quad \bar{S} = 0.107,\quad D\text{-}W = 2.144$$

(xiii) Demand for Money

$$(13.43)\quad M_s = -0.809 + \underset{(0.004)}{0.321}\, PV - \underset{(108.834)}{619.114}\, Z$$

$$\bar{R}^2 = 0.997,\quad \bar{S} = 202.0,\quad D\text{-}W = 1.093$$

(xiv) Investment Allocation

$$(13.44)\quad I_g/I_p = \beta_1$$

(13.45) $I_{g1}/I_{g2} = \beta_2$

(xv) Identities and Technical Definitions

(13.46) $P = \frac{V_1}{V} P_1 + \frac{V_2}{V} P_2$

(13.47) $V_{n1} = P_1 V_1$

(13.48) $V_{n2} = P_2 V_2$

(13.49) $V = V_1 + V_2$

(13.50) $V_n = V_{n1} + V_{n2}$

(13.51) $I_p = I_{p1} + I_{p2}$

(13.52) $I_g = I_{g1} + I_{g2} + I_{gs}$

(13.53) $S = I_p + I_g + I_h + B$

(13.54) $L = L_1 + L_2$

(13.55) $M = M_f + M_m + M_o$

(13.56) $B = E - M$

(13.57) $K_{p1} = I_{p1} + (1-\delta_1)K_{p1,-1}$

(13.58) $K_{p2} = I_{p2} + (1-\delta_2)K_{p2,-1}$

(13.59) $K_h = I_h + (1-\delta_h)K_{h,-1}$

(13.60) $K_{g1} = I_{g1} + (1-\delta_{g1})K_{g1,-1}$

(13.61) $K_{g2} = I_{g2} (1-\delta_{g2})K_{g2,-1}$

(13.62) $K_{gs} = I_{gs} + (1-\delta_{gs})K_{gs,-1}$

(13.63) $K_p = K_{p1} + K_{p2}$

(13.64) $\underline{K_g} = \underline{K_{g1}} + \underline{K_{g2}} + \underline{K_{gs}}$

13.4. Evaluation of the Estimates

Most of the estimated coefficients of the equations seem to be reliable, judged by statistical criteria, and satisfactory or plausible from the standpoint of economic theory. The computed values of the Durbin-Watson coefficient presented along with the equations are used to test the hypothesis of nonautocorrelation. About one-fourth of our estimates have significant autocorrelation as judged by this test.

First we shall examine some properties of the model from the point of view of each equation.

Our production function for the primary sector is assumed to be a Cobb-Douglas type which allows for neutral and continuous technical progress with a time trend. It can be seen that the output elasticities with respect to land, labor, and capital input are 0.360, 0.228, and 0.411, respectively. These output elasticities may be compared with findings by other economists: 0.51-0.62, 0.19-0.28, and 0.16-0.21 for the prewar period by K. Ohkawa and 0.56, 0.19, and 0.25 for the postwar period by K. Tsuchiya.[2] The rate of technical progress for the postwar period is 0.45 percent per year. It follows from our findings that the contribution of capital intensity for the entire period was large.

The production function for the nonprimary sector is a vintage type model which considers explicitly improvements in labor and capital quality. It can be seen from our production function that the output elasticities with respect to labor and capital input are 0.631 and 0.369 for the prewar period, and 0.536 and 0.464 for the postwar period.

Our estimation, as explained in section 13.2 suggests that the rate of improvement in labor quality was roughly 1.0 percent per year over the prewar period, and 0.5 percent per year over the postwar period, and that the rate of improvement in capital quality was 2.2 percent per year over the 1906-1921 period, roughly constant over the 1922-1937 period, and 5.3 percent per year over the 1954-1968 period. The rate of technical progress not directly "embodied" either in capital or labor, which represents improvements in the allocation of resources and better management practices, is 0.8 percent per year for the prewar period, and 2.7 percent per year for the postwar period.

If our estimates of the contribution of improved labor quality and of improved capital quality are roughly correct, then the explanation of growth of total factor productivity of 1.8 percent per year experienced over the prewar period and of 5.8 percent per year over the postwar period can be shown in Table 13.1.

TABLE 13.1. COMPONENTS OF TOTAL FACTOR PRODUCTIVITY (PERCENTAGE ANNUAL GROWTH RATES)

Period	Total Factor Productivity	Improvement in Labor Quality	Improvement in Capital Quality	Disembodied Technical Progress
		$\alpha \underline{q}_L$	$(1-\alpha)\ \underline{q}_K$	γ
1906-1937	1.84	0.63	0.41	0.8
1954-1968	5.76	0.23	2.84	2.7

Our values of $\alpha\underline{q}_L$, $(1-\alpha)\underline{q}_K$, and γ in Table 13.1 may be compared with findings by other economists: 0.75, 0.21, and 1.16 for 1905-1938, and 0.28, 0.81, and 4.37 for 1952-1960 by K. Ohkawa.[3] They seem to be fairly plausible.

It is seen from our savings function that the short-run marginal propensity to save for the postwar period is 0.280. If we put $\underline{S}_t = \underline{S}_{t-1}$ in equation (13.30), we obtain the long-run marginal propensity to save, which turns out to be 0.431.

Equation (13.35) shows that the long-run income elasticity of domestic demand for food is 0.78. This value may be compared with the long-run income elasticity, 0.23, estimated for 1922-1937, by T. Noda, and 0.69, estimated for 1954-1967 by the Economic Research Institute, EPA.[4] Our value may be somewhat overestimated.

From the estimated personal residential construction function we can compute the coefficients of the desired stock and the adjustment equation as follows:

$$(13.65)\quad \underline{K}_{h}^{*} = 4.736 + 1.070\ \underline{V},$$

$$(13.66)\quad \underline{K}_{h} - \underline{K}_{h,-1} = 0.084[\underline{K}_{h}^{*} - \underline{K}_{h,-1}],$$

$$(13.67)\quad \underline{K}_{h} = \underline{I}_{h} + (1 - 0.01)\underline{K}_{h,-1}.$$

These results imply that the marginal capital/output ratio is 1.1 and the depreciation rate is 0.01.

Similarly, from the estimated equation (13.32) we have the following results:

$$(13.68)\quad \log_{e} \underline{K}_{gs}^{*} = 4.676 + 1.838 \log_{e} \underline{V} + 2.643 \log_{e}(\underline{DID}/\underline{N}),$$

$$(13.69)\quad \log_{e} \underline{K}_{gs} - \log_{e} \underline{K}_{gs,-1} = 0.554\ [\log_{e}\underline{K}_{gs}^{*} - \log_{e} \underline{K}_{gs,-1}],$$

$$(13.70)\quad \log_{e} \underline{K}_{gs} = \log_{e} \underline{I}_{gs} + (1 - 0.02) \log_{e} \underline{K}_{gs,-1}.$$

These results mean that the long-term elasticities of capital stock with respect to output and degree of urbanization are 1.8 and 2.6; and that the proportion of the percentage gap between desired and actual stock eliminated during year $\underline{t}$ is 0.55. Consequently, if $\underline{K}_{gs,t}^{*}$ were 110 and $\underline{K}_{gs,t-1}$ were 100, implying a percentage gap of 10 percent, then the capital expansion rate, $\underline{K}_{gs,t}/\underline{K}_{gs,t-1}$ would be 1.054.

From the estimated investment function (13.34) we can compute the coefficients of the desired capital stock and adjustment equations as follows:

$$(13.71)\quad \underline{K}_{p2}^{*} = 1.71\ \underline{V}_{2},$$

$$(13.72)\quad \underline{K}_{p2} - \underline{K}_{p2,-1} = 0.281\ [\underline{K}_{p2}^{*} - \underline{K}_{p2,-1}] + 0.068\ [\underline{K}_{p2,-1}^{*} - \underline{K}_{p2,-2}],$$

$$(13.73)\quad \underline{K}_{p2} = \underline{I}_{p2} + (1 - 0.02)\ \underline{K}_{p2,-1}.$$

Equation (13.72) implies that the capital/output ratio in the nonprimary sector is 1.71. The estimated investment function (13.34) shows that a first-order partial adjustment model in distributed lag form is efficient in explaining investment behavior. It follows from our findings that the estimated average lag is 2.755.

In the export function we estimate a downward shift, postwar as compared with prewar. The elasticities of exports with respect to the world trade variable and the relative labor productivity variable are 1.306 and 0.968 for the postwar period.

In the import equations, it is also noted that the short-run and the long-run elasticities of food import with respect to food consumption are 0.837 and 3.312; and the short-run and the long-run elasticities of other imports with respect to GDP are 0.676 and 1.509.

The calculated values of the endogenous variables in our individual structural equations are very close to their observed values in the sample period. This implies that our estimated structural model of 39 equations (13.26 - 13.64) provides a satisfactory explanation of the Japanese economic growth in terms of direct determinants. However, the coefficients of the structural equations indicate the direct effect of some predetermined variables and some endogenous variables, but not the indirect effect. Consequently, such a structural analysis is only partial in the sense that it does not utilize the full model simultaneously, that is, it does not provide complete evidence on the explanatory effectiveness of the model as a whole.

In order to investigate the explanatory effectiveness of the model as a whole and to evaluate its predictive power, we have to apply the so-called final method to a total analysis of our model's behavior over the sample period. The final method gives the time path of calculated values of the endogenous variables on the basis of actual values of the lagged endogenous variables for only the initial postiion of the sample period, parameter values, and observed values of the exogenous variables over the period.

Our model is blockwise recursive, and the simultaneous block contains nonlinear equations such as the production functions, the wage rate determination equation, and the labor allocation function. The solution of the simultaneous block is made by iterative methods.

The entire system is divided into two blocks. The first

block consists of 8 equations, i.e., (13.26 - 13.29), (13.41), (13.42), (13.49) and (13.54). In this block values for the endogenous variables, V_1, V_2, V, L_1, L_2, w_2, P_1, and P_2 can be simultaneously determined by iterative process, when values for L, $K_{p1,-1}$, $K_{p2,-1}$, $K_{g1,-1}$, $K_{g2,-1}$, A, h, ρ, q_K, q_L, Q, etc., are predetermined.

The second block inclues 31 equations: (13.30-13.40), (13.43 - 13.48), (13.50-13.53), and (13.55-13.64). In this block values for the endogenous variables, S, I_h, I_{p2}, I_{p1}, C_f, O, E, M_f, M_m, M_O, DID, I_{gs}, I_g, I_p, I_{g1}, I_{g_2}, B, M, $\bar{K}_{p1}$, $\bar{K}_{p2}$, K_h, K_{g1}, K_{g2}, K_{gs}, K_p, K_g, M_s, P, V_{n1}, V_{n2}, and V_n can be obtained recursively by substituting predetermined values of all explanatory variables, which are determined either in the first block or exogenously, into these equations.

We can now make a total analysis of the model's behavior over the sample period 1906-1968 by the use of the final method to evaluate the predictive power of the model. Table 13.2 shows the Theil inequality coefficients calculated for the postwar period. The Theil inequality coefficient, U, is a measure for testing the predictive power of model and is given by

$$(13.74)\quad U = \sqrt{\sum_{i=1}^{N} (P_i - A_i)^2 / \sum A_i^2}\ ,$$

where P is the computed value; A is the actual value; and N is the number of sample observations.[5] The closer the Theil inequality coefficient is to zero, the better the prediction is. Although there is no commonly accepted criterion to say how close to zero an "acceptable" or "plausible" prediction is, we do find that most of the values in Table 13.2 are close to zero.

Accordingly, we may conclude that our growth model is effective in explaining the growth of the Japanese economy.

13.5. Ex Ante Extrapolation of the Model to 1969-1985

In this final section we present ex ante forcasts for 1969-1985 by means of simulation experiments with the model.

TABLE 13.2. THEIL INEQUALITY COEFFICIENT OVER THE POSTWAR PERIOD

Variable	Inequality Coefficient	Variable	Inequality Coefficient
V	0.0403	P_2	0.0576
V_1	0.0348	w_2	0.0473
V_2	0.0451	I_p	0.0783
L_1	0.0284	I_g	0.0802
L_2	0.0110	I_h	0.1066
O	0.0659	C_f	0.0410
S	0.0548	M_s	0.0571
E	0.0608	V_n	0.0478
M	0.0521		
P	0.0503		

We try to make an ex ante extrapolation of the model to 1969-1985 by the final method, which is a simulation experiment that is generally dependent on initial conditions, parameters, and time paths of the exogenous variables.

In the calculations of an ex ante extrapolation we make a set of projected values of the exogenous variables. The projected values of the exogenous variables are given in Table 13.3.

In Table 13.3 (1) the rate of growth of world exports, T_w, is expected to be 8.5 percent per year between 1969 and 1975, 8.0 percent per year between 1976 and 1980, and 7.5 percent per year between 1981 and 1985; (2) as for work-hours, h, moderate downward trend for 1961-1967 is projected; (3) a projection of the labor productivity index of six advanced countries, V_{2w}/L_{2w}, is made based on an extrapolation of the past trend of V_{2w}/L_{2w} for 1960-1967; (4) the ratio of total tax revenue to GDP, T, is assumed to remain at the level of 19.5 percent, for 1969-1975, and to rise from 20.0 percent in 1977 to 28.0 percent in 1985; (5) the ratio of I_g to I_p,

β_1, is assumed to remain at the level of 0.420 for 1970-1975, and to rise from 0.430 in 1976 to 0.520 in 1985 on the basis of a trend with the ceiling set to the maximum level of 0.520; and (6) changes in cultivated land, $\underline{A}$, and total labor force, $\underline{L}$, are projected in line with the treatment of the New Economic and Social Development Plan. The rate of capacity utilization, ρ, is assumed to remain at full capacity level over time in order to measure potential output.

With these projected values of exogenous variables and the initial position of the economy as of 1968, the extrapolation of annual values of the endogenous variables has been made. In Table 13.4 we give a compact set of results obtained for the main endogenous variables.

It can be seen from column (I) in Table 13.4 that the average rate of potential growth of gross domestic product in 1965 prices, $\underline{V}$, will be 11.1 percent for 1968-1975 and 9.9 percent for 1975-1985; gross value added in the primary sector, $\underline{V}_1$, 2.2 and 2.6 percent; and gross value added in the non-primary sector, $\underline{V}_2$, 11.1 and 9.8 percent. Employment in the primary sector, $\underline{L}_1$, will decrease from 9.88 million persons in 1968 to 3.53 million persons in 1985. Our results show that the ratio of employment in the primary sector to total labor force will drop below the 10 percent line in 1978, which suggests that the Japanese economy will face a severe labor shortage problem. On the other hand, the percentage share of output of the primary sector in total output will drop from 8.0 percent in 1968 to 4.5 percent in 1975, and to 2.2 percent in 1985.

It is also seen that total exports of goods and services increase by 19.6 percent per year for 1968-1975, 16.0 percent per year for 1975-1980, and 13.7 percent per year for 1980-1985; total imports of goods and services, 15.9, 17.3, and 14.8 percent per year; and GDP deflator, $\underline{P}$, will go up by 4.7 percent per year for 1968-1975, 3.7 percent per year for 1975-1980, and 3.8 percent per year for 1980-1985. Accordingly, it follows from our econometric forecasts that the economic growth will be accompanied by balance of trade surplus and price increase. This implies that it is necessary to consider yen reevaluation in order to realize the economic growth under the condition of balance-of-payments equilibrium and price stability.

In August, 1971, the announcement by President Nixon of new

TABLE 13.3. VALUES OF EXOGENOUS VARIABLES FOR 1969-1985

Calender year	Cultivated Land A	Labor Force L	Work Hours h		World Exports T_W
	(thousand hectares)	(thousand persons)	(hours) I	II	(Million dollars)
1969	6,102	50,790	8.17	8.17	249,600
1970	6,074	51,460	8.08	7.98	270,835
1971	6,051	52,140	8.00	7.78	293,835
1972	6,032	52,650	7.92	7.59	318,811
1973	6,019	53,150	7.83	7.39	345,910
1974	6,016	53,620	7.74	7.20	375,312
1975	6,036	54,080	7.65	7.00	407,214
1976	6,026	54,350	7.60	6.90	439,791
1977	6,041	54,622	7.52	6.80	574,994
1978	6,062	54,895	7.43	6.70	512,972
1979	6,091	55,169	7.35	6.60	554,010
1980	6,127	55,445	7.30	6.50	598,331
1981	6,176	55,723	7.23	6.40	643,206
1982	6,240	56,002	7.13	6.30	691,446
1983	6,316	56,281	7.03	6.20	743,304
1984	6,409	56,563	6.93	6.10	799,052
1985	6,520	56,846	6.83	6.00	858,981

Labor Productivity Index V_{2w}/L_{2w}	β_1 I_g/I_p		Total Tax Revenue GDP %		Savings/GDP S/V
(1963 = 1.000)	(I)	(II)	(I)	(II)	
1.305	0.399	0.391	19.5	19.2	0.385
1.364	0.420	0.367	19.5	19.2	0.402
1.426	0.420	0.415	19.5	19.3	0.384
1.492	0.420	0.495	19.5	19.4	0.392
1.560	0.420	0.506	19.5	19.5	0.401
1.631	0.420	0.512	19.5	19.5	0.411
1.706	0.420	0.518	19.5	19.5	0.420
1.784	0.430	0.524	19.5	19.5	0.412
1.866	0.440	0.530	20.0	19.5	0.404
1.952	0.450	0.536	21.0	20.5	0.396
2.042	0.460	0.542	22.0	21.5	0.388
2.137	0.470	0.548	23.0	22.5	0.380
2.235	0.480	0.554	24.0	23.5	0.372
2.340	0.490	0.560	25.0	24.5	0.365
2.465	0.500	0.566	26.0	25.5	0.358
2.561	0.510	0.572	27.0	26.5	0.351
2.683	0.520	0.580	28.0	27.5	0.344

TABLE 13.4. FORECASTS OF THE JAPANESE ECONOMY FOR 1968-1985 (IN BILLION YEN OF 1965 PRICES)

Calender Year / Variable	1968 Actual Value	1975 Computed Value (I)	(II)	(III)	Increase Rate for 1968-1975 (I)	(II)	(III)
V	45,596	95,520	88,690	84,488	11.1	10.0	9.2
V_1	3,663	4,256	4,253	4,265	2.2	2.1	2.2
V_2	41,932	91,264	84,437	80,223	11.8	10.6	9.7
L (thousand persons)	49,970	54,080	54,080	54,079	1.1	1.1	1.1
L_1 (thousand persons)	9,880	6,442	6,793	6,917	-5.9	-5.2	-5.0
L_2 (thousand persons)	40,090	47,638	47,287	47,162	2.5	2.4	2.4
S	16,078	40,118	37,250	35,485	14.0	12.8	11.0
I_p	9,029	19,320	18,852	18,153	11.8	11.3	10.8
I_g	3,951	8,501	9,766	9,394	11.7	13.8	13.2
I_{gs}	1,684	3,135	7,214	6,860	13.3	24.3	23.4
I_h	2,677	7,154	6,408	5,941	15.6	13.5	12.3
E	5,357	18,084	14,490	13,669	19.6	16.2	15.3
M	4,964	12,041	12,266	11,654	15.9	15.0	14.2
B	411	5,143	2,224	2,016	--	--	--
O (1965=100)	160.4	355.7	328.4	311.4	12.1	10.8	10.0
w_2/P_2 (1965=100)	126.2	202.1	192.7	198.0	7.0	6.2	6.6
$V_n = VP$	51,193	147,600	137,960	133,800	16.3	15.2	14.7
$V_{n1} = V_1P_1$	4,439	6,911	6,906	6,926	6.5	6.5	6.6
$V_{n2} = V_2P_2$	46,754	140,689	131,054	126,874	17.1	15.9	15.4
P (1965 = 100)	112.3	154.5	155.6	158.4	4.7	4.8	5.1
P_1	121.2	162.4	162.4	162.4	4.2	4.2	4.3
P_2	111.5	154.2	155.2	158.2	4.8	4.9	5.1
I_p/V (%)	19.8	20.2	21.3	21.5	--	--	--
M_f/C_f (%)	8.2	18.0	19.9	19.5	--	--	--
DID/N (%)	50.9	62.6	61.7	61.4	--	--	--

1980					
Computed Value			Increase Rate for 1975-1980		
(I)	(II)	(III)	(I)	(II)	(III)
158,180	142,780	132,593	10.6	10.0	9.4
4,830	4,767	4,763	2.6	2.3	2.2
153,350	138,020	127,830	10.9	10.3	9.8
55,445	55,445	55,445	0.5	0.5	0.5
4,670	5,043	5,203	-6.2	-5.8	-5.5
50,775	50,403	50,242	1.3	1.3	1.3
60,109	54,258	50,384	8.4	7.8	7.3
26,685	26,536	24,667	6.7	7.1	6.3
12,809	14,542	13,518	8.5	8.3	7.6
4,690	9,437	8,827	8.4	5.5	5.2
11,353	10,017	9,090	9.7	9.3	8.9
37,965	29,427	26,942	16.0	15.2	14.5
28,703	26,264	23,833	17.3	16.5	15.4
9,262	3,163	3,109	--	--	--
604.1	542.7	502.0	11.2	10.6	10.0
302.2	278.0	288.6	8.4	7.6	7.8
292,500	265,370	254,220	14.7	14.0	13.7
9,588	9,464	9,456	6.8	6.5	6.4
282,912	255,910	244,764	15.0	14.3	14.0
184.9	185.9	191.7	3.7	3.6	3.9
198.5	198.5	198.5	4.1	4.1	4.1
184.5	185.4	191.5	3.7	3.6	3.9
16.9	18.6	18.6	--	--	--
33.1	36.3	33.7	--	--	--
67.4	66.4	66.0	--	--	--

TABLE 13.4. CONTINUED

1985					
Computed Value			Increase Rate for 1980-1985		
(I)	(II)	(III)	(I)	(II)	(III)
244,800	220,720	200,554	9.1	9.1	8.6
5,492	5,427	5,382	2.6	2.6	2.5
239,310	215,293	195,172	9.3	9.3	8.8
56,846	56,846	56,846	0.5	0.5	0.5
3,534	3,842	4,010	-5.4	-5.3	-5.1
53,312	53,004	52,836	1.0	1.0	1.0
84,211	75,926	68,989	7.0	7.0	6.5
34,462	36,293	32,492	5.3	6.5	5.6
18,265	21,050	18,845	7.4	7.7	6.9
6,420	12,553	11,578	6.5	5.9	5.6
16,682	14,955	13,320	8.0	8.3	7.9
72,009	55,682	49,686	13.7	13.6	13.0
57,207	52,053	45,354	14.8	14.7	13.7
14,801	3,629	4,332	--	--	--
947.9	851.8	771.3	9.4	9.4	9.1
443.2	403.7	417.8	8.0	7.7	7.7
545,000	492,640	464,950	13.3	13.2	12.8
13,263	13,105	12,997	6.7	6.7	6.6
531,737	479,530	451,953	13.5	13.4	13.1
222.6	223.2	231.8	3.8	3.7	3.9
241.5	241.5	241.5	4.0	3.9	4.9
222.2	222.7	231.6	3.8	3.7	3.9
14.1	16.4	16.2	--	--	--
58.6	62.8	56.3	--	--	--
70.5	69.7	69.3	--	--	--

economic measures to protect the U.S. balance of payments was released. In December 1971 the multilateral currency realignments aimed at achieving the U.S. balance-of-payments equilibrium and settling the international monetary problem were made. As a result of the currency realignments, Japan was forced to revalue the yen by 16.88 percent and to manage its economy in a new economic environment. Thus, we should reassess the possibilities of Japan's long-term growth in the light of recent currency realignments. The Japanese government adopted monetary and fiscal policies to stablize the economy simultaneously with the revaluation. Special attention will be devoted to examining the impact of the revaluation on the Japanese economy and of the stabilization program by means of simulation experiments with the growth model.

The price elasticity of export demand is the importance in determining the outcome of a revaluation. The estimated export function, (13.37), which includes the relative labor productivity variable as a proxy for the relative price variable, is not sufficient to measure the impact of the currency realignments. We use a new export function for the postwar period estimated by the mixed statistical estimation method,

$$\log_e E = -6.170 + \underset{(0.071)}{1.210} \log_e T_w - \underset{(0.037)}{1.200} \log_e \frac{V_{2w}}{L_{2w}} \Big/ \frac{V_2}{L_2},$$
$$\bar{R} = 0.954, \quad \bar{S} = 0.079, \quad D\text{-}W = 0.975,$$

as an amendment to the system, in order to strengthen the predictive power of the export function.

We assume that the yen is revalued by 11 percent as an effective rate of revaluation in the beginning of 1972. Various assumptions about the I_g/I_p ratio, the total tax revenue / GDP ratio, and work hours are considered from the point of view of long-term economic policy and given experimental treatment in the calculations.

For example, we assume that I_g/I_p ratio (the β_1 ratio) is to increase steadily from 0.391 in 1968 to 0.580 in 1985; and the total tax revenue / GDP ratio (the T ratio) is to remain approximately at the level of 1971 over the year 1972-1977 and then to increase 19.5 to 27.5 percent with a moderate trend.

The columns (II) in Table 13.3 show the numerical values of these exogenous variables used in more realistic forecasting.

Furthermore, we assume that the savings /GDP ratio, S/V, is to rise from 0.385 in 1969 to 0.420 in 1975 in line with the treatment of the New Economic and Social Development Plan and then to decline toward the present German level, which is more realistic for the period.

The results of extrapolation with the revised system of equations in line with assumption (II) are shown in Table 13.4, column (II). It is seen from our realistic forecasts that the average annual rate of growth for V is 10.0 percent, 2.1 percent for V_1, and 10.6 percent for V_2, for 1968-1975, and 9.6, 2.5, and 9.8 percent for 1975-1985, etc. We have a lower level of potential gross domestic product as compared to case (I) in 1975 and 1985.

It is also seen that total exports of goods and services increase by 16.2 percent per year for 1968-1975, 15.2 percent per year for 1975-1980 and 13.6 percent per year for 1980-1985, and total imports of goods and services by 15.0, 16.5, and 14.7 percent per year. It follows that the percentage share of Japanese exports in the world market will be 11.6 percent in 1975 and 21.0 percent in 1985.

It is clear from the results that the trade balance measured in real terms, $B = E - M$, reduces substantially as compared to case (I), implying an improvement in the foreign balance and a successful revaluation. However, our results indicate that exports still exceed imports ($B > 0$) after revaluation. This suggests that it may be necessary to consider yen revaluation again.

If we assume that work hours are to decrease with a sharp trend toward the level of western advanced countries (see h-II in Table 13.3), we have lower level of potential gross domestic product in 1975 and 1985. In Table 13.4, column (III), gross domestic product increases by 9.0 percent per year, gross value added in the primary sector, 2.4, and gross value added in the nonprimary sector, 9.3 for the period 1975-1985. In this case, the percentage share of Japanese exports in the world market will be 18.8 percent in 1985.

13.6. Supplementary Note

The moderate price increase of 1968 to 1972 was accelerated

by various factors such as external price influence on domestic costs and prices (trade price effects), liquidity effects due to massive liquid dollar inflow and easy money policy, and expansive fiscal policy since 1971 in the first half of 1973. As a result of the sharp increase in the wholesale and consumer prices between April and August, 1973, the Bank of Japan raised the official rate of interest from 4.25 percent to 9 percent in quick steps during six months, and the Japanese government took measures to defer the 1973 budget expenses in order to restrain aggregate demand with the intention to curb inflation.

In October, 1973, the fourth Middle East war broke out, and the Arab oil-producing nations took political measures to cut down their petroleum shipments to the advanced market economies and to raise crude petroleum prices substantially. As a result of the oil cutback and the sharp increase in crude oil prices, Japan was forced to reduce the energy supply to sustain its economic activities and to manage its economy in a new economic stiuation.

Thus, we should reassess again the prospects of the level of Japan's economic activity and price trend after 1974 in light of the recent economic environment. The Japanese government decided to keep the present tight monetary and fiscal policy for demand management for a long time to come, though it would be unavoidable that Japanese economic growth would slow down.

There is a wide range of views among forecasters regarding the price performance in the future. The actual outcome will depend on trends in import prices which link to world prices of primary products and on policy developments. Special attention will be devoted to examining the impact of the oil crisis on the Japanese economy and of the price stablization program by means of a simulation with our revised growth model. Results of simulation are summarized in Table 13.5.

Notes

Mr. Yagi of Chubu Electric Co. and Mr. Terui of the Institute of Economic Research, Economic Planning Agency (EPA) rendered

TABLE 13.5. FORECASTS OF THE JAPANESE ECONOMY FOR 1973-1975

(in billion yen of 1965 prices

Variable	1973 Computed	1977 Computed	Increase Rate for 1973-1977	1980 Computed	1985 Computed	Increase Rate for 1981-1985
$\underline{V}$	70,081	93.050	7.0	110,760	143,040	5.2
$\underline{V}_1$	4,044	5,012	6.3	6.010	8,300	6.7
$\underline{V}_2$	66,037	88,038	7.1	104,750	134,740	5.2
$\underline{L}$	5,217	5,434	1.1	5,549	5,746	0.7
$\underline{L}_1$	680	514	-7.3	466	467	0.0
$\underline{L}_2$	4,528	4,920	2.3	5,083	5,279	0.8
$\underline{S}$	28,300	37,335	6.1	46,798	63,941	6.4
$\underline{I}_p$	16,856	20,422	7.0	25,449	34,057	6.0
$\underline{I}_g$	6,483	10,129	6.9	13,463	19.923	8.1
$\underline{I}_h$	4,765	6,630	9.7	7,952	10,521	5.8
$\underline{E}$	10,180	14,767	8.7	18,042	24,268	6.1
$\underline{M}$	9,982	14,613	12.9	18,108	24,827	6.5
$\underline{B}$	198	154	--	-66	-559	--
$\underline{I}_{gs}$	3,350	5,348	8.2	6,232	7,436	3.6
$\underline{I}_g-\underline{I}_{gs}=\underline{I}_{g1}+\underline{I}_{g2}$	3,133	4,781	5.6	7,231	12,488	11.6
$\underline{P}$ (1965 = 100)	164.5	302.1	16.5	408.8	593.9	7.8
$\underline{W}_2$ (1965 = 100)	315.1	721.1	22.8	1,140.1	2,027.4	12.2

invaluable statistical assistance.

1. See Economic Planning Agency, Econometric Models for Medium-Term Economic Plan, 1964-1968 (1965), pp.7-19; H. Ueno, "A Long-Term Model of the Japanese Economy, 1920-1958," International Economic Review, 4 (May 1963), 171-193; H. Ueno and S. Kinoshita, "A Simulation Experiment for Growth with a Long-Term Model of Japan," International Economic Review, 9 (February 1968), 14-48.

2. K. Ohkawa, Theory and Measurement of the Food Economy, 1945, (Tokyo: Nihon, 1945) (in Japanese); K. Tsuchiya, "Studies of the Agricultural Production Function and the Resource Allocation," Quarterly Journal of Agricultural Economy, 9 (January 1955), 209-262 (in Japanese).

3. K. Ohkawa, "Measurement and Analysis of the Residuals: Japanese Economy, 1905-1963," The Economic Review, 14 (April 1968), 133-151 (in Japanese).

4. T. Noda, "Income Elasticities of Demand for Agricultural Products," In S. Tohata and K. Ohkawa (Eds.), Agriculture and the Japanese Economy (Tokyo: Iwamani, 1956), pp. 159-174 (in Japanese): Economic Research Institute, Economic Planning Agency, "The EPA Quarterly Econometric Model for Short-Term Forecasting," Discussion Paper, no. 4 (June 1969).

5. H. Theil, Applied Economic Forecasting (Amsterdam: North Holland, 1966), pp. 26-29.

Part VI
Studies of Business Cycle Stabilization Models

14

A Stabilization Model for the Postwar Japanese Economy, 1954-1962

Masahiro Tatemoto, Tadao Uchida, and Tsunehiko Watanabe

14.1. Introduction

Much experience has recently accumulated both in Japan and elsewhere with the econometric model-building which attempts to explain and also forecast economic characteristics of a national economy in the Tinbergen-Klein tradition. Although these experiences have provided several useful suggestions for understanding the actual economy, there still remains some unsatisfactory feeling among economists. This largely originates from the fact that the econometric models, so far constructed, have highly aggregated totals, and also that the assumption of linear specifications in individual equations are considered to be rather unrealistic. Efforts have been made to overcome these difficulties in the following two ways; first, the disaggregation or sectoralization of a national economy has been pushed ahead, and suitable statistical information has been collected. (One of the significant contributions along this line can be found in the quarterly econometric model for the

---

International Economic Review, vol. 8, no. 1 (February 1967), pp. 13-44. Reprinted by the courtesy of the International Economic Review and the authors.

Japanese economy constructed by Professors S. Ichimura, L. R. Klein, S. Koizumi, Y. Shinkai, and K. Sato at Osaka University.[2]

Secondly, indirect use of nonlinear specifications has been tested extensively (the typical example of this formulation is found in the Central Planning Bureau model of the Netherlands where the nonlinear specification, e.g., the exporting value equation, is linearly expanded by ignoring higher order terms).[3]

In the present paper, our main objective is to provide an answer for the second problem, i.e., an explicit use of the nonlinear specifications which may be of some help to narrow the possible gaps between the econometric model and the economic reality. It may be useful at the outset to distinguish the present model from its predecessors.

1. The present model is far less disaggregative compared with for example, the Osaka University model mentioned above.[4] There are 26 equations and 17 accounting identities in our model. Among those equations, 6 were used for prices and wage adjustments.

2. All components in the distribution side of national income accounts, e.g., wage income, tax revenues, etc. are specified by nominal money terms. Also, the accounting identities in the distribution side are expressed in nominal money terms, which implies that the accounting identities in real terms are used only in the definitions of GNP and of capital stocks. This device was especially useful for avoiding possible distortions caused by the recent sharp price changes in the Japanese economy.

3. Nonlinear specifications among endogenous variables were used whenever found suitable from a theoretical point of view. Though these specifications were minimized because of the difficulties of solving the simultaneous equations, this type of specification was of great help for determining individual structural equations. (This statement was certainly true for constructing the wage adjustment equation and also some of the price equations; see section 14.2).

4. Nonlinear dynamic solutions were directly computed from the structural equations without using any linear approximations, e.g., the Taylor expansion. This implies that there

is no unique reduced form corresponding to this model as a whole and, therefore, that the forecast value can be obtained only through solving the nonlinear simultaneous equations.

5. Special devices were introduced in order to easily obtain the solution, except when those devices disturbed, both theoretically and statistically, the expected relations among economic variables. For example, explanatory variables, which were used in the expenditure side yet definitionally belonged to the distribution side, are specified with suitable time-lags. Those special devices were very useful in deriving solutions according to a blockwise computation scheme (see section 14.2).

6. It has been found that the limited information maximum likelihood estimates are considerably stable in the present model. According to the Klein-Nakamura assertion, the limited information estimates might be quite sensitive in the presence of multicollinearity.[5] In fact, no satisfactory LI estimates have been derived in the case of the Japanese sample. Although the general setup of the present model may be favorable to stability of the LI estimates, the finding (stability of LI estimates) may be significant, at least for Japan's economy.

There are some other points of difference between the present and previous models, as will be explained in the later discussion of each equation, but the preceding points are the major differences where new efforts were made in this research. A fuller description and discussion of the data is reserved for the Appendix.

14.2. The Model

The sample data include the biannual series of the fiscal years 1953 to 1962 (from April to the following March). Since some variables are defined as the relative percentage change from the same half-year period in the preceeding year, (e.g., the money wage earnings), the actual sample size was 18 as a whole. At present, the data for the first half year of 1963 give only available actual values which could be compared with our forecast values of each variable. The estimates are obtained by applying three procedures, i.e., the single-stage least squares (SLS), the limited-information maximum-likelihood (LI) and the two-stage least squares (TSLS).

14.2.1. List of Variables.

*$\underline{V}$ = GNP, (billions of 1960 yen)

*$\underline{C}$ = Personal consumption expenditure (billions of 1960 yen)

*$\underline{I}_p$ = Private investment of producer's plant and equipment (billions of 1960 yen)

*$\underline{J}$ = Inventory investment (billions of 1960 yen)

*$\underline{E}$ = Export total (billions of 1960 yen)

*$\underline{E}_c$ = Exports of commodities (billions of 1960 yen)

$\underline{E}_0$ = Other exports (billions of 1960 yen)

*$\underline{M}_1$ = Imports of raw materials and fuels (billions of 1960 yen)

*$\underline{M}_2$ = Imports of other goods and services (billions of 1960 yen)

$\underline{I}_h$ = Expenditures on private housing construction (billions of 1960 yen)

$\underline{I}_g$ = Government investment expenditure (billions of 1960 yen)

$\underline{C}_g$ = Government consumption expenditure (billions of 1960 yen)

*$\underline{D}_h$ = Capital consumption allowances on private housing (billions of 1960 yen)

*$\underline{D}_p$ = Capital consumption allowances on private capital stocks (billions of 1960 yen)

*$\underline{K}_p$ = Private capital stocks (billions of 1960 yen)

*$\underline{K}_h$ = Private housing stocks (billions of 1960 yen)

*$\underline{K}_j$ = Inventory stocks (billions of 1960 yen)

*$\underline{Y}$ = National income (billions of current yen)

*$\underline{Y}_p$ = Personal income (billions of current yen)

*$\underline{W}$ = Wage, salaries, and other labor income (billions of current yen)

*$\underline{Y}_f$ = Nonwage income in agriculture (including forestries and fisheries) (billions of current yen)

*$\underline{Y}_u$ = Proprietor's income in nonagricultural industries (billions of current yen)

*$\underline{Y}_r$ = Personal property income (billions of current yen)

Y_e = Net income from abroad (billions of current yen)
T_r = Transfer payments (billions of current yen)
S_i = Contributions to social insurances (billions of current yen)
$*Y_d$ = Personal disposable income (billions of current yen)
$*Y_c$ = Corporate income (billions of current yen)
$*S_c$ = Corporate retained earnings (billions of current yen)
$*D_i$ = Dividends (billions of current yen)
$*T_c$ = Corporate income taxes (billions of current yen)
$*T_p$ = Personal income taxes (billions of current yen)
$*T_i$ = Indirect taxes minus subsidies (billions of current yen)
Y_g = Surpluses of government enterprises (billions of current yen)
ϵ = Statistical discrepancies (billions of current yen)
N = Total population (thousands of persons)
N_L = Total labor force (thousands of persons)
$*L$ = Total labor demanded (thousands of persons)
$*L_w$ = Total employees (thousands of persons)
$*L_f$ = Number of persons engaged in agricultural industries, including family workers (thousands of persons)
$*L_u$ = Number of persons engaged in nonagricultural, nonmanufacturing sectors, including family workers (thousands of persons)
$*U$ = Number of unemployed (thousands of persons)
$*u$ = Rate of unemployment (%)
$*w$ = Money wage earnings per capita (thousands of current yen)
$*w_f$ = Money income per capita in agricultural industries (thousands of current yen)
$*w_u$ = Money income per capita in nonagricultural, nonmanufacturing industries (thousands of current yen)
$*p_c$ = Consumer price index (1960 = 100)
$*p_h$ = Price index of private housing investment (1960 = 100)
$*p_i$ = Investment goods price index (1960 = 100)
$*p_w$ = Wholesale price index (1960 = 100)
$*p_e$ = Export price index (1960 = 100)
p_m = Import price index (1960 = 100)
$*p$ = Implicit general deflator (1960 = 100)

$^*\underline{i}$ = Interest rate on loans of all banks (sen (= 1/100 yen) per diem per 100 yen)

$\underline{M}_d$ = Total money supply outstanding (billions of current yen)

δ = Rediscount rate of Bank of Japan (sen (= 1/100 yen) per diem per 100 yen)

$^*\underline{O}$ = Production index in mining and manufacturing industries (1960 = 100)

$\underline{T}_W$ = World exports (excluding Soviet bloc countries (billions of 1960 dollars)

$\underline{p}_e{}^W$ = World export price index of manufactured goods (1960 = 100)

$\underline{t}$ = Time trend (the first half-year of 1954 = 1)

$\underline{z}$ = Dummy variable (the first half-year = 0 and the second half-year = 100)

$\underline{z}^*$ = Dummy variable which represents special tight credit program[6] by the Bank of Japan in the period from the first half-year of 1954 to the first half-year 1955 (when the Bank applied its penalty rate system on excessive borrowing by the Commercial Banks) where $\underline{z}^* = 1$, and in other periods $\underline{z}^* = 0$ denotes endogenous variable.

In each of the equations written below, the first line gives SLS estimates, the second and the third give LI and TSLS estimates, respectively, and the figures in parentheses under each coefficient are sampling errors of parameter estimates. Also, $\bar{\underline{S}}$ represents the estimate of variances in each equation, while $\underline{d}$ (Durbin-Watson ratio) and $\bar{\underline{R}}$ (multiple correlation coefficient adjusted by the degree of freedom) are given only for SLS estimates. When an equation is explained only by exogenous and/or predetermined variables, there are no LI and TSLS estimates.

14.2.2. Estimated Equations.

$$(14.1)\quad \underline{C} = \underline{a}_{1.0} + \underline{a}_{1.1}\left(\frac{\underline{Y}_d}{\underline{p}_c}\right)_{-2}$$

SLS	591.1	0.740 (0.016)	$\bar{\underline{S}} = 57.6$	$\bar{\underline{R}} = 0.996$	$\underline{d} = 1.76$

(14.2) $$J = a_{2.0} + a_{2.1}V + a_{2.2}K_{J-1} + a_{2.3}i_{-1} + a_{2.4}z$$

	$a_{2.0}$	$a_{2.1}$	$a_{2.2}$	$a_{2.3}$	$a_{2.4}$
SLS	1450.0	0.430 (0.061)	-0.425 (0.061)	-813.8 (379.1)	-3.844 (0.881)
			$\bar{S} = 91.3$	$\bar{R} = 0.921$	$d = 1.63$
LI	1914.4	0.351 (0.069)	-0.351 (0.069)	-956.0 (405.2)	-2.848 (0.987)
			$\bar{S} = 97.0$		
TSLS	1554.4	0.412	-0.408	-845.8	-3.620
			$\bar{S} = 91.6$		

(14.3) $$\log_{10}E_c = a_{3.0} + a_{3.1}\log_{10}T_w + a_{3.2}\log\left(\frac{p_e^w}{p_e}\right)_{-1}$$

	$a_{3.0}$	$a_{3.1}$	$a_{3.2}$	
SLS	2.786	1.774 (0.121)	-1.524 (0.258)	
		$\bar{S} = 0.021$	$\bar{R} = 0.990$	$d = 1.60$

(14.4) $$M_1 = a_{4.0} + a_{4.1}O + a_{4.2}J$$

	$a_{4.0}$	$a_{4.1}$	$a_{4.2}$		
SLS	18.36	4.553 (0.328)	0.108 (0.043)		
			$\bar{S} = 34.9$	$\bar{R} = 0.978$	$d = 1.89$
LI	31.19	3.310 (0.942)	0.398 (0.180)		
			$\bar{S} = 70.0$		
TSLS	19.07	4.512	0.116		
			$\bar{S} = 35.0$		

(14.5) $$M_2 = a_{5.0} + a_{5.1}I_p + a_{5.2}(V - I_p) + a_{5.3}z$$

	$a_{5.0}$	$a_{5.1}$	$a_{5.2}$	$a_{5.3}$
SLS	-26.0	0.121 (0.025)	0.042 (0.013)	-0.592 (0.175)
		$\bar{S} = 17.0$	$\bar{R} = 0.989$	$d = 1.81$
LI	-99.6	0.063 (0.039)	0.073 (0.020)	- 0.952 (0.257)
		$\bar{S} = 20.0$		
TSLS	-38.4	0.112	0.047	- 0.652
		$\bar{S} = 17.1$		

(14.6) $$I_p = a_{6.0} + a_{6.1}\left(\frac{Y_c - T_c}{p_i}\right)_{-1} + a_{6.2}i$$

	$a_{6.0}$	$a_{6.1}$	$a_{6.2}$
SLS	1958.4	2.506 (0.181)	- 799.0 (389.5)

$\bar{S} = 108.2 \quad \bar{R} = 0.982 \quad d = 1.01$

(14.7) $D_p = a_{7.0} + a_{7.1}K_{p-1}$

SLS	-211.6	0.094 (0.003)

$\bar{S} = 37.0 \quad \bar{R} = 0.990 \quad d = 2.21$

(14.8) $D_h = a_{8.0} + a_{8.1}K_{h-1}$

SLS	-32.0	0.034 (0.005)

$\bar{S} = 7.6 \quad \bar{R} = 0.852 \quad d = 0.33$

(14.9) $Y_r = a_{9.0} + a_{9.1}Y$

SLS	-103.4	0.075 (0.003)	
		$\bar{S} = 2.5$	$\bar{R} = 0.979$ $d = 1.48$
LI	-105.2	0.076 (0.004)	
		$\bar{S} = 2.5$	
TSLS	-103.6	0.075	
		$\bar{S} = 2.5$	

(14.10) $D_i = a_{10.0} + a_{10.1}Y_c + a_{10.2}Y_{c-2}$

SLS	-2.6	0.046 (0.016)	0.101 (0.018)	
		$\bar{S} = 9.8$	$\bar{R} = 0.979$	$d = 1.48$
LI	-4.02	0.062 (0.018)	0.085 (0.020)	
		$\bar{S} = 9.8$		
TSLS	-2.77	0.048	0.099	
		$\bar{S} = 9.5$		

(14.11) $T_p = a_{11.0} + a_{11.o}(T_p + Y_{p-1})/2$

SLS	-30.0	0.070 (0.007)	
		$\bar{S} = 34.7$	$\bar{R} = 0.933$ $d = 1.68$
LI	-20.9	0.068 (0.007)	

		$\bar{S} = 34.8$	
	-20.3	0.071	
		$\bar{S} = 34.7$	

$$(14.12)\quad T_c = a_{12.0} + a_{12.1} Y_c$$

	$a_{12.0}$	$a_{12.1}$		
SLS	15.30	0.359		
		(0.020)		
		$\bar{S} = 28.6$	$\bar{R} = 0.991$	$d = 1.77$
LI	10.72	0.366		
		(0.020)		
		$\bar{S} = 28.7$		
TSLS	15.03	0.359		
		$\bar{S} = 28.6$		

$$(14.13)\quad T_i = a_{13.0} + a_{13.1}(pV) + a_{13.2} Z$$

	$a_{13.0}$	$a_{13.1}$	$a_{13.2}$	
SLS	67.1	0.088	- 0.560	
		(0.004)	(0.163)	
		$\bar{S} = 32.1$	$\bar{R} = 0.985$	$d = 2.42$
LI	74.4	0.087	- 0.538	
		(0.004)	(0.163)	
		$\bar{S} = 32.2$		
TSLS	68.8	0.088	-0.555	
		$\bar{S} = 32.1$		

$$(14.14)\quad \frac{w \cdot L_w}{pV} = a_{14.0} + a_{14.1}\left(\frac{I_{p-1}}{I_{p-3}}\right) + a_{14.2} Z$$

	$a_{14.0}$	$a_{14.1}$	$a_{14.2}$	
SLS	48.5	-0.0305	- 0.065	
		(0.018)	(0.008)	
		$\bar{S} = 1.5$	$\bar{R} = 0.901$	$d = 1.56$

$$(14.15)\quad \log_{10} L_f = a_{15.0} + a_{15.1}\log_{10} L_w + a_{15.2}\log\left(\frac{w_f}{w}\right)_{-1}$$

	$a_{15.0}$	$a_{15.1}$	$a_{15.2}$	
SLS	5.9	-0.511	0.304	
		(0.033)	(0.019)	
		$\bar{S} = 0.0087$	$\bar{R} = 0.972$	$d = 1.39$
LI	5.9	-0.524	0.303	
		(0.034)	(0.019)	
		$\bar{S} = 0.0087$		
TSLS	5.9	-0.513	0.304	
		$\bar{S} = 0.0087$		

(14.16) $\log_{10}\underline{L} = \underline{a}_{16.0} + \underline{a}_{16.1}\log_{10}\underline{L}_{\underline{w}} + \underline{a}_{16.2}\underline{z}$

	$\underline{a}_{16.0}$	$\underline{a}_{16.1}$	$\underline{a}_{16.2}$	
SLS	3.4	0.283	- 0.0002	
		(0.010)	(0.00001)	
		$\bar{\underline{S}}$ = 0.0025	$\bar{\underline{R}}$ = 0.991	$\underline{d}$ 1.08
LI	3.4	0.281	-0.0002	
		(0.010)	(0.00001)	
		$\bar{\underline{S}}$ = 0.0026		
TSLS	3.4	0.282	-0.0002	
		$\bar{\underline{S}}$ = 0.0026		

(14.17) $\dfrac{\underline{w}-\underline{w}_{-2}}{\underline{w}_{-2}} = \underline{a}_{17.0} + \underline{a}_{17.1}\underline{u} + \underline{a}_{17.2}\left(\dfrac{\underline{p}_{\underline{c}}-\underline{p}_{\underline{c}-2}}{\underline{p}_{\underline{c}-2}}\right) + \underline{a}_{17.3}\underline{z}$

	$\underline{a}_{17.0}$	$\underline{a}_{17.1}$	$\underline{a}_{17.2}$	$\underline{a}_{17.3}$
SLS	14.6	-6.923	0.842	0.0119
		(1.816)	(0.222)	(0.0096)
		$\bar{\underline{S}}$ = 1.99	$\bar{\underline{R}}$ = 0.920	$\underline{d}$ = 1.96
LI	9.93	-4.778	1.348	0.01045
		(2.267)	(0.312)	(0.01125)
		$\bar{\underline{S}}$ = 2.33		
TSLS	13.20	-6.446	0.9576	0.01161
		$\bar{\underline{S}}$ = 2.01		

(14.18) $\log_{10}\underline{w}_{\underline{f}} = \underline{a}_{18.0} + \underline{a}_{18.1}\log_{10}\underline{w}_{\underline{u}} + \underline{a}_{18.2}\underline{z}$

	$\underline{a}_{18.0}$	$\underline{a}_{18.1}$	$\underline{a}_{18.2}$	
SLS	-0.035	0.807	0.0024	
		(0.064)	(0.0001)	
		$\bar{\underline{S}}$ = 0.028	$\bar{\underline{R}}$ = 0.972	$\underline{d}$ =1.31
LI	-0.051	0.816	0.0024	
		(0.064)	(0.0001)	
		$\bar{\underline{S}}$ = 0.028		
TSLS	-0.037	0.808	0.0024	
		$\bar{\underline{S}}$ = 0.028		

(14.19) $\log_{10}\underline{w}_{\underline{u}} = \underline{a}_{19.0} + \underline{a}_{19.1}\log_{10}\underline{w} + \underline{a}_{19.2}\underline{z}$

	$\underline{a}_{19.0}$	$\underline{a}_{19.1}$	$\underline{a}_{19.2}$	
SLS	-0.47	1.193	-0.00023	
		(0.059)	(0.00010)	
		$\bar{\underline{S}}$ = 0.021	$\bar{\underline{R}}$ = 0.984	$\underline{d}$ = 1.43
LI	-0.50	1.203	-0.00023	
		(0.059)	(0.00010)	
		$\bar{\underline{S}}$ = 0.021		
TSLS	-0.48	1.193	-0.00023	
		$\bar{\underline{S}}$ = 0.021		

$$(14.20)\quad \frac{p_c}{p_{c-2}} = a_{20.0} + a_{20.1}\left(\frac{w}{w_{-2}}\right) + a_{20.2}\left(\frac{V/L}{V_{-2}/L_{-2}}\right)$$

	$a_{20.0}$	$a_{20.1}$	$a_{20.2}$	
SLS	55.5	0.603 (0.076)	-0.164 (0.053)	
		$\bar{S}$ = 1.30	$\bar{R}$ = 0.807	d = 1.98
LI	58.8	0.656 (0.086)	-0.248 (0.067)	
		$\bar{S}$ = 1.40		
TSLS	56.8	0.626	-0.199	
		$\bar{S}$ = 1.32		

$$(14.21)\quad p_w = a_{21.0} + a_{21.1}\left(\frac{p_m M}{O}\right) + a_{21.2} i$$

	$a_{21.0}$	$a_{21.1}$	$a_{21.2}$	
SLS	115.37	2.252 (0.341)	-12.21 (3.05)	
		$\bar{S}$ = 1.19	$\bar{R}$ = 0.889	d = 1.68
LI	114.87	2.347 (0.346)	-12.29 (3.06)	
		$\bar{S}$ = 1.20		
TSLS	115.32	2.265	-12.22	
		$\bar{S}$ = 1.19		

$$(14.22)\quad p_i = a_{22.0} + a_{22.1} p_{w-1} + a_{22.2} i$$

	$a_{22.0}$	$a_{22.1}$	$a_{22.2}$	
SLS	92.7	1.230 (0.148)	-51.68 (3.910)	
		$\bar{S}$ = 1.53	$\bar{R}$ = 0.965	d = 1.70

$$(14.23)\quad \frac{p_h - p_{h-2}}{p_{h-2}} = a_{23.0} + a_{23.1}\left(\frac{p_i - p_{i-2}}{p_{i-2}}\right) + a_{23.2}\left(\frac{w - w_{-2}}{w_{-2}}\right)$$

	$a_{23.0}$	$a_{23.1}$		$a_{23.2}$
SLS	-5.0	0.512 (0.175)		1.375 (0.225)
		$\bar{S}$ = 4.1	$\bar{R}$ = 0.873	d = 1.00
LI	-5.1	0.526 (0.180)		1.396 (0.228)
		$\bar{S}$ = 4.2		
TSLS	-5.0	0.515		1.381
		$\bar{S}$ = 4.1		

$$(14.24)\quad \frac{p_e - p_{e-2}}{p_{e-2}} = a_{24.0} + a_{24.1}\left(\frac{p_w - p_{w-2}}{p_{w-2}}\right) + a_{24.2}\left(\frac{K_j}{V} - \frac{K_j^*}{V}\right)$$

	$a_{24.0}$	$a_{24.1}$		$a_{24.2}$
SLS	-0.329	0.996 (0.161)		-0.686 (0.164)
		$\bar{S}$ = 2.4	$\bar{R}$ = 0.865	d = 1.11
LI	-0.275	1.081 (0.168)		-0.795 (0.176)
		$\bar{S}$ = 2.5		
TSLS	-0.319	1.015		-0.705
		$\bar{S}$ = 2.4		

here, K_j^* is defined as follows:

$$\frac{K_j^*}{V} = \underset{}{54.65} + \underset{(0.15)}{1.760}\,t - \underset{(0.018)}{0.121}\,z$$

$$\bar{S} = 3.92 \qquad \bar{R} = 0.947$$

$$(14.25)\quad i = a_{25.0} + a_{25.1}\delta + a_{25.2}\Delta M_{-1}^d + a_{25.3}\bar{z}$$

	$a_{25.0}$	$a_{25.1}$	$a_{25.2}$	$a_{25.3}$
SLS	1.9	0.181 (0.086)	-0.00012 (0.00008)	0.259 (0.053)
		$\bar{S}$ = 0.41	$\bar{R}$ = 0.902	d = 1.89

$$(14.26)\quad O = a_{26.0} + a_{26.1}V + a_{26.2}z$$

	$a_{26.0}$	$a_{26.1}$	$a_{26.2}$	
SLS	-20.30	0.018 (0.0006)	-0.210 (0.020)	
		$\bar{S}$ = 3.9	$\bar{R}$ = 0.993	d = 2.49
LI	-20.30	0.018 (0.0006)	-0.212 (0.023)	
		$\bar{S}$ = 3.9		
TSLS	-2-.46	0.018	-0.211	
		$\bar{S}$ = 3.0		

14.2.3. Identities

$$(14.27)\quad V = C + I_h + I_p + J + E - (M_1 - M_2) + I_g + C_g$$

$$(14.28)\quad pV = p_cC + p_hI_h + p_iI_p + p_wJ + p_eE - p_m(M_1 + M_2) + p_iI_g + p_cC_g$$

(14.29) $\underline{pV} = \underline{Y} + \underline{p_i D_p} + \underline{p_h D_h} + \underline{T_i} + \epsilon$

(14.30) $\underline{Y} = \underline{W} + \underline{Y_u} + \underline{Y_f} + \underline{Y_r} + \underline{Y_c} + \underline{Y_g} + \underline{Y_e}$

(14.31) $\underline{Y_c} = \underline{S_c} + \underline{D_i} + \underline{T_c}$

(14.32) $\underline{Y_p} = \underline{W} + \underline{Y_u} + \underline{Y_f} + \underline{Y_r} + \underline{D_i} + \underline{T_r} + \underline{Y_e} - \underline{S_i}$

(14.33) $\underline{Y_d} = \underline{Y_p} - \underline{T_p}$

(14.34) $\underline{W} = \underline{w} \cdot \underline{L_w}$

(14.35) $\underline{Y_u} = \underline{w_u} \cdot \underline{L_u}$

(14.36) $\underline{Y_f} = \underline{w_f} \cdot \underline{L_f}$

(14.37) $\underline{L} = \underline{L_w} + \underline{L_u} + \underline{L_f}$

(14.38) $\underline{U} = \underline{N_L} - \underline{L}$

(14.39) $\underline{K_p} = \underline{K_{p-1}} + \underline{I_p} - \underline{D_p}$

(14.40) $\underline{K_h} = \underline{K_{h-1}} + \underline{I_h} - \underline{D_h}$

(14.41) $\underline{K_j} = \underline{K_{j-1}} + \underline{J}$

(14.42) $\underline{E} = \underline{E_c} + \underline{E_0}$

The Consumption Equation. Two kinds of qualifications were made in the private consumption function: (i) income should be adjusted for taxes and transfers; thus disposable income was selected as an explanatory variable; and (ii) effects caused by past experience or an existence of the downward rigidity in the consumption expenditure should be taken into consideration. These qualifications were the major findings in the past studies of the Japanese post-war data. The following consumption equation was the first choice:

$$\underline{C} = 294.0 + 0.394 \left(\frac{\underline{Y}_d}{\underline{p}_c}\right) 0.467\ \underline{C}_{-2}$$
$$(0.066) \qquad (0.110)$$
$$\bar{\underline{S}} = 30.0 \quad \bar{\underline{R}} = 0.999 \quad \underline{d} = 2.26.$$

In this equation the long-run marginal propensity to consume is 0.741, which is compatible with the value of 0.741 in equation (14.1). (Also, applying the Koyck transformation, the above equation will be transformed into $\underline{C} = 567.1 + 0.750 \cdot (\underline{Y}_d/\underline{p}_c)_{-2}$, in which the average growth rate of $\underline{Y}_d$ is assumed to be 0.09). This consumption equation, though it may be desirable from a theoretical and statistical viewpoint, was replaced by equation (14.1) for the following two reasons: (i) the use of the variable $(\underline{Y}_d/\underline{p}_c)$ can be a significant obstacle for getting solutions of the nonlinear simultaneous equations, since it is not possible to make a blockwise arrangement with regard to this variable; and (ii) an important economic property, i.e., a stability of the long-run marginal propensity to consume, can be secured even in equation (14.1) as mentioned above.

The Investment Equations. Private capital formation is divided into the producer's plant and equipment, the inventory investment, and the residential construction. Among those components, the last one was treated as exogenous, because during the postwar period, residential construction has been closely related to government policy. In the plant and equipment equation, a monetary variable, i.e., the interest rate on loans, is introduced. According to past experience,[7] the propensity to increase fixed capital assets of private enterprises has been so strong that it was reasonable to rely heavily upon external funds, especially from commercial banks. Because of this, the interest rate can be considered an important policy variable (and it has actually been one of the most effective stabilization measures). The first term of the investment equation for the producers's plant and equipment, i.e., corporate income after tax, confirms the so-called profit motive in investment decisions.

The inventory equation, apart from the usual transaction and stock adjustment variables, is also affected by monetary policy.

The Foreign Trade Equations. Export was explained in terms of world trade effects and price effects, as is usually done.[8] Here the variable of export must contain "other services" and the "factor income from abroad" in addition to the commodities exported," in order to maintain consistency with the definition in the national accounts system. This inclusion may not be appropriate for evaluating price effects, since the price of "other services" is difficult to define, while the amount of the "factor income from abroad" in the early 1950s was very irregular because of the existence of "special procurements" provided by foreign forces. "Commodities exported" were, therefore, treated as a separate endogenous variable. Special attention should be given to the regression coefficient of the relative price, since this variable shows the degree of international competitive strength of Japanese exports.

Import is divided into raw materials (including fuels) and others, because the former component is usually noncompetitive. The elasticity of imported raw materials with respect to manufacturing production is approximately equal to unity according to equation (14.4). In straightforward interpretation this fact, combined with the change in imports caused by inventory adjustments which appeared in the second term of equation (14.4), implies a very difficult condition in the balance of payments because an expansion of production needs a proportional increase in imported raw materials.[9]

Equation (14.5) suggests that the amount of import induced by investment is much larger than that induced by other components of final demand. This suggestion is adequate for explaining past experience in the balance of of payments deficit, because this deficit has frequently occurred after rapid expansion of investment activities.

Capital Consumption Allowances. Although estimated equations are statistically significant, the extrapolations based on equations (14.7) and (14.8) may not be appropriate. During the last couple of years, increases in capital stock have been so rapid that the past trend may well produce systematic bias.

Nonwage Incomes. There are two equations for nonwage income components. One covers corporate dividends, and the other relates to property incomes. Corporate retained earnings will be derived from an accounting identity as a residual. Other components of nonwage income in the commonly accepted national income definition, i.e., proprietors' incomes in the commonly accepted national income definition, i.e., proprietors' incomes in nonagricultural industries are defined as the product of income per proprietor with a corresponding number of self-employed.

Property income is related to the national income by linear relation with the negative intercept which is shown in equation (14.9). This negative intercept implies that the ratio of property income to the total national income is increasing, which may be quite a realistic pattern for a growing economy like Japan's.

The dividend equation (14.10) is derived from the hypothesis that the maintenance of stable dividends has been the prevailing policy for most Japanese enterprises.

The Tax Equations. There are three types of taxes in the present model: direct income tax, corporate tax, and indirect tax. The determination principles of these equations are: (i) taxation procedures are only applicable to nominal money terms, and (ii) direct income tax should be considered on a yearly basis. If the present model is used for policy decisions in national planning, these equations can be treated as exogenous, i.e., tax variables then may well be important policy variables of economic stabilization. (In the actual procedure of formulating the new five-year plan, both treatments were used.)

The Labor Demand Equations. Three types of demand for labor are introduced, i.e., the modern type of labor demand in mostly manufacturing industries ($\underline{L}_{\overline{W}}$), the labor demand in agricultural industries, and the demand in nonagricultural and nonmanufacturing industries. The last two demands are concerned with independent proprietors and family workers. The labor demand $\underline{L}_{\overline{W}}$ is assumed to be a modern type to the extent that its wage earnings can be adjusted through the market mechanism as expressed in equation (14.17). According to conventional procedures used in other econometric model-building, this labor demand would be determined as a solution of a production function (usually the linear homogeneous type, e.g. the Cob-Douglas function) In the case of the Japanese economy, however, nonneutral technological inventions, i.e. the labor-saving type, have prevailed,[10] which implies that the relative share of labor may be considerably influenced by the rate of change in investment expenditures. Equation (14.14), therefore, should be interpreted as the one which determines the labor demand under the existence of nonneutral technological changes. In other words, if neutral technological changes are significant, the relative share of labor will maintain at a level of constancy, i.e., about 45 percent of GNP will be paid to this group of employees according to equation (14.14). It should be noticed here that the general price level $\underline{p}$ is not determined from this equation, although it may be possible to determine $\underline{p}$ if identity (14.28) can be treated in a different way. (In the present model, equation (14.28) determines the general price level $\underline{p}$.)

The labor demand in agricultural industries is strongly related to the strength of the demanding power in the manufacturing sectors and also to the degree of income differentials between agricultural and manufacturing sectors. The incentive for leaving agriculture, therefore, has been high. The third type of labor demand is determined as the residual component from equations (14.16) and (14.37). Equation (14.16) is statistical rather than one which explains labor demand behavioristically. As an alternative to the equation, the following aggregate production function was used in the earlier stage of this experiment:

$$\log_{\underline{e}}\left(\frac{\underline{V}}{\underline{L}}\right) = \underline{b}_{16.0} + \underline{b}_{16.1}\log_{\underline{e}}\left(\frac{\underline{K}_{\underline{p}}}{\underline{L}}\right) + \underline{b}_{16.2}\underline{t} + \underline{b}_{16.3}\underline{z}$$

SLS	2.123	0.481 (0.199)	0.016 (0.011)	0.0022 (0.00022)
				$\bar{\underline{S}} = 0.04$ $\bar{\underline{R}} = 0.986$ $\underline{d} = 1.73$
LI	3.015	0.292 (0.215)	0.026 (0.012)	0.0023 (0.00023)
				$\bar{\underline{S}} = 0.05$
TSLS	2.190	0.467	0.017	0.0022
				$\bar{\underline{S}} = 0.04.$

Although this production function might be considered preferable to equation (14.16) from a theoretical viewpoint, it was not used in the final experiment because of the instability of the coefficients.[11]

The Wage Adjustment Equation. This equation is an extension of the Phillips-Lipsey hypothesis of a reasonably stable "adjustment mechanism" in the labor market.[12] The Phillips-Lipsey hypothesis suggests that the rate of change of money wage is a function of the level of excess supply (demand) in the labor market, which may also be a reflection of the influence of bargaining power. Although the labor market considered here should be a nationwide one instead of specific division such as the market for factory workers, the coverage of labor in the present model is restricted to industrial sectors because of the existence of traditional labor relations in the other sectors, especially with respect to family workers. (Actually, there are almost no trade unions in those sectors.) The second term of this equation, i.e., the change of consumer price, is partly selected as an indicator for expressing a possibility of the potential wage-price spiral. (Although, during the last ten years, this possibility was not positively confirmed, it might become an important problem for the Japanese economy in the future.) In a straightforward interpretation, this second variable should be considered as a result of linearization in the dynamic adjustment function, i.e., $\Delta(\underline{w}/\underline{p}_c) = \underline{f}(\underline{u})$.

The Determination of Per Capita Income. Two types of per capita income are considered here, i.e., the per capita income in agricultural industries and that of nonagricultural industries (excluding wage earnings). According to equations (14.18) and (14.19) per capita income in nonagricultural industries can rise a little higher than the wage earnings per capita, while the per capita income in the agricultural industries is almost stagnant. For example, a 10 percent increase in wages per capita will bring about a 12 percent increase in income per capita in nonagricultural industries, while that in agricultural industries can grow by less than 10 percent.) Combining the result from equation (14.15) with the present pattern in agricultural industries, it is possible to say that stagnation of agriculture has already begun in the Japanese economy.

<u>The Price Equations</u>. Price adjustment is divided into five markets, i.e., consumers, producers, housing, investment goods, and exports. The implicit deflator to GNP can be derived endogenously from the accounting identity (14.28). The consumer price equation (14.20) is explained by two effects, i.e., the income effect expressed by the change in wage rate and the declining effect in terms of the change in labor productivity. When the change of money wage is larger than that of productivity, there is no effective device to stop the rising consumer price in the present model.

The wholesale price which is used as the deflator of inventory investment can be considered noncompetitively determined. As mentioned above, most of the raw materials are imported. The first variable in equation (14.21) represents this situation, On the other hand, a market adjustment mechanism through the demand-supply condition is introduced implicitly and indirectly in terms of the second variable, i.e., the interest rate on loans. For example, the interest rate on loans is used here as an indicator which may reflect the degree of monetary tightness rather than the cost component. Thus, increasing difficulties in business financing, indicated by a rise in the interest rate on loans, will require some adjustments in the wholesale price through inventory pressures.

The price of investment goods is assumed to depend on lagged effects of the wholesale price and the interest rate on loans. The housing price is again the cost-determined one, i.e., the variables which represent construction materials and labor cost are introduced explicitly.

The export price equation is a mixture of the cost-determined and the market-determined formula: i.e., the first variable, $(\underline{p}_W-\underline{p}_{W-2}/\underline{p}_{W-2})$, may represent a key item of the cost, while the second variable, i.e., the deviations of inventory ratio from the normal level will play an active role in promoting exports.

<u>The Interest Rate on Loans</u>. The monetary policies which should be followed by the central bank, i.e., the rediscount policy and the open-market operations, will be the major factors to determine the interest rate on loans from commercial banks.

The last equation (14.26) is added only to close the loop.

Identities. Components of national products, valued in constant prices and also in current prices, will add to the total. The remaining identities are needed to make the model complete.

Overall Features of the Model. The dynamic element in the present model is mostly specified by using the lag structure which, in general, is difficult to be determined. Three qualifications were used to design the lag structure considered here, i.e., (i) theoretical, (ii) statistical, and (iii) computational requirements.

The lag structure in the wage adjustment equation is derived from the first criterion. Assuming that wage changes are made on a twelve-month contractual basis at staggered points during the calender year, an average change in wage earnings of any particular half-year period over the preceding period could be related to price changes and the rate of unemployment with the time-lag. The lag structures in the equations on the expenditure side of GNP are mostly derived from the third criterion, e.g., the consumption equation includes the level of personal disposable income in the previous year in order to facilitate the blockwise computation. The second criterion was used chiefly to avoid possible distortions caused by serial correlations. For example, if the relative difference was not introduced into the export price equation, its Durbin-Watson ratio turned out to be 0.36, which meant that there was a strong serial correlation.

It has to be emphasized here, therefore, that the dynamic properties in the present model are not necessarily economical, as is often seen in other studies; rather they may be chiefly computational. (This may be one of the important drawbacks of the model.)

The nonlinearlity in the model has been considered a great obst acle to solving the simultaneous equation system, especially the problem of the existence of nonlinear combinations of endogenous variables. On the other hand, it is not possible to avoid the use of the nonlinear specifications as long as the model builder allows the coexistence of current-term and real-term variables.

Furthermore, even though it is possible to solve the present simultaneous equations system without making any rearrangements such as a blockwise arrangement, it is impossible to overcome the difficulty of time consumption (or equivalently cost consumption). This kind of difficulty may be a fatal obstacle for our purposes, since the following conjectures will not be tested extensively: (i) because the present system is the nonlinear dynamic one, the sensitivity caused by selection of the initial values could be very large, e.g., the initial values based on the recession period may produce a significantly different path from those based on the boom period; (ii) the transformation into policy models and associated analysis with respect to policy impacts are very desirable, and they strongly depend upon the causal ordering which will be assumed,i.e., the interrelation between the causal ordering and the policy use of the model should be analyzed, especially for planning purposes; and (iii) adjustments of the estimates with respect to constant terms without making any revisions for the slope coefficients could be of some help in improving the accuracy of forecasts.[13]

Here, in the present paper, therefore, one of the mixed ways of handling the nonlinearity is tested, without making any linearizations. A mixed formulation which satisfies these two requirements, theoretical and computation, consists in the use of a blockwise recursive arrangement. The basic principles of determining blocks are as follows: (i) each block should correspond to economic aspects in a national economy; (ii) the nonlinear computations should be done within the same block; (iii) the number of blocks should be minimized; and (iv) the blocks should be arranged recursively.

In the present model, the first block represents the mechanism of determining the variables which belonged to the expenditure side of GNP. The variables of consumption, investment, export, inventory changes, two components of imports, GNP, and the production index were solved as endogenous variables. In order to keep a computational independency of this block from others, the variables which enter into structural equations in this block have to be exogenous or predetermined, with the exception of the endogenous variables which are to be explained within this block. For example, the import equation (14.4) fulfilled the above criterion in the sense that it contained only the variables of the expenditure side of GNP; on the other hand, the consumption equation which was discussed in the second part of this section as an alternative (i.e., $\underline{C} = \underline{a}'_{10} + \underline{a}'_{11}\underline{Y}_d/\underline{p}_c + \underline{a}'_{12}\underline{C}_{-2}$), had to be replaced by equation (14.1), because that alternative contained the variable $\underline{Y}_d$ without any time lags.

After determining the above 8 endogenous variables, the variables $\underline{D}_p$, $\underline{D}_h$, $\underline{K}_p$, and $\underline{K}_j$ will be determined by equations (14.7), (14.8), (14.40), and (14.42). The computed values of these 13 variables will be substituted into the second block where 11 endogenous variables (6 prices, 2 labor variables, unemployment and its ratio, and money wage earnings) should be determined. Equations in this block are (14.14), (14.16), (14.17), (14.20-14.24), (14.28), (14.38), and (14.39). Since this block contains two nonlinear equations, i.e., (14.14) and (14.16), it is impossible to solve them without using the convergence procedure.

Our computation for this nonlinear system is performed as follows: (i) solve equation (14.16) substituting the given initial value of $\underline{L}$, i.e., $\underline{L}^0$ (in practical computations, the actual value in the previous period was used for this $\underline{L}^0$); (ii) equations (14.21), (14.22), and (14.24) determine $\underline{p}_i$, $\underline{p}_w$ and $\underline{p}_e$ successively; (iii) equations (14.14), (14.20), (14.23) and (14.28) can be solved simultaneously, since now $\underline{p}_c$, $\underline{p}_h$, $\underline{p}$, and $\underline{w}$ are linearly related; (iv) three variables of $\underline{u}$, $\underline{U}$, and $\underline{L}$ will be determined from equations (14.17), (14.38) and (14.39) successively; and (v) compare the computed value of $\underline{L}$, i.e., $\underline{L}^1$ with $\underline{L}^0$ and if $(\underline{L}^0 - \underline{L}^1)/\underline{L}^1 > 0.0001$, then continue the same procedure substituting $\underline{L}^1$ into equations (14.16) as the new initial value. If $(\underline{L}^0 - \underline{L}^1)/\underline{L}^1 \leqq 0.0001$, then computations of the convergence will stop. In actual computation, the number of repetitions was around 15 in each sample period. (Although the same type of computation would be possible by using the variable $\underline{u}$ as the initial value, it gave unsatisfactory results because of longer oscillation around a value of $\underline{u}$).

The remaining endogenous variables which largely belong to the distribution side of national income can be determined by introducing the estimated values of endogenous variables determined in the previous two blocks into the third block. Then the same type of recursive procedure for the next period will start again. (The following diagram will give the summarized blockwise arrangement in the present model.)

It has to be emphasized here that the above stated blockwise arrangement may not be a suitable device from the viewpoint of economic theory. It is, however, an unavoidable "necessary evil" in overcoming the computational difficulties.

Finally, it will be of interest to make some remarks on the property of estimates of structural parameters. As shown in the second part of this section, estimates of parameters in individual equations are, in general, considerably stable with respect to different methods of estimation, i.e., the single and two-stage least squares and the limited information methods. So far, the assertion that the presence of multicollinearity among variables will strongly disturb the stability of the simultaneous estimates has been considered to be especially applicable to the postwar Japanese economy, since the speed of economic growth has been so great.[14] Although, in general, this assertion might be true, it may also be possible to state the following conjecture, "instability of LI estimates may be overcome by using suitable techinques for selecting exogenous and predetermined variables," according to our experience in the present experiment.

There are 18 exogenous variables and also 18 predetermined variables in the present model, as were shown in the second part of this section. The number of samples is 18. It is, therefore, necessary to make some selection among those variables to be included in the Mzz matrix in performing a meaningful computation. In the selection, three procedures have been applied, (i) the exogenous variables which are used as explanatory variables in structural equations (not in identities) have to be taken, e.g., the variables of T_w, p_m; (ii) other exogenous variables which appear in identities have to be selected by the degree of importance, e.g., the total supply of labor, N_L, must be explicitly counted, since it affects the wage adjustment equation significantly; and (iii) predetermined variables were selected by considering their mutual interdependence (actually, the simple correlation matrix was computed with regard to those variables and then relatively, mutually independent ones were added as predetermined variables

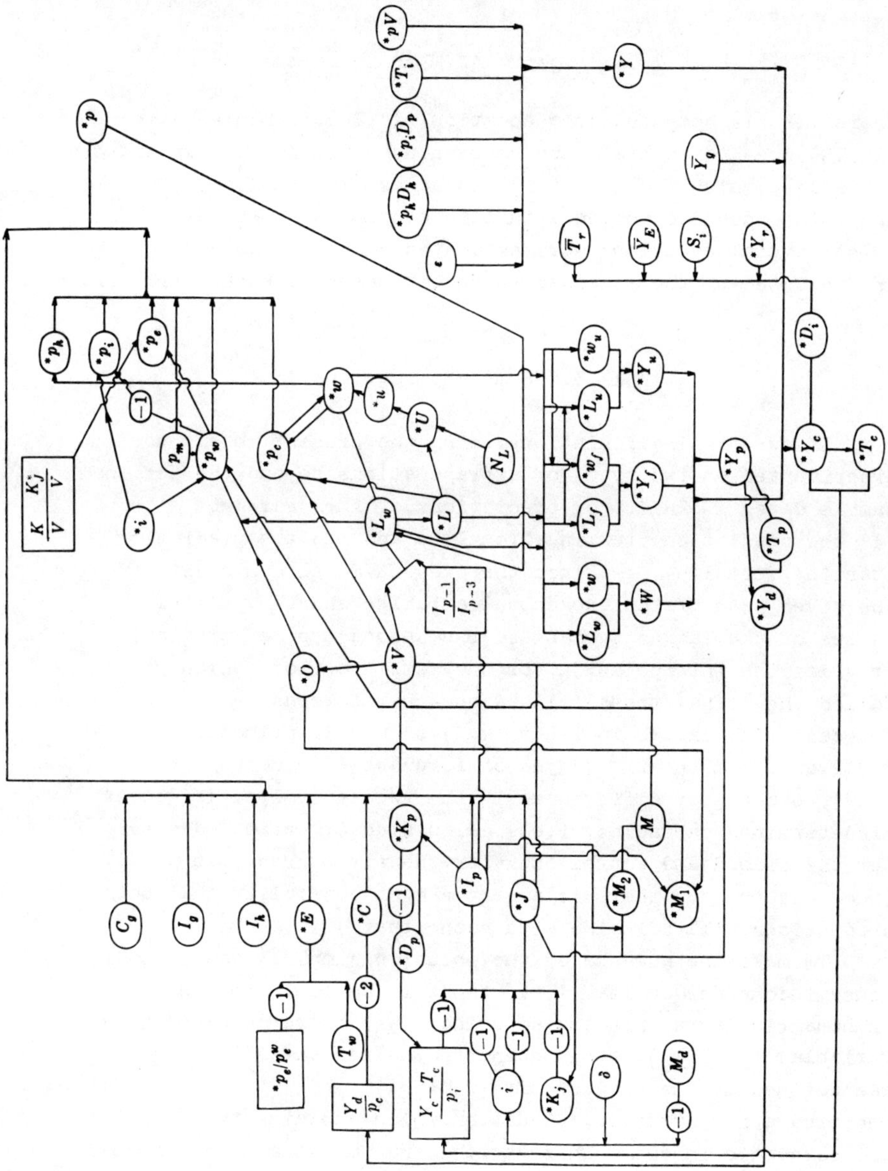

Fig. 14.1.

in the process of estimation). Applying these rules, the following eleven variables were selected:

$$(\underline{I}_g+\underline{C}_g), \underline{t}_w, \underline{p}_m, \underline{z}, \underline{K}_{J-1}, \underline{Y}_{C-2}, \log\left(\frac{\underline{w}_f}{\underline{w}}\right)_{-1}, \underline{p}_{w-2}, \underline{N}_L, \underline{i}_{-1}, \text{ and } \underline{i}^*$$

where $\underline{i}^*$ is computed from equation (14.25), since equation (14.25) does not contain any endogenous variables as explanatory variables, which means that all three estimates, i.e., SLS, LI, and TSLS should coincide with each other. As a matter of fact, 19 structural equations were estimated simultaneously which is indicated by the attached three estimates of each parameter.[15]

14.3. Some Applications

In our trial calculations using the present model, we experimented on two types of extrapolations beyond the terminal sample date, 1962-II, for predictions of the year 1963, i.e., (1) the prediction starting from 1962 and (2) the prediction starting from 1954.[16] Since the present model can be solved with the given path of the exogenous variables and the initial values of the lagged variables, the second type of prediction provides the interpolation for the sample period (which is called the "final test") plus a one-year forecast. The second forecast (Forecast B in Table 14.2) should in principle be different from the first type of forecast (Forecast A in Table 14.2), because of differences in the values of 1962 lagged or predetermined variables, i.e., calculated or estimated ones for the second and actual ones for the first predictions. (needless to say, there is a very slight possiblity that both predictions will coincide with each other.)

To make the algebra of the solution simple, two kinds of money income per capita, i.e., those in agriculture, $\underline{w}_f$ and in nonagriculture, nonmanufacturing, $\underline{w}_u$, were combined as a variable, $(\underline{w}_f + \underline{w}_u)$. Consequently, the new variable, $(\underline{Y}_u + \underline{Y}_f)$ was defined as the product of $(\underline{w}_u + \underline{w}_f)$ and $(\underline{L}_u + \underline{L}_f)$. This required a new structural equation which explains the behavior of "corporate income." (This variable was originally determined as a residual from the accounting identity (14.30).)[17] The equation of "corporate income" used here is

$$\underline{Y}_c = 1248.0 + \underset{(0.034)}{0.077Y} - \underset{(276.9)}{567.2i_{-1}} + \underset{(0.185)}{0.498Y_{c-1}}$$

$$\bar{S} = 68.7 \quad \bar{R} = 0.980 \quad d = 1.05.$$

Using the values of the exogenous variables in Table 14.1, we solved the system for the jointly dependent endogenous variables in 1963-I and 1963-II, and after that yearly totals were calculated. Forecast and actual values are summarized in Table 14.2. On the surface, these appear to have been good forecasts in both types of predictions.

TABLE 14.1. VALUES OF EXOGENOUS VARIABLES, 1963

I_h	538.5	Y_g	126.1
I_g	2,498.7	ϵ	-264.1
C_g	1,813,5	N_L	46,755.0
Y_e	101.1	p_m	100.8
T_r	961.4	T_w	139.3
S_i	687.5	p_e	102.0
E_0	421.3		

Note: Measuring units are given in the text (section 14.1). Necessary division of those yearly totals among the first and the second half-year which were needed to make forecasts were made according to the average pattern in the last three years, i.e., 1960-1962.

Both forecasts gave satisfactory results for almost all variables, the exception being in inventory investment and some prices. It is worth mentioning here that both forecasts succeeded in predicting a sharp upturn in the economy from the low rate of economic growth in the previous year, i.e., 5.1 percent per annum in real GNP through 1962, for the model came out in the correct neighborhood (about 11 percent) while there was strong doubt in the mind of many economists. (For example the official annual projection of GNP growth rate made by the Economic Planning Agency was 6.1 percent for 1963, while the actual one was 12.3 percent.)

A more detailed appraisal requires special attention be given to the performance of price and wage variables, since

TABLE 14.2. COMPARISON OF SELECTED VARIABLES, 1963

	(1) Actual	$(2)^{2}$ Forecast-A	$(3)^{b}$ Forecast-B	$(4)^{c}$ (2)/(1)	$(5)^{c}$ (3)/(1)
$\underline{V}$ (GNP)	19,766.9	19,509.6	19,677.3	98.7	99.5
$\underline{C}$ (Consumption)	9,767.4	9,652.7	9,542.5	98.8	97.7
$\underline{I}^{p}$ (Investment)	4,100.1	4,147.5	4,253.4	101.2	103.7
$\underline{J}$ (Inventory)	1,428.5	1,071.8	1,111.0	75.0	77.8
$\underline{E}$ (Export)	2,407.3	2,506.8	2,570.3	104.1	106.8
$\underline{M}$ (Import)	2,767.1	2,700.0	2,629.5	97.6	95.0
$\underline{pV}$ (GNP, current)	22,542.4	23,000,6	22,274.7	102.0	98.8
$\underline{O}$ (Production index)	149.5	149.6	151.2	100.1	101.1
$\underline{p}_c$ (Consumer price)	121.2	121.8	117.3	100.5	96.8
$\underline{p}_w$ (Wholesale price)	101.5	100.9	100.9	99.4	99.4
$\underline{p}_i$ (Inventory price)	101.3	109.8	106.0	108.4	104.6
$\underline{p}_h$ (Housing price)	138.4	157.0	143.3	113.4	103.5
$\underline{p}_c$ (Export price)	101.4	101.8	99.5	100.4	98.1
$\underline{w}$ (Wage)	374.8	382.5	358.0	102.0	95.5
$\underline{W}$ (Wage income)	9,756.9	9,936.8	9,308.1	101.8	95.4
$\underline{Y}_c$ (Corporate income)	2,714.1	2,759.0	2,694.1	101.7	99.3
$\underline{Y}_p$ (Personal income)	16,058.7	16,214,2	15,626.9	101.0	97.3
$\underline{T}_c + \underline{T}_i + \underline{T}_p$ (Taxes)	4,020.6	4,143.1	4,013.5	103.0	99.8
$\underline{Y}$ (National income)	18,218.8	18,468.5	17,821.5	101.4	97.8
$\underline{p}_e\underline{E}$	2,440.6	2,551.9	2,557.6	104.6	104.8
$\underline{p}_m\underline{M}$	2,791.6	2,721.6	2,650.5	97.5	95.0
$(\overline{V} - \underline{V}_{-2})/\underline{V}_{-2}$ (percent)	12.3	10.8	11.8		

Note: Measuring units are given in the text (section 14.1). a. Forecasts started from 1962. b. Forecasts started from 1954. c. Unit is the percentage.

the use of nonlinearity in the present model has for the most part originated from price-wage relations. As can be observed from Table 14.2, both forecasts provide to some extent significant differences with respect to important price-wage variables, i.e., consumer price, wage rate, and export price. There is an overestimation in forecast-A and vice versa in forecast-B. These over- or underestimations in the price-wage variable are also transferred into the income variables in the distribution account. A straightforward interpretation with regard to the above discrepancy would have to attribute it to the differences in the initial values of the predetermined variables.

An alternative consideration would be the following: From the nature of the present model, the most sensitive part for determining the price-wage relation is the subsystem composed of three equations, i.e., (14.14), (14.17), and (14.20). Furthermore, among three equations, the first one, i.e., the relative share equation (14.14), is the most significant from the computation viewpoint, since equation (14.14) is used for computing the wage rate, and the computed wate rate will then be substituted into the remaining equations. If, therefore, a series of different values is given to the relative share of labor, estimated values of prices, especially consumer price, will become different. In order to test this conjecture empirically, the following simulation test was made: the actual series of (wL_w/pV) were used for solving the system of equations instead of the series of endogenously computed values, although the differences between these two series were not so significant.

V	pV	Y	O	p_c
19,733.0	23,087.6	18,538.6	151.6	123.3

p_w	p_i	p_e	p_h	w
100.9	106.0	99.6	157.9	383.8

These results are almost similar to the forecasts in Table 14.2. Thus, it may be said that the discrepancies of price-wage estimates observed in both forecasts of Table 14.2 have principally originated from the differences in the initial values. This type of simulation test, however, might tell us some interesting points about the quantitative impact of the so-called "incomes policy," if values of the relative share of labor are specified purposively.

Now let us examine the interpolated results briefly, since, as mentioned above, the ex-post prediction for 1955-1962 is ready to be discussed from forecast-B. Among 43 endogenous variables, the following 8 were selected for the present discussion, i.e., GNP ($\underline{V}$), private fixed capital information ($\underline{I}_p$), inventory investment ($\underline{J}$), export ($\underline{E}$), import of raw materials ($\underline{M}_1$), consumer price ($\underline{p}_c$), wage rate ($\underline{w}$), and national income ($\underline{Y}$)[18] (see figs. 14.2-14.9).

As is to be expected, the total aggregative variables such as GNP in real term and national income in current term showed satisfactory results. On the other hand, the difficulty in the ex-post prediction was found in investment variables, i.e., $\underline{I}_p$ and $\underline{J}$, which have also been quite common defects in the past econometric models for the Japanese economy, although there were significant improvements in the present model. Interesting comparisons are shown in Figs. 14.6 and 14.7, i.e., the consumer price and the wage rate. As already mentioned above, the estimated path of these two variables was insufficient to explain changes in the recent couple of years when the rise in consumer price has become a problem of Japan's economic growth. From this unsatisfactory explanation of the price and the wage rate, it may be possible to say that the

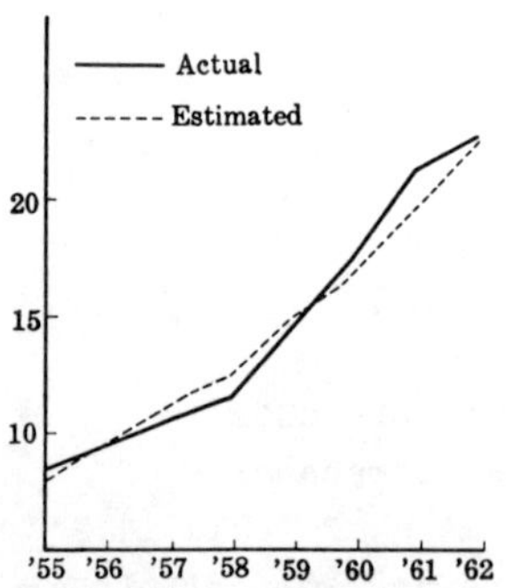

Fig. 14.2. GNP (trillions of 1960 yen)

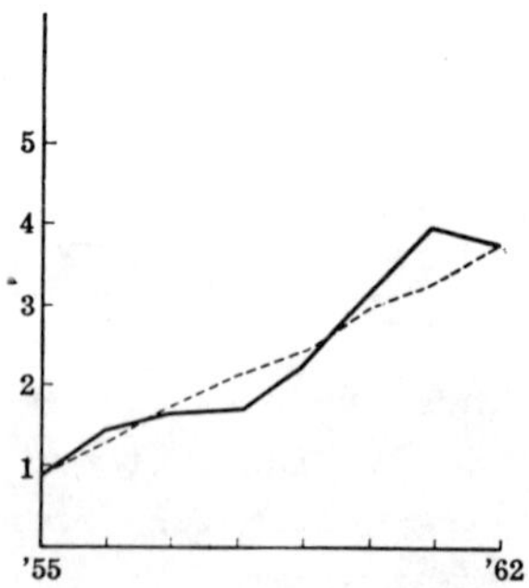

Fig. 14.3. Private Fixed Investment trillions of 1960 yen)

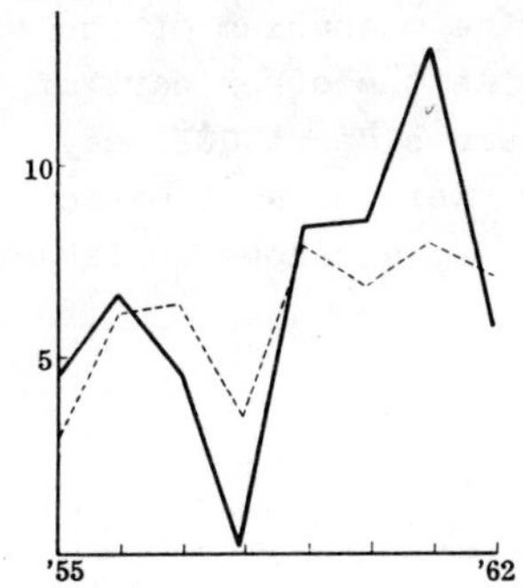

Fig. 14.4. Inventory (hundred billions of 1960 yen)

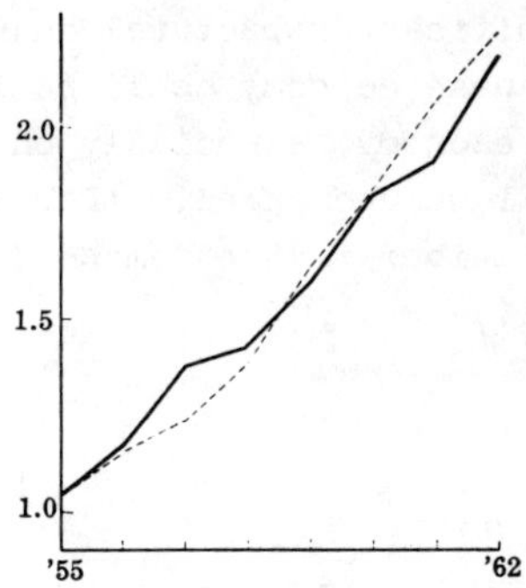

Fig. 14.5 . Total Export (trillions of 1960 yen)

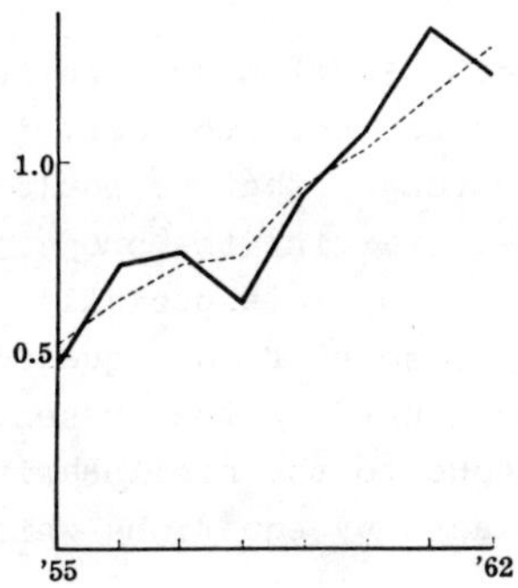

Fig. 14.6. Import of Raw Materials (trillions of 1960 yen)

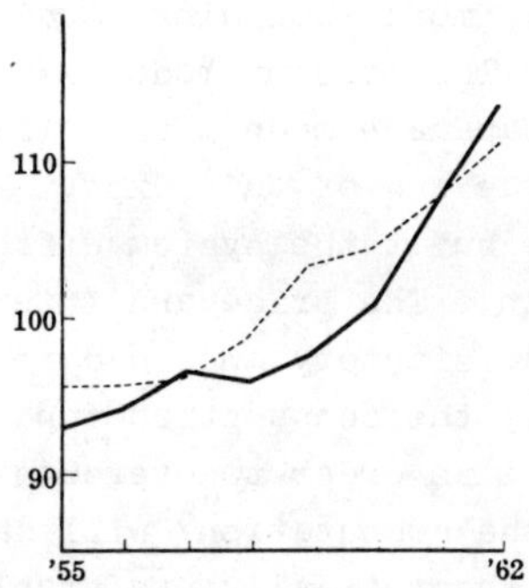

Fig. 14.7. Consumer Price Index (1960 = 100)

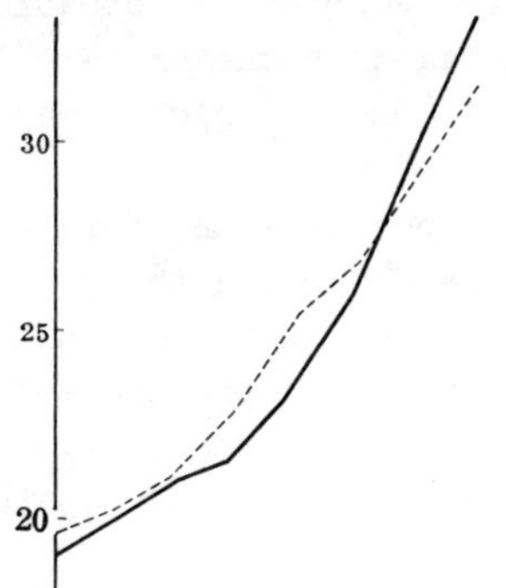

Fig. 14.8. Wage Rate (ten thousands of current yen)

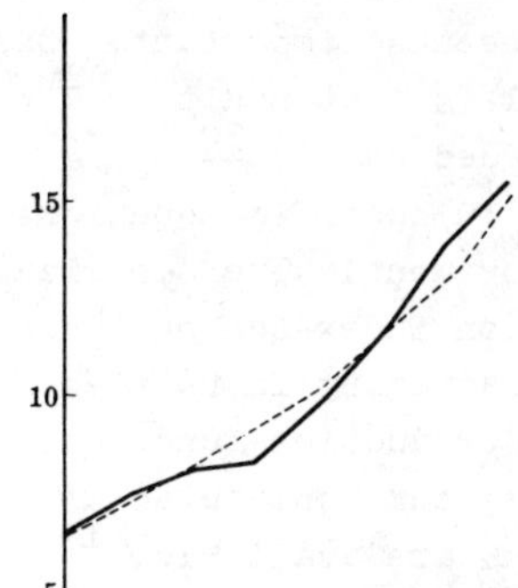

Fig. 14.9. National Income (trillions of current yen)

significant structural change in the price mechanism of the Japanese economy could be identified while the other part of the economy, especially on the expenditure side of GNP, may still be unchanged. (For example, there were no systematic deviations in the demand components of GNP, as shown in Table 14.2.)

14.4. Conclusion

In conclusion, let us indulge in some self-criticism of the present work which would be of some interest to those econometricians who intend to do similar experimental studies, i.e., model-building studies.

The present model is only another contribution to a series of Japanese models and will set the stage for work to come. At the end of this experiment, we felt strongly that we would have built the system differently were we starting the project again. The price and interest rate equations are especially unsatisfactory and need revision.[19] Also, some of the equations, e.g., the consumption function, which were used in the present model in order to overcome difficulties due to the nonlinearities in the computation, will have to be replaced by equations which are theoretically preferable.

It would be desirable to introduce some relation between the amount of money supplied and effective demand, since the role of monetary policy in stabilizing the economic fluctuations has been so important. One of the advantages in the present model is that additional blocks (e.g. the monetary block) may be added easily.[20]

In specific equations there are many possibilities for improvement. The empirical relation between GNP and the production index can be improved by extracting net output in nonmanufacturing industries from GNP, and estimating the aggregate production functions separately for at least manufacturing and nonmanufacturing industries when the data of capital stocks are available.[21]

Inventory might have to be subdivided into farming and nonfarming groups. This kind of subdivision would be necessary especially for imported raw materials and also other imports.

Similarly, housing investment should be included within the model as an endogenous variable, since it is not induced by purely governmental activities, and private motivation has been increasing.

An exogenous treatment of the government sector in the present model, the exception being in the simple tax equations, is not definitely desirable. Separation of the induced part of the governmental activities from the autonomous ones will be needed to test the impact of stabilization policies more carefully.

All these improvements again require time-consuming research work, but they are all capable of being done in the future, and we hope that they will add to the model discussed here.

Appendix 14.A. Sample Data
(For notation see pages 417-419)

Fiscal Year		V	C	I_p	J	E	E_c	E_0	M_1	M_2	u	w	w_f	w_u
1953	I	3,598.2	2,251.7	410.4	209.1	436.0	351.3	84.7	226.4	130.5	1.32	83.0	24.3	70.9
	II	4,338.7	3,609.4	465.1	194.8	424.6	396.0	28.6	240.7	180.2	1.27	90.9	46.4	78.1
1954	I	3,745.4	2,406.1	428.0	218.1	457.2	276.2	181.0	207.1	169.3	1.66	89.9	25.9	68.4
	II	4,421.8	2,666.0	423.1	51.2	495.8	329.4	166.4	203.9	130.9	1.87	95.2	48.5	72.1
1955	I	3,699.8	2,565.1	401.6	-73.1	504.7	340.7	164.0	219.9	158.8	1.79	91.0	31.8	69.5
	II	5,357.2	2,933.6	496.1	533.0	546.4	399.0	147.4	262.3	173.0	1.93	97.6	54.7	79.6
1956	I	4,181.4	2,777.4	641.2	317.9	568.0	413.1	154.9	336.2	181.1	1.53	96.0	30.7	84.3
	II	5,663.6	3,058.8	764.4	351.2	610.4	449.5	160.9	393.9	243.7	1.57	103.4	51.9	85.0
1957	I	4,732.0	2,937.3	846.8	295.0	666.0	495.6	170.4	436.6	261.4	1.26	102.5	32.8	84.5
	II	5,803.7	3,261.4	803.6	173.2	715.0	545.2	169.8	338.1	221.9	1.43	106.3	55.5	87.1
1958	I	4,814.5	3,119.4	828.2	-68.3	681.8	520.7	161.1	307.0	241.7	1.39	104.3	32.9	80.8
	II	6,075.5	3,425.5	869.8	86.2	750.2	570.2	171.0	328.7	264.3	1.64	111.9	61.6	83.8
1959	I	5,603.5	3,340.6	950.4	349.1	777.2	612.5	164.7	424.7	274.4	1.38	110.3	37.2	88.9
	II	7,189.0	3,684.3	1,231.2	494.8	837.4	672.2	165.2	499.4	288.1	1.35	122.9	65.6	95.4
1960	I	6,352.2	3,607.0	1,347.3	312.2	893.3	718.0	175.6	523.1	340.3	1.04	122.1	40.6	105.8
	II	8,220.9	4,019.2	1,720.2	546.9	940.7	757.4	183.3	522.3	289.5	1.06	135.6	73.0	108.6
1961	I	7,478.7	3,937.5	1,885.5	601.9	919.5	736.2	183.3	663.7	444.5	0.88	141.2	44.6	132.2
	II	9,278.3	4,375.7	2,073.9	711.6	1,003.5	805.8	197.7	682.4	456.4	1.00	158.3	81.9	134.7
1962	I	7,792.3	4,288.9	1,913.6	56.9	1,105.4	906.2	199.2	610.7	470.3	0.79	158.9	50.5	143.2
	II	9,808.7	4,713.3	1,852.4	525.2	1,094.1	897.5	196.6	615.1	487.4	1.01	176.2	92.8	146.9

Fiscal Year		p_c	p_h	p_i	p_w	ϵ	N_L	L	L_w	L_f	L_u	U	Y_d
1953	I	87.1	74.3	88.9	99.4	6.7	40,432	39.897	15,483	17.040	7,374	535	2,173.6
	II	91.6	83.3	93.7	102.6	188.9	38,138	38,640	15,990	14,686	7,964	498	2,691.4
1954	I	93.3	81.8	90.1	98.0	75.6	41,593	40,903	16,150	16,784	7,969	690	2,440.7
	II	93.6	80.8	88.5	98.1	75.2	40,073	39,322	16,335	14,552	8,435	751	2,848.3
1955	I	93.3	77.9	86.1	96.9	-322.2	42,980	42,210	16,822	17,096	8,393	770	2,719.9
	II	92.9	77.7	87.0	98.1	423.7	41,628	40,823	17,715	14,422	8,686	805	3,222.1
1956	I	93.8	82.4	93.3	101.5	-379.9	43,638	42,970	18,233	16,731	8,006	668	2,991.4
	II	94.7	86.6	101.3	105.6	377.4	42,393	41,727	19,055	13,972	8,700	666	3,477.0
1957	I	97.0	89.2	104.0	104.7	2-78.1	44,333	43,773	19,428	15,997	8,348	560	3,324.3
	II	96.0	89.1	101.1	101.8	245.6	43,035	42,418	20,113	14,004	8,301	617	3,734.3
1958	I	95.8	88.4	97.2	97.5	-314.6	44,690	44,068	20,453	15,572	8,043	622	3,431.3
	II	96.5	88.5	97.1	97.2	104.6	43,227	42,518	21,058	13,048	3,412	709	4,019.5
1959	I	97.0	89.6	98.1	98.5	-297.9	45,302	44,675	21,613	14,877	8,185	627	3,870.3
	II	98.7	97.1	100.5	100.9	388.7	43,653	43,065	22,018	12,730	8,317	588	4,543.0
1960	I	100.1	98.5	100.0	99.9	-547.8	46,080	45,603	22,830	14,688	8,085	477	4,472.9
	II	101.6	107.8	100.3	99.9	340.5	44,585	44,113	23,297	12,308	8,508	472	5,187.8
1961	I	104.4	123.3	102.9	101.4	-576.0	46,387	45,977	23,593	14,692	7,692	410	5,260.6
	II	109.9	132.9	103.5	100.8	397.6	45,057	44,605	24,583	12.070	7,952	452	6,155.9
1962	I	112.2	131.3	101.9	99.0	-660.6	47,085	46,713	24,938	14,074	7,701	372	6,072.5
	II	115.6	132.8	101.4	99.6	201.1	45,248	44,792	25,220	11,817	7,755	456	6,873.2

Appendix 14.A. Sample Data (continued)

Fiscal Year		Y_c	S_c	D_i	T_c	T_p	T_i	Y_g	I_h	I_g	C_g	D_h	D_p
1953	I	291.7	161.6	31.8	98.3	175.4	316.1	7.4	76.8	361.5	209.6	32.4	209.0
	II	305.6	135.5	36.8	133.2	232.0	352.3	10.5	83.8	343.0	638.8	20.4	254.1
1954	I	258.1	107.3	36.5	114.3	178.5	337.3	-6.8	81.8	254.1	277.2	33.0	248.8
	II	274.1	125.6	21.3	127.2	229.4	396.4	17.3	82.2	411.0	627.3	39.1	311.8
1955	I	260.2	107.3	43.4	109.5	176.3	334.8	-6.0	86.2	302.8	291.2	47.4	309.9
	II	337.1	166.4	46.1	124.6	239.2	429.7	11.0	96.6	522.2	664.5	53.4	350.9
1956	I	415.0	234.3	49.9	130.8	202.5	407.8	-9.8	126.1	21.7	246.4	56.9	346.9
	II	523.9	297.3	53.9	172.7	246.9	465.6	15.1	107.8	662.8	744.0	57.5	369.2
1957	I	532.6	262.2	63.1	207.3	189.3	466.4	29.4	132.2	271.6	281.1	59.9	367.0
	II	457.3	171.8	66.0	219.5	232.0	499.3	39.7	118.3	520.4	771.8	63.2	436.2
1958	I	381.4	121.0	65.7	194.7	205.3	481.8	34.5	137.7	328.0	336.4	68.1	435.7
	II	460.5	210.0	69.5	181.0	231.0	568.9	37.3	130.1	627.3	779.4	69.7	504.4
1959	I	638.9	324.1	78.3	236.5	213.3	565.2	36.4	159.2	353.9	372.0	79.1	500.2
	II	765.2	430.8	81.3	253.1	255.1	617.8	41.5	137.5	764.3	827.0	76.3	622.5
1960	I	930.1	509.4	100.7	320.0	267.1	677.3	45.4	183.6	366.8	505.1	79.8	619.3
	II	1,023.1	549.4	117.8	355.9	335.7	726.6	60.3	150.1	970.4	824.2	75.2	755.7
1961	I	1,159.1	620.4	126.0	411.8	322.4	794.3	72.8	181.3	497.8	553.4	77.0	837.6
	II	1,160.6	576.0	150.6	434.0	420.9	867.4	79.0	160.8	1,172.0	919.6	74.6	970.8
1962	I	1,100.1	468.1	171.4	460.6	419.9	755.3	54.4	212.2	692.5	603.8	76.9	935.0
	II	1,190.7	528.0	183.0	479.9	518.8	987.2	100.5	197.8	1,506,3	1,022.1	78.5	1,085.8

Fiscal Year		K_p	K_h	K_J	Y	Y_p	w	Y_f	Y_u	Y_r	Y_e	T_r
1953	I	5,040.5	2,325.6	1,790.6	2,589.8	2,349.0	1,284.9	414.0	523.1	75.1	- 6.5	94.7
	II	5,251.5	2,379.0	1,985.4	3,157.8	2,923.4	1,454.1	681.9	621.8	88.5	- 4.6	118.1
1954	I	5,430.7	2,427.1	2,203.5	2,760.1	2,619.2	1,451.5	434.5	545.4	94.0	-14.5	150.1
	II	5,542.0	2,470.2	2,254.7	3,262.4	3,077.7	1,555.8	705.8	608.0	113.6	-12.1	180.6
1955	I	5,633.7	2,509.0	2,181.6	3,026.2	2,896.2	1,531.4	543.7	576.5	132.0	-12.4	168.3
	II	5,778.9	2,552.2	2,714.6	3,692.8	3,461.3	1,728.3	790.3	691.5	148.7	-12.9	175.5
1956	I	6,073.2	2,621.4	3,032.5	3,490.3	3,193.9	1,750.7	513.4	674.9	161.4	-15.4	166.0
	II	6,468.4	2,671.7	3,383.7	4,137.3	3,723.9	1,970.7	725.4	739.5	179.6	-16.9	184.6
1957	I	6,948.2	2,744.0	3,678.7	3,957.5	3,513.6	1,991.6	525.1	705.1	191.8	-18.7	171.2
	II	7,315.6	2,799.1	3,851.9	4,326.8	3,966.3	2,137.2	777.7	723.2	211.7	-20.0	208.0
1958	I	7,708.1	2,868.7	3,783.5	3,917.7	3,636.6	2,133.5	512.3	649.8	222.7	-16.9	197.0
	II	8,073.5	2,929.1	3,860.7	4,601.3	4,250.5	2,356.0	804.4	704.7	256.6	-18.2	228.1
1959	I	8,523.7	3,009.2	4,218.8	4,600.6	2,083.6	2,384.1	554.0	727.6	278.5	-18.9	223.2
	II	9,132.4	3,070.4	4,613.6	5,436.6	4,798.1	2,707.0	835.2	793.2	314.0	-19.6	263.3
1960	I	8,860.4	3,174.2	5,025.8	5,526.0	4,740.0	2,786.9	596.0	855.2	333.0	-20.7	266.1
	II	10,824.9	3,248.4	5,572.7	6,411.1	5,523.5	3,160.1	898.2	923.7	380.0	-34.3	296.5
1961	I	11,872.8	3,362.7	6,174.6	6,606.5	5,593.0	3,330.6	654.6	1,016.9	440.0	-27.5	315.0
	II	12,975.9	3,488.9	6,886.2	7,589.9	6,576.8	3,891.0	988.6	1,071.4	438.0	-38.8	353.1
1962	I	13,954.5	3,584.2	6,943.1	7,358.0	6,492.2	3,963.2	711.0	1,102.6	463.4	-26.6	380.0
	II	14,721.1	3,703.5	7,468.3	8,424.3	7,392.0	4,443.0	1,096.4	1,139.0	499.6	-45.8	415.0

Appendix 14.A. Sample Data (continued)

Fiscal Year		S_i	p_e	p_m	p	i	M_d	δ	O	T_w	p_e^W	p_m^W	t	z	z^*
1953	I	68.1	105.7	121.5	86.8	2.46	1,599.2	1.60	40.0	36.8	92.6	104.6	--	0	1
	II	73.2	107.3	117.7	91.3	2.45	1,640.4	1.60	44.5	38.3	91.1	103.1	--	100	1
1954	I	76.3	101.3	116.1	91.4	2.47	1,614.2	1.60	42.9	38.7	91.1	103.1	1	0	1
	II	95.3	110.4	117.6	91.4	2.47	1,741.3	1.60	44.8	41.4	90.6	102.6	2	100	1
1955	I	86.7	102.9	117.4	90.3	2.44	1,790.4	1.60	46.2	41.3	92.6	102.6	3	0	1
	II	105.2	104.9	116.4	91.3	2.38	2,017.1	2.00	57.7	45.6	94.5	104.6	4	100	0
1956	I	107.0	107.4	116.5	93.0	2.29	2,228.4	2.00	57.0	46.3	96.0	105.1	5	0	0
	II	112.9	108.5	121.0	95.4	2.25	2,433.1	2.00	64.5	49.4	98.0	107.1	6	100	0
1957	I	116.2	104.0	118.0	96.8	2.28	2,298.6	2.30	69.2	48.4	99.5	108.7	7	0	0
	II	137.5	96.9	110.0	96.0	2.33	2,451.1	2.30	67.5	47.7	100.0	104.6	8	100	0
1958	I	127.8	94.7	103.3	94.9	2.37	2,544.4	2.30	65.0	46.7	99.0	101.5	9	0	0
	II	150.6	94.5	100.0	95.9	2.24	2,831.2	2.10	71.5	48.8	99.0	99.5	10	100	0
1959	I	143.2	98.3	100.4	96.9	2.21	2,952.3	1.90	79.2	50.7	99.0	99.0	11	0	0
	II	176.3	101.6	101.5	99.4	2.22	3,315.4	2.00	91.7	55.7	100.5	100.0	12	100	0
1960	I	177.2	100.0	100.0	100.0	2.23	3,492.5	2.00	98.9	55.8	100.0	100.0	13	0	0
	II	218.5	98.7	99.6	101.1	2.20	4,128.6	1.90	110.4	58.1	100.0	99.0	14	100	0
1961	I	223.5	100.1	101.6	104.1	2.18	4,368.2	1.80	118.6	58.9	102.0	99.5	15	0	0
	II	277.1	98.1	99.7	107.3	2.24	4,613.9	2.00	129.4	61.7	102.0	99.0	16	0	0
1962	I	262.6	97.9	98.5	109.0	2.25	4,906.8	2.00	128.4	62.0	102.0	98.5	17	0	0
	II	339.1	99.6	99.2	110.3	2.21	6,212.2	1.80	131.3	63.8	102.0	98.0	18	100	0

Notes

The present model was originally prepared in order to provide a consistent basis for the recent Japanese five-year national plan. The authors were members of the supporting committee for the plan and especially shared responsibility for preparing the present model. We are very grateful for the assistance provided by the Economic Planning Agency. Also, our special thanks should be given to Messrs. S. Shishido and S. Kuribayashi, Planning Bureau of the Agency. Without their help and encouragement, it would have been impossible to start such a risky enterprise as the construction of a nonlinear dynamic model with its practical applications. Needless to say, we are responsible for all possible errors in the present text.

1. Although most foreign experiences are easily available, the Japanese ones are not frequently cited because of their linguistic obstacles. In our discussion paper, M. Tatemoto, T. Uchida, and T. Watanabe, "A Stabilization Model for the Postwar Japanese Economy: 1954-1962," Institute of Social and Economic Research, Osaka University, Discussion Paper no. 37 (May 1964), we summarized very briefly the principal characteristics of the main Japanese econometric models.

2. S. Ichimura, L. R. Klein, S. Koizumi, Y. Shinkai, and K. Sato, "Quarterly Econometric Model of Japan: 1952-1959," Osaka Economic Papers, vol. 12, no. 2 (March 1964): pp. 19-36.

3. Other type of treatment of the nonlinear specifications can be found in Ichimura, Klein, Koizumi, Shinkai, and Sato, "Quarterly Econometric Model of Japan: 1952-1959," where the individual structural equations are estimated on the basis of nonlinear specifications, but the Taylor expansions at the specific point are introduced in the final stage to derive the reduced form.

4. Ichimura, Klein, Koizumi, Shinkai, and Sato, "Quarterly Econometric Model of Japan: 1952-1959."

5. L. R. Klein and M. Nakamura, "Singularity in the Equation Systems of Econometrics: Some Aspects of the Problem of Multicollinearity," International Economic Review, 3 (September 1962): 274-299.

6. See E. E. Ehrlich and F. M. Tamagna in B. H. Beckhart, Banking Systems (New York: Columbia University Press, 1953), and H. F. Schiffer The Modern Japanese Banking System (New York: University Publishers, 1962).

7. For example, an investment equation which includes capital stock as an explanatory variable has very often produced a positive coefficient with regard to stock variables, which implies that the bigger the capital stock, the more investment will be needed. It could be a quite plausible phenomenon in rapidly developing economies, such as that of postwar Japan, that ample possibilities exist for expanding investment frontiers.

8. See T. C. Chang, Cyclical Movements in the Balance of Payments (Cambridge: Cambridge University Press, 1951) and J. J. Polak, An International Economic System (Chicago: University of Chicago Press, 1953).

9. Unitary elasticity is, however the average pattern during the sample period, because of introduction of import-substituting technologies. For example, during the first half of this sample period, 1954-1958, the regression coefficient with regard to the production index was objserved as 6.142 compared with the much lower value of 3.940 during the lasthhalf period, 1959-1962. In terms of the elasticity concept, these coefficients correspond to 1.188 and 0.756, respectively; thus some efforts of import substituting in raw materials can be identified.

10. T. Watanabe, "Economic Aspects of Dualism in the Industrial Development of Japan," Economic Development and Cultural Change, 13 (April 1965): 293-312.

11. The equality test (see G. C. Chow, "Tests of Equality between Sets of Coefficients in Two Linear Regressions,"

Econometrica, 28 (July 1960): 591-605) between the successive two periods, i.e., 1954-1958 and 1959-1962, gave very unsatisfactory results with regard to this aggregate production function:

$$1954\text{-}1958: \quad \log_e\left(\frac{V}{L}\right) = 5.323 - \underset{(0.500)}{0.181} \log_e\left(\frac{K_p}{L}\right) + \underset{(0.0207)}{0.034t} + \underset{(0.000367)}{0.0027z}$$

$$\bar{S} = 0.013 \qquad \bar{R} = 0.953$$

$$1959\text{-}1962: \quad \log_e\left(\frac{V}{L}\right) = -4.912 + \underset{(0.974)}{1.088} \log_e\left(\frac{K_p}{L}\right) + \underset{(0.9737)}{0.033t} + \underset{(0.0000742)}{0.0019z}$$

$$\bar{S} = 0.0034 \qquad \bar{R} = 0.986$$

12. S. F. Kalinski, "The Relation Between Unemployment and the Rate of Change of Money Wages in Canada," International Economic Review, 5 (January 1964): 1-33; R. G. Lipsey, "The Relation Between Unemployment and the Rate of Change of Money Wage Rates in the United Kingdom, 1862-1957; A Further Analysis," Economica, new series, 27 (February 1960): 1-31; A. W. Phillips, "The Relation Between Unemployment and Rate of Change of Money Wage Rates in the United Kingdom, 1861-1957, "Economica, new series, 25 (November 1958): 283-299; Phillips, "Price Changes and the Rate of Change of Money Wage Earnings in Japan, 1955-1962," The Quarterly Journal of Economics, 80 (February 1966): 31-47.

13. The detailed investigations about the last two conjectures will be reported in future, though some simple experiments will be discussed in section 14.3.

14. S. Koizumi, "Econometric Models of Japanese Economy" (survey article in Japanese), The Economic Studies Quarterly, The Journal of the Japanese Association of Theoretical Economics, 13 (May 1963): 1-12.

15. Another technically interesting feature of those estimates can be found in the size of the largest characteristic roots of

the **Mzz** matrix in the limited information method; they ranged from 0.04 to 0.59, when most of the values centered around 0.1-0.2.

16. Just before making the present calculation (at the end of September, 1964), the official estimates of the 1963 national income figures became available. Our forecasts, therefore, are compared with the estimates for the whole of 1963, instead of those in the first-half of that year.

17. The nature of equations (14.15), (14.18), and (14.19) was considered to be empirical rather than theoretical in spite of their importance in economic reality. For example, the relation between them decreases in the agricultural share of GNP and the rate of economic growth in the national economy as a whole has been one of the most disputed questions which, however, is not yet formulated sufficiently.

18. The selection was made mainly by the relative importance of variables. Other interpolated results were omitted in the interest of saving space.

19. A transformation of the present model on a quarterly basis is now in progress in which the price equations are quite different

20. This type of extension is also now in progress and will be reported on in the near future.

21. Ichimura, Klein, Koizumi, Shinkai, and Sato, "Quarterly Econometric Model of Japan: 1952-1959."

15

Use of National Accounts for a Short-Term Econometric Model, 1954-1966

S. Shishido, A. Kohno, S. Nagaya, and S. Tanaka

15.1. Introduction

The rapid economic growth of Japan's postwar economy has been accompanied by fairly unstable business fluctuations varying from 3 to 15% in real terms of GNP. The need to stabilize the economy with the aid of more appropriate government policies has increasingly been stressed by various circles. Econometric research has also been dealing with this problem in recent years with quarterly or semiannual models based on national accounts and the related statistical information.[1] A substantial revision of our national accounts made in 1966 by the Economic Research Institute, Economic Planning Agency (EPA), however, forced the research workers to discontinue their projects on model-building based on the old data and to make a fresh start on this new statistical series. They are superior to the old series in terms of international comparability of concepts, consistency with interindustry tables, and statistical accuracy especially related to quarterly movement.

Review of Income and Wealth, series 14, no. 3 (September 1968), pp. 277-309. Reprinted by courtesy of the International Association for Research in Income and Wealth and the authors.

The quarterly model described in the present paper is one of those based on these new data and is designed to serve as a "pilot model" for a more disaggregated "master model" with about a hundred equations. This quarterly model project has been under way since 1966 as a joint project of related studies in the Economic Research Institute, EPA. Accordingly, the present paper is of the nature of an interim report on our short-term econometric research project.

At the beginning, it will be convenient to summarize the features of the present model, in comparison with other models of Japan.

1. The present model fully covers the quarterly national income accounts of the EPA, consisting of six transaction accounts based on the UN-SNA formula. All of our previous quarterly models, however, dealt only with expenditures and some price deflators, thus disregarding income distribution, taxes, and other transfers. The transactions are all seasonally adjusted at annual rates in view of the convenience in short-term economic forecasting. The transactions related to expenditures are expressed in terms of both current and constant prices, while others are only in current prices, as in the case of the Medium-Term Model of the EPA,[2] the Osaka University quarterly model[3] and the several U.S. quarterly models.[4]

2. The present model contains 53 equations, of which 30 are identities. Thus, the size of the model is almost the same as that of the Medium-Term Model, while the disaggregation is now being done in the "master model," especially for investment, consumption, prices and wage rates, etc.

3. As in the case of the Medium-Term Model, nonlinear specifications were used among endogenous variables whenever it was found necessary from theoretical and statistical point of view. The block-wise iteration method was employed to solve the entire system.

4. Although the present model is designed mostly for short-term management of aggregate demand through fiscal and monetary policy, efforts were also made to incorporate longer-run factors such as labor mobility from agriculture to industry, technical progress induced by fixed investment, rate of increase in growth potential, etc.

5. Various tests and simulations were made on the pre-

dictive qualities and workability of the model for projection and policy formulation.

15.2. The Model

First it must be noted that the present model is rather exploratory and that further modification will be made as our research progresses, though its fundamental structure will remain unchanged.

The equations of the model were estimated for the period 1954-1966 covering 48 quarters on the Japanese fiscal year basis[5], i.e., from the second quarter of 1954 through the first quarter of 1966.

The estimates were obtained in principle by the limited-information maximum-likelihood (LI), but two-stage least-squares (TSLS) estimates were used especially in cases where the LI estimates were unstable because of multicollinearity.[6] Needless to say, for those equations explained only by exogenous and/or predetermined variables, ordinary least squares (OLS) were used to derive the estimates.

For all structural equations indicated below, the numbers in parentheses are the standard error estimate of the parameter estimates and $\underline{R}^2$ is the coefficient of determination, $\underline{S}$ is the standard error estimate of the equation, and $\underline{d}$ is the Durbin-Watson statistic.

15.2.1. Structural Equations

Methods of estimation

LI: Limited information maximum likelihood

TSLS: Two stage least squares

OLS: Ordinary least squares

(15.1) Private consumption expenditure (OLS)

$$\underline{C} = 786.15 + \underset{(0.17932)}{0.39366}\left[\frac{1}{4}\sum_{\underline{i}=0}^{3}\underline{C}_{-\underline{i}}\right]_{-1} + \underset{(0.18447)}{0.58221}\left[\frac{\underline{Y}_{\underline{w}} + \underline{T}_{\underline{gp}} - \underline{S}_{\underline{i}}}{\underline{p}_{\underline{c}}}\right]_{-1}$$

$$+ \underset{(0.07656)}{0.24416} \left[\frac{\underline{Y}_r + \underline{Y}_u - \underline{T}_p}{\underline{p}_c}\right]_{-1}$$

$\underline{R}^2 = 0.999 \quad \underline{S} = 93.7 \quad \underline{d} = 1.55$

(15.2) Private housing investment (OLS)

$$\underline{I}_h = 89.88 + \underset{(0.09875)}{0.65776} \underline{I}_{h-1} + \underset{(0.010802)}{0.040513} \left[\frac{\underline{Y}_d}{\underline{p}_c}\right]_{-1} - \underset{(105.45)}{273.24} \frac{\underline{p}_h}{\underline{p}_c}$$

$\underline{R}^2 = 0.995 \quad \underline{S} = 23.7 \quad \underline{d} = 2.11$

(15.3) Gross fixed investment by private enterprises (OLS)

$$\frac{\underline{I}_p}{\underline{V}} = 0.3710 - \underset{(0.02477)}{0.14771} \left[\frac{1}{4} \sum_{\underline{i}=0}^{3} \left(\frac{\underline{K}_p}{\underline{V}}\right)_{-\underline{i}}\right]_{-1}$$

$$+ \underset{(0.0999)}{1.1552} \left[\frac{1}{4} \sum_{\underline{i}=0}^{3} \left(\frac{\underline{Y}_c - \underline{A}_c}{\underline{pV} + \underline{A}_p + \underline{A}_g}\right)_{-\underline{i}}\right]_{-1}$$

$$+ \underset{(0.008223)}{0.031135} \left[\frac{(\underline{S}_c + \underline{A}_c + \underline{D}_p)}{(\underline{S}_c + \underline{A}_c + \underline{D}_p)_{-2}}\right]_{-1}$$

$$- \underset{(0.013200)}{0.063816} \underline{i} + \underset{(0.016175)}{0.053051} \left[\frac{\underline{p}}{\underline{p}_i}\right]_{-2}$$

$\underline{R}^2 = 0.990 \quad \underline{S} = 0.0054 \quad \underline{d} = 2.11$

(15.4) Change in inventories of private enterprises (LI)

$$\underline{J}_p = 5781.2 + \underset{(0.05154)}{0.20700} [\underline{V} + \underline{M}] - \underset{(0.16269)}{0.57451} \underline{K}_{jp-1}$$

$$- \underset{(2696.5)}{4014.9} \left[\frac{\underline{p}_j}{\underline{p}_{j-1}}\right] - \underset{(0.09381)}{0.26219} \left[\sum_{\underline{i}=0}^{1} (\underline{E}_c - \underline{M}_c)_{-\underline{i}}\right]$$

$$+ \underset{(2172.57)}{3440.13} \left[\frac{1}{4} \sum_{\underline{i}=0}^{3} \left(\frac{\underline{L}_c}{\underline{pV}}\right)_{-\underline{i}}\right]_{-1} - \underset{(529.7)}{1013.9} \underline{i}_{-1}$$

$$+ \underset{(0.08644)}{0.24908} \left[\frac{\epsilon}{\underline{p}}\right]$$

$\underline{S} = 155.6 \quad \underline{d} = 1.35$

(15.5) Commodity exports (OLS)

$$\log_{10}\underline{E}_{\underline{c}} = -0.37857 + \underset{(0.0687)}{1.8693} \log_{10}\underline{T}_{\underline{w}} - \underset{(0.33249)}{0.30435} \log_{10}\left[\frac{\underline{p}_{\underline{e}}^{\underline{w}}}{\underline{p}_{\underline{ei}}}\right]_{-1} + \underset{(0.17367)}{0.58805} \log_{10}\left[\frac{\underline{K}_{\underline{jp}-1}}{\underline{V}}\right]_{-1}$$

$\underline{R}^2 = 0.991 \quad \underline{S} = 0.0214 \quad \underline{d} = 1.39$

(15.6) Commodity imports (LI)

$$\underline{M}_{\underline{c}} = -215.87 + \underset{(0.01991)}{0.11798} \underline{J}_{\underline{p}} + \underset{(0.408)}{13.620}(\underline{O}) - \underset{(138.66)}{523.39}[\underline{i}-\underline{i}_{-2}]_{-1} - \underset{(10.311)}{28.183} \underline{t}_{\underline{ic}} + \underset{(235.24)}{341.23} \left[\frac{\underline{p}_{\underline{j}}}{\underline{p}_{\underline{m}}}\right]$$

$\underline{S} = 41.9 \quad \underline{d} = 1.67$

(15.7) Index of mining and manufacturing production (LI)

$$\underline{O} = -18.61 + \underset{(0.001863)}{0.010696} \underline{J}_{\underline{p}} + \underset{(0.002906)}{0.014496} \underline{E}_{\underline{c}} + \underset{(0.001288)}{0.008893} \underline{I}_{\underline{p}} + \underset{(0.000796)}{0.005515} [\underline{C} + \underline{C}_{\underline{g}} + \underline{I}_{\underline{g}} + \underline{I}_{\underline{h}}]$$

$\underline{S} = 2.57 \quad \underline{d} = 1.96$

(15.8) Index of capacity utilization (LI)

$$\rho = -94.06 + \underset{(7.925)}{97.595} \left[\frac{\underline{O}}{\underline{O}_{-1}}\right] - \underset{(0.01236)}{0.05737} \left[\frac{\underline{I}_{\underline{p}} - \underline{I}_{\underline{p}-4}}{\underline{I}_{\underline{p}-4}}\right] + \underset{(0.03100)}{0.94305} \rho_{-1}$$

$\underline{S} = 1.22 \quad \underline{d} = 2.17$

Note: $\dfrac{\underline{I}_{\underline{p}} - \underline{I}_{\underline{p}-4}}{\underline{I}_{\underline{p}-4}}$: %

(15.9) Production function (LI)

$$\log_{10}\left[\frac{\underline{V}}{\underline{hL}}\right] = -\ 1.2127 + \underset{(0.07043)}{0.59725}\ \log_{10}\left[\frac{\rho\underline{K}_{\underline{p}}}{\underline{hL}}\right] + \underset{(0.000707)}{0.003164}\ \underline{t}$$

$\underline{S} = 0.0127 \quad \underline{d} = 0.97$

(15.10) Employees (OLS)

$$\underline{L}_{\underline{W}} = 0.273 - \underset{(0.0013795)}{0.0038341}\ \underline{w}_{-1} + \underset{(0.0049091)}{0.0073697}\ \underline{O}_{-1} + \underset{(0.08443)}{0.31817}\ \underline{N}_{\underline{L}} + \underset{(0.01841)}{0.22498}\ \underline{t}$$

$\underline{R}^2 = 0.998 \quad \underline{S} = 0.174 \quad \underline{d} = 1.11$

(15.11) Unemployment (LI)

$$\underline{U} = -1.942 + \underset{(0.02421)}{0.11673}\ \underline{N}_{\underline{L}} - \underset{(0.013209)}{0.089529}\ \underline{L}_{\underline{W}} - \underset{(0.001358)}{0.008020}\ \rho_{-2}$$

$\underline{S} = 0.044 \quad \underline{d} = 1.34$

(15.12) Wage income per employee (LI)

$$\left[\frac{\underline{w} - \underline{w}_{-4}}{\underline{w}_{-4}}\right] = -4.637 + \underset{(0.16730)}{0.19613}\left[\frac{\underline{p}_{\underline{c}} - \underline{p}_{\underline{c}-4}}{\underline{p}_{\underline{c}-4}}\right]$$

$$- \underset{(2.0021)}{8.1520}\left[\frac{\sum_{\underline{i}=0}^{3} \underline{U}_{-\underline{i}}}{\sum_{\underline{i}=0}^{3} \underline{N}_{\underline{L}-\underline{i}}}\right]_{-2} + \underset{(0.14618)}{0.33431}\left[\frac{\underline{L}_{\underline{ua}}}{\underline{N}_{\underline{L}}}\right]_{-2}$$

$$+ \underset{(0.18022)}{1.10845}\left[\frac{\sum_{\underline{i}=0}^{1} (\underline{Y}_{\underline{c}} + \underline{A}_{\underline{c}})_{-\underline{i}}}{\sum_{\underline{i}=0}^{1} (\underline{Y} + \underline{A}_{\underline{p}} + \underline{A}_{\underline{g}})_{-\underline{i}}}\right]$$

$\underline{S} = 1.79 \quad \underline{d} = 1.96$

Note. All the variables are in percentages.

(15.13) Implicit deflator for private consumption expenditure (LI)

$$\left[\frac{\underline{p}_{c} - \underline{p}_{c-4}}{\underline{p}_{c-4}}\right] = 0.985 + \underset{(0.05151)}{0.33454}\left[\frac{\underline{w} - \underline{w}_{-4}}{\underline{w}_{-4}}\right]$$

$$- \underset{(0.03516)}{0.06811}\left[\frac{\eta - \eta_{-4}}{\eta_{-4}}\right] + \underset{(0.08679)}{0.17165}\left[\frac{\underline{p}_{p} - \underline{p}_{p-4}}{\underline{p}_{p-4}}\right]$$

$$+ \underset{(0.05288)}{0.16976}\left[\frac{\underline{p}_{j} - \underline{p}_{j-4}}{\underline{p}_{j-4}}\right]_{-1}$$

$$+ \underset{(0.09095)}{0.35967}\left[\frac{\underline{p}_{c} - \underline{p}_{c-4}}{\underline{p}_{c-4}}\right]_{-1}$$

$\underline{S} = 0.94 \quad \underline{d} = 1.53$

Note. The variables are in percentages.

(15.14) Implicit deflator for general government expenditure (TSLS)

$$\underline{p}_{cg} = 0.0374 + \underset{(0.0000338)}{0.0025772}\,\underline{w} + \underset{(0.15640)}{0.26655}\,\underline{p}_{j}$$

$\underline{S} = 2.33 \quad \underline{d} = 0.94$

(15.15) Implicit deflator for private housing investment (LI)

$$\left[\frac{\underline{p}_{h} - \underline{p}_{h-4}}{\underline{p}_{h-4}}\right] = -4.164 + \underset{(0.14591)}{0.60140}\left[\frac{\underline{w} - \underline{w}_{-4}}{\underline{w}_{-4}}\right]$$

$$+ \underset{(0.01266)}{0.48548}\left[\frac{\underline{p}_{i} - \underline{p}_{i-4}}{\underline{p}_{i-4}}\right]$$

$$+ \underset{(0.08776)}{0.45327}\left[\frac{\underline{p}_{h} - \underline{p}_{h-4}}{\underline{p}_{h-4}}\right]_{-1}$$

$\underline{S} = 3.38 \quad \underline{d} = 1.42$

Note. The variables are in percentages

(15.16) Implicit deflator for gross fixed investment by private enterprises (OLS)

$$p_i = 0.4987 - \underset{(0.05881)}{0.20097}\left[\frac{4K_p}{\sum_{i=0}^{3} V_{-i}}\right]_{-2} + \underset{(0.050586)}{0.080444}\left[\frac{\sum_{i=0}^{3} w_{-i}}{\sum_{i=0}^{3} \eta_{-i}}\right]_{-1} + \underset{(0.11936)}{0.73378}\left[\frac{p_m M}{V}\right]$$

$$+ \underset{(0.05730)}{0.70122}\, p_{i-1}$$

$R^2 = 0.988$ $S = 0.86$ $d = 1.06$

(15.17) Implicit deflator for gross fixed investment by government (TSLS)

$$\left[\frac{p_{ig} - p_{ig-4}}{p_{ig-4}}\right] = -3.510 + \underset{(0.08619)}{0.50386}\left[\frac{w - w_{-4}}{w_{-4}}\right]$$

$$+ \underset{(0.09264)}{0.70492}\left[\frac{p_i - p_{i-4}}{p_{i-4}}\right]$$

$$+ \underset{(0.09937)}{0.19285}\left[\frac{p_{ig} - p_{ig-4}}{p_{ig-4}}\right]_{-1}$$

$S = 1.64$ $d = 1.44$

Note. The variables are in percentages.

(15.18) Implict deflator for inventories of private enterprises (OLS)

$$p_j = 0.5586 - \underset{(0.04035)}{0.09544}\left[\frac{4K_p}{\sum_{i=0}^{3} V_{-i}}\right]_{-2} - \underset{(0.08012)}{0.36379}\left[\frac{4K_{jp}}{\sum_{i=0}^{3} V_{-i}}\right]_{-1}$$

$$+ \underset{(0.05262)}{0.16489} \left[\frac{\sum_{i=0}^{3} w_{-i}}{\sum_{i=0}^{3} \eta_{-i}} \right]_{-2} + \underset{(0.10615)}{0.76725} \left[\frac{p_m M}{V} \right] + \underset{(0.06182)}{0.49971} p_{j-1}$$

$$R^2 = 0.920 \quad S = 0.64 \quad d = 0.83$$

(15.19) Implicit deflator for exports of goods and services and factor income from abroad (OLS)

$$\left[\frac{p_e - p_{e-4}}{p_{e-4}}\right] = 0.313 + \underset{(0.01604)}{0.12522} \left[\frac{(p_m M/V) - (p_m M/V)_{-4}}{(p_m M/V)_{-4}}\right]$$

$$+ \underset{(0.07672)}{0.12781} \left[\frac{\left(\sum_{i=0}^{3} w_{-i} / \sum_{i=0}^{3} \eta_{-i}\right) - \left(\sum_{i=0}^{3} w_{-i} / \sum_{i=0}^{3} \eta_{-i}\right)_{-4}}{\left(\sum_{i=0}^{3} w_{-i} / \sum_{i=0}^{3} \eta_{-i}\right)_{-4}} \right]_{-4}$$

$$- \underset{(0.016885)}{0.075318} \left[\frac{I_p - I_{p-4}}{I_{p-4}}\right]_{-4}$$

$$R^2 = 0.765 \quad S = 1.66 \quad d = 1.76$$

Note. The variables are in percentages.

(15.20) Personal rental interest income (excluding dividends) (LI)

$$Y_r - D_i = -351.70 + \underset{(0.046200)}{0.094358} Y + \underset{(2.0238)}{1.8853} t$$

$$S = 44.7 \quad d = 0.41$$

(15.21) Personal dividends (LI)

$$D_i = -0.698 + \underset{(0.007600)}{0.023038} (Y_c - T_c) + \underset{(0.02456)}{0.94876} D_{i-1}$$

$$S = 10.1 \quad d = 2.42$$

(15.22) Corporate income (OLS)

$$\left[\frac{\underline{Y}_c + \underline{A}_c}{\underline{Y} + \underline{A}_p + \underline{A}_g}\right] = -0.095166 - \underset{(0.09335)}{0.13219}\left[\frac{\underline{Y}_w}{\underline{pV}}\right]$$

$$+ \underset{(0.02829)}{0.25885}\left[\sum_{\underline{i}=0}^{1}\left(\frac{\underline{I}_p}{\underline{V}}\right)_{-\underline{i}}\right]_{-1} - \underset{(0.015356)}{0.028080}\left[\sum_{\underline{i}=0}^{1}\underline{i}_{-\underline{i}}\right]$$

$$+ \underset{(0.08062)}{0.36230}\left[\frac{\left(\sum_{\underline{i}=0}^{2}\underline{O}_{-\underline{i}}\right)}{\left(\sum_{\underline{i}=0}^{2}\underline{O}_{-\underline{i}}\right)_{-1}}\right] - \underset{(0.11635)}{0.21633}\left[\frac{\underline{K}_{jp}}{\underline{V}}\right]$$

$$\underline{R}^2 = 0.926 \quad \underline{S} = 0.0066 \quad \underline{d} = 1.04$$

(15.23) Inventory valuation adjustment in private incorporated enterprises (OLS)

$$\underline{A}_c = -12.208 + \underset{(0.03869)}{0.73886}\,\underline{A}_p$$

$$\underline{R}^2 = 0.888 \quad \underline{S} = 49.2 \quad \underline{d} = 2.06$$

(Equation for reference)

Direct taxes and charges on households and private nonprofit institutions.

$$\underline{T}_p = -199.61 + \underset{(0.01509)}{0.13378}\,\underline{Y}_{w-1}$$

$$+ \underset{(0.010643)}{0.042476}\left[\sum_{\underline{i}=0}^{2}(\underline{Y}_u + \underline{Y}_r)_{-\underline{i}}\right]_{-3} - \underline{T}'_p$$

$$\underline{R}^2 = 0.999 \quad \underline{S} = 21.9 \quad \underline{d} = 1.82$$

Note. Only used for extrapolation and multiplier simulation, instead of equation (15.46).

Identities:

(15.24) $\underline{E} = \underline{E}_O + \underline{E}_c$

(15.25) $\underline{M} = \underline{M}_O + \underline{M}_c$

(15.26) $\underline{V} = \underline{C} + \underline{C}_g + \underline{I}_h + \underline{I}_p + \underline{I}_g + \underline{J}_p + \underline{J}_g + \underline{E} - \underline{M}$

(15.27) $\underline{L} = \underline{N}_L - \underline{U}$

(15.28) $\underline{L}_u = \underline{L} - \underline{L}_w$

(15.29) $\underline{K}_p = \underline{K}_{p-1} + \frac{1}{4}\underline{I}_p - \frac{1}{4}\underline{R}$

(15.30) $\underline{K}_{jp} = \underline{K}_{jp-1} + \frac{1}{4}\underline{J}_p$

(15.31) $\underline{K}_{jg} = \underline{K}_{jg-1} + \frac{1}{4}\underline{J}_g$

(15.32) $\underline{A}_p = 4[\underline{p}_j\underline{K}_j - (\underline{p}_j\underline{K}_j)_{-1}] - \underline{p}_j\underline{J}_p$

(15.33) $\underline{A}_g = 4[\underline{p}_{jg}\underline{K}_{jg} - (\underline{p}_{jg}\underline{K}_{jg})_{-1}] - \underline{p}_{jg}\underline{J}_g$

(15.34) $\underline{pV} = \underline{p}_c\underline{C} + \underline{p}_{cg}\underline{C} + \underline{p}_h\underline{I}_h + \underline{p}_i\underline{I}_p + \underline{p}_{ig}\underline{I}_g + \underline{p}_j\underline{J}_p + \underline{p}_{jg}\underline{J}_g + \underline{p}_e\underline{E} - \underline{p}_m\underline{M}$

Note. $\underline{p}_{cg}\underline{C}_g$, $\underline{p}_{jg}\underline{J}_g$, and $\underline{p}_{ig}\underline{I}_g$ are exogenous variables.

(15.35) $\underline{Y}_w = \underline{w}\cdot\underline{L}_w$

(15.36) $\underline{Y}_u = \underline{Y} - \underline{Y}_w - \underline{Y}_r - \underline{Y}_c - \underline{Y}_g$

(15.37) $\underline{S}_c = \underline{Y}_c - \underline{T}_c - \underline{D}_i$

(15.38) $\underline{Y} = \underline{pV} - \underline{T}_i + \underline{S}_b - \underline{D}_p - \underline{D}_g - \underline{D}_h - \epsilon$

(15.39) $\underline{Y}_p = \underline{Y}_w + \underline{Y}_u + \underline{Y}_r + \underline{T}_{gp} + \underline{T}_{ap}$

(15.40) $\underline{Y}_d = \underline{Y}_p - \underline{T}_p - \underline{S}_i - \underline{T}_{pa}$

(15.41) $\underline{S}_p = \underline{Y}_p - (\underline{p}_c\underline{C} + \underline{T}_p + \underline{S}_i + \underline{T}_{pa})$

(15.42) $\underline{D}_p = \alpha_1\cdot(\underline{p}_i\underline{K}_p)_{-1}$

(15.43) $\underline{D}_h = \alpha_2\cdot(\underline{p}_h\underline{K}_h)_{-1}$

(15.44) $\underline{p}_i\underline{K}_p = (\underline{p}_i\underline{K}_p)_{-1} + \frac{1}{4}\underline{p}_i\underline{I}_p - \frac{1}{4}\underline{D}_p$

(15.45) $\underline{p}_h\underline{K}_h = (\underline{p}_h\underline{K}_h)_{-1} + \frac{1}{4}\underline{p}_h\underline{I}_h - \frac{1}{4}\underline{D}_h$

(15.46) $\underline{T}_p = \beta_1\cdot\underline{Y}_p$

(15.47) $\underline{T}_c = \beta_2\cdot\underline{Y}_c$

(15.48) $\underline{T}_i - \underline{S}_b = \beta_3\cdot\underline{pV}$

(15.49) $\underline{S} = (\underline{T}_i - \underline{S}_b + \underline{T}_c + \underline{T}_p + \underline{Y}_g + \underline{S}_i + \underline{T}_{ag}) - (\underline{p}_{cg}\underline{C}_g + \underline{T}_{gp} + \underline{T}_{ga})$

(15.50) $\underline{B}_g = (\underline{S}_g + \underline{D}_g) - (\underline{p}_{ig}\underline{I}_g + \underline{p}_{jg}\underline{J}_g)$

(15.51) $$\underline{B_a} = \underline{p_e}\underline{E} - \underline{p_m}\underline{M}$$

(15.52) $$\underline{B_c} = (\underline{S_c} + \underline{D_p}) - (\underline{p_i}\underline{I_p} + \underline{p_j}\underline{J_p})$$

(15.53) $$\eta = \frac{\underline{V}}{\underline{L}}$$

15.2.2. List of Variables

$\underline{A_c}$ = Inventory valuation adjustment in private incorporated enterprises (current thousand million yen)

$\underline{A_g}$ = Inventory valuation adjustment in government enterprises (current thousand million yen)

$\underline{A_p}$ = Inventory valuation adjustment in private enterprises (current thousand million yen)

$\underline{B_a}$ = Current balance in international balance of payments (current thousand million yen)

$\underline{B_c}$ = Balance of saving and capital formation in private enterprises (current thousand million yen)

$\underline{B_g}$ = Balance of saving and capital formation in government (current thousand million yen)

$\underline{C}$ = Private consumption expenditure (1960 thousand million yen)

$\underline{C_g}$ = General government consumption expenditure (1960 thousand million yen)

*$\underline{D_g}$ = Capital consumption allowances in government enterprises (current thousand million yen)

$\underline{D_h}$ = Capital consumption allowances for private dwellings (current thousand million yen)

$\underline{D_i}$ = Personal dividends (current thousand million yen)

$\underline{D_p}$ = Capital consumption allowances in private enterprises (current thousand million yen)

$\underline{E}$ = Exports of goods and services and factor income from abroad (1960 thousand million yen)

$\underline{E_c}$ = Commodity exports (1960 thousand million yen)

*$\underline{E_0}$ = Exports of services and factor income from abroad (1960 thousand million yen)

*$\underline{h}$ = Index of total hours worked (1960 = 100)

*$\underline{i}$ = Average interest rate on loans of all banks (interest rate per diem) ($\frac{1}{10,000}$ (day))

$\underline{I_g}$ = Gross fixed investment by government (1960 thousand million yen)

$\underline{I_h}$ = Private housing investment (1960 thousand million yen)

$\underline{I_p}$ = Gross fixed investment by private enterprises (1960 thousand million yen)

$*\underline{J_g}$ = Change in inventories of government enterprises (1960 thousand million yen)

$\underline{J_p}$ = Change in inventories of private enterprises (1960 thousand million yen)

$\underline{K_{jg}}$ = Inventories of government enterprises (1960 thousand million yen)

$\underline{K_{jp}}$ = Inventories of private enterprises (1960 thousand million yen)

$\underline{K_p}$ = Gross capital stock of private enterprises (1960 thousand million yen)

$\underline{L}$ = Employment (millions of persons)

$*\underline{L_c}$ = Stock of cash currency and short-term deposits in private corporate enterprises (current thousand million yen)

$\underline{L_u}$ = Self-employed (including family workers) (millions of persons)

$*\underline{L_{ua}}$ = Self-employed (including family workers) in agriculture and forestry (millions of persons)

$\underline{L_w}$ = Employees (millions of persons)

$\underline{\overline{M}}$ = Imports of goods and services and factor income paid abroad (1960 thousand million yen)

$\underline{M_c}$ = Commodity imports (1960 thousand million yen)

$*\underline{M_o}$ = Imports of services and factor income paid abroad (1960 thousand million yen)

$*\underline{N_L}$ = Labor force (millions of persons)

$\underline{\overline{O}}$ = Index of mining and manufacturing production (1960 = 100)

$\underline{p}$ = GNP implicit deflator (1960 = 1.0)

$\underline{p_c}$ = Implicit deflator for private consumption expenditure (1960 = 1.0)

$\underline{p_{cg}}$ = Implicit deflator for general government consumption expenditure (1960 = 1.0)

$\underline{p_e}$ = Implicit deflator for exports of goods and services and factor income from abroad (1960 = 1.0)

$*\underline{p}_{ei}{}^{\underline{w}}$ = Export price index of manufactured goods of eleven leading industrial countries (1960 = 1.0)

$\underline{p}_h$ = Implicit deflator for private housing investment (1960 = 1.0)

$\underline{p}_h\underline{K}_h$ = Net capital stock of private dwellings (current thousand million yen)

$\underline{p}_i$ = Implicit deflator for gross fixed investment by private enterprises (1960 = 1.0)

$\underline{p}_i\underline{K}_p$ = Net capital stock of private enterprises (current thousand million yen)

$\underline{p}_{ig}$ = Implicit deflator for gross fixed investment by government (1960 = 1.0)

$\underline{p}_j$ = Implicit deflator for inventories of private enterprises (1960 = 1.0)

$*\underline{p}_{jg}$ = Implicit deflator for inventories of government enterprises (1960 = 1.0)

$*\underline{p}_m$ = Implicit deflator for imports of goods and services and factor income paid abroad (1960 = 1.0)

$*\underline{p}_p$ = Index of prices and changes government can control (1960 = 1.0)

$*\underline{R}$ = Replacement of fixed capital of private enterprises (1960 thousand million yen)

$*\underline{S}_b$ = Current subsidies (current thousand million yen)

$\underline{S}_c$ = Savings of private incorporated enterprises (current thousand million yen)

$\underline{S}_g$ = Saving of general government (current thousand million yen)

$*\underline{S}_i$ = Contributions to social security (current thousand million yen)

$*\underline{t}$ = Trend (1952 2Q = 1)

$*\underline{T}_{ag}$ = Transfers from abroad to general government (current thousand million yen)

$*\underline{T}_{ap}$ = Transfers from abroad to households and private nonprofit institutions (current thousand million yen)

$\underline{T}_c$ = Direct taxes and charges on private corporations (current thousand million yen)

$*\underline{T}_{ga}$ = Transfers from general government to the rest of the world (current thousand million yen)

$*\underline{T}_{gp}$ = Transfers from general government to households and private nonprofit institutions (current thousand million yen)

T_i = Indirect taxes (current thousand million yen)
*t_{ic} = Customs (including tonnage duty) ratio for imported commodities (percent)
T_p = Direct taxes on households and private nonprofit institutions (current thousand million yen)
*T'_p = Personal tax reduction accumulated since 1953 (current thousand million yen)
*T_{pa} = Transfers from households and private nonprofit institutions to the rest of the world (current thousand million yen)
*T_w = Exports from the non-Communist world to the total world (1960 thousand million U. S. dollars, deflated by total export price index)
U = Unemployment (millions of persons)
V = Gross national product (1960 thousand million yen)
w = Wage income per employee (current thousand yen)
Y = National income (current thousand million yen)
Y_c = Corporate income (current thousand million yen)
Y_d = Personal disposable income (current thousand million yen)
*Y_g = Surplus of government enterprises (less interest on the public debt), in current thousand million yen
Y_p = Personal income, (current thousand million yen)
Y_r = Personal rental and interest income (less interest on consumer's debt), in current thousand million yen
Y_u = Proprietor's income (current thousand million yen)
Y_w = Compensation of employees (current thousand million yen)
*α_1 = Rate of depreciation for private fixed capital defined as $D_p/(p_i K_p)_{-1}$
*α_2 = Rate of depreciation for private dwellings, defined as $D_h/(p_h K_h)_{-1}$
*β_1 = Rate of direct taxes on households and private nonprofit institutions defined as T_p/Y_p
*β_2 = Rate of direct taxes and charges on private corporations defined as T_c/Y_c
*β_3 = Rate of indirect taxes (less current subsidies) defined as $(T_i - S_b)/pV$
*ϵ = Statistical discrepancy (current thousand million

yen)

ρ = Index of capacity utilization of manufacturing (1960 = 100)

η = Labor productivity

Notes. 1. * indicates exogenous variable.
2. All variables are seasonally adjusted and expressed in annual rates.

15.2.3. Discussion of the Equations

In the following we discuss briefly the nature of the principal equations.

(i) Consumption

Private consumption expenditure is made dependent on two different income groups lagged by one quarter, i.e., (a) wages and salaries and (b) other personal income with relatively low propensity to consume, and average consumption of the past four quarters. As regards personal tax and transfers, different effects on consumption of these policy variables are also considered, but obviously this treatment should be regarded as temporary. A more elaborate distinction of these variables between wage and nonwage groups is to be made as further detailed data become available.

The long-run marginal propensity to consume is about 0.96 for the wage income group and 0.40 for the nonwage income group. In the past the average propensity to consume out of the total disposable income has continued to be stable, i.e., about 85%, despite the rising share of the wage income group. This clearly reflects the fact that the rising tendency of the propensity to consume has been cancelled by the rapid growth of disposable income in real terms.

(ii) Investment

First, housing investment is explained by personal disposable income, relative price, and the investment in the previous quarter. The long-term elasticity, after adjustment of the distributed lag, is 1.86 with respect to disposable income and -1.12 with respect to relative price, at the average level of each variable.

Our fixed business investment function is specified as an investment ratio to the GNP. Needless to say, this function plays the most dynamic role in analyzing the Japanese economy, as will be seen later in our simulation analysis; and the investment ratio changes widely from 11 to 22% in real terms during the past 12 years.

In specifying our theoretical formula, we first started from the following capital demand function which is based on the familiar Cobb-Douglous production function ($V = AK^{\alpha}L^{1-\alpha}$), as indicated in equation (15.9), and profit-maximum condition as a long-run equilibrium.

$$\frac{K}{V} = \alpha \frac{p}{r} \tag{15.54}$$

where V = GNP, K = capital stock, α = relative factor share of capital, r = price of capital service, p = price of output. This type of function can be transformed and dynamized as below by incorporating the speed of adjustment and replacement approximated by lagged stock-output ratio and supply conditions represented by availability of internal and external funds.[7]

$$\frac{I}{V} = f\left[\frac{P}{pV}, \frac{p}{r}, \left(\frac{K}{V}\right)_{-1}, \frac{\Delta S}{S}, i\right] \tag{15.55}$$

where I = gross investment, P = profit, S = internal cash flow, i.e., corporate gross saving, i = interest rate. Needless to say, the first and second terms are derived from equation (15.54), the third term represents depreciation and the speed of adjustment in capital demand, the fourth term cash-flow effect, and the last term external availability.

In our final version, equation (15.3), the share of profit and the price of capital service are approximated respectively by the share of corporate profit and the price deflator for fixed business investment. The inclusion of the cash flow in our function has two advantages. First, a policy effect of raising the depreciation ratio as an incentive to investment can be explicitly taken into account, which in turn tends to increase the replacement of fixed assets thus leading to a further rise in investment. Second, the effect of corporate tax reduction can be properly incorporated in our model without exaggerating the tax effect on investment. Thus equation (15.3) has four policy instruments directly related to investment: corporate tax, depreciation, replacement, and interest rate.

Inventory investment in equation (15.4) is made dependent on 7 explanatory variables but the error is relatively high. As easily expected, the difficulties in obtaining a good estimate of this function are largely caused by the basic data, especially in the case of quarterly series, speculative behaviors, and other random elements. The first two variables ($\underline{K}_{\underline{j}}$ and $\underline{V} + \underline{M}$) are of ordinary stock-adjustment type and the next two ($\underline{p}_{\underline{j}}$ and $\underline{E}_{\underline{c}} - \underline{M}_{\underline{c}}$) are related to unexpected change in inventories. Because of the high dependency on foreign trade in Japan, the impact of the next increase in exports is negatively associated with the change in inventories. As financial variables affecting inventory investment, we included the liquidity of corporate enterprises

$$(15.55) \qquad [\frac{1}{4} \sum_{\underline{i}=0}^{3} (\frac{\underline{L}_{\underline{c}}}{\underline{pV}})_{-\underline{i}}]_{-1}$$

and the rate of interest ($\underline{i}_{-1}$) as a proxy of external funds availability. The elasticities with respect to these two variables are 0.66 and -3.78, respectively. This lag structure implies that the effect of monetary policy is almost cancelled in the first quarter by the unexpected change in inventories and then becomes significant in the second quarter through the changes in the interest rate and liquidity and that the effect of the latter tends to continue longer than that of the former. The last explanatory variable, statistical discrepancy ϵ, is added to improve the fit of our function by associating the random fluctuations of the data with a residual between the product and income accounts.

(iii) Foreign Trade

The estimation of the export function was started as a demand function for Japanese exports but later it was modified by introducing a supply factor, i.e., the inventory-output ratio. The low price elasticity no doubt reflects this modification. Accordingly, an increase in exogenous expenditure reduces exports through a fall of the inventory-output ratio so that resources are shifted from exports to domestic uses. Our import function uses two policy variables, tariff rate and interest rate, in addition to the ordinary explanation variables such as industrial output, inventory investment, and relative price. The import elasticities are 1.07 with respect to output and 0.23 with respect to relative price.

(iv) Production

The industrial production index (in equation 15.7) is made dependent upon four types of final demand, of which commodity exports have the highest coefficient and those of investment are the next. These results are fairly consistent with those of interindustry analysis. Our production function of the real GNP (equation 15.9) is of the usual Cobb-Douglas type with time trend and indicates that the share of capital, after adjustment for capacity utilization and working hours, is 0.53 and the rate of technical progress is about 4% annually.[8] It is noted that this function is used only for deriving the "production gap" as a difference between actual and potential GNP; and the latter is estimated by assuming a normal trend of working hours and capacity utilization. The potential GNP thus obtained does not feed back into our entire system, unlike some other quarterly models.

(v) Factor Shares

Corporate profit is one of the most important and dynamic variables and also serves as an appropriate indicator of business cycles. In equation (15.22), we explicitly specify this function instead of treating it as a residual between the value of total output and the wage bill. In this latter treatment, various marginal errors are likely to be accumulated in corporate profits and eventually to affect fixed business investment. In our equation (15.22) corporate profit is a function of (a) the fixed investment ratio of the past two quarters (indicating embodied technical progress), (b) the rate of increase in industrial output and the inventory-output ratio (reflecting market conditions), and (c) labor and capital cost, approximated by the labor share and the interest rate. In view of its lower statistical reliability, income of unincorporated business is treated as a residual. Because of a lower marginal propensity to consume, the errors of this income group have little effect on other endogenous variables.

(vi) Employment and Wages

As regards employment in equation (15.10), we started by specifying labor demand for employees as a function of the output level and the wage rate. In view of the imperfection of labor market which has especially been the case with Japan, we modified our original version by adding a supply factor, total labor force, to our equation. Unemployment in equation (15.11) is regressed negatively on labor demand approximated by total employees and positively on total labor force and capacity utilization of equation (15.8). This implies that the number of self-employed and family workers are obtained as a residual, given the total labor force as exogenous. This treatment reflects the existence of a certain amount of hidden unemployment still prevailing in unincorporated business in Japan and it also corresponds to the treatment of its factor share as a residual.

As regards wage rate, equation (15.12) is almost a standard Phillips-type function, except that it introduces labor mobility from agriculture to other sectors as an additional explanatory variable. The implication of this variable is that a fairly rapid migration from agriculture has contributed in the past to check a further wage increase caused by a tightening labor market which is represented by a falling trend of open unemployment. In other words, the wage level in our model is affected in two ways: first through adjustment of open unemployment and second through increased mobility in agricultural migration to other industries. Since the elasticity of wages with respect to this ratio of agricultural employment is 0.33 and the ratio is at present about 25%, a policy toward modernization of agriculture will considerably serve to lighten wage pressure and the wage-cost spiral through increased labor mobility.[9]

(vii) Prices

Since most of our price equations are self-explanatory, we will discuss only the important specifications on prices. First, an attempt was made to include in our functions capacity utilization (K_p/V) in the past four to five quarters. Short-run market conditions of output, represented by K_j/V, were also taken into account in the equation of wholesale price (or inventory price deflator) in equation (15.18). This factor is also introduced indirectly in the consumer price function of equation (15.13). As regards cost, all equations are functions of wages (w) or unit labor cost (wL/V). A special emphasis is given to export price in regard to embodied technical progress, which is approximated by the rate of fixed business investment four quarters before. Special consumer prices and fares controlled by the government, such as prices of rice, liquors and tobacco, railway fares, etc., are treated as exogenous and play an important role in our model as a policy variable in determining price level.

15.3. Ex Post Forecasts, 1954-1966 -- Model Performance

15.3.1. A Short-Run Ex Post Forecast

In order to test the predictive ability of our model, we first started with short run ex post forecasts for two years. The test was done as usually by solving our entire equation system for each successive quarter on the basis of initial values and exogenous variables for 8 quarters. All lagged endogenous variables were those derived from the model rather than actual values. Since we are interested in its pure predictive nature, no adjustment was made for the constant terms of our equations in connection with serial correlations or deviation from initial values. In estimating the errors of our ex post projection, we made 40 cases of this 8-quarter simulation over our observation period, as done by Klein and Evans with their Wharton-EFU model.[10]

Major results of our test are shown in Table 15.1., in

TABLE 15.1. SHORT-RUN EX POST FORECAST ERRORS, IN TERMS OF MEAN ABSOLUTE ERROR AND STANDARD DEVIATION AS PERCENT OF MEAN ACTUAL

	pV		V		C		I_p	
	Mean Absolute Error	Standard Deviation (%)	Mean Absolute Error	Standard Deviation (%)	Mean Absolute Error	Standard Deviation (%)	Mean Absolute Error	Standard Deviation (%)
1Q	215.6	1.8	198.7	1.8	63.4	1.0	78.8	3.9
2Q	198.3	1.7	196.8	1.7	70.5	1.1	70.5	3.3
3Q	180.6	1.6	193.4	1.7	77.2	1.2	75.6	3.5
4Q	188.3	1.5	188.7	1.6	80.4	1.2	75.4	3.2
(1st year)	(92.2)	(0.8)	(124.9)	(1.0)	(50.5)	(0.9)	(47.0)	(2.1)
5Q	232.0	1.8	220.3	1.8	84.9	1.3	83.2	3.6
6Q	248.4	2.0	249.7	2.0	94.9	1.3	84.1	3.7
7Q	259.1	1.9	266.4	2.0	100.4	1.4	90.3	4.0
8Q	258.5	1.8	277.9	2.0	102.1	1.5	102.9	4.3
(2nd year)	(188.1)	(1.3)	(192.3)	(1.5)	(87.5)	(1.2)	(71.7)	(3.1)

	J_p		E		M		O	
	Mean Absolute Error	Standard Deviation (%)	Mean Absolute Error	Standard Deviation (%)	Mean Absolute Error	Standard Deviation (%)	Mean Absolute Error	Standard Deviation (%)
1Q	154.0	35.8	42.3	4.0	45.2	3.7	1.66	2.3
2Q	147.6	34.5	42.7	3.7	46.1	3.6	1.55	2.1
3Q	151.3	33.2	44.1	3.6	47.8	3.6	1.64	2.1
4Q	151.9	32.7	45.1	3.6	51.0	3.7	1.77	2.2
(1st year)	(81.2)	(17.4)	(31.0)	(2.6)	(31.9)	(2.3)	(0.97)	(1.4)
5Q	168.4	36.3	52.8	4.4	58.1	4.2	1.99	2.6
6Q	174.0	37.3	57.4	4.6	57.4	4.0	1.96	2.6
7Q	172.9	36.7	62.6	4.6	57.4	3.8	2.02	2.5
8Q	186.6	38.1	66.0	4.7	60.3	3.8	2.34	2.7
(2nd year)	(115.1)	(23.0)	(46.2)	(3.4)	(38.1)	(2.6)	(1.60)	(1.8)

	p		p_c		w		L_w	
	Mean Absolute Error	Standard Deviation (%)	Mean Absolute Error	Standard Deviation (%)	Mean Absolute Error	Standard Deviation (%)	Mean Absolute Error	Standard Deviation (%)
1Q	0.76	1.0	0.79	1.0	3.84	1.8	0.12	0.8
2Q	0.95	1.2	1.05	1.3	3.73	1.7	0.10	0.7
3Q	1.02	1.3	1.12	1.3	3.60	1.6	0.10	0.6
4Q	1.07	1.3	1.12	1.3	3.78	1.7	0.10	0.6
(1st year)	(0.75)	(0.9)	(0.70)	(0.9)	(2.01)	(0.9)	(0.06)	(0.4)
5Q	1.24	1.4	1.13	1.4	4.13	1.7	0.10	0.6
6Q	1.31	1.6	1.22	1.6	4.19	1.7	0.10	0.6
7Q	1.35	1.6	1.31	1.6	4.87	1.8	0.10	0.6
8Q	1.39	1.5	1.32	1.6	5.14	1.9	0.10	0.6
(2nd year)	(1.07)	(1.3)	(0.99)	(1.2)	(3.08)	(1.2)	(0.06)	(0.3)

Note: For GNP and its components, the figures are in billion yen; for p, p_c, and O in terms of index number (1960 = 100); for w (wage rate) in thousand yen; and for Lw in million persons.

which most of the errors tend to increase as the model estimates for a longer period. This is obviously caused by the increasing tendency of serial correlation, but the extent of such accumulated errors appears to be not so serious as usually expected. The errors of current and real GNP are mostly 1.5 to 2% over the period, those of other variables also being under 5% in most cases. The lowest percentage errors are those for private consumption. However, the errors for the change in inventories are exceptionally high, reflecting its dynamic nature and the weakness of the statistical data.

As regards annual average, most of the errors indicate smaller values because of cancellation of the quarterly errors. The errors of GNP are only 0.8 and 1.3% in current prices for the first and the second years, respectively, while those in constant prices are also 1.0 and 1.5% respectively. This probably indicates the advantage of using our quarterly model for short-run annual forecasting rather than ordinary annual models.

In Table 15.2, the performance of our model is compared in terms of standard deviation as percent of mean and actual with that of a U.S. model, i.e., Wharton-EFU quarterly model with 76 equations based on a sample period, 1948.1-1964.4. Needless to say, qualifications are needed in comparing the two models, especially in regard to differences in economic structure, rate of economic growth, and fluctuations as well as those in the specifications of the models. The table indicates that except for the first quarter the GNP errors of our model are smaller than those of the U.S. model, in both constant and current prices. Generally, the U.S. model indicates a more rapidly increasing tendency of errors as they become more distant from the starting period. As regards GNP components, most of the errors of the Japanese model are again smaller in percentage than those of the U.S. model. For exports, however, the U.S. errors are smaller for the first three quarters, and for consumption, the differences between the two are negligible. The errors of GNP deflator and disposable income, on the other hand, are much smaller in the U.S. model. The larger errors of the price deflator of the Japanese model seem to reflect a wider use of distributed

TABLE 15.2. COMPARISON OF SHORT-RUN EX POST FORECAST ERRORS BETWEEN EPA SHORT-TERM MODEL AND THE WHARTON-EFU MODEL, IN TERMS OF STANDARD ERROR AS PERCENT OF MEAN ACTUAL

	V		pV		p_cC		p_iI_p		pI_h	
	EPA	Wharton-EFU	EPA	Wharton-EFU	EPA	Wharton-EFU	EPA	Wharton-EFU	EPA	Wharton-EFU
1Q	1.8	1.6	1.8	1.7	1.4	1.5	3.7	2.2	4.3	4.8
2Q	1.7	1.8	1.7	1.9	1.5	1.6	3.3	4.3	4.8	4.8
3Q	1.7	1.8	1.6	1.8	1.4	1.5	3.5	4.5	4.7	4.8
4Q	1.6	2.0	1.5	1.9	1.5	1.5	3.4	4.5	4.4	5.5
5Q	1.8	2.2	1.8	2.0	1.4	1.4	3.9	5.2	3.8	6.2
6Q	2.0	2.5	2.0	2.2	1.6	1.5	4.0	5.7	3.9	6.8
7Q	2.0	2.7	1.0	2.2	1.5	1.5	4.3	6.4	4.5	7.2
8Q	2.0	2.8	1.8	2.2	1.4	1.5	4.5	6.9	4.8	7.4

	p_eE		p_mM		Y_d		p	
	EPA	Wharton-EFU	EPA	Wharton-EFU	EPA	Wharton-EFU	EPA	Wharton-EFU
1Q	4.6	3.7	3.8	3.9	2.1	1.1	1.0	0.3
2Q	4.3	3.9	3.6	4.0	2.1	1.2	1.2	0.6
3Q	4.2	4.1	3.6	4.0	2.0	1.0	1.3	0.7
4Q	4.1	4.5	3.7	4.1	1.9	1.0	1.3	0.7
5Q	4.5	4.8	4.2	4.4	2.1	1.0	1.4	0.8
6Q	4.6	5.0	4.0	4.3	2.2	1.1	1.6	0.8
7Q	4.7	5.3	3.7	4.2	2.1	1.1	1.6	0.9
8Q	4.8	5.6	3.8	4.0	2.0	1.1	1.5	0.8

lag, which probably needs to be improved.

In most cases the ex post projections of the turning point of the business cycle with our model were not unsatisfactory. In Fig. 15.1 we indicate 6 cases of ex post forecasts covering our entire period in successive order. Here, each forecast covers 8 quarters. Out of 7 turning points (i.e. 4 upturns and 3 downturns), 6 turning points (3 upturns and 3 downturns) were projected by our model in the neighborhood of the actual turning points in terms of GNP. A failure in timing occurred in the upturn in 1965. This is mostly caused by errors in inventory investment and exports. Thus the recession in this year was somewhat underestimated in terms of its length. However, if business fixed investment is taken as a measure of the turning point, all turning points are closely followed. Though to a lesser extent, our estimates of inventory investment also follow the business fluctuations fairly closely except for the upturn in 1965.

In general, the turning points were better projected, as usually expected, by a shorter-run simulation, such as two or three quarters before the actual turning points. Since the projections described so far are purly ex post ones and there were not adjustments of constant terms, it is clear that analysis of serial correlation and initial values and the resultant adjustments of the constant terms could give a still closer projection as far as the model is estimated properly. In view of the short-run performance of our model described above we can tentatively conclude that the model is fairly workable for the short-run ex ante forecasts as well, especially for the annual estimation.

15.3.2. Long-Run Ex Post Forecast

It is also interesting to examine the long-run performance of our model for analytical and policy uses. To test our model for this end, we simulated it over a long stretch of the sample period, i.e., 48 quarters from 1954.2 through 1966.1, thus covering three and a half cycles. As in the case of the short-run ex post forecasts, all lagged endogenous variables were obtained by the model rather than actual values.

Our result is shown in Table 15.3A and Fig. 15.2. Undoubtedly, the errors of this long-run simulation are larger

Fig. 15.1. Short-Run Ex Post Forecast for Testing Turning Point

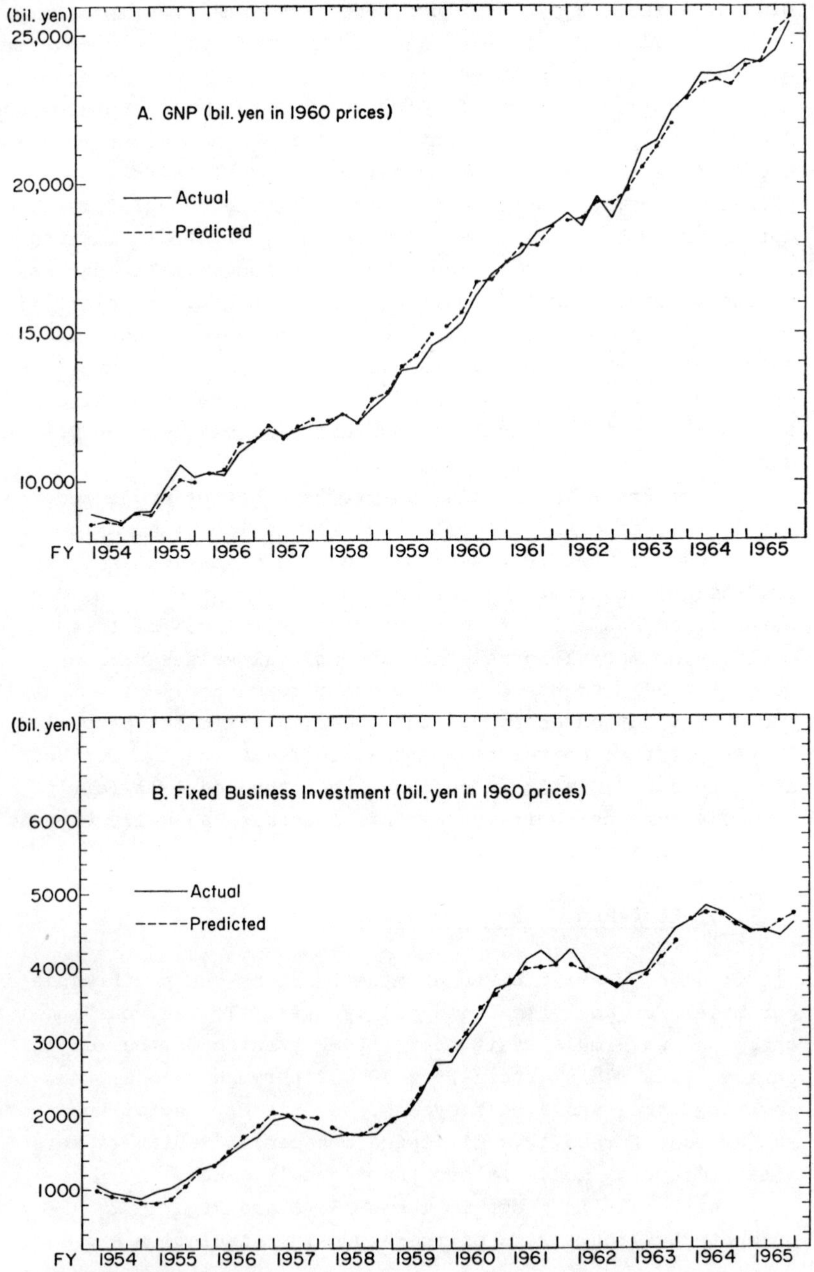

Fig. 15.1 (continued).

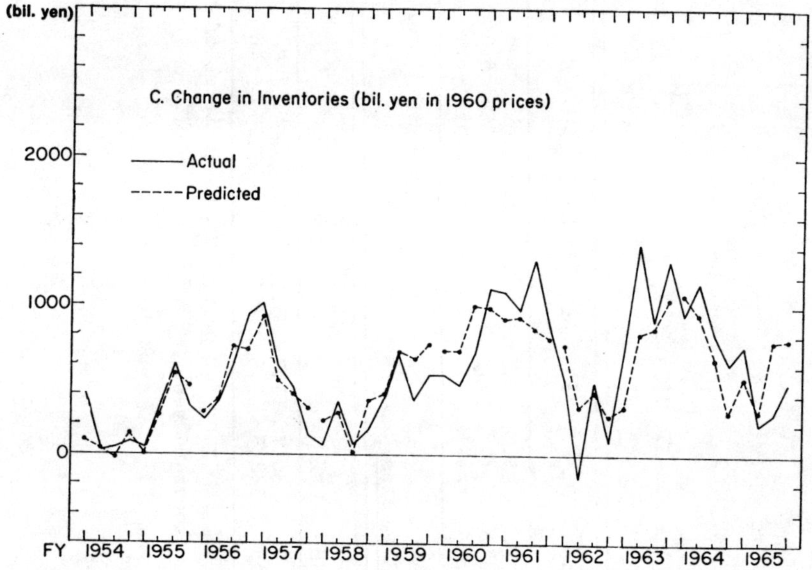

Fig. 15.2. Long-Run Ex post Forecast GNP (bil. yen in 1960 prices)

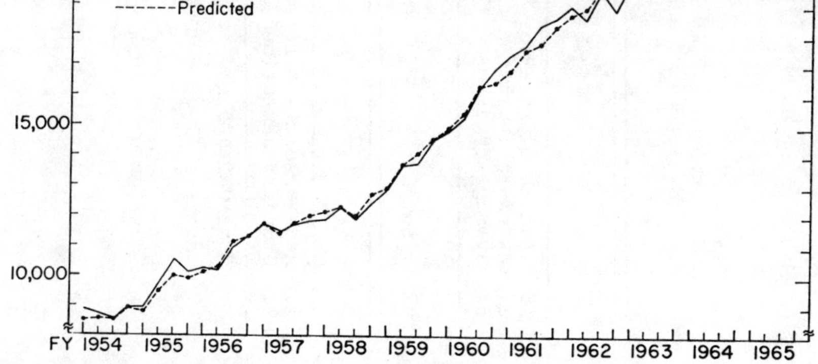

TABLE 15.3. LONG-RUN EX POST FORECAST, 1954.2Q-1966.1Q

A. Quarterly Estimates

	pV	V	C	I_p	J_p	E	M	p	p_c	w	O
1. Mean absolute error (%)	2.0	1.6	0.9	7.7	43.7	2.9	4.3	1.2	1.0	1.7	3.4
2. Standard deviation[a]	480.9	349.3	106.5	283.8	212.0	81.7	83.1	1.41	1.45	6.80	3.79
3. Average error[b]	-64.7	-88.2	-42.5	-52.2	-17.1	0.9	-10.9	0.30	0.55	-0.04	-0.80

B. Annual Estimates

	pV	V	C	I_p	J_p	E	M	p	p_c	w	O
1. Mean absolute error (%)	1.6	1.3	0.7	7.3	30.7	2.3	3.4	0.9	0.9	1.5	2.7
2. Standard deviation[a]	415.3	269.8	85.8	263.4	142.5	53.5	62.4	1.10	1.15	5.46	3.15

[a] For GNP and its components, the figures are in billion yen; for p, p_c, and O in terms of index numbers (1960 = 100); and for w (wage rate) in thousand yen.

[b] Average error = $\frac{1}{T} \cdot \sum_{t=1}^{T} (X_t^{actual} - X_t^{pred.})$.

TABLE 15.4. LONG-RUN EX POST FORECAST ERRORS
(mean absolute percentage error)

	EPA	Wharton-EFU	Brookings
V	1.58	2.32	2.03
pV	1.97	2.79	2.70
p	1.16	1.56	1.46
I_p	7.72	--	8.49
$p_i I_p$	8.39	6.28	--
C	0.93	--	1.55
$p_c C$	1.39	3.19	--
Y_d	1.93	2.90	1.75

Note: Mean absolute percentage error = $\frac{1}{T}\sum_{t=1}^{T}\left|\frac{X_t^{actual}-X_t^{pred}}{X_t^{actual}}\right|\times 100$

than those of short-run simulation described earlier, but the differences are not so great as usually expected. If these quarterly errors are aggregated into annual errors, as indicated in Table 15.3B, we cannot find any significant differences between the long-run forecasts and the short-run forecasts given in Table 15.1. This would imply that accumulated forecasting errors in our model do not tend to rise seriously even during a long period. In other words the model can be used to some extent for medium-term ex ante forecasting as well.

As regards the business-cycle turning point, our chart indicates that the 1954 and 1958 recessions are well picked out by the model, but the 1962 and 1964-1965 recession are depicted less accurately, in particular for the upturn. This tendency of the model is more or less similar to the earlier case of the short-run simulations. There is a slight long-run bias in recent years as indicated in the average error in Table 15.3A which is largely caused by the bias of business fixed investment. As for GNP components, change in inventories again shows the highest percentage errors, accounting for rather insensitive decline in inventories in 1962, whereas consumption has the lowest percentage errors.

In Table 15.4 the errors of our model are compared with two U.S. quarterly models, the Wharton-EFU model and the Brookings model. The latter model has 177 equations and is estimated for the period 1948-1960. Although qualifications are also needed similar to those for Table 15.2, the errors of leading variables in our model are a little smaller than those in the U.S. models except for business fixed investment and disposable income.

15.4. Forecasts for 1966 FY and 1967 FY

15.4.1. Forecast for 1966 FY

After testing our model for short- and long-run ex post forecasts, we extrapolated the model beyond our sample period for ex ante forecasts for the fiscal years (FY) of 1966 and 1967. The forecast for 1966 FY, however, is not a genuine ex ante forecast, since all the exogenous variables except those for the first quarter of 1967 are already known. Thus it should be regarded as a test of the model's performance for short-run forecasting beyond the sample period.

Unlike our ex post forecasts described before, we made slight adjustments of our constant terms in view of the existence of serial correlation, deviation of initial values, unusual factors, etc. The results of this forecast given in Table 15.5 indicate a fairly satisfactory performance of our model. The industrial production index (O), the earliest and the most widely used indicator of business conditions, was estimated almost exactly except for the fourth quarter of 1966. The actual values for GNP and its components are all preliminary figures that are subject to further revisions. Thus the comparison between actual and predicted values of the GNP should also be regarded as rather tentative. Generally there is a slight underestimation for the third quarter and some overestimation for the fourth quarter, which reflects mostly the errors in both fixed and inventory investment. Consumption, on the other hand, was predicted with a small margin of error. For price deflators and wage rate, the model also indicates a fairly good performance.

15.4.2. Forecast for 1967 FY

A genuine ex ante forecast was made for 1967 FY on the basis of two alternative exogenous variables. Our simulation A assumes a constant level in interest rate, while simulation B assumes its rise reflecting a more restrictive monetary policy in response to a rising trend of business investment.

This time we started our simulation from the first quarter of 1967. As shown in Table 15.6, both simulations indicate a high rate of economic growth, with continuous rising trend of business fixed investment and consumption. However, the inventory accumulation reaches its peak in the third quarter of 1967 and starts to decline gradually afterward. The rate of increase in fixed business investment also indicates a leveling-off in the second half of 1967 FY. The rate of increase in exports also declines substantially caused by the change in world trade and that for government investment slightly falls in real terms as compared with the previous year. The price level continues to rise almost at the same pace, whereas the wage rate increases a little faster, reflecting a rapid increase in corporate profits and a rising tendency of consumer prices. As regards the balance of payments, a substantial surplus in 1967 has declined about 30 percent, but there still remains a certain amount of surplus on current account. Finally, the production gap, defined as a difference between actual and potential real GNP derived from our production function of equation (15.9), tends to be narrowed as the economy continues a rapid expansion in both simulations.

The difference between our simulations A and B reflects purely the difference in monetary policy. Thus simulation B indicates a slightly lower rate of economic growth especially in inventory investment and fixed business investment mostly after the latter half of 1967 FY. A larger amount of surplus in the current account of the balance of payments no doubtt reflects the effect of this monetary policy. A rapid and continuous expansion of industrial output is also affected after the fourth quarter of 1967. Similarly, the levelling off of economic expansion causes a larger deficit in the fiscal budget and a wider production gap, while the price levels are hardly affected by this policy measure.

TABLE 15.5. FORECAST FOR 1966 FY

		1966			1967	1966 FY	Rate of Increase (%)
		2Q	3Q	4Q	1Q		
O	P_r	190.7	198.4	207.7	212.9	202.4	14.7
(1960 = 100)	A_c	189.3	200.0	209.0	218.1	204.1	15.6
V	P_r	26,006.3	26,845.2	27,915.3	28,112.5	27,219.8	10.6
(bil. yen)	A_c	26,049.1	27,260.6	27,419.8	28,089.6	27,204.7	10.3
C	P_r	13,969.8	14,346.2	14,648.1	14,983.1	14,486.8	8.2
(bil. yen)	A_c	13,893.8	14,316.6	14,658.0	14,855.5	14,431.0	7.8
I_p	P_r	4,695.1	4,888.2	5,328.3	5,541.5	5,113.3	13.3
(bil. yen)	A_c	4,726.4	4,961.2	5,162.2	5,419.6	5,067.4	12.3
J_p	P_r	608.8	767.9	971.7	916.7	816.3	87.7
(bil. yen)	A_c	436.4	968.8	862.0	1,350.0	904.3	107.9
E	P_r	4,147.3	4,317.7	4,521.8	4,551.0	4,384.5	15.1
(bil. yen)	A_c	4,164.4	4,364.9	4,499.1	4,339.3	4,341.9	14.2
M	P_r	3,564.4	3,684.1	3,865.2	3,949.4	3,765.8	16.9
(bil. yen)	A_c	3,468.4	3,667.4	3,915.1	3,934.0	3,746.2	16.3
pV	P_r	34,232.3	35,699.3	37,387.2	38,187.1	36,376.5	16.2
(bil. yen)	A_c	34,203.9	35,908.5	36,909.5	38,205.5	36,306.9	15.8
Y_c	P_r	2,814.9	3,326.3	3,737.4	3,785.5	3,416.0	29.4
(bil. yen)	A_c	2,918.2	3,466.4	3,753.2	---	---	---

TABLE 15.5. CONTINUED

p	P_r	131.6	133.0	133.9	135.8	133.6	5.1
(1960 = 100)	A_c	131.3	131.7	134.6	136.0	133.5	5.0
p_c	P_r	135.7	136.7	137.9	139.5	137.5	5.0
(1960 = 100)	A_c	136.2	136.4	137.2	139.4	137.3	4.8
w	P_r	546.9	563.6	571.4	580.5	565.5	11.3
(thousand yen)	A_c	548.1	561.8	569.4	---	---	---

Note: P_r = Predicted value, A_c = Actual figure (preliminary estimate).

TABLE 15.6. FORECAST FOR 1967 FY

		1967				1968	1967 FY	Rate of Increase (%)
		1Q	2Q	3Q	4Q	1Q		
O	A	213.1	219.2	227.2	236.4	240.4	230.8	13.8
(1960 = 100)	B	213.1	219.2	227.2	235.6	237.8	230.0	13.4
V	A	28,081.3	29,027.2	29,929.5	30,952.7	31,468.4	30,344.4	11.6
(bil. yen)	B	28,081.3	29,027.2	29,929.5	30,876.1	31,260.1	20,273.2	11.4
C	A	14,933.6	15,236.5	15,547.1	15,998.7	16,318.5	15,775.2	9.5
(bil. yen)	B	14,933.6	15,236.5	15,547.1	15,998.7	16,311.8	15,773.5	9.5
C_g	A	2,052.8	2,005.6	2,014.0	2,025.7	2,031.7	2,019.2	3.3
(bil.yen)	B	2,052.8	2,005.6	2,014.0	2,026.8	2,037.5	2,021.0	3.4
I_p	A	5,569.2	5,631.0	6,064.7	6,498.7	6,585.1	6,194.9	21.4
(bil. yen)	B	5,569.2	5,631.0	6,064.7	6,427.5	6,401.9	6,131.3	20.1
I_g	A	2,822.8	2,992.4	3,080.5	3,091.7	3,187.5	3,087.0	9.1
(bil. yen)	B	2,822.8	2,992.4	3,080.5	3,093.0	3,191.0	3,089.2	9.2
J_p	A	919.0	1,044.5	1,105.7	1,206.2	1,144.5	1,125.2	38.8
(bil. yen)	B	919.0	1,044.5	1,105.7	1,183.9	1,044.9	1,094.8	35.1
E	A	4,575,6	4,683,2	4,722.6	4,882.1	4,978.9	4,829.2	9.7
(bil. yen)	B	4,575.6	4,683.2	4,772.6	4,882.1	4,985.1	4,830.8	9.8
M	A	3,951.2	4,100.3	4,230.0	4,376.2	4,448.6	4,288.8	14.4
(bil. yen)	B	3,951.2	4,100.3	4,230.0	4,361.9	4,387.0	4,269.8	13.9
pV	A	38,090.2	40,033.7	41,351.6	43,456.5	44,816.0	42,414.5	16.9
(bil. yen)	B	38,090.2	40,033.7	41,351.6	43,362.3	44,526.0	43,318.4	16.7
Y_c	A	3,709.3	4,218.8	4,319.4	4,707.4	4,889.8	4,533.8	31.0
(bil. yen)	B	3,709.3	4,218.8	4,319.4	4,645.8	4,702.4	4,471.6	29.2

TABLE 15.6. CONTINUED

p	A	135.6	137.9	138.2	140.4	142.4	139.7	4.8
(1960 = 100)	B	135.6	137.9	138.2	140.4	142.4	139.7	4.8
p_c	A	139.4	143.0	143.1	146.2	148.6	145.2	5.8
(1960 = 100)	B	139.4	143.0	143.1	146.2	148.5	145.2	5.7
w	A	582.3	611.1	628.1	643.4	661.4	636.0	12.5
(thousand yen)	B	582.3	611.1	828.1	642.9	659.3	635.4	12.4
B_g	A	-635.9	-1,218.6	-1,262.6	-1,126.0	-1,141.4	-1,187.1	-12.4
(bil. yen)	B	-635.9	-1,218.6	-1,262.3	-1,159.7	-1,244.5	-1,221.3	-9.9
B_a	A	472.5	395.2	325.8	239.3	240.4	300.2	-35.4
(bil. yen)	B	472.5	395.2	325.8	253.7	305.8	320.1	-31.1
Production gap	A	1,206.1	900.7	724.2	470.3	739.1	708.6	-35.3
(bil. yen)	B	1,206.1	900.7	724.2	540.5	924.7	772.5	-29.5

Note: The rate of interest assumed in A and B are as below.

	1967 1Q	2Q	3Q	4Q	1968 1Q
A -	7.43	7.43	7.43	7.43	7.43
B -	7.43	7.43	7.43	7.53	7.64

15.5 Multipliers for Fiscal and Monetary Policy

In order to analyze the dynamic properties of our model and to measure the effects of exogenous variables for policy-making, we calculated several types of multipliers for the twenty-four quarter period, 1966-1971 FY. For the most important exogenous variables we also calculated long-run multipliers for 1966-1988 FY.

Since our model, being nonlinear, can give different multipliers depending on the level of capacity utilization and unemployment, we first calculated a "standard simulation" or "control solution" mostly based on the exogenous variables used for our five-year economic plan 1966-1971 FY. The multiplier effects were then calculated by assuming a sustained unit increase in the exogenous variables in current prices over the simulation period. Since detailed discussion of the multipliers would take considerable space, we shall confine ourselves only to the principal features of our multipliers.

As indicated in Table 15.7A, the multiplier of government investment, defined as the ratio of the increased expenditure in current prices to the increased GNP in 1960 prices, is 1.08 for the first quarter and then rises gradually up to 2.96 in the eighth quarter, and declines afterwards. On an annual basis, the first year multiplier is 1.68, the second 2.84, and the third 2.62. If these multipliers are expressed in terms of the GNP in current prices, they are raised to 2.17, 4.27, and 5.01 for each year. As regards components of the GNP, the rise in inventories is the most responsive to the rise in the multiplier for the first and the second quarters; gradually it is replaced by the fixed business investment, which reaches its peak in the ninth quarter and starts to fall gradually. Private consumption, on the other hand, starts rising slowly from the second quarter but continues to rise steadily up to the eleventh quarter. Housing investment takes a time path similar to that of fixed business investment, caused not by a kind of stock-adjustment mechanism but rather by an increase in the relative price of housing construction. Exports first decline by 0.07 and then recover, continuing to rise over our simulation period. This reflects a shift from an excess demand for the first 9 quarters due to the rise in government investment to an excess supply, i.e., an export drive, for the

TABLE 15.7. MULTIPLIERS FOR MAJOR EXOGENOUS VARIABLES 1966-1971 FY

A. Government Investment (100 billion yen increase in current prices)

	1	2	3	4	5	6	7	8	9	10	11	12
	$\Delta \underline{V}$	$\Delta \underline{C}$	$\Delta \underline{I}_p$	$\Delta \underline{I}_g$	$\Delta \underline{J}_p$	$\Delta \underline{E}$	$\Delta \underline{M}$	$\Delta(\underline{pv})$	$\Delta \underline{p}$	$\Delta \underline{w}$	$\Delta \underline{B}_g$	$\Delta \underline{B}_a$
1Q	108.3	0.0	19.5	75.7	29.7	0.0	15.8	134.5	-0.03	0.29	-73.3	-16.2
2Q	150.4	17.7	46.1	74.2	43.0	-8.5	22.2	192.0	-0.02	0.68	-62.3	-31.2
3Q	189.6	28.9	73.4	72.5	51.2	-10.2	28.2	245.1	-0.02	0.89	-49.1	-39.2
4Q	224.9	37.5	103.1	69.9	54.7	-10.7	33.2	296.1	-0.01	1.04	-38.8	-45.0
5Q	261.5	47.7	135.4	66.0	57.0	-10.5	38.3	358.5	0.02	1.64	-21.2	-52.3
6Q	281.5	58.9	153.9	60.6	54.7	-9.8	40.5	412.6	0.10	2.46	-2.9	-56.8
7Q	295.5	67.5	168.7	55.7	49.7	-7.4	41.7	456.6	0.17	3.00	12.0	-58.9
8Q	296.2	73.0	173.8	51.5	40.7	-4.5	40.5	480.5	0.23	3.36	19.4	-58.2
9Q	289.7	76.5	174.4	47.3	30.1	-1.0	38.2	499.0	0.30	4.08	24.9	-55.9
10Q	274.4	79.9	167.1	43.1	18.2	2.7	34.6	508.9	0.39	4.89	27.1	-50.4
11Q	255.9	82.1	154.9	40.4	6.8	6.2	30.6	508.0	0.46	5.27	27.8	-44.2
12Q	229.7	80.5	136.4	39.1	-4.9	9.4	25.5	489.0	0.49	5.38	22.3	-36.2
13Q	196.8	76.7	112.9	38.6	-16.7	12.2	19.6	461.7	0.54	5.85	13.0	-27.4
14Q	161.9	73.3	85.8	38.6	-27.3	14.7	13.6	429.9	0.58	6.30	2.5	-17.7
15Q	129.2	69.3	57.6	40.3	-35.2	16.6	8.2	391.9	0.60	6.24	-8.5	-8.8
16Q	95.3	62.3	28.2	43.3	-41.5	17.5	2.8	343.2	0.59	5.92	-23.5	0.1
17Q	60.8	54.3	-1.3	46.5	-46.5	17.8	-2.5	294.4	0.59	5.96	-39.9	8.6
18Q	30.0	47.8	-29.6	49.9	-49.3	17.7	-7.0	249.3	0.58	5.98	-54.6	16.5
19Q	5.5	41.7	-54.9	54.3	-49.2	16.7	-10.3	204.2	0.54	5.52	-67.6	22.3
20Q	-14.6	33.9	-76.3	59.5	-47.1	15.0	-12.8	156.5	0.48	4.87	-81.8	26.7
21Q	-33.1	26.2	-94.8	64.0	-44.3	12.8	-14.9	115.7	0.44	4.61	-96.0	30.3
22Q	-45.0	21.3	-109.4	68.0	-39.8	10.5	-15.9	84.9	0.40	4.42	-105.6	32.7
23Q	-49.4	17.4	-118.8	72.1	-33.4	7.8	-15.8	58.1	0.34	3.82	-112.1	32.5
24Q	-49.3	12.4	-122.7	75.7	-26.2	4.8	-14.9	32.7	0.27	3.10	-118.6	31.2

<u>Notes</u>: (1)-(7) 1.0 billion yen in 1960 prices.
(8), (11), (12) 1.0 billion yen in current prices.
(9) 1960 = 100.
(10) Thousand yen in current prices.

B. Transfer Payments (100 billion yen increase in current prices)

	1 $\Delta \underline{V}$	2 $\Delta \underline{C}$	3 $\Delta \underline{I}_p$	4 $\Delta \underline{I}_g$	5 $\Delta \underline{J}_p$	6 $\Delta \underline{E}$	7 $\Delta \underline{M}$	8 $\Delta(\underline{pv})$	9 $\Delta \underline{p}$	10 $\Delta \underline{w}$	11 $\Delta \underline{B}_g$	12 $\Delta \underline{B}_a$
1Q	0.0	0.0	0.0	0.0	0.0	0.0	0.0	0.0	0.00	0.00	-100.0	0.0
2Q	64.5	42.8	11.6	-0.6	17.7	0.0	9.4	83.1	-0.01	0.18	-83.6	-9.7
3Q	99.3	57.7	29.4	-1.3	28.2	-5.1	14.6	130.1	-0.00	0.43	-74.6	-20.2
4Q	136.0	70.3	50.7	-2.4	37.0	-6.8	20.3	180.6	0.00	0.61	-63.0	-27.7
5Q	171.6	82.4	73.8	-3.7	43.0	-8.0	25.4	231.8	0.00	0.79	-51.9	-34.4
6Q	210.7	96.1	101.4	-6.1	48.5	-8.8	31.0	292.4	0.02	1.23	-36.8	-42.2
7Q	238.3	108.4	122.2	-9.7	50.2	-9.1	34.6	348.2	0.07	1.81	-20.7	-48.3
8Q	259.5	118.4	139.5	-13.2	48.8	-8.1	37.0	397.6	0.13	2.30	-6.2	-52.1
9Q	271.7	126.0	151.6	-16.7	44.2	-6.4	37.8	435.0	0.17	2.77	5.3	-54.4
10Q	276.3	131.7	159.4	-20.6	37.3	-3.9	37.5	463.4	0.24	3.39	13.7	-54.6
11Q	274.1	137.2	161.2	-24.4	28.9	-0.9	36.0	488.2	0.31	4.04	20.7	-52.3
12Q	265.1	140.8	157.0	-27.2	19.4	2.1	33.5	502.4	0.38	4.51	24.9	-48.4
13Q	248.1	141.3	146.5	-29.2	8.9	5.1	29.8	500.6	0.43	4.93	25.0	-43.2
14Q	224.5	139.9	131.3	-30.8	-2.1	8.1	25.3	486.3	0.48	5.37	20.2	-36.4
15Q	197.8	138.5	111.6	-31.7	-12.4	10.9	20.4	469.4	0.53	5.75	14.1	-28.5
16Q	168.8	135.6	88.3	-31.0	-21.6	13.3	15.3	444.5	0.57	5.90	6.0	-20.0
17Q	137.6	130.4	63.1	-29.6	-29.6	14.9	10.0	409.2	0.59	5.98	-4.6	-11.8
18Q	104.6	123.9	36.4	-27.7	-36.6	16.1	4.8	366.0	0.59	6.04	-18.4	-3.2
19Q	73.4	118.1	9.3	-25.2	-41.6	16.8	-0.0	325.9	0.60	6.01	-31.5	5.1
20Q	45.9	111.7	-16.7	-21.4	-44.3	16.7	-4.1	285.3	0.59	5.77	-44.5	12.3
21Q	20.7	104.2	-40.6	-17.1	-45.2	15.9	-7.6	241.0	0.56	5.48	-58.4	18.2
22Q	-2.3	96.7	-62.4	-12.9	-44.8	14.6	-10.7	195.7	0.52	5.22	-72.4	23.3
23Q	-20.8	90.6	-81.5	-8.7	-42.8	12.9	-12.9	158.6	0.48	4.92	-84.1	27.4
24Q	-32.9	84.9	-96.1	-4.3	-38.8	10.8	-14.0	127.0	0.44	4.46	-93.6	30.0

Notes: (1)-(7) 1.0 billion yen in 1960 prices.
(8), (11), (12) 1.0 billion yen in current prices.
(9) 1960 = 100.
(10) 1.0 thousand yen in current prices.

C. Interest Rate on Loans of All Banks (0.365% decrease)

	1 ΔV	2 ΔC	3 ΔI_p	4 ΔI_g	5 ΔJ_p	6 ΔE	7 ΔM	8 $\Delta(pV)$	9 Δp	10 Δw	11 ΔB_g	12 ΔB_a
1Q	214.4	0.0	202.6	-4.8	61.9	0.0	40.2	253.4	-0.11	1.48	82.3	-39.9
2Q	353.3	21.4	293.3	-20.2	238.4	-17.4	147.3	510.3	0.18	4.88	161.4	-155.1
3Q	514.9	50.0	439.9	-37.3	291.9	-28.5	177.5	798.3	0.45	7.80	263.4	-197.2
4Q	711.5	69.0	596.0	-47.1	293.1	-27.7	144.4	1069.1	0.45	9.34	350.9	-171.4
5Q	808.3	88.3	730.2	-58.6	258.2	-24.0	151.9	1242.4	0.54	12.23	388.9	-192.9
6Q	903.8	118.1	847.7	-79.4	238.3	-10.3	163.1	1481.5	0.90	17.27	442.9	-199.3
7Q	974.3	157.5	934.7	-101.1	214.4	-0.7	169.4	1709.0	1.31	21.75	505.2	-210.6
8Q	966.5	184.4	975.9	-117.1	180.3	11.5	167.8	1855.1	1.64	24.58	552.5	-210.5
9Q	969.7	195.3	989.5	-135.1	135.1	25.9	158.8	1948.4	2.00	28.47	578.4	-200.5
10Q	909.5	206.8	976.8	-155.9	84.0	42.4	144.9	2027.6	2.48	33.60	591.8	-180.6
11Q	836.1	220.9	939.9	-172.7	35.2	59.0	129.3	2089.5	2.94	37.49	607.8	-155.8
12Q	739.9	220.1	877.6	-179.3	-12.0	73.1	110.6	2078.1	3.25	39.49	604.5	-123.8
13Q	605.0	204.5	788.1	-183.2	-61.7	84.7	86.5	2004.1	3.53	42.53	578.0	-87.4
14Q	450.5	189.6	680.2	-187.9	-109.6	96.0	60.4	1914.0	3.86	46.32	541.6	-44.9
15Q	300.3	176.2	562.7	-186.8	-148.4	105.1	35.7	1816.7	4.12	48.46	508.7	-2.9
16Q	150.8	151.0	436.5	-174.9	-178.5	110.0	11.9	1666.6	4.24	48.75	461.9	39.4
17Q	-9.5	115.9	306.2	-163.3	-204.1	111.3	-12.5	1487.6	4.32	50.21	402.3	80.1
18Q	-168.9	85.1	176.2	-154.1	-223.8	111.1	-35.8	1320.7	4.42	52.34	342.8	121.5
19Q	-305.3	59.7	53.4	-141.1	-232.4	108.1	-55.0	1171.4	4.46	52.85	296.1	156.0
20Q	-418.1	26.8	-55.7	-120.5	-229.9	101.5	-69.7	1002.3	4.39	51.82	245.5	184.5
21Q	-522.2	-10.2	-151.2	-102.2	-222.0	92.1	-82.2	838.9	4.30	52.17	189.6	208.1
22Q	-611.8	-37.2	-233.0	-90.0	-209.5	81.8	-92.1	715.7	4.24	53.47	147.0	227.0
23Q	-668.6	-56.2	-294.1	-77.6	-188.4	70.4	-96.7	636.4	4.16	53.37	125.3	237.0
24Q	-692.3	-78.5	-330.0	-61.2	-159.0	57.2	-95.8	562.5	4.01	52.07	106.7	240.1

Notes: (1)-(7) 1.0 billion yen in 1960 prices.
(8), (11), (12) 1.0 billion yen in current prices.
(9) 1960 = 100.
(10) Thousand yen in current prices.

rest of our period. A similar tendency can also be observed for imports which rise rapidly in the first quarter in response to the excess demand and then follow a similar time path to the real GNP. Thus, the time path of our multiplier mentioned before is a joint effect of the different time patterns of these GNP components.

For the first year, about two-thirds of the multiplier value is accounted for by inventory investment and business fixed investment, and the rise in the private consumption and other is offset by the increase in the foreign trade deficit which amounts to about 20 percent of the multiplier value. The further increase in the multiplier value for the second year is mostly caused by the rise in consumption and fixed business investment, whereas the share of inventory investment declines substantially. In the third year the share of both fixed and inventory investment declines while those of consumption and housing investment continue to increase.

What would then be the long-run time path and the features of the Japanese multipliers? Our Table 15.8 indicates this time pattern for the period 1966-1988. There is a marked long-run, but damping, cycle of about 9 years, which is mostly generated by our fixed investment function. Our long-run equilibrium value in this table seems to be about 1.8 to 2.0 in real terms which will converge eventually after more than 25 years. A result of comparison of this with the U.S. value in the table seems to suggest an interesting, salient feature of our multiplier distinctive to the Japanese economy. Although qualifications are needed as to the differences in specification of the models,[11] and economic institutions,[12] it can safely be stated that the faster economic expansion accompanied by a higher rate of capacity utilization, keener competition, and stronger factor-substituion in Japan are likely to cause a shorter adjustment of actual to desired capacity output, thus giving a highly dynamic and fluctuating propensity to invest and a long-run swing of output and investment. The length of time needed for the convergence of our multiplier seems to be about 30 years while in the United States it is only 5 to 10 years, although the long-run equilibrium values do not differ very much. It should also be noted that this "Jugler" type investment cycle in Japan would have

TABLE 15.8. LONG-RUN EFFECT OF MULTIPLIER OF GOVERNMENT INVESTMENT IN REAL TERMS

	EPA Model (1966-1988 FY)				Wharton-EFU Model (1966-1975)	
Year	V	C	I_p	J_p	V	I_p
1	2.30	0.29	0.83	0.61	2.37	0.24
2	4.85	1.06	2.70	0.86	1.77	0.34
3	6.18	1.88	3.72	0.30	1.90	0.38
4	3.63	1.75	1.77	-0.75	----	----
5	0.39	0.84	-0.77	-0.91	2.05	0.33
6	-0.63	0.28	-1.59	-0.51	----	----
7	-0.35	0.10	-1.39	-0.09	----	----
8	0.58	0.17	-0.69	0.25	----	----
9	1.90	0.42	0.33	0.47	----	----
10	3.28	0.82	1.38	0.47	2.02	0.27
11	3.86	1.18	1.78	0.16	----	----
12	3.00	1.18	1.06	-0.26	----	----
13	1.57	0.86	-0.06	-0.43	----	----
14	0.70	0.53	-0.71	-0.32	----	----
15	0.53	0.34	-0.80	-0.13	----	----
16	0.81	0.29	-0.55	0.05	----	----
17	1.32	0.35	-0.14	0.17	----	----
18	1.85	0.48	0.26	0.19	----	----
19	2.21	0.61	0.50	0.13	----	----
20	2.25	0.68	0.50	0.02	----	----
21	2.02	0.67	0.29	-0.07	----	----
22	1.70	0.60	0.04	-0.10	----	----
23	1.49	0.52	-0.12	-0.07	----	----

become more unstable had it not been for the higher leakage associated with its higher marginal propensity to save and higher marginal propensity to import. In summing up, we can roughly say that the Japanese multiplier is more investment-oriented and dynamic while the United States' is more consumption-oriented and stable. This more dynamic response of our multiplier to the exogenous stimuli suggests, on the other hand, the need for stronger policy measures to counteract wider business fluctuation and instability, which is discussed later.

As regards to other fiscal policy measures, the multiplier of transfer payments is shown in Table 15.7B. As expected, the multiplier value is much smaller than that of government investment in the first year, but becomes almost at the same level in the second year and surpasses the government investment multiplier in the third year. This clearly reflects a slow but continuous rise in consumption over the first four years, though it tends to decline slowly afterwards. We also note that the share of fixed investment is again larger than in the U.S. case for the earlier period. As easily expected from the specification of our consumption function,the multiplier of personal tax reduction has a slightly smaller value, though it follows a time pattern similar to transfer payments.

Lastly, we shall discuss the multiplier of monetary policy, which is approximated by interest rate on loans of all banks. Over the past period, changes in the interest rate have frequently been made by the central bank, mostly though its discount rate and control of money stock, to counteract the wide fluctuations of business fixed investment and the international balance of payments. Table 15.7C indicates a fairly sensitive response to the change in monetary condition, which is explained largely by the traditional heavy reliance of Japanese firms on external funds associated with the high ratio of business fixed investment to corporate profits and a rapid increase in aggregate demand. As shown in the table, the rise in the interest rate affects business fixed investment, inventory investment, and the balance of payments through an increase in imports in the first quarter. This quick response of fixed investment to changes in the interest rate and the gradual rise over time up to the eighth quarter will reflect behavioral and institutional characteristics of our fixed investment. The elasticity of the real GNP with respect to the interest rate is about -0.35 for the first year according to this simulation. From the view point of monetary policy it should also be noted that the effect is higher in the second than in the first year as in the case of other multipliers. A similar tendency is also found in the U.S. model for monetary policy, though in a much smaller degree.[13] Thus a recession of our economy experienced in 1964-1965 can be explained largely by this time lag of monetary and fiscal policy. A tight money policy, starting in early 1964, continued for one year, and brought about a stronger contracting effect in 1965 than in the previous year. Since fiscal policy in 1964-1965 was not fully prepared for this, government expenditure was not sufficient to cause the economy to recover to the normal output level by the end of 1965. Thus, our simulation analysis suggests the importance of intertemporal consideration of monetary and fiscal policy in particular for a rapidly growing economy with fairly sensitive business investment.

15.6. Data Problems

As noted in the preceding sections, our quarterly model has encountered many difficulties in the statistical data.

First it must be noted that the "statistical discrepancy," obtained as residual between the income and expenditure accounts tends to be greater on the quarterly basis than on the annual basis. The quarterly errors are usually about 1.7% of the GNP in mean absolute, while the annual ones are only 0.6%. These errors represent various elements, but the most significant are those caused by change in inventories, difference between cash and accrual basis of government expenditure, and sampling errors in particular of small business and farmers' income. As noted earlier, we used this discrepancy as one of the explanatory variables in the inventory investment function in view of its strong association with the data errors in inventory statistics. Needless to say, this treatment to prevent exaggerated influence of inventory change on other variables will have to be replaced by the use of a more reliable statistical estimate of this item.

Second, the quarterly GNE needs to be checked against an alternative estimate obtained from value added data. This estimation is now being studied by the Economic Research Institute, EPA. The results will greatly serve not only as an alternative estimate for total output but also for improvement of the present GNE estimates, especially for eliminating volatile fluctuations of inventories caused by data errors.

Lastly, in our experience with model-building, the inventory valuation adjustment was found to be rather inappropriate especially in explaining the changes in corporate profit itself or fixed business investment correlated with the profit. The adjustment is certainly useful for estimating inventory change, but for other purposes it mostly tends to obscure actual business behavior and to miss a critical turning point of the business cycle.

15.7. Concluding Remarks

Our experiment in model-building and its use for short-run quarterly forecasting, described so far, seems to indicate the usefulness of our new quarterly national income accounts for projection and policy-making, despite certain weaknesses inherent in the quarterly accounts. It has been emphasized that the usefulness of these accounts especially for fiscal and monetary policy is enhanced when they are employed for econometric model-building together with other related data. As concluding remarks, we shall make in the following a few comments on the relationship between these accounts and other types of accounts for short-run forecasting.

First, as to the information on the detailed industrial breakdown of total output, our national accounts model can serve as a macroeconomic basis for these analyses. The input-output model developed by the Planning Bureau of the EPA is already available for annual forecasting on a calendar year basis regarding output and imports at the 60-sector level and employment, investment and capital stock at the 20-sector level. Once the aggregate final demand and its components are estimated by our quarterly model, the input-output model can break them down into further details, which can also serve as quite useful information for business planning and market research. In view of the highly dynamic nature of our business fixed investments, such as integrated use of the aggregate and sectoral models will help business to lighten the future risk, thus stabilizing the economy in line with our fast-growing production potential.

For financial variables, the weakness of our model reflects largely the present position of our flow-of-funds accounts. The accounts have not yet been fully integrated with our national income accounts either statistically or conceptually, though the former are also available on a quarterly basis. Thus it seems a little premature to have a completely integrated econometric model including both types of accounts.

As mentioned earlier, our present model is designed as a pilot for a more detailed master model. In the latter model, major emphasis is now being placed on the link between the government and monetary sectors to include more explicitly the interaction between fiscal and monetary policy. Financial variables are also being estimated partly by employing the flow-of-funds accounts. As noted before, variables on wages and prices are to be disaggregated further in line with the breakdown of consumption, exports and imports, etc. This block of wage and prices in the master model will be very useful in formulating medium-term structural policy dealing with specific sectorial prices, employment, productivity, etc.

Notes

The authors are indebted to Professors T. Uchida and T. Watanabe for their valuable comments, and to Miss E. Kawana for computer programming. The views expressed in this paper are entirely personal and do not represent any view of the government.

1. S. Ichimura, L. R. Klein, S. Koizumi, K. Sato, and Y. Shinkai, "Quarterly Econometric Model of Postwar Japanese Economy: 1952-1959," Osaka Economic Papers, vol. 12, no. 2 (March 1964); M. Tatemoto, T. Uchida, and T. Watanabe, "A Stabilization Model for the Post-War Japanese Economy: 1954-1962," International Economic Review, vol. 8, no. 1 (February 1967). Chapter 14 in this volume.

2. Economic Planning Agency, Econometric Models for Medium-Term Economic Plan, 1964-1968 (Tokyo, 1965).

3. Ichimura, Klein, Koizumi, Sato, and Shinkai, "Quarterly Econometric Model of Postwar Japanese Economy: 1952-1959."

4. M. K. Evans, "Multiplier Analysis of a Post-War Quarterly U.S. Model and Comparison with Several Other Models," Review of Economic Studies, vol. 33 (4), no. 96 (October 1966); L. R. Klein, "A Post-War Quarterly Model: Description and Applications," in Models of Income Determination (Princeton University Press, 1963); L. R. Klein, and M. K. Evans, "Experience with Econometric Analysis of the American 'Konjuktur' Position"

in Is the Business Cycle Obsolete? (New York: John Wiley and Sons, Inc., 1969); M. Liebenberg, A. A. Hirsch, and J. Popkin, "A Quarterly Econometric Model of the United States: A Progress Report," Survey of Current Business, vol. 46, no. 5 (May 1966).

5. The Japanese fiscal year relates to the twelve months from April to the following March.

6. Before estimating the structural parameters the equations were grouped into three blocks: (1) expenditure and employment, (2) price and wage, and (3) income distribution. Our simultaneous estimation of structural parameters was made separately for each block in view of the large number of exogenous and predetermined variables.

7. Needless to say, $I/V = [K - (1 - r)K_{-1})/V$, where r = replacement ratio to gross capital stock.

8. The gross capital stock data on a quarterly basis were estimated by the Economic Research Institute on the basis of 1955 and 1960 National Wealth Censuses.

9. T. Watanabe, "Price Changes and the Rate of Change of Money Wage Earnings in Japan, 1955-1962," The Quarterly Journal of Economics, vol. 80 (February 1966). Chapter 7 in this volume.

10. L. R. Klein and M. K. Evans, "Experience with Econometric Analysis of the American 'Konjuktur' Position."

11. If the interest rate i is treated as an endogenous variable and monetary feedbacks are explicitly taken into account, our multiplier value will no doubt be reduced. Similarly, treatment of labor supply as endogenous will also reduce the value. A low multiplier value of the Osaka model is due partly to its inclusion of the interest rate as endogenous (S. Ichimura, "Dynamic Properties of the Osaka Econometric Model of Post-War Japanese Economy, 1952-1961," mimeographed.

12. B. G. Hickman, "Dynamic Properties of Macro-Econometric Models: An International Comparison" (Paper prepared for the SSRC Conference on "Is the Business Cycle Obsolete?" April 1967).

13. L. R. Klein and M. K. Evans, "Experience with Econometric Analysis of the American 'Konjuktur' Position."

Contributors

AKIHIRO AMANO is a Professor on the Faculty of Business Administration, Kobe University.

TUVIA BLUMENTHAL is a Senior Lecturer in Economics at Tel-Aviv University.

HOLLIS B. CHENERY is Vice-President for Development Policy, Internation Bank for Reconstruction and Development.

SHOZABURO FUJINO is a Professor at the Institute of Economic Research, Hitotsubashi University.

FUMIMASA HAMADA is a Professor on the Faculty of Economics, Keio University.

SHINICHI ICHIMURA is Professor and Director of the Center for Southeast Asian Studies, Kyoto University.

LAWRENCE R. KLEIN is Benjamin Franklin Professor of Economics at the University of Pennsylvania.

AKIO KOHNO is Section Chief of the Personnel Division, Daiwa Security Co., Ltd.

RICHARD KOSOBUD is a Professor of Economics at the University of Illinois at Chicago Circle.

RYOSHIN MINAMI is an Associate Professor at the Institute of Economic Research, Hitotsubashi University.

SEIICHI NAGAYA is Chief of the Business Section, Wakayama Branch, Kansai Electric Power, Co., Ltd.

KAZUSHI OHKAWA is a Professor Emeritus of Hitotsubashi University.

AKIRA ONO is a Professor in the Department of Economics, Seikei University.

KAZUO SATO is a Professor of Economics at the State University of New York at Buffalo.

YOICHI SHINKAI is a Professor at the Institute of Social and Economic Research, Osaka University.

SHUNTARO SHISHIDO is a Professor of Economics at Tsukuba University.

SHOSUKE TANAKA is associated with the Asia Institute for Economic Development Planning, Economic Commission for Asia and the Far East.

MASAHIRO TATEMOTO is a Professor on the Faculty of Economics, Osaka University.

TADAO UCHIDA is a Professor in the College of General Education, University of Tokyo.

HIROYA UENO is a Professor in the Department of Economics, Seikei University.

TSUNEHIKO WATANABE is a Professor on the Faculty of Economics, Osaka University.

KUNIO YOSHIHARA is an Associate Professor at the Center for Southeast Asian Studies, Kyoto University.

Index